Reading God's Word
Daily Mass Readings
Church Year C 2001

Living Faith Publications

Living Faith Publications
Creative Communications for the Parish
1564 Fencorp Drive
Fenton, MO 63026
www.livingfaith.com

Reading God's Word
Daily Mass Readings
Church Year C 2001

ISBN Number: 1-889 387-19-3

Published by the authority of the Bishop's Committee on the Liturgy, National Conference of Catholic Bishops.

Cover Design and Art: Sally Beck
Editor: James E. Adams
Editorial assistance: Mark Zimmermann

EDITOR'S NOTE

With so many resources that provide the Mass Scripture readings, why are we offering a book such as this? Aren't there many editions of the Bible, the Lectionary, missals and missalettes available for the Mass readings?

There are indeed many volumes that contain parts of the latest available Church-sanctioned Mass Scripture readings. But there is no other single volume that contains the lectionary's New American Bible text in this particular form— a book of Mass Scripture texts moving through the year calendar day by calendar day.

Featured herein are the Scripture texts from the lectionary for every Sunday and weekday of Church Year 2001 (Cycle C), from December 3, 2000, through December 1, 2001.

Finding the appropriate Scripture reading is as simple as turning to the date you want, and begining to read. What you will be reading is the text that conforms in letter and spirit with the English language liturgy of the worldwide Church.

By means of Scripture proclaimed at Mass, "God speaks to his people, revealing the mystery of their redemption and salvation and offering them spiritual nourishment." (*General Instruction on the Roman Missal*).

The ideal way to absorb the spiritual nourishment of Scripture is through participation in the Liturgy of the Word at Mass. No volume will be more convenient to use in helping prepare one in advance to get the most of the Mass readings. Study, meditation and prayer centered on the readings *prior* to Mass can help one listen more intently as the texts are proclaimed at Mass. (Liturgists are fond of reminding us that we should close our books and *listen* rather than follow along with the printed text in our hands.) And no volume will be more convenient for lectors to use in preparing themselves to properly proclaim Sacred Scripture at Mass.

Those who don't attend Mass daily can nonetheless take in daily spiritual nourishment by meditating and praying with the Scripture texts the liturgy offers to us each day. The thousands of readers of *Living Faith: Daily Catholic Devotions* will surely find this book helpful in their daily prayer, as well as readers of other Catholic publications that integrate the Mass Scripture readings into daily devotional practices.

The discipline of meditating and praying with the Scripture and the psalm verses of Mass stands on its own as a personal devotional practice. Whether done separately or in conjunction with other practices, the advantages of this discipline are threefold: it's based on Scripture, the inspired words that reveal the profound love of God for us; it's based on the particular inspired words about God's love that the Church offers to us for this or that particular day; and it's the same inspired words about God's love being used that same day in the Church around the world.

I strongly urge that this book be used regularly so that daily prayer and meditation on Scripture becomes a habit that leaves a gap if you miss it. The more you reinforce this excellent habit, the more it becomes something you want to do and look forward to doing.

The value of reading each day the Mass Scripture passages for one's personal spiritual life is immense, noted the late spiritual writer Henri J.M. Nouwen.

"Each (daily) passage holds its own treasure for us," he wrote. "For me it has been of immense spiritual value to read each morning the story about Jesus that has been chosen for the day. I have discovered that when I do this over a long period of time, the life of Jesus becomes more and more alive in me and starts to guide me in my daily activities."

May you find a treasure every time you use this book.

James E. Adams

Notice for Lectors

If this book is used to prepare for reading at Mass, please note that the "announcement" formula is: *"A reading from the Book of . . .," "A reading from the Letter of . . .,"* or *"A reading from the holy Gospel according to . . ."* We have placed † before the citation as a reminder for this announcement. At the end of the readings, the lector or celebrant says *"The word of the Lord."* We have placed ✚ at the end of texts as a reminder for that. Also, herein the responsorial psalm is given only once, with an **R.** indicating where repetition is called for; the **R.** at the end of the Gospel Verse indicates that "Alleluia" is repeated once. ∎

DECEMBER 3, 2000
FIRST SUNDAY OF ADVENT

† *Jeremiah 33:14-16*
I will raise up for David a just shoot.

The days are coming, says the LORD,
   when I will fulfill the promise
   I made to the house of Israel and Judah.
In those days, in that time,
   I will raise up for David a just shoot;
   he shall do what is right and just in the land.
In those days Judah shall be safe
   and Jerusalem shall dwell secure;
   this is what they shall call her:
"The LORD our justice." ✠

Psalm 25:4-5, 8-9, 10, 14
R. To you, O Lord, I lift my soul.
Your ways, O LORD, make known to me;
   teach me your paths,
guide me in your truth and teach me,
   for you are God my savior
   and for you I wait all the day. **R.**
Good and upright is the LORD,
   thus he shows sinners the way.
He guides the humble to justice
   and teaches the humble his way. **R.**
All the paths of the LORD are kindness and constancy
   toward those who keep his covenant and his decrees.
The friendship of the LORD is with those who fear him,
   and his covenant for their instruction. **R.**

† *1 Thessalonians 3:12—4:2*
*May the Lord strengthen your hearts
at the coming of our Lord Jesus.*

Brothers and sisters:
May the Lord make you increase and abound in love
   for one another and for all,
   just as we have for you,
   so as to strengthen your hearts,
   to be blameless in holiness before our God and Father

at the coming of our Lord Jesus with all his holy ones.
Amen.

Finally, brothers and sisters,
we earnestly ask and exhort you in the Lord Jesus that,
as you received from us
how you should conduct yourselves to please God
—and as you are conducting yourselves—
you do so even more.
For you know what instructions we gave you through the Lord
Jesus. ✛

Psalm 85:8
R. Alleluia, alleluia.
Show us, Lord, your love;
and grant us your salvation. **R.**

† *Luke 21:25-28, 34-36*
Your redemption is at hand.

Jesus said to his disciples:
"There will be signs in the sun, the moon and the stars,
and on the earth nations will be in dismay,
perplexed by the roaring of the sea and the waves.
People will die of fright
in anticipation of what is coming upon the world,
for the powers of the heavens will be shaken.
And then they will see the Son of Man
coming in a cloud with power and great glory.
But when these signs begin to happen,
stand erect and raise your heads
because your redemption is at hand.

"Beware that your hearts do not become drowsy
from carousing and drunkenness
and the anxieties of daily life,
and that day catch you by surprise like a trap.
For that day will assault everyone
who lives on the face of the earth.
Be vigilant at all times
and pray that you have the strength
to escape the tribulations that are imminent
and to stand before the Son of Man." ✛

MONDAY, DECEMBER 4
ADVENT WEEKDAY, ST. JOHN OF DAMASCENE

† *Isaiah 2:1-5*
*The Lord will gather many nations in an
everlasting peace in the kingdom of heaven.*

This is what Isaiah, son of Amoz, saw concerning Judah and
Jerusalem.
In the days to come,
The mountain of the Lord's house
shall be established as the highest mountain
and raised above the hills.
All nations shall stream toward it;
many peoples shall come and say:
"Come, let us climb the Lord's mountain,
to the house of the God of Jacob,
That he may instruct us in his ways,
and we may walk in his paths."
For from Zion shall go forth instruction,
and the word of the Lord from Jerusalem.
He shall judge between the nations,
and impose terms on many peoples.
They shall beat their swords into plowshares
and their spears into pruning hooks;
One nation shall not raise the sword against another,
nor shall they train for war again.
O house of Jacob, come,
let us walk in the light of the Lord! ✛

Psalm 122:1-2, 3-4 (4-5, 6-7) 8-9
**R. I rejoiced when I heard them say:
let us go to the house of the Lord.**
I rejoiced because they said to me,
"We will go up to the house of the Lord."
And now we have set foot
within your gates, O Jerusalem. **R.**
Jerusalem, built as a city
with compact unity.
To it the tribes go up,
the tribes of the Lord. **R.**
According to the decree for Israel,

to give thanks to the name of the Lord.
In it are set up judgment seats,
   seats for the house of David. **R.**
Pray for the peace of Jerusalem!
   May those who love you prosper!
May peace be within your walls,
   prosperity in your buildings. **R.**
Because of my relatives and friends
   I will say, "Peace be within you!"
Because of the house of the Lord, our God,
   I will pray for your good. **R.**

See Psalm 79:4
R. Alleluia, alleluia.
Come and save us, Lord, our God;
let us see your face, and we shall be saved. **R.**

† *Matthew 8:5-11*
*Many will come from the east and west
and take their place in the kingdom of heaven.*

As Jesus entered Capernaum, a centurion approached him with this request, "Sir, my serving boy is at home in bed paralyzed, suffering painfully." He said to him, "I will come and cure him." "Sir," the centurion said in reply, "I am not worthy to have you under my roof. Just give an order and my boy will get better. I am a man under authority myself and I have troops assigned to me. If I give one man the order, 'Dismissed,' off he goes. If I say to another, 'Come here,' he comes. If I tell my slave, 'Do this,' he does it." Jesus showed amazement on hearing this and remarked to his followers, "I assure you, I have never found this much faith in Israel. Mark what I say! Many will come from the east and the west and will find a place at the banquet in the kingdom of God with Abraham, Isaac, and Jacob. ✛

TUESDAY, DECEMBER 5
ADVENT WEEKDAY

✝ *Isaiah 11:1-10*
The Spirit of the Lord God rests upon him.

On that day,
A shoot shall sprout from the stump of Jesse,
    and from his roots a bud shall blossom.
The spirit of the Lord shall rest upon him:
    a spirit of wisdom and of understanding,
A spirit of counsel and of strength,
    a spirit of knowledge and of fear of the Lord,
    and his delight shall be the fear of the Lord.
Not by appearance shall he judge,
    nor by hearsay shall he decide,
But he shall judge the poor with justice,
    and decide aright for the land's afflicted.
He shall strike the ruthless with the rod of his mouth,
    and with the breath of his lips he shall slay the wicked.
Justice shall be the band around his waist,
    and faithfulness a belt upon his hips.

Then the wolf shall be a guest of the lamb,
    and the leopard shall lie down with the kid;
The calf and the young lion shall browse together,
    with a little child to guide them.
The cow and the bear shall be neighbors,
    together their young shall rest;
    the lion shall eat hay like the ox.
The baby shall play by the cobra's den,
    and the child lay his hand on the adder's lair.
There shall be no harm or ruin on all my holy mountain
    for the earth shall be filled with knowledge of the Lord,
    as water covers the sea.

On that day,
The root of Jesse,
    set up as a signal for the nations,
The Gentiles shall seek out,
    for his dwelling shall be glorious. ✝

Psalm 72:1, 7-8, 12-13, 17

**R. Justice shall flourish in his time,
and fullness of peace for ever.**

O God, with your judgment endow the king,
and with your justice, the king's son;
He shall govern your people with justice
and your afflicted ones with judgment. **R.**
Justice shall flower in his days,
and profound peace, till the moon be no more.
May he rule from sea to sea,
and from the River to the ends of the earth. **R.**
He shall rescue the poor man when he cries out,
and the afflicted when he has no one to help him.
He shall have pity for the lowly and the poor;
the lives of the poor he shall save. **R.**
May his name be blessed forever;
as long as the sun his name shall remain.
In him shall all the tribes of the earth be blessed;
all the nations shall proclaim his happiness. **R.**

Psalm 85:8

R. Alleluia, alleluia.

Lord, let us see your kindness,
and grant us your salvation. **R.**

† *Luke 10:21-24*

Jesus is filled with the Holy Spirit.

Jesus rejoiced in the Holy Spirit and said: "I offer you praise,
O Father, Lord of heaven and earth, because what you have
hidden from the learned and the clever you have revealed to
the merest children.

"Yes, Father, you have graciously willed it so.

"Everything has been given over to me by my Father. No
one knows the Son except the Father and no one knows the
Father except the Son — and anyone to whom the Son wishes
to reveal him."

Turning to his disciples he said to them privately: "Blest
are the eyes that see what you see. I tell you, many prophets
and kings wished to see what you see but did not see it, and to
hear what you hear but did not hear it." ✛

WEDNESDAY, DECEMBER 6
ADVENT WEEKDAY, ST. NICHOLAS

✝ *Isaiah 25: 6-10*
The Lord God has invited us to rejoice with him,
and he will wipe away the tears from every face.

On this mountain the Lord of hosts
    will provide for all peoples
A feast of rich food and choice wines,
    juicy, rich food and pure, choice wines.
On this mountain he will destroy
    the veil that veils all peoples,
The web that is woven over all nations
    he will destroy death forever.
The Lord God will wipe away
    the tears from all faces;
The reproach of his people he will remove
    from the whole earth; for the Lord has spoken.

On that day it will be said:
"Behold our God, to whom we looked to save us!
    This is the Lord for whom we looked;
    let us rejoice and be glad that he has saved us!"
For the hand of the Lord will rest on this mountain. ✝

Psalm 23:1-6
**R. I shall live in the house of the Lord
all the days of my life.**
The Lord is my shepherd; I shall not want.
    In verdant pastures he gives me repose;
Beside restful waters he leads me;
    he refreshes my soul. **R.**
He guides me in right paths
    for his name's sake.
Even though I walk in the dark valley
    I fear no evil; for you are at my side
With your rod and your staff
    that give me courage. **R.**
You spread the table before me
    in the sight of my foes;
You anoint my head with oil;

my cup overflows. **R.**
Only goodness and kindness follow me
    all the days of my life;
And I shall dwell in the house of the Lord
    for years to come. **R.**

Isaiah 33:22
R. Alleluia, alleluia.
The Lord will judge us by his law;
he is our King and Savior. **R.**

† *Matthew 15:29-37*
Jesus healed many and multiplied the bread.

Jesus went along the Sea of Galilee. He went up onto the mountainside and sat down there. Large crowds of people came to him bringing with them cripples, the deformed, the blind, the mute, and many others besides. They laid them at his feet and he cured them. The result was great astonishment in the crowds as they beheld the mute speaking, the deformed made sound, cripples walking about, and the blind seeing. They glorified the God of Israel.

Jesus called his disciples to him and said: "My heart is moved with pity for the crowd. By now they have been with me three days, and have nothing to eat. I do not wish to send them away hungry, for fear they may collapse on the way." His disciples said to him, "How could we ever get enough bread in this deserted spot to satisfy such a crowd?" But Jesus asked them, "How many loaves of bread do you have?" "Seven," they replied, "and a few small fish." Then he directed the crowd to seat themselves on the ground. He took the seven loaves and the fish, and after giving thanks he broke them and gave them to the disciples, who in turn gave them to the crowds. All ate until they were full. When they gathered up the fragments left over, these filled seven hampers. ✝

THURSDAY, DECEMBER 7
ADVENT WEEKDAY, ST. AMBROSE

✛ *Isaiah 26:1-6*
Let the upright nations, the custodians of truth, come in.

On that day they will sing this song in the land of Judah:
"A strong city have we;
    he sets up walls and ramparts to protect us.
Open up the gates
    to let in a nation that is just,
    one that keeps faith.
A nation of firm purpose you keep in peace;
    in peace, for its trust in you."

Trust in the Lord forever!
    For the Lord is an eternal rock.
He humbles those in high places,
    and the lofty city he brings down;
He tumbles it to the ground,
    levels it with the dust.
It is trampled underfoot by the needy,
    by the footsteps of the poor. ✛

Psalm 118:1, 8-9, 19-21, 25-27
R. Blessed is he who comes in the name of the Lord.
Give thanks to the Lord, for he is good,
    for his mercy endures forever.
It is better to take refuge in the Lord
    than to trust in man.
It is better to take refuge in the Lord
    than to trust in princes. **R.**
Open to me the gates of justice;
    I will enter them and give thanks to the Lord.
This gate is the Lord's;
    the just shall enter it.
I will give thanks to you, for you have answered me
    and have been my savior. **R.**
O Lord, grant salvation!
    O Lord, grant prosperity!
Blessed is he who comes in the name of the Lord;
    we bless you from the house of the Lord.

The Lord is God, and he has given us light. **R.**

Isaiah 40:9,10
R. Alleluia, alleluia.
Raise your voice and tell the Good News;
the Lord our God comes in strength. **R.**

† *Matthew 7:21, 24-27*
He who does the will of the Father will enter the kingdom of heaven.

Jesus said to his disciples: "None of those who cry out, 'Lord, Lord,' will enter the kingdom of God but only the one who does the will of my Father in heaven.

"Anyone who hears my words and puts them into practice is like the wise man who built his house on rock. When the rainy season set in, the torrents came and the winds blew and buffeted his house. It did not collapse; it had been solidly set on rock. Anyone who hears my words but does not put them into practice is like the foolish man who built his house on sandy ground. The rains fell, the torrents came, the winds blew and lashed against his house. It collapsed under all this and was completely ruined." ✢

FRIDAY, DECEMBER 8
THE IMMACULATE CONCEPTION
OF THE BLESSED VIRGIN MARY

† *Genesis 3:9-15, 20*
I will put enmity between your offspring and hers.

After the man, Adam, had eaten of the tree, the LORD God called to the man and asked him, "Where are you?" He answered, "I heard you in the garden; but I was afraid, because I was naked, so I hid myself." Then he asked, "Who told you that you were naked? You have eaten, then, from the tree of which I had forbidden you to eat!" The man replied, "The woman whom you put here with me—she gave me fruit from the tree, and so I ate it." The LORD God then asked the woman, "Why did you do such a thing?" The woman answered, "The serpent tricked me into it, so I ate it."

Then the LORD God said to the serpent:
"Because you have done this, you shall be banned
from all the animals

and from all the wild creatures;
on your belly shall you crawl,
    and dirt shall you eat
    all the days of your life.
I will put enmity between you and the woman,
    and between your offspring and hers;
he will strike at your head,
    while you strike at his heel."
The man called his wife Eve, because she became the mother of all the living. ✛

Psalm 98:1-4
R. Sing to the LORD a new song, for he has done marvelous deeds.
Sing to the LORD a new song,
    for he has done wondrous deeds;
his right hand has won victory for him,
    his holy arm. **R.**
The LORD has made his salvation known:
    in the sight of the nations he has revealed his justice.
He has remembered his kindness and his faithfulness
    toward the house of Israel. **R.**
All the ends of the earth have seen
    the salvation by our God.
Sing joyfully to the LORD, all you lands;
    break into song; sing praise. **R.**

† *Ephesians 1:3-6, 11-12*
He chose us in Christ before the foundation of the world.

Brothers and sisters:
Blessed be the God and Father of our Lord Jesus Christ,
    who has blessed us in Christ
    with every spiritual blessing in the heavens,
    as he chose us in him, before the foundation of the world,
    to be holy and without blemish before him.
In love he destined us for adoption to himself
        through Jesus Christ,
in accord with the favor of his will,
    for the praise of the glory of his grace
    that he granted us in the beloved.

In him we were also chosen,
>   destined in accord with the purpose of the One
>   who accomplishes all things according to the intention
>   of his will,
>   so that we might exist for the praise of his glory,
>   we who first hoped in Christ. ✛

cf. Luke 1:28
R. Alleluia, alleluia.
Hail, Mary, full of grace, the Lord is with you;
blessed are you among women. **R.**

† *Luke 1:26-38*
Hail, full of grace! The Lord is with you.

The angel Gabriel was sent from God
>   to a town of Galilee called Nazareth,
>   to a virgin betrothed to a man named Joseph,
>   of the house of David,
>   and the virgin's name was Mary.
And coming to her, he said,
>   "Hail, full of grace! The Lord is with you."
But she was greatly troubled at what was said
>   and pondered what sort of greeting this might be.
Then the angel said to her,
>   "Do not be afraid, Mary,
>   for you have found favor with God.
Behold, you will conceive in your womb and bear a son,
>   and you shall name him Jesus.
He will be great and will be called Son of the Most High,
>   and the Lord God will give him the throne of David his
>   father,
>   and he will rule over the house of Jacob forever,
>   and of his kingdom there will be no end."
But Mary said to the angel,
>   "How can this be,
>   since I have no relations with a man?"
And the angel said to her in reply,
>   "The Holy Spirit will come upon you,
>   and the power of the Most High will overshadow you.
Therefore the child to be born

will be called holy, the Son of God.
And behold, Elizabeth, your relative,
    has also conceived a son in her old age,
    and this is the sixth month for her who was called barren;
    for nothing will be impossible for God."
Mary said, "Behold, I am the handmaid of the Lord.
May it be done to me according to your word."
Then the angel departed from her. ✢

SATURDAY, DECEMBER 9
ADVENT WEEKDAY, BL. JUAN DIEGO

† Isaiah 30:19-21, 23-26
If you have mercy the Lord God will be
gracious to you when he hears your cry.

Thus says the Lord God,
    the Holy One of Israel:
O people of Zion, who dwell in Jerusalem,
    no more will you weep;
He will be gracious to you when you cry out,
    as soon as he hears he will answer you.
The Lord will give you the bread you need
    and the water for which you thirst,
No longer will your Teacher hide himself,
    but with your own eyes you shall see your Teacher,
While from behind, a voice shall sound in your ears:
    "This is the way; walk in it,"
    when you would turn to the right or to the left.

He will give rain for the seed
    that you sow in the ground,
And the wheat that the soil produces
    will be rich and abundant.
On that day your cattle will graze
    in spacious meadows;
The oxen and the asses that till the ground
    will eat silage tossed to them
    with shovel and pitchfork.
Upon every high mountain and lofty hill
    there will be streams of running water.
On the day of the great slaughter,

when the towers fall,
The light of the moon will be like that of the sun
    and the light of the sun will be seven times greater
    [like the light of seven days].
On the day the Lord binds up the wounds of his people,
    he will heal the bruises left by his blows. ✛

Psalm 147:1-6
R. Happy are all who long for the coming of the Lord.
Praise the Lord, for he is good;
    sing praise to our God, for he is gracious;
    it is fitting to praise him.
The Lord rebuilds Jerusalem;
    the dispersed of Israel he gathers. **R.**
He heals the brokenhearted
    and binds up their wounds.
He tells the number of the stars;
    he calls each by name. **R.**
Great is our Lord and mighty in power:
    to his wisdom there is no limit.
The Lord sustains the lowly;
    the wicked he casts to the ground. **R.**

Isaiah 45:8
R. Alleluia, alleluia.
 Let the clouds rain down the Just One,
and the earth bring forth a Savior. **R.**

† Matthew 9:35—10:1, 6-8
When Jesus saw the crowds he felt sorry for them.

Jesus toured all the towns and villages. He taught in their synagogues, he proclaimed the good news of God's reign, and he cured every sickness and disease. At the sight of the crowds, his heart was moved with pity. They were lying prostrate from exhaustion, like sheep without a shepherd. He said to his disciples: "The harvest is good but laborers are scarce. Beg the harvest master to send out laborers to gather his harvest."

Then he summoned his twelve disciples and gave them authority to expel unclean spirits and to cure sickness and disease of every kind. He gave them these instructions: "Go instead after the lost sheep of the house of Israel. As you go, make this announcement: 'The reign of God is at hand!' Cure the sick, raise the dead, heal the leprous, expel demons. The gift you have received, give as a gift." ✛

DECEMBER 10
SECOND SUNDAY OF ADVENT

† *Baruch 5:1-9*
Jerusalem, God will show your splendor.

Jerusalem, take off your robe of mourning and misery;
  put on the splendor of glory from God forever:
Wrapped in the cloak of justice from God,
  bear on your head the mitre
  that displays the glory of the eternal name.
For God will show all the earth your splendor:
  you will be named by God forever
  the peace of justice, the glory of God's worship.

Up, Jerusalem! Stand upon the heights;
  look to the east and see your children
gathered from the east and the west
  at the word of the Holy One,
  rejoicing that they are remembered by God.
Led away on foot by their enemies they left you:
  but God will bring them back to you
  borne aloft in glory as on royal thrones.
For God has commanded
  that every lofty mountain be made low,
and that the age-old depths and gorges
  be filled to level ground,
  that Israel may advance secure in the glory of God.
The forests and every fragrant kind of tree
  have overshadowed Israel at God's command;
for God is leading Israel in joy
  by the light of his glory,
  with his mercy and justice for company. ✛

Psalm 126:1-6
R. **The Lord has done great things for us; we are filled with joy.**
When the LORD brought back the captives of Zion,

we were like men dreaming.
Then our mouth was filled with laughter,
and our tongue with rejoicing. **R.**
Then they said among the nations,
"The LORD has done great things for them."
The LORD has done great things for us;
we are glad indeed. **R.**
Restore our fortunes, O LORD,
like the torrents in the southern desert.
Those who sow in tears
shall reap rejoicing. **R.**
Although they go forth weeping,
carrying the seed to be sown,
They shall come back rejoicing,
carrying their sheaves. **R.**

† *Philippians 1:4-6, 8-11*
Show yourselves pure and blameless for the day of Christ.

Brothers and sisters:
I pray always with joy in my every prayer for all of you,
because of your partnership for the gospel
from the first day until now.
I am confident of this,
that the one who began a good work in you
will continue to complete it
until the day of Christ Jesus.
God is my witness,
how I long for all of you with the affection of Christ Jesus.
And this is my prayer:
that your love may increase ever more and more
in knowledge and every kind of perception,
to discern what is of value,
so that you may be pure and blameless for the day of Christ,
filled with the fruit of righteousness
that comes through Jesus Christ
for the glory and praise of God. ✛

Luke 3:4, 6
R. Alleluia, alleluia.
Prepare the way of the Lord, make straight his paths:
all flesh shall see the salvation of God. **R.**

✝ *Luke 3:1-6*
All flesh shall see the salvation of God.

In the fifteenth year of the reign of Tiberius Caesar,
   when Pontius Pilate was governor of Judea,
   and Herod was tetrarch of Galilee,
   and his brother Philip tetrarch of the region of Ituraea and
      Trachonitis,
   and Lysanias was tetrarch of Abilene,
   during the high priesthood of Annas and Caiaphas,
   the word of God came to John the son of Zechariah
      in the desert.
John went throughout the whole region of the Jordan,
   proclaiming a baptism of repentance for the forgiveness
      of sins,
   as it is written in the book of the words of the prophet
      Isaiah:
A voice of one crying out in the desert:
"Prepare the way of the Lord,
   make straight his paths.
Every valley shall be filled
   and every mountain and hill shall be made low.
The winding roads shall be made straight,
   and the rough ways made smooth,
   and all flesh shall see the salvation of God." ✝

MONDAY, DECEMBER 11
ADVENT WEEKDAY, POPE DAMASUS I

✝ *Isaiah 35:1-10*
God will come and save you.

The desert and the parched land will exult;
   the steppe will rejoice and bloom.
They will bloom with abundant flowers,
   and rejoice with joyful song.
The glory of Lebanon will be given to them,
   the splendor of Carmel and Sharon;
They will see the glory of the Lord,
   the splendor of our God.

Strengthen the hands that are feeble,
   make firm the knees that are weak,

Say to those whose hearts are frightened:
   Be strong, fear not!
Here is your God,
   he comes with vindication;
With divine recompense
   he comes to save you.
Then will the eyes of the blind be opened,
   the ears of the deaf be cleared;
Then will the lame leap like a stag,
   then the tongue of the dumb will sing.

Streams will burst forth in the desert,
   and rivers in the steppe.
The burning sands will become pools,
   and the thirsty ground, springs of water;
The abode where jackals lurk
   will be a marsh for the reed and papyrus.
A highway will be there,
   called the holy way;
No one unclean may pass over it,
   nor fools go astray on it.
No lion will be there,
   nor beast of prey go up to be met upon it.
It is for those with a journey to make,
   and on it the redeemed will walk.
Those whom the Lord has ransomed will return
   and enter Zion singing,
   crowned with everlasting joy;
They will meet with joy and gladness,
   sorrow and mourning will flee. ✢

Psalm 85:9-14
R. Our God will come to save us!
I will hear what the Lord God proclaims;
   the Lord—for he proclaims peace to his people.
Near indeed is his salvation to those who fear him,
   glory dwelling in our land. **R.**
Kindness and truth shall meet;
   justice and peace shall kiss.
Truth shall spring out of the earth,
   and justice shall look down from heaven. **R.**

The Lord himself will give his benefits;
our land shall yield its increase.
Justice shall walk before him,
and salvation, along the way of his steps. **R.**

Luke 3:4, 6
R. Alleluia, alleluia.
Prepare the way for the Lord, make straight his paths:
all mankind shall see the salvation of God. **R.**

✝ Luke 5:17-26
We have seen wonderful things this day.

One day Jesus was teaching, and the power of the Lord made him heal. Sitting close by were Pharisees and teachers of the law who had come from every village of Galilee and from Judea and Jerusalem. Some men came along carrying a paralytic on a mat. They were trying to bring him in and lay him before Jesus; but they found no way of getting him through because of the crowd, so they went up on the roof. There they let him down with his mat through the tiles into the middle of the crowd before Jesus. Seeing their faith, Jesus said, "My friend, your sins are forgiven you."

The scribes and the Pharisees began a discussion, saying: "Who is this man who utters blasphemies? Who can forgive sins but God alone?" Jesus, however, knew their reasoning and answered them by saying: "Why do you harbor these thoughts? Which is easier: to say, 'Your sins are forgiven you,' or to say, 'Get up and walk'? In any case, to make it clear to you that the Son of Man has authority on earth to forgive sins" — he then addressed the paralyzed man: 'I say to you, get up! Take your mat with you, and return to your house."

At once the man stood erect before them. He picked up the mat he had been lying on and went home praising God. At this they were all seized with astonishment. Full of awe, they gave praise to God, saying, "We have seen incredible things today!" ✛

TUESDAY, DECEMBER 12
OUR LADY OF GUADALUPE

† *Zechariah 2:14-17*
Rejoice, daughter of Zion, for I am coming.

Sing and rejoice, O daughter Zion! See, I am coming to dwell among you, says the Lord. Many nations shall join themselves to the Lord on that day, and they shall be his people, and he will dwell among you, and you shall know that the Lord of hosts has sent me to you. The Lord will possess Judah as his portion in the holy land, and he will again choose Jerusalem. Silence, all mankind, in the presence of the Lord! for he stirs forth from his holy dwelling. ✛

Psalm 45:11-12, 14-15, 16-17
R. Listen to me daughter;
see and bend your ear.
Hear, O daughter, and see; turn your ear,
    forget your people and your father's house.
So shall the king desire your beauty;
    for he is your lord, and you must worship him. **R.**
All glorious is the king's daughter as she enters;
    her rainment is threaded with spun gold.
In embroidered apparel she is borne in to the king;
    behind her the virgins of her train are brought to you. **R.**
They are borne in with gladness and joy;
    they enter the palace of the king.
The place of your fathers your sons shall have;
    you shall make them princes through all the land. **R.**

Luke 1:28
R. Alleluia, alleluia.
Hail Mary, full of grace, the Lord is with you;
blessed are you among woman. **R.**

† *Luke 2:27-35*
A sword will pierce your own soul.

Simeon came to the temple, inspired by the Spirit; and when the parents brought in the child Jesus to perform for him the customary ritual of the law, he took him in his arms and blessed God in these words:

"Now, Master, you can dismiss your servant in peace;
   you have fulfilled your word.
For my eyes have witnessed your saving deed
   displayed for all the peoples to see:
A revealing light to the Gentiles,
   the glory of your people Israel."
The child's father and mother were marveling at what was
being said about him. Simeon blessed them and said to Mary
his mother: "This child is destined to be the downfall and the
rise of many in Israel, a sign that will be opposed—and you
yourself shall be pierced with a sword—so that the thoughts of
many hearts may be laid bare." ✛

WENESDAY, DECEMBER 13
St. Lucy

† Isaiah 40:25-31
The Lord God is almighty and gives strength to the weary.

To whom can you liken me as an equal?
   says the Holy One.
Lift up your eyes on high
   and see who has created these things:
He leads out their army and numbers them,
   calling them all by name.
By his great might and the strength of his power
   not one of them is missing!
Why, O Jacob, do you say,
   and declare, O Israel,
"My way is hidden from the Lord,
   and my right is disregarded by my God"?
Do you not know
   or have you not heard?
The Lord is the eternal God,
   creator of the ends of the earth.
He does not faint nor grow weary,
   and his knowledge is beyond scrutiny.
He gives strength to the fainting;
   for the weak he makes vigor abound.
Though young men faint and grow weary,
   and youths stagger and fall,

They that hope in the Lord will renew their strength,
    they will soar as with eagles' wings;
They will run and not grow weary,
    walk and not grow faint. ✢

Psalm 103:1-2, 3-4, 8, 10
R. O bless the Lord, my soul.
Bless the Lord, O my soul;
    and all my being, bless his holy name.
Bless the Lord, O my soul,
    and forget not all his benefits. **R.**
He pardons all your iniquities,
    he heals all your ills.
He redeems your life from destruction,
    he crowns you with kindness and compassion. **R.**
Merciful and gracious is the Lord,
    slow to anger and abounding in kindness.
Not according to our sins does he deal with us,
    nor does he requite us according to our crimes. **R.**

R. Alleluia, alleluia.
Behold, our Lord shall come with power
he will enlighten the eyes of his servants. **R.**

† *Matthew 11:28-30*
Come to me, all you who are overburdened.

Jesus said: "Come to me, all you who are weary and find life
burdensome, and I will refresh you. Take my yoke upon your
shoulders and learn from me, for I am gentle and humble of
heart. Your souls will find rest, for my yoke is easy and my
burden light." ✢

THURSDAY, DECEMBER 14
St. John of the Cross

† *Isaiah 41:13-20*
I am your redeemer, the Holy One of Israel.

I am the Lord, your God,
    who grasp your right hand;
It is I who say to you, "Fear not,

I will help you."
Fear not, O worm Jacob,
   O maggot Israel;
I will help you, says the Lord;
   your redeemer is the Holy One of Israel.
I will make of you a threshing sledge,
   sharp, new, and double-edged,
To thresh the mountains and crush them,
   to make the hills like chaff.
When you winnow them, the wind shall carry them off
   and the storm shall scatter them.
But you shall rejoice in the Lord,
   and glory in the Holy One of Israel.

The afflicted and the needy seek water in vain,
   their tongues are parched with thirst.
I, the Lord, will answer them;
   I, the God of Israel, will not forsake them.
I will open up rivers on the bare heights,
   and fountains in the broad valleys;
I will turn the desert into a marshland,
   and the dry ground into springs of water.
I will plant in the desert the cedar,
   acacia, myrtle, and olive;
I will set in the wasteland the cypress,
   together with the plane tree and the pine,
That all may see and know,
   observe and understand,
That the hand of the Lord has done this,
   the Holy One of Israel has created it. ✛

Psalm 145:1, 9, 10-11, 12-13
R. The Lord is kind and merciful;
   slow to anger, and rich in compassion.
I will extol you, O my God and King,
   and I will bless your name forever and ever.
The Lord is good to all
   and compassionate toward all his works. **R.**
Let all your works give you thanks, O Lord,
   and let your faithful ones bless you.

Let them discourse of the glory of your kingdom
  and speak of your might. **R.**
Let them make known to men your might
  and the glorious splendor of your kingdom.
Your kingdom is a kingdom for all ages,
  and your dominion endures through all generations. **R.**

R. Alleluia, alleluia.
Come, Lord, bring to us your peace;
let us rejoice before you with a perfect heart. **R.**

† *Matthew 11:11-15*
No greater than John the Baptizer has been born.

Jesus said to the crowds: "I solemnly assure you, history has not known a man born of woman greater than John the Baptizer. Yet the least born into the kingdom of God is greater than he. From John the Baptizer's time until now the kingdom of God has suffered violence, and the violent take it by force. All the prophets as well as the law spoke prophetically until John. If you are prepared to accept it, he is Elijah, the one who was certain to come. Heed carefully what you hear!" ✛

FRIDAY, DECEMBER 15
ADVENT WEEKDAY

† *Isaiah 48:17-19*
If only you had listened to my commandments.

Thus says the LORD, your redeemer,
  the Holy One of Israel:
I, the Lord, your God,
  teach you what is for your good,
  and lead you on the way you should go.
If you would hearken to my commandments,
  your prosperity would be like a river,
  and your vindication like the waves of the sea;
Your descendants would be like the sand,
  and those born of your stock like its grains,
Their name never cut off
  or blotted out from my presence. ✛

Psalm 1:1-2, 3, 4, 6

**R. Those who follow you, Lord,
will have the light of life.**

Happy the man who follows not
   the counsel of the wicked
Nor walks in the way of sinners,
   nor sits in the company of the insolent,
But delights in the law of the Lord
   and meditates on his law day and night. **R.**
He is like a tree
   planted near running water,
That yields its fruit in due season,
   and whose leaves never fade.
[Whatever he does, prospers.] **R.**
Not so the wicked, not so;
   they are like chaff which the wind drives away.
For the Lord watches over the way of the just,
   but the way of the wicked vanishes. **R.**

R. Alleluia, alleluia.
Behold, the king will come, the Lord of earth:
and he will set us free. **R.**

✝ *Matthew 11:16-19*
They listened to neither John nor the Son of Man.

Jesus said to the crowds: "What comparison can I use to describe this breed? They are like children squatting in the town squares, calling to their playmates:
   'We piped you a tune but you did not dance!
   We sang you a dirge but you did not wail!'
   In other words, John appeared neither eating nor drinking, and people say, 'He is mad!' The Son of Man appeared eating and drinking, and they say, 'This one is a glutton and drunkard, a lover of tax collectors and those outside the law!' Yet time will prove where wisdom lies." ✝

SATURDAY, DECEMBER 16
ADVENT WEEKDAY

† *Sirach 48:1-4, 9-11*
Elijah came to them.

Like a fire there appeared the prophet Elijah
  whose words were as a flaming furnace.
Their staff of bread he shattered,
  in his zeal he reduced them to straits;
By God's word he shut up the heavens
  and three times brought down fire.
How awesome are you, Elijah!
  Whose glory is equal to yours?
You were taken aloft in a whirlwind,
  in a chariot with fiery horses.
You are destined, it is written, in time to come
  to put an end to wrath before the day of the Lord,
To turn back the hearts of fathers toward their sons,
  and to re-establish the tribes of Jacob.
Blessed is he who shall have seen you before he dies. ✢

Psalm 80:2-3, 15-16, 18-19
**R. Lord, make us turn to you,
  let us see your face and we shall be saved.**
O shepherd of Israel, hearken,
  from your throne upon the cherubim, shine forth.
Rouse your power,
  and come to save us. **R.**
Once again, O Lord of hosts,
  look down from heaven, and see;
Take care of this vine,
  and protect what your right hand has planted
  [the son of man whom you yourself made strong]. **R.**
May your help be with the man of your right hand,
  with the son of man whom you yourself made strong.
Then we will no more withdraw from you;
  give us new life, and we will call upon your name. **R.**

R. Alleluia, alleluia.
The day of the Lord is near;
he comes to save us. **R.**

✛ *Matthew 17:10-13*
Elijah has already come and they did not know him.

As they were coming down the mountainside, the disciples put this question to Jesus: "Why do the scribes claim that Elijah must come first?" In reply he said: "Elijah is indeed coming, and he will restore everything. I assure you, though, that Elijah has already come, but they did not recognize him and they did as they pleased with him. The Son of Man will suffer at their hands in the same way." The disciples then realized that he had been speaking to them about John the Baptizer. ✛

DECEMBER 17
THIRD SUNDAY OF ADVENT

✛ *Zephaniah 3:14-18a*
The Lord will rejoice over you with gladness.

Shout for joy, O daughter Zion!
    Sing joyfully, O Israel!
Be glad and exult with all your heart,
    O daughter Jerusalem!
The LORD has removed the judgment against you
    he has turned away your enemies;
the King of Israel, the LORD, is in your midst,
    you have no further misfortune to fear.
On that day, it shall be said to Jerusalem:
    Fear not, O Zion, be not discouraged!
The LORD, your God, is in your midst,
    a mighty savior;
he will rejoice over you with gladness,
    and renew you in his love,
he will sing joyfully because of you,
    as one sings at festivals. ✛

Isaiah 12:2-6

R. Cry out with joy and gladness: for among you is the great and Holy One of Israel.

God indeed is my savior;
    I am confident and unafraid.
My strength and my courage is the LORD,
    and he has been my savior.
With joy you will draw water
    at the fountain of salvation. **R.**
Give thanks to the LORD, acclaim his name;
    among the nations make known his deeds,
    proclaim how exalted is his name. **R.**
Sing praise to the LORD for his glorious achievement;
    let this be known throughout all the earth.
Shout with exultation, O city of Zion,
    for great in your midst
    is the Holy One of Israel! **R.**

✝ *Philippians 4:4-7*
The Lord is near.

Brothers and sisters:
Rejoice in the Lord always.
I shall say it again: rejoice!
Your kindness should be known to all.
The Lord is near.
Have no anxiety at all, but in everything,
    by prayer and petition, with thanksgiving,
    make your requests known to God.
Then the peace of God that surpasses all understanding
    will guard your hearts and minds in Christ Jesus. ✝

Isaiah 61:1 (cited in Luke 4:18)

R. Alleluia, alleluia.

The Spirit of the Lord is upon me,
because he has anointed me
    to bring glad tidings to the poor. **R.**

† Luke 3:10-18
What should we do?

The crowds asked John the Baptist,
  "What should we do?"
He said to them in reply,
  "Whoever has two cloaks
  should share with the person who has none.
And whoever has food should do likewise."
Even tax collectors came to be baptized and they said to him,
  "Teacher, what should we do?"
He answered them,
  "Stop collecting more than what is prescribed."
Soldiers also asked him,
  "And what is it that we should do?"
He told them,
  "Do not practice extortion,
  do not falsely accuse anyone,
  and be satisfied with your wages."

Now the people were filled with expectation,
  and all were asking in their hearts
  whether John might be the Christ.
John answered them all, saying,
  "I am baptizing you with water,
  but one mightier than I is coming.
I am not worthy to loosen the thongs of his sandals.
He will baptize you with the Holy Spirit and fire.
His winnowing fan is in his hand to clear his threshing floor
  and to gather the wheat into his barn,
  but the chaff he will burn with unquenchable fire."
Exhorting them in many other ways,
  he preached good news to the people. ✝

MONDAY, DECEMBER 18
LATE ADVENT WEEKDAY

† Jeremiah 23:5-8
I will raise a virtuous branch for David.

Behold, the days are coming, says the Lord,
  when I will raise up a righteous shoot to David;

As king he shall reign and govern wisely,
he shall do what is just and right in the land.
In his days Judah shall be saved,
Israel shall dwell in security.
This is the name they give him:
"The Lord our justice."

Therefore, the days will come, says the Lord, when they shall no longer say, "As the Lord lives, who brought the Israelites out of the land of Egypt"; but rather, "As the Lord lives, who brought the descendants of the house of Israel up from the land of the north"—and from all the lands to which I banished them; they shall again live on their own land. ✙

Psalm 72:1, 12-13, 18-19
**R. Justice shall flourish in his time,
and fullness of peace for ever.**
O God, with your judgment endow the king,
and with your justice, the king's son;
He shall govern your people with justice
and your afflicted ones with judgment. **R.**
For he shall rescue the poor man when he cries out,
and the afflicted when he has no one to help him.
He shall have pity for the lowly and the poor;
the lives of the poor he shall save. **R.**
Blessed be the Lord, the God of Israel,
who alone does wondrous deeds.
And blessed forever be his glorious name;
may the whole earth be filled with his glory. Amen. Amen. **R.**

R. Alleluia, alleluia.
Come,
Leader of ancient Israel,
giver of the Law to Moses on Sinai:
rescue us with your mighty power! **R.**

† *Matthew 1:18-24*
Jesus was born of Mary, the betrothed of Joseph, a son of David.

Now this is how the birth of Jesus Christ came about. When his mother Mary was engaged to Joseph, but before they lived together, she was found with child through the power of the Holy Spirit. Joseph her husband, an upright man unwilling to expose her to the law, decided to divorce her quietly. Such was his intention when suddenly the angel of the Lord appeared in a dream and said to him: "Joseph, son of David, have no fear about taking Mary as your wife. It is by the Holy Spirit that she has conceived this child. She is to have a son and you are to name him Jesus because he will save his people from their sins." All this happened to fulfill what the Lord had said through the prophet:

"The virgin shall be with child
and give birth to a son,
and they shall call him Emmanuel,"

a name which means "God is with us." When Joseph awoke he did as the angel of the Lord had directed him and received her into his home as his wife. He had no relations with her at any time before she bore a son, whom he named Jesus. ✛

TUESDAY, DECEMBER 19
LATE ADVENT WEEKDAY

† *Judges 13:2-7, 24-25*
The birth of Samson was announced by an angel.

There was a certain man from Zorah, of the clan of the Danites, whose name was Manoah. His wife was barren and had borne no children. An angel of the Lord appeared to the woman and said to her, "Though you are barren and have had no children, yet you will conceive and bear a son. Now, then, be careful to take no wine or strong drink and to eat nothing unclean. As for the son you will conceive and bear, no razor shall touch his head, for this boy is to be consecrated to God from the womb. It is he who will begin the deliverance of Israel from the power of the Philistines."

The woman went and told her husband, "A man of God came to me; he had the appearance of an angel of God, terrible indeed. I did not ask him where he came from, nor did he tell me his name. But he said to me, 'You will be with child and will bear a son. So take neither wine nor strong drink, and eat nothing unclean. For the boy shall be consecrated to God from the womb, until the day of his death.'"

The woman bore a son and named him Samson. The boy grew up and the Lord blessed him. The spirit of the Lord began to be with him. ✛

Psalm 71:3-6, 16-17

**R. Fill me with your praise
and I will sing your glory!**

Be my rock of refuge,
   a stronghold to give me safety,
   for you are my rock and my fortress.
O my God, rescue me from the hand of the wicked. **R.**
For you are my hope, O Lord;
   my trust, O God, from my youth.
On you I depend from birth;
   from my mother's womb you are my strength. **R.**
I will treat of the mighty works of the Lord;
   O God, I will tell of your singular justice.
O God, you have taught me from my youth,
   and till the present I proclaim your wondrous deeds. **R.**

R. Alleluia, alleluia.
Come,
Flower of Jesse's stem,
sign of God's love for all his people:
save us without delay! **R.**

† *Luke 1:5-25*
The birth of John the Baptizer was announced by Gabriel.

In the days of Herod, king of Judea, there was a priest named
Zechariah of the priestly class of Abijah; his wife was a descendant of Aaron named Elizabeth. Both were just in the eyes of
God, blamelessly following all the commandments and ordinances of the Lord. They were childless, for Elizabeth was
sterile; moreover, both were advanced in years.

   Once, when it was the turn of Zechariah's class and he was
fulfilling his functions as a priest before God, it fell to him by lot
according to priestly usage to enter the sanctuary of the Lord
and offer incense. While the full assembly of people was praying
outside at the incense hour, an angel of the Lord appeared to
him, standing at the right of the altar of incense. Zechariah was
deeply disturbed upon seeing him, and overcome by fear.

   The angel said to him: "Do not be frightened, Zechariah; your
prayer has been heard. Your wife Elizabeth shall bear a son
whom you shall name John. Joy and gladness will be yours, and

many will rejoice at his birth; for he will be great in the eyes of the Lord. He will never drink wine or strong drink, and he will be filled with the Holy Spirit from his mother's womb. Many of the sons of Israel will he bring back to the Lord their God. God himself will go before him, in the spirit and power of Elijah, to turn the hearts of fathers to their children and the rebellious to the wisdom of the just, and to prepare for the Lord a people well-disposed."

Zechariah said to the angel: "How am I to know this? I am an old man; my wife too is advanced in age."

The angel replied: "I am Gabriel, who stand in attendance before God. I was sent to speak to you and bring you this good news. But now you will be mute — unable to speak — until the day when these things take place, because you have not trusted my words. They will all come true in due season." Meanwhile, the people were waiting for Zechariah, wondering at his delay in the temple. When he finally came out he was unable to speak to them, and they realized that he had seen a vision inside. He kept making signs to them, for he remained speechless.

Then, when his period of priestly service was over, he went home.

Afterward, his wife Elizabeth conceived. She went into seclusion for five months, saying, "In these days the Lord is acting on my behalf; he has seen fit to remove my reproach among men." ✝

WEDNESDAY, DECEMBER 20
Late Advent Weekday

† Isaiah 7:10-14
The virgin shall conceive.

The Lord spoke to Ahaz: Ask for a sign from the Lord, your God; let it be deep as the nether world, or high as the sky! But Ahaz answered, "I will not ask! I will not tempt the Lord!" Then he said: Listen, O house of David! Is it not enough for you to weary men, must you also weary my God? Therefore the Lord himself will give you this sign: the virgin shall be with child, and bear a son, and shall name him Immanuel [because "God is with us"]. ✝

Psalm 24:1-6

**R. Let the Lord enter;
he is king of glory.**

The Lord's are the earth and its fullness;
  the world and those who dwell in it.
For he founded it upon the seas
  and established it upon the rivers. **R.**
Who can ascend the mountain of the Lord?
  or who may stand in his holy place?
He whose hands are sinless, whose heart is clean,
  who desires not what is vain. **R.**
He shall receive a blessing from the Lord,
  a reward from God his savior.
Such is the race that seeks for him,
  that seeks the face of the God of Jacob. **R.**

R. Alleluia, alleluia.
Come,
Key of David,
opening the gates of God's eternal Kingdom:
free the prisoners of darkness! **R.**

† *Luke 1:26-38*
You are to conceive and bear a son.

In the sixth month, the angel Gabriel was sent from God to a town of Galilee named Nazareth, to a virgin betrothed to a man named Joseph, of the house of David. The virgin's name was Mary. Upon arriving, the messenger said to her: "Rejoice, O highly favored daughter! The Lord is with you. Blessed are you among women." She was deeply troubled by his words, and wondered what his greeting meant. The messenger went on to say to her: "Do not fear, Mary. You have found favor with God. You shall conceive and bear a son and give him the name Jesus. Great will be his dignity and he will be called Son of the Most High. The Lord God will give him the throne of David his father. He will rule over the house of Jacob forever and his reign will be without end."

Mary said to the angel, "How can this be since I do not know man?" The angel answered her: "The Holy Spirit will come upon you and the power of the Most High will overshadow you;

hence, the holy offspring to be born will be called Son of God. Know that Elizabeth your kinswoman has conceived a son in her old age; she who was thought to be sterile is now in her sixth month, for nothing is impossible with God."

Mary said: "I am the maidservant of the Lord. Let it be done to me as you say." With that the angel left her. ✛

THURSDAY, DECEMBER 21
LATE ADVENT WEEKDAY, ST. PETER CANISIUS

† *The Song of Solomon 2:8-14 (or Zephaniah 3:14-18)*
I hear my beloved, see how he comes leaping on the mountains.

Hark! my lover—here he comes
    springing across the mountains,
    leaping across the hills.
My lover is like a gazelle
    or a young stag.
Here he stands behind our wall,
    gazing through the windows,
    peering through the lattices.
My lover speaks; he says to me,
    "Arise, my beloved, my beautiful one,
    and come!

"For see, the winter is past,
    the rains are over and gone.
The flowers appear on the earth,
    the time of pruning the vines has come,
    and the song of the dove is heard in our land.
The fig tree puts forth its figs,
    and the vines, in bloom, give forth fragrance.
Arise, my beloved, my beautiful one,
    and come!

"O my dove in the clefts of the rock,
    in the secret recesses of the cliff,
Let me see you,
    let me hear your voice,
For your voice is sweet,
    and you are lovely." ✛

Psalm 33:2-3, 11-12, 20-21

**R. Cry out with joy in the Lord, you holy ones;
sing a new song to him.**

Give thanks to the Lord on the harp;
  with the ten-stringed lyre chant his praises.
Sing to him a new song;
  pluck the strings skillfully, with shouts of gladness. **R.**
The plan of the Lord stands forever;
  the design of his heart, through all generations.
Happy the nation whose God is the Lord,
  the people he has chosen for his own inheritance. **R.**
Our soul waits for the Lord,
  who is our help and our shield,
For in him our hearts rejoice;
  in his holy name we trust. **R.**

R. Alleluia, alleluia.
Come,
Radiant Dawn,
splendor of eternal light, sun of justice:
shine on those lost in the darkness of death! **R.**

† Luke 1:39-45
Why should I be honored with a visit from the mother of my Lord?

Mary set out, proceeding in haste into the hill country to a
town of Judah, where she entered Zechariah's house and
greeted Elizabeth. When Elizabeth heard Mary's greeting, the
baby stirred in her womb. Elizabeth was filled with the Holy
Spirit, and cried out in a loud voice: "Blessed are you among
women and blessed is the fruit of your womb. But who am I
that the mother of my Lord should come to me? The moment
your greeting sounded in my ears, the baby stirred in my womb
for joy. Blessed is she who trusted that the Lord's words to her
would be fulfilled." ✛

FRIDAY, DECEMBER 22
LATE ADVENT WEEKDAY

✝ *1 Samuel 1:24-28*
Hannah gave thanks for the birth of Samuel.

Hannah brought Samuel with her, along with a three-year-old bull, an ephah of flour, and a skin of wine, and presented him at the temple of the Lord in Shiloh. After the boy's father had sacrificed the young bull, Hannah, his mother, approached Eli and said: "Pardon, my lord! As you live, my lord, I am the woman who stood near you here, praying to the Lord. I prayed for this child, and the Lord granted my request. Now I, in turn, give him to the Lord; as long as he lives, he shall be dedicated to the Lord." She left him there. ✛

1 Samuel 2:1, 4-8
R. My heart rejoices in the Lord, my Savior.
My heart exults in the Lord,
    my horn is exalted in my God.
I have swallowed up my enemies;
    I rejoice in my victory. **R.**
The bows of the mighty are broken,
    while the tottering gird on strength.
The well-fed hire themselves out for bread,
    while the hungry batten on spoil.
The barren wife bears seven sons,
    while the mother of many languishes. **R.**
The Lord puts to death and gives life;
    he casts down to the nether world;
    he raises up again.
The Lord makes poor and makes rich,
    he humbles, he also exalts. **R.**
He raises the needy from the dust;
    from the ash heap he lifts up the poor,
To seat them with nobles
    and make a glorious throne their heritage. **R.**

R. Alleluia, alleluia.
Come,
King of all nations,

source of your Church's unity and faith:
save all mankind, your own creation! **R.**

† Luke 1:46-56
He who has done great things for me is powerful.

Mary said:
"My being proclaims the greatness of the Lord,
    my spirit finds joy in God my savior,
For he has looked upon his servant in her lowliness;
    all ages to come shall call me blessed.
God who is mighty has done great things for me,
    holy is his name;
His mercy is from age to age
    on those who fear him.
"He has shown might with his arm;
    he has confused the proud in their inmost thoughts.
He has deposed the mighty from their thrones
    and raised the lowly to high places.
The hungry he has given every good thing,
    while the rich he has sent empty away.
He has upheld Israel his servant,
    ever mindful of his mercy;
Even as he promised our fathers,
    promised Abraham and his descendants forever."
    Mary remained with Elizabeth about three months and
then returned home. **✝**

SATURDAY, DECEMBER 23
LATE ADVENT WEEKDAY, ST. JOHN OF KANTY

† Malachi 3:1-4. 23-24
*I shall send you the prophet Elijah as
a sign that the day of the Lord is near.*

Lo, I am sending my messenger
    to prepare the way before me;
And suddenly there will come to the temple
    the Lord whom you seek,
And the messenger of the covenant whom you desire.
    Yes, he is coming, says the Lord of hosts.
But who will endure the day of his coming?

And who can stand when he appears?
For he is like the refiner's fire,
    or like the fuller's lye.
He will sit refining and purifying [silver],
    and he will purify the sons of Levi,
Refining them like gold or like silver
    that they may offer due sacrifice to the Lord.
Then the sacrifice of Judah and Jerusalem
    will please the Lord,
    as in the days of old, as in years gone by.

Lo, I will send you
    Elijah, the prophet,
Before the day of the Lord comes,
    the great and terrible day,
To turn the hearts of the fathers to their children,
    and the hearts of the children to their fathers,
Lest I come and strike
    the land with doom. +

Psalm 25:4-5, 8-9, 10, 14
**R. Lift up your heads and see;
    your redemption is near at hand.**
Your ways, O Lord, make known to me;
    teach me your paths,
Guide me in your truth and teach me,
    for you are God my savior. **R.**
Good and upright is the Lord;
    thus he shows sinners the way.
He guides the humble to justice,
    he teaches the humble his way. **R.**
All the paths of the Lord are kindness and constancy
    toward those who keep his covenant and his decrees.
The friendship of the Lord is with those who fear him,
    and his covenant, for their instruction. **R.**

R. Alleluia, alleluia
Come,
Emmanuel.
God's presence among us, our King, our Judge:
save us, Lord our God! **R.**

† *Luke 1:57-66*
The birth of John the Baptizer.

When Elizabeth's time for delivery arrived, she gave birth to a son. Her neighbors and relatives, upon hearing that the Lord had extended his mercy to her, rejoiced with her. When they assembled for the circumcision of the child on the eighth day, they intended to name him after his father Zechariah. At this his mother intervened, saying, "No, he is to be called John."

They pointed out to her, "None of your relatives has this name." Then, using signs, they asked the father what he wished him to be called.

He signaled for a writing tablet and wrote the words, "His name is John." This astonished them all. At that moment his mouth was opened and his tongue loosed, and he began to speak in praise of God.

Fear descended on all in the neighborhood; throughout the hill country of Judea these happenings began to be recounted to the last detail. All who heard stored these things in their hearts, saying, "What will this child be?" and, "Was not the hand of the Lord upon him?" ✛

DECEMBER 24
FOURTH SUNDAY OF ADVENT

† *Micah 5:1-4a*
From you shall come forth the ruler of Israel.

Thus says the LORD:
You, Bethlehem-Ephrathah
    too small to be among the clans of Judah,
from you shall come forth for me
    one who is to be ruler in Israel;
whose origin is from of old,
    from ancient times.
Therefore the Lord will give them up, until the time
    when she who is to give birth has borne,
and the rest of his kindred shall return
    to the children of Israel.
He shall stand firm and shepherd his flock
    by the strength of the LORD,

in the majestic name of the LORD, his God;
and they shall remain, for now his greatness
    shall reach to the ends of the earth;
    he shall be peace. ✛

Psalm 80:2-3, 15-16, 18-19
**R. Lord, make us turn to you; let us see your face and
we shall be saved.**
O shepherd of Israel, hearken,
    from your throne upon the cherubim, shine forth.
Rouse your power,
    and come to save us. **R.**
Once again, O LORD of hosts,
    look down from heaven, and see;
take care of this vine,
    and protect what your right hand has planted
    the son of man whom you yourself made strong. **R.**
May your help be with the man of your right hand,
    with the son of man whom you yourself made strong.
Then we will no more withdraw from you;
    give us new life, and we will call upon your name. **R.**

† Hebrews 10:5-10
Behold, I come to do your will.

Brothers and sisters:
When Christ came into the world, he said:
    "Sacrifice and offering you did not desire,
        but a body you prepared for me;
    in holocausts and sin offerings you took no delight.
    Then I said, 'As is written of me in the scroll,
    behold, I come to do your will, O God.'"

First he says, "Sacrifices and offerings,
    holocausts and sin offerings,
    you neither desired nor delighted in."
These are offered according to the law.
Then he says, "Behold, I come to do your will."
He takes away the first to establish the second.
By this "will, " we have been consecrated
    through the offering of the body of Jesus
        Christ once for all. ✛

Luke 1:38

R. Alleluia, alleluia.

Behold, I am the handmaid of the Lord.

May it be done to me according to your word. **R.**

† *Luke 1:39-45*

*And how does this happen to me, that
the mother of my Lord should come to me ?*

Mary set out

and traveled to the hill country in haste

to a town of Judah,

where she entered the house of Zechariah

and greeted Elizabeth.

When Elizabeth heard Mary's greeting,

the infant leaped in her womb,

and Elizabeth, filled with the Holy Spirit,

cried out in a loud voice and said,

"Blessed are you among women,

and blessed is the fruit of your womb.

And how does this happen to me,

that the mother of my Lord should come to me?

For at the moment the sound of your greeting reached my ears,

the infant in my womb leaped for joy.

Blessed are you who believed

that what was spoken to you by the Lord

would be fulfilled." ✢

MONDAY, DECEMBER 25
CHRISTMAS, THE NATIVITY OF THE LORD

(These readings are from Mass at Dawn. For Christmas Vigil: Isaiah 62:1-5
• Psalm 89:4-5, 16-17, 27, 29 • Acts 13:16-17, 22-25 • Matthew 1:1-25; For
Midnight Mass: Isaiah 9:1-6 • Psalm 96:1-3, 11-13 • Titus 2:11-14 • Luke 2:1-
14; For Mass during the Day: Isaiah 52:7-10 • Psalm 98:1-6 • Hebrews 1:1-
6 • John 1:1-18 or 1:1-5, 9-14)

† *Isaiah 62:11-12*

Behold, your Savior comes!

See, the LORD proclaims

to the ends of the earth:

say to daughter Zion,

your savior comes!
Here is his reward with him,
  his recompense before him.
They shall be called the holy people,
  the redeemed of the LORD,
and you shall be called "Frequented, "
  a city that is not forsaken. ✛

Psalm 97:1, 6, 11-12
**R. A light will shine on us this day:
the Lord is born for us.**
The LORD is king; let the earth rejoice;
  let the many islands be glad.
The heavens proclaim his justice,
  and all peoples see his glory. **R.**
Light dawns for the just;
  and gladness, for the upright of heart.
Be glad in the LORD, you just,
  and give thanks to his holy name. **R.**

† *Titus 3:4-7*
Because of his mercy, he saved us.

Beloved:
When the kindness and generous love
  of God our savior appeared,
not because of any righteous deeds we had done
  but because of his mercy,
He saved us through the bath of rebirth
  and renewal by the Holy Spirit,
whom he richly poured out on us
  through Jesus Christ our savior,
so that we might be justified by his grace
  and become heirs in hope of eternal life. ✛

Luke 2:14
R. Alleluia, alleluia.
Glory to God in the highest,
and on earth peace to those
on whom his favor rests. **R.**

† *Luke 2:15-20*
The shepherds found Mary and Joseph and the infant.

When the angels went away from them to heaven,
the shepherds said to one another,
"Let us go, then, to Bethlehem
to see this thing that has taken place,
which the Lord has made known to us."
So they went in haste and found Mary and Joseph,
and the infant lying in the manger.
When they saw this,
they made known the message
that had been told them about this child.
All who heard it were amazed
by what had been told them by the shepherds.
And Mary kept all these things,
reflecting on them in her heart.
Then the shepherds returned,
glorifying and praising God
for all they had heard and seen,
just as it had been told to them. ✢

TUESDAY, DECEMBER 26
St. Stephen

† *Acts 6:8-10; 7:54-59*
I can see heaven thrown open.

Stephen was a man filled with grace and power, who worked great wonders and signs among the people. Certain members of the so-called "Synagogue of Roman Freedmen" (that is, the Jews from Cyrene, Alexandria, Cilicia and Asia) would undertake to engage Stephen in debate, but they proved no match for the wisdom and spirit with which he spoke.

Those who listened to his words were stung to the heart; they ground their teeth in anger at him. Stephen meanwhile, filled with the Holy Spirit, looked to the sky above and saw the glory of God, and Jesus standing at God's right hand. "Look!" he exclaimed, "I see an opening in the sky, and the Son of Man standing at God's right hand." The onlookers were shouting aloud, holding their hands over their ears as they did so. Then they rushed at him as one man, dragged him out of the city, and began to stone him. The witnesses meanwhile were piling their cloaks at the feet of a young man named Saul. As Stephen was being stoned he could be heard praying, "Lord Jesus, receive my spirit." ✝

Psalm 31: 3-4, 6,7,8, 17, 21
R. Into your hands, O Lord,
I entrust my spirit.
Be my rock of refuge,
a stronghold to give me safety.
You are my rock and my fortress;
for your name's stake you will lead and guide me. **R.**
Into your hands I commend my spirit;
you will redeem me, O Lord, O faithful God.
But my trust is in the Lord.
I will rejoice and be glad of your kindness. **R.**
Let your face shine upon your servant;
save me in your kindness.
You hide them in the shelter of your presence
from the plottings of men. **R.**

Psalm 118:26, 27
R. Alleluia, alleluia.
Blessed is he who comes in the name of the Lord;
the Lord God shines upon us. **R.**

† *Matthew 10:17-22*
It is not you who will be speaking but the Spirit of your Father.

Jesus said to his apostles: "Be on guard with respect to others. They will hale you into court, they will flog you in their synagogues. You will be brought to trial before rulers and kings, to give witness before them and before the Gentiles on my account. When they hand you over, do not worry about what you will say or how you will say it. When the hour comes, you will be given what you are to say. You yourselves will not be the speakers; the Spirit of your Father will be speaking in you.

"Brother will hand over brother to death, and the father his child; children will turn against parents and have them put to death. You will be hated by all on account of me. But whoever holds out till the end will escape death." ✝

WEDNESDAY, DECEMBER 27
St. John

† 1 John 1:1-4
What we have seen and heard we are making known to you.

This is what we proclaim to you:
what was from the beginning,
what we have heard,
what we have seen with our eyes,
what we have looked upon
and our hands have touched—
we speak of the word of life.
(This life became visible;
we have seen and bear witness to it,
and we proclaim to you the eternal life
that was present to the Father
and became visible to us.)
What we have seen and heard
we proclaim in turn to you
so that you may share life with us.
This fellowship of ours is with the Father
and with his Son, Jesus Christ.
Indeed, our purpose in writing you this
is that our joy may be complete. ✛

Psalm 97:1-2, 5-6, 11-12
R. Let good men rejoice in the Lord.
The Lord is king; let the earth rejoice;
   let the many isles be glad.
Clouds and darkness are round about him,
   justice and judgment are the foundation of his throne. **R.**
The mountains melt like wax before the Lord,
   before the Lord of all the earth.
The heavens proclaim his justice,
   and all peoples see his glory. **R.**
Light dawns for the just;
   and gladness, for the upright of heart.
Be glad in the Lord, you just,
   and give thanks to his holy name. **R.**

R. Alleluia, alleluia.
We praise you, God, we acknowledge you as Lord;
your glorious band of apostles extols you. **R.**

✝ *John 20:2-8*
The other disciple outran Peter and came first to the tomb.

On the first day of the week Mary Magdalene ran off to Simon Peter and the other disciples (the one Jesus loved) and told them, "The Lord has been taken from the tomb! We do not know where they have put him!"

At that, Peter and the other disciple started out on their way toward the tomb. They were running side by side, but then the other disciple outran Peter and reached the tomb first. He did not enter but bent down to peer in, and saw the wrappings lying on the ground. Presently, Simon Peter came along behind him and entered the tomb. He observed the wrappings on the ground and saw the piece of cloth which had covered the head not lying with the wrappings, but rolled up in a place by itself. Then the disciple who had arrived first at the tomb went in. He saw and believed. ✛

THURSDAY, DECEMBER 28
THE HOLY INNOCENTS

✝ *1 John 1:5—2:2*
The blood of Jesus Christ cleanses us of all sin.

Here, then, is the message
we have heard from Jesus Christ
and announced to you:
that God is light;
in him there is no darkness.

If we say, "We have fellowship with him,"
while continuing to walk in darkness,
we are liars and do not act in truth.
But if we walk in light,
as he is in the light,
we have fellowship with one another,
and the blood of his Son Jesus cleanses us from all sin.
If we say, "We are free of the guilt of sin,"

we deceive ourselves; the truth is not to be found in us.
But if we acknowledge our sins,
he who is just can be trusted
to forgive our sins
and cleanse us from every wrong.
If we say, "We have never sinned,"
we make him a liar
and his word finds no place in us.

My little ones,
I am writing this to keep you from sin.
But if anyone should sin,
we have in the presence of the Father,
Jesus Christ, an intercessor who is just.
He is an offering for our sins,
and not for our sins only,
but for those of the whole world. ✛

Psalm 124:2-3, 4-5, 7-8
**R. Our soul has escaped like a bird from
the hunter's net.**
Had not the Lord been with us—
    when men rose up against us,
Then would they have swallowed us alive.
    When their fury was inflamed against us. **R.**
Then would the waters have overwhelmed us;
    the torrent would have swept over us;
Over us then would have swept
    the raging waters. **R.**
Broken was the snare,
    and we were freed.
Our help is in the name of the Lord,
    who made heaven and earth. **R.**

R. Alleluia, alleluia.
We praise you, God; we acknowledge you as Lord;
the radiant army of martyrs acclaims you. **R.**

† *Matthew 2:13-18*

Herod killed all the male children who were in Bethlehem.

After the Magi had left, the angel of the Lord suddenly appeared in a dream to Joseph with the command: "Get up, take the child and his mother, and flee to Egypt. Stay there until I tell you otherwise. Herod is searching for the child to destroy him" Joseph got up and took the child and his mother and left that night for Egypt. He stayed there until the death of Herod, to fulfill what the Lord had said through the prophet: "Out of Egypt I have called my son."
Once Herod realized that he had been deceived by the astrologers, he became furious. He ordered the massacre of all the boys two years old and under in Bethlehem and its environs, making his calculations on the basis of the date he had learned from the astrologers. What was said through Jeremiah the prophet was then fulfilled:
"A cry was heard at Ramah,
    sobbing and loud lamentation:
Rachel bewailing her children;
    no comfort for her, since they are no more." ✝

FRIDAY, DECEMBER 29
FIFTH DAY IN OCTAVE OF CHRISTMAS, ST. THOMAS BECKET

† *1 John 2:3-11*
He who loves his brother lives in the light.

The way we can be sure of our knowledge of Jesus
    is to keep his commandments.
The man who claims, "I have known him,"
    without keeping his commandments,
    is a liar; in such a one there is no truth.
But whoever keeps his word
    truly has the love of God made perfect in him.
The way we can be sure we are in union with him
    is if one who claims to abide in him
    conducts himself just as he did.

Dearly beloved,
    it is no new commandment that I write to you,
    but an old one which you had from the start.

The commandment, now old, is the word you
    have already heard.
On second thought, the commandment that I write you is new,
    as it is realized in him and you,
    for the darkness is over
    and the real light begins to shine.
The man who claims to be in light,
    hating his brother all the while,
    is in darkness even now.
The man who continues in the light
    is the one who loves his brother;
    there is nothing in him to cause a fall.
But the man who hates his brother is in darkness.
He walks in shadows,
    not knowing where he is going,
    since the dark has blinded his eyes. ✝

Psalm 96:1-3, 5-6
R. Let heaven and earth exult in joy.
Sing to the Lord a new song;
    sing to the Lord, all you lands.
Sing to the Lord; bless his name. **R.**
Announce his salvation, day after day
    tell his glory among the nations;
Among all peoples, his wondrous deeds. **R.**
The Lord made the heavens.
    Splendor and majesty go before him;
Praise and grandeur are in his sanctuary. **R.**

John 1:14, 12
R. Alleluia, alleluia.
The Word of God became a man and lived among us.
He enabled those who accepted him
    to become children of God. **R.**

✝ *Luke 2:22-35*
I have seen a light, the glory of your people Israel.

When the day came to purify them according to the law of
Moses, the couple brought Jesus up to Jerusalem so that he
could be presented to the Lord, for it is written in the law of the
Lord, "Every first-born male shall be consecrated to the Lord."

They came to offer in sacrifice "a pair of turtledoves or two young pigeons," in accord with the dictate in the law of the Lord.

There lived in Jerusalem a certain man named Simeon. He was just and pious, and awaited the consolation of Israel, and the Holy Spirit was upon him. It was revealed to him by the Holy Spirit that he would not experience death until he had seen the Anointed of the Lord. He came to the temple now, inspired by the Spirit; and when the parents brought in the child Jesus to perform for him the customary ritual of the law, he took him in his arms and blessed God in these words:

"Now, Master, you can dismiss your servant in peace;
    you have fulfilled your word.
For my eyes have witnessed your saving deed
    displayed for all the peoples to see:
A revealing light to the Gentiles,
    the glory of your people Israel."

The child's father and mother were marveling at what was being said about him. Simeon blessed them and said to Mary his mother: "This child is destined to be the downfall and the rise of many in Israel, a sign that will be opposed—and you yourself shall be pierced with a sword—so that the thoughts of many hearts may be laid bare." ✝

SATURDAY, DECEMBER 30
SIXTH DAY IN OCTAVE OF CHRISTMAS

✝ 1 John 2:12-17
He who does the will of God remains forever.

Little ones, I address you,
    for through his Name your sins have been forgiven.
Fathers, I address you,
    for you have known him who is from the beginning.
Young men, I address you,
    for you have conquered the evil one.
I address you, children,
    for you have known the Father.
I address you, fathers,
    for you have known him who is from the beginning.
I address you, young men,

    for you are strong,
    and the word of God remains in you,
    and you have conquered the evil one.

Have no love for the world,
    nor the things that the world affords.
If anyone loves the world,
    the Father's love has no place in him,
    for nothing that the world affords
    comes from the Father.
Carnal allurements,
    enticements for the eye,
    the life of empty show—
    all these are from the world.
And the world with its seductions is passing away
    but the man who does God's will
    endures forever. ✢

Psalm 96:7-10
R. Let heaven and earth exult in joy.
Give to the Lord, you families of nations,
    give to the Lord glory and praise;
    give to the Lord the glory due his name! **R.**
Bring gifts, and enter his courts;
    worship the Lord in holy attire.
    Tremble before him, all the earth. **R.**
Say among the nations: The Lord is king.
    He has made the world firm, not to be moved;
    he governs the peoples with equity. **R.**

Hebrews 1:1-2
R. Alleluia, alleluia.
In the past God spoke to our fathers through the prophets;
    now he speaks to us through his Son. **R.**

† *Luke 2:36-40*
She spoke of the child to all who looked for the deliverance of Israel.

There was a certain prophetess, Anna by name, daughter of Phanuel of the tribe of Asher. She had seen many days, having lived seven years with her husband after her marriage and then as a widow until she was eighty-four. She was constantly in the temple, worshiping day and night in fasting and prayer. Coming on the scene at this moment, she gave thanks to God and talked about the child to all who looked forward to the deliverance of Jerusalem.

When the pair had fulfilled all the prescriptions of the law of the Lord, they returned to Galilee and their own town of Nazareth. The child grew in size and strength, filled with wisdom, and the grace of God was upon him. ✛

SUNDAY, DECEMBER 31
THE HOLY FAMILY

† Sirach 3:2, 12-14 (or 1 Samuel 1:20-22, 24-28)
Those who fear the Lord honor their parents.

God sets a father in honor over his children;
    a mother's authority he confirms over her sons.
Whoever honors his father atones for sins,
    and preserves himself from them.
When he prays, he is heard;
    he stores up riches who reveres his mother.
Whoever honors his father is gladdened by children,
    and, when he prays, is heard.
Whoever reveres his father will live a long life;
    he who obeys his father brings comfort to his mother.

My son, take care of your father when he is old;
    grieve him not as long as he lives.
Even if his mind fail, be considerate of him;
    revile him not all the days of his life;
kindness to a father will not be forgotten,
    firmly planted against the debt of your sins
    —a house raised in justice to you. ✛

Psalm 128:1-5
R. Blessed are those who fear the Lord and walk in his ways.
Blessed is everyone who fears the LORD,
    who walks in his ways!
For you shall eat the fruit of your handiwork;
    blessed shall you be, and favored. **R.**

Your wife shall be like a fruitful vine
  in the recesses of your home;
your children like olive plants
  around your table. **R.**
Behold, thus is the man blessed
  who fears the LORD.
The LORD bless you from Zion:
  may you see the prosperity of Jerusalem
  all the days of your life. **R.**

† *Colossians 3:12-17*
(or Colossians 3:12-21 or 1 John 3:1-2, 21-24)
Family life in the Lord.

Brothers and sisters:
Put on, as God's chosen ones, holy and beloved,
  heartfelt compassion, kindness, humility, gentleness, and
    patience,
  bearing with one another and forgiving one another,
  if one has a grievance against another;
  as the Lord has forgiven you, so must you also do.
And over all these put on love,
  that is, the bond of perfection.
And let the peace of Christ control your hearts,
  the peace into which you were also called in one body.
And be thankful.
Let the word of Christ dwell in you richly,
  as in all wisdom you teach and admonish one another,
  singing psalms, hymns, and spiritual songs
  with gratitude in your hearts to God.
And whatever you do, in word or in deed,
  do everything in the name of the Lord Jesus,
  giving thanks to God the Father through him. ✛

Colossians 3:15a, 16a
R. Alleluia, alleluia.
Let the peace of Christ control your hearts;
let the word of Christ dwell in you richly. **R.**

✝ *Luke 2:41-52*

His parents found Jesus sitting in the midst of the teachers.

Each year Jesus' parents went to Jerusalem for the feast of
    Passover,
    and when he was twelve years old,
    they went up according to festival custom.
After they had completed its days, as they were returning,
    the boy Jesus remained behind in Jerusalem,
    but his parents did not know it.
Thinking that he was in the caravan,
    they journeyed for a day
    and looked for him among their relatives and
        acquaintances,
    but not finding him,
    they returned to Jerusalem to look for him.
After three days they found him in the temple,
    sitting in the midst of the teachers,
    listening to them and asking them questions,
    and all who heard him were astounded
    at his understanding and his answers.
When his parents saw him,
    they were astonished,
    and his mother said to him,
    "Son, why have you done this to us?
Your father and I have been looking for you with great
    anxiety."
And he said to them,
    "Why were you looking for me?
Did you not know that I must be in my Father's house?"
But they did not understand what he said to them.
He went down with them and came to Nazareth,
    and was obedient to them;
    and his mother kept all these things in her heart.
And Jesus advanced in wisdom and age and favor
    before God and man. ✛

MONDAY, JANUARY 1, 2001
MARY, MOTHER OF GOD

† *Numbers 6:22-27*
*They shall invoke my name upon
the Israelites, and I will bless them.*

The LORD said to Moses:
"Speak to Aaron and his sons and tell them:
    This is how you shall bless the Israelites.
Say to them:
    The LORD bless you and keep you!
    The LORD let his face shine upon
        you, and be gracious to you!
The LORD look upon you kindly and
    give you peace!
So shall they invoke my name upon the Israelites,
    and I will bless them." ✝

Psalm 67:2-3, 5, 6, 8
R. May God bless us in his mercy.
May God have pity on us and bless us;
    may he let his face shine upon us.
So may your way be known upon earth;
    among all nations, your salvation. **R.**
May the nations be glad and exult
    because you rule the peoples in equity;
    the nations on the earth you guide. **R.**
May the peoples praise you, O God;
    may all the peoples praise you!
May God bless us,
    and may all the ends of the earth fear him! **R.**

† *Galatians 4:4-7*
God sent his Son, born of a woman.

Brothers and sisters:
When the fullness of time had come, God sent his Son,
    born of a woman, born under the law,
    to ransom those under the law,
    so that we might receive adoption as sons.
As proof that you are sons,
    God sent the Spirit of his Son into our hearts,

crying out, "Abba, Father!"
So you are no longer a slave but a son,
   and if a son then also an heir, through God. ✛

Hebrews 1:1-2
R. Alleluia, alleluia.
In the past God spoke to our ancestors through the prophets;
in these last days, he has spoken to us through the Son. **R.**

† *Luke 2:16-21*
They found Mary and Joseph and the infant.
When the eight days were completed, he was named Jesus.

The shepherds went in haste to Bethlehem and found Mary
   and Joseph,
   and the infant lying in the manger.
When they saw this,
   they made known the message
   that had been told them about this child.
All who heard it were amazed
   by what had been told them by the shepherds.
And Mary kept all these things,
   reflecting on them in her heart.
Then the shepherds returned,
   glorifying and praising God
   for all they had heard and seen,
   just as it had been told to them.
When eight days were completed for his circumcision,
   he was named Jesus, the name given him by the angel
   before he was conceived in the womb. ✛

TUESDAY, JANUARY 2
St. Basil and St. Gregory

† *1 John 2:22-28*
What you were taught in the beginning remains alive in you.

Who is the liar?
He who denies that Jesus is the Christ.
He is the antichrist,
   denying the Father and the Son.
Anyone who denies the Son
   has no claim on the Father,

but he who acknowledges the Son
can claim the Father as well.

As for you,
let what you heard from the beginning
remain in your hearts.
If what you heard from the beginning
does remain in your hearts,
then you in turn will remain in the Son and in the Father.
He himself made us a promise
and the promise is no less than this:
eternal life.
I have written you these things
about those who try to deceive you.
As for you,
the anointing you received from him
remains in your hearts.
This means you have no need
for anyone to teach you.
Rather, as his anointing teaches you about all things
and is true—free from any lie—
remain in him
as that anointing taught you.
Remain in him now, little ones,
so that when he reveals himself,
we may be fully confident
and not retreat in shame at his coming. ✛

Psalm 98:1-4
R. All the ends of the earth have seen the saving power of God.
Sing to the Lord a new song,
for he has done wondrous deeds;
His right hand has won victory for him,
his holy arm. **R.**
The Lord has made his salvation known:
in the sight of the nations he has revealed his justice.
He has remembered his kindness and his faithfulness
toward the house of Israel. **R.**
All the ends of the earth have seen
the salvation by our God.

Sing joyfully to the Lord, all you lands;
   break into song; sing praise. **R.**

R. Alleluia, alleluia.
A holy day has dawned upon us.
Come, you nations, and adore the Lord.
Today a great light has come upon the earth. **R.**

✝ *John 1:19-28*
There is one to come after me who was created before me.

The testimony John gave when the Jews sent priests and Levites from Jerusalem to ask "Who are you?" was the absolute statement, "I am not the Messiah." They questioned him further, "Who, then? Elijah?" "I am not Elijah," he answered. "Are you the Prophet?" "No," he replied.

Finally they said to him: "Tell us who you are, so that we can give some answer to those who sent us. What do you have to say for yourself?" He said, quoting the prophet Isaiah, "I am 'a voice in the desert, crying out:
   Make straight the way of the Lord!'"

Those whom the Pharisees had sent proceeded to question him further: "If you are not the Messiah, nor Elijah, nor the Prophet, why do you baptize?" John answered them: "I baptize with water. There is one among you whom you do not recognize — the one who is to come after me — the strap of whose sandal I am not worthy to unfasten."

This happened in Bethany, across the Jordan, where John was baptizing. ✛

WEDNESDAY, JANUARY 3
WEEKDAY

✝ *1 John 2:29—3:6*
He who lives in God does not sin.

If you consider the holiness that is God's,
   you can be sure that everyone who acts in holiness
   has been begotten by him.

See what love the Father has bestowed on us
   in letting us be called children of God!
Yet that is what we are.

The reason the world does not recognize us
    is that it never recognized the Son.
Dearly beloved,
    we are God's children now;
    what we shall later be has not yet come to light.
We know that when it comes to light
    we shall be like him,
    for we shall see him as he is.
Everyone who has this hope based on him
    keeps himself pure, as he is pure.
Everyone who sins acts lawlessly,
    for sin is lawlessness.
You know well that the reason he revealed himself
    was to take away sins;
    in him there is nothing sinful.
The man who remains in him does not sin.
The man who sins has not seen him nor known him. ✛

Psalm 98:1, 3-6

**R. All the ends of the earth have seen the saving
power of God.**

Sing to the Lord a new song,
    for he has done wondrous deeds;
His right hand has won victory for him,
    his holy arm. **R.**
All the ends of the earth have seen
    the salvation by our God.
Sing joyfully to the Lord, all you lands;
    break into song; sing praise. **R.**
Sing praise to the Lord with the harp,
    with the harp and melodious song.
With trumpets and the sound of the horn
    sing joyfully before the King, the Lord. **R.**

Hebrews 1:1-2

R. Alleluia, alleluia.

In the past God spoke to our fathers through the prophets;
now he speaks to us through his Son. **R.**

† *John 1:29-34*
This is the Lamb of God.

When John caught sight of Jesus coming toward him, he exclaimed:
"Look there! The Lamb of God
who takes away the sin of the world!
It is he of whom I said:
'After me is to come a man
who ranks ahead of me,
because he was before me.'
I confess I did not recognize him, though the very reason I came baptizing with water was that he might be revealed to Israel."
John gave this testimony also:
"I saw the Spirit descend
like a dove from the sky,
and it came to rest on him.
But I did not recognize him. The one who sent me to baptize with water told me, 'When you see the Spirit descend and rest on someone, it is he who is to baptize with the Holy Spirit.' Now I have seen for myself and have testified, 'This is God's chosen One.'" ✛

THURSDAY, JANUARY 4
St. Elizabeth Ann Seton

† *1 John 3: 7-10*
No one who has been begotten by God sins.

Little ones,
let no one deceive you;
the man who acts in holiness is holy indeed,
even as the Son is holy.
The man who sins belongs to the devil,
because the devil is a sinner from the beginning.
It was to destroy the devil's works
that the Son of God revealed himself.
No one begotten of God acts sinfully
because he remains of God's stock;
he cannot sin

because he is begotten of God.
That is the way to see who are God's children,
    and who are the devil's.
No one whose actions are unholy belongs to God,
    nor anyone who fails to love his brother. ✛

Psalm 98:1, 7-9
**R. All the ends of the earth have seen the saving
power of God.**
Sing to the Lord a new song,
    for he has done wondrous deeds;
His right hand has won victory for him,
    his holy arm. **R.**
Let the sea and what fills it resound,
    the world and those who dwell in it;
Let the rivers clap their hands,
    the mountains shout with them for joy before the Lord. **R.**
The Lord comes;
    he comes to rule the earth;
He will rule the world with justice
    and the peoples with equity. **R.**

R. Alleluia, alleluia.
A holy day has dawned upon us.
Come, you nations, and adore the Lord.
Today a great light has come upon the earth. **R.**

✝ *John 1:35-42*
We have found the Messiah.

John was at Bethany across the Jordan with two of his disciples. As he watched Jesus walk by he said, "Look! There is the Lamb of God!" The two disciples heard what he said, and followed Jesus. When Jesus turned around and noticed them following him, he asked them, "What are you looking for?" They said to him, "Rabbi (which means Teacher), where do you stay?" "Come and see," he answered. So they went to see where he was lodged, and stayed with him that day. (It was about four in the afternoon.)

One of the two who had followed him after hearing John was Simon Peter's brother Andrew. The first thing he did was seek out his brother Simon and tell him, "We have found the Messiah" (which means the Anointed)! He brought him to Jesus, who looked at him and said: "You are Simon, son of John; your name shall be Cephas (which is rendered Peter)." ✛

FRIDAY, JANUARY 5
St. John Neumann

† 1 John 3:11-21
We have passed from death to life, because we love our brothers.

This, remember, is the message
    you heard from the beginning:
    we should love one another.
We should not follow the example of Cain
    who belonged to the evil one
    and killed his brother.
Why did he kill him?
Because his own deeds were wicked
    while his brother's were just.
No need, then, brothers, to be surprised
    if the world hates you.
That we have passed from death to life we know
    because we love the brothers.
The man who does not love is among the living dead.
Anyone who hates his brother is a murderer,
    and you know that eternal life
    abides in no murderer's heart.
The way we came to understand love
    was that he laid down his life for us;
    we too must lay down our lives for our brothers.
I ask you, how can God's love survive in a man
    who has enough of this world's goods
    yet closes his heart to his brother
    when he sees him in need?
Little children,
    let us love in deed and in truth
    and not merely talk about it.
This is our way of knowing we are committed to the truth
    and are at peace before him
    no matter what our consciences may charge us with;

for God is greater than our hearts
and all is known to him.

Beloved,
  if our consciences have nothing to charge us with,
  we can be sure that God is with us. ✢

Psalm 100:1-5
R. Let all the earth cry out to God with joy.
Sing joyfully to the Lord, all you lands;
  serve the Lord with gladness;
  come before him with joyful song. **R.**
Know that the Lord is God;
  he made us, his we are;
  his people, the flock he tends. **R.**
Enter his gates with thanksgiving,
  his courts with praise;
  Give thanks to him; bless his name. **R.**
The Lord is good:
  the Lord, whose kindness endures forever,
  and his faithfulness, to all generations. **R.**

John 1:14, 12
R. Alleluia, alleluia.
The Word of God became a man and lived among us.
He enabled those who accepted him
to become the children of God. **R.**

✝ *John 1:43-51*
You are the Son of God, the king of Israel.

Jesus wanted to set out for Galilee, but first he came upon
Philip. "Follow me," Jesus said to him. Now Philip was from
Bethsaida, the same town as Andrew and Peter. Philip sought
out Nathanael and told him, "We have found the one Moses
spoke of in the law—the prophets too—Jesus, son of Joseph,
from Nazareth." Nathanael's response to that was, "Can
anything good come from Nazareth?" and Philip replied,
"Come, see for yourself." When Jesus saw Nathanael coming
toward him, he remarked: "This man is a real Israelite. There
is no guile in him." "How do you know me?" Nathanael asked
him. "Before Philip called you," Jesus answered, "I saw you

under the fig tree." "Rabbi," said Nathanael, "you are the Son of God; you are the king of Israel." Jesus responded: "Do you believe just because I told you I saw you under the fig tree? You will see much greater things than that."

He went on to tell them, "I solemnly assure you, you shall see the sky opened and the angels of God ascending and descending on the Son of Man." ✝

SATURDAY, JANUARY 6
Bl. André Bessette

✝ 1 John 5:5-13
There are three witnesses: the Spirit and the water and the blood.

Who, then, is conqueror of the world?
The one who believes that Jesus is the Son of God.

Jesus Christ it is who came through water and blood—
    not in water only,
    but in water and in blood.
It is the Spirit who testifies to this,
    and the Spirit is truth.
Thus there are three that testify,
    the Spirit and the water and the blood—
    and these three are of one accord.
Do we not accept human testimony?
The testimony of God is much greater:
    it is the testimony God has given
    on his own Son's behalf.
Whoever believes in the Son of God
    possesses that testimony within his heart.
Whoever does not believe God
    has made God a liar
    by refusing to believe in the testimony
    he has given on his own Son's behalf.
The testimony is this:
    God gave us eternal life,
    and this life is in his Son.
Whoever possesses the Son
    possesses life;
    whoever does not possess the Son of God

does not possess life.

I have written this to you to make you realize that you possess eternal life—you who believe in the name of the Son of God. ✛

Psalm 147:12-15,19-20
R. Praise the Lord, Jerusalem.
Glorify the Lord, O Jerusalem;
 praise your God, O Zion.
For he has strengthened the bars of your gates;
 he has blessed your children within you. **R.**
He has granted peace in your borders;
 with the best of wheat he fills you.
He sends forth his command to the earth;
 swiftly runs his word! **R.**
He has proclaimed his word to Jacob,
 his statutes and his ordinances to Israel.
He has not done thus for any other nation;
 his ordinances he has not made known to them. Alleluia. **R.**

Hebrews 1:1-2
R. Alleluia, alleluia.
In the past God spoke to our fathers through the prophets;
now he speaks to us through his Son. **R.**

† *Mark 1:7-11*
You are my beloved Son in whom I am well pleased.

The theme of John's preaching was: "One more powerful than I is to come after me. I am not fit to stoop and untie his sandal straps. I have baptized you in water; he will baptize you in the Holy Spirit."

During that time, Jesus came from Nazareth in Galilee and was baptized in the Jordan by John. Immediately on coming up out of the water he saw the sky rent in two and the Spirit descending on him like a dove. Then a voice came from the heavens: "You are my beloved Son. On you my favor rests." ✛

SUNDAY, JANUARY 7
THE EPIPHANY OF THE LORD

✝ *Isaiah 60:1-6*
The glory of the Lord shines upon you.

Rise up in splendor, Jerusalem! Your light has come,
    the glory of the Lord shines upon you.
See, darkness covers the earth,
    and thick clouds cover the peoples;
but upon you the LORD shines,
    and over you appears his glory.
Nations shall walk by your light,
    and kings by your shining radiance.
Raise your eyes and look about;
    they all gather and come to you:
your sons come from afar,
    and your daughters in the arms of their nurses.

Then you shall be radiant at what you see,
    your heart shall throb and overflow,
for the riches of the sea shall be emptied out before you,
    the wealth of nations shall be brought to you.
Caravans of camels shall fill you,
    dromedaries from Midian and Ephah;
all from Sheba shall come
    bearing gold and frankincense,
    and proclaiming the praises of the LORD. ✝

Ps 72:1-2, 7-8, 10-11, 12-13
R. LORD, every nation on earth will adore you.
O God, with your judgment endow the king,
    and with your justice, the king's son;
He shall govern your people with justice
    and your afflicted ones with judgment. **R.**
Justice shall flower in his days,
    and profound peace, till the moon be no more.
May he rule from sea to sea,
    and from the River to the ends of the earth. **R.**
The kings of Tarshish and the Isles shall offer gifts;
    the kings of Arabia and Seba shall bring tribute.

All kings shall pay him homage,
    all nations shall serve him. **R.**
For he shall rescue the poor when he cries out,
    and the afflicted when he has no one to help him.
He shall have pity for the lowly and the poor;
    the lives of the poor he shall save. **R.**

† *Ephesians 3:2-3a, 5-6*

Now it has been revealed that the gentiles are coheirs of the promise.

Brothers and sisters:
You have heard of the stewardship of God's grace
        that was given to me for your benefit,
        namely, that the mystery was made known to me
            by revelation.
It was not made known to people in other generations
        as it has now been revealed
        to his holy apostles and prophets by the Spirit:
        that the Gentiles are coheirs, members of the same body,
        and copartners in the promise in Christ Jesus
            through the gospel. ✛

Matthew 2:2
R. Alleluia, alleluia.
We saw his star at its rising
and have come to do him homage. **R.**

† *Matthew 2:1-12*

We saw his star at its rising and have come to do him homage.

When Jesus was born in Bethlehem of Judea,
    in the days of King Herod,
        behold, magi from the east arrived in Jerusalem, saying,
        "Where is the newborn king of the Jews?
We saw his star at its rising
        and have come to do him homage."
When King Herod heard this,
        he was greatly troubled,
        and all Jerusalem with him.
Assembling all the chief priests and the scribes of the people,
        he inquired of them where the Christ was to be born.
They said to him, "In Bethlehem of Judea,

for thus it has been written through the prophet:
And you, Bethlehem, land of Judah,
are by no means least among the rulers of Judah;
since from you shall come a ruler,
who is to shepherd my people Israel."
Then Herod called the magi secretly
and ascertained from them the time of the star's
appearance.
He sent them to Bethlehem and said,
"Go and search diligently for the child.
When you have found him, bring me word,
that I too may go and do him homage."
After their audience with the king they set out.
And behold, the star that they had seen at its rising preceded
them,
until it came and stopped over the place where
the child was.
They were overjoyed at seeing the star,
and on entering the house
they saw the child with Mary his mother.
They prostrated themselves and did him homage.
Then they opened their treasures
and offered him gifts of gold, frankincense, and myrrh.
And having been warned in a dream not to return to Herod,
they departed for their country by another way. ✛

MONDAY, JANUARY 8
The Baptism of the Lord

† *Isaiah 42:1-4, 6-7 (or Isaiah 40:1-5, 9-11)*
Behold my servant with whom I am well pleased.

Thus says the LORD:
Here is my servant whom I uphold,
my chosen one with whom I am pleased,
upon whom I have put my spirit;
he shall bring forth justice to the nations,
not crying out, not shouting,
not making his voice heard in the street.
A bruised reed he shall not break,

and a smoldering wick he shall not quench,
until he establishes justice on the earth;
   the coastlands will wait for his teaching.

I, the LORD, have called you for the victory of justice,
   I have grasped you by the hand;
I formed you, and set you
   as a covenant of the people,
   a light for the nations,
to open the eyes of the blind,
   to bring out prisoners from confinement,
   and from the dungeon, those who live in darkness. ✛

Psalm 29:1-4, 9-10
R. The Lord will bless his people with peace.
Give to the LORD, you sons of God,
   give to the LORD glory and praise,
Give to the LORD the glory due his name;
   adore the LORD in holy attire. **R.**
The voice of the LORD is over the waters,
   the LORD, over vast waters.
The voice of the LORD is mighty;
   the voice of the LORD is majestic. **R.**
The God of glory thunders,
   and in his temple all say, "Glory!"
The LORD is enthroned above the flood;
   the LORD is enthroned as king forever. **R.**

Mark 9:7
R. Alleluia, alleluia.
The heavens were opened and the voice of the Father thun-
   dered:
This is my beloved Son, listen to him. **R.**

✝ *Luke 3:15-16, 21-22*
When Jesus had been baptized and was praying, heaven was opened.

The people were filled with expectation,
   and all were asking in their hearts
   whether John might be the Christ.
John answered them all, saying,
   "I am baptizing you with water,

but one mightier than I is coming.
I am not worthy to loosen the thongs of his sandals.
He will baptize you with the Holy Spirit and fire."

After all the people had been baptized
and Jesus also had been baptized and was praying,
heaven was opened and the Holy Spirit descended upon him
in bodily form like a dove.
And a voice came from heaven,
"You are my beloved Son;
with you I am well pleased." ✛

TUESDAY, JANUARY 9
WEEKDAY

† *Hebrews 2:5-12*
He perfected the author of our salvation through suffering.

For God did not make the world to come—that world of which
we speak—subject to angels. Somewhere this is testified to, in
the passage that says:
"What is man that you should be mindful of him,
or the son of man that you should care for him?
You made him for a little while lower than the angels;
you crowned him with glory and honor,
and put all things under his feet."
In subjecting all things to him, God left nothing
unsubjected. At present we do not see all things thus subject,
but we do see Jesus crowned with glory and honor because he
suffered death: Jesus, who was made for a little while lower
than the angels, that through God's gracious will he might
taste death for the sake of all men. Indeed, it was fitting that
when bringing many sons to glory, God, for whom and through
whom all things exist, should make their leader in the work of
salvation perfect through suffering. He who consecrates and
those who are consecrated have one and the same Father.
Therefore he is not ashamed to call them brothers, saying,
"I will announce your name to my brothers,
I will sing your praise in the midst of the assembly." ✛

Psalm 8:2, 5-9
R. You gave your Son authority over all your creation.
O Lord, our Lord,
   how glorious is your name over all the earth!
What is man that you should be mindful of him,
   or the son of man that you should care for him? **R.**
You have made him little less than the angels,
   and crowned him with glory and honor.
You have given him rule over the works of your hands,
   putting all things under his feet: **R.**
All sheep and oxen,
   yes, and the beasts of the field,
The birds of the air, the fishes of the sea,
   and whatever swims the paths of the seas. **R.**

Psalm 119:27
R. Alleluia, alleluia.
Instruct me in the way of your rules,
and I will reflect on all your wonders. **R.**

† *Mark 1:21-28*
Here was a teaching with authority behind it.

[**I**n the city of Capernaum,] Jesus entered the synagogue on the sabbath and began to teach. The people were spellbound by his teaching because he taught with authority and not like the scribes.

There appeared in their synagogue a man with an unclean spirit that shrieked: "What do you want of us, Jesus of Nazareth? Have you come to destroy us? I know who you are — the holy One of God!" Jesus rebuked him sharply: "Be quiet! Come out of the man!" At that the unclean spirit convulsed the man violently and with a loud shriek came out of him. All who looked on were amazed. They began to ask one another: "What does this mean? A completely new teaching in a spirit of authority! He gives orders to unclean spirits and they obey!" From that point on his reputation spread throughout the surrounding region of Galilee. ✛

WEDNESDAY, JANUARY 10
WEEKDAY

† *Hebrews 2:14-18*
He became like all the brothers that he might share their suffering.

Since the children are men of blood and flesh, Jesus likewise had a full share in ours, that by his death he might rob the devil, the prince of death, of his power, and free those who through fear of death had been slaves their whole life long. Surely he did not come to help angels, but rather the children of Abraham; therefore he had to become like his brothers in every way, that he might be a merciful and faithful high priest before God on their behalf, to expiate the sins of the people. Since he was himself tested through what he suffered, he is able to help those who are tempted. ✛

Psalm 105:1-4, 6-9
R. The Lord remembers his covenant forever.
Give thanks to the Lord, invoke his name;
  make known among the nations his deeds.
Sing to him, sing his praise,
  proclaim all his wondrous deeds. **R.**
Glory in his holy name;
  rejoice, O hearts that seek the Lord!
Look to the Lord in his strength;
  seek to serve him constantly. **R.**
You descendants of Abraham, his servants,
  sons of Jacob, his chosen ones!
He, the Lord, is our God;
  throughout the earth his judgments prevail. **R.**
He remembers forever his covenant
  which he made binding for a thousand generations
Which he entered into with Abraham
  and by his oath to Isaac. **R.**

2 Timothy 1:10
R. Alleluia, alleluia.
Our Savior Jesus Christ has done away with death,
and brought us life through his gospel. **R.**

† *Mark 1:29-39*
He healed many who were suffering from diseases.

Upon leaving the synagogue, Jesus entered the house of Simon and Andrew with James and John. Simon's mother-in-law lay ill with a fever, and the first thing they did was to tell him about her. He went over to her and grasped her hand and helped her up, and the fever left her. She immediately began to wait on them.

After sunset, as evening drew on, they brought him all who were ill and those possessed by demons. Before long the whole town was gathered outside the door. Those whom he cured, who were variously afflicted, were many, and so were the demons he expelled. But he would not permit the demons to speak, because they knew him. Rising early the next morning, he went off to a lonely place in the desert; there he was absorbed in prayer. Simon and his companions managed to track him down, and when they found him, they told him, "Everybody is looking for you!" He said to them: "Let us move on to the neighboring villages so that I may proclaim the good news there also. That is what I have come to do." So he went into their synagogues preaching the good news and expelling demons throughout the whole of Galilee. ✛

THURSDAY, JANUARY 11
WEEKDAY

† *Hebrews 3:7-14*
If only you would listen to him today, and not harden your hearts.

As the Holy Spirit says:
"Today, if you should hear his voice,
    harden not your hearts as at the revolt
    in the day of testing in the desert,
When your fathers tested and tried me,
    and saw my works for forty years.
Because of this I was angered with that generation
    and I said, 'They have always been of erring heart,
    and have never known my ways.'
Thus I swore in my anger,
    'They shall never enter into my rest.'"

Take care, my brothers, lest any of you have an evil and unfaithful spirit and fall away from the living God. Encourage one another daily while it is still "today," so that no one grows hardened by the deceit of sin. We have become partners of Christ if only we maintain to the end that confidence with which we began. ✛

Psalm 95:6-11
**R. If today you hear his voice,
harden not your hearts.**
Come, let us bow down in worship;
let us kneel before the Lord who made us.
For he is our God,
and we are the people he shepherds, the flock he guides. **R.**
Oh, that today you would hear his voice:
"Harden not your hearts as at Meribah,
as in the day of Massah in the desert,
Where your fathers tempted me;
they tested me though they had seen my works. **R.**
Forty years I loathed that generation,
and I said: They are a people of erring heart,
and they know not my ways.
Therefore I swore in my anger:
They shall not enter into my rest." **R.**

Psalm 119:88
R. Alleluia, alleluia.
Give me life, O Lord,
and I will do your commands. **R.**

† Mark 1:40-45
The leper went away from him, cleansed.

A leper approached Jesus with a request, kneeling down as he addressed him: "If you will to do so, you can cure me." Moved with pity, Jesus stretched out his hand, touched him, and said: "I do will it. Be cured." The leprosy left him then and there, and he was cured. Jesus gave him a stern warning and sent him on his way. "Not a word to anyone, now," he said. "Go off and present yourself to the priest and offer for your cure what Moses prescribed. That should be a proof for them." The man went off and began to proclaim the whole matter freely, making the story public. As a result of this, it was no longer possible for Jesus to enter a town openly. He stayed in desert places; yet people kept coming to him from all sides. ✛

FRIDAY, JANUARY 12
WEEKDAY

✝ Hebrews 4:1-5, 11
We must be eager to reach the place of rest.

While the promise of entrance into his rest still holds, we ought to be fearful of disobeying lest any one of you be judged to have lost his chance of entering. We have indeed heard the good news, as they did. But the word which they heard did not profit them, for they did not receive it in faith. It is we, who have believed, who enter into that rest, just as God said:

"Thus I swore in my anger,

'They shall never enter into my rest.'"

Yet God's work was finished when he created the world, for in reference to the seventh day Scripture somewhere says, "And God rested from all his work on the seventh day," and again, in the place we referred to, God says, "They shall never enter into my rest." Let us strive to enter into that rest, so that no one may fall in imitation of the example of Israel's unbelief. ✛

Psalm 78:3-4, 6-8

R. Do not forget the works of the Lord!

What we have heard and know,
  and what our fathers have declared to us,
  we will declare to the generation to come
The glorious deeds of the Lord and his strength
  and the wonders that he wrought. **R.**
That they too may rise and declare to their sons
  that they should put their hope in God,
And not forget the deeds of God
  but keep his commands. **R.**
And not be like their fathers,
  a generation wayward and rebellious,
A generation that kept not its heart steadfast
  nor its spirit faithful toward God. **R.**

Psalm 145:13
R. Alleluia, alleluia.
The Lord is faithful in all his words
and holy in his deeds. **R.**

✛ *Mark 2:1-12*
The Son of Man has authority on earth to forgive sins.

Jesus came back to Capernaum after a lapse of several days and word got around that he was at home. At that they began to gather in great numbers. There was no longer any room for them, even around the door. While he was delivering God's word to them, some people arrived bringing a paralyzed man to him. The four who carried him were unable to bring him to Jesus because of the crowd, so they began to open up the roof over the spot where Jesus was. When they had made a hole, they let down the mat on which the paralytic was lying. When Jesus saw their faith, he said to the paralyzed man, "My son, your sins are forgiven." Now some of the scribes were sitting there asking themselves: "Why does the man talk in that way? He commits blasphemy! Who can forgive sins except God alone?" Jesus was immediately aware of their reasoning, though they kept it to themselves, and he said to them: "Why do you harbor these thoughts? Which is easier, to say to the paralytic, 'Your sins are forgiven,' or to say, 'Stand up, pick up your mat, and walk again'? That you may know that the Son of Man has authority on earth to forgive sins" (he said to the paralyzed man), "I command you: Stand up! Pick up your mat and go home." The man stood and picked up his mat and went outside in the sight of everyone. They were awestruck; all gave praise to God, saying, "We have never seen anything like this!" ✛

SATURDAY, JANUARY 13
St. Hilary

✛ *Hebrews 4:12-16*
Let us approach the throne of grace with confidence.

God's word is living and effective, sharper than any two-edged sword. It penetrates and divides soul and spirit, joints and marrow; it judges the reflections and thoughts of the heart. Nothing is concealed from him; all lies bare and exposed to the eyes of him to whom we must render an account.

Since, then, we have a great high priest who has passed through the heavens, Jesus, the Son of God, let us hold fast to our profession of faith. For we do not have a high priest who is unable to sympathize with our weakness, but one who was tempted in every way that we are, yet never sinned. So let us confidently approach the throne of grace to receive mercy and favor and to find help in time of need. ✝

Psalm 19:8-10, 15
R. Your words, Lord, are spirit and life.
The law of the Lord is perfect,
    refreshing the soul;
The decree of the Lord is trustworthy,
    giving wisdom to the simple. **R.**
The precepts of the Lord are right,
    rejoicing the heart;
The command of the Lord is clear,
    enlightening the eye. **R.**
The fear of the Lord is pure,
    enduring forever;
The ordinances of the Lord are true,
    all of them just. **R.**
Let the words of my mouth and the thought of my heart
    find favor before you,
O Lord, my rock and my redeemer. **R.**

Psalm 119:105
R. Alleluia, alleluia.
Your word is a lamp for my feet,
and a light on my path. **R.**

✝ *Mark 2:13-17*
I have not come to call the just, but sinners.

While Jesus went walking along the lakeshore, people kept coming to him in crowds and he taught them. As he moved on he saw Levi the son of Alphaeus at his tax collector's post, and said to him, "Follow me." Levi got up and became his follower. While Jesus was reclining to eat in Levi's house, many tax collectors and those known as sinners joined him and his disciples at dinner. The number of those who followed him was large. When the scribes who belonged to the Pharisee party saw that he was eating with tax collectors and offenders against the law, they complained to his disciples, "Why does he eat with such as these?" Overhearing the remark, Jesus said to them, "People who are healthy do not need a doctor; sick people do. I have come to call sinners, not the self-righteous." ✝

JANUARY 14
SECOND SUNDAY IN ORDINARY TIME

✝ Isaiah 62:1-5
The bridegroom rejoices in his bride.

For Zion's sake I will not be silent,
    for Jerusalem's sake I will not be quiet,
until her vindication shines forth like the dawn
    and her victory like a burning torch.

Nations shall behold your vindication,
    and all the kings your glory;
you shall be called by a new name
    pronounced by the mouth of the LORD.
You shall be a glorious crown in the hand of the LORD,
    a royal diadem held by your God.
No more shall people call you "Forsaken, "
    or your land "Desolate, "
but you shall be called "My Delight, "
    and your land "Espoused."
For the LORD delights in you
    and makes your land his spouse.
As a young man marries a virgin,
    your Builder shall marry you;
and as a bridegroom rejoices in his bride
    so shall your God rejoice in you. ✝

Psalm 96:1-3, 7-10
R. Proclaim his marvelous deeds to all the nations.
Sing to the LORD a new song;
    sing to the LORD, all you lands.
Sing to the LORD; bless his name. **R.**
Announce his salvation, day after day.

Tell his glory among the nations;
among all peoples, his wondrous deeds. **R.**
Give to the LORD, you families of nations,
give to the LORD glory and praise;
give to the LORD the glory due his name! **R.**
Worship the LORD in holy attire.
Tremble before him, all the earth;
say among the nations: The LORD is king.
He governs the peoples with equity. **R.**

† *1 Corinthians 12:4-11*
One and the same Spirit distributing them
individually to each person as he wishes.

Brothers and sisters:
There are different kinds of spiritual gifts but the same Spirit;
there are different forms of service but the same Lord;
there are different workings but the same God
who produces all of them in everyone.
To each individual the manifestation of the Spirit
is given for some benefit.
To one is given through the Spirit the expression of wisdom;
to another, the expression of knowledge according to the
same Spirit;
to another, faith by the same Spirit;
to another, gifts of healing by the one Spirit;
to another, mighty deeds;
to another, prophecy;
to another, discernment of spirits;
to another, varieties of tongues;
to another, interpretation of tongues.
But one and the same Spirit produces all of these,
distributing them individually to each person
as he wishes. ✢

cf. 2 Thessalonians 2:14
R. Alleluia, alleluia.
God has called us through the Gospel
to possess the glory of our Lord Jesus Christ. **R.**

✝ *John 2:1-11*

Jesus did this as the beginning of his signs at Cana in Galilee.

There was a wedding at Cana in Galilee,
    and the mother of Jesus was there.
Jesus and his disciples were also invited to the wedding.
When the wine ran short,
    the mother of Jesus said to him,
    "They have no wine."
And Jesus said to her,
    "Woman, how does your concern affect me?
My hour has not yet come."
His mother said to the servers,
    "Do whatever he tells you."
Now there were six stone water jars there for Jewish ceremo
        nial washings,
    each holding twenty to thirty gallons.
Jesus told the them,
    "Fill the jars with water."
So they filled them to the brim.
Then he told them,
    "Draw some out now and take it to the headwaiter."
So they took it.
And when the headwaiter tasted the water
        that had become wine,
    without knowing where it came from
    —although the servers who had drawn the water knew—,
    the headwaiter called the bridegroom and said to him,
    "Everyone serves good wine first,
    and then when people have drunk freely, an inferior one;
    but you have kept the good wine until now."
Jesus did this as the beginning of his signs at Cana in Galilee
    and so revealed his glory,
    and his disciples began to believe in him. ✛

MONDAY, JANUARY 15
WEEKDAY

† *Hebrews 5:1-10*
*Since he is the Son of God, he becomes
for all who obey him the source of salvation.*

Every high priest is taken from among men and made their representative before God, to offer gifts and sacrifices for sins. He is able to deal patiently with erring sinners, for he is himself beset by weakness and so must make sin offerings for himself as well as for the people. One does not take this honor on his own initiative, but only when called by God as Aaron was. Even Christ did not glorify himself with the office of high priest; he received it from the One who said to him,

"You are my son;
    today I have begotten you";
just as he says in another place,
"You are a priest forever,
    according to the order of Melchizedek."

In the days when he was in the flesh, he offered prayers and supplications with loud cries and tears to God, who was able to save him from death, and he was heard because of his reverence. Son though he was, he learned obedience from what he suffered; and when perfected, he became the source of eternal salvation for all who obey him, designated by God as high priest according to the order of Melchizedek. ✛

Psalm 110:1-4

R. You are a priest forever, in the line of Melchizedek.

The Lord said to my Lord: "Sit at my right hand
    till I make your enemies your footstool." **R.**

The scepter of your power the Lord will stretch forth from Zion:
    "Rule in the midst of your enemies." **R.**

"Yours is princely power in the day of your birth, in holy splendor;
    before the daystar, like the dew, I have begotten you." **R.**

The Lord has sworn, and he will not repent:
    "You are a priest forever, according to the order of Melchizedek." **R.**

See *Acts 16:14*

R. Alleluia, alleluia.

Open our hearts, O Lord,
to listen to the words of your Son. **R.**

✝ *Mark 2:18-22*
The bridegroom is still with them.

John's disciples and the Pharisees were accustomed to fast. People came to Jesus with the objection, "Why do John's disciples and those of the Pharisees fast while yours do not?" Jesus replied: "How can the guests at a wedding fast as long as the groom is still among them? So long as the groom stays with them, they cannot fast. The day will come, however, when the groom will be taken away from them; on that day they will fast. No one sews a patch of unshrunken cloth on an old cloak. If he should do so, the very thing he has used to cover the hole would pull away — the new from the old — and the tear would get worse. Similarly, no man pours new wine into old wineskins. If he does so, the wine will burst the skins and both wine and skins will be lost. No, new wine is poured into new skins." ✝

TUESDAY, JANUARY 16
WEEKDAY

✝ *Hebrews 6:10-20*
*We have a source of strength to take
firm grip of the hope that is held out to us.*

God is not unjust; he will not forget your work and the love you have shown him by your service, past and present, to his holy people. Our desire is that each of you show the same zeal till the end, fully assured of that for which you hope. Do not grow lazy, but imitate those who, through faith and patience, are inheriting the promises.

When God made his promise to Abraham, he swore by himself, having no one greater to swear by, and said, "I will indeed bless you, and multiply you." And so, after patient waiting, Abraham obtained what God had promised. Men swear by someone greater than themselves; an oath gives firmness to a promise and puts an end to all argument. God, wishing to give the heirs of his promise even clearer evidence that his purpose would not change, guaranteed it by oath, so that, by two things that are unchangeable, in which, he could not lie, we who have taken refuge in him might be strongly encouraged to seize the hope which is placed before us. Like a sure and firm anchor, that hope extends beyond the veil through which Jesus, our forerunner, has entered on our behalf, being made high priest forever according to the order of Melchizedek. ✛

Psalm 111:1-2, 4-5, 9-10
R. The Lord will remember his covenant forever.
I will give thanks to the Lord with all my heart
    in the company and assembly of the just.
Great are the works of the Lord,
    exquisite in all their delights. **R.**
He has won renown for his wondrous deeds;
    gracious and merciful is the Lord.
He has given food to those who fear him;
    he will forever be mindful of his covenant. **R.**
He has sent deliverance to his people;
    he has ratified his covenant forever;
    holy and awesome is his name.
His praise endures forever. **R.**

Psalm 119:34
R. Alleluia, alleluia.
Teach me the meaning of your law, O Lord,
and I will guard it with all my heart. **R.**

† Mark 2:23-28
The sabbath was made for man, not man for the sabbath.

It happened that the Lord was walking through standing grain on the sabbath, and his disciples began to pull off heads of grain as they went along. At this the Pharisees protested: "Look! Why do they do a thing not permitted on the sabbath?" He said to them: "Have you never read what David did when he was in need and he and his men were hungry? How he entered God's house in the days of Abiathar the high priest and ate the holy bread which only the priests were permitted to eat? He even gave it to his men." Then he said to them: "The sabbath was made for man, not man for the sabbath. That is why the Son of Man is lord even of the sabbath." ✛

WEDNESDAY, JANUARY 17
ST. ANTHONY

† *Hebrews 7:1-3, 15-17*
You are a priest forever of the order of Melchizedek.

Melchizedek, king of Salem and priest of the Most High God, met Abraham returning from his defeat of the kings and blessed him. And Abraham apportioned to him one tenth of all his booty. His name means "king of justice"; he was also king of Salem, that is, "king of peace." Without father, mother or ancestry, without beginning of days or end of life, like the Son of God he remains a priest forever.

The matter is clearer still if another priest is appointed according to the likeness of Melchizedek: one who has become a priest, not in virtue of a law expressed in a commandment concerning physical descent, but in virtue of the power of a life which cannot be destroyed. Scripture testifies: "You are a priest forever according to the order of Melchizedek." ✢

Psalm 110:1-4
**R. You are a priest forever,
in the line of Melchizedek.**
The Lord said to my Lord: "Sit at my right hand
till I make your enemies your footstool." **R.**
The scepter of your power the Lord will stretch forth
from Zion:
"Rule in the midst of your enemies." **R.**
"Yours is princely power in the day of your birth, in holy
splendor;
before the daystar, like the dew, I have begotten you." **R.**
The Lord has sworn, and he will not repent:
"You are a priest forever, according to the order of
Melchizedek." **R.**

1 Thessalonians 2:13
R. Alleluia, alleluia.
Receive this message not as the words of man,
but as truly the word of God. **R.**

† *Mark 3:1-6*

*Is it against the law on the sabbath day
to do good — to save life or to kill?*

Jesus returned to the synagogue where there was a man whose hand was shriveled up. The Pharisees kept an eye on Jesus to see whether he would heal him on the sabbath, hoping to be able to bring an accusation against him. He addressed the man with the shriveled hand: "Stand up here in front!" Then he said to them: "Is it permitted to do a good deed on the sabbath — or an evil one? To preserve life—or to destroy it?" At this they remained silent. He looked around at them angrily, for he was deeply grieved that they had closed their minds against him. Then he said to the man, "Stretch out your hand." The man did so and his hand was perfectly restored. When the Pharisees went outside, they immediately began to plot with the Herodians on how they might destroy him. ✢

THURSDAY, JANUARY 18
WEEKDAY

† *Hebrews 7:25—8:6*
He lives forever to intercede for all who came to God through him.

Jesus is always able to save those who approach God through him, since he forever lives to make intercession for them.

It was fitting that we should have such a high priest: holy, innocent, undefiled, separated from sinners, higher than the heavens. Unlike the other high priests, he has no need to offer sacrifice day after day, first for his own sins and then for those of the people; he did that once for all when he offered himself. For the law sets up as high priests men who are weak, but the word of the oath which came after the law appoints as priest the Son, made perfect forever.

The main point in what we are saying is this: we have such a high priest, who has taken his seat at the right hand of the throne of the Majesty in heaven, minister of the sanctuary and of that true tabernacle set up not by man but by the Lord. Now every high priest is appointed to offer gifts and sacrifices; hence the necessity for this one to have something to offer. If he were on earth he would not be a priest, for there are priests already offering the gifts which the law prescribes. They offer worship in a sanctuary which is only a copy and shadow of the heavenly one, for Moses, when about to erect the tabernacle, was warned, "See that you make everything according to the pattern shown you on the mountain." Jesus has obtained a more excellent ministry now, just as he is mediator of a better covenant, founded on better promises. ✛

Psalm 40:7-10, 17
R. Here am I, Lord;
I come to do your will.
Sacrifice or oblation you wished not,
　　but ears open to obedience you gave me.
Holocausts or sin-offerings you sought not;
　　then said I, "Behold I come." **R.**
"In the written scroll it is prescribed for me,
　　to do your will, O my God, is my delight,
And your law is within my heart!" **R.**
I announced your justice in the vast assembly
　　I did not restrain my lips, as you, O Lord, know. **R.**
May all who seek you
　　exult and be glad in you,
And may those who love your salvation
　　say ever, "The Lord be glorified." **R.**

Psalm 130:5
R. Alleluia, alleluia.
I hope in the Lord,
I trust in his word. **R.**

† Mark 3:7-12
The unclean spirits shouted, you are the Son of God,
but he warned them not to make him known.

Jesus withdrew toward the lake with his disciples. A great crowd followed him from Galilee, and an equally great multitude came to him from Judea, Jerusalem, Idumea, Transjordan, and the neighborhood of Tyre and Sidon, because they had heard what he had done. In view of their numbers, he told his disciples to have a fishing boat ready for him so that he could avoid the press of the crowd against him. Because he had cured many, all who had afflictions kept pushing toward him to touch him. Unclean spirits would catch sight of him, fling themselves down at his feet, and shout, "You are the Son of God!", while he kept ordering them sternly not to reveal who he was. ✛

FRIDAY, JANUARY 19
WEEKDAY

† *Hebrews 8:6-13*
He is mediator of a better covenant.

Jesus our high priest has obtained a more excellent ministry now just as he is mediator of a better covenant, founded on better promises.

If that first covenant had been faultless, there would have been no place for a second one. But God, finding fault with them, says:
"Days are coming, says the Lord,
    when I will make a new covenant with the house of Israel
    and with the house of Judah.
It will not be like the covenant I made with their fathers
    the day I took them by the hand
    to lead them forth from the land of Egypt;
For they broke my covenant
    and I grew weary of them, says the Lord.
But this is the covenant I will make with the house of Israel
    after those days, says the Lord:
I will place my laws in their minds
    and I will write them upon their hearts;
I will be their God
    and they shall be my people.
And they shall not teach their fellow citizens
    or their brothers, saying, 'Know the Lord,'
    for all shall know me, from least to greatest.
I will forgive their evildoing,
    and their sins I will remember no more."
When he says, "a new covenant," he declares the first one obsolete. And what has become obsolete and has grown old is close to disappearing. ✛

Psalm 85:8, 10-14
R. Kindness and truth shall meet.
Show us, O Lord, your kindness,
  and grant us your salvation.
Near indeed is his salvation to those who fear him,
  glory dwelling in our land. **R.**
Kindness and truth shall meet;
  justice and peace shall kiss.
Truth shall spring out of the earth,
  and justice shall look down from heaven. **R.**
The Lord himself will give his benefits;
  our land shall yield its increase.
Justice shall walk before him,
  and salvation, along the way of his steps. **R.**

John 15:15
R. Alleluia, alleluia.
I call you my friends, says the Lord,
for I have made know to you all that the
Father has told me. **R.**

† *Mark 3:13-19*
He called those he wanted and they went with him.

Jesus went up the mountain and summoned the men he himself had decided on, who came and joined him. He named twelve as his companions whom he would send to preach the good news; they were likewise to have authority to expel demons. He appointed the Twelve as follows: Simon to whom he gave the name Peter; James, son of Zebedee; and John, the brother of James (he gave these two the name Boanerges, or "sons of thunder"); Andrew, Philip, Bartholomew, Matthew, Thomas, James son of Alphaeus; Thaddaeus, Simon of the Zealot party, and Judas Iscariot, who betrayed him. ✛

SATURDAY, JANUARY 20
St. Fabian and St. Sebastian

† Hebrews 9:2-3,11-14
Through his own blood he has entered into a more perfect covenant.

A tabernacle was constructed, the outer one, in which were the lampstand, and the table, and the showbread; this was called the holy place. Behind the second veil was the tabernacle called the holy of holies.

But when Christ came as high priest of the good things which came to be, he entered once for all into the sanctuary, passing through the greater and more perfect tabernacle not made by hands, that is, not belonging to this creation. He entered not with the blood of goats and calves but with his own blood, and achieved eternal redemption. For if the blood of goats and bulls and the sprinkling of a heifer's ashes can sanctify those who are defiled so that their flesh is cleansed, how much more will the blood of Christ, who through the eternal spirit offered himself up unblemished to God, cleanse our consciences from dead works to worship the living God! ✛

Psalm 47:2-3, 6-9
**R. God mounts his throne to shouts of joy;
a blare of trumpets for the Lord.**
All you peoples, clap your hands,
    shout to God with cries of gladness,
For the Lord, the Most High, the awesome,
    is the great king over all the earth. **R.**
God mounts his throne amid shouts of joy;
    the Lord, amid trumpet blasts.
Sing praise to God, sing praise;
    sing praise to our king, sing praise. **R.**
For king of all the earth is God:
    sing hymns of praise.
God reigns over the nations,
    God sits upon his holy throne. **R.**

Hebrews 4:12
R. Alleluia, alleluia.
The word of God is living and active;
it probes the thoughts and motives of our heart. **R.**

✝ *Mark 3:20-21*

The people said that he was out of his mind.

Jesus returned to the house with his disciples and again the crowd assembled, making it impossible for them to get any food whatever. When his family heard of this they came to take charge of him, saying, "He is out of his mind." ✝

JANUARY 21
THIRD SUNDAY IN ORDINARY TIME

✝ *Nehemiah 8:2-4a, 5-6, 8-10*

They read from the book of the Law and they understood what was read.

Ezra the priest brought the law before the assembly,
    which consisted of men, women,
    and those children old enough to understand.
Standing at one end of the open place that was before the
    Water Gate,
    he read out of the book from daybreak till midday,
    in the presence of the men, the women,
    and those children old enough to understand;
    and all the people listened attentively to the book of the
    law.
Ezra the scribe stood on a wooden platform
    that had been made for the occasion.
He opened the scroll
    so that all the people might see it
    —for he was standing higher up than any of the people—
    and, as he opened it, all the people rose.
Ezra blessed the LORD, the great God,
    and all the people, their hands raised high, answered,
    "Amen, amen!"
Then they bowed down and prostrated themselves before the
    LORD,
    their faces to the ground.
Ezra read plainly from the book of the law of God,
    interpreting it so that all could understand what was read.
Then Nehemiah, that is, His Excellency, and Ezra the priest-
    scribe
    and the Levites who were instructing the people

said to all the people:
"Today is holy to the LORD your God.
Do not be sad, and do not weep"—
    for all the people were weeping as they heard the words of
        the law.
He said further: "Go, eat rich foods and drink sweet drinks,
    and allot portions to those who had nothing prepared;
    for today is holy to our LORD.
Do not be saddened this day,
    for rejoicing in the LORD must be your strength!" ✛

Psalm 19:8-10, 15

R. Your words, Lord, are Spirit and life.

The law of the LORD is perfect,
    refreshing the soul;
the decree of the LORD is trustworthy,
    giving wisdom to the simple. **R.**
The precepts of the LORD are right,
    rejoicing the heart;
the command of the LORD is clear,
    enlightening the eye. **R.**
The fear of the LORD is pure,
    enduring forever;
the ordinances of the LORD are true,
    all of them just. **R.**
Let the words of my mouth and the thought of my heart
    find favor before you,
O LORD, my rock and my redeemer. **R.**

✝ *1 Corinthians 12:12-14, 27* (or *1 Corinthians 12:12-30*)
You are Christ's body and individually parts of it.

Brothers and sisters:
As a body is one though it has many parts,
    and all the parts of the body, though many, are one body,
    so also Christ.
For in one Spirit we were all baptized into one body,
    whether Jews or Greeks, slaves or free persons,
    and we were all given to drink of one Spirit.
Now the body is not a single part, but many.
You are Christ's body, and individually parts of it. ✛

cf. Luke 4:18
R. Alleluia, alleluia.
The Lord sent me to bring glad tidings to the poor,
and to proclaim liberty to captives. **R.**

✝ Luke 1:1-4; 4:14-21
Today this Scripture passage is fulfilled.

Since many have undertaken to compile a narrative of the
  events
  that have been fulfilled among us,
  just as those who were eyewitnesses from the beginning
  and ministers of the word have handed them down to us,
  I too have decided,
  after investigating everything accurately anew,
  to write it down in an orderly sequence for you,
  most excellent Theophilus,
  so that you may realize the certainty of the teachings
  you have received.

Jesus returned to Galilee in the power of the Spirit,
  and news of him spread throughout the whole region.
He taught in their synagogues and was praised by all.

He came to Nazareth, where he had grown up,
  and went according to his custom
  into the synagogue on the sabbath day.
He stood up to read and was handed a scroll of the prophet
  Isaiah.
He unrolled the scroll and found the passage where it was
  written:
  The Spirit of the Lord is upon me,
  because he has anointed me
  to bring glad tidings to the poor.
  He has sent me to proclaim liberty to captives
  and recovery of sight to the blind,
  to let the oppressed go free,
  and to proclaim a year acceptable to the Lord.
Rolling up the scroll, he handed it back to the attendant
  and sat down,
  and the eyes of all in the synagogue looked intently at him.
He said to them,

"Today this Scripture passage is fulfilled in your hearing." ✛

MONDAY, JANUARY 22
St. Vincent

† Hebrews 9:15, 24-28
He offered himself to take the faults of many away; he will
appear a second time to those who are awaiting him.

Christ is mediator of a new covenant: since his death has taken place for deliverance from transgressions committed under the first covenant, those who are called may receive the promised eternal inheritance.

For Christ did not enter into a sanctuary made by hands, a mere copy of the true one; he entered heaven itself that he might appear before God now on our behalf. Not that he might offer himself there again and again, as the high priest enters year after year into the sanctuary with blood that is not his own; were that so, he would have had to suffer death over and over from the creation of the world. But now he has appeared at the end of the ages to take away sins once for all by his sacrifice. Just as it is appointed that men die once, and after death be judged, so Christ was offered up once to take away the sins of many; he will appear a second time not to take away sin but to bring salvation to those who eagerly await him. ✛

Psalm 98:1-6
R. Sing to the Lord a new song,
for he has done marvelous deeds.
Sing to the Lord a new song,
  for he has done wondrous deeds;
His right hand has won victory for him,
  his holy arm. **R.**
The Lord has made his salvation known:
  in the sight of the nations he has revealed his justice.
He has remembered his kindness and his faithfulness
  toward the house of Israel. **R.**
All the ends of the earth have seen
  the salvation by our God.
Sing joyfully to the Lord, all you lands;
  break into song; sing praise. **R.**
Sing praise to the Lord with the harp,

with the harp and melodious song.
With trumpets and the sound of the horn
   sing joyfully before the King, the Lord. **R.**

John 17:17
R. Alleluia, alleluia.
Your word, O Lord, is truth;
make us holy in the truth. **R.**

✝ *Mark 3:22-30*
It is the end of Satan.

The scribes who arrived from Jerusalem said of Jesus, "He is possessed by Beelzebul," and "He expels demons with the help of the prince of demons." Summoning them, Jesus began to speak to them by way of examples: "How can Satan expel Satan? If a kingdom is torn by civil strife, that kingdom cannot last. If a household is divided according to loyalties, that household will not survive. Similarly, if Satan has suffered mutiny in his ranks and is torn by dissension, he cannot endure; he is finished. No one can enter a strong man's house and despoil his property unless he has first put him under restraint. Only then can he plunder his house.

"I give you my word, every sin will be forgiven mankind and all the blasphemies men utter, but whoever blasphemes against the Holy Spirit will never be forgiven. He carries the guilt of his sin without end." He spoke thus because they had said, "He is possessed by an unclean spirit." ✛

TUESDAY, JANUARY 23
WEEKDAY

✝ *Hebrews 10:1-10*
God, I am coming to do your will.

Since the law had only a shadow of the good things to come, and no real image of them, it was never able to perfect the worshipers by the same sacrifices offered continually year after year. Were matters otherwise, the priests would have stopped offering them, for the worshipers, once cleansed, would have had no sin on their conscience. But through those sacrifices there came only a yearly recalling of sins, because it is impossible for the blood of bulls and goats to take sins away.

Wherefore, on coming into the world, Jesus said:
"Sacrifice and offering you did not desire,
but a body you have prepared for me;
Holocausts and sin offerings you took no delight in.
Then I said, 'As is written of me in the book,
I have come to do your will, O God.'"
First he says,
"Sacrifices and offerings, holocausts and sin offerings
you neither desired nor delighted in."
(These are offered according to the prescriptions of the law.) Then he says,
"I have come to do your will."
In other words, he takes away the first covenant to establish the second.

By this "will," we have been sanctified through the offering of the body of Jesus Christ once for all. ✛

Psalm 40:2, 4, 7-8, 10-11
**R. Here am l, Lord;
I come to do your will.**
I have waited, waited for the Lord,
and he stooped toward me.
And he put a new song into my mouth,
a hymn to our God. **R.**
Sacrifice or oblation you wished not,
but ears open to obedience you gave me.
Holocausts or sin-offerings you sought not;
then said I, "Behold I come." **R.**
I announced your justice in the vast assembly;
I did not restrain my lips, as you, O Lord, know. **R.**
Your justice I kept not hid within my heart;
your faithfulness and your salvation I have spoken of;
I have made no secret of your kindness and your truth
in the vast assembly. **R.**

Psalm 119:35, 29
R. Alleluia, alleluia.
Turn my heart to do your will;
teach me your law, O God. **R.**

✝ *Mark 3:31-35*

Here are my mother and my brothers: anyone who does the will of God.

The mother of Jesus and his brothers arrived, and as they stood outside they sent word to him to come out. The crowd seated around him told him, "Your mother and your brothers and sisters are outside asking for you." He said in reply, "Who are my mother and my brothers?" And gazing around him at those seated in the circle he continued, "These are my mother and my brothers. Whoever does the will of God is brother and sister and mother to me." ✝

WEDNESDAY, JANUARY 24
St. Francis de Sales

✝ *Hebrews 10:11-18*

He has achieved the eternal perfection of all whom he is sanctifying.

Every other priest stands ministering day by day, and offering again and again those same sacrifices which can never take away sins. But Jesus offered one sacrifice for sins and took his seat forever at the right hand of God; now he waits until his enemies are placed beneath his feet. By one offering he has forever perfected those who are being sanctified. The Holy Spirit attests this to us, for after saying,

"This is the covenant I will make with them
after those days, says the Lord:
I will put my laws in their hearts
and I will write them on their minds,"

he also says,

"Their sins and their transgressions
I will remember no more."

Once these have been forgiven, there is no further offering for sin. ✝

Psalm 110:1-4

**R. You are a priest forever,
in the line of Melchizedek.**

The Lord said to my Lord: "Sit at my right hand
till I make your enemies your footstool." **R.**

The scepter of your power the Lord will stretch forth from Zion:
"Rule in the midst of your enemies." **R.**

"Yours is princely power in the day of your birth, in holy
    splendor;
    before the daystar, like the dew, I have begotten you." **R.**
The Lord has sworn, and he will not repent:
    "You are a priest forever, according to the order of
    Melchizedek." **R.**

1 Samuel 3:9; John 6:69
R. Alleluia, alleluia.
Speak, O Lord, your servant is listening;
you have the words of everlasting life. **R.**

† *Mark 4:1-20*
The sower goes out to sow.

On one occasion Jesus began to teach beside the lake. Such
a huge crowd gathered around him that he went and sat in a
boat on the water, while the crowd remained on the shore
nearby. He began to instruct them at great length, by the use
of parables, and in the course of his teaching said: "Listen
carefully to this. A farmer went out sowing. Some of what he
sowed landed on the footpath, where the birds came along and
ate it. Some of the seed landed on rocky ground where it had
little soil; it sprouted immediately because the soil had no
depth. Then, when the sun rose and scorched it, it began to
wither for lack of roots. Again, some landed among thorns,
which grew up and choked it off, and there was no yield of
grain. Some seed, finally, landed on good soil and yielded grain
that sprang up to produce at a rate of thirty and sixty and a
hundredfold." Having spoken this parable, he added: "Let him
who has ears to hear me, hear!"

Now when he was away from the crowd, those present with
the Twelve questioned him about the parables. He told them:
"To you the mystery of the reign of God has been confided. To
the others outside it is all presented in parables, so that they
will look intently and not see, listen carefully and not understand, lest perhaps they repent and be forgiven."

He said to them: "You do not understand this parable? How
then are you going to understand other figures like it? What
the sower is sowing is the word. Those on the path are the ones
to whom, as soon as they hear the word, Satan comes to carry

off what was sown in them. Similarly, those sown on rocky ground are people who on listening to the word accept it joyfully at the outset. Being rootless, they last only a while. When some pressure or persecution overtakes them because of the word, they falter. Those sown among thorns are another class. They have listened to the word, but anxieties over life's demands, and the desire for wealth, and cravings of other sorts come to choke it off; it bears no yield. But those sown on good soil are the ones who listen to the word, take it to heart, and yield thirty- and sixty- and a hundred-fold." ✛

THURSDAY, JANUARY 25
THE CONVERSION OF PAUL

✝ Acts 22:3-16 (or Acts 9:1-22)
Rise and be baptized and wash away
your sins, calling on the name of Jesus.

P aul told the people: "I am a Jew, born in Tarsus in Cilicia, but I was brought up in this city. Here I sat at the feel of Gamaliel and was educated strictly in the law of our fathers. I was a staunch defender of God, just as all of you are today. Furthermore I persecuted this new way to the point of death. I arrested and imprisoned both men and women.

"On this point the high priest and the whole council of elders can bear witness, for it was from them that I received letters to our brother Jews in Damascus. I set out with the intention of bringing the prisoners I would arrest back to Jerusalem for punishment. As I was traveling along, approaching Damascus around noon, a great light from the sky suddenly flashed all about me. I fell to the ground and heard a voice say to me, 'Saul, Saul, why do you persecute me?' I answered, 'Who are you, sir?' He said to me, 'I am Jesus the Nazorean whom you are persecuting.' My companions saw the light but did not hear the voice speaking to me. 'What is it I must do, sir?' I asked, and the Lord replied, 'Get up and go into Damascus. There you will be told about everything you are destined to do.' But since I could not see because of the brilliance of the light, I had to be taken by the hand and led into Damascus by my companions.

"A certain Ananias, a devout observer of the law and well

spoken of by all the Jews who lived there, came and stood by me. 'Saul, my brother,' he said, 'recover your sight.' In that instant I regained my sight and looked at him. The next thing he said was, 'The God of our fathers long ago designated you to know his will, to look upon the Just One, and to hear the sound of his voice; before all men you are to be his witness to what you have seen and heard. Why delay, then? Be baptized at once and wash away your sins as you call upon his name.'" ✛

Psalm 117:1-2
**R. Go out to all the world,
and tell the Good News.**
Praise the Lord, all you nations;
glorify him, all you peoples! **R.**
For steadfast is his kindness toward us,
and the fidelity of the Lord endures forever. **R.**

John 15:16
R. Alleluia, alleluia.
I have chosen you from the world, says the Lord,
to go and bear fruit that will last. **R.**

✝ *Mark 16:15-18*
Go out to the whole world and make known the Good News.

Jesus appeared to the Eleven and said to them: "Go into the whole world and proclaim the good news to all creation. The man who believes in it and accepts baptism will be saved; the man who refuses to believe in it will be condemned. Signs like these will accompany those who have professed their faith: they will use my name to expel demons, they will speak entirely new languages, they will be able to handle serpents, they will be able to drink deadly poison without harm, and the sick upon whom they lay their hands will recover." ✛

FRIDAY, JANUARY 26
Sts. Timothy and Titus

✝ *Titus 1:1-5* *(or 2 Timothy 1:1-8)*
To Titus, my beloved son in a common faith.

Paul, servant of God, sent as an apostle of Jesus Christ for the sake of the faith of those whom God has chosen, and to promote their knowledge of the truth as our religion embodies it, in the hope of that eternal life which God, who cannot lie, promised in endless ages past. This he has now manifested in his own good time as his word, in the preaching entrusted to me by the command of God our Savior. Paul to Titus, my own true child in our common faith: May grace and peace from God our Father, and Christ Jesus our Savior, be with you.

My purpose in leaving you in Crete was that you might accomplish what had been left undone, especially the appointment of presbyters in every town, as I instructed you. ✣

Psalm 37:3-6, 23-24, 39-40
R. The salvation of the just comes from the Lord.
Trust in the Lord and do good,
   that you may dwell in the land and enjoy security.
Take delight in the Lord,
   and he will grant you your heart's requests. **R.**
Commit to the Lord your way;
   trust in him, and he will act.
He will make justice dawn for you like the light;
   bright as the noonday shall be your vindication. **R.**
By the Lord are the steps of a man made firm,
   and he approves his way.
Though he fall, he does not lie prostrate,
   for the hand of the Lord sustains him. **R.**
The salvation of the just is from the Lord;
   he is their refuge in time of distress.
And the Lord helps them and delivers them;
   he delivers them from the wicked and saves them,
because they take refuge in him. **R.**

Colossians 3:16,17
R. Alleluia, alleluia.
Give thanks to God our Father through Jesus Christ our Lord,
and may the fullness of his message live within you. **R.**

† Mark 4:26-34
*A man scatters seed and while he sleeps it
grows even though he does not know how.*

Jesus said to the crowd: "This is how it is with the reign of God. A man scatters seed on the ground. He goes to bed and gets up day after day. Through it all the seed sprouts and grows without his knowing how it happens. The soil produces of itself first the blade, then the ear, finally the ripe wheat in the ear. When the crop is ready he 'wields the sickle, for the time is ripe for harvest.'"

He went on to say: "What comparison shall we use for the reign of God? What image will help to present it? It is like mustard seed which, when planted in the soil, is the smallest of all the earth's seeds, yet once it is sown, springs up to become the largest of shrubs, with branches big enough for the birds of the sky to build nests in its shade." By means of many such parables he taught them the message in a way they could understand. To them he spoke only by way of parable, while he kept explaining things privately to his disciples. ✛

SATURDAY, JANUARY 27
St. Angela Merici

† Hebrews 11:1-2, 8-19
They looked forward to a city founded, designed, and built by God.

Faith is confident assurance concerning what we hope for, and conviction about things we do not see. Because of faith the men of old were approved by God. By faith Abraham obeyed when he was called and went forth to the place he was to receive as a heritage; he went forth, moreover, not knowing where he was going. By faith he sojourned in the promised land as in a foreign country, dwelling in tents with Isaac and Jacob, heirs of the same promise; for he was looking forward to the city with foundations, whose designer and maker is God. By faith Sarah received power to conceive though she was past the age, for she thought that the One who had made the promise was worthy of trust. As a result of this faith, there came forth from one man, who was himself as good as dead, descendants as numerous as the stars in the sky and the sands of the seashore.

All of these died in faith. They did not obtain what had been promised but saw and saluted it from afar. By acknowledging themselves to be strangers and foreigners on the earth, they showed that they were seeking a homeland. If they had been thinking back to the place from which they had come, they would have had the opportunity of returning there. But they were searching for a better, a heavenly home. Wherefore God is not ashamed to be called their God, for he has prepared a city for them. By faith Abraham, when put to the test, offered up Isaac; he who had received the promises was ready to sacrifice his only son, of whom it was said, "Through Isaac shall your descendants be called." He reasoned that God was able to raise from the dead, and so he received Isaac back as a symbol. ✛

Luke 1:69-75
R. Blessed be the Lord God of Israel,
for he has visited his people.
He has raised a horn of saving strength for us
    in the house of David his servant,
As he promised through the mouths of his holy ones,
    the prophets of ancient times: **R.**
Salvation from our enemies
    and from the hands of all our foes.
He has dealt mercifully with our fathers
    and remembered the holy covenant. **R.**
The oath he swore to Abraham our father he would grant us:
    that, rid of fear and delivered from the enemy,
We should serve him devoutly, and through all our days,
    be holy in his sight. **R.**

Psalm 111:8
R. Alleluia, alleluia.
Your laws are all made firm, O Lord,
established for ever more. **R.**

† Mark 4:35-41
Who can this be? Even the wind and the sea obey him.

One day as evening drew on Jesus said to his disciples, "Let us cross over to the farther shore." Leaving the crowd, they took him away in the boat in which he was sitting, while the other boats accompanied him. It happened that a bad squall blew up. The waves were breaking over the boat and it began to ship water badly. Jesus was in the stern through it all, sound asleep on a cushion. They finally woke him and said to him, "Teacher, doesn't it matter to you that we are going to

drown?" He awoke and rebuked the wind and said to the sea:
"Quiet! Be still!" The wind fell off and everything grew calm.
Then he said to them, "Why are you so terrified? Why are you
lacking in faith?" A great awe overcame them at this. They
kept saying to one another, "Who can this be that the wind and
the sea obey him?" ✢

<h1 style="text-align:center">JANUARY 28</h1>
<h2 style="text-align:center">FOURTH SUNDAY IN ORDINARY TIME</h2>

† *Jeremiah 1:4-5, 17-19*
A prophet to the nations I appointed you.

The word of the LORD came to me, saying:
Before I formed you in the womb I knew you,
before you were born I dedicated you,
a prophet to the nations I appointed you.

But do you gird your loins;
stand up and tell them
all that I command you.
Be not crushed on their account,
as though I would leave you crushed before them;
for it is I this day
who have made you a fortified city,
a pillar of iron, a wall of brass,
against the whole land:
against Judah's kings and princes,
against its priests and people.
They will fight against you but not prevail over you,
for I am with you to deliver you, says the LORD. ✢

Psalm 71:1-6, 15, 17
R. I will sing of your salvation.
In you, O LORD, I take refuge;
let me never be put to shame.
In your justice rescue me, and deliver me;
incline your ear to me, and save me. **R.**
Be my rock of refuge,
a stronghold to give me safety,
for you are my rock and my fortress.

O my God, rescue me from the hand of the wicked. **R.**
For you are my hope, O Lord;
   my trust, O God, from my youth.
On you I depend from birth;
   from my mother's womb you are my strength. **R.**
My mouth shall declare your justice,
   day by day your salvation.
O God, you have taught me from my youth,
   and till the present I proclaim your wondrous deeds. **R.**

✛ 1 Corinthians 13:4-13 (or 1 Corinthians 12:31—13:13)
So faith, hope, love remain, these three;
but the greatest of these is love.

Brothers and sisters:
Love is patient, love is kind.
It is not jealous, it is not pompous,
   it is not inflated, it is not rude,
   it does not seek its own interests,
   it is not quick-tempered, it does not brood over injury,
   it does not rejoice over wrongdoing
   but rejoices with the truth.
It bears all things, believes all things,
   hopes all things, endures all things.

Love never fails.
If there are prophecies, they will be brought to nothing;
   if tongues, they will cease;
   if knowledge, it will be brought to nothing.
For we know partially and we prophesy partially,
   but when the perfect comes, the partial will pass away.
When I was a child, I used to talk as a child,
   think as a child, reason as a child;
   when I became a man, I put aside childish things.
At present we see indistinctly, as in a mirror,
   but then face to face.
At present I know partially;
   then I shall know fully, as I am fully known.
So faith, hope, love remain, these three;
   but the greatest of these is love. ✛

Luke 4:18

R. Alleluia, alleluia.

The Lord sent me to bring glad tidings to the poor,
to proclaim liberty to captives. **R.**

† *Luke 4:21-30*
Like Elijah and Elisha, Jesus was not sent only to the Jews.

Jesus began speaking in the synagogue, saying:
    "Today this Scripture passage is fulfilled in your hearing."
And all spoke highly of him
        and were amazed at the gracious words that came from his
            mouth.
They also asked, "Isn't this the son of Joseph?"
He said to them, "Surely you will quote me this proverb,
        'Physician, cure yourself,' and say,
        'Do here in your native place
        the things that we heard were done in Capernaum.'"
And he said, "Amen, I say to you,
        no prophet is accepted in his own native place.
Indeed, I tell you,
        there were many widows in Israel in the days of Elijah
        when the sky was closed for three and a half years
        and a severe famine spread over the entire land.
It was to none of these that Elijah was sent,
        but only to a widow in Zarephath in the land of Sidon.
Again, there were many lepers in Israel
        during the time of Elisha the prophet;
        yet not one of them was cleansed, but only Naaman the
            Syrian."
When the people in the synagogue heard this,
        they were all filled with fury.
They rose up, drove him out of the town,
        and led him to the brow of the hill
        on which their town had been built,
        to hurl him down headlong.
But Jesus passed through the midst of them and went away. †

MONDAY, JANUARY 29
WEEKDAY

† *Hebrews 11:32-40*
Through faith they conquered kingdoms.
God will provide for us something better.

What more shall I recount? I have no time to tell of Gideon, Barak, Samson, Jephthah, of David and Samuel and the prophets, who by faith conquered kingdoms, did what was just, obtained the promises; they broke the jaws of lions, put out raging fires, escaped the devouring sword; though weak they were made powerful, became strong in battle, and turned back foreign invaders. Women received back their dead through resurrection. Others were tortured and did not receive deliverance, in order to obtain a better resurrection. Still others endured mockery, scourging, even chains and imprisonment. They were stoned, sawed in two, put to death at sword's point; they went about garbed in the skins of sheep or goats, needy, afflicted, tormented. The world was not worthy of them. They wandered about in deserts and on mountains, they dwelt in caves and in holes of the earth. Yet despite the fact that all of these were approved because of their faith, they did not obtain what had been promised. God had made a better plan, a plan which included us. Without us, they were not to be made perfect. +

Psalm 31:20-24
**R. Let your hearts take comfort,
all who hope in the Lord.**
How great is the goodness, O Lord,
　　which you have in store for those who fear you,
And which, toward those who take refuge in you,
　　you show in the sight of men. **R.**
You hide them in the shelter of your presence
　　from the plottings of men;
You screen them within your abode
　　from the strife of tongues. **R.**
Blessed be the Lord whose wondrous kindness
　　he has shown me in a fortified city. **R.**
Once I said in my anguish,
　　"I am cut off from your sight";

Yet you heard the sound of my pleading
    when I cried out to you. **R.**
Love the Lord, all you his faithful ones!
    The Lord keeps those who are constant,
    but more than requites those who act proudly. **R.**

2 Corinthians 5:19
R. Alleluia, alleluia.
God was in Christ, to reconcile the world to himself;
and the Good News of reconciliation he has entrusted to us. **R.**

† *Mark 5:1-20*
Unclean spirits came out of the man.

Jesus and his disciples came to Gerasene territory on the other side of the lake. As he got out of the boat, he was immediately met by a man from the tombs who had an unclean spirit. The man had taken refuge among the tombs; he could no longer be restrained even with a chain. In fact, he had frequently been secured with handcuffs and chains, but had pulled the chains apart and smashed the fetters. No one had proved strong enough to tame him. Uninterruptedly night and day, amid the tombs and on the hillsides, he screamed and gashed himself with stones. Catching sight of Jesus at a distance, he ran up and did him homage, shrieking in a loud voice, "Why meddle with me, Jesus, Son of God Most High? I implore you in God's name, do not torture me!" (Jesus had been saying to him, "Unclean spirit, come out of the man!") "What is your name?" Jesus asked him. "Legion is my name," he answered. "There are hundreds of us." He pleaded hard with Jesus not to drive them away from that neighborhood.

It happened that a large herd of swine was feeding there on the slope of the mountain. "Send us into the swine," they begged him. "Let us enter them." He gave the word, and with it the unclean spirits came out and entered the swine. The herd of about two thousand went rushing down the bluff into the lake, where they began to drown. The swineherds ran off and brought the news to field and village, and the people came to see what had happened. As they approached Jesus, they caught sight of the man who had been possessed by Legion sitting fully clothed and perfectly sane, and they were seized with fear. The spectators explained what had happened to the possessed man, and told them about the swine. Before long they were begging him to go away from their district. As Jesus was getting into the boat, the man who had been possessed was pressing to accompany him. Jesus did not grant his request, but told him instead: "Go home to your family and make it clear to them how much the Lord in his mercy has done for you." At that the man went off and began to proclaim throughout the Ten Cities what Jesus had done for him. They were all amazed at what they heard. ✛

TUESDAY, JANUARY 30
WEEKDAY

† Hebrews 12:1-4
Through patience we are led to perfection.

Since we for our part are surrounded by a cloud of witnesses, let us lay aside every encumbrance of sin which clings to us and persevere in running the race which lies ahead; let us keep our eyes fixed on Jesus, who inspires and perfects our faith. For the sake of the joy which lay before him he endured the cross, heedless of its shame. He has taken his seat at the right of the throne of God. Remember how he endured the opposition of sinners; hence do not grow despondent or abandon the struggle. In your fight against sin you have not yet resisted to the point of shedding blood. ✛

Psalm 22:26-28, 30-32
R. They will praise you, Lord, who long for you.
I will fulfill my vows before those who fear him.
    The lowly shall eat their fill;
They who seek the Lord shall praise him:
    "May your hearts be ever merry!" **R.**
All the ends of the earth
    shall remember and turn to the Lord;
All the families of the nations
    shall bow down before him.
To him alone shall bow down
    all who sleep in the earth;
Before him shall bend
    all who go down into the dust. **R.**

And to him my soul shall live.
My descendants shall serve him.
Let the coming generation be told of the Lord
that they may proclaim to a people yet to be born
the justice he has shown. **R.**

Psalm 119:18
R. Alleluia, alleluia.
Unveil my eyes, O Lord,
and I will see the marvels of your law. **R.**

† *Mark 5:21-43*
Young woman, I say to you, arise.

When Jesus had crossed back to the other side of the Sea of Galilee in the boat, a large crowd gathered around him and he stayed close to the lake. One of the officials of the synagogue, a man named Jairus, came near. Seeing Jesus, he fell at his feet and made this earnest appeal: "My little daughter is critically ill. Please come and lay your hands on her so that she may get well and live." The two went off together and a large crowd followed, pushing against Jesus.

There was a woman in the area who had been afflicted with a hemorrhage for a dozen years. She had received treatment at the hands of doctors of every sort and exhausted her savings in the process, yet she got no relief; on the contrary, she only grew worse. She had heard about Jesus and came up behind him in the crowd and put her hand to his cloak. "If I just touch his clothing," she thought, "I shall get well." Immediately her flow of blood dried up and the feeling that she was cured of her affliction ran through her whole body. Jesus was immediately conscious that healing power had gone out from him. Wheeling about in the crowd, he began to ask, "Who touched my clothing?" His disciples said to him, "You can see how this crowd hems you in, yet you ask, 'Who touched me?' Despite this, he kept looking around to see the woman who had done it. Fearful and beginning to tremble now as she realized what had happened, the woman came and fell in front of him and told him the whole truth. He said to her, "Daughter, it is your faith that has cured you. Go in peace and be free of this illness."

He had not finished speaking when people from the

official's house arrived saying, "Your daughter is dead. Why bother the Teacher further?" Jesus disregarded the report that had been brought and said to the official: "Fear is useless. What is needed is trust." He would not permit anyone to follow him except Peter, James, and James' brother John. As they approached the house of the synagogue leader, Jesus was struck by the noise of people wailing and crying loudly on all sides. He entered and said to them: "Why do you make this din with your wailing? The child is not dead. She is asleep." At this they began to ridicule him. Then he put them all out.

Jesus took the child's father and mother and his own companions and entered the room where the child lay. Taking her hand he said to her, *"Talitha, koum,"* which means, "Little girl, get up." The girl, a child of twelve, stood up immediately and began to walk around. At this the family's astonishment was complete. He enjoined them strictly not to let anyone know about it, and told them to give her something to eat. ✛

WEDNESDAY, JANUARY 31
St. John Bosco

† Hebrews 12:4-7, 11-15
The Lord disciplines those he loves.

In your fight against sin you have not yet resisted to the point of shedding blood. Moreover, you have forgotten the encouraging words addressed to you as sons:

"My sons, do not disdain the discipline of the Lord
nor lose heart when he reproves you;
For, whom the Lord loves, he disciplines;
he scourges every son he receives."

Endure your trials as the discipline of God, who deals with you as sons. For what son is there whom his father does not discipline? At the time it is administered, all discipline seems a cause for grief and not for joy, but later it brings forth the fruit of peace and justice to those who are trained in its school. So strengthen your drooping hands and your weak knees. Make straight the paths you walk on, that your halting limbs may not be dislocated but healed.

Strive for peace with all men, and for that holiness without which no one can see the Lord. See to it that no one falls away

from the grace of God; that no bitter root springs up through
which many may become defiled. ✛

Psalm 103:1-2, 13-14, 17-18
**R. The Lord's kindness is everlasting to those who
fear him.**
Bless the Lord, O my soul;
  and all my being, bless his holy name.
Bless the Lord, O my soul,
  and forget not all his benefits. **R.**
As a father has compassion on his children,
  so the Lord has compassion on those who fear him,
For he knows how we are formed;
  he remembers that we are dust. **R.**
But the kindness of the Lord is from eternity
  to eternity toward those who fear him,
And his justice toward children's children
  among those who keep his covenant. **R.**

See Ephesians 1:17-18
R. Alleluia, alleluia.
May the Father of our Lord Jesus Christ
enlighten the eyes of our heart
that we might see how great is the hope
to which we are called. **R.**

† *Mark 6:1-6*
A prophet is without honor in his own country.

Jesus went to his own part of the country followed by his
disciples. When the sabbath came he began to teach in the
synagogue in a way that kept his large audience amazed. They
said: "Where did he get all this? What kind of wisdom is he
endowed with? How is it such miraculous deeds are accomplished by his hands? Isn't this the carpenter, the son of Mary,
a brother of James and Joses and Judas and Simon? Aren't his
sisters our neighbors here?" They found him too much for
them. Jesus' response to all this was: "No prophet is without
honor except in his native place, among his own kindred, and
in his own house." He could work no miracle there, apart from
curing a few who were sick by laying hands on them, so much
did their lack of faith distress him. He made the rounds of the
neighboring villages instead, and spent his time teaching. ✛

THURSDAY, FEBRUARY 1
WEEKDAY

† Hebrews 12:18-19, 21-24
You have come to Mount Zion and the city of the living God.

You have not drawn near to an untouchable mountain and a blazing fire, and gloomy darkness and storm and trumpet blast, and a voice speaking words such that those who heard begged that they be not addressed to them. Indeed, so fearful was the spectacle that Moses said, "I am terrified and trembling." No, you have drawn near to Mount Zion and the city of the living God, the heavenly Jerusalem, to myriads of angels in festal gathering, to the assembly of the first-born enrolled in heaven, to God the judge of all, to the spirits of just men made perfect, to Jesus, the mediator of a new covenant, and to the sprinkled blood which speaks more eloquently than that of Abel. ✛

Psalm 48:2-4, 9-11

R. God, in your temple, we ponder your love.

Great is the Lord and wholly to be praised
    in the city of our God.
His holy mountain, fairest of heights,
    is the joy of all the earth. R.
Mount Zion, "the recesses of the North,"
    is the city of the great King.
God is with her castles;
    renowned is he as a stronghold. R.
As we had heard, so have we seen
    in the city of the Lord of hosts,
In the city of our God;
    God makes it firm forever. R.
O God, we ponder your kindness
    within your temple.
As your name, O God, so also your praise
    reaches to the ends of the earth.
Of justice your right hand is full. R.

Philippians 2:15-16
R. Alleluia, alleluia.
Shine on the world like bright stars;
you are offering it the word of life. **R.**

† *Mark 6:7-13*
He summoned the Twelve and sent them out in pairs.

Jesus summoned the Twelve and began to send them out two
by two, giving them authority over unclean spirits. He instructed them to take nothing on the journey but a walking
stick—no food, no traveling bag, not a coin in the purses in
their belts. They were, however, to wear sandals. "Do not bring
a second tunic," he said, and added: "Whatever house you find
yourself in, stay there until you leave the locality. If any place
will not receive you or hear you, shake its dust from your feet
in testimony against them as you leave." With that they went
off, preaching the need of repentance. They expelled many
demons, anointed the sick with oil, and worked many cures. ✛

FRIDAY, FEBRUARY 2
THE PRESENTATION OF THE LORD

† *Malachi 3:1-4*
There will come to the temple the Lord whom you seek.

Thus says the Lord God:
Lo, I am sending my messenger
    to prepare the way before me;
and suddenly there will come to the temple
    the Lord whom you seek,
and the messenger of the covenant whom you desire.
    Yes, he is coming, says the LORD of hosts.
But who will endure the day of his coming?
    And who can stand when he appears?
For he is like the refiner's fire,
    or like the fuller's lye.
He will sit refining and purifying silver,
    and he will purify the sons of Levi,
refining them like gold or like silver
    that they may offer due sacrifice to the LORD.
Then the sacrifice of Judah and Jerusalem

will please the LORD,
as in the days of old, as in years gone by. ✛

Psalm 24:7-10
R. Who is this king of glory? It is the Lord!
Lift up, O gates, your lintels;
    reach up, you ancient portals,
    that the king of glory may come in! **R.**
Who is this king of glory?
    The LORD, strong and mighty,
    the LORD, mighty in battle. **R.**
Lift up, O gates, your lintels;
    reach up, you ancient portals,
    that the king of glory may come in! **R.**
Who is this king of glory?
    The LORD of hosts; he is the king of glory. **R.**

† Hebrews 2:14-18
He had to become like his brothers and sisters in every way.

Since the children share in blood and flesh,
    Jesus likewise shared in them,
    that through death he might destroy the one
    who has the power of death, that is, the devil,
    and free those who through fear of death
    had been subject to slavery all their life.
Surely he did not help angels
    but rather the descendants of Abraham;
    therefore, he had to become like his brothers and sisters
    in every way,
    that he might be a merciful and faithful high priest before
        God
    to expiate the sins of the people.
Because he himself was tested through what he suffered,
    he is able to help those who are being tested. ✛

Luke 2:32
R. Alleluia, alleluia.
A light of revelation to the Gentiles
and glory for your people Israel. **R.**

† Luke 2:22-32 (or Luke 2:22-40)
My eyes have seen your salvation.

When the days were completed for their purification
according to the law of Moses,
Mary and Joseph took Jesus up to Jerusalem
to present him to the Lord,
just as it is written in the law of the Lord,
Every male that opens the womb
shall be consecrated to the Lord,
and to offer the sacrifice of
a pair of turtledoves or two young pigeons,
in accordance with the dictate in the law of the Lord.

Now there was a man in Jerusalem whose name was Simeon.
This man was righteous and devout,
awaiting the consolation of Israel,
and the Holy Spirit was upon him.
It had been revealed to him by the Holy Spirit
that he should not see death
before he had seen the Christ of the Lord.
He came in the Spirit into the temple;
and when the parents brought in the child Jesus
to perform the custom of the law in regard to him,
he took him into his arms and blessed God, saying:
"Now, Master, you may let your servant go
in peace, according to your word,
for my eyes have seen your salvation,
which you prepared in sight of all the peoples,
a light for revelation to the Gentiles,
and glory for your people Israel." ✠

SATURDAY, FEBRUARY 3
St. Blase, St. Ansgar

† Hebrews 13:15-17, 20-21
May the God of peace who brought back from the
dead the great shepherd, lead you in all good things.

Through Jesus let us continually offer God a sacrifice of
praise, that is, the fruit of lips which acknowledge his name.
   Do not neglect good deeds and generosity; God is pleased
by sacrifices of that kind. Obey your leaders and submit to

them, for they keep watch over you as men who must render an account. So act that they may fulfill their task with joy, not with sorrow, for that would be harmful to you.

May the God of peace, who brought up from the dead the great Shepherd of the sheep in the blood of the eternal covenant, Jesus our Lord, furnish you with all that is good, that you may do his will. Through Jesus Christ may he carry out in you all that is pleasing to him. To Christ be glory forever! Amen. ✛

Psalm 23:1-6
R. The Lord is my shepherd;
there is nothing I shall want.
The Lord is my shepherd; I shall not want.
　In verdant pastures he gives me repose;
Beside restful waters he leads me;
　he refreshes my soul. **R.**
He guides me in right paths
　for his name's sake.
Even though I walk in the dark valley
　I fear no evil; for you are at my side
With your rod and your staff
　that give me courage. **R.**
You spread the table before me
　in the sight of my foes;
You anoint my head with oil;
　my cup overflows. **R.**
Only goodness and kindness follow me
　all the days of my life;
And I shall dwell in the house of the Lord
　for years to come. **R.**

John 10:27
R. Alleluia, alleluia.
My sheep listen to my voice, says the Lord;
I know them, and they follow me. **R.**

† *Mark 6:30-34*
They were sheep without a shepherd.

The apostles returned to Jesus and reported to him all that they had done and what they had taught. He said to them, "Come by yourselves to an out-of-the-way place and rest a little." People were coming and going in great numbers, making it impossible for them to so much as eat. So Jesus and the apostles went off in the boat by themselves to a deserted place. People saw them leaving, and many got to know about it. People from all the towns hastened on foot to the place, arriving ahead of them. Upon disembarking Jesus saw a vast crowd. He pitied them, for they were like sheep without a shepherd; and he began to teach them at great length. ✛

FEBRUARY 4
FIFTH SUNDAY IN ORDINARY TIME

✝ *Isaiah 6:1-2a, 3-8*
Here I am! Send me.

In the year King Uzziah died,
  I saw the Lord seated on a high and lofty throne,
  with the train of his garment filling the temple.
Seraphim were stationed above.

They cried one to the other,
  "Holy, holy, holy is the LORD of hosts!
All the earth is filled with his glory!"
At the sound of that cry, the frame of the door shook
  and the house was filled with smoke.

Then I said, "Woe is me, I am doomed!
For I am a man of unclean lips,
  living among a people of unclean lips;
  yet my eyes have seen the King, the LORD of hosts!"
Then one of the seraphim flew to me,
  holding an ember that he had taken with tongs from the
    altar.

He touched my mouth with it, and said,
  "See, now that this has touched your lips,
  your wickedness is removed, your sin purged."

Then I heard the voice of the Lord saying,
  "Whom shall I send? Who will go for us?"
"Here I am, " I said; "send me!" ✛

Psalm 138:1-5, 7-8

**R. In the sight of the angels I will sing
your praises, Lord.**

I will give thanks to you, O LORD, with all my heart,
  for you have heard the words of my mouth;
  in the presence of the angels I will sing your praise;
I will worship at your holy temple
  and give thanks to your name. **R.**

Because of your kindness and your truth;
  for you have made great above all things
  your name and your promise.
When I called, you answered me;
  you built up strength within me. **R.**

All the kings of the earth shall give thanks to you, O LORD,
  when they hear the words of your mouth;
and they shall sing of the ways of the LORD:
  "Great is the glory of the LORD." **R.**

Your right hand saves me.
  The LORD will complete what he has done for me;
your kindness, O LORD, endures forever;
  forsake not the work of your hands. **R.**

✝ 1 Corinthians 15:3-8, 11 (or 1 Corinthians 15:1-11)
So we preached and so you believe.

Brothers and sisters,
  I handed on to you as of first importance what I also
    received:
  that Christ died for our sins
    in accordance with the Scriptures;
  that he was buried;
  that he was raised on the third day
    in accordance with the Scriptures;
  that he appeared to Cephas, then to the Twelve.
After that, he appeared to more
  than five hundred brothers at once,
  most of whom are still living,
  though some have fallen asleep.
After that he appeared to James,
  then to all the apostles.
Last of all, as to one abnormally born,

he appeared to me.
Therefore, whether it be I or they,
so we preach and so you believed. ✛

Matthew 4:19
R. Alleluia, alleluia.
Come after me
and I will make you fishers of men. **R.**

✝ *Luke 5:1-11*
They left everything and followed Jesus.

While the crowd was pressing in on Jesus and listening
to the word of God,
he was standing by the Lake of Gennesaret.
He saw two boats there alongside the lake;
the fishermen had disembarked and were
washing their nets.
Getting into one of the boats, the one belonging to Simon,
he asked him to put out a short distance from the shore.
Then he sat down and taught the crowds from the boat.
After he had finished speaking, he said to Simon,
"Put out into deep water and lower your nets for a catch."
Simon said in reply,
"Master, we have worked hard all night and have caught
nothing,
but at your command I will lower the nets."
When they had done this, they caught a great number of fish
and their nets were tearing.
They signaled to their partners in the other boat
to come to help them.
They came and filled both boats
so that the boats were in danger of sinking.
When Simon Peter saw this, he fell at the knees of Jesus and
said,
"Depart from me, Lord, for I am a sinful man."
For astonishment at the catch of fish they had made seized
him
and all those with him,
and likewise James and John, the sons of Zebedee,
who were partners of Simon.

Jesus said to Simon, "Do not be afraid;
from now on you will be catching men."
When they brought their boats to the shore,
they left everything and followed him. ✛

MONDAY, FEBRUARY 5
ST. AGATHA

† *Genesis 1:1-19*
God spoke, and it was done.

In the beginning, when God created the heavens and the earth, the earth was a formless wasteland, and darkness covered the abyss, while a mighty wind swept over the waters.

Then God said, "Let there be light," and there was light. God saw how good the light was. God then separated the light from the darkness. God called the light "day," and the darkness he called "night." Thus evening came, and morning followed—the first day.

Then God said, "Let there be a dome in the middle of the waters, to separate one body of water from the other." And so it happened: God made the dome, and it separated the water above the dome from the water below it. God called the dome "the sky." Evening came, and morning followed—the second day.

Then God said, "Let the water under the sky be gathered into a single basin, so that the dry land may appear." And so it happened: the water under the sky was gathered into its basin, and the dry land appeared. God called the dry land "the earth," and the basin of the water he called "the sea." God saw how good it was. Then God said, "Let the earth bring forth vegetation: every kind of plant that bears seed and every kind of fruit tree on earth that bears fruit with its seed in it." And so it happened: the earth brought forth every kind of plant that bears seed and every kind of fruit tree on earth that bears fruit with its seed in it. God saw how good it was. Evening came, and morning followed—the third day.

Then God said: "Let there be lights in the dome of the sky, to separate day from night. Let them mark the fixed times, the days and the years, and serve as luminaries in the dome of the sky, to shed light upon the earth." And so it happened: God made the two great lights, the greater one to govern the day, and the lesser one to govern the night; and he made the stars. God set them in the dome of the sky, to shed light upon the earth, to govern the day and the night, and to separate the light from the darkness. God saw how good it was. Evening came, and morning followed—the fourth day. ✛

Psalm 104:1-2, 5-6, 10, 12, 24, 35
R. May the Lord be glad in his works.
Bless the Lord, O my soul!
O Lord, my God, you are great indeed!
You are clothed with majesty and glory,
 robed in light as with a cloak. **R.**
You fixed the earth upon its foundation,
 not to be moved forever;
With the ocean, as with a garment, you covered it;
 above the mountains the waters stood. **R.**
You send forth springs into the watercourses
 that wind among the mountains.
Beside them the birds of heaven dwell;
 from among the branches they send forth their song. **R.**
How manifold are your works, O Lord!
 In wisdom you have wrought them all—
 the earth is full of your creatures;
 Bless the Lord, O my soul! Alleluia. **R.**

Psalm 147:2, 15
R. Alleluia, alleluia.
O praise the Lord, Jerusalem;
he sends out his word to the earth. **R.**

† Mark 6:53-56
All those who touched him were cured.

Jesus and his disciples, after crossing the lake, came ashore at Gennesaret and tied up there. As they were leaving the boat, people immediately recognized him. The crowds scurried about the adjacent area and began to bring in the sick on bedrolls to the place where they heard he was. Wherever he put in an appearance, in villages, in towns, or at crossroads, they laid the sick in the marketplaces and begged him to let them touch just the tassel of his cloak. All who touched him got well. ✛

TUESDAY, FEBRUARY 6
St. Paul Miki and Companions

✝ *Genesis 1:20—2:4*
Let us make man in our own image and likeness.

Then God said, "Let the water teem with an abundance of living creatures, and on the earth let birds fly beneath the dome of the sky." And so it happened: God created the great sea monsters and all kinds of swimming creatures with which the water teems, and all kinds of winged birds. God saw how good it was, and God blessed them, saying, "Be fertile, multiply, and fill the water of the seas; and let the birds multiply on the earth." Evening came, and morning followed—the fifth day.

Then God said, "Let the earth bring forth all kinds of living creatures: cattle, creeping things, and wild animals of all kinds." And so it happened: God made all kinds of wild animals, all kinds of cattle, and all kinds of creeping things of the earth. God saw how good it was. Then God said: "Let us make man in our image, after our likeness. Let them have dominion over the fish of the sea, the birds of the air, and the cattle, and over all the wild animals and all the creatures that crawl on the ground."

God created man in his image;
in the divine image he created him;
male and female he created them.

God blessed them, saying: "Be fertile and multiply; fill the earth and subdue it. Have dominion over the fish of the sea, the birds of the air, and all the living things that move on the earth." God also said: "See, I give you every seed-bearing plant all over the earth and every tree that has seed-bearing fruit on it to be your food; and to all the animals of the land, all the birds of the air, and all the living creatures that crawl on the ground, I give all the green plants for food." And so it happened. God looked at everything he had made, and he found it very good. Evening came, and morning followed—the sixth day.

Thus the heavens and the earth and all their array were completed. Since on the seventh day God was finished with the work he had been doing, he rested on the seventh day from all the work he had undertaken. So God blessed the seventh day and made it holy, because on it he rested from all the work he had done in creation. Such is the story of the heavens and the earth at their creation. ✝

Psalm 8:4-9
R. O Lord, our God,
how wonderful your name in all the earth!
When I behold your heavens, the work of your fingers,
    the moon and the stars which you set in place—
What is man that you should be mindful of him,
    or the son of man that you should care for him? **R.**
You have made him little less than the angels,
    and crowned him with glory and honor.
You have given him rule over the works of your hands,
    putting all things under his feet. **R.**
All sheep and oxen,
    yes, and the beasts of the field,
The birds of the air, the fishes of the sea,
    and whatever swims the paths of the seas. **R.**

James 1:21
R. Alleluia, alleluia.
Receive and submit to the word planted in you;
it can save your souls. **R.**

✝ Mark 7:1-13
You put aside the commandments of God to hold on to human traditions.

The Pharisees and some of the experts in the law who had come from Jerusalem gathered around Jesus. They had observed a few of his disciples eating meals without having purified—that is to say, washed—their hands. The Pharisees, and in fact all Jews, cling to the custom of their ancestors and never eat without scrupulously washing their hands. Moreover, they never eat anything from the market without first sprinkling it. There are many other traditions they observe — for example, the washing of cups and jugs and kettles. So the Pharisees and the scribes questioned him: "Why do your disciples not follow the tradition of our ancestors, but instead take food without purifying their hands?" He said to them: "How accurately Isaiah prophesied about you hypocrites when he wrote,

    'This people pays me lip service

but their heart is far from me.

Empty is the reverence they do me

because they teach as dogmas mere human precepts.'
You disregard God's commandment and cling to what is human tradition."

He went on to say: "You have made a fine art of setting aside God's commandment in the interests of keeping your traditions! For example, Moses said, 'Honor your father and your mother'; and in another place, 'Whoever curses father or mother shall be put to death.' Yet you declare, 'If a person says to his father or mother, Any support you might have had from me is *korban*' (that is, dedicated to God), you allow him to do nothing more for his father or mother. That is the way you nullify God's word in favor of the traditions you have handed on. And you have many other such practices besides." ✛

WEDNESDAY, FEBRUARY 7
WEEKDAY

† *Genesis 2:4-9, 15-17*
The Lord God planted a garden in Eden,
and there he put the man he had formed.

At the time when the Lord God made the earth and the heavens—while as yet there was no field shrub on earth and no grass of the field had sprouted, for the Lord God had sent no rain upon the earth and there was no man to till the soil, but a stream was welling up out of the earth and was watering all the surface of the ground—the Lord God formed man out of the clay of the ground and blew into his nostrils the breath of life, and so man became a living being.

Then the Lord God planted a garden in Eden, in the east, and he placed there the man whom he had formed. Out of the ground the Lord God made various trees grow that were delightful to look at and good for food, with the tree of life in the middle of the garden and the tree of the knowledge of good and bad.

The Lord God then took the man and settled him in the garden of Eden, to cultivate and care for it. The Lord God gave man this order: "You are free to eat from any of the trees of the garden except the tree of the knowledge of good and bad. From that tree you shall not eat; the moment you eat from it you are surely doomed to die." ✛

Psalm 104:1-2, 27-30

R. Oh, bless the Lord, my soul!

Bless the Lord, O my soul!
O Lord, my God, you are great indeed!
You are clothed with majesty and glory,
    robed in light as with a cloak. **R.**
All creatures look to you
    to give them food in due time.
When you give it to them, they gather it;
    when you open your hand, they are filled with
        good things. **R.**
If you take away their breath, they perish
    and return to their dust.
When you send forth your spirit, they are created,
    and you renew the face of the earth. **R.**

Psalm 25:4-5

R. Alleluia, alleluia.

Teach me your paths, my God,
and lead me in your truth. **R.**

† Mark 7:14-23

It is the things that come out of a man that make him unclean.

Jesus summoned the crowd and said to them: "Hear me, all of you, and try to understand. Nothing that enters a man from outside can make him impure; that which comes out of him, and only that, constitutes impurity. Let everyone heed what he hears!"

When he got home, away from the crowd, his disciples questioned him about the proverb. "Are you, too, incapable of understanding?" he asked them. "Do you not see that nothing that enters a man from outside can make him impure? It does not penetrate his being, but enters his stomach only and passes into the latrine." Thus did he render all foods clean. He went on: "What emerges from within a man, that and nothing else is what makes him impure. Wicked designs come from the deep recesses of the heart: acts of fornication, theft, murder, adulterous conduct, greed, maliciousness, deceit, sensuality, envy, blasphemy, arrogance, an obtuse spirit. All these evils come from within and render a man impure." ✛

THURSDAY, FEBRUARY 8
St. Jerome Emiliani

✝ *Genesis 2:18-25*
The Lord God led her to Adam, and they became two in one body.

The Lord God said: "It is not good for the man to be alone. I will make a suitable partner for him." So the Lord God formed out of the ground various wild animals and various birds of the air, and he brought them to the man to see what he would call them; whatever the man called each of them would be its name. The man gave names to all the cattle, all the birds of the air, and all the wild animals; but none proved to be the suitable partner for the man.

So the Lord God cast a deep sleep on the man, and while he was asleep, he took out one of his ribs and closed up its place with flesh. The Lord God then built up into a woman the rib that he had taken from the man. When he brought her to the man, the man said:

"This one, at last, is bone of my bones
    and flesh of my flesh;
This one shall be called 'woman,'
    for out of 'her man' this one has been taken."

That is why a man leaves his father and mother and clings to his wife, and the two of them become one body.

The man and his wife were both naked, yet they felt no shame. ✝

Psalm 128:1-5
R. Happy are those who fear the Lord.
Happy are you who fear the Lord,
    who walk in his ways!
For you shall eat the fruit of your handiwork;
    happy shall you be, and favored. **R.**
Your wife shall be like a fruitful vine
    in the recesses of your home;
Your children like olive plants
    around your table. **R.**
Behold, thus is the man blessed
    who fears the Lord.
The Lord bless you from Zion:

may you see the prosperity of Jerusalem
all the days of your life. **R.**

John 6:64, 69
R. Alleluia, alleluia.
Your words, Lord, are spirit and life,
you have the words of everlasting life. **R.**

† *Mark 7:24-30*
The dogs under the table can eat the children's scraps.

Jesus went to the territory of Tyre and Sidon. He retired to a
certain house and wanted no one to recognize him; however, he
could not escape notice. Soon a woman, whose small daughter
had an unclean spirit, heard about him. She approached him
and crouched at his feet. The woman who was Greek—a Syro-
Phoenician by birth—began to beg him to expel the demon
from her daughter. He told her: "Let the sons of the household
satisfy themselves at table first. It is not right to take the food
of the children and throw it to the dogs." "Please, Lord," she
replied, "even the dogs under the table eat the family's leavings." Then he said to her, "For such a reply, be off now! The
demon has already left your daughter." When she got home,
she found the child lying in bed and the demon gone. ✛

FRIDAY, FEBRUARY 9
WEEKDAY

† *Genesis 3:1-8*
You will be like God, knowing good and evil.

Now the serpent was the most cunning of all the animals that
the Lord God had made. The serpent asked the woman, "Did
God really tell you not to eat from any of the trees in the
garden?" The woman answered the serpent: "We may eat of
the fruit of the trees in the garden; it is only about the fruit of
the tree in the middle of the garden that God said, 'You shall
not eat it or even touch it, lest you die.'" But the serpent said
to the woman: "You certainly will not die! No, God knows well
that the moment you eat of it you will be like gods who know
what is good and what is bad." The woman saw that the tree
was good for food, pleasing to the eyes, and desirable for
gaining wisdom. So she took some of its fruit and ate it; and she

also gave some to her husband, who was with her, and he ate it. Then the eyes of both of them were opened, and they realized that they were naked; so they sewed fig leaves together and made loincloths for themselves.

When they heard the sound of the Lord God moving about in the garden at the breezy time of the day, the man and his wife hid themselves from the Lord God among the trees of the garden. ✛

Psalm 32:1-2, 5-7
R. Happy are those whose sins are forgiven.
Happy is he whose fault is taken away,
    whose sin is covered.
Happy the man to whom the Lord imputes not guilt,
    in whose spirit there is no guile. **R.**
Then I acknowledged my sin to you,
    my guilt I covered not.
I said, "I confess my faults to the Lord,"
    and you took away the guilt of my sin. **R.**
For this shall every faithful man pray to you
    in time of stress.
Though deep waters overflow,
    they shall not reach him. **R.**
You are my shelter; from distress you will preserve me;
    with glad cries of freedom you will ring me round. **R.**

John 14:5
R. Alleluia, alleluia.
I am the way, the truth, and the life, says the Lord;
no one comes to the Father, except through me. **R.**

† Mark 7:31-37
He makes the deaf hear and the dumb speak.

Jesus left Tyrian territory and returned by way of Sidon to the Sea of Galilee, into the district of the Ten Cities. Some people brought him a deaf man who had a speech impediment and begged him to lay his hand on him. Jesus took him off by himself away from the crowd. He put his fingers into the man's ears and, spitting, touched his tongue; then he looked up to heaven and emitted a groan. He said to him, "*Ephphatha!*" (that is, "Be opened!") At once the man's ears were opened; he was freed from the impediment, and began to speak plainly. Then he enjoined them strictly not to tell anyone; but the more he ordered them not to, the more they proclaimed it. Their amazement went beyond all bounds: "He has done everything well! He makes the deaf hear and the mute speak!" ✛

SATURDAY, FEBRUARY 10
St. Scholastica

† *Genesis 3:9-24*
God expelled them from the garden of Eden to toil the earth.

The Lord God called to Adam and asked him, "Where are you?" He answered, "I heard you in the garden; but I was afraid, because I was naked, so I hid myself." Then he asked, "Who told you that you were naked? You have eaten, then, from the tree of which I had forbidden you to eat!" The man replied, "The woman whom you put here with me—she gave me fruit from the tree, and so I ate it." The Lord God then asked the woman, "Why did you do such a thing?" The woman answered, "The serpent tricked me into it, so I ate it."

Then the Lord God said to the serpent:
"Because you have done this, you shall be banned
    from all the animals
    and from all the wild creatures;
On your belly shall you crawl,
    and dirt shall you eat
    all the days of your life.
I will put enmity between you and the woman,
    and between your offspring and hers;
He will strike at your head,
    while you strike at his heel."
To the woman he said:
"I will intensify the pangs of your childbearing;
    in pain shall you bring forth children.
Yet your urge shall be for your husband,
    and he shall be your master."
To the man he said: "Because you listened to your wife and ate from the tree of which I had forbidden you to eat,
"Cursed be the ground because of you!
    In toil shall you eat its yield

all the days of your life.
Thorns and thistles shall it bring forth to you,
    as you eat of the plants of the field.
By the sweat of your face
    shall you get bread to eat,
Until you return to the ground,
    from which you were taken;
For you are dirt,
    and to dirt you shall return."
The man called his wife Eve, because she became the mother of all the living.

For the man and his wife the Lord God made leather garments, with which he clothed them. Then the Lord God said: "See! The man has become like one of us, knowing what is good and what is bad! Therefore, he must not be allowed to put out his hand to take fruit from the tree of life also, and thus eat of it and live forever." The Lord God therefore banished him from the garden of Eden, to till the ground from which he had been taken. When he expelled the man, he settled him east of the garden of Eden; and he stationed the cherubim and the fiery revolving sword, to guard the way to the tree of life. ✛

Psalm 90:2-6, 12-13
R. In every age, O Lord, you have been our refuge.
Before the mountains were begotten
    and the earth and the world were brought forth,
    from everlasting to everlasting you are God. **R.**
You turn man back to dust,
    saying, "Return, O children of men."
For a thousand years in your sight
    are as yesterday, now that it is past,
    or as a watch of the night. **R.**
You make an end of them in their sleep;
    the next morning they are like the changing grass,
Which at dawn springs up anew,
    but by evening wilts and fades. **R.**
Teach us to number our days aright,
    that we may gain wisdom of heart.
Return, O Lord! How long?
    Have pity on your servants! **R.**

Matthew 4:4

R. Alleluia, alleluia.
Man does not live on bread alone,
but on every word that comes from the mouth of God. **R.**

† *Mark 8:1-10*
They ate and were filled.

A large crowd assembled, and they were without anything to eat. Jesus called the disciples over to him and said: "My heart is moved with pity for the crowd. By now they have been with me three days and have nothing to eat. If I send them home hungry, they will collapse on the way. Some of them have come a great distance." His disciples replied, "How can anyone give these people sufficient bread in this deserted spot?" Still he asked them, "How many loaves do you have?" "Seven," they replied. Then he directed the crowd to take their places on the ground. Taking the seven loaves he gave thanks, broke them, and gave them to his disciples to distribute, and they handed them out to the crowd. They also had a few small fishes; asking a blessing on the fish, he told them to distribute these also. The people in the crowd ate until they had their fill; then they gathered up seven wicker baskets of leftovers. Those who had eaten numbered about four thousand.

He dismissed them and got into the boat with his disciples to go to the neighborhood of Dalmanutha. ✝

FEBRUARY 11
SIXTH SUNDAY IN ORDINARY TIME

† *Jeremiah 17:5-8*
Cursed is the one who trusts in human beings;
blessed is the one who trusts in the Lord.

Thus says the LORD:
Cursed is the one who trusts in human beings,
    who seeks his strength in flesh,
    whose heart turns away from the LORD.
He is like a barren bush in the desert
    that enjoys no change of season,
but stands in a lava waste,
    a salt and empty earth.

Blessed is the one who trusts in the LORD,
   whose hope is the LORD.
He is like a tree planted beside the waters
   that stretches out its roots to the stream:
it fears not the heat when it comes;
   its leaves stay green;
in the year of drought it shows no distress,
   but still bears fruit. +

Psalm 1:1-4, 6
R. Blessed are they who hope in the Lord.
Blessed the man who follows not
   the counsel of the wicked,
nor walks in the way of sinners,
   nor sits in the company of the insolent,
but delights in the law of the LORD
   and meditates on his law day and night. **R.**
He is like a tree
   planted near running water,
that yields its fruit in due season,
   and whose leaves never fade.
Whatever he does, prospers. **R.**
Not so the wicked, not so;
   they are like chaff which the wind drives away.
For the LORD watches over the way of the just,
   but the way of the wicked vanishes. **R.**

† *1 Corinthians 15:12, 16-20*
If Christ has not been raised, your faith is in vain.

Brothers and sisters:
If Christ is preached as raised from the dead,
   how can some among you say
      there is no resurrection of the dead?
If the dead are not raised, neither has Christ been raised,
   and if Christ has not been raised, your faith is vain;
      you are still in your sins.
Then those who have fallen asleep in Christ have perished.
If for this life only we have hoped in Christ,
   we are the most pitiable people of all.

But now Christ has been raised from the dead,
   the firstfruits of those who have fallen asleep. +

Luke 6:23ab

R. Alleluia, alleluia.

Rejoice and be glad;
your reward will be great in heaven. **R.**

† *Luke 6:17, 20-26*

Blessed are the poor. Woe to you who are rich.

Jesus came down with the Twelve
and stood on a stretch of level ground
with a great crowd of his disciples
and a large number of the people
from all Judea and Jerusalem
and the coastal region of Tyre and Sidon.
And raising his eyes toward his disciples he said:
"Blessed are you who are poor,
for the kingdom of God is yours.
Blessed are you who are now hungry,
for you will be satisfied.
Blessed are you who are now weeping,
for you will laugh.
Blessed are you when people hate you,
and when they exclude and insult you,
and denounce your name as evil
on account of the Son of Man.
Rejoice and leap for joy on that day!
Behold, your reward will be great in heaven.
For their ancestors treated the prophets in the same way.
But woe to you who are rich,
for you have received your consolation.
Woe to you who are filled now,
for you will be hungry.
Woe to you who laugh now,
for you will grieve and weep.
Woe to you when all speak well of you,
for their ancestors treated the false
prophets in this way." ✝

MONDAY, FEBRUARY 12
WEEKDAY

✝ *Genesis 4:1-15, 25*
Cain set on his brother and killed him.

The man had relations with his wife Eve, and she conceived and bore Cain, saying, "I have produced a man with the help of the Lord." Next she bore his brother Abel. Abel became a keeper of flocks, and Cain a tiller of the soil. In the course of time Cain brought an offering to the Lord from the fruit of the soil, while Abel, for his part, brought one of the best firstlings of his flock. The Lord looked with favor on Abel and his offering, but on Cain and his offering he did not. Cain greatly resented this and was crestfallen. So the Lord said to Cain: "Why are you so resentful and crestfallen? If you do well, you can hold up your head; but if not, sin is a demon lurking at the door: his urge is toward you, yet you can be his master."

Cain said to his brother Abel, "Let us go out in the field." When they were in the field, Cain attacked his brother Abel and killed him. Then the Lord asked Cain, "Where is your brother Abel?" He answered, "I do not know. Am I my brother's keeper?" The Lord then said: "What have you done! Listen: your brother's blood cries out to me from the soil! Therefore you shall be banned from the soil that opened its mouth to receive your brother's blood from your hand. If you till the soil, it shall no longer give you its produce. You shall become a restless wanderer on the earth." Cain said to the Lord: "My punishment is too great to bear. Since you have now banished me from the soil, and I must avoid your presence and become a restless wanderer on the earth, anyone may kill me at sight." "Not so!" the Lord said to him. "If anyone kills Cain, Cain shall be avenged sevenfold." So the Lord put a mark on Cain, lest anyone should kill him at sight.

Adam again had relations with his wife, and she gave birth to a son whom she called Seth. "God has granted me more offspring in place of Abel," she said, "because Cain slew him." ✝

Psalm 50:1, 8, 16-17, 20-21
R. Offer to God a sacrifice of praise.
God the Lord has spoken and summoned the earth,
   from the rising of the sun to its setting.

Not for your sacrifices do I rebuke you,
    for your holocausts are before me always. **R.**
"Why do you recite my statutes,
    and profess my covenant with your mouth
Though you hate discipline
    and cast my words behind you? **R.**
You sit speaking against your brother;
    against your mother's son you spread rumors.
When you do these things, shall I be deaf to it?
    Or think you that I am like yourself?
    I will correct you by drawing them up before your eyes." **R.**

1 Thessalonians 2:13
R. Alleluia, alleluia.
Receive this message not as the words of man,
but as truly the word of God. **R.**

† *Mark 8:11-13*
Why does this generation demand a sign?

The Pharisees came forward and began to argue with Jesus. They were looking for some heavenly sign from him as a test. With a sigh from the depths of his spirit he said, "Why does this age seek a sign? I assure you, no such sign will be given it!" Then he left them, got into the boat again, and went off to the other shore. ✝

TUESDAY, FEBRUARY 13
WEEKDAY

† *Genesis 6:5-8; 7:1-5, 10*
I will rid man, my own creation, from the face of the earth.

When the Lord saw how great was man's wickedness on earth, and how no desire that his heart conceived was ever anything but evil, he regretted that he had made man on the earth, and his heart was grieved.

So the Lord said: "I will wipe out from the earth the men whom I have created, and not only the men, but also the beasts and the creeping things and the birds of the air, for I am sorry that I made them." But Noah found favor with the Lord.

Then the Lord said to Noah: "Go into the ark, you and all your household, for you alone in this age have I found to be truly just. Of every clean animal, take with you seven pairs, a male and its mate; and of the unclean animals, one pair, a male and its mate; likewise, of every clean bird of the air, seven pairs, a male and a female, and of all the unclean birds, one pair, a male and a female. Thus you will keep their issue alive over all the earth. Seven days from now I will bring rain down on the earth for forty days and forty nights, and so I will wipe out from the surface of the earth every moving creature that I have made." Noah did just as the Lord had commanded him.

As soon as the seven days were over, the waters of the flood came upon the earth. ✛

Psalm 29:1-4, 9-10
R. The Lord will bless his people with peace.
Give to the Lord, you sons of God,
    give to the Lord glory and praise,
Give to the Lord the glory due his name;
    adore the Lord in holy attire. **R.**
The voice of the Lord is over the waters,
    the Lord, over vast waters.
The voice of the Lord is mighty;
    the voice of the Lord is majestic. **R.**
The God of glory thunders,
    and in his temple all say, "Glory!"
The Lord is enthroned above the flood;
    the Lord is enthroned as king forever. **R.**

Matthew 11:25
R. Alleluia, alleluia.
Blessed are you, Father, Lord of heaven and earth;
you have revealed to little ones the mysteries of the kingdom. **R.**

† *Mark 8:14-21*
Be on guard against the "yeast" of the Pharisees and the "yeast" of Herod.

The disciples had forgotten to bring any bread along; except for one loaf they had none with them in the boat. So when Jesus instructed them, "Keep your eyes open! Be on your guard against the yeast of the Pharisees and the yeast of Herod," they concluded among themselves that it was because they had no bread. Aware of this he said to them, "Why do you suppose that it is because you have no bread? Do you still not see or comprehend? Are your minds completely blinded? Have you eyes but no sight? Ears but no hearing? Do you remember when I broke the five loaves for the five thousand, how many baskets of fragments you gathered up." They answered, "Twelve." "When I broke the seven loaves for the four thousand, how many full hampers of fragments did you collect?" They answered, "Seven." He said to them again, "Do you still not understand?" ✝

WEDNESDAY, FEBRUARY 14
Sts. Cyril and Methodius

✝ *Genesis 8:6-13, 20-22*
He saw that the waters covered the face of the earth.

At the end of forty days Noah opened the hatch he had made in the ark, and he sent out a raven, to see if the waters had lessened on the earth. It flew back and forth until the waters dried off from the earth. Then he sent out a dove, to see if the waters had lessened on the earth. But the dove could find no place to alight and perch, and it returned to him in the ark, for there was water all over the earth. Putting out his hand, he caught the dove and drew it back to him inside the ark. He waited seven days more and again sent the dove out from the ark. In the evening the dove came back to him, and there in its bill was a plucked-off olive leaf! So Noah knew that the waters had lessened on the earth. He waited still another seven days and then released the dove once more; and this time it did not come back.

In the six hundred and first year of Noah's life, in the first month, on the first day of the month, the water began to dry up on the earth. Noah then removed the covering of the ark and saw that the surface of the ground was drying up.

Noah built an altar to the Lord, and choosing from every clean animal and every clean bird, he offered holocausts on the altar. When the Lord smelled the sweet odor, he said to himself: "Never again will I doom the earth because of man, since the desires of man's heart are evil from the start; nor will I ever again strike down all living beings, as I have done.

As long as the earth lasts,
seedtime and harvest,

cold and heat,
Summer and winter,
and day and night
shall not cease." ✛

Psalm 116:12-15, 18-19
R. To you, Lord, I will offer a sacrifice of praise.
How shall I make a return to the Lord
for all the good he has done for me?
The cup of salvation I will take up,
and I will call upon the name of the Lord. **R.**
My vows to the Lord I will pay
in the presence of all his people.
Precious in the eyes of the Lord
is the death of his faithful ones. **R.**
My vows to the Lord I will pay
in the presence of all his people,
In the courts of the house of the Lord,
in your midst, O Jerusalem. **R.**

Psalm 19:9
R. Alleluia, alleluia.
Your words, O Lord, give joy to my heart,
your teaching is light to my eyes. **R.**

† *Mark 8:22-26*
He restored sight to the blind man and he could see everything clearly.

When Jesus and his disciples arrived at Bethsaida, some people brought him a blind man and begged him to touch him. Jesus took the blind man's hand and led him outside the village. Putting spittle on his eyes he laid his hands on him and asked, "Can you see anything?" The man opened his eyes and said, "I can see people but they look like walking trees!" Then a second time Jesus laid hands on his eyes, and he saw perfectly; his sight was restored and he could see everything clearly. Jesus sent him home with the admonition, "Do not even go into the village." ✛

THURSDAY, FEBRUARY 15
WEEKDAY

† *Genesis 9:1-13*
I set my bow in the clouds and it shall be a sign
of the covenant between me and the earth.

God blessed Noah and his sons and said to them: "Be fertile and multiply and fill the earth. Dread fear of you shall come upon all the animals of the earth and all the birds of the air, upon all the creatures that move about on the ground and all the fishes of the sea; into your power they are delivered. Every creature that is alive shall be yours to eat; I give them all to you as I did the green plants. Only flesh with its lifeblood still in it you shall not eat. For your own lifeblood, too, I will demand an accounting: from every animal I will demand it, and from man in regard to his fellow man I will demand an accounting for human life.

If anyone sheds the blood of man,
    by man shall his blood be shed;
For in the image of God
    has man been made.
Be fertile, then, and multiply; abound on the earth and subdue it."

God said to Noah and to his sons with him: "See, I am now establishing my covenant with you and your descendants after you and with every living creature that was with you: all the birds, and the various tame and wild animals that were with you and came out of the ark. I will establish my covenant with you, that never again shall all bodily creatures be destroyed by the waters of a flood; there shall not be another flood to devastate the earth." God added: "This is the sign that I am giving for all ages to come, of the covenant between me and you and every living creature with you: I set my bow in the clouds to serve as a sign of the covenant between me and the earth." ✚

Psalm 102:16-23, 29
R. **From heaven the Lord looks down on the earth.**
The nations shall revere your name, O Lord,
    and all the kings of the earth your glory,
When the Lord has rebuilt Zion
    and appeared in his glory;

When he has regarded the prayer of the destitute,
and not despised their prayer. **R.**
Let this be written for the generation to come,
and let his future creatures praise the Lord:
"The Lord looked down from his holy height,
from heaven he beheld the earth,
To hear the groaning of the prisoners,
to release those doomed to die." **R.**
The children of your servants shall abide,
and their posterity shall continue in your presence,
That the name of the Lord may be declared in Zion,
and his praise, in Jerusalem,
When the peoples gather together,
and the kingdoms, to serve the Lord. **R.**

John 14:23
R. Alleluia, alleluia.
If anyone loves me, he will hold to my words,
and my Father will love him, and we will come to him. **R.**

† *Mark 8:27-33*
You are the Christ. The Son of Man must suffer many things.

Jesus and his disciples set out for the villages around Caesarea Philippi. On the way he asked his disciples this question: "Who do people say that I am?" They replied, "Some, John the Baptizer, others, Elijah, still others, one of the prophets." "And you," he went on to ask, "who do you say that I am?" Peter answered him, "You are the Messiah!" Then he strictly ordered them not to tell anyone about him.

He then began to teach them that the Son of Man had to suffer much, be rejected by the elders, the chief priests, and the scribes, be put to death, and rise three days later. He said this quite openly. Peter then took him aside and began to remonstrate with him. At this he turned around and, eyeing the disciples, reprimanded Peter in turn: "Get out of my sight, you satan! You are not judging by God's standards but by man's!" ✝

FRIDAY, FEBRUARY 16
WEEKDAY

† *Genesis 11:1-9*
Let us go down and confuse their language.

The whole world spoke the same language, using the same words. While men were migrating in the east, they came upon a valley in the land of Shinar and settled there. They said to one another, "Come, let us mold bricks and harden them with fire." They used bricks for stone, and bitumen for mortar. Then they said, "Come, let us build ourselves a city and a tower with its top in the sky, and so make a name for ourselves; otherwise we shall be scattered all over the earth."

The Lord came down to see the city and the tower that the men had built. Then the Lord said: "If now, while they are one people, all speaking the same language, they have started to do this, nothing will later stop them from doing whatever they presume to do. Let us then go down and there confuse their language, so that one will not understand what another says." Thus the Lord scattered them from there all over the earth, and they stopped building the city. That is why it was called Babel, because there the Lord confused the speech of all the world. It was from that place that he scattered them all over the earth. ✛

Psalm 33:10-15
R. Happy the people the Lord has chosen to be his own.
The Lord brings to nought the plans of nations;
  he foils the designs of peoples.
But the plan of the Lord stands forever;
  the design of his heart, through all generations. **R.**
Happy the nation whose God is the Lord,
  the people he has chosen for his own inheritance.
From heaven the Lord looks down;
  he sees all mankind. **R.**
From his fixed throne he beholds
  all who dwell on the earth,
He who fashioned the heart of each,
  he who knows all their works. **R.**

See Luke 8:15
R. Alleluia, alleluia.
Happy are they who have kept the word with a generous heart, and yield a harvest through perseverance. **R.**

† Mark 8:34—9:1
He who loses his life for my sake and the sake of the gospel will save it.

Jesus summoned the crowd with his disciples and said to them: "If a man wishes to come after me, he must deny his very self, take up his cross and follow in my steps. Whoever would save his life will lose it, but whoever loses his life for my sake and the gospel's will save it. What profit does a man show who gains the whole world and destroys himself in the process? What can a man offer in exchange for his life? If any one in this faithless and corrupt age is ashamed of me and my doctrine, the Son of Man will be ashamed of him when he comes with the holy angels in his Father's glory."

He also said to them: "I assure you, among those standing here there are some who will not taste death until they see the reign of God established in power." ✚

SATURDAY, FEBRUARY 17
SEVEN SERVITE FOUNDERS

† Hebrews 11:1-7
By faith we understand that the world was created by God.

Faith is confident assurance concerning what we hope for, and conviction about things we do not see. Because of faith the men of old were approved by God. Through faith we perceive that the worlds were created by the word of God, and that what is visible came into being through the invisible. By faith Abel offered God a sacrifice greater than Cain's. Because of this he was attested to be just, God himself having borne witness to him on account of his gifts; therefore, although Abel is dead, he still speaks. By faith Enoch was taken away without dying, and "he was seen no more because God took him." Scripture testifies that, before he was taken up, he was pleasing to God— but without faith, it is impossible to please him. Anyone who comes to God must believe that he exists, and that he rewards those who seek him. By faith Noah, warned about things not yet seen, revered God and built an ark that his household might be saved. He thereby condemned the world and inherited the justice which comes through faith. ✙

Psalm 145:2-5, 10-11
R. I will praise your name forever, Lord.
Every day will I bless you,
    and I will praise your name forever and ever.
Great is the Lord and highly to be praised;
    his greatness is unsearchable. **R.**
Generation after generation praises your works
    and proclaims your might.
They speak of the splendor of your glorious majesty
    and tell of your wondrous works. **R.**
Let all your works give you thanks, O Lord,
    and let your faithful ones bless you.
Let them discourse of the glory of your kingdom
    and speak of your might. **R.**

John 8:12
R. Alleluia, alleluia.
I am the light of the world, says the Lord;
the man who follows me will have the light of life. **R.**

✝ Mark 9:2-13
He was transfigured in their presence.

Jesus took Peter, James, and John off by themselves with him and led them up a high mountain. He was transfigured before their eyes and his clothes became dazzlingly white—whiter than the work of any bleacher could make them. Elijah appeared to them along with Moses; the two were in conversation with Jesus. Then Peter spoke to Jesus: "Rabbi, how good it is for us to be here. Let us erect three booths on this site, one for you, one for Moses, and one for Elijah." He hardly knew what to say, for they were all overcome with awe. A cloud came, overshadowing them, and out of the cloud a voice: "This is my Son, my beloved. Listen to him." Suddenly looking around they no longer saw anyone with them—only Jesus.

As they were coming down the mountain, he strictly enjoined them not to tell anyone what they had seen, before the Son of Man had risen from the dead. They kept this word of his to themselves, though they continued to discuss what "to rise from the dead" meant. Finally they put to him this question: "Why do the scribes claim that Elijah must come first?" He told them: "Elijah will indeed come first and restore everything. Yet why does Scripture say of the Son of Man that he must suffer much and be despised? Let me assure you, Elijah has already come. They did entirely as they pleased with him, as the Scriptures say of him." ✛

FEBRUARY 18
SEVENTH SUNDAY IN ORDINARY TIME

† 1 Samuel 26:2, 7-9, 12-13, 22-23
Though the Lord delivered you into my grasp, I would not harm you.

In those days, Saul went down to the desert of Ziph
    with three thousand picked men of Israel,
    to search for David in the desert of Ziph.
So David and Abishai went among Saul's soldiers by night
    and found Saul lying asleep within the barricade,
    with his spear thrust into the ground at his head
    and Abner and his men sleeping around him.

Abishai whispered to David:
    "God has delivered your enemy into your grasp this day.
Let me nail him to the ground with one thrust of the spear;
    I will not need a second thrust!"
But David said to Abishai, "Do not harm him,
    for who can lay hands on the LORD's anointed and remain
        unpunished?"
So David took the spear and the water jug from their place at
        Saul's head,
    and they got away without anyone's seeing or knowing or
        awakening.
All remained asleep,
    because the LORD had put them into a deep slumber.

Going across to an opposite slope,
    David stood on a remote hilltop
    at a great distance from Abner, son of Ner, and the troops.
He said: "Here is the king's spear.
Let an attendant come over to get it.

The LORD will reward each man for his justice and faithfulness.
Today, though the LORD delivered you into my grasp,
   I would not harm the LORD's anointed." ✛

Psalm 103:1-4, 8, 10, 12-13
R. The Lord is kind and merciful.
Bless the LORD, O my soul;
   and all my being, bless his holy name.
Bless the LORD, O my soul,
   and forget not all his benefits. **R.**
He pardons all your iniquities,
   heals all your ills.
He redeems your life from destruction,
   crowns you with kindness and compassion. **R.**
Merciful and gracious is the LORD,
   slow to anger and abounding in kindness.
Not according to our sins does he deal with us,
   nor does he requite us according to our crimes. **R.**
As far as the east is from the west,
   so far has he put our transgressions from us.
As a father has compassion on his children,
   so the LORD has compassion on those who fear him. **R.**

† *1 Corinthians 15:45-49*
Just as we have borne the image of the earthly one,
we shall also bear the image of the heavenly one.

Brothers and sisters:
It is written, *The first man, Adam, became a living being,*
   the last Adam a life-giving spirit.
But the spiritual was not first;
   rather the natural and then the spiritual.
The first man was from the earth, earthly;
   the second man, from heaven.
As was the earthly one, so also are the earthly,
   and as is the heavenly one, so also are the heavenly.
Just as we have borne the image of the earthly one,
   we shall also bear the image of the heavenly one. ✛

John 13:34

R. Alleluia, alleluia.

I give you a new commandment, says the Lord:
love one another as I have loved you. **R.**

† *Luke 6:27-38*

Be merciful, just as your Father is merciful.

Jesus said to his disciples:
"To you who hear I say,
love your enemies, do good to those who hate you,
bless those who curse you, pray for those who mistreat you.
To the person who strikes you on one cheek,
offer the other one as well,
and from the person who takes your cloak,
do not withhold even your tunic.
Give to everyone who asks of you,
and from the one who takes what is yours do not demand it
back.
Do to others as you would have them do to you.
For if you love those who love you,
what credit is that to you?
Even sinners love those who love them.
And if you do good to those who do good to you,
what credit is that to you?
Even sinners do the same.
If you lend money to those from whom you expect repayment,
what credit is that to you?
Even sinners lend to sinners,
and get back the same amount.
But rather, love your enemies and do good to them,
and lend expecting nothing back;
then your reward will be great
and you will be children of the Most High,
for he himself is kind to the ungrateful and the wicked.
Be merciful, just as your Father is merciful.

"Stop judging and you will not be judged.
Stop condemning and you will not be condemned.
Forgive and you will be forgiven.
Give, and gifts will be given to you;
a good measure, packed together, shaken down, and over-

flowing,
will be poured into your lap.
For the measure with which you measure
will in return be measured out to you." ✝

MONDAY, FEBRUARY 19
WEEKDAY

✝ *Sirach 1:1-10*
Before all other things, wisdom was created.

All wisdom comes from the Lord
and with him it remains forever.
The sand of the seashore, the drops of rain,
the days of eternity: who can number these?
Heaven's height, earth's breadth,
the depths of the abyss: who can explore these?
Before all things else wisdom was created;
and prudent understanding, from eternity.
To whom has wisdom's root been revealed?
Who knows her subtleties?
There is but one, wise and truly awe-inspiring,
seated upon his throne:
It is the Lord; he created her,
has seen her and taken note of her.
He has poured her forth upon all his works,
upon every living thing according to his bounty;
he has lavished her upon his friends.

Fear of the Lord is glory and splendor,
gladness and a festive crown.
Fear of the Lord warms the heart,
giving gladness and joy and length of days. ✝

Psalm 93:1-2, 5
R. The Lord is king; he is robed in majesty.
The Lord is king, in splendor robed;
robed is the Lord and girt about with strength. **R.**
And he has made the world firm,
not to be moved.
Your throne stands firm from of old;
from everlasting you are, O Lord. **R.**

Your decrees are worthy of trust indeed:
  holiness befits your house,
  O Lord, for length of days. **R.**

Psalm 119:135
R. Alleluia, alleluia.
Let your face shine on your servant,
and teach me your laws. **R.**

✝ *Mark 9:14-29*
I believe, Lord, help my unbelief.

[As Jesus came down the mountain with Peter, James and John] and approached the disciples, they saw a large crowd standing around, and scribes in lively discussion with them. Immediately on catching sight of Jesus, the whole crowd was overcome with awe. They ran up to greet him. He asked them, "What are you discussing among yourselves?" "Teacher," a man in the crowd replied, "I have brought my son to you because he is possessed by a mute spirit. Whenever it seizes him it throws him down; he foams at the mouth and grinds his teeth and becomes rigid. Just now I asked your disciples to expel him, but they were unable to do so." He replied by saying to the crowd, "What an unbelieving lot you are! How long must I remain with you? How long can I endure you? Bring him to me." When they did so the spirit caught sight of Jesus and immediately threw the boy into convulsions. As he fell to the ground he began to roll around and foam at the mouth. Then Jesus questioned the father: "How long has this been happening to him?" "From childhood," the father replied. "Often it throws him into the fire and into water. You would think it would kill him. If out of the kindness of your heart you can do anything to help us, please do!" Jesus said, " 'If you can?' Everything is possible to a man who trusts." The boy's father immediately exclaimed, "I do believe! Help my lack of trust!" Jesus, on seeing a crowd rapidly gathering, reprimanded the unclean spirit by saying to him, "Mute and deaf spirit, I command you: Get out of him and never enter him again!" Shouting, and throwing the boy into convulsions, it came out of him; the boy became like a corpse, which caused many to say, "He is dead." But Jesus took him by the hand and helped him to his feet. When Jesus arrived at the house his disciples began to ask him privately, "Why is it that we could not expel it?" He told them, "This kind you can drive out only by prayer." ✢

TUESDAY, FEBRUARY 20
WEEKDAY

† *Sirach 2:1-11*
Prepare yourself for the trials.

My son, when you come to serve the Lord,
 prepare yourself for trials.
Be sincere of heart and steadfast,
 undisturbed in time of adversity.
Cling to him, forsake him not;
 thus will your future be great.
Accept whatever befalls you,
 in crushing misfortune be patient;
For in fire gold is tested,
 and worthy men in the crucible of humiliation.
Trust God and he will help you;
 make straight your ways and hope in him.

You who fear the Lord, wait for his mercy,
 turn not away lest you fall.
You who fear the Lord, trust him,
 and your reward will not be lost.
You who fear the Lord, hope for good things,
 for lasting joy and mercy.
Study the generations long past and understand;
 has anyone hoped in the Lord and been disappointed?
Has anyone persevered in his fear and been forsaken?
 has anyone called upon him and been rebuffed?
Compassionate and merciful is the Lord;
 he forgives sins, he saves in time of trouble. ✢

Psalm 37:3-4, 18-19, 27-28, 39-40
R. **Commit your life to the Lord
 and he will help you.**
Trust in the Lord and do good,
 that you may dwell in the land and enjoy security.
Take delight in the Lord,

and he will grant you your heart's requests. **R.**
The Lord watches over the lives of the whole-hearted;
   their inheritance lasts forever.
They are not put to shame in an evil time;
   in days of famine they have plenty. **R.**
Turn from evil and do good,
   that you may abide forever;
For the Lord loves what is right,
   and forsakes not his faithful ones. **R.**
The salvation of the just is from the Lord;
   he is their refuge in time of distress.
And the Lord helps them and delivers them;
   he delivers them from the wicked and saves them,
   because they take refuge in him. **R.**

James 1:18
R. Alleluia, alleluia.
The Father gave us birth by his message of truth,
that we might be as the first fruits of his creation. **R.**

† *Mark 9:30-37*
*The Son of Man will be betrayed. If
anyone wishes to be first he must be last.*

Jesus and his disciples came down the mountain and began a journey through Galilee, but he did not want anyone to know about it. He was teaching his disciples in this vein: "The Son of Man is going to be delivered into the hands of men who will put him to death; three days after his death he will rise." Though they failed to understand his words, they were afraid to question him.

They returned to Capernaum and Jesus, once inside the house, began to ask them, "What were you discussing on the way home?" At this they fell silent, for on the way they had been arguing about who was the most important. So he sat down and called the Twelve around him and said, "If anyone wishes to rank first, he must remain the last one of all and the servant of all." Then he took a little child, stood him in their midst, and putting his arms around him, said to them, "Whoever welcomes a child such as this for my sake welcomes me. And whoever welcomes me welcomes, not me, but him who sent me." ✛

WEDNESDAY, FEBRUARY 21
St. Peter Damian

† *Sirach 4:11-19*
Those who love wisdom, love God.

Wisdom instructs her children
    and admonishes those who seek her.
He who loves her loves life;
    those who seek her out win her favor.
He who holds her fast inherits glory;
    wherever he dwells, the Lord bestows blessings.
Those who serve her serve the Holy One;
    those who love her the Lord loves.
He who obeys her judges nations;
    he who hearkens to her dwells in her inmost chambers.
If one trusts her, he will possess her;
    his descendants too will inherit her.
She walks with him as a stranger,
    and at first she puts him to the test;
Fear and dread she brings upon him
    and tries him with her discipline;
With her precepts she puts him to the proof,
    until his heart is fully with her.
Then she comes back to bring him happiness
    and reveal her secrets to him.
But if he fails her, she will abandon him
    and deliver him into the hands of despoilers. ✛

Psalm 119:165, 168, 171-172, 174-175
R. O Lord, great peace have they who love your law.
Those who love your law have great peace,
    and for them there is no stumbling block. **R.**
I keep your precepts and your decrees,
    for all my ways are before you. **R.**
My lips pour forth your praise,
    because you teach me your statutes. **R.**
May my tongue sing of your promise,
    for all your commands are just. **R.**
I long for your salvation, O Lord,
    and your law is my delight. **R.**

Let my soul live to praise you,
    and may your ordinances help me. **R.**

2 Corinthians 5:19
R. Alleluia, alleluia.
God was in Christ, to reconcile the world to himself;
and the Good News of reconciliation he has entrusted to us. **R.**

† *Mark 9:38-40*
Anyone who is not against us, is for us.

John said to Jesus, "Teacher, we saw a man using your name to expel demons and we tried to stop him because he is not of our company." Jesus said in reply: "Do not try to stop him. No one can perform a miracle in my name and at the same time speak ill of me. Anyone who is not against us is with us." +

THURSDAY, FEBRUARY 22
THE CHAIR OF PETER

† *1 Peter 5:1-4*
I myself am one of your leaders and a witness to the sufferings of Christ.

To the elders among you I, a fellow elder, a witness of Christ's sufferings and sharer in the glory that is to be revealed, make this appeal. God's flock is in your midst; give it a shepherd's care. Watch over it willingly as God would have you do, not under coercion; and not for shameful profit either, but generously. Be examples to the flock, not lording it over those assigned to you, so that when the chief shepherd appears you will win for yourselves the unfading crown of glory. +

Psalm 23:1-6
R. The Lord is my shepherd;
    there is nothing I shall want.
The Lord is my shepherd; I shall not want.
    In verdant pastures he gives me repose;
Beside restful waters he leads me;
    he refreshes my soul. **R.**
He guides me in right paths
    for his name's sake.
Even though I walk in the dark valley

I fear no evil; for you are at my side
With your rod and your staff
    that give me courage. **R.**
You spread the table before me
    in the sight of my foes;
You anoint my head with oil;
    my cup overflows. **R.**
Only goodness and kindness follow me
    all the days of my life;
And I shall dwell in the house of the Lord
    for years to come. **R.**

Matthew 16:18
R. Alleluia, alleluia.
You are Peter, the rock on which I will build my Church;
    the gates of hell will not hold out against it. **R.**

† *Matthew 16:13-19*
You are Peter; and to you I will give the keys of the kingdom of heaven.

When Jesus came to the neighborhood of Caesarea Philippi, he asked his disciples this question: "Who do people say that the Son of Man is?" They replied, "Some say John the Baptizer, others Elijah, still others Jeremiah or one of the prophets." "And you," he said to them, "who do you say that I am?" "You are the Messiah," Simon Peter answered, "the Son of the living God!" Jesus replied, "Blest are you, Simon son of John! No mere man has revealed this to you, but my heavenly Father. I for my part declare to you, you are 'Rock,' and on this rock I will build my church, and the jaws of death shall not prevail against it. I will entrust to you the keys of the kingdom of heaven. Whatever you declare bound on earth shall be bound in heaven; whatever you declare loosed on earth shall be loosed in heaven." ✝

FRIDAY, FEBRUARY 23
St. Polycarp

† *Sirach 6:5-17*
A faithful friend is beyond comparison.

A kind mouth multiplies friends,
    and gracious lips prompt friendly greetings.

Let your acquaintances be many,
  but one in a thousand your confidant.
When you gain a friend, first test him,
  and be not too ready to trust him.
For one sort of friend is a friend when it suits him,
  but he will not be with you in time of distress.
Another is a friend who becomes an enemy,
  and tells of the quarrel to your shame.
Another is a friend, a boon companion,
  who will not be with you when sorrow comes.
When things go well, he is your other self,
  and lords it over your servants;
But if you are brought low, he turns against you
  and avoids meeting you.
Keep away from your enemies;
  be on your guard with your friends.
A faithful friend is a sturdy shelter;
  he who finds one finds a treasure.
A faithful friend is beyond price,
  no sum can balance his worth.
A faithful friend is a life-saving remedy,
  such as he who fears God finds;
For he who fears God behaves accordingly,
  and his friend will be like himself. ✛

Psalm 119:12, 16, 18, 27, 34-35
R. Guide me, Lord, in the way of your commands.
Blessed are you, O Lord;
  teach me your statutes. **R.**
In your statutes I will delight;
  I will not forget your words. **R.**
Open my eyes, that I may consider
  the wonders of your law. **R.**
Make me understand the way of your precepts,
  and I will meditate on your wondrous deeds. **R.**
Give me discernment, that I may observe your law
  and keep it with all my heart. **R.**
Lead me in the path of your commands,
  for in it I delight. **R.**

1 Peter 1:25

R. Alleluia, alleluia.
The word of the Lord stands forever;
it is the word given to you, the Good News. **R.**

† *Mark 10:1-12*
What God has joined together, man must not divide.

Jesus came to the districts of Judea and across the Jordan. Once more crowds gathered around him and as usual he began to teach them. Then some Pharisees came up and as a test began to ask Jesus whether it was permissible for a husband to divorce his wife. In reply he said, "What command did Moses give you?" They answered, "Moses permitted divorce and the writing of a decree of divorce." But Jesus told them: "He wrote that commandment for you because of your stubbornness. At the beginning of creation God made them male and female; for this reason a man shall leave his father and mother and the two shall become as one. They are no longer two but one flesh. Therefore, let no man separate what God has joined." Back in the house again, the disciples began to question him about this. He told them, "Whoever divorces his wife and marries another commits adultery against her; and the woman who divorces her husband and marries another commits adultery." ✛

SATURDAY, FEBRUARY 24
WEEKDAY

† *Sirach 17:1-15*
The Lord made man in his own image.

The Lord from the earth created man,
    and in his own image he made him.
Limited days of life he gives him
    and makes him return to earth again.
He endows man with a strength of his own,
    and with power over all things else on earth.
He puts the fear of him in all flesh,
    and gives him rule over beasts and birds.
He forms men's tongues and eyes and ears,
    and imparts to them an understanding heart.

With wisdom and knowledge he fills them;
good and evil he shows them.
He looks with favor upon their hearts,
and shows them his glorious works,
That they may describe the wonders of his deeds
and praise his holy name.
He has set before them knowledge,
a law of life as their inheritance;
An everlasting covenant he has made with them,
his commandments he has revealed to them.
His majestic glory their eyes beheld,
his glorious voice their ears heard.
He says to them, "Avoid all evil";
each of them he gives precepts about his fellow men.
Their ways are ever known to him,
they cannot be hidden from his eyes.
Over every nation he places a ruler,
but the Lord's own portion is Israel.
All their actions are clear as the sun to him,
his eyes are ever upon their ways. ✛

Psalm 103:13-18
**R. The Lord's kindness is everlasting
to those who fear him.**
As a father has compassion on his children,
so the Lord has compassion on those who fear him,
For he knows how we are formed;
he remembers that we are dust. **R.**
Man's days are like those of grass;
like a flower of the field he blooms;
The wind sweeps over him and he is gone,
and his place knows him no more. **R.**
But the kindness of the Lord is from eternity
to eternity toward those who fear him,
And his justice toward children's children
among those who keep his covenant. **R.**

Matthew 11:25
R. Alleluia, alleluia.
Blessed are you, Father, Lord of heaven and earth;
you have revealed to little ones the mysteries of the kingdom. **R.**

† *Mark 10:13-16*

He who does not accept the kingdom of
heaven like a child will never enter it.

People were bringing their little children to Jesus to have him touch them, but the disciples were scolding them for this. Jesus became indignant when he noticed it and said to them: "Let the children come to me and do not hinder them. It is to just such as these that the kingdom of God belongs. I assure you that whoever does not accept the kingdom of God like a little child shall not enter into it." Then he embraced them and blessed them, placing his hands on them. ✛

FEBRUARY 25
EIGHTH SUNDAY IN ORDINARY TIME

† *Sirach 27:4-7*

Praise no one before he speaks.

When a sieve is shaken, the husks appear;
    so do one's faults when one speaks.
As the test of what the potter molds is in the furnace,
    so in tribulation is the test of the just.
The fruit of a tree shows the care it has had;
    so too does one's speech disclose the bent of one's mind.
Praise no one before he speaks,
    for it is then that people are tested. ✛

Psalm 92:2-3, 13-16
R. Lord, it is good to give thanks to you.
It is good to give thanks to the LORD,
    to sing praise to your name, Most High,
to proclaim your kindness at dawn
    and your faithfulness throughout the night. **R.**
The just one shall flourish like the palm tree,
    like a cedar of Lebanon shall he grow.
They that are planted in the house of the LORD
    shall flourish in the courts of our God. **R.**
They shall bear fruit even in old age;
    vigorous and sturdy shall they be,
declaring how just is the Lord,
    my rock, in whom there is no wrong. **R.**

✛ *1 Corinthians 15:54-58*
God gives us victory through our Lord Jesus Christ.

Brothers and sisters:
When this which is corruptible clothes itself
    with incorruptibility
    and this which is mortal clothes itself with immortality,
    then the word that is written shall come about:
Death is swallowed up in victory.
Where, O death, is your victory?
Where, O death, is your sting?
The sting of death is sin,
    and the power of sin is the law.
But thanks be to God who gives us the victory
    through our Lord Jesus Christ.

Therefore, my beloved brothers and sisters,
    be firm, steadfast, always fully devoted to the work of the
        Lord,
    knowing that in the Lord your labor is not in vain. ✛

Philippians 2:15d, 16a
R. Alleluia, alleluia.
Shine like lights in the world
as you hold on to the word of life. **R.**

✛ *Luke 6:39-45*
From the fullness of the heart the mouth speaks.

Jesus told his disciples a parable,
    "Can a blind person guide a blind person?
Will not both fall into a pit?
No disciple is superior to the teacher;
    but when fully trained,
    every disciple will be like his teacher.
Why do you notice the splinter in your brother's eye,
    but do not perceive the wooden beam in your own?
How can you say to your brother,
    'Brother, let me remove that splinter in your eye,'
    when you do not even notice the wooden beam in your
        own eye?
You hypocrite! Remove the wooden beam from your eye first;

then you will see clearly
to remove the splinter in your brother's eye.

"A good tree does not bear rotten fruit,
nor does a rotten tree bear good fruit.
For every tree is known by its own fruit.
For people do not pick figs from thornbushes,
nor do they gather grapes from brambles.
A good person out of the store of goodness in his heart
produces good,
but an evil person out of a store of evil produces evil;
for from the fullness of the heart the mouth speaks." ✛

MONDAY, FEBRUARY 26
WEEKDAY

✝ Sirach 17:19-27
Turn to the Lord, plead before his face and lessen your offense.

But to the penitent he provides a way back,
he encourages those who are losing hope!
Return to the Lord and give up sin,
pray to him and make your offenses few.
Turn again to the Most High and away from sin,
hate intensely what he loathes;
Who in the nether world can glorify the Most High
in place of the living who offer their praise?
No more can the dead give praise than those who have never
lived;
they glorify the Lord who are alive and well.
How great the mercy of the Lord,
his forgiveness of those who return to him!
The like cannot be found in men,
for not immortal is any son of man.
Is anything brighter than the sun? Yet it can be eclipsed.
How obscure then the thoughts of flesh and blood!
God watches over the hosts of highest heaven,
while all men are dust and ashes. ✛

Psalm 32:1-2, 5-7
R. Let the just exult and rejoice in the Lord.
Happy is he whose fault is taken away,

whose sin is covered.
Happy the man to whom the Lord imputes not guilt,
  in whose spirit there is no guile. **R.**
Then I acknowledged my sin to you,
  my guilt I covered not.
I said, "I confess my faults to the Lord,"
  and you took away the guilt of my sin. **R.**
For this shall every faithful man pray to you
  in time of stress.
Though deep waters overflow,
  they shall not reach him. **R.**
You are my shelter; from distress you will preserve me;
  with glad cries of freedom you will ring me round. **R.**

See Acts 16:14
R. Alleluia, alleluia.
Open our hearts, O Lord,
to listen to the words of your Son. **R.**

✝ Mark 10:17-27
Go, sell everything you have and follow me.

As Jesus was setting out on a journey a man came running
up, knelt down before him and asked, "Good Teacher, what
must I do to share in everlasting life?" Jesus answered, "Why
do you call me good? No one is good but God alone. You know
the commandments:
  'You shall not kill;
  You shall not commit adultery;
  You shall not steal;
  You shall not bear false witness;
  You shall not defraud;
  Honor your father and your mother.'"
He replied, "Teacher, I have kept all these since my childhood."
Then Jesus looked at him with love and told him, "There is one
thing more you must do. Go and sell what you have and give
to the poor; you will then have treasure in heaven. After that,
come and follow me." At these words the man's face fell. He
went away sad, for he had many possessions. Jesus looked
around and said to his disciples, "How hard it is for the rich to
enter the kingdom of God!" The disciples could only marvel at

his words. So Jesus repeated what he had said: "My sons, how hard it is to enter the kingdom of God! It is easier for a camel to pass through a needle's eye than for a rich man to enter the kingdom of God."

They were completely overwhelmed at this, and exclaimed to one another, "Then who can be saved?" Jesus fixed his gaze on them and said, "For man it is impossible but not for God. With God all things are possible." ✛

TUESDAY, FEBRUARY 27
WEEKDAY

† Sirach 35:1-12
A man offers sacrifice by following the law.

To keep the law is a great oblation,
    and he who observes the commandments sacrifices a peace
        offering.
In works of charity one offers fine flour,
    and when he gives alms he presents his sacrifice of praise.
To refrain from evil pleases the Lord,
    and to avoid injustice is an atonement.
Appear not before the Lord empty-handed,
    for all that you offer is in fulfillment of the precepts.
The just man's offering enriches the altar
    and rises as a sweet odor before the Most High.
The just man's sacrifice is most pleasing,
    nor will it ever be forgotten.
In generous spirit pay homage to the Lord,
    be not sparing of freewill gifts.
With each contribution show a cheerful countenance,
    and pay your tithes in a spirit of joy.
Give to the Most High as he has given to you,
    generously, according to your means.

For the Lord is one who always repays,
    and he will give back to you sevenfold.
But offer no bribes, these he does not accept!
    Trust not in sacrifice of the fruits of extortion,
For he is a God of justice,
    who knows no favorites. ✛

Psalm 50:5-8, 14, 23

**R. To the upright I will show
the saving power of God.**

"Gather my faithful ones before me,
   those who have made a covenant with me by sacrifice."
And the heavens proclaim his justice;
   for God himself is the judge. **R.**
"Hear, my people, and I will speak;
   Israel, I will testify against you;
   God, your God, am I.
Not for your sacrifices do I rebuke you,
   for your holocausts are before me always. **R.**
"Offer to God praise as your sacrifice
   and fulfill your vows to the Most High.
He that offers praise as a sacrifice glorifies me;
   and to him that goes the right way I will show the salvation
   of God." **R.**

1 John 2:5

R. Alleluia, alleluia.

He who keeps the word of Christ,
grows perfect in the love of God. **R.**

✝ *Mark 10:28-31*

*Our offerings are acceptable in this present time of
persecution and in the world to come, eternal life.*

Peter was moved to say to Jesus: "We have put aside everything to follow you!" Jesus answered: "I give you my word,
there is no one who has given up home, brothers or sisters,
mother or father, children or property, for me and for the
gospel who will not receive in this present age a hundred times
as many homes, brothers and sisters, mothers, children and
property—and persecution besides—and in the age to come,
everlasting life. Many who are first shall come last, and the
last shall come first." ✝

WEDNESDAY, FEBRUARY 28
ASH WEDNESDAY

† *Joel 2:12-18*
Let your hearts be broken, and not your garments torn.

Even now, says the Lord,
  return to me with your whole heart,
  with fasting, and weeping, and mourning;
Rend your hearts, not your garments,
  and return to the Lord, your God.
For gracious and merciful is he,
  slow to anger, rich in kindness,
  and relenting in punishment.
Perhaps he will again relent
  and leave behind him a blessing,
Offerings and libations
  for the Lord, your God.

Blow the trumpet in Zion!
  proclaim a fast,
  call an assembly;
Gather the people,
  notify the congregation;
Assemble the elders,
  gather the children
  and the infants at the breast;
Let the bridegroom quit his room,
  and the bride her chamber.
Between the porch and the altar
  let the priests, the ministers of the Lord, weep,
And say, "Spare, O Lord, your people,
  and make not your heritage a reproach,
  with the nations ruling over them!
Why should they say among the peoples,
  'Where is their God?'"
    Then the Lord was stirred to concern for his land and took
pity on his people. ✛

Psalm 51:3-6, 12-14, 17

R. Be merciful, O Lord, for we have sinned.

Have mercy on me, O God, in your goodness;
> in the greatness of your compassion wipe out my offense.

Thoroughly wash me from my guilt
> and of my sin cleanse me. **R.**

For I acknowledge my offense,
> and my sin is before me always:

"Against you only have I sinned,
> and done what is evil in your sight." **R.**

A clean heart create for me, O God,
> and a steadfast spirit renew within me.

Cast me not out from your presence,
> and your holy spirit take not from me. **R.**

Give me back the joy of your salvation,
> and a willing spirit sustain in me.

O Lord, open my lips,
> and my mouth shall proclaim your praise. **R.**

✝ 2 Corinthians 5:20—6:2
Be reconciled to God, now is the acceptable time.

We are ambassadors for Christ, God as it were appealing through us. We implore you, in Christ's name: be reconciled to God! For our sakes God made him who did not know sin to be sin, so that in him we might become the very holiness of God.

As your fellow workers we beg you not to receive the grace of God in vain. For he says, "In an acceptable time I have heard you; on a day of salvation I have helped you." Now is the acceptable time! Now is the day of salvation! ✛

Joel 2:12-13

R. Glory and praise to you, Lord Jesus Christ!

With all your heart turn to me
for I am tender and compassionate. **R.**

✝ Matthew 6:1-6, 16-18
Your Father, who sees all that is done in secret, will reward you.

Jesus said to his disciples: "Be on guard against performing religious acts for people to see. Otherwise expect no recompense from your heavenly Father. When you give alms, for example, do not blow a horn before you in synagogues and streets like hypocrites looking for applause. You can be sure of this much, they are already repaid. In giving alms you are not to let your left hand know what your right hand is doing. Keep your deeds of mercy secret, and your Father who sees in secret will repay you.

"When you are praying, do not behave like the hypocrites who love to stand and pray in synagogues or on street corners in order to be noticed. I give you my word, they are already repaid. Whenever you pray, go to your room, close your door, and pray to your Father in private. Then your Father, who sees what no man sees, will repay you.

"When you fast, you are not to look glum as the hypocrites do. They change the appearance of their faces so that others may see they are fasting. I assure you, they are already repaid. When you fast, see to it that you groom your hair and wash your face. In that way no one can see you are fasting but your Father who is hidden; and your Father who sees what is hidden will repay you." ✢

THURSDAY, MARCH 1
LENTEN WEEKDAY

† *Deuteronomy 30:15-20*
I set before you life or death, blessing or curse.

Moses said to the people: "Today I have set before you life and prosperity, death and doom. If you obey the commandments of the Lord, your God, which I enjoin on you today, loving him, and walking in his ways, and keeping his commandments, statutes and decrees, you will live and grow numerous, and the Lord, your God, will bless you in the land you are entering to occupy. If, however, you turn away your hearts and will not listen, but are led astray and adore and serve other gods, I tell you now that you will certainly perish; you will not have a long life on the land which you are crossing the Jordan to enter and occupy. I call heaven and earth today to witness against you: I have set before you life and death, the blessing and the curse. Choose life, then, that you and your descendants may live, by loving the Lord, your God, heeding his voice, and holding fast to him. For that will mean life for you, a long life for you to live on the land which the Lord swore he would give to your fathers Abraham, Isaac and Jacob." ✛

Psalm 1:1-4, 6
R. Happy are they who hope in the Lord.
Happy the man who follows not
    the counsel of the wicked
Nor walks in the way of sinners,
    nor sits in the company of the insolent,
But delights in the law of the Lord
    and meditates on his law day and night. **R.**
He is like a tree
    planted near running water,
That yields its fruit in due season,
    and whose leaves never fade.
    [Whatever he does, prospers.] **R.**
Not so the wicked, not so;
    they are like chaff which the wind drives away.
For the Lord watches over the way of the just,
    but the way of the wicked vanishes. **R.**

Amos 5:14
R. Glory and praise to you, Lord Jesus Christ!
Seek good and not evil
so that you may live,
and the Lord will be with you. **R.**

† *Luke 9:22-25*
He who loses his life for my sake, that man will find salvation.

Jesus said to his disciples: "The Son of Man must first endure many sufferings, be rejected by the elders, the high priests and the scribes, and be put to death, and then be raised up on the third day."

Jesus said to all: "Whoever wishes to be my follower must deny his very self, take up his cross each day, and follow in my steps. Whoever would save his life will lose it, and whoever loses his life for my sake will save it. What profit does he show who gains the whole world and destroys himself in the process?" ✛

FRIDAY, MARCH 2
LENTEN WEEKDAY

† Isaiah 58:1-9
Is this not the sort of fast that pleases me?

Cry out full-throated and unsparingly,
  lift up your voice like a trumpet blast;
Tell my people their wickedness,
  and the house of Jacob their sins.
They seek me day after day,
  and desire to know my ways,
Like a nation that has done what is just
  and not abandoned the law of their God;
They ask me to declare what is due them,
  pleased to gain access to God.
"Why do we fast, and you do not see it?
  afflict ourselves, and you take no note of it?"
Lo, on your fast day you carry out your own pursuits,
  and drive all your laborers.
Yes, your fast ends in quarreling and fighting,
  striking with wicked claw.
Would that today you might fast
  so as to make your voice heard on high!
Is this the manner of fasting I wish,
  of keeping a day of penance:
That a man bow his head like a reed,
  and lie in sackcloth and ashes?
Do you call this a fast,
  a day acceptable to the Lord?
This, rather, is the fasting that I wish:
  releasing those bound unjustly,
  untying the thongs of the yoke;
Setting free the oppressed,
  breaking every yoke;
Sharing your bread with the hungry,
  sheltering the oppressed and the homeless;
Clothing the naked when you see them,
  and not turning your back on your own.

Then your light shall break forth like the dawn,
  and your wound shall quickly be healed.
Your vindication shall go before you,
  and the glory of the Lord shall be your rear guard.
Then you shall call, and the Lord will answer,
  you shall cry for help, and he will say: Here l am!
If you remove from your midst oppression,
  false accusation and malicious speech. ✛

Psalm 51:3-6, 18-19
**R. A broken, humbled heart, O God,
  you will not scorn.**
Have mercy on me, O God, in your goodness;
  in the greatness of your compassion wipe out my offense.
Thoroughly wash me from my guilt
  and of my sin cleanse me. **R.**
For I acknowledge my offense,
  and my sin is before me always:
"Against you only have I sinned,
  and done what is evil in your sight." **R.**
For you are not pleased with sacrifices;
  should I offer a holocaust, you would not accept it.
My sacrifice, O God, is a contrite spirit;
  a heart contrite and humbled, O God, you will not spurn. **R.**

Matthew 4:4
R. Glory and praise to you, Lord Jesus Christ!
Man does not live on bread alone,
but on every word that comes from the mouth of God. **R.**

† *Matthew 9:14-15*
When the bridegroom is taken from them, then they will fast.

When Jesus had crossed over into the territory of the Gerasenes, John's disciples came to him with the objection, "Why is it that while we and the Pharisees fast, your disciples do not?" Jesus said to them: "How can wedding guests go in mourning so long as the groom is with them? When the day comes that the groom is taken away, then they will fast." ✛

SATURDAY, MARCH 3
LENTEN WEEKDAY, ST. KATHERINE DREXEL

† *Isaiah 58:9-14*
You will glory to the Lord God by not going your own way.

Thus says the Lord:
If you remove from your midst oppression,
    false accusation and malicious speech;
If you bestow your bread on the hungry
    and satisfy the afflicted;
Then light shall rise for you in the darkness,
    and the gloom shall become for you like midday;
Then the Lord will guide you always
    and give you plenty even on the parched land.
He will renew your strength,
    and you shall be like a watered garden,
    like a spring whose water never fails.
The ancient ruins shall be rebuilt for your sake,
    and the foundations from ages past you shall raise up;
"Repairer of the breach," they shall call you,
    "Restorer of ruined homesteads."

If you hold back your foot on the sabbath
    from following your own pursuits on my holy day;
If you call the sabbath a delight,
    and the Lord's holy day honorable;
If you honor it by not following your ways,
    seeking your own interests, or speaking with malice—
Then you shall delight in the Lord,
    and I will make you ride on the heights of the earth;
I will nourish you with the heritage of Jacob, your father,
    for the mouth of the Lord has spoken. ✢

Psalm 86:1-6
R. Teach me your way, O Lord,
that I may be faithful in your sight.
Incline your ear, O Lord; answer me,
    for I am afflicted and poor.
Keep my life, for I am devoted to you;
    save your servant who trusts in you. **R.**
You are my God; have pity on me, O Lord,

for to you I call all the day.
Gladden the soul of your servant,
	for to you, O Lord, I lift up my soul. **R.**
For you, O Lord, are good and forgiving,
	abounding in kindness to all who call upon you.
Hearken, O Lord, to my prayer
	and attend to the sound of my pleading. **R.**

Ezekiel 18:31
R. Glory and praise to you, Lord Jesus Christ!
Rid yourselves of all you sins;
and make a new heart and a new spirit. **R.**

† *Luke 5:27-32*
I have not come to call the just, but sinners to repentance.

Jesus saw a tax collector named Levi sitting at his customs post. He said to him, "Follow me." Leaving everything behind, Levi stood up and became his follower. After that Levi gave a great reception for Jesus in his house, in which he was joined by a large crowd of tax collectors and others at dinner. The Pharisees and the scribes of their party said to his disciples, "Why do you eat and drink with tax collectors and non-observers of the law?" Jesus said to them, "The healthy do not need a doctor; sick people do. I have not come to invite the self-righteous to a change of heart, but sinners." ✛

MARCH 4
First Sunday of Lent

† *Deuteronomy 26:4-10*
The confession of faith of the chosen people.

Moses spoke to the people, saying:
	"The priest shall receive the basket from you
	and shall set it in front of the altar of the LORD, your God.
Then you shall declare before the LORD, your God,
	'My father was a wandering Aramean
	who went down to Egypt with a small household
	and lived there as an alien.
But there he became a nation
	great, strong, and numerous.

When the Egyptians maltreated and oppressed us,
  imposing hard labor upon us,
  we cried to the LORD, the God of our fathers,
  and he heard our cry
  and saw our affliction, our toil, and our oppression.
He brought us out of Egypt
  with his strong hand and outstretched arm,
  with terrifying power, with signs and wonders;
  and bringing us into this country,
  he gave us this land flowing with milk and honey.
Therefore, I have now brought you the firstfruits
  of the products of the soil
  which you, O LORD, have given me.'
And having set them before the LORD, your God,
  you shall bow down in his presence. ✛

Psalm 91:1-2, 10-15
R. Be with me, Lord, when I am in trouble.
You who dwell in the shelter of the Most High,
  who abide in the shadow of the Almighty,
say to the LORD, "My refuge and fortress,
  my God in whom I trust." **R.**
No evil shall befall you,
  nor shall affliction come near your tent,
for to his angels he has given command about you,
  that they guard you in all your ways. **R.**
Upon their hands they shall bear you up,
  lest you dash your foot against a stone.
You shall tread upon the asp and the viper;
  you shall trample down the lion and the dragon. **R.**
Because he clings to me, I will deliver him;
  I will set him on high because he acknowledges my name.
He shall call upon me, and I will answer him;
  I will be with him in distress;
I will deliver him and glorify him. **R.**

✝ *Romans 10:8-13*
The confession of faith of all believers in Christ.

Brothers and sisters:
What does Scripture say?

The word is near you,
   in your mouth and in your heart
   —that is, the word of faith that we preach—,
   for, if you confess with your mouth that Jesus is Lord
   and believe in your heart that God raised him from the
      dead,
   you will be saved.
For one believes with the heart and so is justified,
   and one confesses with the mouth and so is saved.
For the Scripture says,
   No one who believes in him will be put to shame.
For there is no distinction between Jew and Greek;
   the same Lord is Lord of all,
   enriching all who call upon him.
For "everyone who calls on the name of the Lord will be saved." ✝

Matthew 4:4b
R. Glory and praise to you, Lord Jesus Christ!
One does not live on bread alone,
but on every word that comes forth from the mouth of God. **R.**

† *Luke 4:1-13*
Jesus was led by the Spirit into the desert and was tempted.

Filled with the Holy Spirit, Jesus returned from the Jordan
   and was led by the Spirit into the desert for forty days,
   to be tempted by the devil.
He ate nothing during those days,
   and when they were over he was hungry.
The devil said to him,
   "If you are the Son of God,
   command this stone to become bread."
Jesus answered him,
   "It is written, *One does not live on bread alone.*"
Then he took him up and showed him
   all the kingdoms of the world in a single instant.
The devil said to him,
   "I shall give to you all this power and glory;
   for it has been handed over to me,
   and I may give it to whomever I wish.
All this will be yours, if you worship me."

Jesus said to him in reply,
"It is written:
*You shall worship the Lord, your God,
and him alone shall you serve.*"
Then he led him to Jerusalem,
made him stand on the parapet of the temple, and said to
him,
"If you are the Son of God,
throw yourself down from here, for it is written:
*He will command his angels concerning you,
to guard you,*
and:
*With their hands they will support you,
lest you dash your foot against a stone.*"
Jesus said to him in reply,
"It also says,
You shall not put the Lord, your God, to the test."
When the devil had finished every temptation,
he departed from him for a time. ✛

MONDAY, MARCH 5
LENTEN WEEKDAY

† *Leviticus 19:1-2, 11-18*
Judge your neighbor justly.

The Lord said to Moses, "Speak to the whole Israelite community and tell them: Be holy, for I, the Lord, your God, am holy.

"You shall not steal. You shall not lie or speak falsely to one another. You shall not swear falsely by my name, thus profaning the name of your God. I am the Lord.

"You shall not defraud or rob your neighbor. You shall not withhold overnight the wages of your day laborer. You shall not curse the deaf, or put a stumbling block in front of the blind, but you shall fear your God. I am the Lord.

"You shall not act dishonestly in rendering judgment. Show neither partiality to the weak nor deference to the mighty, but judge your fellow men justly. You shall not go about spreading slander among your kinsmen; nor shall you stand by idly when your neighbor's life is at stake. I am the Lord.

"You shall not bear hatred for your brother in your heart.

Though you may have to reprove your fellow man, do not incur sin because of him. Take no revenge and cherish no grudge against your fellow countrymen. You shall love your neighbor as yourself. I am the Lord." ✛

Psalm 19:8-10, 15
R. Your words, Lord, are spirit and life.
The law of the Lord is perfect,
    refreshing the soul;
The decree of the Lord is trustworthy,
    giving wisdom to the simple. **R.**
The precepts of the Lord are right,
    rejoicing the heart;
The command of the Lord is clear,
    enlightening the eye. **R.**
The fear of the Lord is pure,
    enduring forever;
The ordinances of the Lord are true,
    all of them just. **R.**
Let the words of my mouth and the thought of my heart
    find favor before you,
O Lord, my rock and my redeemer. **R.**

Psalm 95:8
R. Glory and praise to you, Lord Jesus Christ!
If today you hear his voice,
harden not your hearts. **R.**

† *Matthew 25:31-46*
Whatever you do for one of the
least of these brothers of mine, you do to me.

Jesus said to his disciples: "When the Son of Man comes in his glory, escorted by all the angels of heaven, he will sit upon his royal throne and all the nations will be assembled before him. Then he will separate them into two groups, as a shepherd separates sheep from goats. The sheep he will place on his right hand, the goats on his left. The king will say to those on his right: 'Come, you have my Father's blessing! Inherit the kingdom prepared for you from the creation of the world. For I was hungry and you gave me food, I was thirsty and you gave me drink. I was a stranger and you welcomed me, naked and you clothed me. I was ill and you comforted me, in prison and you came to visit me.' Then the just will ask him: 'Lord, when did we see you hungry and feed you or see you thirsty and give you drink? When did we welcome you away from home or clothe you in your nakedness? When did we visit you when you were ill or in prison?' The king will answer them: 'I assure you, as often as you did it for one of my least brothers, you did it for me.'

"Then he will say to those on his left: 'Out of my sight, you condemned, into that everlasting fire prepared for the devil and his angels! I was hungry and you gave me no food, I was thirsty and you gave me no drink. I was away from home and you gave me no welcome, naked and you gave me no clothing. I was ill and in prison and you did not come to comfort me.' Then they in turn will ask: 'Lord, when did we see you hungry or thirsty or away from home or naked or ill or in prison and not attend you in your needs?' He will answer them: 'I assure you, as often as you neglected to do it to one of these least ones, you neglected to do it to me.' These will go off to eternal punishment and the just to eternal life." ✛

TUESDAY, MARCH 6
LENTEN WEEKDAY

✝ *Isaiah 55:10-11*
My word carries out my will.

For just as from the heavens
    the rain and snow come down
And do not return there
    till they have watered the earth,
    making it fertile and fruitful,
Giving seed to him who sows
    and bread to him who eats,
So shall my word be
    that goes forth from my mouth;
It shall not return to me void,
    but shall do my will,
    achieving the end for which I sent it. ✛

Psalm 34:4-7, 16-19

R. From all their afflictions
God will deliver the just.

Glorify the Lord with me,
    let us together extol his name.
I sought the Lord, and he answered me
    and delivered me from all my fears. **R.**
Look to him that you may be radiant with joy,
    and your faces may not blush with shame.
When the afflicted man called out, the LORD heard,
    and from all his distress he saved him. **R.**
The Lord has eyes for the just,
    and ears for their cry.
The Lord confronts the evildoers,
    to destroy remembrance of them from the earth. **R.**
When the just cry out, the Lord hears them,
    and from all their distress he rescues them.
The Lord is close to the brokenhearted;
    and those who are crushed in spirit he saves. **R.**

Matthew 4:17

R. Glory and praise to you, Lord Jesus Christ!
Repent, says the Lord,
the kingdom of heaven is at hand. **R.**

† *Matthew 6:7-15*
This is how you should pray.

Jesus said to his disciples: "In your prayer do not rattle on like
the pagans. They think they will win a hearing by the sheer
multiplication of words. Do not imitate them. Your Father
knows what you need before you ask him. This is how you are
to pray:
    'Our Father in heaven,
    hallowed be your name,
    your kingdom come,
    your will be done
    on earth as it is in heaven.
    Give us today our daily bread,
    and forgive us the wrong we have done
    as we forgive those who wrong us.

Subject us not to the trial
but deliver us from the evil one.'

"If you forgive the faults of others, your heavenly Father will forgive you yours. If you do not forgive others, neither will your Father forgive you." ✛

WEDNESDAY, MARCH 7
Lenten Weekday, Sts. Perpetua and Felicity

† *Jonah 3:1-10*
Nineveh was converted from its evil ways.

The word of the Lord came to Jonah: "Set out for the great city of Nineveh, and announce to it the message that I will tell you." So Jonah made ready and went to Nineveh, according to the Lord's bidding. Now Nineveh was an enormously large city; it took three days to go through it. Jonah began his journey through the city, and had gone but a single day's walk announcing, "Forty days more and Nineveh shall be destroyed," when the people of Nineveh believed God; they proclaimed a fast and all of them, great and small, put on sackcloth.

When the news reached the king of Nineveh, he rose from his throne, laid aside his robe, covered himself with sackcloth, and sat in the ashes. Then he had this proclaimed throughout Nineveh, by decree of the king and his nobles: "Neither man nor beast, neither cattle nor sheep, shall taste anything; they shall not eat, nor shall they drink water. Man and beast shall be covered with sackcloth and call loudly to God; every man shall turn from his evil way and from the violence he has in hand. Who knows, God may relent and forgive, and withhold his blazing wrath, so that we shall not perish." When God saw by their actions how they turned from their evil way, he repented of the evil that he had threatened to do to them; he did not carry it out. ✛

Psalm 51:3-4, 12-13, 18-19
R. A broken, humbled heart,
   O God, you will not scorn.
Have mercy on me, O God, in your goodness;
   in the greatness of your compassion wipe out my offense.
Thoroughly wash me from my guilt

and of my sin cleanse me. **R.**
A clean heart create for me, O God,
    and a steadfast spirit renew within me.
Cast me not out from your presence,
    and your holy spirit take not from me. **R.**
For you are not pleased with sacrifices;
    should I offer a holocaust, you would not accept it.
My sacrifice, O God, is a contrite spirit;
    a heart contrite and humbled, O God, you will not spurn. **R.**

See Luke 8:15
R. Glory and praise to you, Lord Jesus Christ!
Happy are they who have kept the word with a generous heart,
and yield a harvest through perseverance. **R.**

† *Luke 11:29-32*
No sign will be given to this generation except the sign of Jonah.

While the crowds pressed around Jesus, he began to speak to them in these words: "This is an evil age. It seeks a sign. But no sign will be given it except the sign of Jonah. Just as Jonah was a sign for the Ninevites, so will the Son of Man be a sign for the present age. The queen of the south will rise at the judgment along with the men of this generation, and she will condemn them. She came from the farthest corner of the world to listen to the wisdom of Solomon, but you have a greater than Solomon here. At the judgment, the citizens of Nineveh will rise along with the present generation, and they will condemn it. For at the preaching of Jonah they reformed, but you have a greater than Jonah here." ✛

THURSDAY, MARCH 8
LENTEN WEEKDAY, ST. JOHN OF GOD

† *Esther C:12, 14-16, 23-25*
I have no help other than you, Lord.

Queen Esther, seized with mortal anguish, had recourse to the Lord. She prayed to the Lord, the God of Israel, saying: "My Lord, our King, you alone are God. Help me, who am alone and have no help but you, for I am taking my life in my hand. As a child I was wont to hear from the people of the land of my forefathers that you, O Lord, chose Israel from among all peoples, and our fathers from among all their ancestors, as a lasting heritage, and that you fulfilled all your promises to them. "Be mindful of us, O Lord. Manifest yourself in the time of our distress and give me courage, King of gods and Ruler of every power. Put in my mouth persuasive words in the presence of the lion, and turn his heart to hatred for our enemy, so that he and those who are in league with him may perish. Save us by your power, and help me, who am alone and have no one but you, O Lord. You know all things." ✛

Psalm 138:1-3, 7-8
R. Lord, on the day I called for help,
you answered me.
I will give thanks to you, O Lord, with all my heart,
　　[for you have heard the words of my mouth;]
　　in the presence of the angels I will sing your praise;
I will worship at your holy temple
　　and give thanks to your name, **R.**
Because of your kindness and your truth;
　　for you have made great above all things
　　your name and your promise.
When I called, you answered me;
　　you built up strength within me. **R.**
Your right hand saves me.
The Lord will complete what he has done for me;
Your kindness, O Lord, endures forever;
　　forsake not the work of your hands. **R.**

2 Corinthians 6:2
R. Glory and praise to you, Lord Jesus Christ!
This is the favorable time,
this is the day of salvation. **R.**

† *Matthew 7:7-12*
He who asks, always receives.

Jesus said to his disciples: "Ask, and you will receive. Seek, and you will find. Knock, and it will be opened to you. For the one who asks, receives. The one who seeks, finds. The one who knocks, enters. Would one of you hand his son a stone when he asks for a loaf, or a poisonous snake when he asks for a fish?

If you, with all your sins, know how to give your children what is good, how much more will your heavenly Father give good things to anyone who asks him!

"Treat others the way you would have them treat you: this sums up the law and the prophets." ✚

FRIDAY, MARCH 9
LENTEN WEEKDAY, ST. FRANCES OF ROME

† *Ezekiel 18:21-28*
If a wicked man turns away from his sins, he shall live.

If the wicked man turns away from all the sins he committed, if he keeps all my statutes and does what is right and just, he shall surely live, he shall not die. None of the crimes he committed shall be remembered against him; he shall live because of the virtue he has practiced. Do I indeed derive any pleasure from the death of the wicked? says the Lord God. Do I not rather rejoice when he turns from his evil way that he may live?

And if the virtuous man turns from the path of virtue to do evil, the same kind of abominable things that the wicked man does, can he do this and still live? None of his virtuous deeds shall be remembered, because he has broken faith and committed sin; because of this, he shall die. You say, "The Lord's way is not fair!" Hear now, house of Israel: Is it my way that is unfair, or rather, are not your ways unfair? When a virtuous man turns away from virtue to commit iniquity, and dies, it is because of the iniquity he committed that he must die. But if a wicked man, turning from the wickedness he has committed, does what is right and just, he shall preserve his life; since he has turned away from all the sins which he committed, he shall surely live, he shall not die. ✚

Psalm 130:1-8

**R. If you, O Lord, laid bare our guilt
who could endure it?**
Out of the depths I cry to you, O Lord;
  Lord, hear my voice!
Let your ears be attentive
  to my voice in supplication. **R.**

If you, O Lord, mark iniquities,
     Lord, who can stand?
But with you is forgiveness,
     that you may be revered. **R.**
I trust in the Lord;
     my soul trusts in his word.
My soul waits for the Lord
     more than sentinels wait for the dawn.
Let Israel wait for the Lord. **R.**
For with the Lord is kindness
     and with him is plenteous redemption;
And he will redeem Israel
     from all their iniquities. **R.**

Psalm 130:5, 7
R. Glory and praise to you, Lord Jesus Christ!
I hope in the Lord, I trust in his word;
with him there is mercy and fullness of redemption. **R.**

† *Matthew 5:20-26*
Go first and be reconciled with your brother.

Jesus said to his disciples: "Unless your holiness surpasses that of the scribes and Pharisees you shall not enter the kingdom of God. You have heard the commandment imposed on your forefathers, 'You shall not commit murder; every murderer shall be liable to judgment.' What I say to you is: everyone who grows angry with his brother shall be liable to judgment, any man who uses abusive language toward his brother shall be answerable to the Sanhedrin, and if he holds him in contempt he risks the fires of Gehenna. If you bring your gift to the altar and there recall that your brother has anything against you, leave your gift at the altar, go first to be reconciled with your brother, and then come and offer your gift. Lose no time; settle with your opponent while on your way to court with him. Otherwise your opponent may hand you over to the judge, who will hand you over to the guard, who will throw you into prison. I warn you, you will not be released until you have paid the last penny." ✛

SATURDAY, MARCH 10
LENTEN WEEKDAY

† *Deuteronomy 26:16-19*
You will be a people consecrated to the Lord God.

Moses spoke to the people, saying: "This day the Lord, your God, commands you to observe these statutes and decrees. Be careful, then, to observe them with all your heart and with all your soul. Today you are making this agreement with the Lord: he is to be your God and you are to walk in his ways and observe his statutes, commandments and decrees, and to hearken to his voice. And today the Lord is making this agreement with you: you are to be a people peculiarly his own, as he promised you; and provided you keep all his commandments, he will then raise you high in praise and renown and glory above all other nations he has made, and you will be a people sacred to the Lord, your God, as he promised." ✛

Psalm 119:1-2, 4-5, 7-8
R. Happy are they who follow the law of the Lord.
Happy are they whose way is blameless,
  who walk in the law of the Lord.
Happy are they who observe his decrees,
  who seek him with all their heart. **R.**
You have commanded that your precepts
  be diligently kept.
Oh, that I might be firm in the ways
  of keeping your statutes! **R.**
I will give you thanks with an upright heart,
  when I have learned your just ordinances.
I will keep your statutes;
  do not utterly forsake me. **R.**

Joel 2:12-13
R. Glory and praise to you, Lord Jesus Christ!
With all your heart turn to me
for I am tender and compassionate. **R.**

† *Matthew 5:43-48*
Be perfect as your heavenly Father is perfect.

Jesus said to his disciples: "You have heard the command-ment, 'You shall love your countryman but hate your enemy.' My command to you is: love your enemies, pray for your persecutors. This will prove that you are sons of your heavenly Father, for his sun rises on the bad and the good, he rains on the just and the unjust. If you love those who love you, what merit is there in that? Do not tax collectors do as much? And if you greet your brothers only, what is so praiseworthy about that? Do not pagans do as much? In a word, you must be perfected as your heavenly Father is perfect." ✛

MARCH 11
SECOND SUNDAY OF LENT

† *Genesis 15:5-12, 17-18*
God made a covenant with Abraham, his faithful servant.

The Lord God took Abram outside and said,
   "Look up at the sky and count the stars, if you can.
Just so, " he added, "shall your descendants be."
Abram put his faith in the LORD,
   who credited it to him as an act of righteousness.

He then said to him,
   "I am the LORD who brought you from Ur of the Chaldeans
   to give you this land as a possession."
"O Lord GOD, " he asked,
   "how am I to know that I shall possess it?"
He answered him,
   "Bring me a three-year-old heifer, a three-year-old she-goat,
   a three-year-old ram, a turtledove, and a young pigeon."
Abram brought him all these, split them in two,
   and placed each half opposite the other;
   but the birds he did not cut up.
Birds of prey swooped down on the carcasses,
   but Abram stayed with them.
As the sun was about to set, a trance fell upon Abram,
   and a deep, terrifying darkness enveloped him.

When the sun had set and it was dark,
   there appeared a smoking fire pot and a flaming torch,
   which passed between those pieces.
It was on that occasion that the LORD made a covenant with
      Abram,
   saying: "To your descendants I give this land,
   from the Wadi of Egypt to the Great River, the
   Euphrates." +

Psalm 27:1, 7-9, 13-14
R. The Lord is my light and my salvation.
The LORD is my light and my salvation;
   whom should I fear?
The LORD is my life's refuge;
   of whom should I be afraid? **R.**
Hear, O LORD, the sound of my call;
   have pity on me, and answer me.
Of you my heart speaks; you my glance seeks. **R.**
Your presence, O LORD, I seek.
   Hide not your face from me;
do not in anger repel your servant.
   You are my helper: cast me not off. **R.**
I believe that I shall see the bounty of the LORD
   in the land of the living.
Wait for the LORD with courage;
   be stouthearted, and wait for the LORD. **R.**

† Philippians 3:20—4:1 (or Philippians 3:17—4:1)
Christ will change our lowly body to conform with his glorified body.

Brothers and sisters:
Our citizenship is in heaven,
   and from it we also await a savior, the Lord Jesus Christ.
He will change our lowly body
   to conform with his glorified body
   by the power that enables him also
   to bring all things into subjection to himself.

Therefore, my brothers and sisters,
   whom I love and long for, my joy and crown,
   in this way stand firm in the Lord, beloved. +

cf. Matthew 17:5

R. Glory and praise to you, Lord Jesus Christ!
From the shining cloud the Father's voice is heard:
This is my beloved Son, hear him. **R.**

† *Luke 9:28b-36*
*While he was praying his face changed in
appearance and his clothing became dazzling white.*

Jesus took Peter, John, and James
and went up the mountain to pray.
While he was praying his face changed in appearance
and his clothing became dazzling white.
And behold, two men were conversing with him, Moses and
Elijah,
who appeared in glory and spoke of his exodus
that he was going to accomplish in Jerusalem.
Peter and his companions had been overcome by sleep,
but becoming fully awake,
they saw his glory and the two men standing with him.
As they were about to part from him, Peter said to Jesus,
"Master, it is good that we are here;
let us make three tents,
one for you, one for Moses, and one for Elijah."
But he did not know what he was saying.
While he was still speaking,
a cloud came and cast a shadow over them,
and they became frightened when they entered the cloud.
Then from the cloud came a voice that said,
"This is my chosen Son; listen to him."
After the voice had spoken, Jesus was found alone.
They fell silent and did not at that time
tell anyone what they had seen. ✝

MONDAY, MARCH 12
LENTEN WEEKDAY

† *Daniel 9:4-10*
We have sinned, we have done wrong.

"Lord, great and awesome God, you who keep your merciful
covenant toward those who love you and observe your com-

mandments! We have sinned, been wicked and done evil; we have rebelled and departed from your commandments and your laws. We have not obeyed your servants the prophets, who spoke in your name to our kings, our princes, our fathers, and all the people of the land. Justice, O Lord, is on your side; we are shamefaced even to this day: the men of Judah, the residents of Jerusalem, and all Israel, near and far, in all the countries to which you have scattered them because of their treachery toward you. O Lord, we are shamefaced, like our kings, our princes, and our fathers, for having sinned against you. But yours, O Lord, our God, are compassion and forgiveness! Yet we rebelled against you and paid no heed to your command, O Lord, our God, to live by the law you gave us through your servants the prophets." ✛

Psalm 79:8-9, 11, 13

**R. Lord, do not deal with us
as our sins deserve.**

Remember not against us the iniquities of the past;
    may your compassion quickly come to us,
    for we are brought very low. **R.**
Help us, O God our savior,
    because of the glory of your name;
Deliver us and pardon our sins
    for your name's sake. **R.**
Let the prisoners' sighing come before you;
    with your great power free those doomed to death.
Then we, your people and the sheep of your pasture,
    will give thanks to you forever;
    through all generations we will declare your praise. **R.**

Psalm 51:12, 14

R. Glory and praise to you, Lord Jesus Christ!
Create a clean heart in me, O God;
give back to me the joy of your salvation. **R.**

† *Luke 6:36-38*
Forgive, and you will be forgiven.

Jesus said to his disciples: "Be compassionate, as your Father is compassionate. Do not judge, and you will not be judged. Do not condemn, and you will not be condemned. Pardon, and you shall be pardoned. Give, and it shall be given to you. Good measure pressed down, shaken together, running over, will they pour into the fold of your garment. For the measure you measure with will be measured back to you." ✛

TUESDAY, MARCH 13
LENTEN WEEKDAY

✛ *Isaiah 1:10, 16-20*
Learn to do good, search for justice.

Hear the word of the Lord,
    princes of Sodom!
Listen to the instruction of our God,
    people of Gomorrah!
    Wash yourselves clean!
Put away your misdeeds from before my eyes;
    cease doing evil; learn to do good.
Make justice your aim: redress the wronged,
    hear the orphan's plea, defend the widow.

Come now, let us set things right,
    says the Lord:
Though your sins be like scarlet,
    they may become white as snow;
Though they be crimson red,
    they may become white as wool.
If you are willing, and obey,
    you shall eat the good things of the land;
But if you refuse and resist,
    the sword shall consume you:
    for the mouth of the Lord has spoken! ✛

Psalm 50:8-9, 16-17, 21, 23
**R. To the upright
I will show the saving power of God.**
Not for your sacrifices do I rebuke you,
    for your holocausts are before me always.
I take from your house no bullock,
    no goats out of your fold. **R.**
Why do you recite my statutes,
    and profess my covenant with your mouth,

Though you hate discipline
and cast my words behind you? **R.**
When you do these things, shall I be deaf to it?
Or think you that I am like yourself?
I will correct you by drawing them up before your eyes.
He that offers praise as a sacrifice glorifies me;
and to him that goes the right way I will show the salvation
of God. **R.**

Psalm 95:8
R. Glory and praise to you, Lord Jesus Christ!
If today you hear his voice,
harden not your hearts. **R.**

† *Matthew 23:1-12*
They do not practice what they preach.

Jesus told the crowds and his disciples: "The scribes and the
Pharisees have succeeded Moses as teachers; therefore, do
everything and observe everything they tell you. But do not
follow their example. Their words are bold but their deeds are
few. They bind up heavy loads, hard to carry, to lay on other
men's shoulders, while they themselves will not lift a finger to
budge them. All their works are performed to be seen. They
widen their phylacteries and wear huge tassels. They are fond
of places of honor at banquets and the front seats in synagogues, of marks of respect in public and of being called 'Rabbi.'
As to you, avoid the title 'Rabbi.' One among you is your
teacher, the rest are learners. Do not call anyone on earth your
father. Only one is your father, the One in heaven. Avoid being
called teachers. Only one is your teacher, the Messiah. The
greatest among you will be the one who serves the rest.
Whoever exalts himself shall be humbled, but whoever
humbles himself shall be exalted." ✛

WEDNESDAY, MARCH 14
LENTEN WEEKDAY

† *Jeremiah 18:18-20*
Come, let us persecute him.

The men of Judah and the citizens of Jerusalem said, "Let us
contrive a plot against Jeremiah. It will not mean the loss of

instruction from the priests, nor of counsel from the wise, nor
of messages from the prophets. And so, let us destroy him by
his own tongue; let us carefully note his every word."
Heed me, O Lord,
   and listen to what my adversaries say.
Must good be repaid with evil
   that they should dig a pit to take my life?
Remember that I stood before you
   to speak in their behalf,
   to turn away your wrath from them. ✛

Psalm 31:5-6, 14-16
R. Save me, O Lord, in your steadfast love.
You will free me from the snare they set for me,
   for you are my refuge.
Into your hands I commend my spirit;
   you will redeem me, O Lord, O faithful God. **R.**
I hear the whispers of the crowd, that frighten me from every
   side,
   as they consult together against me, plotting to take my
   life. **R.**
But my trust is in you, O Lord;
   I say, "You are my God."
In your hands is my destiny; rescue me
   from the clutches of my enemies and my persecutors. **R.**

Ezekiel 33:11
R. Glory and praise to you, Lord Jesus Christ!
I do not wish the sinner to die, says the Lord,
but to turn to me and live. **R.**

† *Matthew 20:17-28*
They condemned him to death.

As Jesus was starting to go up to Jerusalem, he took the
Twelve aside on the road and said to them: "We are going up
to Jerusalem now. There the Son of Man will be handed over
to the chief priests and scribes, who will condemn him to
death. They will turn him over to the Gentiles, to be made
sport of and flogged and crucified. But on the third day he will
be raised up."
   The mother of Zebedee's sons came up to him accompanied

by her sons, to do him homage and ask of him a favor. "What is it you want?" he said. She answered, "Promise me that these sons of mine will sit, one at your right hand and the other at your left, in your kingdom." In reply Jesus said, "You do not know what you are asking. Can you drink of the cup I am to drink of?" "We can," they said. He told them, "From the cup I drink of you shall drink. Sitting at my right hand or my left is not mine to give. That is for those for whom it has been reserved by my Father." The other ten, on hearing this, became indignant at the two brothers. Jesus then called them together and said: "You know how those who exercise authority among the Gentiles lord it over them; their great ones make their importance felt. It cannot be like that with you. Anyone among you who aspires to greatness must serve the rest, and whoever wants to rank first among you, must serve the needs of all. Such is the case with the Son of Man who has come, not to be served by others but to serve, to give his own life as a ransom for the many." ✛

THURSDAY, MARCH 15
LENTEN WEEKDAY

† *Jeremiah 17:5-10*
A curse on him who trusts in man;
a blessing on him who trusts in the Lord God.

Thus says the Lord:
Cursed is the man who trusts in human beings,
    who seeks his strength in flesh,
    whose heart turns away from the Lord.
He is like a barren bush in the desert
    that enjoys no change of season,
But stands in a lava waste,
    a salt and empty earth.
Blessed is the man who trusts in the Lord,
    whose hope is the Lord.
He is like a tree planted beside the waters
    that stretches out its roots to the stream:
It fears not the heat when it comes,
    its leaves stay green;
In the year of drought it shows no distress,

but still bears fruit.
More tortuous than all else is the human heart,
   beyond remedy; who can understand it?
I, the Lord, alone probe the mind
   and test the heart,
To reward everyone according to his ways,
   according to the merit of his deeds. ✛

Psalm 1:1-4, 6
R. Happy are they who hope in the Lord.
Happy the man who follows not
   the counsel of the wicked
Nor walks in the way of sinners,
   nor sits in the company of the insolent,
But delights in the law of the Lord
   and meditates on his law day and night. **R.**
He is like a tree
   planted near running water,
That yields its fruit in due season,
   and whose leaves never fade.
   [Whatever he does, prospers.] **R.**
Not so, the wicked, not so;
   they are like chaff which the wind drives away.
For the Lord watches over the way of the just,
   but the way of the wicked vanishes. **R.**

John 11:25, 26
R. Glory and praise to you, Lord Jesus Christ!
I am the resurrection and the life, said the Lord:
he who believes in me will not die forever. **R.**

† *Luke 16:19-31*
Good things came to you and bad things to Lazarus;
now he is comforted while you are in agony.

Jesus said to the Pharisees: "Once there was a rich man who
dressed in purple and linen and feasted splendidly every day.
At his gate lay a beggar named Lazarus, who was covered with
sores. Lazarus longed to eat the scraps that fell from the rich
man's table. The dogs even came and licked his sores. Eventually the beggar died. He was carried by angels to the bosom of
Abraham. The rich man likewise died and was buried. From

the abode of the dead where he was in torment, he raised his eyes and saw Abraham afar off, and Lazarus resting in his bosom.

"He called out, 'Father Abraham, have pity on me. Send Lazarus to dip the tip of his finger in water to refresh my tongue, for I am tortured in these flames.' 'My child,' replied Abraham, 'remember that you were well off in your lifetime, while Lazarus was in misery. Now he has found consolation here, but you have found torment. And that is not all. Between you and us there is fixed a great abyss, so that those who might wish to cross from here to you cannot do so, nor can anyone cross from your side to us.'

"'Father, I ask you, then,' the rich man said, 'send him to my father's house where I have five brothers. Let him be a warning to them so that they may not end in this place of torment.' Abraham answered, 'They have Moses and the prophets. Let them hear them.' 'No, Father Abraham,' replied the rich man. 'But if someone would only go to them from the dead, then they would repent.' Abraham said to him, 'If they do not listen to Moses and the prophets, they will not be convinced even if one should rise from the dead.'" ✛

FRIDAY, MARCH 16
LENTEN WEEKDAY

† Genesis 37:3-4, 12-13, 17-28
Here comes the man of dreams; let us kill him.

Israel loved Joseph best of all his sons, for he was the child of his old age; and he had made him a long tunic. When his brothers saw that their father loved him best of all his sons, they hated him so much that they would not even greet him.

One day, when his brothers had gone to pasture their father's flocks at Shechem, Israel said to Joseph, "Your brothers, you know, are tending our flocks at Shechem. Get ready; I will send you to them."

So Joseph went after his brothers and caught up with them in Dothan. They noticed him from a distance, and before he came up to them, they plotted to kill him. They said to one another: "Here comes that master dreamer! Come on, let us kill him and throw him into one of the cisterns here; we could say that a wild beast devoured him. We shall then see what comes of his dreams."

When Reuben heard this, he tried to save him from their hands, saying: "We must not take his life. Instead of shedding blood," he continued, "just throw him into that cistern there in the desert; but don't kill him outright." His purpose was to rescue him from their hands and restore him to his father. So when Joseph came up to them, they stripped him of the long tunic he had on; then they took him and threw him into the cistern, which was empty and dry.

They then sat down to their meal. Looking up, they saw a caravan of Ishmaelites coming from Gilead, their camels laden with gum, balm, and resin to be taken down to Egypt. Judah said to his brothers: "What is to be gained by killing our brother and concealing his blood? Rather, let us sell him to these Ishmaelites, instead of doing away with him ourselves. After all, he is our brother, our own flesh." His brothers agreed. They sold Joseph to the Ishmaelites for twenty pieces of silver. ✛

Psalm 105:16-21
R. Remember the marvels the Lord has done.
When the Lord called down a famine on the land
and ruined the crop that sustained them,
He sent a man before them,
Joseph, sold as a slave. **R.**
They had weighed him down with fetters,
and he was bound with chains,
Till his prediction came to pass
and the word of the Lord proved him true. **R.**
The king sent and released him,
the ruler of the peoples set him free.
He made him lord of his house
and ruler of all his possessions. **R.**

John 3:16
R. Glory and praise to you, Lord Jesus Christ!
God loved the world so much, he gave us his only Son,
that all who believe in him might have eternal life. **R.**

✝ *Matthew 21:33-43, 45-46*
This is the heir; let us kill him.

Jesus said to the chief priests and elders of the people: "Listen to this parable. There was a property owner who planted a vineyard, put a hedge around it, dug out a vat, and erected a tower. Then he leased it out to tenant farmers and went on a journey. When vintage time arrived he dispatched his slaves to the tenants to obtain his share of the grapes. The tenants responded by seizing the slaves. They beat one, killed another, and stoned a third. A second time he dispatched even more slaves than before, but they treated them the same way. Finally he sent his son to them, thinking, 'They will respect my son.' When they saw the son, the tenants said to one another, 'Here is the one who will inherit everything. Let us kill him and then we shall have his inheritance!' With that they seized him, dragged him outside the vineyard, and killed him. What do you suppose the owner of the vineyard will do to those tenants when he comes?" They replied, "He will bring that wicked crowd to a bad end and lease his vineyard out to others, who will see to it that he has grapes at vintage time." Jesus said to them, "Did you never read in the Scriptures,

'The stone which the builders rejected
has become the keystone of the structure.
It was the Lord who did this
and we find it marvelous to behold'?

For this reason, I tell you, the kingdom of God will be taken away from you and given to a nation that will yield a rich harvest."

When the chief priests and the Pharisees heard these parables, they realized he was speaking about them. Although they sought to arrest him they had reason to fear the crowds who regarded him as a prophet. ✛

SATURDAY, MARCH 17
LENTEN WEEKDAY, ST. PATRICK

✝ *Micah 7:14-15, 18-20*
Once again tread down all our sins to the bottom of the sea.

Shepherd your people with your staff,
the flock of your inheritance,

That dwells apart in a woodland,
    in the midst of Carmel.
Let them feed in Bashan and Gilead,
    as in the days of old;
As in the days when you came from the land of Egypt,
    show us wonderful signs.

Who is there like you, the God who removes guilt
    and pardons sin for the remnant of his inheritance;
Who does not persist in anger forever,
    but delights rather in clemency,
And will again have compassion on us,
    treading underfoot our guilt?
You will cast into the depths of the sea
    all our sins;
You will show faithfulness to Jacob,
    and grace to Abraham,
As you have sworn to our fathers
    from days of old. ✛

Psalm 103:1-4, 9-12
R. The Lord is kind and merciful.
Bless the Lord, O my soul;
    and all my being, bless his holy name.
Bless the Lord, O my soul,
    and forget not all his benefits. **R.**
He pardons all your iniquities,
    he heals all your ills.
He redeems your life from destruction,
    he crowns you with kindness and compassion. **R.**
He will not always chide,
    nor does he keep his wrath forever.
Not according to our sins does he deal with us,
    nor does he requite us according to our crimes. **R.**
For as the heavens are high above the earth,
    so surpassing is his kindness toward those who fear him.
As far as the east is from the west,
    so far has he put our transgressions from us. **R.**

Luke 15:18

R. Glory and praise to you, Lord Jesus Christ!
I will rise and go to my father and tell him:
Father, I have sinned against heaven and against you. **R.**

† *Luke 15:1-3, 11-32*
Your brother here was dead, and has come to life.

The tax collectors and sinners were all gathering around Jesus to hear him, at which the Pharisees and the scribes murmured, "This man welcomes sinners and eats with them." At this Jesus addressed this parable to them: "A man had two sons. The younger of them said to his father, 'Father, give me the share of the estate that is coming to me.' So the father divided up the property. Some days later this younger son collected all his belongings and went off to a distant land, where he squandered his money on dissolute living. After he had spent everything, a great famine broke out in that country and he was in dire need. So he attached himself to one of the propertied class of the place, who sent him to his farm to take care of the pigs. He longed to fill his belly with the husks that were fodder for pigs, but no one made a move to give him anything. Coming to his senses at last, he said: 'How many hired hands at my father's place have more than enough to eat, while here I am starving! I will break away and return to my father, and say to him, "Father, I have sinned against God and against you; I no longer deserve to be called your son. Treat me like one of your hired hands."' With that he set off for his father's house. While he was still a long way off, his father caught sight of him and was deeply moved. He ran out to meet him, threw his arms around his neck, and kissed him. The son said to him, 'Father, I have sinned against God and against you; I no longer deserve to be called your son.' The father said to his servants: 'Quick! bring out the finest robe and put it on him; put a ring on his finger and shoes on his feet. Take the fatted calf and kill it. Let us eat and celebrate because this son of mine was dead and has come back to life. He was lost and is found.' Then the celebration began.

"Meanwhile the elder son was out on the land. As he neared the house on his way home, he heard the sound of music and dancing. He called one of the servants and asked him the reason for the dancing and the music. The servant answered, 'Your brother is home, and your father has killed the fatted calf because he has him back in good health.' The son grew angry at this and would not go in; but his father came out and began to plead with him.

"He said to his father in reply: 'For years now I have slaved for you. I never disobeyed one of your orders, yet you never gave me so much as a kid goat to celebrate with my friends. Then, when this son of yours returns after having gone through your property with loose women, you kill the fatted calf for him.'

"'My son,' replied the father, 'you are with me always, and everything I have is yours. But we must celebrate and rejoice! This brother of yours was dead, and has come back to life. He was lost, and is found.'" ✛

MARCH 18
THIRD SUNDAY OF LENT

✝ Exodus 3:1-8a, 13-15 (or Exodus 17:3-7)
"I AM" sent me to you.

Moses was tending the flock of his father-in-law Jethro,
    the priest of Midian.
Leading the flock across the desert, he came to Horeb,
    the mountain of God.
There an angel of the LORD appeared to Moses in fire
    flaming out of a bush.
As he looked on, he was surprised to see that the bush,
    though on fire, was not consumed.
So Moses decided,
    "I must go over to look at this remarkable sight,
    and see why the bush is not burned."

When the LORD saw him coming over to look at it more closely,
    God called out to him from the bush, "Moses! Moses!"
He answered, "Here I am."
God said, "Come no nearer!
Remove the sandals from your feet,
    for the place where you stand is holy ground.
I am the God of your fathers, " he continued,

"the God of Abraham, the God of Isaac, the God of Jacob."
Moses hid his face, for he was afraid to look at God.
But the LORD said,
"I have witnessed the affliction of my people in Egypt
and have heard their cry of complaint against their slave
drivers,
so I know well what they are suffering.
Therefore I have come down to rescue them
from the hands of the Egyptians
and lead them out of that land into a good and spacious land,
a land flowing with milk and honey."

Moses said to God, "But when I go to the Israelites
and say to them, 'The God of your fathers has sent me to you,'
if they ask me, 'What is his name?' what am I to tell them?"
God replied, "I am who am."
Then he added, "This is what you shall tell the Israelites:
I AM sent me to you."

God spoke further to Moses, "Thus shall you say to the
Israelites:
The LORD, the God of your fathers,
the God of Abraham, the God of Isaac, the God of Jacob,
has sent me to you.

"This is my name forever;
thus am I to be remembered through all generations." ✛

Psalm 103:1-4, 6-8, 11 (or Psalm 95:1-2, 6-7, 8-9)
R. The Lord is kind and merciful.
Bless the LORD, O my soul;
and all my being, bless his holy name.
Bless the LORD, O my soul,
and forget not all his benefits. **R.**
He pardons all your iniquities,
heals all your ills,
He redeems your life from destruction,
crowns you with kindness and compassion. **R.**
The LORD secures justice
and the rights of all the oppressed.
He has made known his ways to Moses,
and his deeds to the children of Israel. **R.**

Merciful and gracious is the LORD,
    slow to anger and abounding in kindness.
For as the heavens are high above the earth,
    so surpassing is his kindness toward those who fear him. **R.**

† *1 Corinthians 10:1-6, 10-12* (or Romans 5:1-2, 5-8)
*The life of the people with Moses in the desert
was written down as a warning to us.*

I do not want you to be unaware, brothers and sisters,
    that our ancestors were all under the cloud
    and all passed through the sea,
    and all of them were baptized into Moses
    in the cloud and in the sea.
All ate the same spiritual food,
    and all drank the same spiritual drink,
    for they drank from a spiritual rock that followed them,
    and the rock was the Christ.
Yet God was not pleased with most of them,
    for they were struck down in the desert.

These things happened as examples for us,
    so that we might not desire evil things, as they did.
Do not grumble as some of them did,
    and suffered death by the destroyer.
These things happened to them as an example,
    and they have been written down as a warning to us,
    upon whom the end of the ages has come.
Therefore, whoever thinks he is standing secure
    should take care not to fall. ✛

Matthew 4:17
R. Glory and praise to you, Lord Jesus Christ!
Repent, says the Lord;
the kingdom of heaven is at hand. **R.**

† *Luke 13:1-9* (or John 4:5-42 or 4:5-15, 19-26, 39, 40-42)
If you do not repent, you will all perish as they did.

Some people told Jesus about the Galileans
    whose blood Pilate had mingled with the blood
        of their sacrifices.
Jesus said to them in reply,

"Do you think that because these Galileans suffered
in this way
they were greater sinners than all other Galileans?
By no means!
But I tell you, if you do not repent,
you will all perish as they did!
Or those eighteen people who were killed
when the tower at Siloam fell on them—
do you think they were more guilty
than everyone else who lived in Jerusalem?
By no means!
But I tell you, if you do not repent,
you will all perish as they did!"

And he told them this parable:
"There once was a person who had a fig tree planted
in his orchard,
and when he came in search of fruit on it but found none,
he said to the gardener,
'For three years now I have come in search of fruit
on this fig tree
but have found none.
So cut it down.
Why should it exhaust the soil?'
He said to him in reply,
'Sir, leave it for this year also,
and I shall cultivate the ground around it and fertilize it;
it may bear fruit in the future.
If not you can cut it down.'" ✛

MONDAY, MARCH 19
St. Joseph

✝ 2 Samuel 7:4-5a, 12-14a, 16
The Lord God will give him the throne of David his father.

The Lord spoke to Nathan and said:
"Go, tell my servant David,
'When your time comes and you rest with your ancestors,
I will raise up your heir after you, sprung from your loins,
and I will make his kingdom firm.

It is he who shall build a house for my name.
And I will make his royal throne firm forever.
I will be a father to him,
    and he shall be a son to me.
Your house and your kingdom shall endure forever before me;
    your throne shall stand firm forever.'" ✛

Psalm 89:2-5, 27, 29
R. The son of David will live forever.
The promises of the LORD I will sing forever,
    through all generations my mouth
        will proclaim your faithfulness,
for you have said, "'My kindness is established forever";
    in heaven you have confirmed your faithfulness. **R.**
"I have made a covenant with my chosen one;
    I have sworn to David my servant:
forever will I confirm your posterity
    and establish your throne for all generations." **R.**
"He shall say of me, 'You are my father,
    my God, the Rock my savior!'
Forever I will maintain my kindness toward him,
    my covenant with him stands firm." **R.**

† *Romans 4:13, 16-18, 22*
Abraham believed, hoping against hope.

Brothers and sisters:
It was not through the law
    that the promise was made to Abraham and his descen
        dants
    that he would inherit the world,
    but through the righteousness that comes from faith.
For this reason, it depends on faith,
    so that it may be a gift,
    and the promise may be guaranteed to all his descendants,
not to those who only adhere to the law
    but to those who follow the faith of Abraham,
    who is the father of all of us, as it is written,
    I have made you father of many nations.
He is our father in the sight of God,
    in whom he believed, who gives life to the dead

and calls into being what does not exist.
He believed, hoping against hope,
    that he would become "the father of many nations, "
    according to what was said, "Thus shall your descendants be."
That is why "it was credited to him as righteousness." ✢

Psalm 84:5
R. Glory and praise to you, Lord Jesus Christ.
Blessed are those who dwell in your house, O Lord,
they never cease to praise you. **R.**

    † Luke 2:41-51a (or Matthew 1:16, 18-21, 24a)
    Your father and I have been looking for you with great anxiety.

Each year Jesus' parents went to Jerusalem for the feast of
    Passover,
    and when he was twelve years old,
    they went up according to festival custom.
After they had completed its days, as they were returning,
    the boy Jesus remained behind in Jerusalem,
    but his parents did not know it.
Thinking that he was in the caravan,
    they journeyed for a day
    and looked for him among their relatives and
        acquaintances,
    but not finding him,
    they returned to Jerusalem to look for him.
After three days they found him in the temple,
    sitting in the midst of the teachers,
    listening to them and asking them questions,
    and all who heard him were astounded
    at his understanding and his answers.
When his parents saw him,
    they were astonished,
    and his mother said to him,
    "Son, why have you done this to us?
Your father and I have been looking for you with great
        anxiety."
And he said to them,
    "Why were you looking for me?
Did you not know that I must be in my Father's house?"

But they did not understand what he said to them.
He went down with them and came to Nazareth,
   and was obedient to them. ✢

TUESDAY, MARCH 20
LENTEN WEEKDAY

† *Daniel 3:25, 34-43*
We ask you to receive us with humble and contrite hearts.

Azariah stood up in the fire and prayed aloud:
"For your name's sake, O Lord, do not deliver us up forever,
   or make void your covenant.
Do not take away your mercy from us,
   for the sake of Abraham, your beloved,
   Isaac your servant, and Israel your holy one,
To whom you promised to multiply their offspring
   like the stars of heaven,
   or the sand on the shore of the sea.
For we are reduced, O Lord, beyond any other nation,
   brought low everywhere in the world this day
   because of our sins.
We have in our day no prince, prophet, or leader,
   no holocaust, sacrifice, oblation, or incense,
   no place to offer first fruits, to find favor with you.
But with contrite heart and humble spirit
   let us be received;
As though it were holocausts of rams and bullocks,
   or thousands of fat lambs,
So let our sacrifice be in your presence today
   as we follow you unreservedly;
   for those who trust in you cannot be put to shame.
And now we follow you with our whole heart,
   we fear you and we pray to you.
Do not let us be put to shame,
   but deal with us in your kindness and great mercy.
Deliver us by your wonders,
   and bring glory to your name, O Lord." ✢

Psalm 25:4-9

R. Remember your mercies, O Lord.

Your ways, O Lord, make known to me;
    teach me your paths,
Guide me in your truth and teach me,
    for you are God my savior. **R.**
Remember that your compassion, O Lord,
    and your kindness are from of old.
In your kindness remember me,
    because of your goodness, O Lord. **R.**
Good and upright is the Lord;
    thus he shows sinners the way.
He guides the humble to justice,
    he teaches the humble his way. **R.**

Amos 5:14

R. Glory and praise to you, Lord Jesus Christ!

Seek good and not evil
so that you may live,
and the Lord will be with you. **R.**

† *Matthew 18:21-35*

Unless each of you forgive your brother, the Father will not forgive you.

Peter came up and asked Jesus, "Lord, when my brother wrongs me, how often must I forgive him? Seven times?" "No," Jesus replied, "not seven times; I say, seventy times seven times. That is why the reign of God may be said to be like a king who decided to settle accounts with his officials. When he began his auditing, one was brought in who owed him a huge amount. As he had no way of paying it, his master ordered him to be sold, along with his wife, his children, and all his property, in payment of the debt. At that the official prostrated himself in homage and said, 'My lord, be patient with me and I will pay you back in full.' Moved with pity, the master let the official go and wrote off the debt. But when that same official went out he met a fellow servant who owed him a mere fraction of what he himself owed. He seized him and throttled him. 'Pay back what you owe,' he demanded. His fellow servant dropped to his knees and began to plead with him, 'Just give me time and I will pay you back in full.' But he would hear none of it.

Instead, he had him put in jail until he paid back what he owed. When his fellow servants saw what had happened they were badly shaken, and went to their master to report the whole incident. His master sent for him and said, 'You worthless wretch! I canceled your entire debt when you pleaded with me. Should you not have dealt mercifully with your fellow servant, as I dealt with you?' Then in anger the master handed him over to the torturers until he paid back all that he owed. My heavenly Father will treat you in exactly the same way unless each of you forgives his brother from his heart." ✝

WEDNESDAY, MARCH 21
LENTEN WEEKDAY

✝ *Deuteronomy 4:1, 5-9*
Keep the commandments and your work will be complete.

These are the words which Moses spoke to the people: "Now, Israel, hear the statutes and decrees which I am teaching you to observe, that you may live, and may enter in and take possession of the land which the Lord, the God of your fathers, is giving you. Therefore, I teach you the statutes and decrees as the Lord, my God, has commanded me, that you may observe them in the land you are entering to occupy. Observe them carefully, for thus will you give evidence of your wisdom and intelligence to the nations, who will hear of all these statutes and say, 'This great nation is truly a wise and intelligent people.' For what great nation is there that has gods so close to it as the Lord, our God, is to us whenever we call upon him? Or what great nation has statutes and decrees that are as just as this whole law which I am setting before you today?

"However, take care and be earnestly on your guard not to forget the things which your own eyes have seen, nor let them slip from your memory as long as you live, but teach them to your children and to your children's children." ✝

Psalm 147:12-13, 15-16, 19-20
R. Praise the Lord, Jerusalem.
Glorify the Lord, O Jerusalem;
    praise your God, O Zion.
For he has strengthened the bars of your gates;

he has blessed your children within you. **R.**
He sends forth his command to the earth;
    swiftly runs his word!
He spreads snow like wool;
    frost he strews like ashes. **R.**
He has proclaimed his word to Jacob,
    his statutes and his ordinances to Israel.
He has not done thus for any other nation;
    his ordinances he has not made known to them. **R.**

Matthew 4:4
R. Glory and praise to you, Lord Jesus Christ!
Man does not live on bread alone,
but on every word that comes from the mouth of God. **R.**

✝ *Matthew 5:17-19*
The man who keeps and teaches the law will be called great.

Jesus said to his disciples: "Do not think that I have come to abolish the law and the prophets. I have come, not to abolish them, but to fulfill them. Of this much I assure you: until heaven and earth pass away, not the smallest letter of the law, not the smallest part of a letter shall be done away with until it all comes true. That is why whoever breaks the least significant of these commands and teaches others to do so shall be called least in the kingdom of God. Whoever fulfills and teaches these commands shall be great in the kingdom of God." ✛

THURSDAY, MARCH 22
LENTEN WEEKDAY

✝ *Jeremiah 7:23-28*
This is the nation that will not listen to the voice of the Lord God.

Thus says the Lord: This is what I commanded my people: Listen to my voice; then I will be your God and you shall be my people. Walk in all the ways that I command you, so that you may prosper.

But they obeyed not, nor did they pay heed. They walked in the hardness of their evil hearts and turned their backs, not their faces, to me. From the day that your fathers left the land of Egypt even to this day, I have sent you untiringly all my servants the prophets. Yet they have not obeyed me nor paid heed; they have stiffened their necks and done worse than their fathers. When you speak all these words to them, they will not listen to you either; when you call to them, they will not answer you. Say to them: This is the nation which does not listen to the voice of the Lord, its God, or take correction. Faithfulness has disappeared; the word itself is banished from their speech. ✛

Psalm 95:1-2, 6-9
**R. If today you hear his voice,
harden not your hearts.**
Come, let us sing joyfully to the Lord;
　let us acclaim the Rock of our salvation.
Let us greet him with thanksgiving;
　let us joyfully sing psalms to him. **R.**
Come, let us bow down in worship;
　let us kneel before the Lord who made us.
For he is our God,
　and we are the people he shepherds, the flock he guides. **R.**
Oh, that today you would hear his voice:
　"Harden not your hearts as at Meribah,
　as in the day of Massah in the desert,
Where your fathers tempted me;
　they tested me though they had seen my works." **R.**

John 6:64, 69
R. Glory and praise to you, Lord Jesus Christ!
Your words, Lord, are spirit and life;
you have the message of eternal life. **R.**

✝ *Luke 11:14-23*
He who is not with me is against me.

Jesus was casting out a devil which was mute, and when the devil was cast out the dumb man spoke. The crowds were amazed at this. Some of them said, "It is by Beelzebul, the prince of devils, that he casts out devils." Others, to test him, were demanding of him a sign from heaven.

Because he knew their thoughts, he said to them: "Every kingdom divided against itself is laid waste. Any house torn by dissension falls. If Satan is divided against himself, how can his kingdom last?—since you say it is by Beelzebul that I cast out devils. If I cast out devils by Beelzebul, by whom do your people cast them out? In such case, let them act as your judges. But if it is by the finger of God that I cast out devils, then the reign of God is upon you.

"When a strong man fully armed guards his courtyard, his possessions go undisturbed. But when someone stronger than he comes and overpowers him, such a one carries off the arms on which he was relying and divides the spoils. The man who is not with me is against me. The man who does not gather with me scatters." ✛

FRIDAY, MARCH 23
Lenten Weekday, St. Toribio de Mogrovejo

✝ Hosea 14:2-10
We will not say to the work of our hands: Our God.

Return, O Israel, to the Lord, your God;
  you have collapsed through your guilt.
Take with you words,
  and return to the Lord;
Say to him, "Forgive all iniquity,
  and receive what is good, that we may render
  as offerings the bullocks from our stalls.
Assyria will not save us,
  nor shall we have horses to mount;
We shall say no more, 'Our god,'
  to the work of our hands;
  for in you the orphan finds compassion."

I will heal their defection,
  I will love them freely;
  for my wrath is turned away from them.
I will be like the dew for Israel:
  he shall blossom like the lily;
He shall strike root like the Lebanon cedar,
  and put forth his shoots.
His splendor shall be like the olive tree
  and his fragrance like the Lebanon cedar.
Again they shall dwell in his shade
  and raise grain;

They shall blossom like the vine
and his fame shall be like the wine of Lebanon.

Ephraim! What more has he to do with idols?
I have humbled him, but I will prosper him.
"I am like a verdant cypress tree"—
Because of me you bear fruit!

Let him who is wise understand these things;
let him who is prudent know them.
Straight are the paths of the Lord,
in them the just walk,
but sinners stumble in them. ✝

Psalm 81:6-11, 14, 17
**R. I am the Lord, your God:
hear my voice.**
An unfamiliar speech I hear:
"I relieved his shoulder of the burden;
his hands were freed from the basket.
In distress you called, and I rescued you. **R.**
Unseen, I answered you in thunder;
I tested you at the waters of Meribah.
Hear, my people, and I will admonish you;
O Israel, will you not hear me? **R.**
There shall be no strange god among you
nor shall you worship any alien god.
I, the Lord, am your God
who led you forth from the land of Egypt. **R.**
If only my people would hear me,
and Israel walk in my ways,
I would feed them with the best of wheat,
and with honey from the rock I would fill them." **R.**

Ezekiel 18:31
R. Glory and praise to you, Lord Jesus Christ!
Rid yourselves of all your sins;
and make a new heart and a new spirit. **R.**

† *Mark 12:28-34*

The Lord your God is one Lord and you must love him.

One of the scribes came up to Jesus and asked him, "Which is the first of all the commandments?" Jesus replied: "This is the first:

'Hear, O Israel! The Lord our God is Lord alone!
Therefore you shall love the Lord your God
with all your heart,
with all your soul,
with all your mind,
and with all your strength.'

This is the second,

'You shall love your neighbor as yourself.'

There is no other commandment greater than these." The scribe said to him: "Excellent, Teacher! you are right in saying, 'He is the One, there is no other than he.' Yes, 'to love him with all our heart, with all our thoughts and with all our strength, and to love our neighbor as ourselves' is worth more than any burnt offering or sacrifice." Jesus approved the insight of this answer and told him, "You are not far from the reign of God." And no one had the courage to ask him any more questions. ✛

SATURDAY, MARCH 24

LENTEN WEEKDAY

† *Hosea 6:1-6*

What I want is love, not sacrifice.

In their affliction, they shall look for me:
"Come, let us return to the Lord,
For it is he who has rent, but he will heal us;
he has struck us, but he will bind our wounds.
He will revive us after two days;
on the third day he will raise us up,
to live in his presence.
Let us know, let us strive to know the Lord;
as certain as the dawn is his coming,
and his judgment shines forth like the light of day!
He will come to us like the rain,
like spring rain that waters the earth."

What can I do with you, Ephraim?
What can I do with you, Judah?
Your piety is like a morning cloud,
like the dew that early passes away.
For this reason I smote them through the prophets,
I slew them by the words of my mouth;
For it is love that I desire, not sacrifice,
and knowledge of God rather than holocausts. ✛

Psalm 51:3-4, 18-21
**R. It is steadfast love, not sacrifice,
that God desires.**
Have mercy on me, O God, in your goodness;
in the greatness of your compassion wipe out my offense.
Thoroughly wash me from my guilt
and of my sin cleanse me. **R.**
For you are not pleased with sacrifices;
should I offer a holocaust, you would not accept it.
My sacrifice, O God, is a contrite spirit;
a heart contrite and humbled, O God, you will not spurn. **R.**
Be bountiful, O Lord, to Zion in your kindness
by rebuilding the walls of Jerusalem;
Then shall you be pleased with due sacrifices,
burnt offerings and holocausts. **R.**

Psalm 51:12, 14
R. Glory and praise to you, Lord Jesus Christ!
Create a clean heart in me, O God;
give back to me the joy of your salvation. **R.**

† *Luke 18:9-14*
The publican went home justified, not the Pharisee.

Jesus spoke this parable addressed to those who believed in their own self-righteousness while holding everyone else in contempt: "Two men went up to the temple to pray; one was a Pharisee, the other a tax collector. The Pharisee with head unbowed prayed in this fashion: 'I give you thanks, O God, that I am not like the rest of men—grasping, crooked, adulterous—or even like this tax collector. I fast twice a week. I pay tithes on all I possess.' The other man, however, kept his distance, not even daring to raise his eyes to heaven. All he did was beat his breast and say, 'O God, be merciful to me, a sinner.' Believe me, this man went home from the temple justified but the other did not. For everyone who exalts himself shall be humbled while he who humbles himself shall be exalted." +

MARCH 25
FOURTH SUNDAY OF LENT

† *Joshua 5:9a, 10-12 (or 1 Samuel 16:1, 6-7, 10-13)*
The people of God entered the promised land and there kept the Passover.

The LORD said to Joshua,
"Today I have removed the reproach of Egypt from you."

While the Israelites were encamped at Gilgal on the plains of
Jericho,
they celebrated the Passover
on the evening of the fourteenth of the month.
On the day after the Passover,
they ate of the produce of the land
in the form of unleavened cakes and parched grain.
On that same day after the Passover,
on which they ate of the produce of the land, the manna
ceased.
No longer was there manna for the Israelites,
who that year ate of the yield of the land of Canaan. +

Psalm 34:2-7 (or Psalm 23:1-6)
R. Taste and see the goodness of the Lord.
I will bless the LORD at all times;
his praise shall be ever in my mouth.
Let my soul glory in the LORD;
the lowly will hear me and be glad. **R.**
Glorify the LORD with me,
let us together extol his name.
I sought the LORD, and he answered me
and delivered me from all my fears. **R.**
Look to him that you may be radiant with joy,
and your faces may not blush with shame.
When the poor one called out, the LORD heard,
and from all his distress he saved him. **R.**

† *2 Corinthians 5:17-21* (or Ephesians 5:8-14)
God reconciled us to himself through Christ.

Brothers and sisters:
Whoever is in Christ is a new creation:
 the old things have passed away;
 behold, new things have come.
And all this is from God,
 who has reconciled us to himself through Christ
 and given us the ministry of reconciliation,
 namely, God was reconciling the world to himself in Christ,
 not counting their trespasses against them
 and entrusting to us the message of reconciliation.
So we are ambassadors for Christ,
 as if God were appealing through us.
We implore you on behalf of Christ,
 be reconciled to God.
For our sake he made him to be sin who did not know sin,
 so that we might become the righteousness of God in him. ✛

Luke 15:18
R. Glory and praise to you, Lord Jesus Christ!
I will get up and go to my Father and shall say to him:
Father, I have sinned against heaven and against you. **R.**

† *Luke 15:1-3, 11-32* (or John 9:1-41 or 9:1,6-9,13-17,34-38)
Your brother was dead and has come to life again.

Tax collectors and sinners were all drawing near to listen to
 Jesus,
 but the Pharisees and scribes began to complain, saying,
 "This man welcomes sinners and eats with them."
So to them Jesus addressed this parable:
"A man had two sons, and the younger son said to his father,
 'Father give me the share of your estate that should come to
 me.'
So the father divided the property between them.
After a few days, the younger son collected all his belongings
 and set off to a distant country
 where he squandered his inheritance on a life of dissipation.
When he had freely spent everything,
 a severe famine struck that country,

and he found himself in dire need.
So he hired himself out to one of the local citizens
who sent him to his farm to tend the swine.
And he longed to eat his fill of the pods on which the swine fed,
but nobody gave him any.
Coming to his senses he thought,
'How many of my father's hired workers
have more than enough food to eat,
but here am I, dying from hunger.
I shall get up and go to my father and I shall say to him,
"Father, I have sinned against heaven and against you.
I no longer deserve to be called your son;
treat me as you would treat one of your hired workers."'
So he got up and went back to his father.
While he was still a long way off,
his father caught sight of him, and was filled with
compassion.
He ran to his son, embraced him and kissed him.
His son said to him,
'Father, I have sinned against heaven and against you;
I no longer deserve to be called your son.'
But his father ordered his servants,
'Quickly bring the finest robe and put it on him;
put a ring on his finger and sandals on his feet.
Take the fattened calf and slaughter it.
Then let us celebrate with a feast,
because this son of mine was dead, and has come to life
again;
he was lost, and has been found.'
Then the celebration began.
Now the older son had been out in the field
and, on his way back, as he neared the house,
he heard the sound of music and dancing.
He called one of the servants and asked what this might mean.
The servant said to him,
'Your brother has returned
and your father has slaughtered the fattened calf
because he has him back safe and sound.'
He became angry,
and when he refused to enter the house,

his father came out and pleaded with him.
He said to his father in reply,
    'Look, all these years I served you
    and not once did I disobey your orders;
    yet you never gave me even a young goat to feast on
        with my friends.
But when your son returns
    who swallowed up your property with prostitutes,
    for him you slaughter the fattened calf.'
He said to him,
    'My son, you are here with me always;
    everything I have is yours.
But now we must celebrate and rejoice,
    because your brother was dead and has come to life again;
    he was lost and has been found.'" ✝

MONDAY, MARCH 26
THE ANNUNCIATION OF THE LORD

✝ Isaiah 7:10-14; 8:10
Behold, the virgin shall conceive.

The LORD spoke to Ahaz, saying:
    Ask for a sign from the LORD, your God;
    let it be deep as the netherworld, or high as the sky!
But Ahaz answered,
    "I will not ask! I will not tempt the LORD!"
Then Isaiah said:
    Listen, O house of David!
Is it not enough for you to weary people,
    must you also weary my God?
Therefore the Lord himself will give you this sign:
    the virgin shall conceive, and bear a son,
    and shall name him Emmanuel,
    which means "God is with us!" ✝

Psalm 40:7-11
R. Here am I, Lord; I come to do your will.
Sacrifice or offering you wished not,
    but ears open to obedience you gave me.
Holocausts and sin-offerings you sought not;

then said I, "Behold, I come;" **R.**
"In the written scroll it is prescribed for me.
To do your will, O God, is my delight,
    and your law is within my heart!" **R.**
I announced your justice in the vast assembly;
    I did not restrain my lips, as you, O LORD, know. **R.**
Your justice I kept not hid within my heart;
    your faithfulness and your salvation I have spoken of;
I have made no secret of your kindness and your truth
    in the vast assembly. **R.**

✝ *Hebrews 10:4-10*

As is written of me in the scroll, behold, I come to do your will, O God.

Brothers and sisters:
It is impossible that the blood of bulls and goats
    takes away sins.
For this reason, when Christ came into the world, he said:
    "Sacrifice and offering you did not desire,
        but a body you prepared for me;
    in holocausts and sin offerings you took no delight.
    Then I said, 'As is written of me in the scroll,
    behold, I come to do your will, O God.'"

First Christ says, "Sacrifices and offerings,
    holocausts and sin offerings,
    you neither desired nor delighted in."
These are offered according to the law.
Then he says, "Behold, I come to do your will."
He takes away the first to establish the second.
By this "will," we have been consecrated
    through the offering of the body of Jesus Christ
        once for all. ✢

John 1:14ab
R. Glory and praise to you, Lord Jesus Christ.
The Word became flesh and made his dwelling among us
and we saw his glory. **R.**

† *Luke 1:26-38*
Behold, you will conceive in your womb and bear a son.

The angel Gabriel was sent from God
    to a town of Galilee called Nazareth,
    to a virgin betrothed to a man named Joseph,
    of the house of David,
    and the virgin's name was Mary.
And coming to her, he said,
    "Hail, full of grace! The Lord is with you."
But she was greatly troubled at what was said
    and pondered what sort of greeting this might be.
Then the angel said to her,
    "Do not be afraid, Mary,
    for you have found favor with God.
Behold, you will conceive in your womb and bear a son,
    and you shall name him Jesus.
He will be great and will be called Son of the Most High,
    and the Lord God will give him the throne of David his
        father,
    and he will rule over the house of Jacob forever,
    and of his kingdom there will be no end."
But Mary said to the angel,
    "How can this be,
    since I have no relations with a man?"
And the angel said to her in reply,
    "The Holy Spirit will come upon you,
    and the power of the Most High will overshadow you.
Therefore the child to be born
    will be called holy, the Son of God.
And behold, Elizabeth, your relative,
    has also conceived a son in her old age,
    and this is the sixth month for her who was called barren;
    for nothing will be impossible for God."
Mary said, "Behold, I am the handmaid of the Lord.
May it be done to me according to your word."
Then the angel departed from her. ✛

TUESDAY, MARCH 27
LENTEN WEEKDAY

✝ *Ezekiel 47:1-9, 12*
I saw water coming forth from the temple,
and all those were saved to whom that water came.

The angel brought me back to the entrance of the temple of the Lord, and I saw water flowing out from beneath the threshold of the temple toward the east, for the facade of the temple was toward the east; the water flowed down from the southern side of the temple, south of the altar. He led me outside by the north gate, and around to the outer gate facing the east, where I saw water trickling from the southern side. Then when he had walked off to the east with a measuring cord in his hand, he measured off a thousand cubits and had me wade through the water, which was ankle-deep. He measured off another thousand and once more had me wade through the water, which was now knee-deep. Again he measured off a thousand and had me wade; the water was up to my waist. Once more he measured off a thousand, but there was now a river through which I could not wade; for the water had risen so high it had become a river that could not be crossed except by swimming. He asked me, "Have you seen this, son of man?" Then he brought me to the bank of the river, where he had me sit. Along the bank of the river I saw very many trees on both sides. He said to me, "This water flows into the eastern district down upon the Arabah, and empties into the sea, the salt waters, which it makes fresh. Wherever the river flows, every sort of living creature that can multiply shall live, and there shall be abundant fish, for wherever this water comes the sea shall be made fresh. Along both banks of the river, fruit trees of every kind shall grow; their leaves shall not fade, nor their fruit fail. Every month they shall bear fresh fruit, for they shall be watered by the flow from the sanctuary. Their fruit shall serve for food, and their leaves for medicine." ✝

Psalm 46:2-3, 5-6, 8-9
R. The mighty Lord is with us;
the God of Jacob is our refuge.
God is our refuge and our strength,
    an ever-present help in distress.

Therefore we fear not, though the earth be shaken
  and mountains plunge into the depths of the sea. **R.**
There is a stream whose runlets gladden the city of God,
  the holy dwelling of the Most High.
God is in its midst; it shall not be disturbed;
  God will help it at the break of dawn. **R.**
The Lord of hosts is with us;
  our stronghold is the God of Jacob.
Come! behold the deeds of the Lord,
  the astounding things he has wrought on earth. **R.**

John 8:12
R. Glory and praise to you, Lord Jesus Christ!
I am the light of the world, says the Lord;
he who follows me will have the light of life. **R.**

† *John 5:1-3, 5-16*
He was cured at once by that man.

On the occasion of a Jewish feast, Jesus went up to Jerusalem. Now in Jerusalem by the Sheep Pool there is a place with the Hebrew name Bethesda. Its five porticoes were crowded with sick people lying there blind, lame or disabled [waiting for the movement of the waters]. There was one man who had been sick for thirty-eight years. Jesus, who knew he had been sick a long time, said when he saw him lying there, "Do you want to be healed?" "Sir," the sick man answered, "I don't have anyone to plunge me into the pool once the water has been stirred up. By the time I get there, someone else has gone in ahead of me." Jesus said to him, "Stand up! Pick up your mat and walk!" The man was immediately cured; he picked up his mat and began to walk.

The day was a sabbath. Consequently, some of the Jews began telling the man who had been cured, "It is the sabbath, and you are not allowed to carry that mat around." He explained: "It was the man who cured me who told me, 'Pick up your mat and walk.'" "This person who told you to pick it up and walk," they asked, "who is he?" The man who had been restored to health had no idea who it was. The crowd in that place was so great that Jesus had been able to slip away.

Later on, Jesus found him in the temple precincts and said

to him: "Remember, now, you have been cured. Give up your sins so that something worse may not overtake you." The man went off and informed the Jews that Jesus was the one who had cured him.

It was because Jesus did things such as this on the sabbath that they began to persecute him. ✛

WEDNESDAY, MARCH 28
LENTEN WEEKDAY

† Isaiah 49:8-15
I have given you as covenant of the people to establish the land.

Thus says the Lord:
In a time of favor I answer you,
    on the day of salvation I help you,
To restore the land
    and allot the desolate heritages,
Saying to the prisoners: Come out!
To those in darkness: Show yourselves!
Along the ways they shall find pasture,
    on every bare height shall their pastures be.
They shall not hunger or thirst,
    nor shall the scorching wind or the sun strike them;
For he who pities them leads them
    and guides them beside springs of water.
I will cut a road through all my mountains,
    and make my highways level.
See, some shall come from afar,
    others from the north and the west,
    and some from the land of Syene.

Sing out, O heavens, and rejoice, O earth,
    break forth into song, you mountains.
For the Lord comforts his people
    and shows mercy to his afflicted.

But Zion said, "The Lord has forsaken me;
    my Lord has forgotten me."
Can a mother forget her infant,
    be without tenderness for the child of her womb?
Even should she forget,
    I will never forget you. ✛

Psalm 145:8-9, 13-14, 17-18

R. The Lord is kind and merciful.

The Lord is gracious and merciful,
  slow to anger and of great kindness.
The Lord is good to all
  and compassionate toward all his works. **R.**
The Lord is faithful in all his words
  and holy in all his works.
The Lord lifts up all who are falling
  and raises up all who are bowed down. **R.**
The Lord is just in all his ways
  and holy in all his works.
The Lord is near to all who call upon him,
  to all who call upon him in truth. **R.**

John 3:16

R. Glory and praise to you, Lord Jesus Christ!
God loved the world so much, he gave us his only Son,
that all who believe in him might have eternal life. **R.**

† John 5:17-30
*As the Father raises the dead and gives them life,
so the Son gives life to those he chooses.*

Jesus said to the Jews:
  "My Father is at work until now,
  and I am at work as well."
The reason why the Jews were even more determined to kill
him was that he not only was breaking the sabbath but, worse
still, was speaking of God as his own Father, thereby making
himself God's equal.
  This was Jesus' answer:
  "I solemnly assure you,
    the Son cannot do anything by himself—
  he can do only what he sees the Father doing.
  For whatever the Father does,
    the Son does likewise.
  For the Father loves the Son
    and everything the Father does he shows him.
  Yes, to your great wonderment,
    he will show him even greater works than these.
  Indeed, just as the Father raises the dead and grants life,

so the Son grants life to those to whom he wishes.
The Father himself judges no one,
but has assigned all judgment to the Son,
so that all men may honor the Son
just as they honor the Father.
He who refuses to honor the Son
refuses to honor the Father who sent him.
I solemnly assure you,
the man who hears my word
and has faith in him who sent me
possesses eternal life.
He does not come under condemnation,
but has passed from death to life.
I solemnly assure you,
an hour is coming, has indeed come,
when the dead shall hear the voice of God's Son,
and those who have heeded it shall live.
Indeed, just as the Father possesses life in himself,
so has he granted it to the Son to have life in himself.
The Father has given over to him power to pass
    judgment
because he is Son of Man;
no need for you to be surprised at this,
for an hour is coming
in which all those in the tombs
shall hear his voice and come forth.
Those who have done right shall rise to live;
the evildoers shall rise to be damned.
I cannot do anything of myself.
I judge as I hear,
and my judgment is honest
because I am not seeking my own will
but the will of him who sent me." ✛

THURSDAY, MARCH 29
LENTEN WEEKDAY

† *Exodus 32:7-14*
Relent, Lord, and do not bring disaster on your people.

The Lord said to Moses, "Go down at once to your people, whom you brought out of the land of Egypt, for they have become depraved. They have soon turned aside from the way I pointed out to them, making for themselves a molten calf and worshiping it, sacrificing to it and crying out, 'This is your God, O Israel, who brought you out of the land of Egypt!' I see how stiff-necked this people is," continued the Lord to Moses. "Let me alone, then, that my wrath may blaze up against them to consume them. Then I will make of you a great nation."

But Moses implored the Lord, his God, saying, "Why, O Lord, should your wrath blaze up against your own people, whom you brought out of the land of Egypt with such great power and with so strong a hand? Why should the Egyptians say, 'With evil intent he brought them out, that he might kill them in the mountains and exterminate them from the face of the earth'? Let your blazing wrath die down; relent in punishing your people. Remember your servants Abraham, Isaac and Israel, and how you swore to them by your own self, saying, 'I will make your descendants as numerous as the stars in the sky; and all this land that I promised, I will give your descendants as their perpetual heritage.'" So the Lord relented in the punishment he had threatened to inflict on his people. ✛

Psalm 106:19-23
R. Lord, remember us,
for the love you bear your people.
Our fathers made a calf in Horeb
and adored a molten image;
They exchanged their glory
for the image of a grass-eating bullock. **R.**
They forgot the God who had saved them,
who had done great deeds in Egypt,
Wondrous deeds in the land of Ham,
terrible things at the Red Sea. **R.**
Then he spoke of exterminating them,

but Moses, his chosen one,
Withstood him in the breach
to turn back his destructive wrath. **R.**

John 6:64, 69
R. Glory and praise to you, Lord Jesus Christ!
Your words, Lord, are spirit and life;
you have the message of eternal life. **R.**

† *John 5:31-47*
It is Moses who will be your accuser in whom you hoped.

Jesus said to the Jews:
"If I witness on my own behalf,
you cannot verify my testimony;
but there is another who is testifying on my behalf,
and the testimony he renders me
I know can be verified.
You have sent to John,
who has testified to the truth.
(Not that I myself accept such human testimony —
I refer to these things only for your salvation.)
He was the lamp, set aflame and burning bright,
and for a while you exulted willingly in his light.
Yet I have testimony greater than John's,
namely, the works the Father has given me to accomplish.
These very works which I perform
testify on my behalf
that the Father has sent me.
Moreover, the Father who sent me
has himself given testimony on my behalf.
His voice you have never heard,
his form you have never seen,
neither do you have his word abiding in your hearts
because you do not believe
the one he has sent.
Search the Scriptures
in which you think you have eternal life—
they also testify on my behalf.
Yet you are unwilling to come to me
to possess that life.

"It is not that I accept human praise—
it is simply that I know you,
and you do not have the love of God in your hearts.
I have come in my Father's name,
yet you do not accept me.
But let someone come in his own name
and him you will accept.
How can people like you believe,
when you accept praise from one another
yet do not seek the glory that comes from the One [God]?
Do not imagine that I will be your accuser
     before the Father;
the one to accuse you is Moses
on whom you have set your hopes.
If you believed Moses
you would then believe me,
for it was about me that he wrote.
But if you do not believe what he wrote,
how can you believe what I say?" ✢

FRIDAY, MARCH 30
LENTEN WEEKDAY

† Wisdom 2:1, 12-22
Let us condemn him to a shameful death.

The wicked said among themselves, thinking not aright:
"Let us beset the just one, because he is obnoxious to us;
     he sets himself against our doings,
Reproaches us for transgressions of the law
     and charges us with violations of our training.
He professes to have knowledge of God
     and styles himself a child of the Lord.
To us he is the censure of our thoughts;
     merely to see him is a hardship for us,
Because his life is not like other men's,
     and different are his ways.
He judges us debased;
     he holds aloof from our paths as from things impure.
He calls blest the destiny of the just
     and boasts that God is his Father.

Let us see whether his words be true;
  let us find out what will happen to him.
For if the just one be the son of God, he will defend him
  and deliver him from the hand of his foes.
With revilement and torture let us put him to the test
  that we may have proof of his gentleness
  and try his patience.
Let us condemn him to a shameful death;
  for according to his own words, God will take care of him."
These were their thoughts, but they erred;
  for their wickedness blinded them,
And they knew not the hidden counsels of God;
  neither did they count on a recompense of holiness
  nor discern the innocent souls' reward. ✝

Psalm 34:17-21, 23
R. The Lord is near to broken hearts.
The Lord confronts the evildoers,
  to destroy remembrance of them from the earth.
When the just cry out, the Lord hears them,
  and from all their distress he rescues them. **R.**
The Lord is close to the brokenhearted;
  and those who are crushed in spirit he saves.
Many are the troubles of the just man,
  but out of them all the Lord delivers him. **R.**
He watches over all his bones;
  not one of them shall be broken.
The Lord redeems the lives of his servants;
  no one incurs guilt who takes refuge in him. **R.**

Psalm 95:8
R. Glory and praise to you, Lord Jesus Christ!
If today you hear his voice,
harden not your hearts. **R.**

† *John 7:1-2, 10, 25-30*
They would have arrested him but his hour had not come.

Jesus moved about within Galilee. He had decided not to travel in Judea because some of the Jews were looking for a chance to kill him. The Jewish feast of Booths drew near. Once his brothers had gone up to the festival he too went up, but as if in secret and not for all to see.

Some of the people of Jerusalem remarked, "Is this not the one they want to kill? Here he is speaking in public and they don't say a word to him! Perhaps even the authorities have decided that this is the Messiah. Still, we know where this man is from. When the Messiah comes, no one is supposed to know his origins."

At this, Jesus, who was teaching in the temple area, cried out:
"So you know me,
and you know my origins?
The truth is, I have not come of myself.
I was sent by One who has the right to send,
and him you do not know.
I know him
because it is from him I come:
he sent me."
At this they tried to seize him, but no one laid a finger on him because his hour had not yet come. ✝

SATURDAY, MARCH 31
Lenten Weekday

✝ Jeremiah 11:18-20
I am like the trustful lamb, being led to the slaughter.

I knew their plot because the Lord informed me; at that time you, O Lord, showed me their doings. Yet I, like a trusting lamb led to slaughter, had not realized that they were hatching plots against me: "Let us destroy the tree in its vigor; let us cut him off from the land of the living, so that his name will be spoken no more."

But, you, O Lord of hosts, O just Judge,
searcher of mind and heart,
Let me witness the vengeance you take on them,
for to you I have entrusted my cause! ✝

Psalm 7:2-3, 9-12
R. Lord, my God, I take shelter in you.
O Lord, my God, in you I take refuge;
save me from all my pursuers and rescue me,
Lest I become like the lion's prey,

to be torn to pieces, with no one to rescue me. **R.**
Do me justice, O Lord, because I am just,
 and because of the innocence that is mine.
Let the malice of the wicked come to an end,
 but sustain the just,
 O searcher of heart and soul, O just God. **R.**
A shield before me is God,
 who saves the upright of heart;
A just judge is God,
 a God who punishes day by day. **R.**

Joel 2:12-13
R. Glory and praise to you, Lord Jesus Christ!
With all your heart turn to me
for I am tender and compassionate. **R.**

✝ *John 7:40-53*
Would the Christ be from Galilee?

Some in the crowd who heard the words of Jesus began to say,
"This must be the Prophet." Others were claiming, "He is the
Messiah." But an objection was raised: "Surely the Messiah is
not to come from Galilee? Does not Scripture say that the
Messiah, being of David's family, is to come from Bethlehem,
the village where David lived?" In this fashion the crowd was
sharply divided over him. Some of them even wanted to
apprehend him. However, no one laid hands on him.

When the temple guards came, the chief priests and
Pharisees asked them, "Why did you not bring him in?" "No
man ever spoke like that before," the guards replied. "Do not
tell us you too have been taken in!" the Pharisees retorted.
"You do not see any of the Sanhedrin believing in him, do you?
Or the Pharisees? Only this lot, that knows nothing about the
law—and they are lost anyway!" One of their own number,
Nicodemus (the man who had come to him), spoke up to say,
"Since when does our law condemn any man without first
hearing him and knowing the facts?" "Do not tell us you are a
Galilean too," they taunted him. "Look it up. You will not find
the Prophet coming from Galilee."

Then each went off to his own house. ✛

APRIL 1
FIFTH SUNDAY OF LENT

† Isaiah 43:16-21 (or Ezekiel 37:12-14)
See, I am doing something new and I give my people drink.

Thus says the LORD,
    who opens a way in the sea
    and a path in the mighty waters,
who leads out chariots and horsemen,
    a powerful army,
till they lie prostrate together, never to rise,
    snuffed out and quenched like a wick.
Remember not the events of the past,
    the things of long ago consider not;
see, I am doing something new!
    Now it springs forth, do you not perceive it?
In the desert I make a way,
    in the wasteland, rivers.
Wild beasts honor me,
    jackals and ostriches,
for I put water in the desert
    and rivers in the wasteland
    for my chosen people to drink,
the people whom I formed for myself,
    that they might announce my praise. ✛

Psalm 126:1-6 (or Psalm 130:1-8)
R. The Lord has done great things for us;
we are filled with joy.
When the LORD brought back the captives of Zion,
    we were like men dreaming.
Then our mouth was filled with laughter,
    and our tongue with rejoicing. **R.**
Then they said among the nations,
    "The LORD has done great things for them."
The LORD has done great things for us;
    we are glad indeed. **R.**
Restore our fortunes, O LORD,
    like the torrents in the southern desert.
Those that sow in tears
    shall reap rejoicing. **R.**

Although they go forth weeping,
 carrying the seed to be sown,
They shall come back rejoicing,
 carrying their sheaves. **R.**

*✝ **Philippians 3:8-14** (or Romans 8:8-11)*
Because of Christ, I consider everything
as a loss, being conformed to his death.

Brothers and sisters:
I consider everything as a loss
 because of the supreme good of knowing
  Christ Jesus my Lord.
For his sake I have accepted the loss of all things
 and I consider them so much rubbish,
 that I may gain Christ and be found in him,
 not having any righteousness of my own based on the law
 but that which comes through faith in Christ,
 the righteousness from God,
 depending on faith to know him and the power of his
  resurrection
 and the sharing of his sufferings by being conformed
  to his death,
 if somehow I may attain the resurrection from the dead.

It is not that I have already taken hold of it
 or have already attained perfect maturity,
 but I continue my pursuit in hope that I may possess it,
 since I have indeed been taken possession of by Christ
  Jesus.
Brothers and sisters, I for my part
 do not consider myself to have taken possession.
Just one thing: forgetting what lies behind
 but straining forward to what lies ahead,
 I continue my pursuit toward the goal,
 the prize of God's upward calling, in Christ Jesus. ✛

Joel 2:12-13
R. Glory and praise to you, Lord Jesus Christ!
Even now, says the Lord,
return to me with your whole heart;
for I am gracious and merciful. **R.**

† John 8:1-11 (or John 11:1-45 or 11:3-7,17,20-27,33b-45)
*Let the one among you who is without
sin be the first to throw a stone at her.*

Jesus went to the Mount of Olives.
But early in the morning he arrived again in the temple area,
    and all the people started coming to him,
    and he sat down and taught them.
Then the scribes and the Pharisees brought a woman
    who had been caught in adultery
    and made her stand in the middle.
They said to him,
    "Teacher, this woman was caught
    in the very act of committing adultery.
Now in the law, Moses commanded us to stone such women.
So what do you say?"
They said this to test him,
    so that they could have some charge to bring against him.
Jesus bent down and began to write on the ground with his
        finger.
But when they continued asking him,
    he straightened up and said to them,
    "Let the one among you who is without sin
    be the first to throw a stone at her."
Again he bent down and wrote on the ground.
And in response, they went away one by one,
    beginning with the elders.
So he was left alone with the woman before him.
Then Jesus straightened up and said to her,
    "Woman, where are they?
Has no one condemned you?"
She replied, "No one, sir."
Then Jesus said, "Neither do I condemn you.
Go, and from now on do not sin any more." ✛

MONDAY, APRIL 2
LENTEN WEEKDAY

✝ *Daniel 13:41-62* (or Daniel 13:1-9, 15-17, 19-30, 33-62)
Be aware of death, since we know not the hour when it comes.

The assembly condemned Susanna to death. But Susanna cried aloud: "O eternal God, you know what is hidden and are aware of all things before they come to be: you know that they have testified falsely against me. Here I am about to die, though I have done none of the things with which these wicked men have charged me."

The Lord heard her prayer. As she was being led to execution, God stirred up the holy spirit of a young boy named Daniel, and he cried aloud: "I will have no part in the death of this woman." All the people turned and asked him, "What is this you are saying?" He stood in their midst and continued, "Are you such fools, O Israelites! To condemn a woman of Israel without examination and without clear evidence? Return to court, for they have testified falsely against her."

Then all the people returned in haste. To Daniel the elders said, "Come, sit with us and inform us, since God has given you the prestige of old age." But he replied, "Separate these two far from one another that I may examine them."

After they were separated one from the other, he called one of them and said: "How you have grown evil with age! Now have your past sins come to term: passing unjust sentences, condemning the innocent, and freeing the guilty, although the Lord says, 'The innocent and the just you shall not put to death.' Now, then, if you were a witness, tell me under what tree you saw them together." "Under a mastic tree," he answered. "Your fine lie has cost you your head," said Daniel; "for the angel of God shall receive the sentence from him and split you in two." Putting him to one side, he ordered the other one to be brought. "Offspring of Canaan, not of Judah," Daniel said to him, "beauty has seduced you, lust has subverted your conscience. This is how you acted with the daughters of Israel, and in their fear they yielded to you; but a daughter of Judah did not tolerate your wickedness. Now, then, tell me under what tree you surprised them together." "Under an oak," he said. "Your fine lie has cost you also your head," said Daniel;

"for the angel of God waits with a sword to cut you in two so as
to make an end of you both."

The whole assembly cried aloud, blessing God who saves
those that hope in him. They rose up against the two elders, for
by their own words Daniel had convicted them of perjury.
According to the law of Moses, they inflicted on them the
penalty they had plotted to impose on their neighbor: they put
them to death. Thus was innocent blood spared that day. ✦

Psalm 23:1-6
**R. Though I walk in the valley of darkness,
I fear no evil, for you are with me.**
The Lord is my shepherd; I shall not want.
    In verdant pastures he gives me repose.
Beside restful waters he leads me;
    he refreshes my soul. **R.**
He guides me in right paths
    for his name's sake.
Even though I walk in the dark valley
    I fear no evil; for you are at my side
With your rod and your staff
    that give me courage. **R.**
You spread the table before me
    in the sight of my foes;
You anoint my head with oil;
    my cup overflows. **R.**
Only goodness and kindness
    follow me all the days of my life;
And I shall dwell in the house of the Lord
    for years to come. **R.**

Matthew 4:17
R. Glory and praise to you, Lord Jesus Christ!
Repent, says the Lord,
the kingdom of heaven is at hand. **R.**

† *John 8:12-20*
I am the light of the world.

Jesus said to the Jews:
"I am the light of the world.
No follower of mine shall ever walk in darkness;
    no, he shall possess the light of life."
This caused the Pharisees to break in with: "You are your
own witness. Such testimony cannot be valid." Jesus answered:
"What if I am my own witness?
My testimony is valid nonetheless,
    because I know where I came from
    and where I am going;
    you know neither the one nor the other.
You pass judgment according to appearances
    but I pass judgment on no man.
Even if I do judge,
    that judgment of mine is valid
    because I am not alone:
    I have at my side the One who sent me, the Father.
It is laid down in your law
    that evidence given by two persons is valid.
I am one of those testifying in my behalf,
    the Father who sent me is the other."
They pressed him: "And where is this 'Father' of yours?"
Jesus replied:
"You know neither me nor my Father.
If you knew me, you would know my Father too."
He spoke these words while teaching at the temple trea-
sury. Still, he went unapprehended, because his hour had not
yet come. ✦

TUESDAY, APRIL 3
LENTEN WEEKDAY

† *Numbers 21:4-9*
Whoever looks at the fiery serpent shall live.

From Mount Hor the Israelites set out on the Red Sea road,
to by-pass the land of Edom. But with their patience worn out
by the journey, the people complained against God and Moses,

"Why have you brought us up from Egypt to die in this desert, where there is no food or water? We are disgusted with this wretched food!"

In punishment the Lord sent among the people saraph serpents, which bit the people so that many of them died. Then the people came to Moses and said, "We have sinned in complaining against the Lord and you. Pray the Lord to take the serpents from us." So Moses prayed for the people, and the Lord said to Moses, "Make a saraph and mount it on a pole, and if anyone who has been bitten looks at it, he will recover." Moses accordingly made a bronze serpent and mounted it on a pole, and whenever anyone who had been bitten by a serpent looked at the bronze serpent, he recovered. ✛

Psalm 102:2-3, 16-21
R. O Lord, hear my prayer,
and let my cry come to you.
O Lord, hear my prayer,
and let my cry come to you.
Hide not your face from me
in the day of my distress.
Incline your ear to me;
in the day when I call, answer me speedily. **R.**
The nations shall revere your name, O Lord,
and all the kings of the earth your glory,
When the Lord has rebuilt Zion
and appeared in his glory;
When he has regarded the prayer of the destitute,
and not despised their prayer. **R.**
Let this be written for the generation to come,
and let his future creatures praise the Lord:
"The Lord looked down from his holy height,
from heaven he beheld the earth,
To hear the groaning of the prisoners,
to release those doomed to die." **R.**

Psalm 130:5, 7
R. Glory and praise to you, Lord Jesus Christ!
I hope in the Lord, I trust in his word;
with him there is mercy and fullness of redemption. **R.**

† *John 8:21-30*
When you have lifted up the Son of Man, then you will know that I am he.

Jesus said to the Pharisees:
  "I am going away. You will look for me
  but you will die in your sins.
  Where I am going you cannot come."
At this some of the Jews began to ask, "Does he mean he will
kill himself when he claims, 'Where I am going you cannot
come'? He went on:
  "You belong to what is below;
  I belong to what is above.
  You belong to this world—
  a world which cannot hold me.
  That is why I said you would die in your sins.
  You will surely die in your sins
  unless you come to believe that I AM."
"Who are you, then?" they asked him. Jesus answered:
  "What I have been telling you from the beginning.
  I could say much about you in condemnation,
  but no, I only tell the world
  what I have heard from him,
  the truthful One, who sent me."
They did not grasp that he was speaking to them of the Father.
Jesus continued:
  "When you lift up the Son of Man,
  you will come to realize that I AM
  and that I do nothing by myself.
  I say only what the Father has taught me.
  The One who sent me is with me.
  He has not deserted me
  since I always do what pleases him."
Because he spoke this way, many came to believe in him. ✛

WEDNESDAY, APRIL 4
LENTEN WEEKDAY, ST. ISIDORE

† *Daniel 3:14-20, 91-92, 95*
He has sent his angel to rescue his servants.

King Nebuchadnezzar said: "Is it true, Shadrach, Meshach,
and Abednego, that you will not serve my god, or worship the

golden statue that I set up? Be ready now to fall down and worship the statue I had made, whenever you hear the sound of the trumpet, flute, lyre, harp, psaltery, bagpipe, and all the other musical instruments; otherwise, you shall be instantly cast into the white-hot furnace; and who is the God that can deliver you out of my hands?" Shadrach, Meshach, and Abednego answered King Nebuchadnezzar, "There is no need for us to defend ourselves before you in this matter. If our God, whom we serve, can save us from the white-hot furnace and from your hands, O king, may he save us! But even if he will not, know, O king, that we will not serve your god or worship the golden statue which you set up."

Nebuchadnezzar's face became livid with utter rage against Shadrach, Meshach, and Abednego. He ordered the furnace to be heated seven times more than usual and had some of the strongest men in his army bind Shadrach, Meshach, and Abednego and cast them into the white-hot furnace.

Nebuchadnezzar rose in haste and asked his nobles, "Did we not cast three men bound into the fire?" "Assuredly, O king," they answered. "But," he replied, "I see four men unfettered and unhurt, walking in the fire, and the fourth looks like a son of God." Nebuchadnezzar exclaimed, "Blessed be the God of Shadrach, Meshach, and Abednego, who sent his angel to deliver the servants that trusted in him; they disobeyed the royal command and yielded their bodies rather than serve or worship any god except their own God." ✛

Daniel 3:52-56
R. Glory and praise forever!
Blessed are you, O Lord, the God of our fathers,
    praiseworthy and exalted above all forever;
And blessed is your holy and glorious name,
    praiseworthy and exalted above all for all ages. **R.**
Blessed are you in the temple of your holy glory,
    praiseworthy and glorious above all forever. **R.**
Blessed are you on the throne of your kingdom,
    praiseworthy and exalted above all forever. **R.**
Blessed are you who look into the depths
    from your throne upon the cherubim,

praiseworthy and exalted above all forever. **R.**
Blessed are you in the firmament of heaven,
praiseworthy and glorious forever. **R.**

Matthew 4:17
R. Glory and praise to you, Lord Jesus Christ!
Repent, says the Lord,
the kingdom of heaven is at hand. **R.**

✝ *John 8:31-42*
If the Son makes you free, you will be free indeed.

Jesus said to those Jews who believed in him:
"If you live according to my teaching,
you are truly my disciples;
then you will know the truth,
and the truth will set you free."
"We are descendants of Abraham," was their answer. "Never
have we been slaves to anyone. What do you mean by saying,
'You will be free'?" Jesus answered them:
"I give you my assurance,
everyone who lives in sin
is the slave of sin.
(No slave has a permanent place in the family,
but the son has a place there forever.)
That is why, if the son frees you,
you will really be free.
I realize you are of Abraham's stock.
Nonetheless, you are trying to kill me
because my word finds no hearing among you.
I tell what I have seen in the Father's presence;
you do what you have heard from your father."
They retorted, "Our father is Abraham." Jesus told them:
"If you were Abraham's children,
you would be following Abraham's example.
The fact is, you are trying to kill me,
a man who has told you the truth
which I have heard from God.
Abraham did nothing like that.
Indeed you are doing your father's works!"
They cried, "We are no illegitimate breed! We have but one

father and that is God himself." Jesus answered:
"Were God your father
you would love me,
for I came forth from God, and am here.
I did not come of my own will;
it was he who sent me." ✛

THURSDAY, APRIL 5
LENTEN WEEKDAY, ST. VINCENT FERRER

† *Genesis 17:3-9*
He will be the father of a multitude of nations.

When Abram prostrated himself, God spoke to him: "My covenant with you is this: you are to become the father of a host of nations. No longer shall you be called Abram; your name shall be Abraham, for I am making you the father of a host of nations. I will render you exceedingly fertile; I will make nations of you; kings shall stem from you. I will maintain my covenant with you and your descendants after you throughout the ages as an everlasting pact, to be your God and the God of your descendants after you. I will give to you and to your descendants after you the land in which you are now staying, the whole land of Canaan, as a permanent possession; and I will be their God."

God also said to Abraham: "On your part, you and your descendants after you must keep my covenant throughout the ages." ✛

Psalm 105:4-9
R. The Lord remembers his covenant forever.
Look to the Lord in his strength;
    seek to serve him constantly.
Recall the wondrous deeds that he has wrought,
    his portents, and the judgments he has uttered. **R.**
You descendants of Abraham, his servants,
    sons of Jacob, his chosen ones!
He, the Lord, is our God;
    throughout the earth his judgments prevail. **R.**
He remembers forever his covenant
    which he made binding for a thousand generations—

Which he entered into with Abraham
and by his oath to Isaac. **R.**

Amos 5:14
R. Glory and praise to you, Lord Jesus Christ!
Seek good and not evil
so that you may live,
and the Lord will be with you. **R.**

✝ *John 8:51-59*
Your father, Abraham, rejoiced because he saw my day.

Jesus said to the Jews:
"I solemnly assure you,
if a man is true to my word
he shall never see death."
"Now we are sure you are possessed," the Jews retorted.
"Abraham is dead. The prophets are dead. Yet you claim, 'A
man shall never know death if he keeps my word.' Surely you
do not pretend to be greater than our father Abraham, who
died! Or the prophets, who died! Whom do you make yourself
out to be?" Jesus answered:
"If I glorify myself,
that glory comes to nothing.
He who gives me glory is the Father,
the very one you claim for your God,
even though you do not know him.
But I know him.
Were I to say I do not know him,
I would be no better than you—a liar!
Yes, I know him well,
and I keep his word.
Your father Abraham rejoiced
that he might see my day.
He saw it and was glad."
At this the Jews objected: "You are not yet fifty! How can you
have seen Abraham?" Jesus answered them:
"I solemnly declare it:
before Abraham came to be, I AM."
At that they picked up rocks to throw at Jesus, but he hid
himself and slipped out of the temple precincts. ✛

FRIDAY, APRIL 6
LENTEN WEEKDAY

† *Jeremiah 20:10-13*
The Lord God is with me, a mighty hero.

I hear the whisperings of many:
   "Terror on every side!
   Denounce! let us denounce him!"
All those who were my friends
   are on the watch for any misstep of mine.
"Perhaps he will be trapped; then we can prevail,
   and take our vengeance on him."
But the Lord is with me, like a mighty champion;
   my persecutors will stumble, they will not triumph.
In their failure they will be put to utter shame,
   to lasting, unforgettable confusion.
O Lord of hosts, you who test the just,
   who probe mind and heart,
Let me witness the vengeance you take on them,
   for to you I have entrusted my cause.
Sing to the Lord
   praise the Lord,
For he has rescued the life of the poor
   from the power of the wicked! ✛

Psalm 18:2-7
**R. In my distress I called upon the Lord,
and he heard my voice.**
I love you, O Lord, my strength,
   O Lord, my rock, my fortress, my deliverer. **R.**
My God, my rock of refuge,
   my shield, the horn of my salvation, my stronghold!
Praised be the Lord, I exclaim,
   and I am safe from my enemies. **R.**
The breakers of death surged round about me,
   the destroying floods overwhelmed me;
The cords of the nether world enmeshed me,
   the snares of death overtook me. **R.**
In my distress I called upon the Lord
   and cried out to my God;

From his temple he heard my voice,
  and my cry to him reached his ears. **R.**

See Luke 8:15
R. Glory and praise to you, Lord Jesus Christ!
Happy are they who have kept the word with a generous heart,
and yield a harvest through perseverance. **R.**

✝ John 10:31-42
They wanted to arrest him but he eluded them.

When the Jews reached for rocks to stone him, Jesus protested to them, "Many good deeds have I shown you from the Father. For which of these do you stone me?" "It is not for any 'good deed' that we are stoning you," the Jews retorted, "but for blaspheming. You who are only a man are making yourself God." Jesus answered:
  "Is it not written in your law,
  'I have said, You are gods'?
  If it calls those men gods
  to whom God's word was addressed—
  and Scripture cannot lose its force—
  do you claim that I blasphemed
  when, as he whom the Father consecrated
  and sent into the world,
  I said, 'I am God's Son'?
  If I do not perform my Father's works,
  put no faith in me.
  But if I do perform them,
  even though you put no faith in me,
  put faith in these works,
  so as to realize what it means
  that the Father is in me
  and I in him."
At these words they again tried to arrest him, but he eluded their grasp.
  Then he went back across the Jordan to the place where John had been baptizing earlier, and while he stayed there many people came to him. "John may never have performed a sign," they commented, "but whatever John said about this man was true." In that place, many came to believe in him. ✝

SATURDAY, APRIL 7
LENTEN WEEKDAY

† *Ezekiel 37:21-28*
I will make them into one nation.

Thus speaks the Lord God: I will take the Israelites from among the nations to which they have come, and gather them from all sides to bring them back to their land. I will make them one nation upon the land, in the mountains of Israel, and there shall be one prince for them all. Never again shall they be two nations, and never again shall they be divided into two kingdoms.

No longer shall they defile themselves with their idols, their abominations, and all their transgressions. I will deliver them from all their sins of apostasy, and cleanse them so that they may be my people and I may be their God. My servant David shall be prince over them, and there shall be one shepherd for them all; they shall live by my statutes and carefully observe my decrees. They shall live on the land which I gave to my servant Jacob, the land where their fathers lived; they shall live on it forever, they, and their children, and their children's children, with my servant David their prince forever. I will make with them a covenant of peace; it shall be an everlasting covenant with them, and I will multiply them, and put my sanctuary among them forever. My dwelling shall be with them; I will be their God, and they shall be my people. Thus the nations shall know that it is I, the Lord, who make Israel holy, when my sanctuary shall be set up among them forever. ✛

Jeremiah 31:10-13
**R. The Lord will guard us,
like a shepherd guarding his flock.**
Hear the word of the Lord, O nations,
　proclaim it on distant coasts, and say:
He who scattered Israel, now gathers them together,
　he guards them as a shepherd his flock. **R.**
The Lord shall ransom Jacob,
　he shall redeem him from the hand of his conqueror.
Shouting, they shall mount the heights of Zion,
　they shall come streaming to the Lord's blessings:

The grain, the wine, and the oil,
   the sheep and the oxen. **R.**
Then the virgins shall make merry and dance,
   and young men and old as well.
I will turn their mourning into joy,
   I will console and gladden them after their sorrows. **R.**

Psalm 95:8
R. Glory and praise to you, Lord Jesus Christ!
If today you hear his voice,
harden not your hearts. **R.**

✝ *John 11:45-57*
He gathered together in unity the scattered children of God.

Many of the Jews who had come to visit Mary, and had seen what Jesus did, put their faith in him. Some others, however, went to the Pharisees and reported what Jesus had done. The result was that the chief priests and the Pharisees called a meeting of the Sanhedrin. "What are we to do," they said, "with this man performing all sorts of signs? If we let him go on like this, the whole world will believe in him. Then the Romans will come in and sweep away our sanctuary and our nation." One of their number named Caiaphas, who was high priest that year, addressed them at this point: "You have no understanding whatever! Can you not see that it is better for you to have one man die [for the people] than to have the whole nation destroyed?" (He did not say this on his own. It was rather as high priest for that year that he prophesied that Jesus would die for the nation—and not for this nation only, but to gather into one all the dispersed children of God.)

From that day onward there was a plan afoot to kill him. In consequence, Jesus no longer moved about freely in Jewish circles. He withdrew instead to a town called Ephraim in the region near the desert, where he stayed with his disciples.

The Jewish Passover was near, which meant that many people from the country went up to Jerusalem for Passover purification. They were on the lookout for Jesus, various people in the temple vicinity saying to each other, "What do you think? Is he likely to come for the feast?" (The chief priests and the Pharisees had given orders that anyone who knew where he was should report it, so that they could apprehend him.) ✛

APRIL 8
PALM SUNDAY OF THE LORD'S PASSION

† *Luke 19:28-40*
(At the Procession with Palms)
Blessed is he who comes in the name of the Lord.

Jesus proceeded on his journey up to Jerusalem.
As he drew near to Bethphage and Bethany
    at the place called the Mount of Olives,
    he sent two of his disciples.
He said, "Go into the village opposite you,
    and as you enter it you will find a colt tethered
    on which no one has ever sat.
Untie it and bring it here.
And if anyone should ask you,
    'Why are you untying it?'
    you will answer,
    'The Master has need of it.'"
So those who had been sent went off
    and found everything just as he had told them.
And as they were untying the colt, its owners said to them,
    "Why are you untying this colt?"
They answered,
    "The Master has need of it."
So they brought it to Jesus,
    threw their cloaks over the colt,
    and helped Jesus to mount.
As he rode along,
    the people were spreading their cloaks on the road;
    and now as he was approaching the slope of the Mount of
        Olives,
    the whole multitude of his disciples
    began to praise God aloud with joy
    for all the mighty deeds they had seen.
They proclaimed:
    "Blessed is the king who comes
        in the name of the Lord.
    Peace in heaven
        and glory in the highest."
Some of the Pharisees in the crowd said to him,

"Teacher, rebuke your disciples."
He said in reply,
"I tell you, if they keep silent,
the stones will cry out!" ✛

(At the Mass)
† Isaiah 50:4-7
*My face I did not shield from buffets and spitting,
knowing that I shall not be put to shame.*

The Lord GOD has given me
a well-trained tongue,
that I might know how to speak to the weary
a word that will rouse them.
Morning after morning
he opens my ear that I may hear;
and I have not rebelled,
have not turned back.
I gave my back to those who beat me,
my cheeks to those who plucked my beard;
my face I did not shield
from buffets and spitting.
The Lord GOD is my help,
therefore I am not disgraced;
I have set my face like flint,
knowing that I shall not be put to shame. ✛

Psalm 22:8-9, 17-20, 23-24.
R. My God, my God, why have you abandoned me?
All who see me scoff at me;
they mock me with parted lips, they wag their heads:
"He relied on the LORD; let him deliver him,
let him rescue him, if he loves him." **R.**
Indeed, many dogs surround me,
a pack of evildoers closes in upon me;
they have pierced my hands and my feet;
I can count all my bones. **R.**
They divide my garments among them,
and for my vesture they cast lots.
But you, O LORD, be not far from me;
O my help, hasten to aid me. **R.**
I will proclaim your name to my brethren;
in the midst of the assembly I will praise you:

"You who fear the LORD, praise him;
 all you descendants of Jacob, give glory to him;
revere him, all you descendants of Israel!" **R.**

† *Philippians 2:6-11*
Christ humbled himself. Because of this God greatly exalted him.

Christ Jesus, though he was in the form of God,
 did not regard equality with God
  something to be grasped.
Rather, he emptied himself,
 taking the form of a slave,
 coming in human likeness;
 and found human in appearance,
 he humbled himself,
 becoming obedient to the point of death,
  even death on a cross.
Because of this, God greatly exalted him
 and bestowed on him the name
 which is above every name,
 that at the name of Jesus
 every knee should bend,
 of those in heaven and on earth and under the earth,
 and every tongue confess that
 Jesus Christ is Lord,
 to the glory of God the Father. ✛

Philippians 2:8-9
R. Glory and praise to you, Lord Jesus Christ!
Christ became obedient to the point of death,
even death on a cross.
Because of this, God greatly exalted him
and bestowed on him the name which is above every name. **R.**

† *Luke 23:1-49* (or *Luke 22:14—23:56*)
The Passion of our Lord Jesus Christ.

The elders of the people, chief priests and scribes,
 arose and brought Jesus before Pilate.
They brought charges against him, saying,
 "We found this man misleading our people;
 he opposes the payment of taxes to Caesar

and maintains that he is the Christ, a king."
Pilate asked him, "Are you the king of the Jews?"
He said to him in reply, "You say so."
Pilate then addressed the chief priests and the crowds,
    "I find this man not guilty."
But they were adamant and said,
    "He is inciting the people with his teaching
        throughout all Judea,
    from Galilee where he began even to here."

On hearing this Pilate asked if the man was a Galilean;
    and upon learning that he was under Herod's jurisdiction,
    he sent him to Herod who was in Jerusalem at that time.
Herod was very glad to see Jesus;
    he had been wanting to see him for a long time,
    for he had heard about him
    and had been hoping to see him perform some sign.
He questioned him at length,
    but he gave him no answer.
The chief priests and scribes, meanwhile,
    stood by accusing him harshly.
Herod and his soldiers treated him contemptuously and
        mocked him,
    and after clothing him in resplendent garb,
    he sent him back to Pilate.
Herod and Pilate became friends that very day,
    even though they had been enemies formerly.
Pilate then summoned the chief priests,
        the rulers, and the people
    and said to them, "You brought this man to me
    and accused him of inciting the people to revolt.
I have conducted my investigation in your presence
    and have not found this man guilty
    of the charges you have brought against him,
    nor did Herod, for he sent him back to us.
So no capital crime has been committed by him.
Therefore I shall have him flogged and then release him."
But all together they shouted out,
    "Away with this man!
    Release Barabbas to us."
—Now Barabbas had been imprisoned for a rebellion

that had taken place in the city and for murder.—
Again Pilate addressed them, still wishing to release Jesus,
    but they continued their shouting,
    "Crucify him! Crucify him!"
Pilate addressed them a third time,
    "What evil has this man done?
    I found him guilty of no capital crime.
Therefore I shall have him flogged and then release him."
With loud shouts, however,
    they persisted in calling for his crucifixion,
    and their voices prevailed.
The verdict of Pilate was that their demand should be granted.
So he released the man who had been imprisoned
    for rebellion and murder, for whom they asked,
    and he handed Jesus over to them to deal with as they
        wished.

As they led him away
    they took hold of a certain Simon, a Cyrenian,
    who was coming in from the country;
    and after laying the cross on him,
    they made him carry it behind Jesus.
A large crowd of people followed Jesus,
    including many women who mourned and lamented him.
Jesus turned to them and said,
    "Daughters of Jerusalem, do not weep for me;
    weep instead for yourselves and for your children
    for indeed, the days are coming when people will say,
    'Blessed are the barren,
    the wombs that never bore
    and the breasts that never nursed.'
At that time people will say to the mountains,
    'Fall upon us!'
    and to the hills, 'Cover us!'
    for if these things are done when the wood is green
    what will happen when it is dry?"
Now two others, both criminals,
    were led away with him to be executed.

When they came to the place called the Skull,
    they crucified him and the criminals there,

one on his right, the other on his left.
Then Jesus said,
"Father, forgive them, they know not what they do."
They divided his garments by casting lots.
The people stood by and watched;
the rulers, meanwhile, sneered at him and said,
"He saved others, let him save himself
if he is the chosen one, the Christ of God."
Even the soldiers jeered at him.
As they approached to offer him wine they called out,
"If you are King of the Jews, save yourself."
Above him there was an inscription that read,
"This is the King of the Jews."

Now one of the criminals hanging there reviled Jesus, saying,
"Are you not the Christ?
Save yourself and us."
The other, however, rebuking him, said in reply,
"Have you no fear of God,
for you are subject to the same condemnation?
And indeed, we have been condemned justly,
for the sentence we received corresponds to our crimes,
but this man has done nothing criminal."
Then he said,
"Jesus, remember me when you come into your kingdom."
He replied to him,
"Amen, I say to you,
today you will be with me in Paradise."

It was now about noon and darkness came over the whole land
until three in the afternoon
because of an eclipse of the sun.
Then the veil of the temple was torn down the middle.
Jesus cried out in a loud voice,
"Father, into your hands I commend my spirit";
and when he had said this he breathed his last.
(Here all kneel and pause for a short time.)
The centurion who witnessed what had happened glorified
God and said,
"This man was innocent beyond doubt."
When all the people who had gathered for this spectacle
saw what had happened,

they returned home beating their breasts;
>   but all his acquaintances stood at a distance,
>   including the women who had followed him from Galilee
>   and saw these events. ✛

APRIL 9
MONDAY OF HOLY WEEK

† Isaiah 42:1-7

He will not cry out, nor make his voice heard in the streets.
(First song of the servant of Yahweh)

Here is my servant whom I uphold,
>   my chosen one with whom I am pleased,
Upon whom I have put my spirit;
>   he shall bring forth justice to the nations,
Not crying out, not shouting,
>   not making his voice heard in the street.
A bruised reed he shall not break,
>   and a smoldering wick he shall not quench,
Until he establishes justice on the earth;
>   the coastlands will wait for his teaching.

Thus says God, the Lord,
>   who created the heavens and stretched them out,
>   who spreads out the earth with its crops,
Who gives breath to its people
>   and spirit to those who walk on it:
I, the Lord, have called you for the victory of justice,
>   I have grasped you by the hand;
I formed you, and set you
>   as a covenant of the people,
>   a light for the nations,
To open the eyes of the blind,
>   to bring out prisoners from confinement,
>   and from the dungeon, those who live in darkness. ✛

Psalm 27:1-3, 13-14

R. The Lord is my light and my salvation.
The Lord is my light and my salvation;
>   whom should I fear?
The Lord is my life's refuge;
>   of whom should I be afraid? **R.**

When evildoers come at me
  to devour my flesh,
My foes and my enemies
  themselves stumble and fall. **R.**
Though an army encamp against me,
  my heart will not fear;
Though war be waged upon me,
  even then will I trust. **R.**
I believe that I shall see the bounty of the Lord
  in the land of the living.
Wait for the Lord with courage;
  be stouthearted, and wait for the Lord. **R.**

R. Glory and praise to you, Lord Jesus Christ!
Let us greet our king;
he alone showed mercy for our sins. **R.**

† *John 12:1-11*
Let her keep it for the day of my burial.

Six days before Passover Jesus came to Bethany, the village
of Lazarus whom Jesus had raised from the dead. There they
gave him a banquet, at which Martha served. Lazarus was one
of those at table with him. Mary brought a pound of costly
perfume made from genuine aromatic nard, with which she
anointed Jesus' feet. Then she dried his feet with her hair, and
the house was filled with the ointment's fragrance. Judas
Iscariot, one of his disciples (the one about to hand him over),
protested: "Why was this perfume not sold? It could have
brought three hundred silver pieces, and the money have been
given to the poor." (He did not say this out of concern for the
poor, but because he was a thief. He held the purse, and used
to help himself to what was deposited there.) To this Jesus
replied, "Leave her alone. Let her keep it against the day they
prepare me for burial. The poor you always have with you, but
me you will not always have."

The great crowd of Jews discovered he was there and came
out, not only because of Jesus but also to see Lazarus, whom
he had raised from the dead. The fact was, the chief priests
planned to kill Lazarus too, because many Jews were going
over to Jesus and believing in him on account of Lazarus. ✝

APRIL 10
TUESDAY OF HOLY WEEK

† Isaiah 49:1-6

*I have made you the light of nations so that my
salvation may reach to the ends of the earth.
(Second song of the servant of Yahweh)*

Hear me, O coastlands,
  listen, O distant peoples.
The Lord called me from birth,
  from my mother's womb he gave me my name.
He made of me a sharp-edged sword
  and concealed me in the shadow of his arm.
He made me a polished arrow,
  in his quiver he hid me.
You are my servant, he said to me,
  Israel, through whom I show my glory.
Though I thought I had toiled in vain,
  and for nothing, uselessly, spent my strength,
Yet my reward is with the Lord,
  my recompense is with my God.
For now the Lord has spoken
  who formed me as his servant from the womb,
That Jacob may be brought back to him
  and Israel gathered to him;
And I am made glorious in the sight of the Lord,
  and my God is now my strength!
It is too little, he says, for you to be my servant,
  to raise up the tribes of Jacob,
  and restore the survivors of Israel;
I will make you a light to the nations,
  that my salvation may reach to the ends of the earth. ✛

Psalm 71:1-6, 15, 17
R. **I will sing of your salvation.**
In you, O Lord, I take refuge;
  let me never be put to shame.
In your justice rescue me, and deliver me;
  incline your ear to me, and save me. **R.**
Be my rock of refuge,
  a stronghold to give me safety,

for you are my rock and my fortress.
O my God, rescue me from the hand of the wicked. **R.**
For you are my hope, O Lord;
   my trust, O God, from my youth.
On you I depend from birth;
   from my mother's womb you are my strength. **R.**
My mouth shall declare your justice,
   day by day your salvation,
   though I know not their extent.
O God, you have taught me from my youth,
   and till the present I proclaim your wondrous deeds. **R.**

R. Glory and praise to you, Lord Jesus Christ!
Hail to our king, obedient to his Father;
he went to his crucifixion like a gentle lamb. **R.**

† *John 13:21-33, 36-38*
*One of you will betray me; before the cock crows,
you will have disowned me three times.*

Jesus, reclining with his disciples, grew deeply troubled. He went on to give this testimony:
   "I tell you solemnly,
   one of you will betray me."
The disciples looked at one another, puzzled as to whom he could mean. One of them, the disciple whom Jesus loved, reclined close to him as they ate. Simon Peter signaled him to ask Jesus whom he meant. He leaned back against Jesus' chest and said to him, "Lord, who is he?" Jesus answered, "The one to whom I give the bit of food I dip in the dish." He dipped the morsel, then took it and gave it to Judas, son of Simon Iscariot. Immediately after, Satan entered his heart. Jesus addressed himself to him, "Be quick about what you are to do." (Naturally, none of those reclining at table understood why Jesus said this to him. A few had the idea that, since Judas held the common purse, Jesus was telling him to buy what was needed for the feast, or to give something to the poor.) No sooner had Judas eaten the morsel than he went out. It was night.
   Once Judas had left, Jesus said:
   "Now is the Son of Man glorified
   and God is glorified in him.

[If God has been glorified in him,]
God will, in turn, glorify him in himself,
and will glorify him soon.
My children, I am not to be with you much longer.
You will look for me,
but I say to you now
what I once said to the Jews:
'Where I am going, you cannot come.'"

"Lord," Simon Peter said to him, "where do you mean to go?" Jesus answered:

"I am going where you cannot follow me now;
later on you shall come after me."

"Lord," Peter said to him, "why can I not follow you now? I will lay down my life for you!" "You will lay down your life for me, will you?" Jesus answered. "I tell you truly, the cock will not crow before you have three times disowned me!" ✛

APRIL 11
WEDNESDAY OF HOLY WEEK

† Isaiah 50:4-9
I did not cover my face against insult and spittle.
(Third song of the servant of Yahweh)

The Lord God has given me
    a well-trained tongue,
That I might know how to speak to the weary
    a word that will rouse them.
Morning after morning
    he opens my ear that I may hear;
And I have not rebelled,
    have not turned back.
I gave my back to those who beat me,
    my cheeks to those who plucked my beard;
My face I did not shield
    from buffets and spitting.

The Lord God is my help,
    therefore I am not disgraced;
I have set my face like flint,
    knowing that I shall not be put to shame.
He is near who upholds my right;

if anyone wishes to oppose me,
let us appear together.
Who disputes my right?
Let him confront me.
See, the Lord God is my help. ✛

Psalm 69:8-10, 21-22, 31, 33-34
R. Lord, in your great love, answer me.
For your sake I bear insult,
and shame covers my face.
I have become an outcast to my brothers,
a stranger to my mother's sons,
Because zeal for your house consumes me,
and the insults of those who blaspheme you fall upon me. **R.**
Insult has broken my heart, and I am weak,
I looked for sympathy, but there was none;
for comforters, and I found none.
Rather they put gall in my food,
and in my thirst they gave me vinegar to drink. **R.**
I will praise the name of God in song,
and I will glorify him with thanksgiving:
"See, you lowly ones, and be glad;
you who seek God, may your hearts be merry!
For the Lord hears the poor,
and his own who are in bonds he spurns not." **R.**

R. Glory and praise to you, Lord Jesus Christ!
Hail to our king, obedient to his Father;
he went to his crucifixion like a gentle lamb. **R.**

† Matthew 26:14-25
*The Son of Man is going the way scripture says,
but alas for that man by whom the Son of Man is betrayed.*

One of the Twelve whose name was Judas Iscariot went off
to the chief priests and said, "What are you willing to give me
if I hand him over to you?" They paid him thirty pieces of silver,
and from that time on he kept looking for an opportunity to
hand him over.

On the first day of the feast of Unleavened Bread, the
disciples came up to Jesus and said, "Where do you wish us to
prepare the Passover supper for you?" He said, "Go to this man

in the city and tell him, 'The Teacher says, My appointed time
draws near. I am to celebrate the Passover with my disciples
in your house.'"

The disciples then did as Jesus had ordered, and prepared
the Passover supper.

When it grew dark he reclined at table with the Twelve. In
the course of the meal he said, "I give you my word, one of you
is about to betray me." Distressed at this, they began to say to
him one after another, "Surely it is not I, Lord?" He replied:
"The man who has dipped his hand into the dish with me is the
one who will hand me over. The Son of Man is departing, as
Scripture says of him, but woe to that man by whom the Son
of Man is betrayed. Better for him if he had never been born."

Then Judas, his betrayer, spoke: "Surely it is not I, Rabbi?"
Jesus answered, "It is you who have said it." ✝

APRIL 12
HOLY THURSDAY: MASS OF THE LORD'S SUPPER

✝ *Exodus 12:1-8, 11-14*
The law regarding the Passover meal.

The LORD said to Moses and Aaron in the land of Egypt,
    "This month shall stand at the head of your calendar;
    you shall reckon it the first month of the year.
Tell the whole community of Israel:
    On the tenth of this month every one of your families
    must procure for itself a lamb, one apiece for each house-
        hold.
If a family is too small for a whole lamb,
    it shall join the nearest household in procuring one
    and shall share in the lamb
    in proportion to the number of persons who partake of it.
The lamb must be a year-old male and without blemish.
You may take it from either the sheep or the goats.
You shall keep it until the fourteenth day of this month,
    and then, with the whole assembly of Israel present,
    it shall be slaughtered during the evening twilight.
They shall take some of its blood
    and apply it to the two doorposts and the lintel

of every house in which they partake of the lamb.
That same night they shall eat its roasted flesh
with unleavened bread and bitter herbs.

"This is how you are to eat it:
with your loins girt, sandals on your feet and your staff in
hand,
you shall eat like those who are in flight.
It is the Passover of the LORD.
For on this same night I will go through Egypt,
striking down every firstborn of the land, both man and
beast,
and executing judgment on all the gods of Egypt—I, the
LORD!
But the blood will mark the houses where you are.
Seeing the blood, I will pass over you;
thus, when I strike the land of Egypt,
no destructive blow will come upon you.

"This day shall be a memorial feast for you,
which all your generations shall celebrate
with pilgrimage to the LORD, as a perpetual institution." ✛

Psalm 116:12-13, 15-16bc, 17-18
**R. Our blessing-cup is a
communion with the Blood of Christ.**
How shall I make a return to the LORD
for all the good he has done for me?
The cup of salvation I will take up,
and I will call upon the name of the LORD. **R.**
Precious in the eyes of the LORD
is the death of his faithful ones.
I am your servant, the son of your handmaid;
you have loosed my bonds. **R.**
To you will I offer sacrifice of thanksgiving,
and I will call upon the name of the LORD.
My vows to the LORD I will pay
in the presence of all his people. **R.**

† 1 Corinthians 11:23-26

For as often as you eat this bread and drink the cup,
you proclaim the death of the Lord.

Brothers and sisters:
I received from the Lord what I also handed on to you,
    that the Lord Jesus, on the night he was handed over,
    took bread, and, after he had given thanks,
    broke it and said, "This is my body that is for you.
Do this in remembrance of me."
In the same way also the cup, after supper, saying,
    "This cup is the new covenant in my blood.
Do this, as often as you drink it, in remembrance of me."
For as often as you eat this bread and drink the cup,
    you proclaim the death of the Lord until he comes. ✢

John 13:34

R. Glory and praise to you, Lord Jesus Christ!
I give you a new commandment, says the Lord:
love one another as I have loved you. **R.**

† John 13:1-15

Jesus loved them to the end.

Before the feast of Passover, Jesus knew that his hour had
    come
    to pass from this world to the Father.
He loved his own in the world and he loved them to the end.
The devil had already induced Judas, son of Simon the
    Iscariot, to hand him over.
So, during supper,
    fully aware that the Father had put everything into his
      power
    and that he had come from God and was returning to God,
    he rose from supper and took off his outer garments.
He took a towel and tied it around his waist.
Then he poured water into a basin
    and began to wash the disciples' feet
    and dry them with the towel around his waist.
He came to Simon Peter, who said to him,
    "Master, are you going to wash my feet?"
Jesus answered and said to him,

"What I am doing, you do not understand now,
but you will understand later."
Peter said to him, "You will never wash my feet."
Jesus answered him,
"Unless I wash you, you will have no inheritance with me."
Simon Peter said to him,
"Master, then not only my feet, but my hands and head as
well."
Jesus said to him,
"Whoever has bathed has no need except to have his feet
washed,
for he is clean all over;
so you are clean, but not all."
For he knew who would betray him;
for this reason, he said, "Not all of you are clean."
So when he had washed their feet
and put his garments back on and reclined at table again,
he said to them, "Do you realize what I have done for you?
You call me 'teacher' and 'master,' and rightly so, for indeed
I am.
If I, therefore, the master and teacher, have washed your feet,
you ought to wash one another's feet.
I have given you a model to follow,
so that as I have done for you, you should also do." ✚

APRIL 13
GOOD FRIDAY OF THE LORD'S PASSION

† Isaiah 52:13—53:12
He himself was wounded for our sins.
(Fourth oracle of the Servant of the Lord)

See, my servant shall prosper,
he shall be raised high and greatly exalted.
Even as many were amazed at him—
so marred was his look beyond human semblance
and his appearance beyond that of the sons of man—
so shall he startle many nations,
because of him kings shall stand speechless;
for those who have not been told shall see,
those who have not heard shall ponder it.

Who would believe what we have heard?
  To whom has the arm of the LORD been revealed?
He grew up like a sapling before him,
  like a shoot from the parched earth;
there was in him no stately bearing to make us look at him,
  nor appearance that would attract us to him.
He was spurned and avoided by people,
  a man of suffering, accustomed to infirmity,
one of those from whom people hide their faces,
  spurned, and we held him in no esteem.

Yet it was our infirmities that he bore,
  our sufferings that he endured,
while we thought of him as stricken,
  as one smitten by God and afflicted.
But he was pierced for our offenses,
  crushed for our sins;
upon him was the chastisement that makes us whole,
  by his stripes we were healed.
We had all gone astray like sheep,
  each following his own way;
but the LORD laid upon him
  the guilt of us all.

Though he was harshly treated, he submitted
  and opened not his mouth;
like a lamb led to the slaughter
  or a sheep before the shearers,
  he was silent and opened not his mouth.
Oppressed and condemned, he was taken away,
  and who would have thought any more of his destiny?
When he was cut off from the land of the living,
  and smitten for the sin of his people,
a grave was assigned him among the wicked
  and a burial place with evildoers,
though he had done no wrong
  nor spoken any falsehood.
But the LORD was pleased
  to crush him in infirmity.

If he gives his life as an offering for sin,
  he shall see his descendants in a long life,
  and the will of the LORD shall be accomplished through him.

Because of his affliction
  he shall see the light
    in fullness of days;
through his suffering, my servant shall justify many,
  and their guilt he shall bear.
Therefore I will give him his portion among the great,
  and he shall divide the spoils with the mighty,
because he surrendered himself to death
  and was counted among the wicked;
and he shall take away the sins of many,
  and win pardon for their offenses. ✝

Psalm 31:2, 6, 12-13, 15-17, 25
**R. Father, into your hands
  I commend my spirit.**
In you, O LORD, I take refuge;
  let me never be put to shame.
In your justice rescue me.
  Into your hands I commend my spirit;
you will redeem me, O LORD, O faithful God. **R.**
For all my foes I am an object of reproach,
  a laughingstock to my neighbors, and a dread to my
    friends;
  they who see me abroad flee from me.
I am forgotten like the unremembered dead;
  I am like a dish that is broken. **R.**
But my trust is in you, O LORD;
  I say, "You are my God.
In your hands is my destiny; rescue me
  from the clutches of my enemies and my persecutors." **R.**
Let your face shine upon your servant;
  save me in your kindness.
Take courage and be stouthearted,
  all you who hope in the LORD. **R.**

† *Hebrews 4:14-16; 5:7-9*

*Jesus learned obedience and became
the source of salvation for all who obey him.*

Brothers and sisters:
Since we have a great high priest who has passed through the
heavens,
Jesus, the Son of God,
let us hold fast to our confession.
For we do not have a high priest
who is unable to sympathize with our weaknesses,
but one who has similarly been tested in every way,
yet without sin.
So let us confidently approach the throne of grace
to receive mercy and to find grace for timely help.

In the days when Christ was in the flesh,
he offered prayers and supplications with loud cries and
tears
to the one who was able to save him from death,
and he was heard because of his reverence.
Son though he was, he learned obedience from what he suffered;
and when he was made perfect,
he became the source of eternal salvation for all who obey
him. ✛

Philippians 2:8-9
R. Glory and praise to you, Lord Jesus Christ!
Christ became obedient to the point of death,
even death on a cross.
Because of this, God greatly exalted him
and bestowed on him the name which is above every other
name. **R.**

† *John 18:1—19:42*
The Passion of our Lord Jesus Christ.

Jesus went out with his disciples across the Kidron valley
to where there was a garden,
into which he and his disciples entered.
Judas his betrayer also knew the place,
because Jesus had often met there with his disciples.
So Judas got a band of soldiers and guards

from the chief priests and the Pharisees
and went there with lanterns, torches, and weapons.
Jesus, knowing everything that was going to happen to him,
went out and said to them, "Whom are you looking for?"
They answered him, "Jesus the Nazorean."
He said to them, "I AM."
Judas his betrayer was also with them.
When he said to them, "I AM, "
they turned away and fell to the ground.
So he again asked them,
"Whom are you looking for?"
They said, "Jesus the Nazorean."
Jesus answered,
"I told you that I AM.
So if you are looking for me, let these men go."
This was to fulfill what he had said,
"I have not lost any of those you gave me."
Then Simon Peter, who had a sword, drew it,
struck the high priest's slave, and cut off his right ear.
The slave's name was Malchus.
Jesus said to Peter,
"Put your sword into its scabbard.
Shall I not drink the cup that the Father gave me?"
So the band of soldiers, the tribune, and the Jewish guards
seized Jesus,
bound him, and brought him to Annas first.
He was the father-in-law of Caiaphas,
who was high priest that year.
It was Caiaphas who had counseled the Jews
that it was better that one man should die rather than the
people.

Simon Peter and another disciple followed Jesus.
Now the other disciple was known to the high priest,
and he entered the courtyard of the high priest with Jesus.
But Peter stood at the gate outside.
So the other disciple, the acquaintance of the high priest,
went out and spoke to the gatekeeper and brought Peter in.
Then the maid who was the gatekeeper said to Peter,
"You are not one of this man's disciples, are you?"
He said, "I am not."

Now the slaves and the guards were standing around a
    charcoal fire
    that they had made, because it was cold,
    and were warming themselves.
Peter was also standing there keeping warm.

The high priest questioned Jesus
    about his disciples and about his doctrine.
Jesus answered him,
    "I have spoken publicly to the world.
I have always taught in a synagogue
    or in the temple area where all the Jews gather,
    and in secret I have said nothing. Why ask me?
Ask those who heard me what I said to them.
They know what I said."
When he had said this,
    one of the temple guards standing there struck Jesus and said,
    "Is this the way you answer the high priest?"
Jesus answered him,
    "If I have spoken wrongly, testify to the wrong;
    but if I have spoken rightly, why do you strike me?"
Then Annas sent him bound to Caiaphas the high priest.

Now Simon Peter was standing there keeping warm.
And they said to him,
    "You are not one of his disciples, are you?"
He denied it and said,
    "I am not."
One of the slaves of the high priest,
    a relative of the one whose ear Peter had cut off, said,
    "Didn't I see you in the garden with him?"
Again Peter denied it.
And immediately the cock crowed.

Then they brought Jesus from Caiaphas to the praetorium.
It was morning.
And they themselves did not enter the praetorium,
    in order not to be defiled so that they could eat the
        Passover.
So Pilate came out to them and said,
    "What charge do you bring against this man?"
They answered and said to him,

"If he were not a criminal,
we would not have handed him over to you."
At this, Pilate said to them,
"Take him yourselves, and judge him according to your law."
The Jews answered him,
"We do not have the right to execute anyone, "
in order that the word of Jesus might be fulfilled
that he said indicating the kind of death he would die.
So Pilate went back into the praetorium
and summoned Jesus and said to him,
"Are you the King of the Jews?"
Jesus answered,
"Do you say this on your own
or have others told you about me?"
Pilate answered,
"I am not a Jew, am I?
Your own nation and the chief priests handed you over to me.
What have you done?"
Jesus answered,
"My kingdom does not belong to this world.
If my kingdom did belong to this world,
my attendants would be fighting
to keep me from being handed over to the Jews.
But as it is, my kingdom is not here."
So Pilate said to him,
"Then you are a king?"
Jesus answered,
"You say I am a king.
For this I was born and for this I came into the world,
to testify to the truth.
Everyone who belongs to the truth listens to my voice."
Pilate said to him, "What is truth?"

When he had said this,
he again went out to the Jews and said to them,
"I find no guilt in him.
But you have a custom that I release one prisoner
to you at Passover.
Do you want me to release to you the King of the Jews?"
They cried out again,
"Not this one but Barabbas!"

Now Barabbas was a revolutionary.
Then Pilate took Jesus and had him scourged.
And the soldiers wove a crown out of thorns and placed it on
      his head,
    and clothed him in a purple cloak,
    and they came to him and said,
    "Hail, King of the Jews!"
And they struck him repeatedly.
Once more Pilate went out and said to them,
    "Look, I am bringing him out to you,
    so that you may know that I find no guilt in him."
So Jesus came out,
    wearing the crown of thorns and the purple cloak.
And he said to them, "Behold, the man!"
When the chief priests and the guards saw him they cried out,
    "Crucify him, crucify him!"
Pilate said to them,
    "Take him yourselves and crucify him.
I find no guilt in him."
The Jews answered,
    "We have a law, and according to that law he ought to die,
    because he made himself the Son of God."
Now when Pilate heard this statement,
    he became even more afraid,
    and went back into the praetorium and said to Jesus,
    "Where are you from?"
Jesus did not answer him.
So Pilate said to him,
    "Do you not speak to me?
Do you not know that I have power to release you
    and I have power to crucify you?"
Jesus answered him,
    "You would have no power over me
    if it had not been given to you from above.
For this reason the one who handed me over to you
    has the greater sin."
Consequently, Pilate tried to release him; but the Jews cried out,
    "If you release him, you are not a Friend of Caesar.
Everyone who makes himself a king opposes Caesar."

When Pilate heard these words he brought Jesus out
  and seated him on the judge's bench
  in the place called Stone Pavement, in Hebrew, Gabbatha.
It was preparation day for Passover, and it was about noon.
And he said to the Jews,
  "Behold, your king!"
They cried out,
  "Take him away, take him away! Crucify him!"
Pilate said to them,
  "Shall I crucify your king?"
The chief priests answered,
  "We have no king but Caesar."
Then he handed him over to them to be crucified.
So they took Jesus, and, carrying the cross himself,
  he went out to what is called the Place of the Skull,
  in Hebrew, Golgotha.
There they crucified him, and with him two others,
  one on either side, with Jesus in the middle.
Pilate also had an inscription written and put on the cross.
It read,
  "Jesus the Nazorean, the King of the Jews."
Now many of the Jews read this inscription,
  because the place where Jesus
    was crucified was near the city;
  and it was written in Hebrew, Latin, and Greek.
So the chief priests of the Jews said to Pilate,
  "Do not write 'The King of the Jews,'
  but that he said, 'I am the King of the Jews'."
Pilate answered,
  "What I have written, I have written."

When the soldiers had crucified Jesus,
  they took his clothes and divided them into four shares,
  a share for each soldier.
They also took his tunic, but the tunic was seamless,
  woven in one piece from the top down.
So they said to one another,
  "Let's not tear it, but cast lots for it to see whose it will be,"
  in order that the passage of Scripture
    might be fulfilled that says:

They divided my garments among them,
 and for my vesture they cast lots.
This is what the soldiers did.
Standing by the cross of Jesus were his mother
 and his mother's sister, Mary the wife of Clopas,
 and Mary of Magdala.
When Jesus saw his mother
and the disciple there whom he loved
 he said to his mother, "Woman, behold, your son."
Then he said to the disciple,
 "Behold, your mother."
And from that hour the disciple took her into his home.

After this, aware that everything was now finished,
 in order that the Scripture might be fulfilled,
 Jesus said, "I thirst."
There was a vessel filled with common wine.
So they put a sponge soaked in wine on a sprig of hyssop
 and put it up to his mouth.
When Jesus had taken the wine, he said,
 "It is finished."
And bowing his head, he handed over the spirit.
 (Here all kneel and pause for a short time.)
Now since it was preparation day,
 in order that the bodies might not remain
  on the cross on the sabbath,
 for the sabbath day of that week was a solemn one,
 the Jews asked Pilate that their legs be broken
 and that they be taken down.
So the soldiers came and broke the legs of the first
 and then of the other one who was crucified with Jesus.
But when they came to Jesus and saw that he was already dead,
 they did not break his legs,
 but one soldier thrust his lance into his side,
 and immediately blood and water flowed out.
An eyewitness has testified, and his testimony is true;
 he knows that he is speaking the truth,
 so that you also may come to believe.
For this happened so that
 the Scripture passage might be fulfilled:
 Not a bone of it will be broken.

And again another passage says:
They will look upon him whom they have pierced.

After this, Joseph of Arimathea,
  secretly a disciple of Jesus for fear of the Jews,
  asked Pilate if he could remove the body of Jesus.
And Pilate permitted it.
So he came and took his body.
Nicodemus, the one who had first come to him at night,
  also came bringing a mixture of myrrh and aloes
  weighing about one hundred pounds.
They took the body of Jesus
  and bound it with burial cloths along with the spices,
  according to the Jewish burial custom.
Now in the place where he had been crucified
    there was a garden,
  and in the garden a new tomb,
    in which no one had yet been buried.
So they laid Jesus there because of the Jewish preparation day;
  for the tomb was close by. ✛

APRIL 14
HOLY SATURDAY: EASTER VIGIL MASS

(Other readings for the Easter Vigil liturgy are: Genesis 1:1—2:2 or 1:1, 26-31a •
Psalm 104:1-2, 5-6, 10, 12-14, 24, 35 or Psalm 33:4-7, 12-13, 20-22 • Genesis 22:1-18
or 22:1-2, 9a, 10-13, 15-18 • Psalm 16:5, 8-11 • Isaiah 54:5-14 • Psalm 30:2, 4-6, 11-
13 • Isaiah 55:1-11 • Isaiah 12:2-6 • Baruch 3:9-15, 32—4:4 • Psalm 19:8-11 • Ezekiel
36:16-17a, 18-28 • Psalm 42:3, 5;43:3-4 or Psalm 51:12-15, 18-19 or Isaiah 12:2-6)

† *Exodus 14:15—15:1*
The Israelites marched on dry land through the midst of the sea.

The LORD said to Moses, "Why are you crying out to me?
Tell the Israelites to go forward.
And you, lift up your staff and, with hand outstretched over the sea,
  split the sea in two,
  that the Israelites may pass through it on dry land.
But I will make the Egyptians so obstinate
  that they will go in after them.
Then I will receive glory through Pharaoh and all his army,
  his chariots and charioteers.
The Egyptians shall know that I am the LORD,
  when I receive glory through Pharaoh

and his chariots and charioteers."

The angel of God, who had been leading Israel's camp,
    now moved and went around behind them.

The column of cloud also, leaving the front,
    took up its place behind them,
    so that it came between the camp of the Egyptians
    and that of Israel.

But the cloud now became dark, and thus the night passed
    without the rival camps coming any closer together
        all night long.

Then Moses stretched out his hand over the sea,
    and the LORD swept the sea
    with a strong east wind throughout the night
    and so turned it into dry land.

When the water was thus divided,
    the Israelites marched into the midst of the sea
        on dry land,
    with the water like a wall to their right and to their left.

The Egyptians followed in pursuit;
    all Pharaoh's horses and chariots and charioteers went
        after them
    right into the midst of the sea.

In the night watch just before dawn
    the LORD cast through the column of the fiery cloud
    upon the Egyptian force a glance that threw it into a panic;
    and he so clogged their chariot wheels
    that they could hardly drive.

With that the Egyptians sounded the retreat before Israel,
    because the LORD was fighting for them against the
        Egyptians.

Then the LORD told Moses, "Stretch out your hand over the sea,
    that the water may flow back upon the Egyptians,
    upon their chariots and their charioteers."

So Moses stretched out his hand over the sea,
    and at dawn the sea flowed back to its normal depth.

The Egyptians were fleeing head on toward the sea,
    when the LORD hurled them into its midst.

As the water flowed back,
    it covered the chariots and the charioteers of Pharaoh's

whole army
which had followed the Israelites into the sea.
Not a single one of them escaped.
But the Israelites had marched on dry land
through the midst of the sea,
with the water like a wall to their right and to their left.
Thus the LORD saved Israel on that day
from the power of the Egyptians.
When Israel saw the Egyptians lying dead on the seashore
and beheld the great power that the LORD
had shown against the Egyptians,
they feared the LORD and believed in him and in his servant
Moses.
Then Moses and the Israelites sang this song to the LORD:
I will sing to the LORD, for he is gloriously triumphant;
horse and chariot he has cast into the sea. ✛

Exodus 15:1-6, 17-18
R. Let us sing to the Lord;
he has covered himself in glory.
I will sing to the LORD, for he is gloriously triumphant;
horse and chariot he has cast into the sea.
My strength and my courage is the LORD,
and he has been my savior.
He is my God, I praise him;
the God of my father, I extol him. **R.**
The LORD is a warrior,
LORD is his name!
Pharaoh's chariots and army he hurled into the sea;
the elite of his officers were submerged in the Red Sea. **R.**
The flood waters covered them,
they sank into the depths like a stone.
Your right hand, O LORD, magnificent in power,
your right hand, O LORD, has shattered the enemy. **R.**
You brought in the people you redeemed
and planted them on the mountain of your inheritance—
the place where you made your seat, O LORD,
the sanctuary, LORD, which your hands established.
The LORD shall reign forever and ever. **R.**

† *Romans 6:3-11*

Christ, raised from the dead, dies no more.

Brothers and sisters:

Are you unaware that we who were baptized into Christ Jesus
were baptized into his death?

We were indeed buried with him through baptism into death,
so that, just as Christ was raised from the dead
by the glory of the Father,
we too might live in newness of life.

For if we have grown into union with him through a death like
his,
we shall also be united with him in the resurrection.
We know that our old self was crucified with him,
so that our sinful body might be done away with,
that we might no longer be in slavery to sin.
For a dead person has been absolved from sin.
If, then, we have died with Christ,
we believe that we shall also live with him.
We know that Christ, raised from the dead, dies no more;
death no longer has power over him.
As to his death, he died to sin once and for all;
as to his life, he lives for God.
Consequently, you too must think of yourselves as being dead
to sin
and living for God in Christ Jesus. ✢

Psalm 118:1-2, 16-17, 22-23

R. Alleluia, alleluia.

Give thanks to the LORD, for he is good,
for his mercy endures forever.
Let the house of Israel say,
"His mercy endures forever." **R.**
The right hand of the LORD has struck with power;
the right hand of the LORD is exalted.
I shall not die, but live,
and declare the works of the LORD. **R.**
The stone the builders rejected
has become the cornerstone.
By the LORD has this been done;
it is wonderful in our eyes. **R.**

† Luke 24:1-12
Why do you seek the Living One among the dead?

At daybreak on the first day of the week
the women who had come from Galilee with Jesus
took the spices they had prepared
and went to the tomb.
They found the stone rolled away from the tomb;
but when they entered,
they did not find the body of the Lord Jesus.
While they were puzzling over this, behold,
two men in dazzling garments appeared to them.
They were terrified and bowed their faces to the ground.
They said to them,
"Why do you seek the living one among the dead?
He is not here, but he has been raised.
Remember what he said to you while he was still in Galilee,
that the Son of Man must be handed over to sinners
and be crucified, and rise on the third day."
And they remembered his words.
Then they returned from the tomb
and announced all these things to the eleven
and to all the others.
The women were Mary Magdalene, Joanna, and Mary the
mother of James;
the others who accompanied them also told this to
the apostles,
but their story seemed like nonsense
and they did not believe them.
But Peter got up and ran to the tomb,
bent down, and saw the burial cloths alone;
then he went home amazed at what had happened. ✛

ɪ

APRIL 15
EASTER SUNDAY, RESURRECTION OF THE LORD

† Acts 10:34a, 37-43
We ate and drank with him after he rose from the dead.

Peter proceeded to speak and said:
"You know what has happened all over Judea,
beginning in Galilee after the baptism
that John preached,
how God anointed Jesus of Nazareth
with the Holy Spirit and power.
He went about doing good
and healing all those oppressed by the devil,
for God was with him.
We are witnesses of all that he did
both in the country of the Jews and in Jerusalem.
They put him to death by hanging him on a tree.
This man God raised on the third day and granted that he be
visible,
not to all the people, but to us,
the witnesses chosen by God in advance,
who ate and drank with him after he rose from the dead.
He commissioned us to preach to the people
and testify that he is the one appointed by God
as judge of the living and the dead.
To him all the prophets bear witness,
that everyone who believes in him
will receive forgiveness of sins through his name. ✛

Psalm 118:1-2, 16-17, 22-23
**R. This is the day the Lord has made;
let us rejoice and be glad.** *(or* **Alleluia.***)*
Give thanks to the LORD, for he is good,
for his mercy endures forever.
Let the house of Israel say,
"His mercy endures forever." **R.**
"The right hand of the LORD has struck with power;
the right hand of the LORD is exalted.
I shall not die, but live,
and declare the works of the LORD. **R.**

The stone which the builders rejected
    has become the cornerstone.
By the LORD has this been done;
    it is wonderful in our eyes. **R.**

✝ *Colossians 3:1-4 (or 1 Corinthians 5:6b-8)*
Seek what is above, where Christ is.

Brothers and sisters:
If then you were raised with Christ, seek what is above,
    where Christ is seated at the right hand of God.
Think of what is above, not of what is on earth.
For you have died, and your life is hidden with Christ in God.
When Christ your life appears,
    then you too will appear with him in glory. ✚

cf. 1 Corinthians 5:7b-8a
R. Alleluia, alleluia.
Christ, our paschal lamb, has been sacrificed;
let us then feast with joy in the Lord. **R.**

✝ *John 20:1-9 (or Luke 24:1-13; or Luke 24:13-35)*
He had to rise from the dead.

On the first day of the week,
    Mary of Magdala came to the tomb early in the morning,
    while it was still dark,
    and saw the stone removed from the tomb.
So she ran and went to Simon Peter
    and to the other disciple whom Jesus loved, and told them,
    "They have taken the Lord from the tomb,
    and we don't know where they put him."
So Peter and the other disciple went out and came to the tomb.
They both ran, but the other disciple ran faster than Peter
    and arrived at the tomb first;
    he bent down and saw the burial cloths there,
        but did not go in.
When Simon Peter arrived after him,
    he went into the tomb and saw the burial cloths there,
    and the cloth that had covered his head,
    not with the burial cloths but rolled up in a separate place.
Then the other disciple also went in,

the one who had arrived at the tomb first,
and he saw and believed.
For they did not yet understand the Scripture
that he had to rise from the dead. ✝

MONDAY, APRIL 16
OCTAVE OF EASTER

✝ Acts 2:14, 22-33
God raised this Jesus; of this we are all witnesses.

On the day of Pentecost, Peter stood up with the Eleven,
  raised his voice, and proclaimed:
  "You who are Jews, indeed all of you staying in Jerusalem.
Let this be known to you, and listen to my words.
You who are Israelites, hear these words.
Jesus the Nazarene was a man commended to you by God
  with mighty deeds, wonders, and signs,
    which God worked through him in your midst, as you
      yourselves know.
This man, delivered up by the set plan and foreknowledge of
      God,
    you killed, using lawless men to crucify him.
But God raised him up, releasing him from the throes of death,
  because it was impossible for him to be held by it.
For David says of him:
  I saw the Lord ever before me,
    with him at my right hand I shall not be disturbed.
  Therefore my heart has been glad and my tongue has
      exulted;
    my flesh, too, will dwell in hope,
  because you will not abandon my soul to the netherworld,
    nor will you suffer your holy one to see corruption.
  You have made known to me the paths of life;
    you will fill me with joy in your presence.

"My brothers, one can confidently say to you
  about the patriarch David that he died and was buried,
  and his tomb is in our midst to this day.
But since he was a prophet and knew that God had sworn an
      oath to him
  that he would set one of his descendants upon his throne,

he foresaw and spoke of the resurrection of the Christ,
that neither was he abandoned to the netherworld
nor did his flesh see corruption.
God raised this Jesus;
of this we are all witnesses.
Exalted at the right hand of God,
he received the promise of the Holy Spirit from the Father
and poured it forth, as you both see and hear." ✝

Psalm 16:1-2, 5, 7-11
R. You are my inheritance, O Lord. *(or* **Alleluia.***)*
Keep me, O God, for in you I take refuge,
I say to the LORD, "My Lord are you."
O LORD, my allotted portion and cup,
you it is who hold fast my lot. **R.**
I bless the LORD who counsels me;
even in the night my heart exhorts me.
I set the LORD ever before me;
with him at my right hand, I shall never be disturbed. **R.**
Therefore my heart is glad and my soul rejoices;
my body, too, abides in confidence,
because you will not abandon my soul to the netherworld,
nor will you suffer your faithful one to undergo
corruption. **R.**
You will show me the path to life,
fullness of joys in your presence,
the delights of your right hand forever. **R.**

Psalm 118:24
R. Alleluia, alleluia.
This is the day the Lord has made;
let us rejoice in it and be glad. **R.**

✝ *Matthew 28:8-15*
Go tell my brothers to go to Galilee, and there they will see me.

The women went away quickly from the tomb,
fearful yet overjoyed,
and ran to announce the news to his disciples..
And behold, Jesus met them on their way and greeted them.
They approached, embraced his feet, and did him homage.
Then Jesus said to them, "Do not be afraid.

Go tell my brothers to go to Galilee,
  and there they will see me."

While they were going, some of the guard went into the city
  and told the chief priests all that had happened.
They assembled with the elders and took counsel;
  then they gave a large sum of money to the soldiers,
  telling them, "You are to say,
  'His disciples came by night and stole him while we were
    asleep.'
And if this gets to the ears of the governor,
  we will satisfy him and keep you out of trouble."
The soldiers took the money and did as they were instructed.
And this story has circulated among the Jews to the present
  day. ✛

TUESDAY, APRIL 17
OCTAVE OF EASTER

† Acts 2:36-41
Repent and be baptized, every one of you, in the name of Jesus.

On the day of Pentecost, Peter said to the Jews,
  "Let the whole house of Israel know for certain
  that God has made him both Lord and Christ,
  this Jesus whom you crucified."

Now when they heard this, they were cut to the heart,
  and they asked Peter and the other apostles,
  "What are we to do, my brothers?"
Peter said to them,
  "Repent and be baptized, every one of you,
  in the name of Jesus Christ, for the forgiveness of your
    sins;
  and you will receive the gift of the Holy Spirit.
For the promise is made to you and to your children
  and to all those far off,
  whomever the Lord our God will call."
He testified with many other arguments, and was exhorting
  them,
  "Save yourselves from this corrupt generation."
Those who accepted his message were baptized,
  and about three thousand persons were added that day. ✛

Psalm 33:4-5, 18-20, 22

R. The earth is full of the goodness of the Lord.
(or **Alleluia.***)*

Upright is the word of the Lᴏʀᴅ,
    and all his works are trustworthy.
He loves justice and right;
    of the kindness of the Lᴏʀᴅ the earth is full. **R.**
See, the eyes of the Lᴏʀᴅ are upon those who fear him,
    upon those who hope for his kindness,
to deliver them from death,
    and preserve them in spite of famine. **R.**
Our soul waits for the Lᴏʀᴅ,
    who is our help and our shield.
May your kindness, O Lᴏʀᴅ, be upon us;
    who have put our hope in you. **R.**

Psalm 118:24

R. Alleluia, alleluia.
This is the day the Lord has made;
let us rejoice in it and be glad. **R.**

† *John 20:11-18*

"I have seen the Lord," she said, and then reported what he had told her.

Mary stayed outside the tomb weeping.
And as she wept, she bent over into the tomb
    and saw two angels in white sitting there,
    one at the head and one at the feet
    where the body of Jesus had been.
And they said to her, "Woman, why are you weeping?"
She said to them, "They have taken my Lord,
    and I don't know where they laid him."
When she had said this, she turned around and saw Jesus
        there,
    but did not know it was Jesus.
Jesus said to her, "Woman, why are you weeping?
Whom are you looking for?"
She thought it was the gardener and said to him,
    "Sir, if you carried him away,
    tell me where you laid him,
    and I will take him."
Jesus said to her, "Mary!"

She turned and said to him in Hebrew, "*Rabbouni*, "
    which means Teacher.
Jesus said to her, "Stop holding on to me,
    for I have not yet ascended to the Father.
But go to my brothers and tell them,
    'I am going to my Father and your Father,
    to my God and your God.'"
Mary of Magdala went and announced to the disciples,
    "I have seen the Lord, "
    and then reported what he had told her. ✛

WEDNESDAY, APRIL 18
OCTAVE OF EASTER

† *Acts 3:1-10*
What I do have, I give you: in the name of Jesus, rise and walk.

Peter and John were going up to the temple area
    for the three o'clock hour of prayer.
And a man crippled from birth was carried
    and placed at the gate of the temple called "the Beautiful
        Gate"
    every day to beg for alms from the people who entered the
        temple.
When he saw Peter and John about to go into the temple,
    he asked for alms.
But Peter looked intently at him, as did John,
    and said, "Look at us."
He paid attention to them, expecting to receive something
        from them.
Peter said, "I have neither silver nor gold,
    but what I do have I give you:
    in the name of Jesus Christ the Nazarene, rise and walk."
Then Peter took him by the right hand and raised him up,
    and immediately his feet and ankles grew strong.
He leaped up, stood, and walked around,
    and went into the temple with them,
    walking and jumping and praising God.
When all the people saw him walking and praising God,
    they recognized him as the one
    who used to sit begging at the Beautiful Gate of the temple,

and they were filled with amazement and astonishment
at what had happened to him. ✛

Psalm 105:1-4, 6-9
R. Let all who seek the Lord rejoice.
Give thanks to the LORD, invoke his name;
    make known among the nations his deeds.
Sing praise, sing his praise,
    proclaim all his wondrous deeds. **R.**
Glory in his holy name;
    rejoice, O hearts that seek the LORD!
Look to the LORD in his strength;
    constantly seek his face. **R.**
You descendants of Abraham, his servants,
    sons of Jacob, his chosen ones!
He, the LORD, is our God
    throughout the earth his judgements prevail. **R.**
He remembers forever his covenant,
    which he made binding for a thousand generations—
which he entered into with Abraham,
    and by his oath with Isaac. **R.**

Psalm 118:24
R. Alleluia, alleluia.
This is the day the Lord has made;
let us rejoice in it and be glad. **R.**

† *Luke 24:13-35*
The Lord was made known to them in the breaking of bread.

That very day, the first day of the week,
    two of Jesus' disciples were going
    to a village seven miles from Jerusalem called Emmaus
and they were conversing about all the things that had
    occurred.
And it happened that while they were conversing and debat-
    ing,
    Jesus himself drew near and walked with them,
    but their eyes were prevented from recognizing him.
He asked them,
    "What are you discussing as you walk along?"
They stopped, looking downcast.

One of them, named Cleopas, said to him in reply,
"Are you the only visitor to Jerusalem
who does not know of the things
that have taken place there in these days?"
And he replied to them, "What sort of things?"
They said to him,
"The things that happened to Jesus the Nazarene,
who was a prophet mighty in deed and word
before God and all the people,
how our chief priests and rulers both handed him over
to a sentence of death and crucified him.
But we were hoping that he would be the one to redeem Israel;
and besides all this,
it is now the third day since this took place.
Some women from our group, however, have astounded us:
they were at the tomb early in the morning
and did not find his body;
they came back and reported
that they had indeed seen a vision of angels
who announced that he was alive.
Then some of those with us went to the tomb
and found things just as the women had described,
but him they did not see."
And he said to them, "Oh, how foolish you are!
How slow of heart to believe all that the prophets spoke!
Was it not necessary that the Christ should suffer these things
and enter into his glory?"
Then beginning with Moses and all the prophets,
he interpreted to them what referred to him
in all the Scriptures.
As they approached the village to which they were going,
he gave the impression that he was going on farther.
But they urged him, "Stay with us,
for it is nearly evening and the day is almost over."
So he went in to stay with them.
And it happened that, while he was with them at table,
he took bread, said the blessing,
broke it, and gave it to them.
With that their eyes were opened and they recognized him,
but he vanished from their sight.

Then they said to each other,
"Were not our hearts burning within us
while he spoke to us on the way and opened the Scriptures
to us?"
So they set out at once and returned to Jerusalem
where they found gathered together
the eleven and those with them, who were saying,
"The Lord has truly been raised and has appeared to
Simon!"
Then the two recounted to them
what had taken place on the way
and how he was made known to them in the breaking of
bread. ✛

THURSDAY, APRIL 19
OCTAVE OF EASTER

† Acts 3:11-26
The author of life you put death, but God raised him from the dead.

As the crippled man who had been cured clung to Peter and
John,
all the people hurried in amazement toward them
in the portico called "Solomon's Portico."
When Peter saw this, he addressed the people,
"You Israelites, why are you amazed at this,
and why do you look so intently at us
as if we had made him walk by our own power or piety?
The God of Abraham, the God of Isaac, and the God of Jacob,
the God of our fathers, has glorified his servant Jesus
whom you handed over and denied in Pilate's presence,
when he had decided to release him.
You denied the Holy and Righteous One
and asked that a murderer be released to you.
The author of life you put to death,
but God raised him from the dead; of this we are witnesses.
And by faith in his name,
this man, whom you see and know, his name has made
strong,
and the faith that comes through it
has given him perfect health,

in the presence of all of you.
Now I know, brothers,
    that you acted out of ignorance, just as your leaders did;
    but God has thus brought to fulfillment
    what he had announced beforehand
    through the mouth of all the prophets,
    that his Christ would suffer.
Repent, therefore, and be converted, that your sins may be
        wiped away,
    and that the Lord may grant you times of refreshment
    and send you the Christ already appointed for you, Jesus,
    whom heaven must receive until the times of universal
        restoration
    of which God spoke through the mouth
    of his holy prophets from of old.
For Moses said:
    A prophet like me will the Lord, your God, raise up for you
        from among your own kinsmen;
        to him you shall listen in all that he may say to you.
    Everyone who does not listen to that prophet
        will be cut off from the people.

"Moreover, all the prophets who spoke,
    from Samuel and those afterwards, also announced
        these days.
You are the children of the prophets
    and of the covenant that God made with your ancestors
    when he said to Abraham,
'In your offspring all the families of the earth shall be
        blessed.'
For you first, God raised up his servant and sent him to
        bless you
    by turning each of you from your evil ways." ✢

Psalm 8:2, 5-9
R. O Lord, our God, how wonderful your name in all
    the earth! *(or* **Alleluia.***)*
O LORD, our Lord,
    how glorious is your name over all the earth!
What is man that you should be mindful of him,
    or the son of man that you should care for him? **R.**

You have made him little less than the angels,
and crowned him with glory and honor.
You have given him rule over the works of your hands,
putting all things under his feet. **R.**
All sheep and oxen,
yes, and the beasts of the field,
the birds of the air, the fishes of the sea,
and whatever swims the paths of the seas. **R.**

Psalm 118:24
R. Alleluia, alleluia.
This is the day the Lord has made;
let us rejoice in it and be glad. **R.**

✝ *Luke 24:35-48*

Thus it is written that the Christ would
suffer and rise from the dead on the third day.

The two disciples of Jesus recounted
what had taken place on the way to Emmaus,
and how he was made known to them in the breaking of
bread.
While they were still speaking about this,
he stood in their midst and said to them,
"Peace be with you."
But they were startled and terrified
and thought that they were seeing a ghost.
Then he said to them, "Why are you troubled?
And why do questions arise in your hearts?
Look at my hands and my feet, that it is I myself.
Touch me and see, because a ghost does not have flesh and
bones
as you can see I have."
And as he said this,
he showed them his hands and his feet.
While they were still incredulous for joy and were amazed,
he asked them, "Have you anything here to eat?"
They gave him a piece of baked fish;
he took it and ate it in front of them.

He said to them,
"These are my words that I spoke to you while I was still
with you,

that everything written about me in the law of Moses
and in the prophets and psalms must be fulfilled."
Then he opened their minds to understand the Scriptures.
And he said to them,
"Thus it is written that the Christ would suffer
and rise from the dead on the third day
and that repentance, for the forgiveness of sins,
would be preached in his name
to all the nations, beginning from Jerusalem.
You are witnesses of these things." ✛

FRIDAY, APRIL 20
OCTAVE OF EASTER

✝ Acts 4:1-12
Nor is there any other name by which we are to be saved.

While Peter and John were still speaking to the people,
the priests, the captain of the temple guard,
and the Sadducees confronted them,
disturbed that they were teaching the people
and proclaiming in Jesus the resurrection of the dead.
They laid hands on them
and put them in custody until the next day,
since it was already evening.
But many of those who heard the word came to believe
and the number of men grew to about five thousand.

On the next day, their leaders, elders, and scribes
were assembled in Jerusalem, with Annas the high priest,
Caiaphas, John, Alexander,
and all who were of the high-priestly class.
They brought them into their presence and questioned them,
"By what power or by what name have you done this?"
Then Peter, filled with the Holy Spirit, answered them,
"Leaders of the people and elders:
If we are being examined today
about a good deed done to a cripple,
namely, by what means he was saved,
then all of you and all the people of Israel should know
that it was in the name of Jesus Christ the Nazarene
whom you crucified, whom God raised from the dead;

in his name this man stands before you healed.
He is 'the stone rejected by you, the builders,
    which has become the cornerstone.'
There is no salvation through anyone else,
    nor is there any other name under heaven
    given to the human race by which we are to be saved." ✚

Psalm 118:1-2, 4, 22-27
R. **The stone rejected by the builders has become the
cornerstone.** *(or* **Alleluia.***)*
Give thanks to the LORD, for he is good,
    for his mercy endures forever.
Let the house of Israel say:
    "His mercy endures forever."
Let those who fear the LORD say,
    "His mercy endures forever." **R.**
The stone which the builders rejected
    has become the cornerstone.
By the LORD has this been done;
    it is wonderful in our eyes.
This is the day the LORD has made;
    let us be glad and rejoice in it. **R.**
O LORD, grant salvation!
    O LORD, grant prosperity!
Blessed is he who comes in the name of the LORD;
    we bless you from the house of the LORD.
The LORD is God and he has given us light. **R.**

Psalm 118:24
R. **Alleluia, alleluia.**
This is the day the Lord has made;
let us rejoice in it and be glad. **R.**

† *John 21:1-14*
*Jesus came and took the bread and
gave it to them, and in like manner the fish.*

Jesus revealed himself again to his disciples at the Sea of
    Tiberias.
He revealed himself in this way.
Together were Simon Peter, Thomas called Didymus,
    Nathanael from Cana in Galilee,

Zebedee's sons, and two others of his disciples.
Simon Peter said to them, "I am going fishing."
They said to him, "We also will come with you."
So they went out and got into the boat,
    but that night they caught nothing.
When it was already dawn, Jesus was standing on the shore;
    but the disciples did not realize that it was Jesus.
Jesus said to them, "Children, have you caught anything to
      eat?"
They answered him, "No."
So he said to them, "Cast the net over the right side of the boat
    and you will find something."
So they cast it, and were not able to pull it in
    because of the number of fish.
So the disciple whom Jesus loved said to Peter, "It is the Lord."
When Simon Peter heard that it was the Lord,
    he tucked in his garment, for he was lightly clad,
    and jumped into the sea.
The other disciples came in the boat,
    for they were not far from shore, only about a hundred
      yards,
    dragging the net with the fish.
When they climbed out on shore,
    they saw a charcoal fire with fish on it and bread.
Jesus said to them, "Bring some of the fish you just caught."
So Simon Peter went over and dragged the net ashore
    full of one hundred fifty-three large fish.
Even though there were so many, the net was not torn.
Jesus said to them, "Come, have breakfast."
And none of the disciples dared to ask him, "Who are you?"
    because they realized it was the Lord.
Jesus came over and took the bread and gave it to them,
    and in like manner the fish.
This was now the third time Jesus was revealed to his disciples
    after being raised from the dead. ✙

SATURDAY, APRIL 21
OCTAVE OF EASTER

✝ *Acts 4:13-21*
It is impossible for us not to speak about what we have seen and heard.

Observing the boldness of Peter and John
and perceiving them to be uneducated, ordinary men,
the Jews were amazed,
and they recognized them as the companions of Jesus.
Then when they saw the man who had been cured standing
there with them,
they could say nothing in reply.
So they ordered them to leave the Sanhedrin,
and conferred with one another, saying,
"What are we to do with these men?
Everyone living in Jerusalem knows that a remarkable sign
was done through them, and we cannot deny it.
But so that it may not be spread any further among the people,
let us give them a stern warning
never again to speak to anyone in this name."
So they called them back
and ordered them not to speak or teach at all in the name
of Jesus.
Peter and John, however, said to them in reply,
"Whether it is right in the sight of God
for us to obey you rather than God, you be the judges.
It is impossible for us not to speak about what we have seen
and heard."
After threatening them further,
the Jews released them,
finding no way to punish them,
on account of the people who were all praising God
for what had happened. ✝

Psalm 118:1, 14-21
R. I praise you, Lord, for you have answered me.
(or **Alleluia.***)*
Give thanks to the LORD, for he is good,
for his mercy endures forever.
My strength and my courage is the LORD,
and he has been my savior.

The joyful shout of victory
    in the tents of the just. **R.**
The right hand of the L<small>ORD</small> is exalted;
    "The right hand of the L<small>ORD</small> has struck with power."
I shall not die, but live,
    and declare the works of the L<small>ORD</small>.
Though the L<small>ORD</small> has chastised me,
yet he has not delivered me to death. **R.**
Open to me the gates of justice;
    I will enter them and give thanks to the L<small>ORD</small>.
This is the gate of the L<small>ORD</small>;
    the just shall enter it.
I will give thanks to you, for you have answered me
    and have been my savior. **R.**

Psalm 118:24
R. Alleluia, alleluia.
This is the day the Lord has made;
let us rejoice in it and be glad. **R.**

† *Mark 16:9-15*
Go into the whole world and proclaim the Gospel.

When Jesus had risen, early on the first day of the week,
    he appeared first to Mary Magdalene,
    out of whom he had driven seven demons.
She went and told his companions who were mourning and
        weeping.
When they heard that he was alive
    and had been seen by her, they did not believe.

After this he appeared in another form
    to two of them walking along on their way to the country.
They returned and told the others;
    but they did not believe them either.

But later, as the eleven were at table, Jesus appeared to them
    and rebuked them for their unbelief and hardness of heart
    because they had not believed those
    who saw him after he had been raised.
He said to them, "Go into the whole world
    and proclaim the gospel to every creature." ✛

APRIL 22
SECOND SUNDAY OF EASTER

† *Acts 5:12-16*
More than ever, believers in the Lord,
great numbers of men and women, were added to them.

Many signs and wonders were done among the people
 at the hands of the apostles.
They were all together in Solomon's portico.
None of the others dared to join them, but the people esteemed
 them.
Yet more than ever, believers in the Lord,
 great numbers of men and women, were added to them.
Thus they even carried the sick out into the streets
 and laid them on cots and mats
 so that when Peter came by,
 at least his shadow might fall on one or another of them.
A large number of people from the towns
 in the vicinity of Jerusalem also gathered,
 bringing the sick and those disturbed by unclean spirits,
 and they were all cured. ✣

Psalm 118:2-4, 13-15, 22-24
**R. Give thanks to the Lord for he is good,
 his love is everlasting.** *(or* **Alleluia.***)*
Let the house of Israel say,
 "His mercy endures forever."
Let the house of Aaron say,
 "His mercy endures forever."
Let those who fear the LORD say,
 "His mercy endures forever." **R.**
I was hard pressed and was falling,
 but the LORD helped me.
My strength and my courage is the LORD,
 and he has been my savior.
The joyful shout of victory
 in the tents of the just: **R.**
The stone which the builders rejected
 has become the cornerstone.
By the LORD has this been done;

it is wonderful in our eyes.
This is the day the LORD has made;
let us be glad and rejoice in it. **R.**

† *Revelation 1:9-11a, 12-13, 17-19*
I was dead, but now I am alive forever and ever.

I, John, your brother, who share with you
the distress, the kingdom, and the endurance we have in
Jesus,
found myself on the island called Patmos
because I proclaimed God's word and gave testimony to
Jesus.
I was caught up in spirit on the Lord's day
and heard behind me a voice as loud as a trumpet,
which said,
"Write on a scroll what you see."
Then I turned to see whose voice it was that spoke to me,
and when I turned, I saw seven gold lampstands
and in the midst of the lampstands one like a son of man,
wearing an ankle-length robe, with a gold sash around his
chest.

When I caught sight of him, I fell down at his feet as though
dead.
He touched me with his right hand and said, "Do not be afraid.
I am the first and the last, the one who lives.
Once I was dead, but now I am alive forever and ever.
I hold the keys to death and the netherworld.
Write down, therefore, what you have seen,
and what is happening, and what will happen
afterwards." ✛

John 20:29
R. Alleluia, alleluia.
You believe in me, Thomas, because you have seen me, says
the Lord;
Blessed are they who have not seen me, but still believe! **R.**

✝ *John 20:19-31*
Eight days later Jesus came and stood in their midst.

On the evening of that first day of the week,
    when the doors were locked, where the disciples were,
    for fear of the Jews,
    Jesus came and stood in their midst
    and said to them, "Peace be with you."
When he had said this, he showed them his hands and his side.
The disciples rejoiced when they saw the Lord.
Jesus said to them again, "Peace be with you.
As the Father has sent me, so I send you."
And when he had said this, he breathed on them
        and said to them,
    "Receive the Holy Spirit.
Whose sins you forgive are forgiven them,
    and whose sins you retain are retained."

Thomas, called Didymus, one of the Twelve,
    was not with them when Jesus came.
So the other disciples said to him, "We have seen the Lord."
But he said to them,
    "Unless I see the mark of the nails in his hands
    and put my finger into the nailmarks
    and put my hand into his side, I will not believe."

Now a week later his disciples were again inside
    and Thomas was with them.
Jesus came, although the doors were locked,
    and stood in their midst and said, "Peace be with you."
Then he said to Thomas, "Put your finger here and see my
        hands,
    and bring your hand and put it into my side,
    and do not be unbelieving, but believe."
Thomas answered and said to him, "My Lord and my God!"
Jesus said to him, "Have you come to believe because you have
        seen me?
Blessed are those who have not seen and have believed."

Now Jesus did many other signs in the presence of his disciples
    that are not written in this book.
But these are written that you may come to believe

that Jesus is the Christ, the Son of God,
and that through this belief you may have life in
his name. ✝

MONDAY, APRIL 23
EASTER WEEKDAY, ST. GEORGE, ST. ADALBERT

† *Acts 4:23-31*
*When they had prayed they were filled with the Holy
Spirit and began to proclaim the word of God boldly.*

Peter and John, after being released, went back to their own
people and told them what the priests and elders had said. All
raised their voices in prayer to God on hearing the story:
"Sovereign Lord, 'who made heaven and earth, and sea and all
that is in them,' you have said by the Holy Spirit through the
lips of our father David your servant:
'Why did the Gentiles rage,
    the peoples conspire in folly?
The kings of the earth were aligned,
    the princes gathered together
    against the Lord and against his anointed.'
Indeed, they gathered in this very city against your holy
Servant, Jesus, 'whom you anointed' — Herod and Pontius
Pilate in league with 'the Gentiles' and 'the peoples' of Israel.
They have brought about the very things which in your
powerful providence you planned long ago. But now, O Lord,
look at the threats they are leveling against us. Grant to your
servants, even as they speak your words, complete assurance
by stretching forth your hand in cures and signs and wonders
to be worked in the name of Jesus, your holy Servant."
    The place where they were gathered shook as they prayed.
They were filled with the Holy Spirit and continued to speak
God's word with confidence. ✝

Psalm 2:1-9
R. **Happy are all who put their trust in the Lord.**
(or **Alleluia.***)*
Why do the nations rage
    and the peoples utter folly?
The kings of the earth rise up,
    and the princes conspire together
    against the Lord and against his anointed:

"Let us break their fetters
and cast their bonds from us!" **R.**
He who is throned in heaven laughs;
the Lord derides them.
Then in anger he speaks to them;
he terrifies them in his wrath:
"I myself have set up my king
on Zion, my holy mountain."
I will proclaim the decree of the Lord. **R.**
The Lord said to me, "You are my son;
this day I have begotten you.
Ask of me and I will give you
the nations for an inheritance
and the ends of the earth for your possession.
You shall rule them with an iron rod;
you shall shatter them like an earthen dish." **R.**

R. Alleluia, alleluia.
Christ had to suffer and to rise from the dead,
and so to enter into his glory. **R.**

✝ *John 3:1-8*
Unless a man has been born again, he cannot see the kingdom of God.

A certain Pharisee named Nicodemus, a member of the
Jewish Sanhedrin, came to Jesus at night. "Rabbi," he said,
"we know you are a teacher come from God, for no man can
perform signs and wonders such as you perform unless God is
with him." Jesus gave him this answer:
"I solemnly assure you,
no one can see the rule of God
unless he is begotten from above."
"How can a man be born again once he is old?" retorted
Nicodemus. "Can he return to his mother's womb and be born
all over again?" Jesus replied:
"I solemnly assure you,
no one can enter into God's kingdom
without being begotten of water and Spirit.
Flesh begets flesh,
Spirit begets spirit.
Do not be surprised that I tell you

you must all be begotten from above.
The wind blows where it will.
You hear the sound it makes
but you do not know where it comes from,
or where it goes.
So it is with everyone begotten of the Spirit." ✛

TUESDAY, APRIL 24
EASTER WEEKDAY, ST. FIDELIS

† Acts 4:32-37
Be of one heart and one mind.

The community of believers were of one heart and one mind.
None of them ever claimed anything as his own; rather, everything was held in common. With power the apostles bore witness
to the resurrection of the Lord Jesus, and great respect was paid
to them all; nor was there anyone needy among them, for all who
owned property or houses sold them and donated the proceeds.
They used to lay them at the feet of the apostles to be distributed
to everyone according to his need.

There was a certain Levite from Cyprus named Joseph, to
whom the apostles gave the name Barnabas (meaning "son of
encouragement"). He sold a farm that he owned and made a
donation of the money, laying it at the apostles' feet. ✛

Psalm 93:1-2, 5
R. **The Lord is king;**
he is robed in majesty. *(or* **Alleluia.***)*
The Lord is king, in splendor robed;
    robed is the Lord and girt about with strength. **R.**
And he has made the world firm,
    not to be moved.
Your throne stands firm from of old;
    from everlasting you are, O Lord. **R.**
Your decrees are worthy of trust indeed:
    holiness befits your house,
    O Lord, for length of days. **R.**

R. **Alleluia, alleluia.**
Nailed to the cross for our sake,
the Lord is now risen from the grave. **R.**

✝ *John 3:7-15*

*No one has gone to heaven, except the one
who came from heaven, the Son of Man.*

Jesus said to Nicodemus:
  "I solemnly assure you,
  do not be surprised that I tell you
  you must all be begotten from above.
  The wind blows where it will.
  You hear the sound it makes
  but you do not know where it comes from,
  or where it goes.
  So it is with everyone begotten of the Spirit."
  "How can such a thing happen?" asked Nicodemus. Jesus
responded: "You hold the office of teacher of Israel and still you
do not understand these matters?
  "I solemnly assure you,
  we are talking about what we know,
  we are testifying to what we have seen.
  You are the ones who do not accept our testimony.
  If you do not believe
  when I tell you about earthly things,
  how are you to believe
  when I tell you about those of heaven?
  No one has gone up to heaven
  except the One who came down from there_
  the Son of Man [who is in heaven].
  Just as Moses lifted up the serpent in the desert,
  so must the Son of Man be lifted up,
  that all who believe
  may have eternal life in him." ✝

WEDNESDAY, APRIL 25
St. Mark

✝ *1 Peter 5:5-14*
My son, Mark, sends you greetings.

In your relations with one another, clothe yourselves with
humility, because God "is stern with the arrogant but to the
humble he shows kindness." Bow humbly under God's mighty
hand, so that in due time he may lift you high. Cast all your cares

on him because he cares for you. Stay sober and alert. Your opponent the devil is prowling like a roaring lion looking for someone to devour. Resist him, solid in your faith, realizing that the brotherhood of believers is undergoing the same sufferings throughout the world. The God of all grace, who called you to his everlasting glory in Christ, will himself restore, confirm, strengthen and establish those who have suffered a little while. Dominion be his throughout the ages! Amen.

I am writing briefly through Silvanus, whom I take to be a faithful brother to you. Herewith are expressed my encouragement and my testimony that this is the true grace of God. Be steadfast in it. The church in Babylon sends you greetings, as does Mark my son. Greet one another with the embrace of true love. To all of you who are in Christ, peace. ✛

Psalm 89:2-3, 6-7, 16-17
R. Forever I will sing the goodness of the Lord.
(or **Alleluia.***)*
The favors of the Lord I will sing forever;
    through all generations my mouth shall proclaim your
        faithfulness.
For you have said, "My kindness is established forever";
    in heaven you have confirmed your faithfulness. **R.**
The heavens proclaim your wonders, O Lord,
    and your faithfulness, in the assembly of the holy ones.
For who in the skies can rank with the Lord?
    Who is like the Lord among the sons of God? **R.**
Happy the people who know the joyful shout;
    in the light of your countenance, O Lord, they walk.
At your name they rejoice all the day,
    and through your justice they are exalted. **R.**

1 Corinthians 1:23-24
R. Alleluia, alleluia.
We preach a Christ who was crucified;
he is the power and the wisdom of God. **R.**

✝ *Mark 16:15-20*
Make known the Good News to every creature.

Jesus appeared to the Eleven and told them; "Go into the world and proclaim the good news to all creation. The man who believes in it and accepts baptism will be saved; the man who refuses to believe in it will be condemned. Signs like these will accompany those who have professed their faith: they will use my name to expel demons, they will speak entirely new languages, they will be able to handle serpents, they will be able to drink deadly poison without harm, and the sick upon whom they lay their hands will recover." Then, after speaking to them, the Lord Jesus was taken up into heaven and took his seat at God's right hand. The Eleven went forth and preached everywhere. The Lord continued to work with them throughout and confirm the message through the signs which accompanied them. ✛

THURSDAY, APRIL 26
EASTER WEEKDAY

† Acts 5:27-33
We are witnesses of these words, and so is the Holy Spirit.

When the attendants had led the apostles in and made them stand before the Sanhedrin, the high priest began the interrogation in this way: "We gave you strict orders not to teach about that name, yet you have filled Jerusalem with your teaching and are determined to make us responsible for that man's blood." To this, Peter and the apostles replied: "Better for us to obey God than men! The God of our fathers has raised up Jesus whom you put to death, 'hanging him on a tree.' He whom God has exalted at his right hand as ruler and savior is to bring repentance to Israel and forgiveness of sins. We testify to this. So too does the Holy Spirit, whom God has given to those that obey him."

When the Sanhedrin heard this, they were stung to fury and wanted to kill them. ✛

Psalm 34:2, 9, 17-20
R. The Lord hears the cry of the poor. *(or* **Alleluia.***)*
I will bless the Lord at all times;
    his praise shall be ever in my mouth.
Taste and see how good the Lord is;
    happy the man who takes refuge in him. **R.**
The Lord confronts the evildoers,
    to destroy remembrance of them from the earth.
When the just cry out, the Lord hears them,

and from all their distress he rescues them. **R.**
The Lord is close to the brokenhearted;
  and those who are crushed in spirit he saves.
Many are the troubles of the just man,
  but out of them all the Lord delivers him. **R.**

R. Alleluia, alleluia.
Christ is risen, and makes all things new;
he has shown pity to all mankind. **R.**

† *John 3:31-36*
The Father loves the Son, and gave all things into his hands.

Jesus said to Nicodemus:
  "The One who comes from above is above all;
  the one who is of the earth is earthly,
  and he speaks on an earthly plane.
  The One who comes from heaven [who is above all]
  testifies to what he has seen and heard,
  but no one accepts his testimony.
  Whoever does accept this testimony
  certifies that God is truthful.
  For the One whom God has sent
  speaks the words of God;
  he does not ration his gift of the Spirit.
  The Father loves the Son
  and has given everything over to him.

  Whoever believes in the Son
  has life eternal.
  Whoever disobeys the Son
  will not see life,
  but must endure the wrath of God." ✛

FRIDAY, APRIL 27
EASTER WEEKDAY

† *Acts 5:34-42*
They went out rejoicing that they had the honor of
suffering humiliation for the sake of the name of Jesus.

A certain member of the Sanhedrin stood up and had the
apostles ordered out of court for a few minutes, and then said

to the assembly, "Fellow Israelites, think twice about what you are going to do with these men. Not long ago a certain Theudas came on the scene and tried to pass himself off as someone of importance. About four hundred men joined him. However he was killed, and all those who had been so easily convinced by him were disbanded. In the end it came to nothing. Next came Judas the Galilean at the time of the census. He too built up quite a following, but likewise died, and all his followers were dispersed. The present case is similar. My advice is that you have nothing to do with these men. Let them alone. If their purpose or activity is human in its origins it will destroy itself. If, on the other hand, it comes from God, you will not be able to destroy them without fighting God himself."

This speech persuaded them. In spite of it, however, the Sanhedrin called in the apostles and had them whipped. They ordered them not to speak again about the name of Jesus, and afterward dismissed them. The apostles for their part left the Sanhedrin full of joy that they had been judged worthy of ill-treatment for the sake of the Name. Day after day, both in the temple and at home, they never stopped teaching and proclaiming the good news of Jesus the Messiah. ✛

Psalm 27:1, 4, 13-14
**R. One thing I seek:
to dwell in the house of the Lord.** (*or* **Alleluia.**)
The Lord is my light and my salvation;
     whom should I fear?
The Lord is my life's refuge;
     of whom should I be afraid? **R.**
One thing I ask of the Lord;
     this I seek:
To dwell in the house of the Lord
     all the days of my life,
That I may gaze on the loveliness of the Lord
     and contemplate his temple. **R.**
I believe that I shall see the bounty of the Lord
     in the land of the living.
Wait for the Lord with courage;
     be stouthearted, and wait for the Lord. **R.**

R. Alleluia, alleluia.

I am the good shepherd, says the Lord;
I know my sheep and mine know me. **R.**

† *John 6:1-15*

*He gave the food to those who were
sitting around, as much as they wanted.*

Jesus crossed the Sea of Galilee [to the shore] of Tiberias; a vast crowd kept following him because they saw the signs he was performing for the sick. Jesus then went up the mountain and sat down there with his disciples. The Jewish feast of Passover was near; when Jesus looked up and caught sight of a vast crowd coming toward him, he said to Philip, "Where shall we buy bread for these people to eat?" (He knew well what he intended to do but he asked this to test Philip's response.) Philip replied, "Not even with two hundred days' wages could we buy loaves enough to give each of them a mouthful."

One of Jesus' disciples, Andrew, Simon Peter's brother, remarked to him, "There is a lad here who has five barley loaves and a couple of dried fish, but what good is that for so many?" Jesus said, "Get the people to recline." Even though the men numbered about five thousand, there was plenty of grass for them to find a place on the ground. Jesus then took the loaves of bread, gave thanks, and passed them around to those reclining there; he did the same with the dried fish, as much as they wanted. When they had had enough, he told his disciples, "Gather up the crusts that are left over so that nothing will go to waste." At this, they gathered twelve baskets full of pieces left over by those who had been fed with the five barley loaves.

When the people saw the sign he had performed they began to say, "This is undoubtedly the Prophet who is to come into the world." At that, Jesus realized that they would come and carry him off to make him king, so he fled back to the mountain alone. ✝

SATURDAY, APRIL 28
EASTER WEEKDAY, ST. PETER CHANEL, ST. LOUIS DE MONTFORT

✝ *Acts 6:1-7*
They chose seven men who were filled with the Holy Spirit.

In those days as the number of disciples grew, the ones who spoke Greek complained that their widows were being neglected in the daily distribution of food, as compared with the widows of those who spoke Hebrew. The Twelve assembled the community of the disciples and said, "It is not right for us to neglect the word of God in order to wait on the tables. Look around among your own number, brothers, for seven men acknowledged to be deeply spiritual and prudent, and we shall appoint them to this task. This will permit us to concentrate on prayer and the ministry of the word." The proposal was unanimously accepted by the community. Following this they selected Stephen, a man filled with faith and the Holy Spirit; Philip, Prochorus, Nicanor, Timon, Parmenas and Nicolaus of Antioch, who had been a convert to Judaism. They presented these men to the apostles, who first prayed over them and then imposed hands on them.

The word of God continued to spread, while at the same time the number of the disciples in Jerusalem enormously increased. There were many priests among those who embraced the faith. ✝

Psalm 33:1-2, 4-5, 18-19
**R. Lord, let your mercy be on us,
    as we place our trust in you.** *(or* **Alleluia.***)*
Exult, you just, in the Lord;
    praise from the upright is fitting.
Give thanks to the Lord on the harp;
    with the ten-stringed lyre chant his praises. **R.**
Upright is the word of the Lord,
    and all his works are trustworthy.
He loves justice and right;
    of the kindness of the Lord the earth is full. **R.**
See, the eyes of the Lord are upon those who fear him,
    upon those who hope for his kindness,
To deliver them from death

and preserve them in spite of famine. **R.**

R. Alleluia, alleluia.
Christ now raised from the dead will never die again;
death no longer has power over him. **R.**

† *John 6:16-21*
They saw Jesus, walking upon the water.

As evening drew on, the disciples of Jesus came down to the lake. They embarked, intending to cross the lake toward Capernaum. By this time it was dark, and Jesus had still not joined them; moreover, with a strong wind blowing, the sea was becoming rough. Finally, when they had rowed three or four miles, they sighted Jesus approaching the boat, walking on the water. They were frightened, but he told them, "It is I; do not be afraid." They wanted to take him into the boat, but suddenly it came aground on the shore they had been approaching. ✢

APRIL 29
THIRD SUNDAY OF EASTER

† *Acts 5:27-32, 40b-41*
We are witnesses of these words as is the Holy Spirit.

When the captain and the court officers had brought the
    apostles in
  and made them stand before the Sanhedrin,
  the high priest questioned them,
  "We gave you strict orders, did we not,
  to stop teaching in that name?
Yet you have filled Jerusalem with your teaching
  and want to bring this man's blood upon us."
But Peter and the apostles said in reply,
  "We must obey God rather than men.
The God of our ancestors raised Jesus,
  though you had him killed by hanging him on a tree.
God exalted him at his right hand as leader and savior
  to grant Israel repentance and forgiveness of sins.
We are witnesses of these things,
  as is the Holy Spirit whom God has given to those who obey
    him."

The Sanhedrin ordered the apostles
  to stop speaking in the name of Jesus, and dismissed them.
So they left the presence of the Sanhedrin,
  rejoicing that they had been found worthy
  to suffer dishonor for the sake of the name. ✛

Psalm 30:2, 4-6, 11-13
R. I will praise you, Lord, for you have rescued me.
(or **Alleluia.***)*
I will extol you, O LORD, for you drew me clear
  and did not let my enemies rejoice over me.
O LORD, you brought me up from the netherworld;
  you preserved me from among those going down
        into the pit. **R.**
Sing praise to the LORD, you his faithful ones,
  and give thanks to his holy name.
For his anger lasts but a moment;
  a lifetime, his good will.
At nightfall, weeping enters in,
  but with the dawn, rejoicing. **R.**
Hear, O LORD, and have pity on me;
  O LORD, be my helper.
You changed my mourning into dancing;
  O LORD, my God, forever will I give you thanks. **R.**

† *Revelation 5:11-14*
Worthy is the Lamb that was slain to receive power and riches.

I, John, looked and heard the voices of many angels
  who surrounded the throne
  and the living creatures and the elders.
They were countless in number, and they cried out in a loud
        voice:
    "Worthy is the Lamb that was slain
        to receive power and riches, wisdom and strength,
        honor and glory and blessing."
Then I heard every creature in heaven and on earth
  and under the earth and in the sea,
  everything in the universe, cry out:
    "To the one who sits on the throne and to the Lamb
      be blessing and honor, glory and might,
      forever and ever."

The four living creatures answered, "Amen, "
and the elders fell down and worshiped. ✛

R. Alleluia, alleluia.
Christ is risen, creator of all;
he has shown pity on all people. **R.**

*✝ **John 21:1-14** (or John 21:1-19)*
Jesus came and took the bread and
gave it to them and in like manner the fish.

At that time, Jesus revealed himself to his disciples at the Sea
of Tiberias.
He revealed himself in this way.
Together were Simon Peter, Thomas called Didymus,
Nathanael from Cana in Galilee,
Zebedee's sons, and two others of his disciples.
Simon Peter said to them, "I am going fishing."
They said to him, "We also will come with you."
So they went out and got into the boat,
but that night they caught nothing.
When it was already dawn, Jesus was standing on the shore;
but the disciples did not realize that it was Jesus.
Jesus said to them, "Children, have you caught anything to eat?"
They answered him, "No."
So he said to them, "Cast the net over the right side of the boat
and you will find something."
So they cast it, and were not able to pull it in
because of the number of fish.
So the disciple whom Jesus loved said to Peter, "It is the Lord."
When Simon Peter heard that it was the Lord,
he tucked in his garment, for he was lightly clad,
and jumped into the sea.
The other disciples came in the boat,
for they were not far from shore, only about a hundred yards,
dragging the net with the fish.
When they climbed out on shore,
they saw a charcoal fire with fish on it and bread.
Jesus said to them, "Bring some of the fish you just caught."
So Simon Peter went over and dragged the net ashore
full of one hundred fifty-three large fish.

Even though there were so many, the net was not torn.
Jesus said to them, "Come, have breakfast."
And none of the disciples dared to ask him, "Who are you?"
  because they realized it was the Lord.
Jesus came over and took the bread and gave it to them,
  and in like manner the fish.
This was now the third time Jesus was revealed to his disciples
  after being raised from the dead. ✛

MONDAY, APRIL 30
EASTER WEEKDAY, POPE PIUS V

✝ Acts 6:8-15
They could not withstand the wisdom and the Spirit with which he spoke.

Stephen, filled with grace and power, worked great wonders and signs among the people. Certain members of the so-called "Synagogue of Roman Freedmen" (that is, the Jews from Cyrene, Alexandria, Cilicia and Asia) would undertake to engage Stephen in debate, but they proved no match for the wisdom and spirit with which he spoke. They persuaded some men to make the charge that they had heard him speaking blasphemies against Moses and God, and in this way they incited the people, the elders, and the scribes. All together they confronted him, seized him, and led him off to the Sanhedrin. There they brought in false witnesses, who said: "This man never stops making statements against the holy place and the law. We have heard him claim that Jesus the Nazorean will destroy this place and change the customs which Moses handed down to us." The members of the Sanhedrin who sat there stared at him intently. Throughout, Stephen's face seemed like that of an angel. ✛

Psalm 119:23-24, 26-27, 29-30
R. Happy are those of blameless life. *(or* **Alleluia.***)*
Though princes meet and talk against me,
  your servant meditates on your statutes.
Yes, your decrees are my delight;
  they are my counselors. **R.**
I declared my ways, and you answered me;
  teach me your statutes.

Make me understand the way of your precepts,
  and I will meditate on your wondrous deeds. **R.**
Remove from me the way of falsehood,
  and favor me with your law.
The way of truth I have chosen;
  I have set your ordinances before me. **R.**

R. Alleluia, alleluia.
My sheep listen to my voice, says the Lord;
I know them and they follow me. **R.**

† John 6:22-29

*Do not work for food which cannot last,
but for food which endures to eternal life.*

The crowd remained on the other side of the lake. The next day they realized that there had been only one boat there and that Jesus had not left in it with his disciples; rather, they had set out by themselves. Then some boats came out from Tiberias near the place where they had eaten the bread after the Lord had given thanks. Once the crowd saw that neither Jesus nor his disciples were there, they too embarked in the boats and went to Capernaum looking for Jesus.

When they found him on the other side of the lake, they said to him, "Rabbi, when did you come here?" Jesus answered them:
  "I assure you,
  you are not looking for me because you have seen signs
  but because you have eaten your fill of the loaves.
  You should not be working for perishable food
  but for food that remains unto life eternal,
  food which the Son of Man will give you;
  it is on him that God the Father has set his seal."
At this they said to him, "What must we do to perform the works of God?" Jesus replied:
  "This is the work of God:
  have faith in the One whom he sent." **✝**

TUESDAY, MAY 1

Easter Weekday, St. Joseph the Worker

(Below are Weekday readings. Readings for St. Joseph Memorial are: Genesis 1:26—
2:3 or Colossians 3:14-15, 17, 23-24 • Psalm 90:2-4, 12-14, 16 • Matthew 13:54-58.)

† *Acts 7:51—8:1*
Jesus, Lord, receive my spirit.

Stephen said to the people and elders and scribes: "You stiff-
necked people, uncircumcised in heart and ears, you are
always opposing the Holy Spirit just as your fathers did before
you. Was there ever any prophet whom your fathers did not
persecute? In their day, they put to death those who foretold
the coming of the Just One; now you in your turn have become
his betrayers and murderers. You who received the law
through the ministry of angels have not observed it."

Those who listened to his words were stung to the heart;
they ground their teeth in anger at him. Stephen meanwhile,
filled with the Holy Spirit, looked to the sky above and saw the
glory of God, and Jesus standing at God's right hand. "Look!"
he exclaimed, "I see an opening in the sky, and the Son of Man
standing at God's right hand." The onlookers were shouting
aloud, holding their hands over their ears as they did so. Then
they rushed at him as one man, dragged him out of the city,
and began to stone him. The witnesses meanwhile were piling
their cloaks at the feet of a young man named Saul. As Stephen
was being stoned he could be heard praying, "Lord Jesus,
receive my spirit." He fell to his knees and cried out in a loud
voice, "Lord, do not hold this sin against them." And with that
he died.

Saul, for his part, concurred in the act of killing. ✛

Psalm 31:3-4, 6-8, 17, 21

**R. Into your hands, O Lord,
I entrust my spirit.**

Be my rock of refuge,
  a stronghold to give me safety.
You are my rock and my fortress;
  for your name's sake you will lead and guide me.
Into your hands I commend my spirit;
  you will redeem me, O Lord, O faithful God.
My trust is in the Lord;
  I will rejoice and be glad of your kindness. **R.**

Let your face shine upon your servant;
    save me in your kindness.
You hide them in the shelter of your presence
    from the plottings of men. **R.**

R. Alleluia, alleluia.
We know that Christ is truly risen from the dead;
victorious king, deal kindly with us. **R.**

† *John 6:30-35*
It was not Moses, but my Father who gave you bread from heaven.

The crowd said to Jesus: "What sign are you going to perform for us to see so that we can put faith in you? What is the 'work' you do? Our ancestors had manna to eat in the desert; according to Scripture, 'He gave them bread from the heavens to eat.'" Jesus said to them:
    "I solemnly assure you,
    it was not Moses who gave you bread from the heavens;
    it is my Father who gives you the real heavenly bread.
    God's bread
    comes down from heaven
    and gives life to the world."
"Sir, give us this bread always," they besought him.
Jesus explained to them:
    "I myself am the bread of life.
    No one who comes to me shall ever be hungry,
    no one who believes in me shall thirst again." ✚

WEDNESDAY, MAY 2
St. Athanasius

† *Acts 8:1-8*
They went from place to place preaching the Good News.

A certain day saw the beginning of a great persecution of the church in Jerusalem. All except the apostles scattered throughout the countryside of Judea and Samaria. Devout men buried Stephen, bewailing him loudly as they did so. After that, Saul began to harass the church. He entered house after house, dragged men and women out, and threw them into jail.
    The members of the church who had been dispersed went

about preaching the word. Philip, for example, went down to the town of Samaria and there proclaimed the Messiah. Without exception, the crowds that heard Philip and saw the miracles he performed attended closely to what he had to say. There were many who had unclean spirits, which came out shrieking loudly. Many others were paralytics or cripples, and these were cured. The rejoicing in that town rose to fever pitch. +

Psalm 66:1-7
R. Let all the earth cry out to God with joy.
(or **Alleluia.***)*
Shout joyfully to God, all you on earth,
    sing praise to the glory of his name;
    proclaim his glorious praise.
Say to God, "How tremendous are your deeds! **R.**
Let all on earth worship and sing praise to you,
    sing praise to your name!"
Come and see the works of God,
    his tremendous deeds among men. **R.**
He has changed the sea into dry land;
    through the river they passed on foot;
    therefore let us rejoice in him.
He rules by his might forever. **R.**

R. Alleluia, alleluia.
You believe in me, Thomas, because you have seen me;
happy those who have not seen me, but still believe! **R.**

† *John 6:35-40*
*This is the will of my Father, that
whoever sees the Son will have eternal life.*

Jesus explained to the crowd:
    "I myself am the bread of life.
    No one who comes to me shall ever be hungry,
    no one who believes in me shall thirst again.
    But as I told you—
    though you have seen me, you still do not believe.
    All that the Father gives me shall come to me;
    no one who comes will I ever reject,
    because it is not to do my own will
    that I have come down from heaven,
    but to do the will of him who sent me.

It is the will of him who sent me
that I should lose nothing of what he has given me;
rather, that I should raise it up on the last day.
Indeed, this is the will of my Father,
that everyone who looks upon the Son
and believes in him
shall have eternal life.
Him I will raise up on the last day." ✛

THURSDAY, MAY 3
STS. PHILIP AND JAMES

† *1 Corinthians 15:1-8*
The Lord appeared to James, then to all the Apostles.

Brothers, I want to remind you of the gospel I preached to you, which you received and in which you stand firm. You are being saved by it at this very moment if you retain it as I preached it to you. Otherwise you have believed in vain. I handed on to you first of all what I myself received, that Christ died for our sins in accord with Scriptures; that he was buried and, in accord with the Scriptures, rose on the third day; that he was seen by Cephas, then by the Twelve. After that he was seen by five hundred brothers at once, most of whom are still alive, although some have fallen asleep. Next he was seen by James; then by all the apostles. Last of all he was seen by me, as one born out of the normal course. ✛

Psalm 19:2-5
R. Their message goes out through all the earth.
(or **Alleluia.***)*
The heavens declare the glory of God,
    and the firmament proclaims his handiwork.
Day pours out the word to day,
    and night to night imparts knowledge. **R.**
Not as a word or a discourse
    while voice is not heard;
Through all the earth their voice resounds,
    and to the ends of the world, their message. **R.**

John 14:6, 9
R. Alleluia, alleluia.
I am the way, the truth, and the life, says the Lord;
Philip, whoever sees me sees the Father. **R.**

✝ *John 14:6-14*
Have I been with you so long and yet you do not know me?

Jesus told Thomas:
"I am the way, and the truth, and the life;
no one comes to the Father but through me.
If you really knew me, you would know my Father also.
From this point on you know him; you have seen him."
"Lord," Philip said to him, "show us the Father and that
will be enough for us." "Philip," Jesus replied, "after I have
been with you all this time, you still do not know me?
"Whoever has seen me has seen the Father.
How can you say, 'Show us the Father'?
Do you not believe that I am in the Father
and the Father is in me?
The words I speak are not spoken of myself;
It is the Father who lives in me accomplishing his works.
Believe me that I am in the Father
and the Father is in me,
or else, believe because of the works I do.
I solemnly assure you,
the man who has faith in me
will do the works I do,
and greater far than these.
Why? Because I go to the Father,
and whatever you ask in my name
I will do
so as to glorify the Father in the Son.
Anything you ask me in my name
I will do." ✚

FRIDAY, MAY 4
EASTER WEEKDAY

† *Acts 9:1-20*
This man is my chosen instrument to bring my name before the gentiles.

Saul, breathing murderous threats against the Lord's disciples, went to the high priest and asked him for letters to the synagogues in Damascus which would empower him to arrest and bring to Jerusalem anyone he might find, man or woman, living according to the new way. As he traveled along and was approaching Damascus, a light from the sky suddenly flashed about him. He fell to the ground and at the same time heard a voice saying, "Saul, Saul, why do you persecute me?" "Who are you, sir?" he asked. The voice answered, "I am Jesus, the one you are persecuting. Get up and go into the city, where you will be told what to do." The men who were traveling with him stood there speechless. They had heard the voice but could see no one. Saul got up from the ground unable to see, even though his eyes were open. They had to take him by the hand and lead him into Damascus. For three days he continued blind, during which time he neither ate nor drank.

There was a disciple in Damascus named Ananias to whom the Lord had appeared in a vision. "Ananias!" he said. "Here I am, Lord," came the answer. The Lord said to him, "Go at once to Straight Street, and at the house of Judas ask for a certain Saul of Tarsus. He is there praying." (Saul saw in a vision a man named Ananias coming to him and placing his hands on him so that he might recover his sight.) But Ananias protested: "Lord, I have heard from many sources about this man and all the harm he has done to your holy people in Jerusalem. He is here now with authorization from the chief priests to arrest any who invoke your name." The Lord said to him: "You must go! This man is the instrument I have chosen to bring my name to the Gentiles and their kings and to the people of Israel. I myself shall indicate to him how much he will have to suffer for my name." With that Ananias left. When he entered the house he laid his hands on Saul and said, "Saul, my brother, I have been sent by the Lord Jesus who appeared to you on the way here, to help you recover your sight and be filled with the Holy Spirit." Immediately something like scales fell from his eyes and he regained his sight. He got up and was baptized, and his strength returned to him after he had taken food.

Saul stayed some time with the disciples in Damascus, and soon began to proclaim in the synagogues that Jesus was the Son of God. ✝

Psalm 117:1-2
**R. Go out to all the world,
and tell the Good News.** *(or* **Alleluia.***)*
Praise the Lord, all you nations;
    glorify him, all you peoples! **R.**
For steadfast is his kindness toward us,
    and the fidelity of the Lord endures forever. **R.**

R. Alleluia, alleluia.
Christ has risen and shines upon us,
whom he has redeemed by his blood. **R.**

† *John 6:52-59*
My flesh is real food and my blood is real drink.

The Jews quarreled among themselves, saying, "How can this man give us his flesh to eat?" Thereupon Jesus said to them:
"Let me solemnly assure you,
if you do not eat the flesh of the Son of Man
and drink his blood,
you have no life in you.
He who feeds on my flesh
and drinks my blood
has life eternal,
and I will raise him up on the last day.
For my flesh is real food
and my blood real drink.
The man who feeds on my flesh
and drinks my blood
remains in me, and I in him.
Just as the Father who has life sent me
and I have life because of the Father,
so the man who feeds on me
will have life because of me.
This is the bread that came down from heaven.

Unlike your ancestors who ate and died nonetheless,
the man who feeds on this bread shall live forever."
He said this in a synagogue instruction at Capernaum. ✙

SATURDAY, MAY 5
Easter Weekday

✝ Acts 9:31-42
*The Church became established and in the
presence of the Holy Spirit grew in numbers.*

Throughout all Judea, Galilee and Samaria the church was
at peace. It was being built up and was making steady progress
in the fear of the Lord; at the same time it enjoyed the
increased consolation of the Holy Spirit.

Once when Peter was making numerous journeys, he went
—among other places—to God's holy people living in Lydda.
There he found a man named Aeneas, a paralytic who had
been bedridden for eight years. Peter said to him, "Aeneas,
Jesus Christ cures you! Get up and make your bed." The man
got up at once. All the inhabitants of Lydda and Sharon, upon
seeing him, were converted to the Lord.

Now in Joppa there was a certain woman convert named
Tabitha (in Greek *Dorcas*, meaning a gazelle). Her life was
marked by constant good deeds and acts of charity. At about
that time she fell ill and died. They washed her body and laid
it out in an upstairs room. Since Lydda was near Joppa, the
disciples who had heard that Peter was there sent two men to
him with the urgent request, "Please come over to us without
delay." Peter set out with them as they asked. Upon his arrival
they took him upstairs to the room. All the widows came to him
in tears and showed him the various garments Dorcas had
made when she was still with them. Peter first made everyone
go outside; then he knelt down and prayed. Turning to the
dead body, he said, "Tabitha, stand up." She opened her eyes,
then looked at Peter and sat up. He gave her his hand and
helped her to her feet. The next thing he did was to call in those
who were believers and the widows to show them that she was
alive. This became known all over Joppa, and because of it,
many came to believe in the Lord. ✙

Psalm 116:12-17

**R. What return can I make to the Lord
for all that he gives to me?** *(or* **Alleluia.***)*

How shall I make a return to the Lord
   for all the good he has done for me?
The cup of salvation I will take up,
   and I will call upon the name of the Lord. **R.**

My vows to the Lord I will pay
   in the presence of all his people.
Precious in the eyes of the Lord
   is the death of his faithful ones. **R.**

O Lord, I am your servant;
   I am your servant, the son of your handmaid;
   you have loosed my bonds.
To you will I offer sacrifice of thanksgiving,
   and I will call upon the name of the Lord. **R.**

R. Alleluia, alleluia.

Nailed to the cross for our sake,
the Lord is now risen from the grave. **R.**

† *John 6:60-69*
To whom shall we go? You have the words of eternal life.

Many of the disciples of Jesus remarked, "This sort of talk is
hard to endure! How can anyone take it seriously?" Jesus was
fully aware that his disciples were murmuring in protest at
what he had said. "Does it shake your faith?" he asked them.
   "What, then, if you were to see the Son of Man
   ascend to where he was before . . . ?
   It is the spirit that gives life;
   the flesh is useless.
   The words I spoke to you
   are spirit and life.
   Yet among you there are some who do not believe."
(Jesus knew from the start, of course, the ones who refused to
believe, and the one who would hand him over.) He went on to
say:
   "This is why I have told you
   that no one can come to me
   unless it is granted him by the Father."

From this time on, many of his disciples broke away and would not remain in his company any longer. Jesus then said to the Twelve, "Do you want to leave me too?" Simon Peter answered him, "Lord, to whom shall we go? You have the words of eternal life. We have come to believe; we are convinced that you are God's holy one." ✝

MAY 6
FOURTH SUNDAY OF EASTER

✝ *Acts 13:14, 43-52*
We now turn to the Gentiles.

Paul and Barnabas continued on from Perga
and reached Antioch in Pisidia.
On the sabbath they entered the synagogue and took their seats.
Many Jews and worshipers who were converts to Judaism
followed Paul and Barnabas, who spoke to them
and urged them to remain faithful to the grace of God.

On the following sabbath almost the whole city gathered
to hear the word of the Lord.
When the Jews saw the crowds, they were filled with jealousy
and with violent abuse contradicted what Paul said.
Both Paul and Barnabas spoke out boldly and said,
"It was necessary that the word of God be spoken to you first,
but since you reject it
and condemn yourselves as unworthy of eternal life,
we now turn to the Gentiles.
For so the Lord has commanded us,
I have made you a light to the Gentiles,
that you may be an instrument of salvation
to the ends of the earth."

The Gentiles were delighted when they heard this
and glorified the word of the Lord.
All who were destined for eternal life came to believe,
and the word of the Lord continued to spread
through the whole region.
The Jews, however, incited the women of prominence who
were worshipers

and the leading men of the city,
stirred up a persecution against Paul and Barnabas,
and expelled them from their territory.
So they shook the dust from their feet in protest against them,
and went to Iconium.
The disciples were filled with joy and the Holy Spirit. ✛

Psalm 100:1-3, 5
R. We are his people, the sheep of his flock.
Sing joyfully to the LORD, all you lands;
serve the LORD with gladness;
come before him with joyful song. **R.**
Know that the LORD is God;
he made us, his we are;
his people, the flock he tends. **R.**
The LORD is good:
his kindness endures forever,
and his faithfulness, to all generations. **R.**

† *Revelation 7:9, 14b-17*
*The Lamb will shepherd them and lead
them to springs of life-giving water.*

I, John, had a vision of a great multitude,
which no one could count,
from every nation, race, people, and tongue.
They stood before the throne and before the Lamb,
wearing white robes and holding palm branches
in their hands.

Then one of the elders said to me,
"These are the ones who have survived
the time of great distress;
they have washed their robes
and made them white in the blood of the Lamb.

"For this reason they stand before God's throne
and worship him day and night in his temple.
The one who sits on the throne will shelter them.
They will not hunger or thirst anymore,
nor will the sun or any heat strike them.
For the Lamb who is in the center of the throne

will shepherd them
and lead them to springs of life-giving water,
and God will wipe away every tear from their
eyes." ✝

John 10:14

R. Alleluia, alleluia.
I am the good shepherd, says the Lord;
I know my sheep, and mine know me. **R.**

✝ *John 10:27-30*
I give my sheep eternal life.

Jesus said:
"My sheep hear my voice;
I know them, and they follow me.
I give them eternal life, and they shall never perish.
No one can take them out of my hand.
My Father, who has given them to me, is greater than all,
and no one can take them out of the Father's hand.
The Father and I are one." ✝

MONDAY, MAY 7
EASTER WEEKDAY

✝ *Acts 11:1-18*
God can give even the gentiles the repentance that leads to eternal life.

The apostles and the brothers heard that Gentiles, too, had accepted the word of God. As a result, when Peter went up to Jerusalem some among the circumcised took issue with him, saying, "You entered the house of uncircumcised men and ate with them." Peter then explained the whole affair to them step by step from the beginning: "I was at prayer in the city of Joppa when, in a trance, I saw a vision. An object like a big canvas came down; it was lowered down to me from the sky by its four corners. As I stared at it I could make out four-legged creatures of the earth, wild beasts and reptiles, and birds of the sky. I listened as a voice said to me, 'Get up, Peter! Slaughter, then eat.' I replied: 'Not for a moment, sir! Nothing unclean or impure has ever entered my mouth!' A second time the voice from the heavens spoke out: 'What God has purified you are not to call unclean.' This happened three times; then the canvas with everything in it was drawn up again into the sky.

"Immediately after that, the three men who had been sent to me from Caesarea came to the house where we were staying. The Spirit instructed me to accompany them without hesitation. These six brothers came along with me, and we entered the man's house. He informed us that he had seen an angel standing in his house and that the angel had said: 'Send someone to Joppa and fetch Simon, known also as Peter. In the light of what he will tell you, you shall be saved, and all your household.' As I began to address them the Holy Spirit came upon them, just as it had upon us at the beginning. Then I remembered what the Lord had said: 'John baptized with water but you will be baptized with the Holy Spirit.' If God was giving them the same gift he gave us when we first believed in the Lord Jesus Christ, who was I to interfere with him?" When they heard this they stopped objecting, and instead began to glorify God in these words: "If this be so, then God has granted life-giving repentance even to the Gentiles." ✛

Psalms 42:2-3; 43:3-4
R. My soul is thirsting for the living God.
(or **Alleluia.***)*
As the hind longs for the running waters,
    so my soul longs for you, O God.
Athirst is my soul for God, the living God.
    When shall I go and behold the face of God? **R.**
Send forth your light and your fidelity;
    they shall lead me on
And bring me to your holy mountain,
    to your dwelling-place. **R.**
Then will I go in to the altar of God,
    the God of my gladness and joy;
Then will I give you thanks upon the harp,
    O God, my God! **R.**

R. Alleluia, alleluia.
Christ now raised from the dead will never die again;
death no longer has power over him. **R.**

† *John 10:1-10*
I am the gate of the sheepfold.

Jesus said:
> "Truly I assure you:
> Whoever does not enter the sheepfold through the gate
> but climbs in some other way
> is a thief and a marauder.
> The one who enters through the gate
> is shepherd of the sheep;
> the keeper opens the gate for him.
> The sheep hear his voice
> as he calls his own by name
> and leads them out.
> When he has brought out [all] those that are his,
> he walks in front of them,
> and the sheep follow him
> because they recognize his voice.
> They will not follow a stranger
> such a one they will flee,
> because they do not recognize a stranger's voice."

Even though Jesus used this figure with them, they did not grasp what he was trying to tell them. He therefore said [to them again]:
> "My solemn word is this:
> I am the sheepgate.
> All who came before me
> were thieves and marauders
> whom the sheep did not heed.

> "I am the gate.
> Whoever enters through me
> will be safe.
> He will go in and out,
> and find pasture.
> The thief comes
> only to steal and slaughter and destroy.
> I came
> that they might have life
> and have it to the full." ✛

TUESDAY, MAY 8
EASTER WEEKDAY

✝ Acts 11:19-26
They preached to the Greeks proclaiming the Lord Jesus.

Those in the community who had been dispersed by the persecution that arose because of Stephen went as far as Phoenicia, Cyprus and Antioch, making the message known to none but Jews. However, some men of Cyprus and Cyrene among them who had come to Antioch began to talk even to the Greeks, announcing the good news of the Lord Jesus to them. The hand of the Lord was with them and a great number of them believed and were converted to the Lord. News of this eventually reached the ears of the church in Jerusalem, resulting in Barnabas' being sent to Antioch. On his arrival he rejoiced to see the evidence of God's favor. He encouraged them all to remain firm in their commitment to the Lord, since he himself was a good man filled with the Holy Spirit and faith. Thereby large numbers were added to the Lord. Then Barnabas went off to Tarsus to look for Saul; once he had found him, he brought him back to Antioch. For a whole year they met with the church and instructed great numbers. It was in Antioch that the disciples were called Christians for the first time. ✛

Psalm 87:1-7
R. All you nations, praise the Lord. *(or* **Alleluia.***)*
His foundation upon the holy mountains
    the Lord loves:
The gates of Zion,
    more than any dwelling of Jacob.
Glorious things are said of you,
    O city of God! **R.**
I tell of Egypt and Babylon
    among those that know the Lord;
Of Philistia, Tyre, Ethiopia:
    "This man was born there."
And of Zion they shall say:
    "One and all were born in her;
And he who has established her
    is the Most High Lord." **R.**

They shall note, when the peoples are enrolled:
"This man was born there."
And all shall sing, in their festive dance:
"My home is within you." **R.**

R. Alleluia, alleluia.
I am the good shepherd, says the Lord;
I know my sheep and mine know me. **R.**

✝ John 10:22-30
My Father and I are one.

It was winter, and the time came for the feast of the Dedication in Jerusalem. Jesus was walking in the temple area, in Solomon's Portico, when the Jews gathered around him and said, "How long are you going to keep us in suspense? If you really are the Messiah, tell us so in plain words." Jesus answered:
"I did tell you, but you do not believe.
The works I do in my Father's name
give witness in my favor,
but you refuse to believe
because you are not my sheep.
My sheep hear my voice.
I know them,
and they follow me.
I give them eternal life,
and they shall never perish.
No one shall snatch them out of my hand.
My Father is greater than all, in what he has given me,
and there is no snatching out of his hand.
The Father and I are one." ✝

WEDNESDAY, MAY 9
Easter Weekday

✝ Acts 12:24—13:5
I want Saul and Barnabas set aside.

The word of the Lord continued to spread and increase.
Barnabas and Saul returned to Jerusalem upon completing the relief mission, taking with them John Mark.

There were in the church at Antioch certain prophets and teachers: Barnabas, Symeon known as Niger, Lucius of Cyrene, Manaen (who had been brought up with Herod the tetrarch), and Saul. On one occasion, while they were engaged in the liturgy of the Lord and were fasting, the Holy Spirit spoke to them: "Set apart Barnabas and Saul for me to do the work for which I have called them." Then, after they had fasted and prayed, they imposed hands on them and sent them off.

These two, sent forth by the Holy Spirit, went down to the port of Seleucia and set sail from there for Cyprus. On their arrival in Salamis they proclaimed the word of God in the Jewish synagogues. +

Psalm 67:2-3, 5-6, 8
R. O God, let all the nations praise you! *(or* **Alleluia.***)*
May God have pity on us and bless us;
may he let his face shine upon us.
So may your way be known upon earth;
among all nations, your salvation. **R.**
May the nations be glad and exult
because you rule the peoples in equity;
the nations on the earth you guide. **R.**
May the peoples praise you, O God;
may all the peoples praise you!
May God bless us,
and may all the ends of the earth fear him! **R.**

R. Alleluia, alleluia.
Christ has risen and makes all things new;
he has shown pity to all mankind. **R.**

† *John 12:44-50*
I the light have come into the world.

Jesus proclaimed aloud:
"Whoever puts faith in me
believes not so much in me
as in him who sent me;
and whoever looks on me
is seeing him who sent me.
I have come to the world as its light,
to keep anyone who believes in me

from remaining in the dark.
If anyone hears my words and does not keep them,
I am not the one to condemn him,
for I did not come to condemn the world
but to save it.
Whoever rejects me and does not accept my words
already has his judge,
namely, the word I have spoken—
It is that which will condemn him on the last day.
For I have not spoken on my own;
no, the Father who sent me
has commanded me
what to say and how to speak.
Since I know that his commandment means eternal life,
whatever I say
is spoken just as he instructed me." ✝

THURSDAY, MAY 10
EASTER WEEKDAY

✝ *Acts 13:13-25*
God has raised up one of David's descendants, Jesus, as Savior.

From Paphos, Paul and his companions put out to sea and sailed to Perga in Pamphylia. There John left them and returned to Jerusalem. They continued to travel on from Perga and came to Antioch in Pisidia. On the sabbath day they entered the synagogue and sat down. After the reading of the law and of the prophets, the leading men of the synagogue sent this message to them: "Brothers, if you have any exhortation to address to the people please speak up."

So Paul arose, motioned to them for silence, and began: "Fellow Israelites and you others who reverence our God, listen to what I have to say! The God of the people Israel once chose our fathers. He made this people great during their sojourn in the land of Egypt, and 'with an outstretched arm' he led them out of it. For forty years 'he put up with them in the desert'; then he destroyed 'seven nations' in the land of Canaan to give them that country as their heritage at the end of some four hundred and fifty years. Later on he set up judges to rule them until the time of the prophet Samuel. When they asked for a king, God gave them Saul son of Kish, of the tribe of Benjamin, who ruled for forty years. Then God removed him and raised up David as their king; on his behalf God testified, 'I have found David son of Jesse to be a man after my own heart who will fulfill my every wish.'

"According to his promise, God has brought forth from this man's descendants Jesus, a savior for Israel. John heralded the coming of Jesus by proclaiming a baptism of repentance to all the people of Israel. As John's career was coming to an end, he would say, 'What you suppose me to be I am not. Rather, look for the one who comes after me. I am not worthy to unfasten the sandals on his feet.'" +

Psalm 89:2-3, 21-22, 25, 27
R. Forever I will sing the goodness of the Lord.
The favors of the Lord I will sing forever;
    through all generations my mouth shall proclaim your
        faithfulness.
For you have said, "My kindness is established forever";
    in heaven you have confirmed your faithfulness. **R.**
I have found David, my servant;
    with my holy oil I have anointed him,
That my hand may be always with him,
    and that my arm may make him strong. **R.**
My faithfulness and my kindness shall be with him,
    and through my name shall his horn be exalted.
"He shall say of me, 'You are my father,
    my God, the Rock, my savior.'" **R.**

R. Alleluia, alleluia.
Christ now raised from the dead will never die again;
death no longer has power over him. **R.**

† *John 13:16-20*
Whoever receives the one I send, receives me.

[After Jesus had washed the feet of the disciples he said:]
"I solemnly assure you,
    no slave is greater than his master;
    no messenger outranks the one who sent him.
Once you know all these things,
    blest will you be if you put them into practice.

What I say is not said of all,
for I know the kind of men I chose.
My purpose here is the fulfillment of Scripture:
'He who partook of bread with me
has raised his heel against me.'
I tell you this now, before it takes place,
so that when it takes place you may believe
that I AM.
I solemnly assure you,
he who accepts anyone I send
accepts me,
and in accepting me
accepts him who sent me." ✝

FRIDAY, MAY 11
EASTER WEEKDAY

✝ Acts 13:26-33
God has fulfilled his promise by raising Jesus from the dead.

[When Paul came to Antioch in Pisidia, he said in the synagogue:] "My brothers, children of the family of Abraham and you others who reverence our God, it was to us that this message of salvation was sent forth. The inhabitants of Jerusalem and their rulers failed to recognize him, and in condemning him they fulfilled the words of the prophets which we read sabbath after sabbath. Even though they found no charge against him which deserved death, they begged Pilate to have him executed. Once they had thus brought about all that had been written of him, they took him down from the tree and laid him in a tomb. Yet God raised him from the dead, and for many days thereafter Jesus appeared to those who had come up with him from Galilee to Jerusalem. These are his witnesses now before the people.

"We ourselves announce to you the good news that what God promised our fathers he has fulfilled for us, their children, in raising up Jesus, according to what is written in the second psalm, 'You are my son; this day I have begotten you.'" ✝

Psalm 2:6-11

R. You are my Son;
this day have I begotten you. *(or* **Alleluia.***)*

"I myself have set up my king
on Zion, my holy mountain."
I will proclaim the decree of the Lord:
The Lord said to me, "You are my son;
this day I have begotten you." **R.**
"Ask of me and I will give you
the nations for an inheritance
and the ends of the earth for your possession.
You shall rule them with an iron rod;
you shall shatter them like an earthen dish." **R.**
And now, O kings, give heed;
take warning, you rulers of the earth.
Serve the Lord with fear, and rejoice before him;
with trembling pay homage to him. **R.**

R. Alleluia, alleluia.
Christ had to suffer and to rise from the dead,
and so to enter into his glory. **R.**

✝ *John 14:1-6*
I am the way, the truth, and the life.

Jesus said to his disciples,
"Do not let your hearts be troubled.
Have faith in God
and faith in me.
In my Father's house there are many dwelling places;
otherwise, how could I have told you
that I was going to prepare a place for you?
I am indeed going to prepare a place for you,
and then I shall come back to take you with me,
that where I am you also may be.
You know the way that leads where I go."
"Lord," said Thomas, "we do not know where you are going.
How can we know the way?" Jesus told him:
"I am the way, and the truth, and the life;
no one comes to the Father but through me." ✝

SATURDAY, MAY 12
Easter Weekday, Sts. Nereus & Achilleus, St. Pancras

† Acts 13:44-52
Now he must turn to the gentiles.

On another sabbath, almost the entire city gathered to hear the word of God. When the Jews saw the crowds, they became very jealous and countered with violent abuse whatever Paul said. Paul and Barnabas spoke out fearlessly, nonetheless: "The word of God has to be declared to you first of all; but since you reject it and thus convict yourselves as unworthy of everlasting life, we now turn to the Gentiles. For thus were we instructed by the Lord: 'I have made you a light to the nations, a means of salvation to the ends of the earth.'" The Gentiles were delighted when they heard this and responded to the word of the Lord with praise. All who were destined for life everlasting believed in it. Thus the word of the Lord was carried throughout that area.

But some of the Jews stirred up their influential women sympathizers and the leading men of the town, and in that way got a persecution started against Paul and Barnabas. The Jews finally expelled them from their territory. So the two shook the dust from their feet in protest and went on to Iconium. The disciples could not but be filled with joy and the Holy Spirit. ✢

Psalm 98:1-4
**R. All the ends of the earth have seen
the saving power of God.** *(or* **Alleluia.***)*
Sing to the Lord a new song,
for he has done wondrous deeds;
His right hand has won victory for him,
his holy arm. **R.**
The Lord has made his salvation known:
in the sight of the nations he has revealed his justice.
He has remembered his kindness and his faithfulness
toward the house of Israel. **R.**
All the ends of the earth have seen
the salvation by our God.
Sing joyfully to the Lord, all you lands;

break into song; sing praise. **R.**

R. Alleluia, alleluia.
We know that Christ is truly risen from the dead;
victorious king, deal kindly with us. **R.**

✝ *John 14:7-14*
He who sees me, also sees the Father.

Jesus said to his disciples,
    "If you really knew me, you would know my Father also.
From this point on you know him; you have seen him."
    "Lord," Philip said to him, "show us the Father and that
will be enough for us." "Philip," Jesus replied, "after I have
been with you all this time, you still do not know me?
    "Whoever has seen me has seen the Father.
How can you say, 'Show us the Father'?
Do you not believe that I am in the Father
and the Father is in me?
The words I speak are not spoken of myself;
it is the Father who lives in me accomplishing his works.
Believe me that I am in the Father
and the Father is in me, or else, believe because of the
    works I do.
I solemnly assure you,
the man who has faith in me
will do the works I do,
and greater far than these.
Why? Because I go to the Father,
and whatever you ask in my name
I will do,
so as to glorify the Father in the Son.
Anything you ask me in my name
I will do." ✛

MAY 13
FIFTH SUNDAY OF EASTER

† Acts 14:21-27
They called the Church together and
reported what God had done with them.

After Paul and Barnabas had proclaimed the good news
  to that city
  and made a considerable number of disciples,
    they returned to Lystra and to Iconium and to Antioch.
They strengthened the spirits of the disciples
  and exhorted them to persevere in the faith, saying,
    "It is necessary for us to undergo many hardships
    to enter the kingdom of God."
They appointed elders for them in each church and,
  with prayer and fasting, commended them to the Lord
  in whom they had put their faith.
Then they traveled through Pisidia and reached Pamphylia.
After proclaiming the word at Perga they went down to
        Attalia.
From there they sailed to Antioch,
  where they had been commended to the grace of God
  for the work they had now accomplished.
And when they arrived, they called the church together
  and reported what God had done with them
  and how he had opened the door of faith to the Gentiles. ✛

Psalm 145:8-13
**R. I will praise your name forever,
  my king and my God. (or Alleluia.)**
The LORD is gracious and merciful,
  slow to anger and of great kindness.
The LORD is good to all
  and compassionate toward all his works. **R.**
Let all your works give you thanks, O LORD,
  and let your faithful ones bless you.
Let them discourse of the glory of your kingdom
  and speak of your might. **R.**
Let them make known your might to the children of Adam,
  and the glorious splendor of your kingdom.

Your kingdom is a kingdom for all ages,
and your dominion endures through all generations. **R.**

✝ *Revelation 21:1-5a*
God will wipe every tear from their eyes.

Then I, John, saw a new heaven and a new earth.
The former heaven and the former earth had passed away,
and the sea was no more.
I also saw the holy city, a new Jerusalem,
coming down out of heaven from God,
prepared as a bride adorned for her husband.
I heard a loud voice from the throne saying,
"Behold, God's dwelling is with the human race.
He will dwell with them and they will be his people
and God himself will always be with them as their God.
He will wipe every tear from their eyes,
and there shall be no more death or mourning, wailing or
pain,
for the old order has passed away."

The One who sat on the throne said,
"Behold, I make all things new." ✝

John 13:34
R. Alleluia, alleluia.
I give you a new commandment, says the Lord:
love one another as I have loved you. **R.**

✝ *John 13:31-33a, 34-35*
I give you a new commandment: love one another.

When Judas had left them, Jesus said,
"Now is the Son of Man glorified, and God is glorified in
him.
If God is glorified in him,
God will also glorify him in himself,
and God will glorify him at once.
My children, I will be with you only a little while longer.
I give you a new commandment: love one another.
As I have loved you, so you also should love one another.
This is how all will know that you are my disciples,
if you have love for one another." ✝

MONDAY, MAY 14
St. Matthias

† Acts 1:15-17, 20-26
The lot fell to Matthias and he was numbered with the eleven Apostles.

In those days, Peter stood up in the center of the brothers; there must have been a hundred and twenty gathered together. "Brothers," he said, "the saying in Scripture uttered long ago by the Holy Spirit through the mouth of David was destined to be fulfilled in Judas, the one that guided those who arrested Jesus. He was one of our number and he had been given a share in this ministry of ours.

"It is written in the Book of Psalms,
'Let his encampment be desolate.
May no one dwell on it.'
And again,
'May another take his office.'
It is entirely fitting, therefore, that one of those who was of our company while the Lord Jesus moved among us, from the baptism of John until the day he was taken up from us, should be named as witness with us to his resurrection." At that they nominated two, Joseph (called Barsabbas, also known as Justus) and Matthias. Then they prayed: "O Lord, you read the hearts of men. Make known to us which of these two you choose for this apostolic ministry, replacing Judas, who deserted the cause and went the way he was destined to go." They then drew lots between the two men. The choice fell to Matthias, who was added to the eleven apostles. ✛

Psalm 113:1-8
**R. The Lord will give him a seat
with the leaders of his people.**
Praise, you servants of the Lord,
  praise the name of the Lord.
Blessed be the name of the Lord
  both now and forever. **R.**
From the rising to the setting of the sun
  is the name of the Lord to be praised.
High above all nations is the Lord;
  above the heavens is his glory. **R**

Who is like the Lord, our God, who is enthroned on high
and looks upon the heavens and the earth below? **R.**
He raises up the lowly from the dust;
from the dunghill he lifts up the poor
To seat them with princes,
with the princes of his own people. **R.**

John 15:16
R. Alleluia, alleluia.
I have chosen you from the world, says the Lord.
to go out and bear fruit that will last. **R.**

✝ *John 15:9-17*
I shall no longer call you servants; I call you my friends.

Jesus said to his disciples:
"As the Father has loved me,
so I have loved you.
Live on in my love.
You will live in my love
if you keep my commandments,
even as I have kept my Father's commandments
and live in his love.
All this I tell you
that my joy may be yours
and your joy may be complete.
This is my commandment:
love one another
as I have loved you.
There is no greater love than this:
to lay down one's life for one's friends.
You are my friends
if you do what I command you.
I no longer speak of you as slaves,
for a slave does not know what his master is about.
Instead, I call you friends,
since I have made known to you all
that I heard from my Father.
It was not you who chose me,
it was I who chose you
to go forth and bear fruit.

Your fruit must endure,
so that all you ask the Father in my name
he will give you.
The command I give you is this,
that you love one another." ✛

TUESDAY, MAY 15
EASTER WEEKDAY

† Acts 14:19-28
They assembled the Church and gave an
account of all that God had done with them.

In those days some Jews from Antioch and Iconium arrived
and won the people over. They stoned Paul and dragged him
out of the town, leaving him there for dead. His disciples
quickly formed a circle about him, and before long he got up
and went back into the town. The next day he left with
Barnabas for Derbe. After they had proclaimed the good news
in that town and made numerous disciples, they retraced their
steps to Lystra and Iconium first, then to Antioch. They gave
their disciples reassurances, and encouraged them to persevere in the faith with this instruction: "We must undergo
many trials if we are to enter into the reign of God." In each
church they installed elders and, with prayer and fasting,
commended them to the Lord in whom they had put their faith.

Then they passed through Pisidia and came to Pamphylia.
After preaching the message in Perga, they went down to
Attalia. From there they sailed back to Antioch, where they had
first been commended to the favor of God for the task they had
now completed. On their arrival, they called the congregation
together and related all that God had helped them accomplish,
and how he had opened the door of faith to the Gentiles. Then
they spent some time there with the disciples. ✛

Psalm 145:10-13, 21
R. Your friends tell the glory of your kingship, Lord.
Let all your works give you thanks, O Lord,
    and let your faithful ones bless you.
Let them discourse of the glory of your kingdom
    and speak of your might. **R.**

Making known to men your might
    and the glorious splendor of your kingdom.
Your kingdom is a kingdom for all ages,
    and your dominion endures through all generations. **R.**
May my mouth speak the praise of the Lord,
    and may all flesh bless his holy name forever and ever. **R.**

R. Alleluia, alleluia.
I am the good shepherd, says the Lord;
I know my sheep and mine know me. **R.**

† *John 14:27-31*
My peace I give to you

Jesus said to his disciples:
    "'Peace' is my farewell to you,
    my peace is my gift to you;
    I do not give it to you as the world gives peace.
    Do not be distressed or fearful.
    You have heard me say,
    'I go away for a while and I come back to you.'
    If you truly loved me
    you would rejoice to have me go to the Father,
    for the Father is greater than I.
    I tell you this now, before it takes place,
    so that when it takes place you may believe.
    I shall not go on speaking to you longer;
    the Prince of this world is at hand.
    He has no hold on me,
    but the world must know that I love the Father
    and do as the Father has commanded." ✛

WEDNESDAY, MAY 16
EASTER WEEKDAY

† *Acts 15:1-6*
They arranged to go to the apostles and elders
in Jerusalem and consider the problem with them.

Some men came down to Antioch from Judea and began to teach the brothers: "Unless you are circumcised according to Mosaic practice, you cannot be saved." This created dissension and much controversy between them and Paul and Barnabas.

Finally it was decided that Paul, Barnabas, and some others should go up to see the apostles and elders in Jerusalem about this question.

The church saw them off and they made their way through Phoenicia and Samaria, telling everyone about the conversion of the Gentiles as they went. Their story caused great joy among the brothers. When they arrived in Jerusalem they were welcomed by that church, as well as by the apostles and the elders, to whom they reported all that God had helped them accomplish. Some of the converted Pharisees then got up and demanded that such Gentiles be circumcised and told to keep the Mosaic law.

The apostles and the elders accordingly convened to look into the matter. ✛

Psalm 122:1-5
R. I rejoiced when I heard them say:
   let us go to the house of the Lord. *(or* **Alleluia.***)*
I rejoiced because they said to me,
   "We will go up to the house of the Lord."
And now we have set foot
   within your gates, O Jerusalem. **R.**
Jerusalem, built as a city
   with compact unity.
To it the tribes go up,
   the tribes of the Lord. **R.**
According to the decree for Israel,
   to give thanks to the name of the Lord.
In it are set up judgment seats,
   seats for the house of David. **R.**

R. Alleluia, alleluia.
Christ has risen and shines upon us,
whom he has redeemed by his blood. **R.**

† John 15:1-8
Whoever remains in me and I in him, this man bears much fruit.

Jesus said to his disciples:
   "I am the true vine
   and my Father is the vinegrower.
   He prunes away

every barren branch,
but the fruitful ones
he trims clean
to increase their yield.
You are clean already,
thanks to the word I have spoken to you.
Live on in me, as I do in you.
No more than a branch can bear fruit of itself
apart from the vine,
can you bear fruit
apart from me.
I am the vine, you are the branches.
He who lives in me and I in him,
will produce abundantly,
for apart from me you can do nothing.
A man who does not live in me
is like a withered, rejected branch,
picked up to be thrown in the fire and burnt.
If you live in me,
and my words stay part of you,
you may ask what you will—
it will be done for you.
My Father has been glorified
in your bearing much fruit
and becoming my disciples." ✝

THURSDAY, MAY 17
EASTER WEEKDAY

✝ Acts 15:7-21
*I judge that we should not make things more
difficult for those gentiles who have turned to God.*

After much discussion, Peter took the floor and said to the apostles and the elders: "Brothers, you know well enough that from the early days God selected me from your number to be the one from whose lips the Gentiles would hear the message of the gospel and believe. God, who reads the hearts of men, showed his approval by granting the Holy Spirit to them just as he did to us. He made no distinction between them and us, but purified their hearts by means of faith also. Why, then, do you put God to the test by trying to place on the shoulders of these converts a yoke which neither we nor our fathers were able to bear? Our belief is rather that we are saved by the favor of the Lord Jesus and so are they." At that the whole assembly fell silent. They listened to Barnabas and Paul as the two described all the signs and wonders God had worked among the Gentiles through them.

When they concluded their presentation, James spoke up: "Brothers, listen to me. Symeon has told you how God first concerned himself with taking from among the Gentiles a people to bear his name. The words of the prophets agree with this, where it says in Scripture, 'Hereafter I will return and rebuild the fallen hut of David: from its ruins I will rebuild it and set it up again, so that all the rest of mankind and all the nations that bear my name may seek out the Lord. Thus says the Lord who accomplishes these things known to him from of old.' It is my judgment, therefore, that we ought not to cause God's Gentile converts any difficulties. We should merely write to them to abstain from anything contaminated by idols, from illicit sexual union, from the meat of strangled animals, and from eating blood. After all, for generations now Moses has been proclaimed in every town and has been read aloud in the synagogues on every sabbath." ✝

Psalm 96:1-3, 10
**R. Proclaim his marvelous deeds
to all the nations.**
Sing to the Lord a new song;
    sing to the Lord, all you lands.
    Sing to the Lord; bless his name. **R.**
Announce his salvation, day after day.
    Tell his glory among the nations;
    among all peoples, his wondrous deeds. **R.**
Say among the nations: The Lord is king.
    He has made the world firm, not to be moved;
    he governs the peoples with equity. **R.**

R. Alleluia, alleluia.
Christ is risen, and makes all things new;
he has shown pity to all mankind. **R.**

✝ John 15:9-11

Remain in my love that your joy may be increased.

Jesus said to his disciples:
"As the Father has loved me,
so I have loved you.
Live on in my love.
You will live in my love
if you keep my commandments,
even as I have kept my Father's commandments,
and live in his love.
All this I tell you
that my joy may be yours
and your joy may be complete." ✛

FRIDAY, MAY 18

EASTER WEEKDAY, POPE JOHN I

✝ Acts 15:22-31

*It has been decided by the Holy Spirit and
ourselves not to burden you beyond what is essential.*

It was resolved by the apostles and elders, in agreement with the whole Jerusalem church, that representatives be chosen from among their number and sent to Antioch along with Paul and Barnabas. Those chosen were leading men of the community, Judas, known as Barsabbas, and Silas. They were to deliver this letter:

"The apostles and the elders, your brothers, send greetings to the brothers of Gentile origin in Antioch, Syria and Cilicia. We have heard that some of our number without any instructions from us have upset you with their discussions and disturbed your peace of mind. Therefore we have unanimously resolved to choose representatives and send them to you, along with our beloved Barnabas and Paul, who have dedicated themselves to the cause of our Lord Jesus Christ. Those whom we are sending you are Judas and Silas, who will convey this message by word of mouth: 'It is the decision of the Holy Spirit, and ours too, not to lay on you any burden beyond that which is strictly necessary, namely, to abstain from meat sacrificed to idols, from blood, from the meat of strangled animals, and from illicit sexual union. You will be well advised to avoid these things. Farewell.'"

Thus were the representatives sent on their way to Antioch; and upon their arrival there they called the assembly together to deliver the letter. When it was read there was great delight at the encouragement it gave. ✛

Psalm 57:8-12
R. I will praise you among the nations, O Lord.
(or **Alleluia.***)*
My heart is steadfast, O God; my heart is steadfast;
    I will sing and chant praise.
Awake, O my soul; awake, lyre and harp!
    I will wake the dawn. **R.**
I will give thanks to you among the peoples, O Lord,
    I will chant your praise among the nations.
Be exalted above the heavens, O God;
    above all the earth be your glory! **R.**

R. Alleluia, alleluia.
I am the good shepherd, says the Lord;
I know my sheep and mine know me. **R.**

† *John 15:12-17*
This I command you, that you love one another.

Jesus said to his disciples,
    'This is my commandment:
    love one another
    as I have loved you.
    There is no greater love than this:
    to lay down one's life for one's friends.
    You are my friends
    if you do what I command you.
    I no longer speak of you as slaves,
    for a slave does not know what his master is about.
    Instead I call you friends,
    since I have made known to you all
        that I heard from my Father.
    It was not you who chose me,
    it was I who chose you
    to go forth and bear fruit.
    Your fruit must endure,

so that all you ask the Father in my name
he will give you.
The command I give you is this,
that you love one another." ✛

SATURDAY, MAY 19
EASTER WEEKDAY

✝ Acts 16:1-10
Come to Macedonia and help us.

Paul arrived at Derbe; then he came to Lystra, where there
was a disciple named Timothy, whose mother was a Jew and
a believer, and whose father was a Greek. Since the brothers
in Lystra and Iconium spoke highly of him, Paul was anxious
to have him come along on the journey. Paul had him circumcised because of the Jews of that region, for they all knew that
it was only his father who was Greek. As they made their way
from town to town, they transmitted to the people for obser-
vance the decisions which the apostles and elders had made in
Jerusalem.

Through all this, the congregations grew stronger in faith
and daily increased in numbers.

They next traveled through Phrygia and Galatian territory because they had been prevented by the Holy Spirit from
preaching the message in the province of Asia. When they
came to Mysia they tried to go on into Bithynia, but again the
Spirit of Jesus would not allow them. Crossing through Mysia
instead, they came down to Troas. There one night Paul had
a vision. A man of Macedonia stood before him and invited
him, "Come over to Macedonia and help us."

After this vision, we immediately made efforts to get across
to Macedonia, concluding that God had summoned us to
proclaim the good news there. ✛

Psalm 100:1-3, 5
R. Let all the earth cry out to God with joy.
(or Alleluia.)
Sing joyfully to the Lord, all you lands;
    serve the Lord with gladness;
    come before him with joyful song. **R.**
Know that the Lord is God;

he made us, his we are;
his people, the flock he tends. **R.**
The Lord is good:
his kindness endures forever,
and his faithfulness, to all generations. **R.**

R. Alleluia, alleluia.
I am the good shepherd, says the Lord;
I know my sheep and mine know me. **R.**

† *John 15:18-21*
You do not belong to the world because I have chosen you out of it.

Jesus said to his disciples:
"If you find that the world hates you,
know it has hated me before you.
If you belonged to the world,
it would love you as its own;
the reason it hates you
is that you do not belong to the world.
But I chose you out of the world.
Remember what I told you:
no slave is greater than his master.
They will harry you
as they harried me.
They will respect your words
as much as they respected mine.
All this they will do to you because of my name,
for they know nothing of him who sent me." **✝**

MAY 20
Sixth Sunday of Easter

(If the Ascension is celebrated on May 27, the following Second Reading,
Alleluia verse, and Gospel may be used today: Revelation 22:12-14, 16-17, 20
• cf. John 14:18 • John 17:20-26.)

† *Acts 15:1-2, 22-29*
*It is the decision of the Holy Spirit and of us not
to place on you any burden beyond these necessities.*

Some who had come down from Judea were instructing the
brothers,
"Unless you are circumcised according to the Mosaic practice,

you cannot be saved."
Because there arose no little dissension and debate
    by Paul and Barnabas with them,
    it was decided that Paul, Barnabas, and some of the others
    should go up to Jerusalem to the apostles and elders
    about this question.

The apostles and elders, in agreement with the whole church,
    decided to choose representatives
    and to send them to Antioch with Paul and Barnabas.
The ones chosen were Judas, who was called Barsabbas,
    and Silas, leaders among the brothers.
This is the letter delivered by them:

"The apostles and the elders, your brothers,
    to the brothers in Antioch, Syria, and Cilicia
    of Gentile origin: greetings.
Since we have heard that some of our number
    who went out without any mandate from us
    have upset you with their teachings
    and disturbed your peace of mind,
    we have with one accord decided to choose representatives
    and to send them to you along with our beloved Barnabas
        and Paul,
    who have dedicated their lives to the name of our Lord Jesus
        Christ.
So we are sending Judas and Silas
    who will also convey this same message by word of mouth:
    'It is the decision of the Holy Spirit and of us
    not to place on you any burden beyond these necessities,
    namely, to abstain from meat sacrificed to idols,
    from blood, from meats of strangled animals,
    and from unlawful marriage.
If you keep free of these,
    you will be doing what is right. Farewell.'" ✛

Psalm 67:2-3, 5, 6, 8
R. O God, let all the nations praise you! *(or* **Alleluia.***)*
May God have pity on us and bless us;
    may he let his face shine upon us.
So may your way be known upon earth;

among all nations, your salvation. **R.**
May the nations be glad and exult
  because you rule the peoples in equity;
  the nations on the earth you guide. **R.**
May the peoples praise you, O God;
  may all the peoples praise you!
May God bless us,
  and may all the ends of the earth fear him! **R.**

† *Revelation 21:10-14, 22-23*
The angel showed me the holy city coming down out of heaven.

The angel took me in spirit to a great, high mountain
  and showed me the holy city Jerusalem
  coming down out of heaven from God.
It gleamed with the splendor of God.
Its radiance was like that of a precious stone,
  like jasper, clear as crystal.
It had a massive, high wall,
  with twelve gates where twelve angels were stationed
  and on which names were inscribed,
  the names of the twelve tribes of the Israelites.
There were three gates facing east,
  three north, three south, and three west.
The wall of the city had twelve courses of stones as its
    foundation,
  on which were inscribed the twelve names
  of the twelve apostles of the Lamb.

I saw no temple in the city
  for its temple is the Lord God almighty and the Lamb.
The city had no need of sun or moon to shine on it,
  for the glory of God gave it light,
  and its lamp was the Lamb. ✢

John 14:23
R. Alleluia, alleluia.
Whoever loves me will keep my word, says the Lord,
and my Father will love him and we will come to him. **R.**

✝ *John 14:23-29*

The Holy Spirit will teach you everything
and remind you of all that I told you.

J esus said to his disciples:
"Whoever loves me will keep my word,
and my Father will love him,
and we will come to him and make our dwelling with him.
Whoever does not love me does not keep my words;
yet the word you hear is not mine
but that of the Father who sent me.

"I have told you this while I am with you.
The Advocate, the Holy Spirit,
whom the Father will send in my name,
will teach you everything
and remind you of all that I told you.
Peace I leave with you; my peace I give to you.
Not as the world gives do I give it to you.
Do not let your hearts be troubled or afraid.
You heard me tell you,
'I am going away and I will come back to you.'
If you loved me,
you would rejoice that I am going to the Father;
for the Father is greater than I.
And now I have told you this before it happens,
so that when it happens you may believe." ✛

MONDAY, MAY 21
EASTER WEEKDAY

✝ *Acts 16:11-15*
The Lord opened her heart to accept those things which Paul taught.

W e put out to sea from Troas and set a course straight for
Samothrace, and the next day on to Neapolis; from there we
went to Philippi, a leading city in the district of Macedonia and
a Roman colony. We spent some time in that city. Once, on the
sabbath, we went outside the city gate to the bank of the river,
where we thought there would be a place of prayer. We sat down
and spoke to the women who were gathered there. One who
listened was a woman named Lydia, a dealer in purple goods

from the town of Thyatira. She already reverenced God, and the Lord opened her heart to accept what Paul was saying. After she and her household had been baptized, she extended us an invitation: "If you are convinced that I believe in the Lord, come and stay at my house." She managed to prevail on us. ✛

Psalm 149:1-6, 9
R. The Lord takes delight in his people. *(or* **Alleluia.***)*
Sing to the Lord a new song
    of praise in the assembly of the faithful.
Let Israel be glad in their maker,
    let the children of Zion rejoice in their king. **R.**
Let them praise his name in the festive dance,
    let them sing praise to him with timbrel and harp.
For the Lord loves his people,
    and he adorns the lowly with victory. **R.**
Let the faithful exult in glory;
    let them sing for joy upon their couches.
Let the high praises of God be in their throats.
    This is the glory of all his faithful. Alleluia. **R.**

R. Alleluia, alleluia.
If then you have been raised with Christ,
    seek the things that are above,
where Christ is seated at the right hand of God. **R.**

† *John 15:26—16:4*
The Spirit of truth will bear witness to me.

Jesus said to his disciples:
    "When the Paraclete comes,
    the Spirit of truth who comes from the Father—
    and whom I myself will send from the Father—
    he will bear witness on my behalf.
    You must bear witness as well,
    for you have been with me from the beginning.
    I have told you all this
    to keep your faith from being shaken.
    Not only will they expel you from synagogues;
    a time will come
    when anyone who puts you to death
    will claim to be serving God!

All this they will do [to you]
because they know neither the Father nor me.
But I have told you these things
that when their hour comes
you may remember my telling you of them." ✛

TUESDAY, MAY 22
EASTER WEEKDAY

† Acts 16:22-34
Believe in the Lord Jesus, and you will be saved, and your household too.

The crowd [of Philippians] joined in the attack on Paul and Silas, and the magistrates stripped them and ordered them to be flogged. After receiving many lashes they were thrown into prison, and the jailer was given instructions to guard them well. Upon receipt of these instructions he put them in maximum security, going so far as to chain their feet to a stake.

About midnight, while Paul and Silas were praying and singing hymns to God as their fellow prisoners listened, a severe earthquake suddenly shook the place, rocking the prison to its foundations. Immediately all the doors flew open and everyone's chains were pulled loose. The jailer woke up to see the prison gates wide open. Thinking that the prisoners had escaped, he drew his sword to kill himself; but Paul shouted to him, "Do not harm yourself! We are all still here." The jailer called for a light, then rushed in and fell trembling at the feet of Paul and Silas. After a brief interval he led them out and said, "Men, what must I do to be saved?" Their answer was, "Believe in the Lord Jesus and you will be saved, and all your household." They proceeded to announce the word of God to him and to everyone in his house. At that late hour of the night he took them in and bathed their wounds; then he and his whole household were baptized. He led them up into his house, spread a table before them, and joyfully celebrated with his whole family his newfound faith in God. ✛

Psalm 138:1-3, 7-8
R. Your right hand has saved me, O Lord.
I will give thanks to you, O Lord, with all my heart,
　　[for you have heard the words of my mouth;]
In the presence of the angels I will sing your praise;

I will worship at your holy temple,
and give thanks to your name. **R.**
Because of your kindness and your truth,
you have made great above all things
your name and your promise.
When I called, you answered me;
you built up strength within me. **R.**
Your right hand saves me.
The Lord will complete what he has done for me;
Your kindness, O Lord, endures forever;
forsake not the work of your hands. **R.**

R. Alleluia, alleluia.
I am the good shepherd, says the Lord;
I know my sheep and mine know me. **R.**

† John 16:5-11

Unless I go away, the Advocate will not come to you.

Jesus said to his disciples,
"Now that I go back to him who sent me,
not one of you asks me, 'Where are you going?'
Because I have had all this to say to you,
you are overcome with grief.
Yet I tell you the sober truth:
It is much better for you that I go.
If I fail to go,
the Paraclete will never come to you,
whereas if I go,
I will send him to you.
When he comes,
he will prove the world wrong
about sin,
about justice,
about condemnation.
About sin—
In that they refuse to believe in me;
about justice—
from the fact that I go to the Father
and you can see me no more;
about condemnation—
for the prince of this world has been condemned." **✚**

WEDNESDAY, MAY 23
EASTER WEEKDAY

✝ *Acts 17:15, 22—18:1*
The God I proclaim to you, you already worship without knowing it.

Paul was taken as far as Athens by an escort, who then returned with instructions for Silas and Timothy to join him as soon as possible.

Then Paul stood up in the Areopagus and delivered this address: "Men of Athens, I note that in every respect you are scrupulously religious. As I walked around looking at your shrines, I even discovered an altar inscribed, 'To a God Unknown.' Now, what you are thus worshiping in ignorance I intend to make known to you. For the God who made the world and 'all that is in it,' the Lord of heaven and earth, does not dwell in sanctuaries made by human hands; no more does he receive man's service as if he were in need of it. Rather, it is he 'who gives' to all life and 'breath' and everything else. From one stock he made every nation of mankind to dwell on the face of the earth. It is he who set limits to their epochs and 'fixed the boundaries' of their regions. They were to seek God, yes, to grope for him and perhaps eventually to find him—though he is not really far from any one of us. 'In him we live and move and have our being,' as some of your own poets have put it, 'for we too are his offspring.' If we are in fact God's offspring, we ought not to think of divinity as something like a statue of gold or silver or stone, a product of man's genius and his art. God may well have overlooked bygone periods when men did not know him; but now he calls on all men everywhere to reform their lives. He has set the day on which he is going to 'judge the world with justice' through a man he has appointed — one whom he has endorsed in the sight of all by raising him from the dead."

When they heard about the raising of the dead, some sneered, while others said, "We must hear you on this topic some other time." At that point, Paul left them. A few did join him, however, to become believers. Among these were Dionysius, a member of the court of the Areopagus, a woman named Damaris, and a few others.

After that, Paul left Athens and went to Corinth. ✝

Psalm 148:1-2, 11-14

R. Heaven and earth are filled with your glory.
(or **Alleluia.***)*

Praise the Lord from the heavens,
    praise him in the heights;
Praise him, all you his angels,
    praise him, all you his hosts. **R.**
Let the kings of the earth and all peoples,
    the princes and all the judges of the earth,
Young men too, and maidens,
    old men and boys, **R.**
Praise the name of the Lord,
    for his name alone is exalted;
His majesty is above earth and heaven. **R.**
He has lifted up the horn of his people;
    be this his praise from all his faithful ones,
From the children of Israel, the people close to him.
    Alleluia. **R.**

R. Alleluia, alleluia.
I am the good shepherd, says the Lord;
I know my sheep and mine know me. **R.**

† *John 16:12-15*

The spirit of truth will lead you to the complete truth.

Jesus said to his disciples,
    "I have much more to tell you,
    but you cannot bear it now.
    When he comes, however,
    being the Spirit of truth
    he will guide you to all truth.
    He will not speak on his own,
    but will speak only what he hears,
    and will announce to you the things to come.
    In doing this he will give glory to me,
    because he will have received from me
    what he will announce to you.
    All that the Father has belongs to me.
    That is why I said that what he will announce to you
    he will have from me." ✛

THURSDAY, MAY 24
THE ASCENSION OF THE LORD

(If Ascension is celebrated on May 27, the readings today are:
Acts 18:1-8 • Psalm 98:1-4 • John 16:16-20.)

✝ *Acts 1:1-11*

As the Apostles were looking on, Jesus was taken up.

In the first book, Theophilus,
   I dealt with all that Jesus did and taught
   until the day he was taken up,
   after giving instructions through the Holy Spirit
   to the apostles whom he had chosen.
He presented himself alive to them
   by many proofs after he had suffered,
   appearing to them during forty days
   and speaking about the kingdom of God.
While meeting with them,
   he enjoined them not to depart from Jerusalem,
   but to wait for "the promise of the Father
   about which you have heard me speak;
   for John baptized with water,
   but in a few days you will be baptized with the Holy Spirit."

When they had gathered together they asked him,
   "Lord, are you at this time going to restore the kingdom to
      Israel?"
He answered them, "It is not for you to know the times or seasons
that the Father has established by his own authority.
But you will receive power when the Holy Spirit comes upon you,
   and you will be my witnesses in Jerusalem,
   throughout Judea and Samaria,
   and to the ends of the earth."
When he had said this, as they were looking on,
   he was lifted up, and a cloud took him from their sight.
While they were looking intently at the sky as he was going,
   suddenly two men dressed in white garments stood beside
      them.
They said, "Men of Galilee,
   why are you standing there looking at the sky?
This Jesus who has been taken up from you into heaven
   will return in the same way as you have seen him going into
      heaven." ✝

Psalm 47:2-3, 6-9

R. God mounts his throne to shouts of joy:
a blare of trumpets for the Lord.

All you peoples, clap your hands,
  shout to God with cries of gladness,
For the LORD, the Most High, the awesome,
  is the great king over all the earth. **R.**
God mounts his throne amid shouts of joy;
  the LORD, amid trumpet blasts.
Sing praise to God, sing praise;
  sing praise to our king, sing praise. **R.**
For king of all the earth is God;
  sing hymns of praise.
God reigns over the nations,
  God sits upon his holy throne. **R.**

† *Ephesians 1:17-23* *(or Hebrews 9:24-28; 10:19-23)*
Christ has entered into heaven itself.

Brothers and sisters:
May the God of our Lord Jesus Christ, the Father of glory,
  give you a Spirit of wisdom and revelation
  resulting in knowledge of him.
May the eyes of your hearts be enlightened,
  that you may know what is the hope that belongs to his call,
  what are the riches of glory
  in his inheritance among the holy ones,
  and what is the surpassing greatness of his power
  for us who believe,
  in accord with the exercise of his great might:
  which he worked in Christ,
  raising him from the dead
  and seating him at his right hand in the heavens,
  far above every principality, authority,
    power, and dominion,
  and every name that is named
  not only in this age but also in the one to come.
And he put all things beneath his feet
  and gave him as head over all things to the church,
  which is his body,
  the fullness of the one who fills all things in every way. **✛**

Matthew 28:19a, 20b

R. Alleluia, alleluia.

Go and teach all nations, says the Lord;
I am with you always, until the end of the world. **R.**

✝ *Luke 24:46-53*
As he blessed them, he was taken up to heaven.

Jesus said to his disciples:
　　"Thus it is written that the Christ would suffer
　　and rise from the dead on the third day
　　and that repentance, for the forgiveness of sins,
　　would be preached in his name
　　to all the nations, beginning from Jerusalem.
You are witnesses of these things.
And behold I am sending the promise of my Father upon you;
　　but stay in the city
　　until you are clothed with power from on high."

Then he led them out as far as Bethany,
　　raised his hands, and blessed them.
As he blessed them he parted from them
　　and was taken up to heaven.
They did him homage
　　and then returned to Jerusalem with great joy,
　　and they were continually in the temple praising God. ✛

FRIDAY, MAY 25
EASTER WEEKDAY, STS. BEDE, GREGORY, AND MARY MAGDALENE DE PAZZI

✝ *Acts 18:9-18*
Many people in this city are with me.

[When Paul was in Corinth] one night in a vision the Lord said to him: "Do not be afraid. Go on speaking and do not be silenced, for I am with you. No one will attack you or harm you. There are many of my people in this city." Paul ended by settling there for a year and a half, teaching them the word of God.

　　During Gallio's proconsulship in Achaia, the Jews rose in a body against Paul and brought him before the bench. "This fellow," they charged, "is influencing people to worship God in ways that are against the law." Paul was about to speak in self-defense when Gallio said to the Jews: "If it were a crime or a serious fraud, I would give you Jews a patient and reasonable hearing. But since this is a dispute about terminology and titles and your own law, you must see to it yourselves. I refuse to judge such matters." With that, he dismissed them from the court. Then they all pounced on Sosthenes, a leading man of the synagogue, and beat him in full view of the bench; but Gallio paid no attention to it.

Paul stayed on in Corinth for quite a while; but eventually he took leave of the brothers and sailed for Syria, in the company of Priscilla and Aquila. At the port of Cenchreae he shaved his head because of a vow he had taken. ✛

Psalm 47:2-7
R. God is king of all the earth. *(or* **Alleluia.***)*
All you peoples, clap your hands,
    shout to God with cries of gladness,
For the Lord, the Most High, the awesome,
    is the great king over all the earth. **R.**
He brings peoples under us;
    nations under our feet.
He chooses for us our inheritance,
    the glory of Jacob, whom he loves. **R.**
God mounts his throne amid shouts of joy;
    the Lord, amid trumpet blasts.
Sing praise to God, sing praise;
    sing praise to our king, sing praise. **R.**

R. Alleluia, alleluia.
The Lord said: I will not leave you orphans.
I will come back to you, and your hearts will rejoice. **R.**

† *John 16:20-23*
Your joy no man will take from you.

Jesus said to his disciples:
    "I tell you truly:
    you will weep and mourn
    while the world rejoices;
    you will grieve for a time,
    but your grief will be turned into joy.
    When a woman is in labor

she is sad that her time has come.
When she has borne her child,
she no longer remembers her pain
for joy that a man has been born into the world.
In the same way, you are sad for a time,
but I shall see you again;
then your hearts will rejoice
with a joy no one can take from you.
On that day you will have no questions to ask me." ✛

SATURDAY, MAY 26
EASTER WEEKDAY, ST. PHILIP NERI

† *Acts 18:23-28*
Apollos demonstrated from the scriptures that Jesus was Christ.

After spending some time in Antioch, Paul set out again, traveling systematically through the Galatian country and Phrygia to reassure all his disciples.

A Jew named Apollos, a native of Alexandria and a man of eloquence, arrived by ship at Ephesus. He was both an authority on Scripture and instructed in the new way of the Lord. Apollos was a man full of spiritual fervor. He spoke and taught accurately about Jesus, although he knew only of John's baptism. He too began to express himself fearlessly in the synagogue. When Priscilla and Aquila heard him, they took him home and explained to him God's new way in greater detail. He wanted to go on to Achaia, and so the brothers encouraged him by writing the disciples there to welcome him. When he arrived, he greatly strengthened those who through God's favor had become believers. He was vigorous in his public refutation of the Jewish party as he went about establishing from the Scriptures that Jesus is the Messiah. ✛

Psalm 47: 2-3, 8-10
R. **God is king of all the earth.** *(or* **Alleluia.***)*
All you peoples, clap your hands,
　　shout to God with cries of gladness,
For the Lord, the Most High, the awesome,
　　is the great king over all the earth. **R.**
For king of all the earth is God;

sing hymns of praise.
God reigns over the nations,
 God sits upon his holy throne. **R.**
The princes of the peoples are gathered together
 with the people of the God of Abraham.
For God's are the guardians of the earth;
 he is supreme. **R.**

R. Alleluia, alleluia.
I went from the Father and came into the world;
and now I leave the world to return to the Father. **R.**

† *John 16:23-28*

My Father loves you because you have loved me and believed in me.

Jesus said to his disciples,
 "I give you my assurance,
 whatever you ask the Father,
 he will give you in my name.
 Until now you have not asked for anything in my name.
 Ask and you shall receive,
 that your joy may be full.
 I have spoken these things to you in veiled language.
 A time will come when I shall no longer do so,
 but shall tell you about the Father in plain speech.
 On that day you will ask in my name
 and I do not say that I will petition the Father for you.
 The Father already loves you,
 because you have loved me
 and have believed that I came from God.
 [I did indeed come from the Father;]
 I came into the world.
 Now I am leaving the world
 to go to the Father." ✛

MAY 27
SEVENTH SUNDAY OF EASTER
(If Ascension is celebrated today, use the readings given for May 24.)

✝ *Acts 7:55-60*
I see the Son of Man standing at the right hand of God.

Stephen, filled with the Holy Spirit,
  looked up intently to heaven and saw the glory of God
  and Jesus standing at the right hand of God,
  and Stephen said, "Behold, I see the heavens opened
  and the Son of Man standing at the right hand of God."
But they cried out in a loud voice,
  covered their ears, and rushed upon him together.
They threw him out of the city, and began to stone him.
The witnesses laid down their cloaks
  at the feet of a young man named Saul.
As they were stoning Stephen, he called out,
  "Lord Jesus, receive my spirit."
Then he fell to his knees and cried out in a loud voice,
  "Lord, do not hold this sin against them;"
  and when he said this, he fell asleep. ✝

Psalm 97:1-2, 6-7, 9

R. The Lord is king, the most high over all the earth.
(or **Alleluia.***)*

The LORD is king; let the earth rejoice;
  let the many islands be glad.
Justice and judgment are the foundation of his throne. **R.**
The heavens proclaim his justice,
  and all peoples see his glory.
All gods are prostrate before him. **R.**
You, O LORD, are the Most High over all the earth,
  exalted far above all gods. **R.**

✝ *Revelation 22:12-14, 16-17, 20*
Come, Lord Jesus!

I, John, heard a voice saying to me:
  "Behold, I am coming soon.
I bring with me the recompense I will give to each
  according to his deeds.
I am the Alpha and the Omega, the first and the last,

the beginning and the end."

Blessed are they who wash their robes
    so as to have the right to the tree of life
    and enter the city through its gates.

"I, Jesus, sent my angel to give you this testimony
       for the churches.
I am the root and offspring of David,
    the bright morning star."

The Spirit and the bride say, "Come."
Let the hearer say, "Come."
Let the one who thirsts come forward,
    and the one who wants it receive the gift of life-giving water.

The one who gives this testimony says, "Yes, I am coming
      soon."
Amen! Come, Lord Jesus! ✛

    cf. John 14:18
R. Alleluia, alleluia.
I will not leave you orphans, says the Lord.
I will come back to you, and your hearts will rejoice. **R.**

        ✝ *John 17:20-26*
      That they may be brought to perfection as one!

Lifting up his eyes to heaven, Jesus prayed saying:
    "Holy Father, I pray not only for them,
    but also for those who will believe in me through their word,
    so that they may all be one,
    as you, Father, are in me and I in you,
    that they also may be in us,
    that the world may believe that you sent me.
And I have given them the glory you gave me,
    so that they may be one, as we are one,
    I in them and you in me,
    that they may be brought to perfection as one,
    that the world may know that you sent me,
    and that you loved them even as you loved me.
Father, they are your gift to me.
I wish that where I am they also may be with me,

that they may see my glory that you gave me,
because you loved me before the foundation of the world.
Righteous Father, the world also does not know you,
but I know you, and they know that you sent me.
I made known to them your name and I will make it known,
that the love with which you loved me
may be in them and I in them." ✝

MONDAY, MAY 28
EASTER WEEKDAY

✝ Acts 19:1-8
Did you receive the Holy Spirit when you became believers?

While Apollos was in Corinth, Paul passed through the interior of the country and came to Ephesus. There he found some disciples to whom he put the question, "Did you receive the Holy Spirit when you became believers?" They answered, "We have not so much as heard that there is a Holy Spirit." "Well, how were you baptized?" he persisted. They replied, "With the baptism of John." Paul then explained, "John's baptism was a baptism of repentance. He used to tell the people about the one who would come after him in whom they were to believe — that is, Jesus." When they heard this, they were baptized in the name of the Lord Jesus. As Paul laid his hands on them, the Holy Spirit came down on them and they began to speak in tongues and to utter prophecies. There were in the company about twelve men in all.

Paul entered the synagogue, and over a period of three months debated fearlessly, with persuasive arguments, about the kingdom of God. ✝

Psalm 68:2-7
R. Sing to God, O kingdoms of the earth. *(or* **Alleluia.***)*
God arises; his enemies are scattered,
    and those who hate him flee before him.
As smoke is driven away, so are they driven;
    as wax melts before the fire. **R.**
But the just rejoice and exult before God;
    they are glad and rejoice.
Sing to God, chant praise to his name;

his name is the Lord; exult before him. **R.**
The father of orphans and the defender of widows
   is God in his holy dwelling.
God gives a home to the forsaken;
   he leads forth prisoners to prosperity. **R.**

R. Alleluia, alleluia.
The Lord said: I will not leave you orphans.
I will come back to you, and your hearts will rejoice. **R.**

† John 16:29-33
Be brave, I have conquered the world.

The disciples said to Jesus:
   "At last you are speaking plainly without talking in veiled language! We are convinced that you know everything. There is no need for anyone to ask you questions. We do indeed believe you came from God."
   Jesus answered them:
      "Do you really believe?
      An hour is coming—has indeed already come—
      when you will be scattered and each will go his way,
      leaving me quite alone.
      (Yet I can never be alone;
      the Father is with me.)
      I tell you all this
      that in me you may find peace.
      You will suffer in the world.
      But take courage!
      I have overcome the world." ✛

TUESDAY, MAY 29
EASTER WEEKDAY

† Acts 20:17-27
*I have run the race and borne witness
to the world, a task I accepted from the Lord Jesus.*

Paul sent word from Miletus to Ephesus, summoning the elders of that church. When they came to him he delivered this address: "You know how I lived among you from the first day I set foot in the province of Asia—how I served the Lord in humility through the sorrows and trials that came my way from the plottings of certain Jews. Never did I shrink from telling you what was for your own good, or from teaching you in public or in private. With Jews and Greeks alike I insisted solemnly on repentance before God and on faith in our Lord Jesus. But now, as you see, I am on my way to Jerusalem, compelled by the Spirit and not knowing what will happen to me there—except that the Holy Spirit has been warning me from city to city that chains and hardships await me. I put no value on my life if only I can finish my race and complete the service to which I have been assigned by the Lord Jesus, bearing witness to the gospel of God's grace. I know as I speak these words that none of you among whom I went about preaching the kingdom will ever see my face again. Therefore I solemnly declare this day that I take the blame for no man's conscience, for I have never shrunk from announcing to you God's design in its entirety." ✛

Psalm 68:10-11. 20-21
R. Sing to God, O kingdoms of the earth.
A bountiful rain you showered down, O God, upon your
     inheritance;
     you restored the land when it languished;
Your flock settled in it;
     in your goodness, O God, you provided it for the needy. **R.**
Blessed day by day be the Lord,
     who bears our burdens; God, who is our salvation.
God is a saving God for us;
     the Lord, my Lord, controls the passageways of death. **R.**

R. Alleluia, alleluia.
The Holy Spirit will teach you all things,
and remind you of all I have said to you. **R.**

† *John 17:1-11*
Father, glorify your Son.

Jesus looked up to heaven and said:
   "Father, the hour has come!
   Give glory to your Son
   that your Son may give glory to you,
   inasmuch as you have given him authority over all mankind,
   that he may bestow eternal life on those you gave him.

(Eternal life is this:
to know you, the only true God,
and him whom you have sent, Jesus Christ.)
I have given you glory on earth
by finishing the work you gave me to do.
Do you now, Father, give me glory at your side,
a glory I had with you before the world began.
I have made your name known
to those you gave me out of the world.
These men you gave me were yours;
they have kept your word.
Now they realize
that all that you gave me comes from you.
I entrusted to them
the message you entrusted to me,
and they received it.
They have known that in truth I came from you,
they have believed it was you who sent me.

"For these I pray—
not for the world
but for these you have given me,
for they are really yours.
(Just as all that belongs to me is yours,
so all that belongs to you is mine.)
It is in them that I have been glorified.
I am in the world no more,
but these are in the world
as I come to you." ✢

WEDNESDAY, MAY 30
Easter Weekday

† Acts 20:28-38
*I commend you to God, who has power
to build you up and to give you an inheritance.*

Paul spoke to the elders of the church of Ephesus: "Keep
watch over yourselves, and over the whole flock the Holy Spirit
has given you to guard. Shepherd the church of God, which he
has acquired at the price of his own blood. I know that when
I am gone, savage wolves will come among you who will not

spare the flock. From your own number, men will present themselves distorting the truth and leading astray any who follow them. Be on guard, therefore. Do not forget that for three years, night and day, I never ceased warning you individually even to the point of tears. I commend you now to the Lord, and to that gracious word of his which can enlarge you, and give you a share among all who are consecrated to him. Never did I set my heart on anyone's silver or gold or envy the way he dressed. You yourselves know that these hands of mine have served both my needs and those of my companions. I have always pointed out to you that it is by such hard work that you must help the weak. You need to recall the words of the Lord Jesus himself, who said, 'There is more happiness in giving than receiving.'"

After this discourse, Paul knelt down with them all and prayed. They began to weep without restraint, throwing their arms around him and kissing him, for they were deeply distressed to hear that they would never see his face again. Then they escorted him to the ship. ✦

Psalm 68:29-30, 33-36
R. Sing to God, O kingdoms of the earth.
(or **Alleluia.***)*
Show forth, O God, your power,
    the power, O God, with which you took our part;
For your temple in Jerusalem
    let the kings bring you gifts. **R.**
You kingdoms of the earth, sing to God,
    chant praise to the Lord
    who rides on the heights of the ancient heavens.
Behold, his voice resounds, the voice of power:
    "Confess the power of God!" **R.**
Over Israel is his majesty;
    his power is in the skies.
Awesome in his sanctuary is God, the God of Israel;
    he gives power and strength to his people. **R.**

R. Alleluia, alleluia.
The Lord said: I will not leave you orphans.
I will come back to you, and your hearts will rejoice. **R.**

† *John 17:11-19*
May they be one as we are one.

Jesus looked up to heaven and prayed:
"O Father most holy,
protect them with your name which you have given me,
[that they may be one, even as we are one.]
As long as I was with them,
I guarded them with your name which you gave me.
I kept careful watch,
and not one of them was lost,
none but him who was destined to be lost —
in fulfillment of Scripture.
Now, however, I come to you;
I say all this while I am still in the world
that they may share my joy completely.
I gave them your word,
and the world has hated them for it;
they do not belong to the world,
[any more than I belong to the world].
I do not ask you to take them out of the world,
but to guard them from the evil one.
They are not of the world,
any more than I am of the world.
Consecrate them by means of truth—
'Your word is truth.'
As you have sent me into the world,
so I have sent them into the world;
I consecrate myself for their sakes now,
that they may be consecrated in truth." ✛

THURSDAY, MAY 31
THE VISITATION OF MARY

† *Romans 12:9-16* (or *Zephaniah 3:14-18*)
Contribute to the needs of God's people, and practice hospitality.

Your love must be sincere. Detest what is evil, cling to what
is good. Love one another with the affection of brothers.
Anticipate each other in showing respect. Do not grow slack
but be fervent in spirit; he whom you serve is the Lord. Rejoice
in hope, be patient under trial, persevere in prayer. Look on

the needs of the saints as your own; be generous in offering hospitality. Bless your persecutors; bless and do not curse them. Rejoice with those who rejoice, weep with those who weep. Have the same attitude toward all. Put away ambitious thoughts and associate with those who are lowly. ✝

Isaiah 12: 2-6
R. Among you is the great and Holy One of Israel.
God indeed is my savior;
    I am confident and unafraid.
My strength and my courage is the Lord,
    and he has been my savior.
With joy you will draw water
    at the fountain of salvation. **R.**
Give thanks to the Lord, acclaim his name;
    among the nations make known his deeds,
    proclaim how exalted is his name. **R.**
Sing praise to the Lord for his glorious achievement;
    let this be known throughout all the earth.
Shout with exultation, O city of Zion,
    for great in your midst
    is the Holy One of Israel! **R.**

Luke 1:45
R. Alleluia, alleluia.
Blessed are you, O Virgin Mary, for your firm believing, that the promises of the Lord would be fulfilled. **R.**

† Luke 1:39-56
Why should I be honored with a visit from the mother of my Lord?

Mary set out, proceeding in haste into the hill country to a town of Judah, where she entered Zechariah's house and greeted Elizabeth. When Elizabeth heard Mary's greeting, the baby stirred in her womb. Elizabeth was filled with the Holy Spirit and cried out in a loud voice: "Blessed are you among women and blessed is the fruit of your womb. But who am I that the mother of my Lord should come to me? The moment your greeting sounded in my ears, the baby stirred in my womb for joy. Blessed is she who trusted that the Lord's words to her would be fulfilled."
Then Mary said:

"My being proclaims the greatness of the Lord,
my spirit finds joy in God my savior,
For he has looked upon his servant in her lowliness;
all ages to come shall call me blessed
God who is mighty has done great things for me,
holy is his name;
His mercy is from age to age
on those who fear him.

"He has shown might with his arm;
he has confused the proud in their inmost thoughts.
He has deposed the mighty from their thrones
and raised the lowly to high places.
The hungry he has given every good thing,
while the rich he has sent empty away.
He has upheld Israel his servant,
ever mindful of his mercy;
Even as he promised our fathers,
promised Abraham and his descendants forever."

Mary remained with Elizabeth about three months and then returned home. ✛

FRIDAY, JUNE 1
EASTER WEEKDAY, ST. JUSTIN

✝ *Acts 25:13-21*
Jesus was dead, whom Paul claimed to be alive.

King Agrippa and Bernice arrived in Caesarea and paid Festus a courtesy call. Since they were to spend several days there, Festus referred Paul's case to the king. "There is a prisoner here," he said, "whom Felix left behind in custody. While I was in Jerusalem the chief priests and the elders of the Jews presented their case against this man and demanded his condemnation. I replied that it was not the Roman practice to hand an accused man over before he had been confronted with his accusers and given a chance to defend himself against their charges. When they came here with me, I did not delay the matter. The very next day I took my seat on the bench and ordered the man brought in. His accusers surrounded him but they did not charge him with any of the crimes I expected. Instead they differed with him over issues in their own religion, and about a certain Jesus who had died but who Paul claimed is alive. Not knowing how to decide the case, I asked whether the prisoner was willing to go to Jerusalem and stand trial there on these charges. Paul appealed to be kept here until there would be an imperial investigation of his case, so I issued orders that he be kept in custody until I could send him to the emperor." ✛

Psalm 103:1-2. 11-12. 19-20
R. The Lord has set his throne in heaven.
(or **Alleluia.***)*
Bless the Lord, O my soul;
    and all my being, bless his holy name.
Bless the Lord, O my soul,
    and forget not all his benefits; **R.**
For as the heavens are high above the earth,
    so surpassing is his kindness toward those who fear him.
As far as the east is from the west,
    so far has he put our transgressions from us. **R.**
The Lord has established his throne in heaven,
    and his kingdom rules over all.
Bless the Lord, all you his angels,
    you mighty in strength, who do his bidding. **R.**

R. Alleluia, alleluia.
God and teach all people my gospel;
I am with you always, until the end of the world. **R.**

† *John 21:15-19*
Feed my lambs, feed my sheep.

When [Jesus manifested himself to his disciples and] they had eaten their meal, he said to Simon Peter, "Simon, son of John, do you love me more than these?" "Yes, Lord," Peter said, "you know that I love you." At which Jesus said, "Feed my lambs."

A second time he put his question, "Simon, son of John, do you love me?" "Yes, Lord," Peter said, "you know that I love you." Jesus replied, "Tend my sheep."

A third time Jesus asked him, "Simon, son of John, do you love me?" Peter was hurt because he had asked a third time, "Do you love me?" So he said to him: "Lord, you know everything. You know well that I love you." Jesus told him, "Feed my sheep."

"I tell you solemnly:

as a young man
you fastened your belt
and went about as you pleased;
but when you are older
you will stretch out your hands,
and another will tie you fast
and carry you off against your will."
(What he said indicated the sort of death by which Peter was
to glorify God.) When Jesus had finished speaking he said to
him, "Follow me." ✟

SATURDAY, JUNE 2
Easter Weekday, Sts. Marcellinus and Peter

† Acts 28:16-20, 30-31
He remained at Rome, proclaiming the kingdom of God.

Upon entry into Rome, Paul was allowed to take a lodging of his
own, although a soldier was assigned to keep guard over him.

Three days later Paul invited the prominent men of the
Jewish community to visit him. When they had gathered he
said: "My brothers, I have done nothing against our people or
our ancestral customs; yet in Jerusalem I was handed over to
the Romans as a prisoner. The Romans tried my case and
wanted to release me because they found nothing against me
deserving of death. When the Jews objected, I was forced to
appeal to the emperor, though I had no cause to make accusa-
tions against my own people. This is the reason, then, why I
have asked to see you and speak with you. I wear these chains
solely because I share the hope of Israel."

For two full years Paul stayed on in his rented lodgings,
welcoming all who came to him. With full assurance, and
without any hindrance whatever, he preached the reign of God
and taught about the Lord Jesus Christ. ✟

Psalm 11:4-5, 7
R. **The just will gaze on your face, O Lord.**
The Lord is in his holy temple;
    the Lord's throne is in heaven.
His eyes behold,
    his searching glance is on mankind. R.

The Lord searches the just and the wicked;
the lover of violence he hates.
For the Lord is just, he loves just deeds
the upright shall see his face. **R.**

R. Alleluia, alleluia.
Go and teach all people my gospel;
I am with you always, until the end of the world. **R.**

† John 21:20-25
This is the disciple who has written these facts and his testimony is true.

As Peter followed Jesus, he turned around and noticed that the disciple whom Jesus loved was following (the one who had leaned against Jesus' chest during the supper and said, "Lord, which one will hand you over?"). Seeing him, Peter was prompted to ask Jesus, "But Lord, what about him?" "Suppose I want him to stay until I come," Jesus replied, "how does that concern you? Your business is to follow me." This is how the report spread among the brothers that this disciple was not going to die. Jesus never told him, as a matter of fact, that the disciple was not going to die; all he said was, "Suppose I want him to stay until I come. [How does that concern you]?"

It is this same disciple who is the witness to these things; it is he who wrote them down and his testimony, we know, is true. There are still many other things that Jesus did, yet if they were written about in detail, I doubt there would be room enough in the entire world to hold the books to record them. ✛

JUNE 3
PENTECOST SUNDAY
(The Pentecost Vigil readings are: Genesis 11:1-9 or Exodus 19:3-8a, 16-20b or Ezekiel 37:1-14 or Joel 3:1-5 • Psalm 104:1-2, 24, 35, 27-30 • Romans 8:22-27 • John 7:37-39)

† Acts 2:1-11
They were filled with the Holy Spirit and began to speak.

When the time for Pentecost was fulfilled,
they were all in one place together.
And suddenly there came from the sky
a noise like a strong driving wind,
and it filled the entire house in which they were.

Then there appeared to them tongues as of fire,
    which parted and came to rest on each one of them.
And they were all filled with the Holy Spirit
    and began to speak in different tongues,
    as the Spirit enabled them to proclaim.

Now there were devout Jews from every nation under heaven
    staying in Jerusalem.
At this sound, they gathered in a large crowd,
    but they were confused
    because each one heard them speaking in his own language.
They were astounded, and in amazement they asked,
    "Are not all these people who are speaking Galileans?
Then how does each of us hear them in his native language?
We are Parthians, Medes, and Elamites,
    inhabitants of Mesopotamia, Judea and Cappadocia,
    Pontus and Asia, Phrygia and Pamphylia,
    Egypt and the districts of Libya near Cyrene,
    as well as travelers from Rome,
    both Jews and converts to Judaism, Cretans and Arabs,
    yet we hear them speaking in our own tongues
    of the mighty acts of God." ✛

Psalm 104:1, 24, 29-30, 31, 34
**R. Lord, send out your Spirit,
    and renew the face of the earth.** *(or **Alleluia.**)*
Bless the LORD, O my soul!
    O LORD, my God, you are great indeed!
How manifold are your works, O LORD!
    the earth is full of your creatures; **R.**
May the glory of the LORD endure forever;
    may the LORD be glad in his works!
Pleasing to him be my theme;
    I will be glad in the LORD. **R.**
If you take away their breath, they perish
    and return to their dust.
When you send forth your spirit, they are created,
    and you renew the face of the earth. **R.**

✝ 1 Corinthians 12:3b-7, 12-13 *(or Romans 8:8-17)*
In one Spirit we were all baptized into one body.

Brothers and sisters:
No one can say, "Jesus is Lord," except by the Holy Spirit.
There are different kinds of spiritual gifts but the same Spirit;
    there are different forms of service but the same Lord;
    there are different workings but the same God
    who produces all of them in everyone.
To each individual the manifestation of the Spirit
    is given for some benefit.

As a body is one though it has many parts,
    and all the parts of the body, though many, are one body,
    so also Christ.
For in one Spirit we were all baptized into one body,
    whether Jews or Greeks, slaves or free persons,
    and we were all given to drink of one Spirit. ✛

R. Alleluia, alleluia.
Come, Holy Spirit, fill the hearts of your faithful
and kindle in them the fire of your love. **R.**

✝ John 14:15-16, 23b-26 *(or John 20:19-23)*
The Holy Spirit will teach you everything.

Jesus said to his disciples:
"If you love me, you will keep my commandments.
And I will ask the Father,
    and he will give you another Advocate
    to be with you always.

"Whoever loves me will keep my word,
    and my Father will love him,
    and we will come to him and make our dwelling with him.
Those who do not love me do not keep my words;
    yet the word you hear is not mine
    but that of the Father who sent me.

"I have told you this while I am with you.
The Advocate, the Holy Spirit whom the Father
        will send in my name,
    will teach you everything
    and remind you of all that I told you." ✛

MONDAY, JUNE 4
WEEKDAY

† *Tobit 1:1-2; 2:1-9*
Tobiah feared the Lord more than the king.

This book tells the story of Tobit of the tribe of Naphtali, who during the reign of Shalmaneser, king of Assyria, was taken captive from Thisbe, which is south of Kedesh Naphtali in upper Galilee, above and to the west of Asser, north of Phogor.

On our festival of Pentecost, the feast of Weeks, a fine dinner was prepared for me, and I reclined to eat. The table was set for me, and when many different dishes were placed before me, I said to my son Tobiah: "My son, go out and try to find a poor man from among our kinsmen exiled here in Nineveh. If he is a sincere worshiper of God, bring him back with you, so that he can share this meal with me. Indeed, son, I shall wait for you to come back."

Tobiah went out to look for some poor kinsman of ours. When he returned he exclaimed, "Father!" I said to him, "What is it, son?" He answered, "Father, one of our people has been murdered! His body lies in the market place where he was just strangled!" I sprang to my feet, leaving the dinner untouched; and I carried the dead man from the street and put him in one of the rooms, so that I might bury him after sunset. Returning to my own quarters, I washed myself and ate my food in sorrow. I was reminded of the oracle pronounced by the prophet Amos against Bethel:
"Your festivals shall be turned into mourning,
And all your songs into lamentation."
And I wept. Then at sunset I went out, dug a grave, and buried him.

The neighbors mocked me, saying to one another: "Will this man never learn! Once before he was hunted down for execution because of this very thing; yet now that he has escaped, here he is again burying the dead!"

That same night I bathed, and went to sleep next to the wall of my courtyard. Because of the heat I left my face uncovered. ✟

Psalm 112:1-6
R. Happy the man who fears the Lord. *(or* **Alleluia.***)*
Happy the man who fears the Lord,
　who greatly delights in his commands.
His posterity shall be mighty upon the earth;
　the upright generation shall be blessed. **R.**
Wealth and riches shall be in his house;
　his generosity shall endure forever.
The Lord dawns through the darkness, a light for the upright;
　he is gracious and merciful and just. **R.**
Well for the man who is gracious and lends,
　who conducts his affairs with justice;
He shall never be moved;
　the just man shall be in everlasting remembrance. **R.**

Psalm 19:9
R. Alleluia, alleluia.
Your words, O Lord, give joy to my heart,
your teaching is light to my eyes. **R.**

† *Mark 12:1-12*
They seized the beloved son, killed him,
and threw him out of the vineyard.

Jesus began to address the chief priests, the scribes and the
elders once more in parables: "A man planted a vineyard, put
a hedge around it, dug out a vat, and erected a tower. Then he
leased it to tenant farmers and went on a journey. In due time
he dispatched a man in his service to the tenants to obtain
from them his share of produce from the vineyard. But they
seized him, beat him, and sent him off empty handed. The
second time he sent them another servant; him too they beat
over the head and treated shamefully. He sent yet another and
they killed him. So too with many others: some they beat; some
they killed. He still had one to send—the son whom he loved.
He sent him to them as a last resort, thinking, 'They will have
to respect my son.' But those tenants said to one another, 'Here
is the one who will inherit everything. Come, let us kill him,
and the inheritance will be ours.' Then they seized and killed
him and dragged him outside the vineyard. What do you
suppose the owner of the vineyard will do? He will come and
destroy those tenants and turn his vineyard over to others. Are

you not familiar with this passage of Scripture:
'The stone rejected by the builders
has become the keystone of the structure.
It was the Lord who did it
and we find it marvelous to behold'?"
They wanted to arrest him at this, yet they had reason to fear
the crowd. (They knew well enough that he meant the parable
for them.) Finally they left him and went off. ✙

TUESDAY, JUNE 5
St. Boniface

† *Tobit 2:9-14*
Even though he was blind he did not turn against God.

One night I (Tobit) [fatigued from burying the dead] went to
sleep next to the wall of my courtyard. Because of the heat I left
my face uncovered. I did not know there were birds perched on
the wall above me, till their warm droppings settled in my
eyes, causing cataracts. I went to see some doctors for a cure,
but the more they anointed my eyes with various salves, the
worse the cataracts became, until I could see no more. For four
years I was deprived of eyesight, and all my kinsmen were
grieved at my condition. Ahiqar, however, took care of me for
two years, until he left for Elymais.

At that time my wife Anna worked for hire at weaving
cloth, the kind of work women do. When she sent back the
goods to their owners, they would pay her. Late in winter she
finished the cloth and sent it back to the owners. They paid her
the full salary, and also gave her a young goat for the table. On
entering my house the goat began to bleat. I called to my wife
and said: "Where did this goat come from? Perhaps it was
stolen! Give it back to its owners; we have no right to eat stolen
food!" But she said to me, "It was given to me as a bonus over
and above my wages." Yet I would not believe her, and told her
to give it back to its owners. I became very angry with her over
this. So she retorted: "Where are your charitable deeds now?
Where are your virtuous acts? See! Your true character is
finally showing itself!" ✙

Psalm 112:1-2, 7-9

R. The heart of the just man is secure,
trusting in the Lord. *(or* **Alleluia.***)*

Happy the man who fears the Lord,
   who greatly delights in his commands.
His posterity shall be mighty upon the earth;
   the upright generation shall be blessed. **R.**
An evil report he shall not fear;
   his heart is firm, trusting in the Lord.
His heart is steadfast; he shall not fear
   till he looks down upon his foes. **R.**
Lavishly he gives to the poor;
   his generosity shall endure forever;
   his horn shall be exalted in glory. **R.**

Psalm 19:9

R. Alleluia, alleluia.

Your words, O Lord, give joy to my heart,
your teaching is light to my eyes. **R.**

† *Mark 12:13-17*

Give to Caesar what belongs to Caesar and to God what belongs to God.

Some Pharisees and Herodians were sent after Jesus to catch him in his speech. The two groups came and said to him: "Teacher, we know you are a truthful man, unconcerned about anyone's opinion. It is evident you do not act out of human respect but teach God's way of life sincerely. Is it lawful to pay the tax to the emperor or not? Are we to pay or not to pay?" Knowing their hypocrisy he said to them, "Why are you trying to trip me up? Bring me a coin and let me see it." When they brought one, he said to them, "Whose head is this and whose inscription is it?" "Caesar's," they told him. At that Jesus said to them, "Give to Caesar what is Caesar's but give to God what is God's." Their amazement at him knew no bounds. +

WEDNESDAY, JUNE 6
WEEKDAY, ST. NORBERT

† *Tobit 3:1-11, 16*
Their prayers were heard by the Lord and found favor in his sight.

Grief-stricken in spirit, Tobit groaned and wept aloud. Then
with sobs he began to pray:
"You are righteous, O Lord,
    and all your deeds are just;
All your ways are mercy and truth;
    you are the judge of the world.
And now, O Lord, may you be mindful of me,
    and look with favor upon me.
Punish me not for my sins,
    nor for my inadvertent offenses,
    nor for those of my fathers.

"They sinned against you,
    and disobeyed your commandments.
So you handed us over to plundering, exile, and death,
    till we were an object lesson, a byword, a reproach
    in all the nations among whom you scattered us.

"Yes, your judgments are many and true
    in dealing with me as my sins
    and those of my fathers deserve.
For we have not kept your commandments,
    nor have we trodden the paths of truth before you.

"So now, deal with me as you please,
    and command my life breath to be taken from me,
    that I may go from the face of the earth into dust.
It is better for me to die than to live,
    because I have heard insulting calumnies,
    and I am overwhelmed with grief.

"Lord, command me to be delivered from such anguish;
    let me go to the everlasting abode;
    Lord, refuse me not.
For it is better for me to die
    than to endure so much misery in life,
    and to hear these insults!"

On the same day, at Ecbatana in Media, it so happened that Raguel's daughter Sarah also had to listen to abuse, from one of her father's maids. For she had been married to seven husbands, but the wicked demon Asmodeus killed them off before they could have intercourse with her, as it is prescribed for wives. So the maid said to her: "You are the one who strangles your husbands! Look at you! You have already been married seven times, but you have had no joy with any one of your husbands. Why do you beat us? Because your husbands are dead? Then why not join them! May we never see a son or daughter of yours!"

That day she was deeply grieved in spirit. She went in tears to an upstairs room in her father's house with the intention of hanging herself. But she reconsidered, saying to herself: "No! People would level this insult against my father: 'You had only one beloved daughter, but she hanged herself because of ill fortune!' And thus would I cause my father in his old age to go down to the nether world laden with sorrow. It is far better for me not to hang myself, but to beg the Lord to have me die, so that I need no longer live to hear such insults."

At that time, then, she spread out her hands, and facing the window, poured out her prayer.

At that very time, the prayer of these two suppliants was heard in the glorious presence of Almighty God. So Raphael was sent to heal them both. ✛

Psalm 25:2-9
R. To you, O Lord, I lift my soul.
O Lord, my God
In you I trust; let me not be put to shame,
let not my enemies exult over me.
No one who waits for you shall be put to shame;
those shall be put to shame who heedlessly break faith. **R.**
Your ways, O Lord, make known to me;
teach me your paths,
Guide me in your truth and teach me,
for you are God my savior. **R.**
Remember that your compassion, O Lord,
and your kindness are from of old.
In your kindness remember me,

because of your goodness, O Lord. **R.**
Good and upright is the Lord;
   thus he show sinners the way.
He guides the humble to justice,
   he teaches the humble his way. **R.**

Psalm 19:9
R. Alleluia, alleluia.
Your words, O Lord, give joy to my heart,
your teaching is light to my eyes. **R.**

† *Mark 12:18-27*
He is the God not of the dead, but of the living.

Then some Sadducees who hold there is no resurrection came to Jesus with a question: "Teacher, we were left this in writing by Moses: 'If anyone's brother dies leaving a wife but no child, his brother must take the wife and produce offspring for his brother.' There were these seven brothers. The eldest took a wife and died, leaving no children. The second took the woman, and he too died childless. The same thing happened to the third; in fact none of the seven left any children behind. Last of all, the woman also died. At the resurrection, when they all come back to life, whose wife will she be? All seven married her." Jesus said: "You are badly misled, because you fail to understand the Scriptures or the power of God. When people rise from the dead, they neither marry nor are given in marriage but live like angels in heaven. As to the raising of the dead, have you not read in the book of Moses, in the passage about the burning bush, how God told him,
   'I am the God of Abraham, the God of Isaac,
      the God of Jacob'?
He is the God of the living, not of the dead. You are very much mistaken." ✛

THURSDAY, JUNE 7
WEEKDAY

† Tobit 6:11; 7:1,9-14; 8:4-7
The Lord made you come to me that we might be joined together.

The angel Raphael spoke thus to Tobiah, "Tonight we must stay with Raguel, who is a relative of yours. He has a daughter named Sarah." So he brought him to the house of Raguel, whom they found seated by his courtyard gate. They greeted him first. He said to them, "Greetings to you too, brothers! Good health to you and welcome!"

Afterward, Raguel slaughtered a ram from the flock and gave them a cordial reception. When they had bathed and reclined to eat, Tobiah said to Raphael, "Brother Azariah, ask Raguel to let me marry my kinswoman Sarah." Raguel overheard the words; so he said to the boy: "Eat and drink and be merry tonight, for no man is more entitled to marry my daughter Sarah than you, brother. Besides, not even I have the right to give her to anyone but you, because you are my closest relative. But I will explain the situation to you very frankly. I have given her in marriage to seven men, all of whom were kinsmen of ours, and all died on the very night they approached her. But now, son, eat and drink. I am sure the Lord will look after you both." Tobiah answered, "I will eat or drink nothing until you set aside what belongs to me."

Raguel said to him: "I will do it. She is yours according to the decree of the Book of Moses. Your marriage to her has been decided in heaven! Take your kinswoman; from now on you are her love, and she is your beloved. She is yours today and ever after. And tonight, son, may the Lord of heaven prosper you both. May he grant you mercy and peace." Then Raguel called his daughter Sarah, and she came to him. He took her by the hand and gave her to Tobiah with the words: "Take her according to the law. According to the decree written in the Book of Moses she is your wife. Take her and bring her back safely to your father. And may the God of heaven grant both of you peace and prosperity." He then called her mother and told her to bring a scroll, so that he might draw up a marriage contract stating that he gave Sarah to Tobiah as his wife according to the decree of the Mosaic law. Her mother brought the scroll, and he drew up the contract, to which they affixed their seals. Afterward they began to eat and drink.

Tobiah arose from bed and said to his wife, "My love, get up. Let us pray and beg our Lord to have mercy on us and to grant us deliverance." She got up, and they started to pray and beg that deliverance might be theirs. He began with these words:

"Blessed are you, O God of our fathers;
    praised be your name forever and ever.
Let the heavens and all your creation
    praise you forever.
You made Adam and you gave him his wife Eve
    to be his help and support;
    and from these two the human race descended.
You said, 'It is not good for the man to be alone;
    let us make him a partner like himself.'
Now, Lord, you know that I take this wife of mine
    not because of lust,
    but for a noble purpose.
Call down your mercy on me and on her,
    and allow us to live together to a happy old age." ✛

Psalm 128:1-5
R. Happy are those who fear the Lord.
Happy are you who fear the Lord,
    who walk in his ways!
For you shall eat the fruit of your handiwork;
    happy shall you be, and favored. **R.**
Your wife shall be like a fruitful vine
    in the recesses of your home;
Your children like olive plants
    around your table. **R.**
Behold, thus is the man blessed
    who fears the Lord.
The Lord bless you from Zion:
    may you see the prosperity of Jerusalem
    all the days of your life. **R.**

Psalm 19:9
R. Alleluia, alleluia.
Your words, O Lord, give joy to my heart,
your teaching is light to my eyes. **R.**

† *Mark 12:28-34*
This is the first commandment. The second is similar to it.

One of the scribes came up to ask Jesus, "Which is the first of all the commandments?" Jesus replied: "This is the first:
'Hear, O Israel! The Lord our God is Lord alone!
Therefore you shall love the Lord your God
    with all your heart,
    with all your soul,
    with all your mind,
    and with all your strength.'
This is the second,
    'You shall love your neighbor as yourself.'
There is no other commandment greater than these." The scribe said to him: "Excellent, Teacher! You are right in saying, 'He is the One, there is no other than he.' Yes, 'to love him with all our heart, with all our thoughts and with all our strength, and to love our neighbor as ourselves' is worth more than any burnt offering or sacrifice." Jesus approved the insight of this answer and told him, "You are not far from the reign of God." And no one had the courage to ask him any more questions. ✤

FRIDAY, JUNE 8
WEEKDAY

† *Tobit 11:5-15*
*You have scourged me and now you
have saved me, Lord; I can see my son.*

Anna sat watching the road by which her son was to come. When she saw him coming, she exclaimed to his father, "Tobit, your son is coming, and the man who traveled with him!"

Raphael said to Tobiah before he reached his father: "I am certain that his eyes will be opened. Smear the fish gall on them. This medicine will make the cataracts shrink and peel off from his eyes; then your father will again be able to see the light of day."

Then Anna ran up to her son, threw her arms around him, and said to him, "Now that I have seen you again, son, I am ready to die!" And she sobbed aloud. Tobit got up and stumbled out through the courtyard gate. Tobiah went up to him with

the fish gall in his hand, and holding him firmly, blew into his eyes. "Courage, father," he said. Next he smeared the medicine on his eyes, and it made them smart. Then, beginning at the corners of Tobit's eyes, Tobiah used both hands to peel off the cataracts. When Tobit saw his son, he threw his arms around him and wept. He exclaimed, "I can see you, son, the light of my eyes!" Then he said:
"Blessed be God,
　　and praised be his great name,
　　and blessed be all his holy angels.
May his holy name be praised
　　throughout all the ages,
Because it was he who scourged me,
　　and it is he who has had mercy on me.
　　Behold, I now see my son Tobiah!" ✛

Psalm 146:2,7-10
R. Praise the Lord, my soul! *(or* **Alleluia.***)*
Praise the Lord, O my soul;
　　I will praise the Lord all my life;
　　I will sing praise to my God while I live. **R.**
The Lord keeps faith forever,
　　secures justice for the oppressed,
　　gives food to the hungry.
The Lord sets captives free. **R.**
The Lord gives sight to the blind.
　　The Lord raises up those that were bowed down;
The Lord loves the just.
　　The Lord protects strangers. **R.**
The fatherless and the widow he sustains,
　　but the way of the wicked he thwarts.
The Lord shall reign forever;
　　your God, O Zion, through all generations. Alleluia. **R.**

Psalm 19:9
R. Alleluia, alleluia.
Your words, O Lord, give joy to my heart,
your teaching is light to my eyes. **R.**

† *Mark 12:35-37*
How can the scribes maintain that Christ is the son of David?

As Jesus was teaching in the temple precincts he went on to say: "How can the scribes claim, 'The Messiah is David's son'? David himself, inspired by the Holy Spirit, said,

'The Lord said to my Lord: Sit at my right hand
until I make your enemies your footstool.'

If David himself addresses him as 'Lord,' in what sense can he be his son?" The majority of the crowd heard this with delight. ✚

SATURDAY, JUNE 9
WEEKDAY, ST. EPHREM

† *Tobit 12:1,5-15,20*
I will return to him who sent me; bless the Lord.

Tobit called his son Tobiah and said to him, "Son, see to it that you give what is due to the man who made the journey with you; give him a bonus too." So Tobiah called Raphael and said, "Take as your wages half of all that you have brought back, and go in peace."

Raphael called the two men aside privately and said to them: "Thank God! Give him the praise and the glory. Before all the living, acknowledge the many good things he has done for you, by blessing and extolling his name in song. Before all men, honor and proclaim God's deeds, and do not be slack in praising him. A king's secret it is prudent to keep, but the works of God are to be declared and made known. Praise them with due honor. Do good, and evil will not find its way to you. Prayer and fasting are good, but better than either is almsgiving accompanied by righteousness. A little with righteousness is better than abundance with wickedness. It is better to give alms than to store up gold; for almsgiving saves one from death and expiates every sin. Those who regularly give alms shall enjoy a full life; but those habitually guilty of sin are their own worst enemies.

"I will now tell you the whole truth; I will conceal nothing at all from you. I have already said to you, 'A king's secret it is prudent to keep, but the works of God are to be made known with due honor.' I can now tell you that when you, Tobit, and Sarah prayed, it was I who presented and read the record of your prayer before the Glory of the Lord; and I did the same thing when you used to bury the dead. When you did not hesitate to get up and leave your dinner in order to go and bury the dead, I was sent to put you to the test. At the same time, however, God commissioned me to heal you and your daughter-in-law Sarah. I am Raphael, one of the seven angels who enter and serve before the Glory of the Lord.

"So now get up from the ground and praise God. Behold, I am about to ascend to him who sent me; write down all these things that have happened to you." ✛

Tobit 13:2, 6
R. Blessed be God, who lives forever.
God scourges and then has mercy;
    he casts down to the depths of the nether world,
    and he brings up from the great abyss.
No one can escape his hand. **R.**
So now consider what he has done for you,
    and praise him with full voice.
Bless the Lord of righteousness,
    and exalt the King of the ages. **R.**
In the land of my exile I praise him,
    and show his power and majesty to a sinful nation. **R.**
Turn back, you sinners! do the right before him:
    perhaps he may look with favor upon you
    and show you mercy. **R.**

Psalm 19:9
R. Alleluia, alleluia.
Your words, O Lord, give joy to my heart,
your teaching is light to my eyes. **R.**

† Mark 12:38-44
This poor widow has given more than all others.

In the course of his teaching Jesus said: "Be on guard against the scribes, who like to parade around in their robes and accept marks of respect in public, front seats in the synagogues, and places of honor at banquets. These men devour the savings of widows and recite long prayers for appearance' sake; it is they who will receive the severest sentence."

Taking a seat opposite the treasury, he observed the crowd putting money into the collection box. Many of the wealthy put in sizable amounts; but one poor widow came and put in two small copper coins worth about a cent. He called his disciples over and told them: "I want you to observe that this poor widow contributed more than all the others who donated to the treasury. They gave from their surplus wealth, but she gave from her want, all that she had to live on." ✛

JUNE 10
TRINITY SUNDAY

† Proverbs 8:22-31
Before the earth was made, Wisdom was conceived.

Thus says the wisdom of God:
"The LORD possessed me, the beginning of his ways,
    the forerunner of his prodigies of long ago;
from of old I was poured forth,
    at the first, before the earth.
When there were no depths I was brought forth,
    when there were no fountains or springs of water;
before the mountains were settled into place,
    before the hills, I was brought forth;
while as yet the earth and fields were not made,
    nor the first clods of the world.

"When the Lord established the heavens I was there,
    when he marked out the vault over the face of the deep;
when he made firm the skies above,
    when he fixed fast the foundations of the earth;
when he set for the sea its limit,
    so that the waters should not transgress his command;
then was I beside him as his craftsman,
    and I was his delight day by day,
playing before him all the while,
    playing on the surface of his earth;
    and I found delight in the human race." ✛

Psalm 8:4-9

**R. O Lord, our God, how wonderful
your name in all the earth!**

When I behold your heavens, the work of your fingers,
    the moon and the stars which you set in place—
What is man that you should be mindful of him,
    or the son of man that you should care for him? **R.**
You have made him little less than the angels,
    and crowned him with glory and honor.
You have given him rule over the works of your hands,
    putting all things under his feet: **R.**
All sheep and oxen,
    yes, and the beasts of the field,
the birds of the air, the fishes of the sea,
    and whatever swims the paths of the seas. **R.**

† *Romans 5:1-5*

To God, through Christ, in love poured out through the Holy Spirit.

Brothers and sisters:

Therefore, since we have been justified by faith,
    we have peace with God through our Lord Jesus Christ,
    through whom we have gained access by faith
    to this grace in which we stand,
    and we boast in hope of the glory of God.
Not only that, but we even boast of our afflictions,
    knowing that affliction produces endurance,
    and endurance, proven character,
    and proven character, hope,
    and hope does not disappoint,
    because the love of God has been poured out into our hearts
    through the Holy Spirit that has been given to us. ✝

cf. Revelation 1:8

R. Alleluia, alleluia.

Glory to the Father, the Son, and the Holy Spirit;
to God who is, who was, and who is to come. **R.**

✝ *John 16:12-15*

Everything that the Father has is mine;
the Spirit will take from what is mine and declare it to you.

Jesus said to his disciples:
"I have much more to tell you, but you cannot bear it now.
But when he comes, the Spirit of truth,
    he will guide you to all truth.
He will not speak on his own,
    but he will speak what he hears,
    and will declare to you the things that are coming.
He will glorify me,
    because he will take from what is mine and declare it to you.
Everything that the Father has is mine;
    for this reason I told you that he will take from what is mine
    and declare it to you." ✝

MONDAY, JUNE 11
ST. BARNABAS

✝ *Acts 11:21-26;13:1-3*

He was a good man, filled with the Holy Spirit and with faith.

A great number believed and were converted to the Lord. News of this eventually reached the ears of the church in Jerusalem, resulting in Barnabas' being sent to Antioch. On his arrival he rejoiced to see the evidence of God's favor. He encouraged them all to remain firm in their commitment to the Lord, since he himself was a good man filled with the Holy Spirit and faith. Thereby large numbers were added to the Lord. Then Barnabas went off to Tarsus to look for Saul; once he had found him, he brought him back to Antioch. For a whole year they met with the church and instructed great numbers. It was in Antioch that the disciples were called Christians for the first time.

There were in the church at Antioch certain prophets and teachers: Barnabas, Symeon known as Niger, Lucius of Cyrene, Manaen (who had been brought up with Herod the tetrarch), and Saul. On one occasion, while they were engaged in the liturgy of the Lord and were fasting, the Holy Spirit spoke to them: "Set apart Barnabas and Saul for me to do the work for which I have called them." Then, after they had fasted and prayed, they imposed hands on them and sent them off. ✝

Psalm 98:1-6

**R. The Lord has revealed to the nations
his saving power.**

Sing to the Lord a new song,
    for he has done wondrous deeds;
His right hand has won victory for him,
    his holy arm. **R.**
The Lord has made his salvation known:
    in the sight of the nations he has revealed his justice.
He has remembered his kindness and his faithfulness
    toward the house of Israel. **R.**
All the ends of the earth have seen
    the salvation by our God.
Sing joyfully to the Lord, all you lands;
    break into song; sing praise. **R.**
Sing praise to the Lord with the harp,
    with the harp and melodious song.
With trumpets and the sound of the horn
    sing joyfully before the King, the LORD. **R.**

R. Alleluia, alleluia.
We praise you, God; we acknowledge you as Lord;
your glorious band of apostles extols you. **R.**

† *Matthew 10:7-13*
You received without charge, give without charge.

Jesus said to his disciples: "As you go, make this announcement: 'The reign of God is at hand!' Cure the sick, raise the dead, heal the leprous, expel demons. The gift you have received, give as a gift. Provide yourselves with neither gold nor silver nor copper in your belts; no traveling bag, no change of shirt, no sandals, no walking staff. The workman, after all, is worth his keep.

"Look for a worthy citizen in every town or village you come to and stay with him until you leave. As you enter his home bless it. If the home is deserving, your blessing will descend on it. If it is not, your blessing will return to you. ✝

TUESDAY, JUNE 12
WEEKDAY

† *2 Corinthians 1:18-22*
The Son of God, Jesus Christ was not yes and no, in him it is always yes.

As God keeps his word, I declare that my word to you is not "yes" one minute and "no" the next. Jesus Christ, whom Silvanus, Timothy, and I preached to you as Son of God, was not alternately "yes" and "no"; he was never anything but "yes." Whatever promises God has made have been fulfilled in him; therefore it is through him that we address our Amen to God when we worship together. God is the one who firmly establishes us along with you in Christ; it is he who anointed us and has sealed us, thereby depositing the first payment, the Spirit in our hearts. ✦

Psalm 119:129-133,135
R. Lord, let your face shine on me.
Wonderful are your decrees;
    therefore I observe them. **R.**
The revelation of your words sheds light,
    giving understanding to the simple. **R.**
I gasp with open mouth
    in my yearning for your commands. **R.**
Turn to me in pity
    as you turn to those who love your name. **R.**
Steady my footsteps according to your promise,
    and let no iniquity rule over me. **R.**
Let your countenance shine upon your servant,
    and teach me your statutes. **R.**

Psalm 130:5
R. Alleluia, alleluia.
I hope in the Lord,
I trust in his word. **R.**

† *Matthew 5:13-16*
You are the light of the world.

Jesus said to his disciples: "You are the salt of the earth. But what if salt goes flat? How can you restore its flavor? Then it is good for nothing but to be thrown out and trampled underfoot.

"You are the light of the world. A city set on a hill cannot be hidden. Men do not light a lamp and then put it under a bushel basket. They set it on a stand where it gives light to all in the house. In the same way, your light must shine before men so that they may see goodness in your acts and give praise to your heavenly Father." ✦

WEDNESDAY, JUNE 13
St. Anthony

† 2 Corinthians 3:4-11
He made us ministers of the new covenant,
a covenant of spirit not of letters.

This great confidence in God is ours, through Christ. It is not that we are entitled of ourselves to take credit for anything. Our sole credit is from God, who has made us qualified ministers of a new covenant, a covenant not of a written law but of spirit. The written law kills, but the Spirit gives life.

If the ministry of death, carved in writing on stone, was inaugurated with such glory that the Israelites could not look on Moses' face because of the glory that shone on it (even though it was a fading glory), how much greater will be the glory of the ministry of the Spirit? If the ministry of the covenant that condemned had glory, greater by far is the glory of the ministry that justifies. Indeed, when you compare that limited glory with this surpassing glory, the former should be declared no glory at all. If what was destined to pass away was given in glory, greater by far is the glory that endures. ✦

Psalm 99:5-9
R. Holy is the Lord our God.
Extol the Lord, our God,
 and worship at his footstool;
  holy is he! **R.**
Moses and Aaron were among his priests,
 and Samuel, among those who called upon his name;
  they called upon the Lord, and he answered them. **R.**
From the pillar of cloud he spoke to them;
 they heard his decrees and the law he gave them. **R.**
O Lord, our God, you answered them;
 a forgiving God you were to them,

though requiting their misdeeds. **R.**
Extol the Lord, our God,
and worship at his holy mountain;
for holy is the Lord, our God. **R.**

Psalm 130:5
R. Alleluia, alleluia.
I hope in the Lord,
I trust in his word. **R.**

✝ *Matthew 5:17-19*
I have come not to abolish the law, but to complete it.

Jesus said to his disciples: "Do not think that I have come to abolish the law and the prophets. I have come, not to abolish them, but to fulfill them. Of this much I assure you: until heaven and earth pass away, not the smallest letter of the law, not the smallest part of a letter, shall be done away with until it all comes true. That is why whoever breaks the least significant of these commands and teaches others to do so shall be called least in the kingdom of God. Whoever fulfills and teaches these commands shall be great in the kingdom of God." ✝

THURSDAY, JUNE 14
WEEKDAY

✝ *2 Corinthians 3:15—4:1, 3-6*
God has shone in our minds to radiate the light of God's glory.

Even now, when Moses is read a veil covers the understanding of the Israelites. "But whenever Israel turns to the Lord, the veil will be removed." The Lord is the Spirit, and where the Spirit of the Lord is, there is freedom. All of us, gazing on the Lord's glory with unveiled faces, are being transformed from glory to glory into his very image by the Lord who is the Spirit.

Because we possess this ministry through God's mercy, we do not give in to discouragement. If our gospel can be called "veiled" in any sense, it is such only for those who are headed toward destruction. Their unbelieving minds have been blinded by the god of the present age so that they do not see the splendor of the gospel showing forth the glory of Christ, the image of God. It is not ourselves we preach but Christ Jesus as

Lord, and ourselves as your servants for Jesus' sake. For God, who said, "Let light shine out of darkness," has shone in our hearts, that we in turn might make known the glory of God shining on the face of Christ. ✛

Psalm 85:9-14
R. The glory of the Lord will dwell in our land.
I will hear what God proclaims;
　the Lord—for he proclaims peace to his people.
Near indeed is his salvation to those who fear him,
　glory dwelling in our land. **R.**
Kindness and truth shall meet;
　justice and peace shall kiss.
Truth shall spring out of the earth,
　and justice shall look down from heaven. **R.**
The Lord himself will give his benefits;
　our land shall yield its increase.
Justice shall walk before him,
　and salvation, along the way of his steps. **R.**

Psalm 130:5
R. Alleluia, alleluia.
I hope in the Lord,
I trust in his word. **R.**

† *Matthew 5:20-26*
He who is angry with his brother will be judged for it.

Jesus said to his disciples: "I tell you, unless your holiness surpasses that of the scribes and Pharisees you shall not enter the kingdom of God.

"You have heard the commandment imposed on your forefathers, 'You shall not commit murder; every murderer shall be liable to judgment.' What I say to you is: everyone who grows angry with his brother shall be liable to judgment; any man who uses abusive language toward his brother shall be answerable to the Sanhedrin, and if he holds him in contempt he risks the fires of Gehenna. If you bring your gift to the altar and there recall that your brother has anything against you, leave your gift at the altar, go first to be reconciled with your brother, and then come and offer your gift. Lose no time; settle with your opponent while on your way to court with him.

Otherwise your opponent may hand you over to the judge, who will hand you over to the guard, who will throw you into prison. I warn you, you will not be released until you have paid the last penny." +

FRIDAY, JUNE 15
WEEKDAY

† 2 Corinthians 4:7-15
He who raised the Lord Jesus to life will raise us with him in our turn.

The treasure [of the knowledge of the glory of God] we possess in earthen vessels to make it clear that its surpassing power comes from God and not from us. We are afflicted in every way possible, but we are not crushed; full of doubts, we never despair. We are persecuted but never abandoned; we are struck down but never destroyed. Continually we carry about in our bodies the dying of Jesus, so that in our bodies the life of Jesus also may be revealed. While we live we are constantly being delivered to death for Jesus' sake, so that the life of Jesus may be revealed in our mortal flesh. Death is at work in us, but life in you. We have that spirit of faith of which the Scripture says, "Because I believed, I spoke out." We believe and so we speak, knowing that he who raised up the Lord Jesus will raise us up along with Jesus and place both us and you in his presence. Indeed, everything is ordered to your benefit, so that the grace bestowed in abundance may bring greater glory to God because they who give thanks are many. +

Psalm 116:10-11,15-18
R. To you, Lord, I will offer a sacrifice of praise.
*(or **Alleluia.**)*
I believed, even when I said,
"I am greatly afflicted";
I said in my alarm,
"No man is dependable." **R.**
Precious in the eyes of the Lord
is the death of his faithful ones.
O Lord, I am your servant;
I am your servant, the son of your handmaid;
you have loosed my bonds. **R.**
To you will I offer sacrifice of thanksgiving,
and I will call upon the name of the Lord.

My vows to the Lord I will pay
in the presence of all his people. **R.**

Psalm 130:5
R. Alleluia, alleluia.
I hope in the Lord,
I trust in his word. **R.**

† *Matthew 5:27-32*
If a man looks at a woman lustfully, he has already sinned.

Jesus said to his disciples: "You have heard the command-ment, 'You shall not commit adultery.' What I say to you is: anyone who looks lustfully at a woman has already committed adultery with her in his thoughts. If your right eye is your trouble, gouge it out and throw it away! Better to lose part of your body than to have it all cast into Gehenna. Again, if your right hand is your trouble, cut it off and throw it away! Better to lose part of your body than to have it all cast into Gehenna.

"It was also said, 'Whenever a man divorces his wife, he must give her a decree of divorce.' What I say to you is: everyone who divorces his wife—lewd conduct is a separate case—forces her to commit adultery. The man who marries a divorced woman likewise commits adultery." ✛

SATURDAY, JUNE 16
WEEKDAY

† *2 Corinthians 5:14-21*
For our sake God made the sinless one into sin.

The love of Christ impels us who have reached the conviction that since one died for all, all died. He died for all so that those who live might live no longer for themselves, but for him who for their sakes died and was raised up.

Because of this we no longer look on anyone in terms of mere human judgment. If at one time we so regarded Christ, we no longer know him by this standard. This means that if anyone is in Christ, he is a new creation. The old order has passed away; now all is new! All this has been done by God, who has reconciled us to himself through Christ and has given us the ministry of reconciliation. I mean that God, in Christ, was reconciling the world to himself, not counting men's transgressions against them, and that he has entrusted the message of reconciliation to us. This makes us ambassadors for Christ, God as it were appealing through us. We implore you, in Christ's name: be reconciled to God! For our sakes God made him who did not know sin to be sin, so that in him we might become the very holiness of God. ✛

Psalm 103:1-4, 8-9,11-12
R. The Lord is kind and merciful.
Bless the Lord, O my soul;
    and all my being, bless his holy name.
Bless the Lord, O my soul,
    and forget not all his benefits. **R.**
He pardons all your iniquities,
    he heals all your ills.
He redeems your life from destruction,
    he crowns you with kindness and compassion. **R.**
Merciful and gracious is the Lord,
    slow to anger and abounding in kindness.
He will not always chide,
    nor does he keep his wrath forever. **R.**
For as the heavens are high above the earth,
    so surpassing is his kindness toward those who fear him.
As far as the east is from the west,
    so far has he put our transgressions from us. **R.**

Psalm 130:5
R. Alleluia, alleluia.
I hope in the Lord,
I trust in his word. **R.**

† *Matthew 5:33-37*
I say to you do not swear at all.

Jesus said to his disciples: "You have heard the commandment imposed on your forefathers, 'Do not take a false oath; rather, make good to the Lord all your pledges.' What I tell you is: do not swear at all. Do not swear by heaven (it is God's throne), nor by the earth (it is his footstool), nor by Jerusalem (it is the city of the great King); do not swear by your head (you cannot make a single hair white or black). Say, 'Yes' when you mean 'Yes' and 'No' when you mean 'No.' Anything beyond that is from the evil one." ✝

SUNDAY, JUNE 17
THE BODY AND BLOOD OF CHRIST

✝ Genesis 14:18-20
Melchizedek brought out bread and wine.

In those days, Melchizedek, king of Salem, brought out bread
   and wine,
   and being a priest of God Most High,
   he blessed Abram with these words:
   "Blessed be Abram by God Most High,
      the creator of heaven and earth;
   and blessed be God Most High,
      who delivered your foes into your hand."
Then Abram gave him a tenth of everything. ✝

Psalm 110:1-4
**R. You are a priest forever, in the line of
   Melchizedek.**
The LORD said to my Lord: "Sit at my right hand
   till I make your enemies your footstool." **R.**
The scepter of your power the LORD will stretch forth from Zion:
   "Rule in the midst of your enemies." **R.**
"Yours is princely power in the day of your birth, in holy
      splendor;
   before the daystar, like the dew, I have begotten you." **R.**
The LORD has sworn, and he will not repent:
   "You are a priest forever, according to the order of
      Melchizedek." **R.**

✝ 1 Corinthians 11:23-26
For as often as you eat and drink, you proclaim the death of the Lord.

Brothers and sisters:
I received from the Lord what I also handed on to you,
   that the Lord Jesus, on the night he was handed over,
   took bread, and, after he had given thanks,
   broke it and said, "This is my body that is for you.
Do this in remembrance of me."

In the same way also the cup, after supper, saying,
"This cup is the new covenant in my blood.
Do this, as often as you drink it, in remembrance of me."
For as often as you eat this bread and drink the cup,
you proclaim the death of the Lord until he comes. ✛

John 6:51
R. Alleluia, alleluia.
I am the living bread that came down from heaven, says the
Lord;
whoever eats this bread will live forever. **R.**

† *Luke 9:11b-17*
They all ate and were satisfied.

Jesus spoke to the crowds about the kingdom of God,
and he healed those who needed to be cured.
As the day was drawing to a close,
the Twelve approached him and said,
"Dismiss the crowd
so that they can go to the surrounding villages and farms
and find lodging and provisions;
for we are in a deserted place here."
He said to them, "Give them some food yourselves."
They replied, "Five loaves and two fish are all we have,
unless we ourselves go and buy food for all these people."
Now the men there numbered about five thousand.
Then he said to his disciples,
"Have them sit down in groups of about fifty."
They did so and made them all sit down.
Then taking the five loaves and the two fish,
and looking up to heaven,
he said the blessing over them, broke them,
and gave them to the disciples to set before the crowd.
They all ate and were satisfied.
And when the leftover fragments were picked up,
they filled twelve wicker baskets. ✛

MONDAY, JUNE 18
WEEKDAY

† *2 Corinthians 6:1-10*
We have shown that we are the servants of God.

As your fellow workers we beg you not to receive the grace of God in vain. For he says, "In an acceptable time I have heard you; on a day of salvation I have helped you." Now is the acceptable time! Now is the day of salvation!

We avoid giving anyone offense so that our ministry may not be blamed. On the contrary, in all that we do we strive to present ourselves as ministers of God, acting with patient endurance amid trials, difficulties, distresses, beatings, imprisonments, and riots; as men familiar with hard work, sleepless nights, and fastings; conducting ourselves with innocence, knowledge, and patience, in the Holy Spirit, in sincere love; as men with the message of truth and the power of God, wielding the weapons of righteousness with right hand and left, whether honored or dishonored, spoken of well or ill. We are called imposters, yet we are truthful; nobodies who in fact are well known; dead, yet here we are alive; punished, but not put to death; sorrowful, though we are always rejoicing; poor, yet we enrich many. We seem to have nothing, yet everything is ours! ✛

Psalm 98:1-4
R. The Lord has made known his salvation.
Sing to the Lord a new song,
    for he has done wondrous deeds;
His right hand has won victory for him,
    his holy arm. **R.**
The Lord has made his salvation known:
    in the sight of the nations he has revealed his justice.
He has remembered his kindness and his faithfulness
    toward the house of Israel. **R.**
All the ends of the earth have seen
    the salvation by our God.
Sing joyfully to the Lord, all you lands;
    break into song; sing praise. **R.**

John 17:17
R. Alleluia, alleluia.
Your word, O Lord, is truth;
make us holy in the truth. **R.**

✝ *Matthew 5:38-42*
I say to you, offer the wicked man no resistance.

Jesus said to his disciples: "You have heard the commandment, 'An eye for an eye, a tooth for a tooth.' But what I say to you is: offer no resistance to injury. When a person strikes you on the right cheek, turn and offer him the other. If anyone wants to go to law over your shirt, hand him your coat as well. Should anyone press you into service for one mile, go with him two miles. Give to the man who begs from you. Do not turn your back on the borrower." ✝

TUESDAY, JUNE 19
WEEKDAY, ST. ROMUALD

✝ *2 Corinthians 8:1-9*
Christ became poor for our sake.

Brothers, I should like you to know of the grace of God conferred on the churches of Macedonia. In the midst of severe trial their overflowing joy and deep poverty have produced an abundant generosity. According to their means—indeed I can testify even beyond their means—and voluntarily, they begged us insistently for the favor of sharing in this service to members of the church. Beyond our hopes they first gave themselves to God and then to us by the will of God. That is why I have exhorted Titus, who had already begun this work of charity among you, to bring it to successful completion: that just as you are rich in every respect, in faith and discourse, in knowledge, in total concern, and in our love for you, you may also abound in this charity.

I am not giving an order but simply testing your generous love against the concern which others show. You are well acquainted with the favor shown you by our Lord Jesus Christ: how for your sake he made himself poor though he was rich, so that you might become rich by his poverty. ✝

Psalm 146:2, 5-9
R. Praise the Lord, my soul! *(or* **Alleluia.***)*
I will praise the Lord all my life;
    I will sing praise to my God while I live. **R.**
Happy he whose help is the God of Jacob,
    whose hope is in the Lord, his God,
Who made heaven and earth,
    the sea and all that is in them. **R.**
Who keeps faith forever,
    secures justice for the oppressed,
    gives food to the hungry.
The Lord sets captives free. **R.**
The Lord gives sight to the blind.
    The Lord raises up those that were bowed down;
The Lord loves the just.
    The Lord protects strangers. **R.**

John 17:17
R. Alleluia, alleluia.
Your word, O Lord, is truth;
make us holy in the truth. **R.**

† *Matthew 5:43-48*
Love your enemies.

Jesus said to his disciples: "You have heard the commandment, 'You shall love your countryman but hate your enemy.' My command to you is: love your enemies, pray for your persecutors. This will prove that you are sons of your heavenly Father, for his sun rises on the bad and the good, he rains on the just and the unjust. If you love those who love you, what merit is there in that? Do not tax collectors do as much? And if you greet your brothers only, what is so praiseworthy about that? Do not pagans do as much? In a word, you must be perfected as your heavenly Father is perfect." ✠

WEDNESDAY, JUNE 20
WEEKDAY

✝ 2 Corinthians 9:6-11
God loves a cheerful giver.

Let me say this much: He who sows sparingly will reap sparingly, and he who sows bountifully will reap bountifully. Everyone must give according to what he has inwardly decided; not sadly, not grudgingly, for God loves a cheerful giver. God can multiply his favors among you so that you may always have enough of everything and even a surplus for good works, as it is written:
"He scattered abroad and gave to the poor,
   his justice endures forever."
He who supplies seed for the sower and bread for the eater will provide in abundance; he will multiply the seed you sow and increase your generous yield. In every way your liberality is enriched; through us it results in thanks offered to God. ✝

Psalm 112:1-4, 9
R. Happy the man who fears the Lord.
Happy the man who fears the Lord,
   who greatly delights in his commands.
His posterity shall be mighty upon the earth;
   the upright generation shall be blessed. **R.**
Wealth and riches shall be in his house;
   his generosity shall endure forever.
The Lord dawns through the darkness, a light for the upright;
   he is gracious and merciful and just. **R.**
Lavishly he gives to the poor;
   his generosity shall endure forever;
   his horn shall be exalted in glory. **R.**

John 17:17
R. Alleluia, alleluia.
Your word, O Lord, is truth;
make us holy in the truth. **R.**

† *Matthew 6:1-6, 16-18*

Your Father who sees all that is done in secret will reward you.

Jesus said to his disciples: "Be on guard against performing religious acts for people to see. Otherwise expect no recompense from your heavenly Father. When you give alms, for example, do not blow a horn before you in synagogues and streets like hypocrites looking for applause. You can be sure of this much, they are already repaid. In giving alms you are not to let your left hand know what your right hand is doing. Keep your deeds of mercy secret, and your Father who sees in secret will repay you.

"When you are praying, do not behave like the hypocrites who love to stand and pray in synagogues or on street corners in order to be noticed. I give you my word, they are already repaid. Whenever you pray, go to your room, close your door, and pray to your Father in private.

"When you fast, you are not to look glum as the hypocrites do. They change the appearance of their faces so that others may see they are fasting. I assure you, they are already repaid. When you fast, see to it that you groom your hair and wash your face. In that way no one can see you are fasting but your Father who is hidden; and your Father who sees what is hidden will repay you." ✛

THURSDAY, JUNE 21
St. Aloysius Gonzaga

† *2 Corinthians 11:1-11*

I preached the gospel of God to you freely.

You must endure a little of my folly. Put up with me, I beg you! I am jealous of you with the jealousy of God himself, since I have given you in marriage to one husband, presenting you as a chaste virgin to Christ. My fear is that, just as the serpent seduced Eve by his cunning, your thoughts may be corrupted and you may fall away from your sincere and complete devotion to Christ. I say this because when someone comes preaching another Jesus than the one we preached, or when you receive a different spirit than the one you have received, or a gospel other than the gospel you accepted, you seem to endure it quite well. I consider myself inferior to the "super apostles" in nothing. I may be unskilled in speech but I know that I am not lacking in knowledge. We have made this evident to you in every conceivable way.

Could I have done wrong when I preached the gospel of God to you free of charge, humbling myself with a view to exalting you? I robbed other churches, I accepted support from them in order to minister to you. When I was with you and in want I was a burden to none of you, for the brothers who came from Macedonia supplied my needs. In every way possible I kept myself from being burdensome to you, and I shall continue to do so. I swear by the Christ who is in me that this boast of mine will not cease in the regions of Achaia! Why? Because I do not love you? God knows I do. +

Psalm 111:1-4, 7-8

R. Your works, O Lord, are justice and truth.
(or **Alleluia.***)*
I will give thanks to the Lord with all my heart
    in the company and assembly of the just.
Great are the works of the Lord,
    exquisite in all their delights. **R.**
Majesty and glory are his work,
    and his justice endures forever.
He has won renown for his wondrous deeds;
    gracious and merciful is the Lord. **R.**
The works of his hands are faithful and just;
    sure are all his precepts,
Reliable forever and ever,
    wrought in truth and equity. **R.**

John 17:17

R. Alleluia, alleluia.
Your word, O Lord, is truth;
make us holy in the truth. **R.**

† *Matthew 6:7-15*
You should pray like this: Our Father ...

Jesus said to his disciples: "In your prayer do not rattle on like the pagans. They think they will win a hearing by the sheer multiplication of words. Do not imitate them. Your Father knows what you need before you ask him. This is how you are to pray:

'Our Father in heaven,
hallowed be your name,
your kingdom come,
your will be done
on earth as it is in heaven.
Give us today our daily bread,
and forgive us the wrong we have done
as we forgive those who wrong us.
Subject us not to the trial
but deliver us from the evil one.'
"If you forgive the faults of others, your heavenly Father will forgive you yours. If you do not forgive others, neither will your Father forgive you." ✛

FRIDAY, JUNE 22
SACRED HEART OF JESUS

† Ezekiel 34:11-16
I myself will pasture my sheep and I myself will give them rest.

Thus says the Lord GOD:
I myself will look after and tend my sheep.
As a shepherd tends his flock
when he finds himself among his scattered sheep,
so will I tend my sheep.
I will rescue them from every place where they were scattered
when it was cloudy and dark.
I will lead them out from among the peoples
and gather them from the foreign lands;
I will bring them back to their own country
and pasture them upon the mountains of Israel
in the land's ravines and all its inhabited places.
In good pastures will I pasture them,
and on the mountain heights of Israel
shall be their grazing ground.
There they shall lie down on good grazing ground,
and in rich pastures shall they be pastured
on the mountains of Israel.
I myself will pasture my sheep;
I myself will give them rest, says the Lord GOD.

The lost I will seek out,
> the strayed I will bring back,
> the injured I will bind up,
> the sick I will heal,
> but the sleek and the strong I will destroy,
> shepherding them rightly. ✛

Psalm 23:1-6
**R. The Lord is my shepherd;
there is nothing I shall want.**

The LORD is my shepherd; I shall not want.
> In verdant pastures he gives me repose;
beside restful waters he leads me;
> he refreshes my soul. **R.**
He guides me in right paths
> for his name's sake.
Even though I walk in the dark valley
> I fear no evil; for you are at my side
with your rod and your staff
> that give me courage. **R.**
You spread the table before me
> in the sight of my foes;
you anoint my head with oil;
> my cup overflows. **R.**
Only goodness and kindness follow me
> all the days of my life;
and I shall dwell in the house of the LORD
> for years to come. **R.**

† *Romans 5:5b-11*
God proves his love for us.

Brothers and sisters:
The love of God has been poured out into our hearts
> through the Holy Spirit that has been given to us.
For Christ, while we were still helpless,
> died at the appointed time for the ungodly.
Indeed, only with difficulty does one die for a just person,
> though perhaps for a good person
> one might even find courage to die.
But God proves his love for us

in that while we were still sinners Christ died for us.
How much more then, since we are now justified by his blood,
    will we be saved through him from the wrath.
Indeed, if, while we were enemies,
    we were reconciled to God through the death of his Son,
    how much more, once reconciled,
    will we be saved by his life.
Not only that,
    but we also boast of God through our Lord Jesus Christ,
    through whom we have now received reconciliation. ✛

John 10:14 (or Matthew 11:29ab)
R. Alleluia, alleluia.
I am the good shepherd, says the Lord;
I know my sheep, and mine know me. **R.**

† Luke 15:3-7
Rejoice with me because I have found my lost sheep.

Jesus addressed this parable to the Pharisees and scribes:
"What man among you having a hundred sheep and losing one
        of them
    would not leave the ninety-nine in the desert
    and go after the lost one until he finds it?
And when he does find it,
    he sets it on his shoulders with great joy
    and, upon his arrival home,
    he calls together his friends and neighbors and says to them,
    'Rejoice with me because I have found my lost sheep.'
I tell you, in just the same way
    there will be more joy in heaven over one sinner who repents
    than over ninety-nine righteous people
    who have no need of repentance." ✛

SATURDAY, JUNE 23
IMMACULATE HEART OF MARY

† 2 Corinthians 12:1-10
Gladly will I boast of my weaknesses.

I must go on boasting, however useless it may be, and speak
of visions and revelations of the Lord. I know a man in Christ
who, fourteen years ago—whether he was in or outside his

body I cannot say, only God can say—a man who was snatched up to the third heaven. I know that this man—whether in or outside his body I do not know, God knows—was snatched up to Paradise to hear words which cannot be uttered, words which no man may speak. About this man I will boast; but I will do no boasting about myself unless it be about my weaknesses. And even if I were to boast it would not be folly in me because I would only be telling the truth.

But I refrain, lest anyone think more of me than what he sees in me or hears from my lips. As to the extraordinary revelations, in order that I might not become conceited I was given a thorn in the flesh, an angel of Satan to beat me and keep me from getting proud. Three times I begged the Lord that this might leave me. He said to me, "My grace is enough for you, for in weakness power reaches perfection." And so I willingly boast of my weaknesses instead, that the power of Christ may rest upon me.

Therefore I am content with weakness, with mistreatment, with distress, with persecutions and difficulties for the sake of Christ; for when I am powerless, it is then that I am strong. ✛

Psalm 34:8-13
R. Taste and see the goodness of the LORD.
The angel of the LORD encamps
    around those who fear him, and delivers them.
Taste and see how good the LORD is;
    happy the man who takes refuge in him. **R.**
Fear the LORD, you his holy ones,
    for nought is lacking to those who fear him.
The great grow poor and hungry;
    but those who seek the LORD want for no good thing. **R.**
Come, children, hear me;
    I will teach you the fear of the LORD.
Which of you desires life,
    and takes delight in prosperous days? **R.**

John 17:17
R. Alleluia, alleluia.
Your word, O Lord, is truth;
make us holy in the truth. **R.**

† *Luke 2:41-51*
She stored all these things in her heart.

The parents of Jesus used to go every year to Jerusalem for the feast of the Passover, and when he was twelve they went up for the celebration as was their custom. As they were returning at the end of the feast, the child Jesus remained behind unknown to his parents. Thinking he was in the party, they continued their journey for a day, looking for him among their relatives and acquaintances.

Not finding him, they returned to Jerusalem in search of him. On the third day they came upon him in the temple sitting in the midst of the teachers, listening to them and asking them questions. All who heard him were amazed at his intelligence and his answers.

When his parents saw him they were astonished, and his mother said to him: "Son, why have you done this to us? You see that your father and I have been searching for you in sorrow." He said to them: "Why did you search for me? Did you not know I had to be in my Father's house?" But they did not grasp what he said to them.

He went down with them then, and came to Nazareth, and was obedient to them. His mother meanwhile kept all these things in memory. ✥

SUNDAY, JUNE 24
THE BIRTH OF JOHN THE BAPTIST
(Readings for The Birth Of John The Baptist Vigil liturgy are: Jeremiah 1:4-10 • Psalm 71:1-6, 15, 17 • 1 Peter 1:8-12 • Luke 1:5-17)

† *Isaiah 49:1-6*
I will make you a light to the nations.

Hear me, O coastlands
    listen, O distant peoples.
The LORD called me from birth,
    from my mother's womb he gave me my name.
He made of me a sharp-edged sword
    and concealed me in the shadow of his arm.
He made me a polished arrow,
    in his quiver he hid me.
You are my servant, he said to me,
    Israel, through whom I show my glory.

Though I thought I had toiled in vain,
    and for nothing, uselessly, spent my strength,
yet my reward is with the LORD,
    my recompense is with my God.
For now the LORD has spoken
    who formed me as his servant from the womb,
that Jacob may be brought back to him
    and Israel gathered to him;
and I am made glorious in the sight of the Lord,
    and my God is now my strength!
It is too little, he says, for you to be my servant,
    to raise up the tribes of Jacob,
    and restore the survivors of Israel;
I will make you a light to the nations,
    that my salvation may reach to the ends of the earth. ✝

Psalm 139:1-3,13-15
R. I praise you for I am wonderfully made.
O LORD you have probed me and you know me;
    you know when I sit and when I stand;
    you understand my thoughts from afar.
My journeys and my rest you scrutinize,
    with all my ways you are familiar. **R.**
Truly you have formed my inmost being;
    you knit me in my mother's womb.
I give you thanks that I am fearfully, wonderfully made;
    wonderful are your works. **R.**
My soul also you knew full well;
    nor was my frame unknown to you
when I was made in secret,
    when I was fashioned in the depths of the earth. **R.**

✝ Acts 13:22-26
John heralded his coming by proclaiming a baptism of repentance.

In those days, Paul said:
    "God raised up David as their king;
    of him he testified,
    'I have found David, son of Jesse, a man after my own
        heart;
    he will carry out my every wish.'

From this man's descendants God, according to his promise,
  has brought to Israel a savior, Jesus.
John heralded his coming by proclaiming a baptism of repen
    tance
  to all the people of Israel;
  and as John was completing his course, he would say,
  'What do you suppose that I am? I am not he.
Behold, one is coming after me;
  I am not worthy to unfasten the sandals of his feet.'

"My brothers, children of the family of Abraham,
  and those others among you who are God-fearing,
  to us this word of salvation has been sent." ✛

cf. Luke 1:76
R. Alleluia, alleluia.
You, child, will be called prophet of the Most High,
for you will go before the Lord to prepare his way. **R.**

† *Luke 1:57-66, 80*
John is his name.

When the time arrived for Elizabeth to have her child
  she gave birth to a son.
Her neighbors and relatives heard
  that the Lord had shown his great mercy toward her,
  and they rejoiced with her.
When they came on the eighth day to circumcise the child,
  they were going to call him Zechariah after his father,
  but his mother said in reply,
  "No. He will be called John."
But they answered her,
  "There is no one among your relatives who has this name."
So they made signs, asking his father what he wished him to
    be called.
He asked for a tablet and wrote, "John is his name, "
  and all were amazed.
Immediately his mouth was opened, his tongue freed,
  and he spoke blessing God.
Then fear came upon all their neighbors,
  and all these matters were discussed
  throughout the hill country of Judea.

All who heard these things took them to heart, saying,
"What, then, will this child be?"
For surely the hand of the Lord was with him.

The child grew and became strong in spirit,
and he was in the desert until the day
of his manifestation to Israel. ✛

MONDAY, JUNE 25
WEEKDAY

✝ *Genesis 12:1-9*
Abraham went out as God told him.

The Lord said to Abram: "Go forth from the land of your kinsfolk and from your father's house to a land that I will show you.
"I will make of you a great nation,
and I will bless you;
I will make your name great,
so that you will be a blessing.
I will bless those who bless you
and curse those who curse you.
All the communities of the earth
shall find blessing in you."
Abram went as the Lord directed him, and Lot went with him. Abram was seventy-five years old when he left Haran. Abram took his wife Sarai, his brother's son Lot, all the possessions that they had accumulated, and the persons they had acquired in Haran, and they set out for the land of Canaan. When they came to the land of Canaan, Abram passed through the land as far as the sacred place at Shechem, by the terebinth of Moreh. (The Canaanites were then in the land.)
The Lord appeared to Abram and said, "To your descendants I will give this land." So Abram built an altar there to the Lord who had appeared to him. From there he moved on to the hill country east of Bethel, pitching his tent with Bethel to the west and Ai to the east, He built an altar there to the Lord and invoked the Lord by name. Then Abram journeyed on by stages to the Negeb. ✛

Psalm 33:12-13,18-20, 22

**R. Happy the people the Lord has chosen
to be his own.**

Happy the nation whose God is the Lord,
    the people he has chosen for his own inheritance.
From heaven the Lord looks down;
    he sees all mankind. **R.**
See, the eyes of the Lord are upon those who fear him,
    upon those who hope for his kindness,
To deliver them from death
    and preserve them in spite of famine. **R.**
Our soul waits for the Lord,
    who is our help and our shield.
May your kindness, O Lord, be upon us
    who have put our hope in you. **R.**

Psalm 119:135

R. Alleluia, alleluia.

Let your face shine on your servant,
and teach me your laws. **R.**

† *Matthew 7:1-5*
Take the beam out of your own eye first.

Jesus said to his disciples: "If you want to avoid judgment, stop passing judgment. Your verdict on others will be the verdict passed on you. The measure with which you measure will be used to measure you. Why look at the speck in your brother's eye when you miss the plank in your own? How can you say to your brother, 'Let me take that speck out of your eye,' while all the time the plank remains in your own? You hypocrite! Remove the plank from your own eye first; then you will see clearly to take the speck from your brother's eye." ✛

TUESDAY, JUNE 26
WEEKDAY

† *Genesis 13:2, 5-18*
Let there be no dispute between me and you, for we are brothers.

Abram was very rich in livestock, silver, and gold.
    Lot, who went with Abram, also had flocks and herds and

tents, so that the land could not support them if they stayed together; their possessions were so great that they could not dwell together. There were quarrels between the herdsmen of Abram's livestock and those of Lot's. (At this time the Canaanites and the Perizzites were occupying the land.)

So Abram said to Lot: "Let there be no strife between you and me, or between your herdsmen and mine, for we are kinsmen. Is not the whole land at your disposal? Please separate from me. If you prefer the left, I will go to the right; if you prefer the right, I will go to the left." Lot looked about and saw how well watered the whole Jordan Plain was as far as Zoar, like the Lord's own garden, or like Egypt. (This was before the Lord had destroyed Sodom and Gomorrah.) Lot, therefore, chose for himself the whole Jordan Plain and set out eastward. Thus they separated from each other; Abram stayed in the land of Canaan, while Lot settled among the cities of the Plain, pitching his tents near Sodom. Now the inhabitants of Sodom were very wicked in the sins they committed against the Lord.

After Lot had left, the Lord said to Abram: "Look about you, and from where you are, gaze to the north and south, east and west; all the land that you see I will give to you and your descendants forever. I will make your descendants like the dust of the earth; if anyone could count the dust of the earth, your descendants too might be counted. Set forth and walk about in the land, through its length and breadth, for to you I will give it." Abram moved his tents and went on to settle near the terebinth of Mamre, which is at Hebron. There he built an altar to the Lord. ✝

Psalm 15:2-5
**R. He who does justice
will live in the presence of the Lord.**
He who walks blamelessly and does justice;
    who thinks the truth in his heart
    and slanders not with his tongue. **R.**
Who harms not his fellow man,
    nor takes up a reproach against his neighbor;
By whom the reprobate is despised,
    while he honors those who fear the Lord. **R.**

Who lends not his money at usury
  and accepts no bribe against the innocent,
He who does these things
  shall never be disturbed. **R.**

Psalm 119:135
R. Alleluia, alleluia.
Let your face shine on your servant,
and teach me your laws. **R.**

† *Matthew 7: 6, 12-14*
Always treat others as you would like them to treat you.

Jesus said to his disciples: "Do not give what is holy to dogs or toss your pearls before swine. They will trample them under foot, at best, and perhaps even tear you to shreds.

"Treat others the way you would have them treat you: this sums up the law and the prophets.

"Enter through the narrow gate. The gate that leads to damnation is wide, the road is clear, and many choose to travel it. But how narrow is the gate that leads to life, how rough the road, and how few there are who find it!" ✛

WEDNESDAY, JUNE 27
WEEKDAY, ST. CYRIL OF ALEXANDRIA

† *Genesis 15:1-12, 17-18*
Abraham put his faith in the Lord God,
who counted this as making him justified.

The word of the Lord came to Abram in a vision:
  "Fear not, Abram!
    I am your shield;
    I will make your reward very great,"
But Abram said, "O Lord God, what good will your gifts be, if I keep on being childless and have as my heir the steward of my house, Eliezer?" Abram continued, "See, you have given me no offspring, and so one of my servants will be my heir." Then the word of the Lord came to him: "No, that one shall not be your heir; your own issue shall be your heir." He took him outside and said: "Look up at the sky and count the stars, if you can. Just so," he added, "shall your descendants be." Abram put his faith in the Lord, who credited it to him as an act of

righteousness.

He then said to him, "I am the Lord who brought you from Ur of the Chaldeans to give you this land as a possession." "O Lord God," he asked, "how am I to know that I shall possess it?" He answered him, "Bring me a three-year-old heifer, a three-year-old she-goat, a three-year-old ram, a turtledove, and a young pigeon." He brought him all these, split them in two, and placed each half opposite the other; but the birds he did not cut up. Birds of prey swooped down on the carcasses, but Abram stayed with them. As the sun was about to set, a trance fell upon Abram, and a deep, terrifying darkness enveloped him.

When the sun had set and it was dark, there appeared a smoking brazier and a flaming torch, which passed between those pieces. It was on that occasion that the Lord made a covenant with Abram, saying: "To your descendants I give this land, from the Wadi of Egypt to the Great River [the Euphrates]." ✛

Psalm 105:1-4, 6-9
R. The Lord remembers his covenant forever.
(or **Alleluia.***)*
Give thanks to the Lord, invoke his name;
　　make known among the nations his deeds.
Sing to him, sing his praise,
　　proclaim all his wondrous deeds. **R.**
Glory in his holy name;
　　rejoice, O hearts that seek the Lord!
Look to the Lord in his strength;
　　seek to serve him constantly. **R.**
You descendants of Abraham, his servants,
　　sons of Jacob, his chosen ones!
He, the Lord, is our God;
　　throughout the earth his judgments prevail. **R.**
He remembers forever his covenant
　　which he made binding for a thousand generations—
Which he entered into with Abraham
　　and by his oath to Isaac. **R.**

Psalm 119:135

R. Alleluia, alleluia.

Let your face shine on your servant,
and teach me your laws. **R.**

† *Matthew 7:15-20*
By their fruits you will know them.

Jesus said to his disciples: "Be on your guard against false prophets, who come to you in sheep's clothing but underneath are wolves on the prowl. You will know them by their deeds. Do you ever pick grapes from thornbushes, or figs from prickly plants? Never! Any sound tree bears good fruit, while a decayed tree bears bad fruit. A sound tree cannot bear bad fruit any more than a decayed tree can bear good fruit. Every tree that does not bear good fruit is cut down and thrown into the fire. You can tell a tree by its fruit." †

THURSDAY, JUNE 28
St. Irenaeus

† *Genesis 16:6-12,15-16 (or Genesis 16:1-12, 15-16)*
Hagar bore Abraham a son and he called him Ishmael.

Abram told Sarai: "Your maid is in your power. Do to her whatever you please." Sarai then abused her so much that Hagar ran away from her. The Lord's messenger found her by a spring in the wilderness, the spring on the road to Shur, and he asked, "Hagar, maid of Sarai, where have you come from and where are you going?" She answered, "I am running away from my mistress, Sarai." But the Lord's messenger told her: "Go back to your mistress and submit to her abusive treatment. I will make your descendants so numerous," added the Lord's messenger, "that they will be too many to count. Besides," the Lord's messenger said to her:

"You are now pregnant and shall bear a son;
  you shall name him Ishmael,
For the Lord has heard you,
  God has answered you.
He shall be a wild ass of a man,
  his hand against everyone,
  and everyone's hand against him;

In opposition to all his kin
  shall he encamp."
Hagar bore Abram a son, and Abram named the son whom
Hagar bore him Ishmael. Abram was eighty-six years old
when Hagar bore him Ishmael. ✢

Psalm 106:1-5
R. Give thanks to the Lord for he is good.
(or **Alleluia.***)*
Give thanks to the Lord, for he is good,
  for his kindness endures forever.
Who can tell the mighty deeds of the Lord,
  or proclaim all his praises? **R.**
Who can tell the mighty deeds of the Lord,
  or proclaim all his praises?
Happy are they who observe what is right,
  who do always what is just.
Remember us, O Lord, as you favor your people. **R.**
Visit me with your saving help,
  that I may see the prosperity of your chosen ones,
Rejoice in the joy of your people,
  and glory with your inheritance. **R.**

Psalm 119:135
R. Alleluia, alleluia.
Let your face shine on your servant,
and teach me your laws. **R.**

† *Matthew 7:21-29*
The house built on rock is compared to the house built on sand.

Jesus said to his disciples: "None of those who cry out, 'Lord,
Lord,' will enter the kingdom of God but only the one who does
the will of my Father in heaven. When that day comes, many
will plead with me, 'Lord, Lord, have we not prophesied in your
name? Have we not exorcised demons by its power? Did we not
do many miracles in your name as well?' Then I will declare to
them solemnly, 'I never knew you. Out of my sight, you
evildoers!'"

"Anyone who hears my words and puts them into practice
is like the wise man who built his house on rock. When the
rainy season set in, the torrents came and the winds blew and

buffeted his house. It did not collapse; it had been solidly set on rock. Anyone who hears my words but does not put them into practice is like the foolish man who built his house on sandy ground. The rains fell, the torrents came, the winds blew and lashed against his house. It collapsed under all this and was completely ruined."

Jesus finished this discourse and left the crowds spellbound at his teaching. The reason was that he taught with authority and not like their scribes. ✛

FRIDAY, JUNE 29
STS. PETER AND PAUL

(Readings for the Sts. Peter and Paul Vigil Mass are: Acts 3:1-10 • Psalm 19:2-5 • Galatians 1:11-20 • John 21:15-19)

†Acts 12:1-11
Now I know for certain that the Lord rescued me from the hand of Herod.

In those days, King Herod laid hands upon some members of
 the church to harm them.
He had James, the brother of John, killed by the sword,
 and when he saw that this was pleasing to the Jews
 he proceeded to arrest Peter also.
—It was the feast of Unleavened Bread.—
He had him taken into custody and put in prison
 under the guard of four squads of four soldiers each.
He intended to bring him before the people after Passover.
Peter thus was being kept in prison,
 but prayer by the church was fervently being made
 to God on his behalf.

On the very night before Herod was to bring him to trial,
 Peter, secured by double chains,
 was sleeping between two soldiers,
 while outside the door guards kept watch on the prison.
Suddenly the angel of the Lord stood by him
 and a light shone in the cell.
He tapped Peter on the side and awakened him, saying,
 "Get up quickly."
The chains fell from his wrists.
The angel said to him, "Put on your belt and your sandals."
He did so.
Then he said to him, "Put on your cloak and follow me."

So he followed him out,
>not realizing that what was happening through the angel
>>was real;
>he thought he was seeing a vision.
They passed the first guard, then the second,
>and came to the iron gate leading out to the city,
>which opened for them by itself.
They emerged and made their way down an alley,
>and suddenly the angel left him. ✝

Psalm 34:2-9

**R. The angel of the Lord will rescue
those who fear him.**

I will bless the LORD at all times;
>his praise shall be ever in my mouth.
Let my soul glory in the LORD;
>the lowly will hear me and be glad. **R.**
Glorify the LORD with me,
>let us together extol his name.
I sought the LORD, and he answered me
>and delivered me from all my fears. **R.**
Look to him that you may be radiant with joy,
>and your faces may not blush with shame.
When the poor one called out, the LORD heard,
>and from all his distress he saved him. **R.**
The angel of the LORD encamps
>around those who fear him, and delivers them.
Taste and see how good the LORD is;
>blessed the man who takes refuge in him. **R.**

✝ *2 Timothy 4:6-8,17-18*
From now on the crown of righteousness awaits me.

I, Paul, am already being poured out like a libation,
>and the time of my departure is at hand.
I have competed well; I have finished the race;
>I have kept the faith.
From now on the crown of righteousness awaits me,
>which the Lord, the just judge,
>>will award to me on that day, and not only to me,
>>but to all who have longed for his appearance.

The Lord stood by me and gave me strength,
    so that through me the proclamation might be completed
    and all the Gentiles might hear it.
And I was rescued from the lion's mouth.
The Lord will rescue me from every evil threat
    and will bring me safe to his heavenly kingdom.
To him be glory forever and ever. Amen. ✛

Matthew 16:18
R. Alleluia. alleluia.
You are Peter and upon this rock I will build my church,
and the gates of the netherworld shall not prevail
    against it. **R.**

† *Matthew 16:13-19*
You are Peter, and I will give you the keys to the kingdom of heaven.

When Jesus went into the region of Caesarea Philippi
    he asked his disciples,
    "Who do people say that the Son of Man is?"
They replied, "Some say John the Baptist, others Elijah,
    still others Jeremiah or one of the prophets."
He said to them, "But who do you say that I am?"
Simon Peter said in reply,
    "You are the Christ, the Son of the living God."
Jesus said to him in reply, "Blessed are you, Simon son of
    Jonah.
For flesh and blood has not revealed this to you, but my
    heavenly Father.
And so I say to you, you are Peter,
    and upon this rock I will build my church,
    and the gates of the netherworld shall not prevail
    against it.
I will give you the keys to the kingdom of heaven.
Whatever you bind on earth shall be bound in heaven;
    and whatever you loose on earth shall be loosed in
    heaven." ✛

SATURDAY, JUNE 30
WEEKDAY, THE FIRST MARTYRS OF THE CHURCH OF ROME

✝ *Genesis 18:1-15*
Is anything too difficult for the Lord God? I will
visit you again and Sarah will have a son.

The Lord appeared to Abraham by the terebinth of Mamre, as he sat in the entrance of his tent, while the day was growing hot. Looking up, he saw three men standing nearby. When he saw them, he ran from the entrance of the tent to greet them; and bowing to the ground, he said: "Sir, if I may ask you this favor, please do not go on past your servant. Let some water be brought, that you may bathe your feet, and then rest yourselves under the tree. Now that you have come this close to your servant, let me bring you a little food, that you may refresh yourselves; and afterward you may go on your way." "Very well," they replied, "do as you have said."

Abraham hastened into the tent and told Sarah, "Quick, three seahs of fine flour! Knead it and make rolls." He ran to the herd, picked out a tender, choice steer, and gave it to a servant, who quickly prepared it. Then he got some curds and milk, as well as the steer that had been prepared, and set these before them; and he waited on them under the tree while they ate.

"Where is your wife Sarah?" they asked him. "There in the tent," he replied. One of them said, "I will surely return to you about this time next year, and Sarah will then have a son." Sarah was listening at the entrance of the tent, just behind him. Now Abraham and Sarah were old, advanced in years, and Sarah had stopped having her womanly periods. So Sarah laughed to herself and said, "Now that I am so withered and my husband is so old, am I still to have sexual pleasure?" But the Lord said to Abraham: "Why did Sarah laugh and say, 'Shall I really bear a child, old as I am?' Is anything too marvelous for the Lord to do? At the appointed time, about this time next year, I will return to you, and Sarah will have a son." Because she was afraid, Sarah dissembled, saying," I didn't laugh." But he said, "Yes you did." ✝

Luke 1:46-50, 53-55

R. The Lord has remembered his mercy.

My being proclaims the greatness of the Lord,
   my spirit finds joy in God my savior. **R.**
For he has looked upon his servant in her lowliness;
   all ages to come shall call me blessed.
God who is mighty has done great things for me,
   holy is his name. **R.**
His mercy is from age to age
   on those who fear him.
The hungry he has given every good thing,
   while the rich he has sent away empty. **R.**
He has upheld Israel his servant,
   ever mindful of his mercy;
Even as he promised our fathers,
   promised and his descendants forever. **R.**

Psalm 119:135

R. Alleluia, alleluia.

Let your face shine on your servant,
and teach me your laws. **R.**

† *Matthew 8:5-17*

*Many will come from east and west and take their
places with Abraham, Isaac, and Jacob at the feast.*

As Jesus entered Capernaum, a centurion approached him
with this request: "Sir, my serving boy is at home in bed
paralyzed, suffering painfully." He said to him, "I will come
and cure him." "Sir," the centurion said in reply, "I am not
worthy to have you under my roof. Just give an order and my
boy will get better. I am a man under authority myself and I
have troops assigned to me. If I give one man the order,
'Dismissed,' off he goes. If I say to another, 'Come here,' he
comes. If I tell my slave, 'Do this,' he does it." Jesus showed
amazement on hearing this and remarked to his followers, "I
assure you, I have never found this much faith in Israel. Mark
what I say! Many will come from the east and the west and will
find a place at the banquet in the kingdom of God with
Abraham, Isaac, and Jacob, while the natural heirs of the
kingdom will be driven out into the dark. Wailing will be heard
there, and the grinding of teeth." To the centurion Jesus said,

"Go home. It shall be done because you trusted." That very moment the boy got better.

Jesus entered Peter's house and found Peter's mother-in-law in bed with a fever. He took her by the hand and the fever left her. She got up at once and began to wait on him.

As evening drew on, they brought him many who were possessed. He expelled the spirits by a simple command and cured all who were afflicted, thereby fulfilling what had been said through Isaiah the prophet:
"It was our infirmities he bore,
our sufferings he endured." ✛

JULY 1
THIRTEENTH SUNDAY IN ORDINARY TIME

† *1 Kings 19:16b,19-21*
Then Elisha left and followed Elijah as his attendant.

The LORD said to Elijah:
"You shall anoint Elisha, son of Shaphat of Abelmeholah,
as prophet to succeed you."

Elijah set out and came upon Elisha, son of Shaphat,
as he was plowing with twelve yoke of oxen;
he was following the twelfth.
Elijah went over to him and threw his cloak over him.
Elisha left the oxen, ran after Elijah, and said,
"Please, let me kiss my father and mother goodbye,
and I will follow you."
Elijah answered, "Go back!
Have I done anything to you?"
Elisha left him, and taking the yoke of oxen, slaughtered them;
he used the plowing equipment for fuel to boil their flesh,
and gave it to his people to eat.
Then Elisha left and followed Elijah as his attendant. ✛

Psalm 16:1-2, 5, 7-11
R. You are my inheritance, O Lord.
Keep me, O God, for in you I take refuge;
I say to the Lord, "My LORD are you.
O LORD, my allotted portion and my cup,
you it is who hold fast my lot." **R.**

I bless the LORD who counsels me;
   even in the night my heart exhorts me.
I set the LORD ever before me;
   with him at my right hand I shall not be disturbed. **R.**
Therefore my heart is glad and my soul rejoices,
   my body, too, abides in confidence
because you will not abandon my soul to the netherworld,
   nor will you suffer your faithful one to undergo
      corruption. **R.**
You will show me the path to life,
   fullness of joys in your presence,
      the delights at your right hand forever. **R.**

† *Galatians 5:1,13-18*
You were called for freedom.

Brothers and sisters:
For freedom Christ set us free;
   so stand firm and do not submit again to the yoke of slavery.

For you were called for freedom, brothers and sisters.
But do not use this freedom
   as an opportunity for the flesh;
   rather, serve one another through love.
For the whole law is fulfilled in one statement,
   namely, *You shall love your neighbor as yourself.*
But if you go on biting and devouring one another,
   beware that you are not consumed by one another.

I say, then: live by the Spirit
   and you will certainly not gratify the desire of the flesh.
For the flesh has desires against the Spirit,
   and the Spirit against the flesh;
   these are opposed to each other,
   so that you may not do what you want.
But if you are guided by the Spirit, you are not under the law. ✝

1 Samuel 3:9; John 6:68c
R. Alleluia, alleluia.
Speak, Lord, your servant is listening;
you have the words of everlasting life. **R.**

† *Luke 9:51-62*

*He resolutely determined to journey to
Jerusalem. I will follow you wherever you go.*

When the days for Jesus' being taken up were fulfilled,
   he resolutely determined to journey to Jerusalem,
   and he sent messengers ahead of him.
On the way they entered a Samaritan village
   to prepare for his reception there,
   but they would not welcome him
   because the destination of his journey was Jerusalem.
When the disciples James and John saw this they asked,
   "Lord, do you want us to call down fire from heaven
   to consume them?"
Jesus turned and rebuked them, and they journeyed to an
   other village.

As they were proceeding on their journey someone said to him,
   "I will follow you wherever you go."
Jesus answered him,
   "Foxes have dens and birds of the sky have nests,
   but the Son of Man has nowhere to rest his head."

And to another he said, "Follow me."
But he replied, "Lord, let me go first and bury my father."
But he answered him, "Let the dead bury their dead.
But you, go and proclaim the kingdom of God."
And another said, "I will follow you, Lord,
   but first let me say farewell to my family at home."
To him Jesus said, "No one who sets a hand to the plow
   and looks to what was left behind is fit for the kingdom of
   God." ✦

MONDAY, JULY 2
WEEKDAY

† *Genesis 18:16-33*

Are you going to destroy the just man with the sinner?

The men set out from the valley of Mamre and looked down
toward Sodom; Abraham was walking with them, to see them
on their way. The Lord reflected: "Shall I hide from Abraham
what I am about to do, now that he is to become a great and

populous nation, and all the nations of the earth are to find blessing in him? Indeed, I have singled him out that he may direct his sons and his posterity to keep the way of the Lord by doing what is right and just, so that the Lord may carry into effect for Abraham the promises he made about him." Then the Lord said: "The outcry against Sodom and Gomorrah is so great, and their sin so grave, that I must go down and see whether or not their actions fully correspond to the cry against them that comes to me. I mean to find out."

While the two men walked on farther toward Sodom, the Lord remained standing before Abraham. Then Abraham drew nearer to him and said: "Will you sweep away the innocent with the guilty? Suppose there were fifty innocent people in the city; would you wipe out the place, rather than spare it for the sake of the fifty innocent people within it? Far be it from you to do such a thing, to make the innocent die with the guilty, so that the innocent and the guilty would be treated alike! Should not the judge of all the world act with justice?" The Lord replied, "If I find fifty innocent people in the city of Sodom, I will spare the whole place for their sake." Abraham spoke up again: "See how I am presuming to speak to my Lord, though I am but dust and ashes! What if there are five less than fifty innocent people? Will you destroy the whole city because of those five?" "I will not destroy it," he answered, "if I find forty-five there." But Abraham persisted, saying, "What if only forty are found there?" He replied, "I will forbear doing it for the sake of the forty." Then he said, "Let not my Lord grow impatient if I go on. What if only thirty are found there?" He replied, "I will forbear doing it if I can find but thirty there." Still he went on, "Since I have thus dared to speak to my Lord, what if there are no more than twenty?" "I will not destroy it," he answered, "for the sake of the twenty." But he still persisted: "Please, let not my Lord grow angry if I speak up this last time. What if there are at least ten there?" "For the sake of those ten," he replied, "I will not destroy it."

The Lord departed as soon as he had finished speaking with Abraham, and Abraham returned home. ✢

Psalm 103:1-4, 8-11

R. The Lord is kind and merciful.

Bless the Lord, O my soul;
   and all my being, bless his holy name.
Bless the Lord, O my soul,
   and forget not all his benefits. **R.**
He pardons all your iniquities,
   he heals all your ills.
He redeems your life from destruction,
   he crowns you with kindness and compassion. **R.**
Merciful and gracious is the Lord,
   slow to anger and abounding in kindness.
He will not always chide,
   nor does he keep his wrath forever. **R.**
Not according to our sins does he deal with us,
   nor does he requite us according to our crimes.
For as the heavens are high above the earth,
   so surpassing is his kindness toward those who fear him. **R.**

See Acts 16:14

R. Alleluia, alleluia.

Open our hearts, O Lord,
to listen to the words of your Son. **R.**

† *Matthew 8:18-22*
Follow me.

Jesus, seeing the people crowd around him, gave orders to cross the lake to the other shore. A scribe approached him and said, "Teacher, wherever you go I will come after you." Jesus said to him, "The foxes have lairs, the birds in the sky have nests, but the Son of Man has nowhere to lay his head." Another, a disciple, said to him, "Lord, let me go and bury my father first." But Jesus told him, "Follow me, and let the dead bury their dead." +

TUESDAY, JULY 3
St. Thomas

† *Ephesians 2:19-22*
You are part of the building built on the foundation of the apostles.

You are strangers and aliens no longer. No, you are fellow citizens of the saints and members of the household of God. You form a building which rises on the foundation of the apostles and prophets, with Christ Jesus himself as the capstone. Through him the whole structure is fitted together and takes shape as a holy temple in the Lord; in him you are being built into this temple, to become a dwelling place for God in the Spirit. ✛

Psalm 117:1-2
**R. Go out to all the world,
and tell the Good News.**
Praise the Lord, all you nations;
glorify him, all you peoples! **R.**
For steadfast is his kindness toward us,
and the fidelity of the Lord endures forever. **R.**

John 20:29
R. Alleluia, alleluia.
You believed in me, Thomas, because you have seen me;
happy those who have not seen me, but still believe!

† *John 20:24-29*
My Lord and my God.

Thomas (the name means "Twin"), one of the Twelve, was absent when Jesus came into the room. The other disciples kept telling him: "We have seen the Lord!" His answer was, "I'll never believe it without probing the nailprints in his hands, without putting my finger in the nailmarks and my hand into his side."

A week later, the disciples were once more in the room, and this time Thomas was with them. Despite the locked doors, Jesus came and stood before them. "Peace be with you," he said; then, to Thomas: "Take your finger and examine my hands. Put your hand into my side. Do not persist in your unbelief, but believe!" Thomas said in response, "My Lord and

my God!" Jesus then said to him:
"You became a believer because you saw me.
Blest are they who have not seen and have believed." ✛

WEDNESDAY, JULY 4
WEEKDAY, ST. ELIZABETH OF PORTUGAL, INDEPENDENCE DAY

† Genesis 21:5,8-20
The slave girl's son will not share the inheritance with my son Isaac.

Abraham was a hundred years old when his son Isaac was born to him. Isaac grew, and on the day of the child's weaning, Abraham held a great feast.

Sarah noticed the son whom Hagar the Egyptian had borne to Abraham playing with her son Isaac; so she demanded of Abraham: "Drive out that slave and her son! No son of that slave is going to share the inheritance with my son Isaac!" Abraham was greatly distressed, especially on account of his son Ishmael. But God said to Abraham: "Do not be distressed about the boy or about your slave woman. Heed the demands of Sarah, no matter what she is asking of you; for it is through Isaac that descendants shall bear your name. As for the son of the slave woman, I will make a great nation of him also, since he too is your offspring."

Early the next morning Abraham got some bread and a skin of water and gave them to Hagar. Then, placing the child on her back, he sent her away. As she roamed aimlessly in the wilderness of Beer-sheba, the water in the skin was used up. So she put the child down under a shrub, and then went and sat down opposite him, about a bowshot away; for she said to herself, "Let me not watch the child die." As she sat opposite him, he began to cry. God heard the boy's cry, and God's messenger called to Hagar from heaven: "What is the matter, Hagar? Don't be afraid; God has heard the boy's cry in this plight of his. Arise, lift up the boy and hold him by the hand; for I will make of him a great nation." Then God opened her eyes, and she saw a well of water. She went and filled the skin with water, and then let the boy drink.

God was with the boy as he grew up. ✛

Psalm 34:7-8,10-13

R. The Lord hears the cry of the poor.

When the afflicted man called out, the Lord heard,
> and from all his distress he saved him.
The angel of the Lord encamps
> around those who fear him, and delivers them. **R.**
Fear the Lord, you his holy ones,
> for nought is lacking to those who fear him.
The great grow poor and hungry;
> but those who seek the Lord want for no good thing. **R.**
Come, children, hear me;
> I will teach you the fear of the Lord.
Which of you desires life,
> and takes delight in prosperous days? **R.**

See Acts 16:14

R. Alleluia, alleluia.

Open our hearts, O Lord,
to listen to the words of your Son. **R.**

† *Matthew 8:28-34*
He came before the appointed time to torture the demons.

As Jesus approached the Gadarene boundary, he encountered two men coming out of the tombs. They were possessed by demons and were so savage that no one could travel along the road. With a sudden shriek they cried: "Why meddle with us, Son of God? Have you come to torture us before the appointed time?" Some distance away a large herd of swine was feeding. The demons kept appealing to him, "If you expel us, send us into the herd of swine." He answered, "Out with you!" At that they came forth and entered the swine. The whole herd went rushing down the bluff into the sea and were drowned.

The swineherds took to their heels, and upon their arrival in the town related everything that had happened, including the story about the two possessed men. The upshot was that the entire town came out to meet Jesus. When they caught sight of him, they begged him to leave their neighborhood. ✛

THURSDAY, JULY 5
WEEKDAY, ST. ANTHONY MARY ZACCARIA

† *Genesis 22:1-19*
The sacrifice of Abraham, our father in faith.

God put Abraham to the test. He called to him, "Abraham!" "Ready!" he replied. Then God said: "Take your son Isaac, your only one, whom you love, and go to the land of Moriah. There you shall offer him up as a holocaust on a height that I will point out to you." Early the next morning Abraham saddled his donkey, took with him his son Isaac, and two of his servants as well, and with the wood that he had cut for the holocaust, set out for the place of which God had told him.

On the third day Abraham got sight of the place from afar. Then he said to his servants: "Both of you stay here with the donkey, while the boy and I go on over yonder. We will worship and then come back to you." Thereupon Abraham took the wood for the holocaust and laid it on his son Isaac's shoulders, while he himself carried the fire and the knife. As the two walked on together, Isaac spoke to his father Abraham. "Father!" he said. "Yes, son," he replied. Isaac continued, "Here are the fire and the wood, but where is the sheep for the holocaust?" "Son," Abraham answered, "God himself will provide the sheep for the holocaust." Then the two continued going forward.

When they came to the place of which God had told him, Abraham built an altar there and arranged the wood on it. Next he tied up his son Isaac, and put him on top of the wood on the altar. Then he reached out and took the knife to slaughter his son. But the Lord's messenger called to him from heaven, "Abraham, Abraham!" "Yes, Lord," he answered. "Do not lay your hand on the boy," said the messenger. "Do not do the least thing to him. I know now how devoted you are to God, since you did not withhold from me your own beloved son." As Abraham looked about, he spied a ram caught by its horns in the thicket. So he went and took the ram and offered it up as a holocaust in place of his son. Abraham named the site Yahweh-yireh; hence people now say, "On the mountain the Lord will see."

Again the Lord's messenger called to Abraham from heaven

and said: "I swear by myself, declares the Lord, that because you acted as you did in not withholding from me your beloved son, I will bless you abundantly and make your descendants as countless as the stars of the sky and the sands of the seashore; your descendants shall take possession of the gates of their enemies, and in your descendants all the nations of the earth shall find blessing—all this because you obeyed my command."

Abraham then returned to his servants, and they set out together for Beer-sheba, where Abraham made his home. ✝

Psalm 115:1-6, 8-9
**R. I will walk in the presence of the Lord,
in the land of the living.**
Not to us, O Lord, not to us
but to your name give glory
because of your kindness, because of your truth.
Why should the pagans say,
"Where is their God?" **R.**
Our God is in heaven;
whatever he wills, he does.
Their idols are silver and gold,
the handiwork of men. **R.**
They have mouths but speak not;
they have eyes but see not;
They have ears but hear not;
they have noses but smell not. **R.**
Their makers shall be like them,
everyone that trusts in them.
The house of Israel trusts in the LORD;
he is their help and their shield. **R.**

See Acts 16:14
R. Alleluia, alleluia.
Open our hearts, O Lord,
to listen to the words of your Son. **R.**

✝ *Matthew 9:1-8*
They praised God for giving such power to men.

Jesus entered a boat, made the crossing, and came back to his own town. There the people at once brought to him a paralyzed man lying on a mat. When Jesus saw their faith he said to the paralytic, "Have courage, son, your sins are forgiven." At that some of the scribes said to themselves, "The man blasphemes." Jesus was aware of what they were thinking and said: "Why do you harbor evil thoughts? Which is less trouble to say, 'Your sins are forgiven' or 'Stand up and walk'? To help you realize that the Son of Man has authority on earth to forgive sins"— he then said to the paralyzed man—"Stand up! Roll up your mat, and go home." The man stood up and went toward his home. At the sight, a feeling of awe came over the crowd, and they praised God for giving such authority to men. ✛

FRIDAY, JULY 6
Weekday, St. Maria Goretti

✝ *Genesis 23:1-4,19; 24:1-8, 62-67*
Isaac loved Rebekah—he made her his wife,
and was consoled for the loss of his mother.

The span of Sarah's life was one hundred and twenty-seven years. She died in Kiriatharba (that is, Hebron) in the land of Canaan, and Abraham performed the customary mourning rites for her. Then he left the side of his dead one and addressed the Hittites: "Although I am a resident alien among you, sell me from your holdings a piece of property for a burial ground, that I may bury my dead wife."

After this transaction, Abraham buried his wife Sarah in the cave of the field of Machpelah, facing Mamre (that is, Hebron) in the land of Canaan.

Abraham had now reached a ripe old age, and the Lord had blessed him in every way. Abraham said to the senior servant of his household, who had charge of all his possessions: "Put your hand under my thigh, and I will make you swear by the Lord, the God of heaven and the God of earth, that you will not procure a wife for my son from the daughters of the Canaanites among whom I live, but that you will go to my own land and to my kindred to get a wife for my son Isaac." The servant asked him: "What if the woman is unwilling to follow me to this land? Should I then take your son back to the land from which you migrated?" "Never take my son back there for any reason," Abraham told him. "The Lord, the God of heaven, who took me from my father's house and the land of my kin, and who confirmed by oath the promise he then made to me, 'I will give this land to your descendants'—he will send his messenger before you, and you will obtain a wife for my son there. If the woman is unwilling to follow you, you will be released from this oath. But never take my son back there!"

[A long time later, Isaac went] to live in the region of the Negeb. One day toward evening he went out . . . in the field, and as he looked around, he noticed that camels were approaching. Rebekah, too, was looking about, and when she saw him, she alighted from her camel and asked the servant, "Who is the man out there, walking through the fields toward us?" "That is my master," replied the servant. Then she covered herself with her veil.

The servant recounted to Isaac all the things he had done. Then Isaac took Rebekah into his tent; he married her, and thus she became his wife. In his love for her Isaac found solace after the death of his mother Sarah. ✛

Psalm 106:1-5
R. Give thanks to the Lord for he is good.
 (or **Alleluia.***)*
Give thanks to the Lord, for he is good,
 for his kindness endures forever.
Who can tell the mighty deeds of the Lord,
 or proclaim all his praises? **R.**
Happy are they who observe what is right,
 who do always what is just.
Remember me, O Lord, as you favor your people. **R.**
Visit me with your saving help,
 that I may see the prosperity of your chosen ones,
Rejoice in the joy of your people,
 and glory with your inheritance. **R.**

See Acts 16:14
R. Alleluia, alleluia.
Open our hearts, O Lord,
to listen to the words of your Son. **R.**

✝ *Matthew 9:9-13*
It is not the healthy who need the doctor;
what I want is mercy, not sacrifice.

As Jesus moved about, he saw a man named Matthew at his post where taxes were collected. He said to him, "Follow me." Matthew got up and followed him. Now it happened that, while Jesus was at table in Matthew's home, many tax collectors and those known as sinners came to join Jesus and his disciples at dinner. The Pharisees saw this and complained to his disciples, "What reason can the Teacher have for eating with tax collectors and those who disregard the law?" Overhearing the remark, he said: "People who are in good health do not need a doctor; sick people do. Go and learn the meaning of the words, 'It is mercy I desire and not sacrifice.' I have come to call, not the self-righteous, but sinners." ✛

SATURDAY, JULY 7
WEEKDAY

✝ *Genesis 27:1-5,15-29*
Jacob took his brother's place and by fraud received the blessing.

When Isaac was so old that his eyesight had failed him, he called his older son Esau and said to him, "Son!" "Yes, father!" he replied. Isaac then said, "As you can see, I am so old that I may now die at any time. Take your gear, therefore — your quiver and bow — and go out into the country to hunt some game for me. With your catch prepare an appetizing dish for me, such as I like, and bring it to me to eat, so that I may give you my special blessing before I die."

Rebekah had been listening while Isaac was speaking to his son Esau, who went out into the country to carry out his father's orders.

Rebekah then took the best clothes of her older son Esau that she had in the house, and gave them to her younger son Jacob to wear; and with the skins of the kids she covered up his hands and the hairless parts of his neck. Then she handed her son Jacob the appetizing dish and the bread she had prepared.

Bringing them to his father, Jacob said, "Father!" "Yes?" replied Isaac. "Which of my sons are you?" Jacob answered his father: "I am Esau, your first-born. I did as you told me. Please sit up and eat some of my game, so that you may give me your special blessing." But Isaac asked, "How did you succeed so quickly, son?" He answered, "The Lord, your God, let things turn out well with me." Isaac then said to Jacob, "Come closer, son, that I may feel you, to learn whether you really are my son Esau or not." So Jacob moved up closer to his father. When Isaac felt him, he said, "Although the voice is Jacob's, the hands are Esau's." (He failed to identify him because his hands were hairy, like those of his brother Esau; so in the end he gave him his blessing.) Again he asked him, "Are you really my son Esau?" "Certainly," he replied. Then Isaac said, "Serve me your game, son, that I may eat of it and then give you my blessing." Jacob served it to him, and Isaac ate; he brought him wine, and he drank. Finally his father Isaac said to him, "Come closer, son, and kiss me." As Jacob went up and kissed him, Isaac smelled the fragrance of his clothes. With that, he blessed him, saying,

"Ah, the fragrance of my son
    is like the fragrance of a field
    that the Lord has blessed!

"May God give to you
    of the dew of the heavens
And of the fertility of the earth
    abundance of grain and wine.

"Let peoples serve you,
    and nations pay you homage;
Be master of your brothers,
    and may your mother's sons bow down to you.
Cursed be those who curse you,
    and blessed be those who bless you." ✛

Psalm 135:1-6
R. Praise the Lord for he is good! *(or* **Alleluia.***)*
Praise the name of the Lord;
    Praise, you servants of the Lord
Who stand in the house of the Lord,
    in the courts of the house of our God. **R.**
Praise the Lord, for the Lord is good;
    sing praise to his name, which we love;

For the Lord has chosen Jacob for himself,
    Israel for his own possession. **R.**
For I know that the Lord is great;
    our Lord is greater than all gods.
All that the Lord wills he does
      in heaven and on earth,
      in the seas and in all the deeps. **R.**

See Acts 16:14
R. Alleluia, alleluia.
Open our hearts, O Lord,
to listen to the words of your Son. **R.**

† *Matthew 9:14-17*
The wedding guests would never mourn
while the bridegroom is still with them.

John's disciples came to Jesus with the objection, "Why is it
that while we and the Pharisees fast, your disciples do not?"
Jesus said to them: "How can wedding guests go in mourning
so long as the groom is with them? When the day comes that
the groom is taken away, then they will fast. Nobody sews a
piece of unshrunken cloth on an old cloak; the very thing he
has used to cover the hole will pull, and the rip only get worse.
People do not pour new wine into old wineskins. If they do, the
skins burst, the wine spills out, and the skins are ruined. No,
they pour new wine into new wineskins, and in that way both
are preserved." ✛

JULY 8
FOURTEENTH SUNDAY IN ORDINARY TIME

† *Isaiah 66:10-14c*
Behold, I will spread prosperity over her like a river.

Thus says the LORD:
Rejoice with Jerusalem and be glad because of her,
    all you who love her;
exult, exult with her,
    all you who were mourning over her!
Oh, that you may suck fully
    of the milk of her comfort,

that you may nurse with delight
    at her abundant breasts!
    For thus says the LORD:
Lo, I will spread prosperity over Jerusalem like a river,
    and the wealth of the nations like an overflowing torrent.
As nurslings, you shall be carried in her arms,
    and fondled in her lap;
as a mother comforts her child,
    so will I comfort you;
    in Jerusalem you shall find your comfort.

When you see this, your heart shall rejoice
    and your bodies flourish like the grass;
the LORD's power shall be known to his servants. ✝

Psalm 66:1-7, 16, 20
R. Let all the earth cry out to God with joy.
Shout joyfully to God, all the earth,
    sing praise to the glory of his name;
    proclaim his glorious praise.
Say to God, "How tremendous are your deeds!" **R.**
"Let all on earth worship and sing praise to you,
    sing praise to your name!"
Come and see the works of God,
    his tremendous deeds among the children of Adam. **R.**
He has changed the sea into dry land;
    through the river they passed on foot;
    therefore let us rejoice in him.
He rules by his might forever. **R.**
Hear now, all you who fear God, while I declare
    what he has done for me.
Blessed be God who refused me not
    my prayer or his kindness! **R.**

† *Galatians 6:14-18*
I bear the marks of Jesus on my body.

Brothers and sisters:
May I never boast except in the cross of our Lord Jesus Christ,
    through which the world has been crucified to me,
    and I to the world.
For neither does circumcision mean anything, nor does

uncircumcision,
but only a new creation.
Peace and mercy be to all who follow this rule
and to the Israel of God.

From now on, let no one make troubles for me;
for I bear the marks of Jesus on my body.

The grace of our Lord Jesus Christ be with your spirit,
brothers and sisters. Amen. ✙

Colossians 3:15a, 16a
R. Alleluia, alleluia.
Let the peace of Christ control your hearts;
let the word of Christ dwell in you richly. **R.**

† *Luke 10:1-9 (or Luke 10:1-12, 17-20)*
Your peace will rest on that person.

At that time the Lord appointed seventy-two others
whom he sent ahead of him in pairs
to every town and place he intended to visit.
He said to them,
"The harvest is abundant but the laborers are few;
so ask the master of the harvest
to send out laborers for his harvest.
Go on your way;
behold, I am sending you like lambs among wolves.
Carry no money bag, no sack, no sandals;
and greet no one along the way.
Into whatever house you enter, first say,
'Peace to this household.'
If a peaceful person lives there,
your peace will rest on him;
but if not, it will return to you.
Stay in the same house and eat and drink what is offered to you,
for the laborer deserves his payment.
Do not move about from one house to another.
Whatever town you enter and they welcome you,
eat what is set before you,
cure the sick in it and say to them,
'The kingdom of God is at hand for you.'" ✙

MONDAY, JULY 9
WEEKDAY

† *Genesis 28:10-22*
*He saw a ladder standing there, angels of God
going up and coming down, and God speaking.*

Jacob departed from Beer-sheba and proceeded toward Haran. When he came upon a certain shrine, as the sun had already set, he stopped there for the night. Taking one of the stones at the shrine, he put it under his head and lay down to sleep at that spot. Then he had a dream: a stairway rested on the ground, with its top reaching to the heavens; and God's messengers were going up and down on it. And there was the Lord standing beside him and saying:

"I, the Lord, am the God of your forefather Abraham and the God of Isaac; the land on which you are lying I will give to you and your descendants. These shall be as plentiful as the dust of the earth, and through them you shall spread out east and west, north and south. In you and your descendants all the nations of the earth shall find blessing. Know that I am with you; I will protect you wherever you go, and bring you back to this land. I will never leave you until I have done what I promised you."

When Jacob awoke from his sleep, he exclaimed, "Truly, the Lord is in this spot, although I did not know it!" In solemn wonder he cried out: "How awesome is this shrine! This is nothing else but an abode of God, and that is the gateway to heaven!" Early the next morning Jacob took the stone that he had put under his head, set it up as a memorial stone, and poured oil on top of it. He called that site Bethel, whereas the former name of the town had been Luz.

Jacob then made this vow: "If God remains with me, to protect me on this journey I am making and to give me enough bread to eat and clothing to wear, and I come back safe to my father's house, the Lord shall be my God. This stone that I have set up as a memorial stone shall be God's abode." ✛

Psalm 91:1-4,14-15
R. In you, my God, I place my trust.
You who dwell in the shelter of the Most High,
    who abide in the shadow of the Almighty,

Say to the Lord, "My refuge and my fortress,
  my God, in whom I trust." **R.**
For he will rescue you from the snare of the fowler,
  from the destroying pestilence.
With his pinions he will cover you,
  and under his wings you shall take refuge. **R.**
Because he clings to me, I will deliver him;
  I will set him on high because he acknowledges my name.
He shall call upon me, and I will answer him;
  I will be with him in distress. **R.**

See Ephesians 1:17-18
R. Alleluia, alleluia.
May the Father of our Lord Jesus Christ
enlighten the eyes of our heart
that we might see how great is the hope
to which we are called. **R.**

† *Matthew 9:18-26*
My daughter has just died, but come to her and she will live.

As Jesus was speaking, a synagogue leader came up, did him reverence and said: "My daughter has just died. Please come and lay your hand on her and she will come back to life." Jesus stood up and followed him, and his disciples did the same. As they were going, a woman who had suffered from hemorrhages for twelve years came up behind him and touched the tassel on his cloak. "If only I can touch his cloak," she thought, "I shall get well." Jesus turned around and saw her and said, "Courage, daughter! Your faith has restored you to health." That very moment the woman got well.

When Jesus arrived at the synagogue leader's house and saw the flute players and the crowd who were making a din, he said, "Leave, all of you! The little girl is not dead. She is asleep." At this they began to ridicule him. When the crowd had been put out he entered and took her by the hand, and the little girl got up. News of this circulated throughout the district. ✛

TUESDAY, JULY 10
WEEKDAY

† *Genesis 32:23-33*
*Your name shall be called Israel,
because you have been strong against God.*

In the course of the night, Jacob arose, took his two wives, with the two maidservants and his eleven children, and crossed the ford of the Jabbok. After he had taken them across the stream and had brought over all his possessions, Jacob was left there alone. Then some man wrestled with him until the break of dawn. When the man saw that he could not prevail over him, he struck Jacob's hip at its socket, so that the hip socket was wrenched as they wrestled. The man then said, "Let me go, for it is daybreak." But Jacob said, "I will not let you go until you bless me." "What is your name?" the man asked. He answered, "Jacob." Then the man said, "You shall no longer be spoken of as Jacob, but as Israel, because you have contended with divine and human beings and have prevailed." Jacob then asked him, "Do tell me your name, please." He answered, "Why should you want to know my name?" With that, he bade him farewell. Jacob named the place Peniel, "Because I have seen God face to face," he said, "yet my life has been spared."

At sunrise, as he left Penuel, Jacob limped along because of his hip. That is why, to this day, the Israelites do not eat the sciatic muscle that is on the hip socket, inasmuch as Jacob's hip socket was struck at the sciatic muscle. ✦

Psalm 17:1-3, 6-8,15
R. In my justice, I shall see your face, O Lord.
Hear, O Lord, a just suit;
    attend to my outcry;
    hearken to my prayer from lips without deceit. **R.**
From you let my judgment come;
    your eyes behold what is right.
Though you test my heart, searching it in the night,
    though you try me with fire, you shall find
        no malice in me. **R.**
I call upon you, for you will answer me, O God;

incline your ear to me; hear my word.
Show your wondrous kindness,
   O savior of those who flee. **R.**
Hide me in the shadow of your wings.
   I in justice shall behold your face;
On waking, I shall be content in your presence. **R.**

See Ephesians 1:17-18
R. Alleluia, alleluia.
May the Father of our Lord Jesus Christ
enlighten the eyes of our heart
that we might see how great is the hope
to which we are called. **R.**

✝ *Matthew 9:32-38*
The harvest is rich but the laborers are few.

Some people brought Jesus a mute who was possessed by a demon. Once the demon was expelled the mute began to speak, to the great surprise of the crowds. "Nothing like this has ever been seen in Israel!" they exclaimed. But the Pharisees were saying, "He casts out demons through the prince of demons."

Jesus continued his tour of all the towns and villages. He taught in their synagogues, he proclaimed the good news of God's reign, and he cured every sickness and disease. At the sight of the crowds, his heart was moved with pity. They were lying prostrate from exhaustion, like sheep without a shepherd. He said to his disciples: "The harvest is good but laborers are scarce. Beg the harvest master to send out laborers to gather his harvest." ✝

WEDNESDAY, JULY 11
St. Benedict

✝ *Genesis 41:55-57; 42:5-7, 17-24*
We have merited this misery because we have sinned against our brother

When hunger came to be felt throughout the land of Egypt and the people cried to Pharaoh for bread, Pharaoh directed all the Egyptians to go to Joseph and do whatever he told them. When the famine had spread throughout the land, Joseph opened all the cities that had grain and rationed it to the

Egyptians, since the famine had gripped the land of Egypt. In fact, all the world came to Joseph to obtain rations of grain, for famine had gripped the whole world.

The sons of Israel were among those who came to Egypt to procure rations. It was Joseph, as governor of the country, who dispensed the rations to all the people. When Joseph's brothers came and knelt down before him with their faces to the ground, he recognized them as soon as he saw them. But he concealed his own identity from them and spoke sternly to them.

With that, he locked them up in the guardhouse for three days.

On the third day Joseph said to them: "Do this, and you shall live; for I am a God-fearing man. If you have been honest, only one of your brothers need be confined in this prison, while the rest of you may go and take home provisions for your starving families. But you must come back to me with your youngest brother. Your words will thus be verified, and you will not die." To this they agreed.

To one another, however, they said: "Alas, we are being punished because of our brother. We saw the anguish of his heart when he pleaded with us, yet we paid no heed; that is why this anguish has now come upon us." "Didn't I tell you," broke in Reuben, "not to do wrong to the boy? But you wouldn't listen! Now comes the reckoning for his blood." They did not know, of course, that Joseph understood what they said, since he spoke with them through an interpreter. But turning away from them, he wept. ✢

Psalm 33:2-3,10-11,18-19
**R. Lord, let your mercy be on us,
as we place our trust in you.**
Give thanks to the Lord on the harp;
    with the ten-stringed lyre chant his praises.
Sing to him a new song;
    pluck the strings skillfully, with shouts of gladness. **R.**
The Lord brings to nought the plans of nations;
    he foils the designs of peoples.
But the plan of the Lord stands forever;
    the design of his heart, through all generations. **R.**
But see, the eyes of the Lord are upon those who fear him,

upon those who hope for his kindness,
To deliver them from death
and preserve them in spite of famine. **R.**

See Ephesians 1:17-18
R. Alleluia, alleluia.
May the Father of our Lord Jesus Christ
enlighten the eyes of our heart
that we might see how great is the hope
to which we are called. **R.**

† *Matthew 10:1-7*
Go to the lost sheep of the house of Israel.

Jesus summoned his twelve disciples and gave them authority to expel unclean spirits and to cure sickness and disease of every kind.

The names of the twelve apostles are these: first Simon, now known as Peter, and his brother Andrew; James, Zebedee's son, and his brother John; Philip and Bartholomew, Thomas and Matthew the tax collector; James, son of Alphaeus, and Thaddaeus; Simon the Zealot Party member, and Judas Iscariot, who betrayed him. Jesus sent these men on mission as the Twelve, after giving them the following instructions:

"Do not visit pagan territory and do not enter a Samaritan town. Go instead after the lost sheep of the house of Israel. As you go, make this announcement: 'The reign of God is at hand!'" ✛

THURSDAY, JULY 12
WEEKDAY

† *Genesis 44:18-21, 23-29; 45:1-5*
God sent me before you into Egypt to preserve your lives.

Judah approached Joseph and said: "I beg you, my lord, let your servant speak earnestly to my lord, and do not become angry with your servant, for you are the equal of Pharaoh. My lord asked your servants, 'Have you a father, or another brother?' So we said to my lord, 'We have an aged father, and a young brother, the child of his old age. This one's full brother is dead, and since he is the only one by that mother who is left, his father dotes on him.' Then you told your servants, 'Bring him down to me that my eyes may look on him. Unless your youngest brother comes back with you, you shall not come into my presence again.' When we returned to your servant our father, we reported to him the words of my lord.

"Later, our father told us to come back and buy some food for the family. So we reminded him, 'We cannot go down there; only if our youngest brother is with us can we go, for we may not see the man if our youngest brother is not with us.' Then your servant our father said to us, 'As you know, my wife bore me two sons. One of them, however, disappeared, and I had to conclude that he must have been torn to pieces by wild beasts; I have not seen him since. If you now take this one away from me too, and some disaster befalls him, you will send my white head down to the nether world in grief.'"

Joseph could no longer control himself in the presence of all his attendants, so he cried out, "Have everyone withdraw from me!" Thus no one else was about when he made himself known to his brothers. But his sobs were so loud that the Egyptians heard him, and so the news reached Pharaoh's palace. "I am Joseph," he said to his brothers. "Is my father still in good health?" But his brothers could give him no answer, so dumbfounded were they at him.

"Come closer to me," he told his brothers. When they had done so, he said: "I am your brother Joseph, whom you once sold into Egypt. But now do not be distressed, and do not reproach yourselves for having sold me here. It was really for the sake of saving lives that God sent me here ahead of you." ✠

Psalm 105:16-21
R. **Remember the marvels the Lord has done.**
   (*or* **Alleluia.**)
When he called down a famine on the land
   and ruined the crop that sustained them,
He sent a man before them,
   Joseph, sold as a slave. **R.**
They had weighed him down with fetters,
   and he was bound with chains,
Till his prediction came to pass
   and the word of the Lord proved him true. **R.**
The king sent and released him,

the ruler of the peoples set him free.
He made him lord of his house
   and ruler of all his possessions. **R.**

See Ephesians 1:17-18
R. Alleluia, alleluia.
May the Father of our Lord Jesus Christ
enlighten the eyes of our heart
that we might see how great is the hope
to which we are called. **R.**

† *Matthew 10:7-15*
You received without charge, give without charge.

Jesus said to his disciples: "As you go, make this announcement: 'The reign of God is at hand!' Cure the sick, raise the
dead, heal the leprous, expel demons. The gift you have
received, give as a gift. Provide yourselves with neither gold
nor silver nor copper in your belts; no traveling bag, no change
of shirt, no sandals, no walking staff. The workman, after all,
is worth his keep.

"Look for a worthy citizen in every town or village you come
to and stay with him until you leave. As you enter his home bless
it. If the home is deserving, your blessing will descend on it. If
it is not, your blessing will return to you. If anyone does not
receive you or listen to what you have to say, leave that house
or town, and once outside it shake its dust from your feet. I
assure you, it will go easier for the region of Sodom and
Gomorrah on the day of judgment than it will for that town." ✛

FRIDAY, JULY 13
WEEKDAY, ST. HENRY

† *Genesis 46:1-7, 28-30*
Now I can die, because I have seen you again.

Israel set out with all that was his. When he arrived at Beer-
sheba, he offered sacrifices to the God of his father Isaac.
There God, speaking to Israel in a vision by night, called,
"Jacob! Jacob!" "Here I am," he answered. Then he said: "I am
God, the God of your father. Do not be afraid to go down to
Egypt, for there I will make you a great nation. Not only will

I go down to Egypt with you; I will also bring you back here, after Joseph has closed your eyes."

So Jacob departed from Beer-sheba, and the sons of Israel put their father and their wives and children on the wagons that Pharaoh had sent for his transport. They took with them their livestock and the possessions they had acquired in the land of Canaan. Thus Jacob and all his descendants migrated to Egypt. His sons and his grandsons, his daughters and his granddaughters—all his descendants—he took with him to Egypt.

Israel had sent Judah ahead to Joseph, so that he might meet him in Goshen. On his arrival in the region of Goshen, Joseph hitched the horses to his chariot and rode to meet his father Israel in Goshen. As soon as he saw him, he flung himself on his neck and wept a long time in his arms. And Israel said to Joseph, "At last I can die, now that I have seen for myself that Joseph is still alive." ✛

Psalm 37:3-4, 18-19, 27-28, 39-40
R. The salvation of the just comes from the Lord.
Trust in the Lord and do good,
    that you may dwell in the land and enjoy security.
Take delight in the Lord,
    and he will grant you your heart's requests. **R.**
The Lord watches over the lives of the whole-hearted;
    their inheritance lasts forever.
They are not put to shame in an evil time;
    in days of famine they have plenty. **R.**
Turn from evil and do good,
    that you may abide forever;
For the Lord loves what is right,
    and forsakes not his faithful ones.
Criminals are destroyed,
    and the posterity of the wicked is cut off. **R.**
The salvation of the just is from the Lord;
    he is their refuge in time of distress.
And the Lord helps them and delivers them;
    he delivers them from the wicked and saves them,
    because they take refuge in him. **R.**

See *Ephesians 1:17-18*

R. Alleluia, alleluia.

May the Father of our Lord Jesus Christ
enlighten the eyes of our heart
that we might see how great is the hope
to which we are called. **R.**

† *Matthew 10:16-23*

It is not you who speak, but the Spirit speaking in you.

Jesus said to his disciples: "I am sending you out like sheep among wolves. You must be clever as snakes and innocent as doves. Be on your guard with respect to others. They will hale you into court, they will flog you in their synagogues. You will be brought to trial before rulers and kings, to give witness before them and the Gentiles on my account. When they hand you over, do not worry about what you will say or how you will say it. When the hour comes, you will be given what you are to say. You yourselves will not be the speakers; the Spirit of your Father will be speaking in you.

"Brother will hand over brother to death, and the father his child; children will turn against parents and have them put to death. You will be hated by all on account of me. But whoever holds out till the end will escape death. When they persecute you in one town, flee to the next. I solemnly assure you, you will not have covered the towns of Israel before the Son of Man comes." +

SATURDAY, JULY 14

Bl. Kateri Tekakwitha, St. Camillus de Lellis

† *Genesis 49:29-33; 50:15-24*

God will visit you and bring about the deliverance of many people.

Jacob gave this charge to his sons: "Since I am about to be taken to my kindred, bury me with my fathers in the cave that lies in the field of Ephron the Hittite, the cave in the field of Machpelah, facing on Mamre, in the land of Canaan, the field that Abraham bought from Ephron the Hittite for a burial ground. There Abraham and his wife Sarah are buried, and so are Isaac and his wife Rebekah, and there, too, I buried Leah— the field and the cave in it that had been purchased from the

Hittites."

When Jacob had finished giving these instructions to his sons, he drew his feet into the bed, breathed his last, and was taken to his kindred.

Now that their father was dead, Joseph's brothers became fearful and thought, "Suppose Joseph has been nursing a grudge against us and now plans to pay us back in full for all the wrong we did him!" So they approached Joseph and said: "Before your father died, he gave us these instructions: 'You shall say to Joseph, Jacob begs you to forgive the criminal wrongdoing of your brothers, who treated you so cruelly.' Please, therefore, forgive the crime that we, the servants of your father's God, committed." When they spoke these words to him, Joseph broke into tears. Then his brothers proceeded to fling themselves down before him and said, "Let us be your slaves!" But Joseph replied to them: "Have no fear. Can I take the place of God? Even though you meant harm to me, God meant it for good, to achieve his present end, the survival of many people. Therefore have no fear. I will provide for you and for your children." By thus speaking kindly to them, he reassured them.

Joseph remained in Egypt, together with his father's family. He lived a hundred and ten years. He saw Ephraim's children to the third generation, and the children of Manasseh's son Machir were also born on Joseph's knees.

Joseph said to his brothers: "I am about to die. God will surely take care of you and lead you out of this land to the land that he promised on oath to Abraham, Isaac and Jacob." ✝

Psalm 105:1-4, 6-7
**R. Turn to the Lord in your need
and you will live.**
Give thanks to the Lord, invoke his name;
    make known among the nations his deeds.
Sing to him, sing his praise,
    proclaim all his wondrous deeds. **R.**
Glory in his holy name;
    rejoice, O hearts that seek the Lord!
Look to the Lord in his strength;
    seek to serve him constantly. **R.**

You descendants of Abraham, his servants,
    sons of Jacob, his chosen ones!
He, the Lord, is our God;
    throughout the earth his judgments prevail. **R.**

See Ephesians 1:17-18
R. Alleluia, alleluia.
May the Father of our Lord Jesus Christ
enlighten the eyes of our heart
that we might see how great is the hope
to which we are called. **R.**

✝ *Matthew 10:24-33*
Do not be afraid of those who can kill the body.

Jesus said to his apostles: "No pupil outranks his teacher, no slave his master. The pupil should be glad to become like his teacher, the slave like his master. If they call the head of the house Beelzebul, how much more the members of his household! Do not let them intimidate you. Nothing is concealed that will not be revealed, and nothing hidden that will not become known. What I tell you in darkness, speak in the light. What you hear in private, proclaim from housetops.

"Do not fear those who deprive the body of life but cannot destroy the soul. Rather, fear him who can destroy both body and soul in Gehenna. Are not two sparrows sold for next to nothing? Yet not a single sparrow falls to the ground without your Father's consent. As for you, every hair of your head has been counted; so do not be afraid of anything. You are worth more than an entire flock of sparrows. Whoever acknowledges me before men I will acknowledge before my Father in heaven. Whoever disowns me before men I will disown before my Father in heaven." ✙

JULY 15
FIFTEENTH SUNDAY IN ORDINARY TIME

✝ *Deuteronomy 30:10-14*
The word is very near to you: you have only to carry it out.

Moses said to the people:
    "If only you would heed the voice of the LORD, your God,

and keep his commandments and statutes
that are written in this book of the law,
when you return to the LORD, your God,
with all your heart and all your soul.

"For this command that I enjoin on you today
is not too mysterious and remote for you.
It is not up in the sky, that you should say,
'Who will go up in the sky to get it for us
and tell us of it, that we may carry it out?'
Nor is it across the sea, that you should say,
'Who will cross the sea to get it for us
and tell us of it, that we may carry it out?'
No, it is something very near to you,
already in your mouths and in your hearts;
you have only to carry it out." ✛

Psalm 69:14, 17, 30-31, 33-34, 36-37 (or Psalm 19:8-11)
R. Turn to the Lord in your need, and you will live.
I pray to you, O LORD,
for the time of your favor, O God!
In your great kindness answer me
with your constant help.
Answer me, O LORD, for bounteous is your kindness:
in your great mercy turn toward me. **R.**
I am afflicted and in pain;
let your saving help, O God, protect me.
I will praise the name of God in song,
and I will glorify him with thanksgiving. **R.**
"See, you lowly ones, and be glad;
you who seek God, may your hearts revive!
For the LORD hears the poor,
and his own who are in bonds he spurns not." **R.**
For God will save Zion
and rebuild the cities of Judah.
The descendants of his servants shall inherit it,
and those who love his name shall inhabit it. **R.**

✝ Colossians 1:15-20
All things were created through him and for him.

Christ Jesus is the image of the invisible God,
 the firstborn of all creation.
For in him were created all things in heaven and on earth,
 the visible and the invisible,
 whether thrones or dominions or principalities or powers;
 all things were created through him and for him.
He is before all things,
 and in him all things hold together.
He is the head of the body, the church.
He is the beginning, the firstborn from the dead,
 that in all things he himself might be preeminent.
For in him all the fullness was pleased to dwell,
 and through him to reconcile all things for him,
 making peace by the blood of his cross
 through him, whether those on earth or those in heaven. ✛

cf. John 6:63c, 68c
R. Alleluia, alleluia.
Your words, Lord, are Spirit and life;
you have the words of everlasting life. **R.**

✝ Luke 10:25-37
Who is my neighbor?

There was a scholar of the law who stood up to test him and
 said,
 "Teacher, what must I do to inherit eternal life?"
Jesus said to him, "What is written in the law?
How do you read it?"
He said in reply,
 You shall love the Lord, your God,
 with all your heart,
 with all your being,
 with all your strength,
 and with all your mind,
 and your neighbor as yourself."
He replied to him, "You have answered correctly;
 do this and you will live."

But because he wished to justify himself, he said to Jesus,
"And who is my neighbor?"
Jesus replied,
"A man fell victim to robbers
as he went down from Jerusalem to Jericho.
They stripped and beat him and went off leaving him half-dead.
A priest happened to be going down that road,
but when he saw him, he passed by on the opposite side.
Likewise a Levite came to the place,
and when he saw him, he passed by on the opposite side.
But a Samaritan traveler who came upon him
was moved with compassion at the sight.
He approached the victim,
poured oil and wine over his wounds and bandaged them.
Then he lifted him up on his own animal,
took him to an inn, and cared for him.
The next day he took out two silver coins
and gave them to the innkeeper with the instruction,
'Take care of him.
If you spend more than what I have given you,
I shall repay you on my way back.'
Which of these three, in your opinion,
was neighbor to the robbers' victim?"
He answered, "The one who treated him with mercy."
Jesus said to him, "Go and do likewise." ✝

MONDAY, JULY 16
WEEKDAY, OUR LADY OF MOUNT CARMEL

✝ Exodus 1:8-14, 22
We must move against Israel lest they become greater in number.

A new king, who knew nothing of Joseph, came to power in Egypt. He said to his subjects, "Look how numerous and powerful the Israelite people are growing, more so than we ourselves! Come, let us deal shrewdly with them to stop their increase; otherwise, in time of war they too may join our enemies to fight against us, and so leave our country."

Accordingly, taskmasters were set over the Israelites to oppress them with forced labor. Thus they had to build for Pharaoh the supply cities of Pithom and Raamses. Yet the more they were oppressed, the more they multiplied and spread. The Egyptians, then, dreaded the Israelites and reduced them to cruel slavery, making life bitter for them with hard work in mortar and brick and all kinds of field work—the whole cruel fate of slaves.

Pharaoh then commanded all his subjects, "Throw into the river every boy that is born to the Hebrews, but you may let all the girls live." ✚

Psalm 124:1-8
R. Our help is in the name of the Lord.
Had not the Lord been with us—
    let Israel say,
    had not the Lord been with us—
When men rose up against us,
    then would they have swallowed us alive,
When their fury was inflamed against us. **R.**
Then would the waters have overwhelmed us;
The torrent would have swept over us;
    over us then would have swept
    the raging waters.
Blessed be the Lord, who did not leave us
    a prey to their teeth. **R.**
We were rescued like a bird
    from the fowlers' snare;
Broke was the snare,
    and we were freed.
Our help is in the name of the Lord,
    who made heaven and earth. **R.**

See Luke 8:15
R. Alleluia, alleluia.
Happy are they who have kept the word with a generous heart, and yield a harvest through perseverance. **R.**

† *Matthew 10:34—11:1*
I have not come to bring peace, but the sword.

Jesus said to his apostles: "Do not suppose that my mission on earth is to spread peace. My mission is to spread, not peace, but division. I have come to set a man at odds with his father, a daughter with her mother, a daughter-in-law with her mother-in-law: in short, to make a man's enemies those of his own household. Whoever loves father or mother, son or daughter more than me, is not worthy of me. He who will not take up his cross and come after me is not worthy of me. He who seeks only himself brings himself to ruin, whereas he who brings himself to nought for me discovers who he is.

"He who welcomes you welcomes me, and he who welcomes me welcomes him who sent me. He who welcomes a prophet because he bears the name of prophet receives a prophet's reward; he who welcomes a holy man because he is known as holy receives a holy man's reward. And I promise you that whoever gives a cup of cold water to one of these lowly ones because he is a disciple will not want for his reward."

When Jesus had finished instructing his twelve disciples, he left that locality to teach and preach in their towns. ✝

TUESDAY, JULY 17
WEEKDAY

✝ Exodus 2:1-15
He was called by the name Moses because he was taken from the water.
Afterwards he grew up to lead his brothers.

A certain man of the house of Levi married a Levite woman, who conceived and bore a son. Seeing that he was a goodly child, she hid him for three months. When she could hide him no longer, she took a papyrus basket, daubed it with bitumen and pitch, and putting the child in it, placed it among the reeds on the river bank. His sister stationed herself at a distance to find out what would happen to him.

Pharaoh's daughter came down to the river to bathe, while her maids walked along the river bank. Noticing the basket among the reeds, she sent her handmaid to fetch it. On opening it, she looked and lo, there was a baby boy, crying! She was moved with pity for him and said, "It is one of the Hebrews' children." Then his sister asked Pharaoh's daughter, "Shall I go and call one of the Hebrew women to nurse the child for you?" "Yes, do so," she answered. So the maiden went and called the child's own mother. Pharaoh's daughter said to her, "Take this child and nurse it for me, and I will repay you." The woman therefore took the child and nursed it. When the child grew, she brought him to Pharaoh's daughter, who adopted him as her son and called him Moses; for she said, "I drew him out of the water."

On one occasion, after Moses had grown up, when he visited his kinsmen and witnessed their forced labor, he saw an Egyptian striking a Hebrew, one of his own kinsmen. Looking about and seeing no one, he slew the Egyptian and hid him in the sand. The next day he went out again, and now two Hebrews were fighting! So he asked the culprit, "Why are you striking your fellow Hebrew?" But he replied, "Who has appointed you ruler and judge over us? Are you thinking of killing me as you killed the Egyptian?" Then Moses became afraid and thought, "The affair must certainly be known."

Pharaoh, too, heard of the affair and sought to put him to death. But Moses fled from him and stayed in the land of Midian. +

Psalm 69:3, 14, 30-31, 33-34
R. Turn to the Lord in your need, and you will live.
I am sunk in the abysmal swamp
    where there is no foothold;
I have reached the watery depths;
    the flood overwhelms me. **R.**
But I pray to you, O Lord,
    for the time of your favor, O God!
In your great kindness answer me
    with your constant help. **R.**
But I am afflicted and in pain;
    let your saving help, O God, protect me.
I will praise the name of God in song,
    and I will glorify him with thanksgiving; **R.**
See, you lowly ones, and be glad;
    you who seek God, may your hearts be merry!
For the Lord hears the poor,
    and his own who are in bonds he spurns not. **R.**

See Luke 8:15
R. Alleluia, alleluia.
Happy are they who have kept the word with a generous heart,
and yield a harvest through perseverance. **R.**

† *Matthew 11:20-24*
*It will not go as hard with Tyre and Sidon and the
land of Sodom on Judgment Day as with you.*

Jesus began to reproach the towns where most of his miracles
had been worked, with their failure to reform: "It will go ill
with you, Chorazin! And just as ill with you, Bethsaida! If the
miracles worked in you had taken place in Tyre and Sidon,
they would have reformed in sackcloth and ashes long ago. I
assure you, it will go easier for Tyre and Sidon than for you on
the day of judgment. As for you, Capernaum,
'Are you to be exalted to the skies?
You shall go down to the realm of death!'
If the miracles worked in you had taken place in Sodom, it
would be standing today. I assure you, it will go easier for
Sodom than for you on the day of judgment." ✛

WEDNESDAY, JULY 18
WEEKDAY

† *Exodus 3:1-6, 9-12*
The Lord appeared to Moses in the form of fire in the midst of a bush.

Moses was tending the flock of his father-in-law Jethro, the
priest of Midian. Leading the flock across the desert, he came
to Horeb, the mountain of God. There an angel of the Lord
appeared to him in fire flaming out of a bush. As he looked on,
he was surprised to see that the bush, though on fire, was not
consumed. So Moses decided, "I must go over to look at this
remarkable sight, and see why the bush is not burned."

When the Lord saw him coming over to look at it more
closely, God called out to him from the bush, "Moses! Moses!"
He answered, "Here I am." God said, "Come no nearer! Remove
the sandals from your feet, for the place where you stand is
holy ground. I am the God of your father," he continued, "the
God of Abraham, the God of Isaac, the God of Jacob." Moses hid
his face, for he was afraid to look at God.

The Lord said, "So indeed the cry of the Israelites has
reached me, and I have truly noted that the Egyptians are
oppressing them. Come, now! I will send you to Pharaoh to
lead my people, the Israelites, out of Egypt."

But Moses said to God, "Who am I that I should go to

Pharaoh and lead the Israelites out of Egypt?" He answered, "I will be with you; and this shall be your proof that it is I who have sent you: when you bring my people out of Egypt, you will worship God on this very mountain." ✙

Psalm 103:1-4, 6-7
R. The Lord is kind and merciful.
Bless the Lord, O my soul;
    and all my being, bless his holy name.
Bless the Lord, O my soul,
    and forget not all his benefits. **R.**
He pardons all your iniquities,
    he heals all your ills.
He redeems your life from destruction,
    he crowns you with kindness and compassion. **R.**
The Lord secures justice
    and the rights of all the oppressed.
He has made known his ways to Moses,
    and his deeds to the children of Israel. **R.**

See Luke 8:15
R. Alleluia, alleluia.
Happy are they who have kept the word with a generous heart,
and yield a harvest through perseverance. **R.**

† *Matthew 11:25-27*
The Lord hides these things from the wise and reveals them to children.

On one occasion Jesus spoke thus: "Father, Lord of heaven and earth, to you I offer praise; for what you have hidden from the learned and the clever you have revealed to the merest children. Father, it is true. You have graciously willed it so. Everything has been given over to me by my Father. No one knows the Son but the Father, and no one knows the Father but the Son—and anyone to whom the Son wishes to reveal him." ✙

THURSDAY, JULY 19
WEEKDAY

† *Exodus 3:11-20*
I am who am. I am has sent me to you.

Moses, hearing the voice from the burning bush, said to God, "Who am I that I should go to Pharaoh and lead the Israelites out of Egypt?" He answered, "I will be with you; and this shall be your proof that it is I who have sent you: when you bring my people out of Egypt, you will worship God on this very mountain."

"But," said Moses to God, "when I go to the Israelites and say to them, 'The God of your fathers has sent me to you,' if they ask me, 'What is his name?' what am I to tell them?" God replied, "I am who am." Then he added, "This is what you shall tell the Israelites: I AM sent me to you."

God spoke further to Moses, "Thus shall you say to the Israelites: The Lord, the God of your fathers, the God of Abraham, the God of Isaac, the God of Jacob, has sent me to you.

"This is my name forever;
this is my title for all generations.

"Go and assemble the elders of the Israelites, and tell them: The Lord, the God of your fathers, the God of Abraham, Isaac and Jacob, has appeared to me and said: I am concerned about you and about the way you are being treated in Egypt; so I have decided to lead you up out of the misery of Egypt into the land of the Canaanites, Hittites, Amorites, Perizzites, Hivites and Jebusites, a land flowing with milk and honey.

"Thus they will heed your message. Then you and the elders of Israel shall go to the king of Egypt and say to him: The Lord, the God of the Hebrews, has sent us word. Permit us, then, to go a three days' journey in the desert, that we may offer sacrifice to the Lord, our God.

"Yet I know that the king of Egypt will not allow you to go unless he is forced. I will stretch out my hand, therefore, and smite Egypt by doing all kinds of wondrous deeds there. After that he will send you away." ✝

Psalm 105:1, 5, 8-9, 24-27

R. The Lord remembers his covenant forever.
(or **Alleluia.***)*

Give thanks to the Lord, invoke his name;
  make known among the nations his deeds.
Recall the wondrous deeds that he has wrought,
  his portents, and the judgments he has uttered. **R.**
He remembers forever his covenant
  which he made binding for a thousand generations—
Which he entered into with Abraham
  and by his oath to Isaac. **R.**
He greatly increased his people
  and made them stronger than their foes,
Whose hearts he changed, so that they hated his people,
  and dealt deceitfully with his servants. **R.**
He sent Moses his servant;
  Aaron, whom he had chosen.
They wrought his signs among them,
  and wonders in the land of ham. **R.**

See Luke 8:15

R. Alleluia, alleluia.
Happy are they who have kept the word with a generous heart,
and yield a harvest through perseverance. **R.**

✝ Matthew 11:28-30
I am gentle and humble in heart.

Jesus spoke thus: "Come to me, all you who are weary and
find life burdensome, and I will refresh you. Take my yoke
upon your shoulders and learn from me, for I am gentle and
humble of heart. Your souls will find rest, for my yoke is easy
and my burden light." ✛

FRIDAY, JULY 20
WEEKDAY

✝ Exodus 11:10—12:14
The lamb must be slain in the evening;
when I see the blood I will pass over it.

Moses and Aaron performed various wonders in Pharaoh's
presence, but the Lord made Pharaoh obstinate, and he would
not let the Israelites leave his land.

The Lord said to Moses and Aaron in the land of Egypt, "This month shall stand at the head of your calendar; you shall reckon it the first month of the year. Tell the whole community of Israel: On the tenth of this month every one of your families must procure for itself a lamb, one apiece for each household. If a family is too small for a whole lamb, it shall join the nearest household in procuring one and shall share in the lamb in proportion to the number of persons who partake of it. The lamb must be a year-old male and without blemish. You may take it from either the sheep or the goats. You shall keep it until the fourteenth day of this month, and then, with the whole assembly of Israel present, it shall be slaughtered during the evening twilight. They shall take some of its blood and apply it to the two doorposts and the lintel of every house in which they partake of the lamb. That same night they shall eat its roasted flesh with unleavened bread and bitter herbs. It shall not be eaten raw or boiled, but roasted whole, with its head and shanks and inner organs. None of it must be kept beyond the next morning; whatever is left over in the morning shall be burned up.

"This is how you are to eat it: with your loins girt, sandals on your feet and your staff in hand, you shall eat like those who are in flight. It is the Passover of the Lord. For on this same night I will go through Egypt, striking down every first-born of the land, both man and beast, and executing judgment on all the gods of Egypt—I, the Lord! But the blood will mark the houses where you are. Seeing the blood, I will pass over you; thus, when I strike the land of Egypt, no destructive blow will come upon you.

"This day shall be a memorial feast for you, which all your generations shall celebrate with pilgrimage to the Lord, as a perpetual institution." ✛

Psalm 116:12-13,15-18
**R. I will take the cup of salvation,
and call on the name of the Lord.**
How shall I make a return to the Lord
    for all the good he has done for me?
The cup of salvation I will take up,
    and I will call upon the name of the Lord. **R.**

Precious in the eyes of the Lord
  is the death of his faithful ones.
I am your servant, the son of your handmaid;
  you have loosed my bonds. **R.**
To you will I offer sacrifice of thanksgiving,
  and I will call upon the name of the Lord.
My vows to the Lord I will pay
  in the presence of all his people. **R.**

See Luke 8:15
R. Alleluia, alleluia.
Happy are they who have kept the word with a generous heart,
and yield a harvest through perseverance. **R.**

✝ *Matthew 12:1-8*
The Son of Man is master of the Sabbath.

Once on a sabbath Jesus walked through the standing grain. His disciples felt hungry, so they began to pull off the heads of grain and eat them. When the Pharisees spied this, they protested: "See here! Your disciples are doing what is not permitted on the sabbath." He replied: "Have you not read what David did when he and his men were hungry, how he entered God's house and ate the holy bread, a thing forbidden to him and his men or anyone other than priests? Have you not read in the law how the priests on temple duty can break the sabbath rest without incurring guilt? I assure you, there is something greater than the temple here. If you understood the meaning of the text, 'It is mercy I desire and not sacrifice,' you would not have condemned these innocent men. The Son of Man is indeed the Lord of the sabbath." ✛

SATURDAY, JULY 21
WEEKDAY, ST. LAWRENCE OF BRINDISI

✝ *Exodus 12:37-42*
The night is here when the Lord will lead Israel out of the land of Egypt.

The Israelites set out from Rameses for Succoth, about six hundred thousand men on foot, not counting the children. A crowd of mixed ancestry also went up with them, besides their livestock, very numerous flocks and herds. Since the dough they had brought out of Egypt was not leavened, they baked it into unleavened loaves. They had been rushed out of Egypt and had no opportunity even to prepare food for the journey.

The time the Israelites had stayed in Egypt was four hundred and thirty years. At the end of four hundred and thirty years, all the hosts of the Lord left the land of Egypt on this very date. This was a night of vigil for the Lord, as he led them out of the land of Egypt; so on this same night all the Israelites must keep a vigil for the Lord throughout their generations. ✝

Psalm 136:1, 23-24, 10-15
R. His love is everlasting.
Give thanks to the Lord, for he is good,
    for his mercy endures forever;
Who remembered us in our abjection,
    for his mercy endures forever;
And freed us from our foes,
    for his mercy endures forever. **R.**
Who smote the Egyptians in their first-born,
    for his mercy endures forever;
And brought out Israel from their midst,
    for his mercy endures forever;
With a mighty hand and an outstretched arm,
    for his mercy endures forever. **R.**
Who split the Red Sea in twain,
    for his mercy endures forever;
And led Israel through its midst,
    for his mercy endures forever;
But swept Pharaoh and his army into the Red Sea,
    for his mercy endures forever. **R.**

See Luke 8:15
R. Alleluia, alleluia.
Happy are they who have kept the word with a generous heart, and yield a harvest through perseverance. **R.**

✝ *Matthew 12:14-21*
*He did not show himself to them that
what had been said would be fulfilled.*

When the Pharisees were outside they began to plot against
Jesus to find a way to destroy him. Jesus was aware of this, and
so he withdrew from that place.

Many people followed him and he cured them all, though
he sternly ordered them not to make public what he had done.
This was to fulfill what had been said through Isaiah the
prophet:

"Here is my servant whom I have chosen,
my loved one in whom I delight.
I will endow him with my spirit
and he will proclaim justice to the Gentiles.
He will not contend or cry out,
nor will his voice be heard in the streets.
The bruised reed he will not crush;
The smoldering wick he will not quench
until judgment is made victorious.
In his name, the Gentiles will find hope." ✝

JULY 22
Sixteenth Sunday in Ordinary Time

✝ *Genesis 18:1-10a*
Lord, do not go on past your servant.

The LORD appeared to Abraham by the terebinth of Mamre,
as he sat in the entrance of his tent,
while the day was growing hot.
Looking up, Abraham saw three men standing nearby.
When he saw them, he ran from the entrance of the tent to
greet them;
and bowing to the ground, he said:
"Sir, if I may ask you this favor,
please do not go on past your servant.
Let some water be brought, that you may bathe your feet,
and then rest yourselves under the tree.
Now that you have come this close to your servant,
let me bring you a little food, that you may refresh yourselves;

and afterward you may go on your way."
The men replied, "Very well, do as you have said."

Abraham hastened into the tent and told Sarah,
"Quick, three measures of fine flour! Knead it and make
rolls."
He ran to the herd, picked out a tender, choice steer,
and gave it to a servant, who quickly prepared it.
Then Abraham got some curds and milk,
as well as the steer that had been prepared,
and set these before the three men;
and he waited on them under the tree while they ate.

They asked Abraham, "Where is your wife Sarah?"
He replied, "There in the tent."
One of them said, "I will surely return to you about this time
next year,
and Sarah will then have a son." ✛

Psalm 15:2-5
**R. He who does justice will live in
the presence of the Lord.**
One who walks blamelessly and does justice;
who thinks the truth in his heart
and slanders not with his tongue. **R.**
Who harms not his fellow man,
nor takes up a reproach against his neighbor;
by whom the reprobate is despised,
while he honors those who fear the LORD. **R.**
Who lends not his money at usury
and accepts no bribe against the innocent.
One who does these things
shall never be disturbed. **R.**

† *Colossians 1:24-28*
The mystery hidden from ages has now been manifested to his holy ones.

Brothers and sisters:
Now I rejoice in my sufferings for your sake,
and in my flesh I am filling up
what is lacking in the afflictions of Christ
on behalf of his body, which is the church,

of which I am a minister
in accordance with God's stewardship given to me
to bring to completion for you the word of God,
the mystery hidden from ages and from generations past.
But now it has been manifested to his holy ones,
to whom God chose to make known the riches of the glory
of this mystery among the Gentiles;
it is Christ in you, the hope for glory.
It is he whom we proclaim,
admonishing everyone and teaching everyone with all
wisdom,
that we may present everyone perfect in Christ. ✝

cf. Luke 8:15
R. Alleluia, alleluia.
Blessed are they who have kept the word with a generous
heart,
and yield a harvest through perseverance. **R.**

† *Luke 10:38-42*
Martha welcomed him. Mary has chosen the better part.

Jesus entered a village
where a woman whose name was Martha welcomed him.
She had a sister named Mary
who sat beside the Lord at his feet listening to him speak.
Martha, burdened with much serving, came to him and said,
"Lord, do you not care
that my sister has left me by myself to do the serving?
Tell her to help me."
The Lord said to her in reply,
"Martha, Martha, you are anxious and worried about
many things.
There is need of only one thing.
Mary has chosen the better part
and it will not be taken from her." ✝

MONDAY, JULY 23
WEEKDAY, ST. BRIDGET OF SWEDEN

† *Exodus 14:5-18*
They will know that I am the Lord God
when I glorify myself at the expense of Pharaoh.

When it was reported to the king of Egypt that the people had fled, Pharaoh and his servants changed their minds about them. "What have we done!" they exclaimed. "Why, we have released Israel from our service!" So Pharaoh made his chariots ready and mustered his soldiers—six hundred first-class chariots and all the other chariots of Egypt, with warriors on them all. So obstinate had the Lord made Pharaoh that he pursued the Israelites even while they were marching away in triumph. The Egyptians, then, pursued them; Pharaoh's whole army, his horses, chariots and charioteers, caught up with them as they lay encamped by the sea, at Pi-hahiroth, in front of Baal-zephon.

Pharaoh was already near when the Israelites looked up and saw that the Egyptians were on the march in pursuit of them. In great fright they cried out to the Lord. And they complained to Moses, "Were there no burial places in Egypt that you had to bring us out here to die in the desert? Why did you do this to us? Why did you bring us out of Egypt? Did we not tell you this in Egypt, when we said, 'Leave us alone. Let us serve the Egyptians'? Far better for us to be the slaves of the Egyptians than to die in the desert." But Moses answered the people, "Fear not! Stand your ground, and you will see the victory the Lord will win for you today. These Egyptians whom you see today you will never see again. The Lord himself will fight for you; you have only to keep still."

Then the Lord said to Moses, "Why are you crying out to me? Tell the Israelites to go forward. And you, lift up your staff and, with hand outstretched over the sea, split the sea in two, that the Israelites may pass through it on dry land. But I will make the Egyptians so obstinate that they will go in after them. Then I will receive glory through Pharaoh and all his army, his chariots and charioteers. The Egyptians shall know that I am the Lord, when I receive glory through Pharaoh and his chariots and charioteers." ✛

Exodus 15:1-6
**R. Let us sing to the Lord;
he has covered himself in glory.**
I will sing to the Lord, for he is gloriously triumphant;
 horse and chariot he has cast into the sea.
My strength and my courage is the Lord,
 and he has been my savior.
He is my God, I praise him;
 the God of my father, I extol him. **R.**
The Lord is a warrior,
 Lord is his name!
Pharaoh's chariots and army he hurled into the sea;
 the elite of his officers were submerged in the Red Sea. **R.**
The flood waters covered them,
 they sank into the depths like a stone.
Your right hand, O Lord, magnificent in power,
 your right hand, O Lord, has shattered the enemy. **R.**

John 6:64, 69
R. Alleluia, alleluia.
Your words, Lord, are spirit and life,
you have the words of everlasting life. **R.**

✝ *Matthew 12:38-42*
*On Judgment Day the Queen of the South will
rise up with this generation and condemn it.*

Some of the scribes and Pharisees then spoke up, saying, "Teacher, we want to see you work some signs." Jesus answered: "An evil and unfaithful age is eager for a sign! No sign will be given it but that of the prophet Jonah. Just as Jonah spent three days and three nights in the belly of the whale, so will the Son of Man spend three days and three nights in the bowels of the earth. At the judgment, the citizens of Nineveh will rise with the present generation and be the ones to condemn it. At the preaching of Jonah they reformed their lives; but you have a greater than Jonah here. At the judgment, the queen of the South will rise with the present generation and be the one to condemn it. She came from the farthest corner of the earth to listen to the wisdom of Solomon; but you have a greater than Solomon here." ✛

TUESDAY, JULY 24
WEEKDAY

† *Exodus 14:21—15:1*
The sons of Israel went on dry ground right into the sea.

Moses stretched out his hand over the sea, and the Lord swept the sea with a strong east wind throughout the night and so turned it into dry land. When the water was thus divided, the Israelites marched into the midst of the sea on dry land, with the water like a wall to their right and to their left.

The Egyptians followed in pursuit; all Pharaoh's horses and chariots and charioteers went after them right into the midst of the sea. In the night watch just before dawn the Lord cast through the column of the fiery cloud upon the Egyptian force a glance that threw it into a panic; and he so clogged their chariot wheels that they could hardly drive. With that the Egyptians sounded the retreat before Israel, because the Lord was fighting for them against the Egyptians.

Then the Lord told Moses, "Stretch out your hand over the sea, that the water may flow back upon the Egyptians, upon their chariots and their charioteers." So Moses stretched out his hand over the sea, and at dawn the sea flowed back to its normal depth. The Egyptians were fleeing head on toward the sea, when the Lord hurled them into its midst. As the water flowed back, it covered the chariots and the charioteers of Pharaoh's whole army which had followed the Israelites into the sea. Not a single one of them escaped. But the Israelites had marched on dry land through the midst of the sea, with the water like a wall to their right and to their left. Thus the Lord saved Israel on that day from the power of the Egyptians. When Israel saw the Egyptians lying dead on the seashore and beheld the great power that the Lord had shown against the Egyptians, they feared the Lord and believed in him and in his servant Moses.

Then Moses and the Israelites sang this song to the Lord:
I will sing to the Lord, for he is gloriously triumphant;
horse and chariot he has cast into the sea. ✛

Exodus 15:8-10,12,17

R. Let us sing to the Lord;
he has covered himself in glory.

At the breath of your anger the waters piled up,
   the flowing waters stood like a mound,
   the flood waters congealed in the midst of the sea.
The enemy boasted, "I will pursue and overtake them;
   I will divide the spoils and have my fill of them;
   I will draw my sword; my hand shall despoil them!" **R.**
When your wind blew, the sea covered them;
   like lead they sank in the mighty waters.
When you stretched out your right hand,
   the earth swallowed them! **R.**
And you brought them in and planted them on the mountain
      of your inheritance—
   the place where you made your seat, O Lord,
   the sanctuary, O Lord, which your hands established. **R.**

John 6:64, 69

R. Alleluia, alleluia.

Your words, Lord, are spirit and life,
you have the words of everlasting life. **R.**

✝ *Matthew 12:46-50*

Extending his hands toward the disciples, he said:
Here are my mother and my brothers.

Jesus was addressing the crowds when his mother and his
brothers appeared outside to speak with him. Someone said to
him, "Your mother and your brothers are standing out there
and they wish to speak to you." He said to the one who had told
him, "Who is my mother? Who are my brothers?" Then extending his hands to his disciples, he said, "There are my mother
and my brothers. Whoever does the will of my heavenly Father
is brother and sister and mother to me." ✝

WEDNESDAY, JULY 25
St. James

† *2 Corinthians 4:7-15*
We carry always in our bodies the death of Jesus.

We possess a treasure in earthen vessels to make it clear that its surpassing power comes from God and not from us. We are afflicted in every way possible, but we are not crushed; full of doubts, we never despair. We are persecuted but never abandoned; we are struck down but never destroyed. Continually we carry about in our bodies the dying of Jesus, so that in our bodies the life of Jesus may also be revealed. While we live we are constantly being delivered to death for Jesus' sake, so that the life of Jesus may be revealed in our mortal flesh. Death is at work in us, but life in you. We have that spirit of faith of which the Scripture says, "Because I believed, I spoke out." We believe and so we speak, knowing that he who raised up the Lord Jesus will raise us up along with Jesus and place both us and you in his presence. Indeed, everything is ordered to your benefit, so that the grace bestowed in abundance may bring greater glory to God because they who give thanks are many. ✢

Psalm 126:1-6

**R. Those who sow in tears, shall reap
with shouts of joy.**

When the Lord brought back the captives of Zion,
    we were like men dreaming.
Then our mouth was filled with laughter,
    and our tongue with rejoicing. **R.**
Then they said among the nations,
    "The Lord has done great things for them."
The Lord has done great things for us;
    we are glad indeed. **R.**
Restore our fortunes, O Lord,
    like the torrents in the southern desert.
Those that sow in tears
    shall reap rejoicing. **R.**
Although they go forth weeping,
    carrying the seed to be sown,
They shall come back rejoicing,
    carrying their sheaves. **R.**

John 15:16

R. Alleluia, alleluia.

I have chosen you from the world, says the Lord,
to go and bear fruit that will last. **R.**

✝ *Matthew 20:20-28*
You shall indeed drink my cup.

The mother of Zebedee's sons came up to Jesus accompanied by her sons, to do him homage and ask of him a favor. "What is it you want?" he said. She answered, "Promise me that these sons of mine will sit, one at your right hand and the other at your left, in your kingdom." In reply Jesus said, "You do not know what you are asking. Can you drink of the cup I am to drink of?" "We can," they said. He told them, "From the cup I drink of you shall drink. Sitting at my right hand or my left is not mine to give. That is for those for whom it has been reserved by my Father." The other ten, on hearing this, became indignant at the two brothers. Jesus then called them together and said: "You know how those who exercise authority among the Gentiles lord it over them; their great ones make their importance felt. It cannot be like that with you. Anyone among you who aspires to greatness must serve the rest, and whoever wants to rank first among you must serve the needs of all. Such is the case with the Son of Man who has come, not to be served by others but to serve, to give his own life as a ransom for the many." ✝

THURSDAY, JULY 26
STS. JOACHIM AND ANN

✝ *Sirach 44:1, 10-15*
Their name lives on for all generations.

Now will I praise those godly men,
　　our ancestors, each in his own time:
These were godly men
　　whose virtues have not been forgotten;
Their wealth remains in their families,
　　their heritage with their descendants;
Through God's covenant with them their family endures,
　　their prosperity, for their sake.

And for all time their progeny will endure,
  their glory will never be blotted out;
Their bodies are peacefully laid away,
  but their name lives on and on.
At gatherings their wisdom is retold,
  and the assembly proclaims their praise. ✛

Psalm 132:11, 13-14, 17-18
R. God will give him the throne of David, his father.
The Lord swore to David
  a firm promise from which he will not withdraw:
"Your own offspring
  I will set upon your throne." **R.**
For the Lord has chosen Zion;
  he prefers her for his dwelling.
"Zion is my resting place forever;
  in her will I dwell, for I prefer her. **R.**
"In her will I make a horn to sprout forth for David;
  I will place a lamp for my anointed.
His enemies I will clothe with shame,
  but upon him my crown shall rise. **R.**

Luke 2:25
R. Alleluia, alleluia.
They yearned for the comforting of Israel,
and the Holy Spirit dwelt in them. **R.**

† Matthew 13:16-17
Many prophets and just men have longed to see what you see.

Jesus said to his disciples: "Blest are your eyes because they
see and blest are your ears because they hear. I assure you,
many a prophet and many a saint longed to see what you see
but did not see it, to hear what you hear but did not hear it. ✛

FRIDAY, JULY 27
WEEKDAY

† Exodus 20:1-17
The law was given through Moses.

God delivered all these commandments:
"I, the Lord, am your God, who brought you out of the land

of Egypt, that place of slavery. You shall not have other gods besides me. You shall not carve idols for yourselves in the shape of anything in the sky above or on the earth below or in the waters beneath the earth; you shall not bow down before them or worship them. For I, the Lord, your God, am a jealous God, inflicting punishment for their fathers' wickedness on the children of those who hate me, down to the third and fourth generation; but bestowing mercy down to the thousandth generation, on the children of those who love me and keep my commandments.

"You shall not take the name of the Lord, your God, in vain. For the Lord will not leave unpunished him who takes his name in vain.

"Remember to keep holy the sabbath day. Six days you may labor and do all your work, but the seventh day is the sabbath of the Lord, your God. No work may be done then either by you, or your son or daughter, or your male or female slave, or your beast, or by the alien who lives with you. In six days the Lord made the heavens and the earth, the sea and all that is in them; but on the seventh day he rested. That is why the Lord has blessed the sabbath day and made it holy.

"Honor your father and your mother, that you may have a long life in the land which the Lord, your God, is giving you.

"You shall not kill.

"You shall not commit adultery.

"You shall not steal.

"You shall not bear false witness against your neighbor.

"You shall not covet your neighbor's house. You shall not covet your neighbor's wife, nor his male or female slave, nor his ox or ass, nor anything else that belongs to him." ✝

Psalm 19:8-11
R. Lord, you have the words of everlasting life.
The law of the Lord is perfect,
    refreshing the soul;
The decree of the Lord is trustworthy,
    giving wisdom to the simple. **R.**
The precepts of the Lord are right,
    rejoicing the heart;

The command of the Lord is clear,
 enlightening the eye; **R.**
The fear of the Lord is pure,
 enduring forever;
The ordinances of the Lord are true,
 all of them just. **R.**
They are more precious than gold,
 than a heap of purest gold;
Sweeter also than syrup
 or honey from the comb. **R.**

John 6:64, 69
R. Alleluia, alleluia.
Your words, Lord, are spirit and life,
you have the words of everlasting life. **R.**

† *Matthew 13:18-23*
He who hears the word of God and understands it, yields much fruit.

Jesus said to his disciples, "Mark well the parable of the sower. The seed along the path is the man who hears the message about God's reign without understanding it The evil one approaches him to steal away what was sown in his mind. The seed that fell on patches of rock is the man who hears the message and at first receives it with joy. But he has no roots, so he lasts only for a time. When some setback or persecution involving the message occurs, he soon falters. What was sown among briers is the man who hears the message, but then worldly anxiety and the lure of money choke it off. Such a one produces no yield. But what was sown on good soil is the man who hears the message and takes it in. He it is who bears a yield of a hundred- or sixty- or thirty-fold." ✛

SATURDAY, JULY 28
WEEKDAY

† *Exodus 24:3-8*
This is the blood of the covenant which the Lord God has made with you.

When Moses came to the people and related all the words and ordinances of the Lord, they all answered with one voice, "We will do everything that the Lord has told us." Moses then wrote down all the words of the Lord and, rising early the next day, he erected at the foot of the mountain an altar and twelve pillars for the twelve tribes of Israel. Then, having sent certain young men of the Israelites to offer holocausts and sacrifice young bulls as peace offerings to the Lord, Moses took half of the blood and put it in large bowls; the other half he splashed on the altar. Taking the book of the covenant, he read it aloud to the people, who answered, "All that the Lord has said, we will heed and do." Then he took the blood and sprinkled it on the people, saying, "This is the blood of the covenant which the Lord has made with you in accordance with all these words of his." ✛

Psalm 50:1-2, 5-6, 14-15
R. Offer to God a sacrifice of praise.
God the Lord has spoken and summoned the earth,
 from the rising of the sun to its setting.
From Zion, perfect in beauty,
 God shines forth. **R.**
"Gather my faithful ones before me,
 those who have made a covenant with me by sacrifice."
And the heavens proclaim his justice;
 for God himself is the judge. **R.**
"Offer to God praise as your sacrifice
 and fulfill your vows to the Most High;
Then call upon me in time of distress;
 I will rescue you, and you shall glorify me." **R.**

John 6:64, 69
R. Alleluia, alleluia.
Your words, Lord, are spirit and life,
you have the words of everlasting life. **R.**

† Matthew 13:24-30
Let them both grow until the harvest time.

Jesus proposed to the crowds another parable: "The reign of God may be likened to a man who sowed good seed in his field. While everyone was asleep, his enemy came and sowed weeds through his wheat, and then made off. When the crop began to mature and yield grain, the weeds made their appearance as well. The owner's slaves came to him and said, 'Sir, did you not sow good seed in your field? Where are the weeds coming from?' He answered, 'I see an enemy's hand in this.' His slaves said to him, 'Do you want us to go out and pull them up?' 'No,' he replied, 'pull up the weeds and you might take the wheat along with them. Let them grow together until harvest; then at harvest time I will order the harvesters, first collect the weeds and bundle them up to burn, then gather the wheat into my barn.'" ✛

JULY 29
SEVENTEENTH SUNDAY IN ORDINARY TIME

✝ *Genesis 18:20-32*
Let not my Lord grow angry if I speak.

In those days, the LORD said: "The outcry against Sodom and
    Gomorrah is so great,
    and their sin so grave,
    that I must go down and see whether or not their actions
    fully correspond to the cry against them that comes to me.
I mean to find out."

While Abraham's visitors walked on farther toward Sodom,
    the LORD remained standing before Abraham.
Then Abraham drew nearer and said:
    "Will you sweep away the innocent with the guilty?
Suppose there were fifty innocent people in the city;
    would you wipe out the place, rather than spare it
    for the sake of the fifty innocent people within it?
Far be it from you to do such a thing,
    to make the innocent die with the guilty
    so that the innocent and the guilty would be treated alike!
Should not the judge of all the world act with justice?"
The LORD replied,
    "If I find fifty innocent people in the city of Sodom,
    I will spare the whole place for their sake."
Abraham spoke up again:
    "See how I am presuming to speak to my Lord,
    though I am but dust and ashes!
What if there are five less than fifty innocent people?
Will you destroy the whole city because of those five?"
He answered, "I will not destroy it, if I find forty-five there."

But Abraham persisted, saying "What if only forty are found
there?"
He replied, "I will forbear doing it for the sake of the forty."
Then Abraham said, "Let not my Lord grow impatient if I go
on.
What if only thirty are found there?"
He replied, "I will forbear doing it if I can find but thirty there."
Still Abraham went on,
"Since I have thus dared to speak to my Lord,
what if there are no more than twenty?"
The LORD answered, "I will not destroy it, for the sake of the
twenty."
But he still persisted:
"Please, let not my Lord grow angry if I speak up this last
time.
What if there are at least ten there?"
He replied, "For the sake of those ten, I will not destroy it." ✛

Psalm 138:1-3, 6-8
R. LORD, on the day I called for help, you answered me.
I will give thanks to you, O LORD, with all my heart,
for you have heard the words of my mouth;
in the presence of the angels I will sing your praise;
I will worship at your holy temple
and give thanks to your name. **R.**
Because of your kindness and your truth;
for you have made great above all things
your name and your promise.
When I called you answered me;
you built up strength within me. **R.**
The LORD is exalted, yet the lowly he sees,
and the proud he knows from afar.
Though I walk amid distress, you preserve me;
against the anger of my enemies you raise your hand. **R.**
Your right hand saves me.
The LORD will complete what he has done for me;
your kindness, O LORD, endures forever;
forsake not the work of your hands. **R.**

† *Colossians 2:12-14*

God has brought you to life along with Christ,
having forgiven us all our transgressions.

Brothers and sisters:
You were buried with him in baptism,
    in which you were also raised with him
    through faith in the power of God,
    who raised him from the dead.
And even when you were dead
    in transgressions and the uncircumcision of your flesh,
    he brought you to life along with him,
    having forgiven us all our transgressions;
obliterating the bond against us, with its legal claims,
    which was opposed to us,
    he also removed it from our midst, nailing it to the cross. ✝

Romans 8:15bc
R. Alleluia, alleluia.
You have received a Spirit of adoption,
through which we cry, Abba, Father. **R.**

† *Luke 11:1-13*

Ask and you will receive.

Jesus was praying in a certain place, and when he had
        finished,
    one of his disciples said to him,
    "Lord, teach us to pray just as John taught his disciples."
He said to them, "When you pray, say:
    Father, hallowed be your name,
        your kingdom come.
        Give us each day our daily bread
        and forgive us our sins
        for we ourselves forgive everyone in debt to us,
        and do not subject us to the final test."

And he said to them, "Suppose one of you has a friend
    to whom he goes at midnight and says,
    'Friend, lend me three loaves of bread,
    for a friend of mine has arrived at my house from a journey
    and I have nothing to offer him,'

and he says in reply from within,
'Do not bother me; the door has already been locked
and my children and I are already in bed.
I cannot get up to give you anything.'
I tell you,
if he does not get up to give the visitor the loaves
because of their friendship,
he will get up to give him whatever he needs
because of his persistence.

"And I tell you, ask and you will receive;
seek and you will find;
knock and the door will be opened to you.
For everyone who asks, receives;
and the one who seeks, finds;
and to the one who knocks, the door will be opened.
What father among you would hand his son a snake
when he asks for a fish?
Or hand him a scorpion when he asks for an egg?
If you then, who are wicked,
know how to give good gifts to your children,
how much more will the Father in heaven
give the Holy Spirit to those who ask him?" ✝

MONDAY, JULY 30
WEEKDAY, ST. PETER CHRYSOLOGUS

† *Exodus 32:15-24, 30-34*
This people has committed a grave sin, making themselves gods of gold.

Moses turned and came down the mountain with the two tablets of the commandments in his hands, tablets that were written on both sides, front and back; tablets that were made by God, having inscriptions on them that were engraved by God himself. Now, when Joshua heard the noise of the people shouting, he said to Moses, "That sounds like a battle in the camp." But Moses answered, "It does not sound like cries of victory, nor does it sound like cries of defeat; the sounds that I hear are cries of revelry." As he drew near the camp, he saw the calf and the dancing. With that, Moses' wrath flared up, so that he threw the tablets down and broke them on the base of the mountain. Taking the calf they had made, he fused it in the fire and then ground it down to powder, which he scattered on the water and made the Israelites drink.

Moses asked Aaron, "What did this people ever do to you that you should lead them into so grave a sin?" Aaron replied, "Let not my lord be angry. You know well enough how prone the people are to evil. They said to me, 'Make us a god to be our leader; as for the man Moses who brought us out of the land of Egypt, we do not know what has happened to him.' So I told them, 'Let anyone who has gold jewelry take it off.' They gave it to me, and I threw it into the fire, and this calf came out."

On the next day Moses said to the people, "You have committed a grave sin. I will go up to the Lord, then; perhaps I may be able to make atonement for your sin." So Moses went back to the Lord and said, "Ah, this people has indeed committed a grave sin in making a god of gold for themselves! If you would only forgive their sin! If you will not, then strike me out of the book that you have written." The Lord answered, "Him only who has sinned against me will I strike out of my book. Now, go and lead the people whither I have told you. My angel will go before you. When it is time for me to punish, I will punish them for their sin." ✛

Psalm 106:19-23
R. Give thanks to the Lord for he is good.
(or **Alleluia.***)*
They made a calf in Horeb
    and adored a molten image;
They exchanged their glory
    for the image of a grass-eating bullock. **R.**
They forgot the God who had saved them,
    who had done great deeds in Egypt,
Wondrous deeds in the land of Ham,
    terrible things at the Red sea. **R.**
Then he spoke of exterminating them,
    but Moses, his chosen one,
Withstood him in the breach
    to turn back his destructive wrath.

Psalm 145:13

R. Alleluia, alleluia.

The Lord is faithful in all his words
and holy in all his deeds. **R.**

✝ *Matthew 13:31-35*

*When the seed grows it is the biggest shrub of all
and the birds of the air come and nest in its branches.*

Jesus proposed to the crowds another parable: "The reign of God is like a mustard seed which someone took and sowed in his field. It is the smallest seed of all, yet when full-grown it is the largest of plants. It becomes so big a shrub that the birds of the sky come and build their nests in its branches."

He offered them still another image: "The reign of God is like yeast which a woman took and kneaded into three measures of flour. Eventually the whole mass of dough began to rise." All these lessons Jesus taught the crowds in the form of parables. He spoke to them in parables only, to fulfill what had been said through the prophet:

"I will open my mouth in parables,
    I will announce what has lain hidden since the creation
    of the world." ✝

TUESDAY, JULY 31
St. Ignatius of Loyola

✝ *Exodus 33:7-11; 34:5-9, 28*
The Lord God spoke to Moses face to face.

The tent, which was called the meeting tent, Moses used to pitch at some distance away, outside the camp. Anyone who wished to consult the Lord would go to this meeting tent outside the camp. Whenever Moses went out to the tent, the people would all rise and stand at the entrance of their own tents, watching Moses until he entered the tent. As Moses entered the tent, the column of cloud would come down and stand at its entrance while the Lord spoke with Moses. On seeing the column of cloud stand at the entrance of the tent, all the people would rise and worship at the entrance of their own tents. The Lord used to speak to Moses face to face, as one man speaks to another. Moses would then return to the camp, but his young assistant, Joshua, son of Nun, would not move out of the tent.

Moses invoked the name of the Lord who stood with him there and proclaimed his name, "Lord." Thus the Lord passed before him and cried out, "The Lord, the Lord, a merciful and gracious God, slow to anger and rich in kindness and fidelity, continuing his kindness for a thousand generations, and forgiving wickedness and crime and sin; yet not declaring the guilty guiltless, but punishing children and grandchildren to the third and fourth generation for their fathers' wickedness!" Moses at once bowed down to the ground in worship. Then he said, "If I find favor with you, O Lord, do come along in our company. This is indeed a stiff-necked people; yet pardon our wickedness and sins, and receive us as your own."

So Moses stayed there with the Lord for forty days and forty nights, without eating any food or drinking any water, and he wrote on the tablets the words of the covenant, the ten commandments. ✛

Psalm 103:6-13
R. The Lord is kind and merciful.
The Lord secures justice
    and the rights of all the oppressed.
He has made known his ways to Moses,
    and his deeds to the children of Israel. **R.**
Merciful and gracious is the Lord,
    slow to anger and abounding in kindness.
He will not always chide,
    nor does he keep his wrath forever. **R.**
Not according to our sins does he deal with us,
    nor does he requite us according to our crimes.
For as the heavens are high above the earth,
    so surpassing is his kindness toward those who fear him. **R.**
As far as the east is from the west,
    so far has he put our transgressions from us.
As a father has compassion on his children,
    so the Lord has compassion on those who fear him. **R.**

Psalm 145:13

R. Alleluia, alleluia.
The Lord is faithful in all his words
and holy in all his deeds. **R.**

✝ Matthew 13:35-43
*Just as the weeds are gathered up and burnt
in the fire, so it will be at the end of time.*

Jesus dismissed the crowds and went home. His disciples came to him with the request, "Explain to us the parable of the weeds in the field." He said in answer: "The farmer sowing good seed is the Son of Man; the field is the world, the good seed the citizens of the kingdom. The weeds are the followers of the evil one and the enemy who sowed them is the devil. The harvest is the end of the world, while the harvesters are the angels. Just as weeds are collected and burned, so it will be at the end of the world. The Son of Man will dispatch his angels to collect from his kingdom all who draw others to apostasy, and all evildoers. The angels will hurl them into the fiery furnace where they will wail and grind their teeth. Then the saints will shine like the sun in their Father's kingdom. Let everyone heed what he hears!" ✝

WEDNESDAY, AUGUST 1
St. Alphonsus Liguori

✝ Exodus 34:29-35
Seeing Moses' face, they would not approach him.

As Moses came down from Mount Sinai with the two tablets of the commandments in his hands, he did not know that the skin of his face had become radiant while he conversed with the Lord. When Aaron, then, and the other Israelites saw Moses and noticed how radiant the skin of his face had become, they were afraid to come near him. Only after Moses called to them did Aaron and all the rulers of the community come back to him. Moses then spoke to them. Later on, all the Israelites came up to him, and he enjoined on them all that the Lord had told him on Mount Sinai. When he finished speaking with them, he put a veil over his face. Whenever Moses entered the presence of the Lord to converse with him, he removed the veil

until he came out again. On coming out, he would tell the
Israelites all that had been commanded. Then the Israelites
would see that the skin of Moses' face was radiant; so he would
again put the veil over his face until he went in to converse
with the Lord. ✛

Psalm 99:5-7, 9
R. Holy is the Lord our God.
Extol the Lord, our God,
    and worship at his footstool;
    holy is he! **R.**
Moses and Aaron were among his priests,
    and Samuel, among those who called upon his name;
    they called upon the Lord, and he answered them. **R.**
From the pillar of cloud he spoke to them;
    they heard his decrees and the law he gave them. **R.**
Extol the Lord, our God,
    and worship at his holy mountain;
    for holy is the Lord, our God. **R.**

Matthew 11:25
R. Alleluia, alleluia.
Blessed are you, Father, Lord of heaven and earth;
you have revealed to little ones the mysteries
    of the kingdom. **R.**

† *Matthew 13:44-46*
He sold everything he had and went and bought the field.

Jesus said to the crowds: "The reign of God is like a buried
treasure which a man found in a field. He hid it again, and
rejoicing at his find went and sold all he had and bought that
field. Or again, the kingdom of heaven is like a merchant's
search for fine pearls. When he found one really valuable
pearl, he went back and put up for sale all that he had and
bought it." ✛

THURSDAY, AUGUST 2
WEEKDAY, ST. EUSEBIUS OF VERCELLI

† *Exodus 40:16-21, 34-38*
*The cloud covered the tent of meeting
and the glory of the Lord God filled the tabernacle.*

Moses did all that the Lord had commanded him. On the first day of the first month of the second year the Dwelling was erected. It was Moses who erected the Dwelling. He placed its pedestals, set up its boards, put in its bars, and set up its columns. He spread the tent over the Dwelling and put the covering on top of the tent, as the Lord had commanded him. He took the commandments and put them in the ark; he placed poles alongside the ark and set the propitiatory upon it. He brought the ark into the Dwelling and hung the curtain veil, thus screening off the ark of the commandments, as the Lord had commanded him.

Then the cloud covered the meeting tent, and the glory of the Lord filled the Dwelling. Moses could not enter the meeting tent, because the cloud settled down upon it and the glory of the Lord filled the Dwelling. Whenever the cloud rose from the Dwelling, the Israelites would set out on their journey. But if the cloud did not lift, they would not go forward; only when it lifted did they go forward. In the daytime the cloud of the Lord was seen over the Dwelling; whereas at night, fire was seen in the cloud by the whole house of Israel in all the stages of their journey. ✝

Psalm 84:3-6, 8, 11
**R. How lovely is your dwelling-place,
Lord, mighty God!**
My soul yearns and pines
　for the courts of the Lord.
My heart and my flesh
　cry out for the living God. **R.**
Even the sparrow finds a home,
　and the swallow a nest
　in which she puts her young—
Your altars, O Lord of hosts,
　my king and my God. **R.**

Happy they who dwell in your house!
  continually they praise you.
Happy the men whose strength you are!
They go from strength to strength; **R.**
I had rather one day in your courts
  than a thousand elsewhere;
I had rather lie at the threshold of the house of my God
  than dwell in the tents of the wicked. **R.**

Matthew 11:25
R. Alleluia, alleluia.
Blessed are you, Father, Lord of heaven and earth;
you have revealed to little ones the mysteries
  of the kingdom. **R.**

† *Matthew 13:47-53*
They gather the good ones in a basket, the bad are thrown away.

Jesus said to the crowds: "The reign of God is also like a dragnet thrown into the lake, which collected all sorts of things. When it was full they hauled it ashore and sat down to put what was worthwhile into containers. What was useless they threw away. That is how it will be at the end of the world. Angels will go out and separate the wicked from the just and hurl the wicked into the fiery furnace, where they will wail and grind their teeth.

"Have you understood all this?" "Yes," they answered; to which he replied, "Every scribe who is learned in the reign of God is like the head of a household who can bring from his storeroom both the new and the old." When Jesus had finished this parable he moved on from that district. ✛

FRIDAY, AUGUST 3
WEEKDAY

† *Leviticus 23:1, 4-11, 15-16, 27, 34-37*
The solemn feasts of the Lord God are sacred assemblies.

The Lord said to Moses, "These are the festivals of the Lord which you shall celebrate at their proper time with a sacred assembly. The Passover of the Lord falls on the fourteenth day of the first month, at the evening twilight. The fifteenth day of this month is the Lord's feast of Unleavened Bread. For seven days you shall eat unleavened bread. On the first of these days you shall hold a sacred assembly and do no sort of work. On each of the seven days you shall offer an oblation to the Lord. Then on the seventh day you shall again hold a sacred assembly and do no sort of work."

The Lord said to Moses, "Speak to the Israelites and tell them: When you come into the land which I am giving you, and reap your harvest, you shall bring a sheaf of the first fruits of your harvest to the priest, who shall wave the sheaf before the Lord that it may be acceptable for you.

"Beginning with the day after the sabbath, the day on which you bring the wave-offering sheaf, you shall count seven full weeks, and then on the day after the seventh week, the fiftieth day, you shall present the new cereal offering to the Lord. The tenth of this seventh month is the Day of Atonement, when you shall hold a sacred assembly and mortify yourselves and offer an oblation to the Lord. The fifteenth day of this seventh month is the Lord's feast of Booths, which shall continue for seven days. On the first day there shall be a sacred assembly, and you shall do no sort of work. For seven days you shall offer an oblation to the Lord, and on the eighth day you shall again hold a sacred assembly and offer an oblation to the Lord. On that solemn closing you shall do no sort of work.

"These, therefore, are the festivals of the Lord on which you shall proclaim a sacred assembly, and offer as an oblation to the Lord holocausts and cereal offerings, sacrifices and libations, as prescribed for each day." ✝

Psalm 81:3-6,10-11
R. Sing with joy to God our help.
Take up a melody, and sound the timbrel,
    the pleasant harp and the lyre.
Blow the trumpet at the new moon,
    at the full moon, on our solemn feast; **R.**
For it is a statute in Israel,
    an ordinance of the God of Jacob,
Who made it a decree for Joseph
    when he came forth from the land of Egypt. **R.**
There shall be no strange god among you

nor shall you worship any alien god.
I, the Lord, am your God
who led you forth from the land of Egypt. **R.**

Matthew 11:25
R. Alleluia, alleluia.
Blessed are you, Father, Lord of heaven and earth;
you have revealed to little ones the mysteries
of the kingdom. **R.**

† *Matthew 13:54-58*
Is this not the son of the carpenter? Where did he get all his wisdom?

Jesus went to his native place and spent his time teaching the people in their synagogue. They were filled with amazement, and said to one another, "Where did this man get such wisdom and miraculous powers? Isn't this the carpenter's son? Isn't Mary known to be his mother and James, Joseph, Simon, and Judas his brothers? Aren't his sisters our neighbors? Where did he get all this?" They found him altogether too much for them. Jesus said to them, "No prophet is without honor except in his native place, indeed in his own house." And he did not work many miracles there because of their lack of faith. ✛

SATURDAY, AUGUST 4
St. John Mary Vianney

† *Leviticus 25:1, 8-17*
In the jubilee year you will reap all you possess.

The Lord said to Moses on Mount Sinai, "Seven weeks of years shall you count—seven times seven years—so that the seven cycles amount to forty-nine years. Then, on the tenth day of the seventh month let the trumpet resound; on this, the Day of Atonement, the trumpet blast shall re-echo throughout your land. This fiftieth year you shall make sacred by proclaiming liberty in the land for all its inhabitants. It shall be a jubilee for you, when every one of you shall return to his own property, every one to his own family estate. In this fiftieth year, your year of jubilee, you shall not sow, nor shall you reap the aftergrowth or pick the grapes from the untrimmed vines. Since this is the jubilee, which shall be sacred for you, you may not eat of its produce, except as taken directly from the field.

"In this year of jubilee, then, every one of you shall return to his own property. Therefore, when you sell any land to your neighbor or buy any from him, do not deal unfairly. On the basis of the number of years since the last jubilee shall you purchase the land from him; and so also, on the basis of the number of years for crops, shall he sell it to you. When the years are many, the price shall be so much the more; when the years are few, the price shall be so much the less. For it is really the number of crops that he sells you. Do not deal unfairly, then; but stand in fear of your God. I, the Lord, am your God." ✛

Psalm 67:2-3, 5, 7-8
R. O God, let all the nations praise you!
May God have pity on us and bless us;
    may he let his face shine upon us.
So may your way be known upon earth;
    among all nations, your salvation. **R.**
May the nations he glad and exult
    because you rule the peoples in equity;
    the nations on the earth you guide. **R.**
The earth has yielded its fruits;
    God, our God, has blessed us.
May God bless us,
    and may all the ends of the earth fear him. **R.**

Matthew 11:25
R. Alleluia, alleluia.
Blessed are you, Father, Lord of heaven and earth;
you have revealed to little ones the mysteries
    of the kingdom. **R.**

† Matthew 14:1-12
Herod had John beheaded; the disciples went and told Jesus.

On one occasion Herod the tetrarch, having heard of Jesus' reputation, exclaimed to his courtiers, "This man is John the Baptizer—it is he in person, raised from the dead; that is why such miraculous powers are at work in him!" Recall that Herod had had John arrested, put in chains, and imprisoned on account of Herodias, the wife of his brother Philip. That was because John had told him, "It is not right for you to live with her." Herod wanted to kill John but was afraid of the people, who regarded him as a prophet Then on Herod's birthday Herodias' daughter performed a dance before the court which delighted Herod so much that he swore he would grant her anything she asked for. Prompted by her mother she said, "Bring me the head of John the Baptizer on a platter." The king immediately had his misgivings, but because of his oath and the guests who were present he gave orders that the request be granted. He sent the order to have John beheaded in prison. John's head was brought in on a platter and given to the girl, who took it to her mother. Later his disciples presented themselves to carry his body away and bury it. Afterward, they came and informed Jesus. ✛

AUGUST 5
EIGHTEENTH SUNDAY IN ORDINARY TIME

† *Ecclesiastes 1:2; 2:21-23*
What profit comes to a man from all his toil?

Vanity of vanities, says Qoheleth,
    vanity of vanities! All things are vanity!

Here is one who has labored with wisdom
        and knowledge and skill,
    and yet to another who has not labored over it,
        he must leave property.
This also is vanity and a great misfortune.
For what profit comes to man from all the toil and anxiety of
        heart
    with which he has labored under the sun?
All his days sorrow and grief are their occupation;
    even at night his mind is not at rest.
This also is vanity. ✛

Psalm 90:3-6,12-14,17
**R. If today you hear his voice,
    harden not you hearts.**
You turn man back to dust,
    saying, "Return, O children of men."
For a thousand years in your sight
    are as yesterday, now that it is past,

or as a watch of the night. **R.**
You make an end of them in their sleep;
  the next morning they are like the changing grass,
which at dawn springs up anew,
  but by evening wilts and fades. **R.**
Teach us to number our days aright,
  that we may gain wisdom of heart.
Return, O LORD! How long?
  Have pity on your servants! **R.**
Fill us at daybreak with your kindness,
  that we may shout for joy and gladness all our days.
And may the gracious care of the LORD our God be ours;
  prosper the work of our hands for us!
Prosper the work of our hands! **R.**

✝ *Colossians 3:1-5, 9-11*
Seek what is above, where Christ is.

Brothers and sisters:
If you were raised with Christ, seek what is above,
  where Christ is seated at the right hand of God.
Think of what is above, not of what is on earth.
For you have died,
  and your life is hidden with Christ in God.
When Christ your life appears,
  then you too will appear with him in glory.

Put to death, then, the parts of you that are earthly:
  immorality, impurity, passion, evil desire,
  and the greed that is idolatry.
Stop lying to one another,
  since you have taken off the old self with its practices
  and have put on the new self,
  which is being renewed, for knowledge,
  in the image of its creator.
Here there is not Greek and Jew,
  circumcision and uncircumcision,
  barbarian, Scythian, slave, free;
  but Christ is all and in all. ✝

Matthew 5:3

R. Alleluia, alleluia.
Blessed are the poor in spirit,
for theirs is the kingdom of heaven. **R.**

† *Luke 12:13-21*
The things you have prepared, to whom will they belong?

Someone in the crowd said to Jesus,
"Teacher, tell my brother to share the inheritance with me."
He replied to him,
"Friend, who appointed me as your judge and arbitrator?"
Then he said to the crowd,
"Take care to guard against all greed,
for though one may be rich,
one's life does not consist of possessions."

Then he told them a parable.
"There was a rich man whose land produced a bountiful
harvest.
He asked himself, 'What shall I do,
for I do not have space to store my harvest?'
And he said, 'This is what I shall do:
I shall tear down my barns and build larger ones.
There I shall store all my grain and other goods
and I shall say to myself, "Now as for you,
you have so many good things stored up for many years,
rest, eat, drink, be merry!"'
But God said to him,
'You fool, this night your life will be demanded of you;
and the things you have prepared,
to whom will they belong?'
Thus will it be for all who store up treasure for themselves
but are not rich in what matters to God." ✢

MONDAY, AUGUST 6
THE TRANSFIGURATION OF THE LORD

† *Daniel 7:9-10,13-14*
His clothing was snow bright.

As I watched:
Thrones were set up
and the Ancient One took his throne.
His clothing was snow bright,
and the hair on his head as white as wool;
his throne was flames of fire,
with wheels of burning fire.
A surging stream of fire
flowed out from where he sat;
thousands upon thousands were ministering to him,
and myriads upon myriads attended him.
The court was convened and the books were opened.

As the visions during the night continued, I saw
one like a Son of man coming,
on the clouds of heaven;
when he reached the Ancient One
and was presented before him,
the one like a Son of man received dominion, glory, and
kingship;
all peoples, nations, and languages serve him.
His dominion is an everlasting dominion
that shall not be taken away,
his kingship shall not be destroyed. ✛

Psalm 97:1-2, 5-6, 9
R. The Lord is king, the most high over all the earth.
The LORD is king; let the earth rejoice;
let the many islands be glad.
Clouds and darkness are round about him;
justice and judgment are the foundation of his throne. **R.**
The mountains melt like wax before the LORD,
before the LORD of all the earth.
The heavens proclaim his justice;
all peoples see his glory. **R.**

Because you, O LORD, are the Most High over all the earth,
exalted far above all gods. **R.**

† *2 Peter 1:16-19*
We ourselves heard this voice come from heaven.

Beloved:
We did not follow cleverly devised myths
    when we made known to you
    the power and coming of our Lord Jesus Christ,
    but we had been eyewitnesses of his majesty.
For he received honor and glory from God the Father
    when that unique declaration came to him from the majes
        tic glory,
    "This is my Son, my beloved, with whom I am well pleased."
We ourselves heard this voice come from heaven
    while we were with him on the holy mountain.
Moreover, we possess the prophetic message that is altogether
        reliable.
You will do well to be attentive to it,
    as to a lamp shining in a dark place,
    until day dawns and the morning star rises in your
        hearts. ✛

Matthew 17:5c
R. Alleluia, alleluia.
This is my beloved Son with whom I am well pleased;
listen to him. **R.**

† *Luke 9:28b-36*
While Jesus was praying his face changed in appearance.

Jesus took Peter, John, and James
    and went up a mountain to pray.
While he was praying his face changed in appearance
    and his clothing became dazzling white.
And behold, two men were conversing with him, Moses and
        Elijah,
    who appeared in glory and spoke of his exodus
    that he was going to accomplish in Jerusalem.
Peter and his companions had been overcome by sleep,
    but becoming fully awake,

they saw his glory and the two men standing with him.
As they were about to part from him, Peter said to Jesus,
    "Master, it is good that we are here;
    let us make three tents,
    one for you, one for Moses, and one for Elijah."
But he did not know what he was saying.
While he was still speaking,
    a cloud came and cast a shadow over them,
    and they became frightened when they entered the cloud.
Then from the cloud came a voice that said,
    "This is my chosen Son; listen to him."
After the voice had spoken, Jesus was found alone.
They fell silent and did not at that time
    tell anyone what they had seen. ✛

TUESDAY, AUGUST 7
WEEKDAY, SIXTUS II AND COMPANIONS, ST. CAJETAN

† *Numbers 12:1-13*
Moses is at home in my house. How have you dared to speak against him?

Miriam and Aaron spoke against Moses on the pretext of the marriage he had contracted with a Cushite woman. They complained, "Is it through Moses alone that the Lord speaks? Does he not speak through us also?" And the Lord heard this. Now, Moses himself was by far the meekest man on the face of the earth. So at once the Lord said to Moses and Aaron and Miriam, "Come out, you three, to the meeting tent." And the three of them went. Then the Lord came down in the column of cloud, and standing at the entrance of the tent, called Aaron and Miriam. When both came forward, he said, "Now listen to the words of the Lord:
    Should there be a prophet among you,
        in visions will I reveal myself to him,
        in dreams will I speak to him;
    Not so with my servant Moses!
    Throughout my house he bears my trust:
        face to face I speak to him,
        plainly and not in riddles.
    The presence of the Lord he beholds.
Why, then, did you not fear to speak against my servant

Moses?"

So angry was the Lord against them that when he departed, and the cloud withdrew from the tent, there was Miriam, a snow-white leper! When Aaron turned and saw her a leper, "Ah, my lord!" he said to Moses, "please do not charge us with the sin that we have foolishly committed! Let her not thus be like the stillborn babe that comes forth from its mother's womb with its flesh half consumed." Then Moses cried to the Lord, "Please, not this! Pray, heal her!" ✛

Psalm 51:3-7,12-13
R. Be merciful, O Lord, for we have sinned.
Have mercy on me, O God, in your goodness;
    in the greatness of your compassion wipe out my offense.
Thoroughly wash me from my guilt
    and of my sin cleanse me. **R.**
For I acknowledge my offense,
    and my sin is before me always:
"Against you only have I sinned
    and done what is evil in your sight"— **R.**
That you may be justified in your sentence,
    vindicated when you condemn.
Indeed, in guilt was I born,
    and in sin my mother conceived me. **R.**
A clean heart create for me, O God,
    and a steadfast spirit renew within me.
Cast me not out from your presence,
    and your holy spirit take not from me. **R.**

2 Timothy 1:10
R. Alleluia, alleluia.
Our Savior Jesus Christ has done away with death,
and brought us life through his gospel. **R.**

† *Matthew 14:22-36*
Order me to come to you across the water.

After the crowds had eaten their fill Jesus insisted that his disciples get into a boat and precede him to the other side. When he had sent them away, he went up on the mountain by himself to pray, remaining there alone as evening drew on. Meanwhile the boat, already several hundred yards out from shore, was being tossed about in the waves raised by strong head winds. At about three in the morning, he came walking toward them on the lake. When the disciples saw him walking on the water, they were terrified. "It is a ghost!" they said, and in their fear they began to cry out. Jesus hastened to reassure them: "Get hold of yourselves! It is I. Do not be afraid!" Peter spoke up and said, "Lord, if it is really you, tell me to come to you across the water." "Come!" he said. So Peter got out of the boat and began to walk on the water, moving toward Jesus. But when he perceived how strong the wind was, becoming frightened, he began to sink and cried out, "Lord, save me!" Jesus at once stretched out his hand and caught him. "How little faith you have!" he exclaimed. "Why did you falter?" Once they had climbed into the boat, the wind died down. Those who were in the boat showed him reverence, declaring, "Undoubtedly you are the Son of God!"

After making the crossing they reached the shore at Gennesaret; and when the men of that place recognized him they spread the word throughout the region. People brought him all the afflicted, with the plea that he let them do no more than touch the tassel of his cloak. As many as touched it were fully restored to health. ✛

WEDNESDAY, AUGUST 8
ST. DOMINIC

† Numbers 13:1-2, 25;14:1, 26-29, 34-35
They will have nothing of the land they desired.

The Lord said to Moses in the desert of Pharan, "Send men to reconnoiter the land of Canaan, which I am giving the Israelites." After reconnoitering the land for forty days they returned, met Moses and Aaron and the whole community of the Israelites in the desert of Paran at Kadesh, made a report to them all, and showed them the fruit of the country. They told Moses: "We went into the land to which you sent us. It does indeed flow with milk and honey, and here is its fruit. However, the people who are living in the land are fierce, and the towns are fortified and very strong. Besides, we saw descendants of the Anakim there. Amalekites live in the region of the Negeb; Hittites, Jebusites and Amorites dwell in the highlands, and Canaanites along the seacoast and the banks of the Jordan."

Caleb, however, to quiet the people toward Moses, said, "We ought to go up and seize the land, for we can certainly do so." But the men who had gone up with him said, "We cannot attack these people; they are too strong for us." So they spread discouraging reports among the Israelites about the land they had scouted, saying, "The land that we explored is a country that consumes its inhabitants. And all the people we saw there are huge men, veritable giants [the Anakim were a race of giants]; we felt like mere grasshoppers, and so we must have seemed to them."

At this, the whole community broke out with loud cries, and even in the night the people wailed.

The Lord said to Moses and Aaron: "How long will this wicked community grumble against me? I have heard the grumblings of the Israelites against me. Tell them: By my life, says the Lord, I will do to you just what I have heard you say. Here in the desert shall your dead bodies fall. Forty days you spent in scouting the land; forty years shall you suffer for your crimes: one year for each day. Thus you will realize what it means to oppose me. I, the Lord, have sworn to do this to all this wicked community that conspired against me: here in the desert they shall die to the last man." ✛

Psalm 106:6-7, 13-14, 21-23
**R. Lord, remember us,
for the love you bear your people.** *(or* **Alleluia.***)*
We have sinned, we and our fathers;
    we have committed crimes; we have done wrong.
Our fathers in Egypt
    considered not your wonders. **R.**
But soon they forgot his works;
    they waited not for his counsel.
They gave way to craving in the desert
    and tempted God in the wilderness. **R.**
They forgot the God who had saved them,
    who had done great deeds in Egypt,
Wondrous deeds in the land of Ham,
    terrible things at the Red Sea. **R.**
Then he spoke of exterminating them,

but Moses, his chosen one,
Withstood him in the breach
to turn back his destructive wrath. **R.**

2 Timothy 1:10
R. Alleluia, alleluia.
Our Savior Jesus Christ has done away with death,
and brought us life through his gospel. **R.**

† *Matthew 15:21-28*
Woman, you have great faith.

Jesus withdrew to the district of Tyre and Sidon. It happened
that a Canaanite woman living in that locality presented
herself, crying out to him, "Lord, Son of David, have pity on me!
My daughter is terribly troubled by a demon." He gave her no
word of response. His disciples came up and began to entreat
him, "Get rid of her. She keeps shouting after us." "My mission
is only to the lost sheep of the house of Israel," Jesus replied.
She came forward then and did him homage with the plea,
"Help me, Lord!" But he answered, "It is not right to take the
food of sons and daughters and throw it to the dogs." "Please,
Lord," she insisted, "even the dogs eat the leavings that fall
from their masters' tables." Jesus then said in reply, "Woman,
you have great faith! Your wish will come to pass." That very
moment her daughter got better. +

THURSDAY, AUGUST 9
WEEKDAY

† *Numbers 20:1-13*
He showed them his treasure, the font of living water.

The whole Israelite community arrived in the desert of Zin in
the first month, and the people settled at Kadesh. It was here
that Miriam died, and here that she was buried.

As the community had no water, they held a council
against Moses and Aaron. The people contended with Moses,
exclaiming, "Would that we too had perished with our kinsmen in the Lord's presence! Why have you brought the Lord's
community into this desert where we and our livestock are
dying? Why did you lead us out of Egypt, only to bring us to this

wretched place which has neither grain nor figs nor vines nor pomegranates? Here there is not even water to drink!" But Moses and Aaron went away from the assembly to the entrance of the meeting tent, where they fell prostrate.

Then the glory of the Lord appeared to them, and the Lord said to Moses, "Take the staff and assemble the community, you and your brother Aaron, and in their presence order the rock to yield its waters. From the rock you shall bring forth water for the community and their livestock to drink." So Moses took the staff from its place before the Lord, as he was ordered. He and Aaron assembled the community in front of the rock, where he said to them, "Listen to me, you rebels! Are we to bring water for you out of this rock?" Then, raising his hand, Moses struck the rock twice with his staff, and water gushed out in abundance for the community and their livestock to drink. But the Lord said to Moses and Aaron, "Because you were not faithful to me in showing forth my sanctity before the Israelites, you shall not lead this community into the land I will give them."

These are the waters of Meribah, where the Israelites contended against the Lord, and where he revealed his sanctity among them. ✝

Psalm 95:1-2, 6-9
**R. If today you hear his voice,
    harden not your hearts.**
Come, let us sing joyfully to the Lord;
    let us acclaim the Rock of our salvation.
Let us greet him with thanksgiving;
    let us joyfully sing psalms to him. **R.**
Come, let us bow down in worship;
    let us kneel before the Lord who made us.
For he is our God,
    and we are the people he shepherds, the flock he guides. **R.**
Oh, that today you would hear his voice:
    "Harden not your hearts as at Meribah,
    as in the day of Massah in the desert,
Where your fathers tempted me;
    they tested me though they had seen my works." **R.**

2 Timothy 1:10
R. Alleluia, alleluia.
Our Savior Jesus Christ has done away with death,
and brought us life through his gospel. **R.**

✝ *Matthew 16:13-23*
You are Peter, to you I will give the keys of the kingdom of heaven.

When Jesus came to the neighborhood of Caesarea Philippi, he asked his disciples this question: "Who do people say that the Son of Man is?" They replied, "Some say John the Baptizer, others Elijah, still others Jeremiah or one of the prophets." "And you," he said to them, "who do you say that I am?" "You are the Messiah," Simon Peter answered, "the Son of the living God!" Jesus replied, "Blest are you, Simon son of John! No mere man has revealed this to you, but my heavenly Father. I for my part declare to you, you are 'Rock,' and on this rock I will build my church, and the jaws of death shall not prevail against it. I will entrust to you the keys of the kingdom of heaven. Whatever you declare bound on earth shall be bound in heaven; whatever you declare loosed on earth shall be loosed in heaven." Then he strictly ordered his disciples not to tell anyone that he was the Messiah.

From then on Jesus [the Messiah] started to indicate to his disciples that he must go to Jerusalem to suffer greatly there at the hands of the elders, the chief priests, and the scribes, and to be put to death, and raised up on the third day. At this, Peter took him aside and began to remonstrate with him. "May you be spared, Master! God forbid that any such thing ever happen to you!" Jesus turned on Peter and said, "Get out of my sight, you satan! You are trying to make me trip and fall. You are not judging by God's standards but by man's." ✝

FRIDAY, AUGUST 10
St. Lawrence

✝ *2 Corinthians 9:6-10*
God loves a cheerful giver.

He who sows sparingly will reap sparingly, and he who sows bountifully will reap bountifully. Everyone must give according to what he has inwardly decided; not sadly, not grudgingly,

for God loves a cheerful giver. God can multiply his favors among you so that you may always have enough of everything and even a surplus for good works, as it is written:
"He scattered abroad and gave to the poor,
his justice endures forever."
He who supplies seed for the sower and bread for the eater will provide in abundance; he will multiply the seed you sow and increase your generous yield. ✛

Psalm 112:1-2, 5-9
**R. Happy the man who is merciful
and lends to those in need.**
Happy the man who fears the Lord,
who greatly delights in his commands.
His posterity shall be mighty upon the earth;
the upright generation shall be blessed. **R.**
Well for the man who is gracious and lends,
who conducts his affairs with justice;
He shall never be moved;
the just man shall be in everlasting remembrance. **R.**
An evil report he shall not fear;
his heart is firm, trusting in the Lord.
His heart is steadfast; he shall not fear
till he looks down upon his foes. **R.**
Lavishly he gives to the poor;
his generosity shall endure forever;
his horn shall be exalted in glory. **R.**

John 8:12
R. Alleluia, alleluia.
I am the light of the world, says the Lord;
the man who follows me will have the light of life. **R.**

† *John 12:24-26*
If anyone serves me the Father will honor him.

Jesus said to his disciples:
"I solemnly assure you,
unless the grain of wheat falls to the earth and dies,
it remains just a grain of wheat.
But if it dies,
it produces much fruit.

The man who loves his life
loses it,
while the man who hates his life in this world
preserves it to life eternal.
If anyone would serve me,
let him follow me;
where I am,
there will my servant be.
Anyone who serves me,
the Father will honor." ✛

SATURDAY, AUGUST 11
St. Clare

† *Deuteronomy 6:4-13*
You shall love the Lord your God with your whole heart.

Moses said to the people: "Hear, O Israel! The Lord is our God, the Lord alone! Therefore, you shall love the Lord, your God, with all your heart, and with all your soul, and with all your strength. Take to heart these words which I enjoin on you today. Drill them into your children. Speak of them at home and abroad, whether you are busy or at rest. Bind them at your wrist as a sign and let them be as a pendant on your forehead. Write them on the doorposts of your houses and on your gates.

"When the Lord, your God, brings you into the land which he swore to your fathers, Abraham, Isaac and Jacob, that he would give you, a land with fine, large cities that you did not build, with houses full of goods of all sorts that you did not garner, with cisterns that you did not dig, with vineyards and olive groves that you did not plant; and when, therefore, you eat your fill, take care not to forget the Lord, who brought you out of the land of Egypt, that place of slavery. The Lord, your God, shall you fear; him shall you serve, and by his name shall you swear." ✛

Psalm 18:2-4, 47, 51
R. I love you, Lord, my strength.
I love you, O Lord, my strength,
    O Lord, my rock, my fortress, my deliverer. **R.**
My God, my rock of refuge,

my shield, the horn of my salvation, my stronghold!
Praised be the Lord, I exclaim,
    and I am safe from my enemies. **R.**
The Lord live! And blessed be my rock!
    Extolled be God my savior.
You who gave great victories to your king
    and showed kindness to your anointed,
    to David and his posterity forever. **R.**

2 Timothy 1:10
R. Alleluia, alleluia.
Our Savior Jesus Christ has done away with death,
and brought us life through his gospel. **R.**

† *Matthew 17:14-20*
If you have faith, nothing is impossible for you.

A man came up to Jesus and knelt before him. "Lord," he said, "take pity on my son, who is demented and in a serious condition. For example, he often falls into the fire and frequently into the water. I have brought him to your disciples but they could not cure him." In reply Jesus said: "What an unbelieving and perverse lot you are! How long must I remain with you? How long can I endure you? Bring him here to me!" Then Jesus reprimanded him, and the demon came out of him. That very moment the boy was cured.

The disciples approached Jesus at that point and asked him privately, "Why could we not expel it?" "Because you have so little trust," he told them. "I assure you, if you had faith the size of a mustard seed, you would be able to say to this mountain, 'Move from here to there,' and it would move. Nothing would be impossible for you." ✝

AUGUST 12
NINETEENTH SUNDAY IN ORDINARY TIME

† *Wisdom 18:6-9*
*Just as you punished our adversaries,
you glorified us whom you had summoned.*

T he night of the passover was known beforehand to our
    fathers,

that, with sure knowledge of the oaths in which they put
   their faith,
they might have courage.
Your people awaited the salvation of the just
   and the destruction of their foes.
For when you punished our adversaries,
   in this you glorified us whom you had summoned.
For in secret the holy children of the good were offering
      sacrifice
   and putting into effect with one accord the
      divine institution. ✝

Psalm 33:1,12,18-22
**R. Blessed the people the Lord has chosen
to be his own.**
Exult, you just, in the LORD;
   praise from the upright is fitting.
Blessed the nation whose God is the LORD,
   the people he has chosen for his own inheritance. **R.**
See, the eyes of the LORD are upon those who fear him,
   upon those who hope for his kindness,
to deliver them from death
   and preserve them in spite of famine. **R.**
Our soul waits for the LORD,
   who is our help and our shield.
May your kindness, O LORD, be upon us
   who have put our hope in you. **R.**

*† **Hebrews 11:1-2, 8-19** (or Hebrews 11:1-2, 8-12)*
Abraham looked forward to the city whose architect and maker is God.

Brothers and sisters:
Faith is the realization of what is hoped for
   and evidence of things not seen.
Because of it the ancients were well attested.

By faith Abraham obeyed when he was called to go out to a place
   that he was to receive as an inheritance;
   he went out, not knowing where he was to go.
By faith he sojourned in the promised land as in a foreign
      country,
   dwelling in tents with Isaac and Jacob,

heirs of the same promise;
for he was looking forward to the city with foundations,
whose architect and maker is God.
By faith he received power to generate,
even though he was past the normal age
—and Sarah herself was sterile—
for he thought that the one who had made the promise was
trustworthy.
So it was that there came forth from one man,
himself as good as dead,
descendants as numerous as the stars in the sky
and as countless as the sands on the seashore.

All these died in faith.
They did not receive what had been promised
but saw it and greeted it from afar
and acknowledged themselves to be strangers
and aliens on earth,
for those who speak thus show that they are seeking a
homeland.
If they had been thinking of the land from which they had come,
they would have had opportunity to return.
But now they desire a better homeland, a heavenly one.
Therefore, God is not ashamed to be called their God,
for he has prepared a city for them.

By faith Abraham, when put to the test, offered up Isaac,
and he who had received the promises was ready to offer
his only son,
of whom it was said,
"Through Isaac descendants shall bear your name."
He reasoned that God was able to raise even from the dead,
and he received Isaac back as a symbol. ✠

Matthew 24:42a, 44
R. Alleluia, alleluia.
Stay awake and be ready!
For you do not know on what day the Son of Man will come. **R.**

† *Luke 12:32-48 (or Luke 12:35-40)*
You also must be prepared.

Jesus said to his disciples:
"Do not be afraid any longer, little flock,
for your Father is pleased to give you the kingdom.
Sell your belongings and give alms.
Provide money bags for yourselves that do not wear out,
an inexhaustible treasure in heaven
that no thief can reach nor moth destroy.
For where your treasure is, there also will your heart be.

"Gird your loins and light your lamps
and be like servants who await their master's return from a
wedding,
ready to open immediately when he comes and knocks.
Blessed are those servants
whom the master finds vigilant on his arrival.
Amen, I say to you, he will gird himself,
have them recline at table, and proceed to wait on them.
And should he come in the second or third watch
and find them prepared in this way,
blessed are those servants.
Be sure of this:
if the master of the house had known the hour
when the thief was coming,
he would not have let his house be broken into.
You also must be prepared, for at an hour you do not expect,
the Son of Man will come."

Then Peter said,
"Lord, is this parable meant for us or for everyone?"
And the Lord replied,
"Who, then, is the faithful and prudent steward
whom the master will put in charge of his servants
to distribute the food allowance at the proper time?
Blessed is that servant whom his master on arrival finds doing
so.
Truly, I say to you, the master will put the servant
in charge of all his property.
But if that servant says to himself,
'My master is delayed in coming,'

and begins to beat the menservants and the maidservants,
to eat and drink and get drunk,
then that servant's master will come
on an unexpected day and at an unknown hour
and will punish the servant severely
and assign him a place with the unfaithful.
That servant who knew his master's will
but did not make preparations nor act in accord with his
will
shall be beaten severely;
and the servant who was ignorant of his master's will
but acted in a way deserving of a severe beating
shall be beaten only lightly.
Much will be required of the person entrusted with much,
and still more will be demanded of the person entrusted
with more." ✝

MONDAY, AUGUST 13
WEEKDAY, POPE PONTIAN AND ST. HIPPOLYTUS

✝ Deuteronomy 10:12-22
*Circumcise your hearts. Love the strangers, for
you yourselves were strangers in the land of Egypt.*

Moses said to the people: "And now, Israel, what does the
Lord, your God, ask of you but to fear the Lord, your God, and
follow his ways exactly, to love and serve the Lord, your God,
with all your heart and all your soul, to keep the commandments and statutes of the Lord which I enjoin on you today for
your own good? Think! The heavens, even the highest heavens, belong to the Lord, your God, as well as the earth and
everything on it. Yet in his love for your fathers the Lord was
so attached to them as to choose you, their descendants, in
preference to all other peoples, as indeed he has now done.
Circumcise your hearts, therefore, and be no longer stiff-
necked. For the Lord, your God, is the God of gods, the Lord of
lords, the great God, mighty and awesome, who has no favor-
ites, accepts no bribes; who executes justice for the orphan and
the widow, and befriends the alien, feeding and clothing him.
So you too must befriend the alien, for you were once aliens
yourselves in the land of Egypt. The Lord, your God, shall you

fear, and him shall you serve; hold fast to him and swear by his name. He is your glory, he, your God, who has done for you those great and terrible things which your own eyes have seen. Your ancestors went down to Egypt seventy strong, and now the Lord, your God, has made you as numerous as the stars of the sky." ✛

Psalm 147:12-15,19-20
R. Praise the Lord, Jerusalem. *(or* **Alleluia.***)*
Glorify the Lord, O Jerusalem;
  praise your God, O Zion.
For he has strengthened the bars of your gates;
  he has blessed your children within you. **R.**
He has granted peace in your borders;
  with the best of wheat he fills you.
He sends forth his command to the earth;
  swiftly runs his word! **R.**
He has proclaimed his word to Jacob,
  his statutes and his ordinances to Israel.
He has not done thus for any other nation;
  his ordinances he has not made known to them. Alleluia. **R.**

James 1:21
R. Alleluia. alleluia.
Receive and submit to the word planted in you;
it can save your souls. **R.**

† Matthew 17:22-27
They put him to death and he rose. The sons are freed from tribute.

When Jesus and the disciples met in Galilee, he said to them, "The Son of Man is going to be delivered into the hands of men who will put him to death, and he will be raised up on the third day." At these words they were overwhelmed with grief.

When they entered Capernaum, the collectors of the temple tax approached Peter and said, "Does your master not pay the temple tax?" "Of course he does," Peter replied. Then Jesus on entering the house asked, without giving him time to speak: "What is your opinion, Simon? Do the kings of the world take tax or toll from their sons, or from foreigners?" When he replied, "From foreigners," Jesus observed: "Then their sons are exempt. But for fear of disedifying them go to the lake, throw in a line, and take out the first fish you catch. Open its mouth and you will discover there a coin worth twice the temple tax. Take it and give it to them for you and me." ✢

TUESDAY, AUGUST 14
St. Maximilian Kolbe

† *Deuteronomy 31:1-8*
Be strong, Joshua, stand firm, you will lead
this people into the land of promise.

When Moses finished speaking to all Israel, he said to them, "I am now one hundred and twenty years old and am no longer able to move about freely; besides, the Lord has told me that I shall not cross this Jordan. It is the Lord, your God, who will cross before you; he will destroy these nations before you, that you may supplant them. [It is Joshua who will cross before you, as the Lord promised.] The Lord will deal with them just as he dealt with Sihon and Og, the kings of the Amorites whom he destroyed, and with their country. When, therefore, the Lord delivers them up to you, you must deal with them exactly as I have ordered you. Be brave and steadfast; have no fear or dread of them, for it is the Lord, your God, who marches with you; he will never fail you or forsake you."

Then Moses summoned Joshua and in the presence of all Israel said to him, "Be brave and steadfast, for you must bring this people into the land which the Lord swore to their fathers he would give them; you must put them in possession of their heritage. It is the Lord who marches before you; he will be with you and will never fail you or forsake you. So do not fear or be dismayed." ✢

Deuteronomy 32:3-4, 7-9, 12
R. The portion of the Lord is his people.
For I will sing the Lord's renown.
  Oh, proclaim the greatness of our God!
The Rock—how faultless are his deeds,
  how right all his ways! **R.**
Think back on the days of old,
  reflect on the years of age upon age.
Ask your father and he will inform you,

ask your elders and they will tell you. **R.**
When the Most High assigned the nations their heritage,
    when he parceled out the descendants of Adam,
He set up the boundaries of the peoples
    after the number of the sons of God. **R.**
While the Lord's own portion was Jacob,
    his hereditary share was Israel.
The Lord alone was their leader,
    no strange god was with him. **R.**

James 1:21
R. Alleluia, alleluia.
Receive and submit to the word planted in you;
it can save your souls. **R.**

† Matthew 18:1-5, 10, 12-14
Be careful never to despise one of these little ones.

The disciples came up to Jesus with the question, "Who is of greatest importance in the kingdom of God?" He called a little child over and stood him in their midst and said: "I assure you, unless you change and become like little children, you will not enter the kingdom of God. Whoever makes himself lowly, becoming like this child, is of greatest importance in that heavenly reign.

"Whoever welcomes one such child for my sake welcomes me. See that you never despise one of these little ones. I assure you their angels in heaven constantly behold my heavenly Father's face.

"What is your thought on this: A man owns a hundred sheep and one of them wanders away; will he not leave the ninety-nine out on the hills and go in search of the stray? If he succeeds in finding it, believe me he is happier about this one than about the ninety-nine that did not wander away. Just so, it is no part of your heavenly Father's plan that a single one of these little ones shall ever come to grief." ✣

WEDNESDAY, AUGUST 15
THE ASSUMPTION OF THE BLESSED VIRGIN MARY

(Readings for the Assumption Vigil Mass are: 1 Chronicles 15:3-4, 15-16; 15:1-2 •
Psalm 132:6-7, 9-10, 13-14 • 1 Corinthians 15:54-57 • Luke 11:27-28)

† *Revelation 11:19a; 12:1-6a, 10ab*
A woman clothed with the sun, with the moon beneath her feet.

God's temple in heaven was opened,
> and the ark of his covenant could be seen in the temple.

A great sign appeared in the sky, a woman clothed with the sun,
> with the moon beneath her feet,
> and on her head a crown of twelve stars.

She was with child and wailed aloud in pain as she labored to
> give birth.

Then another sign appeared in the sky;
> it was a huge red dragon, with seven heads and ten horns,
> and on its heads were seven diadems.

Its tail swept away a third of the stars in the sky
> and hurled them down to the earth.

Then the dragon stood before the woman about to give birth,
> to devour her child when she gave birth.

She gave birth to a son, a male child,
> destined to rule all the nations with an iron rod.

Her child was caught up to God and his throne.
The woman herself fled into the desert
> where she had a place prepared by God.

Then I heard a loud voice in heaven say:
> "Now have salvation and power come,
>> and the kingdom of our God
>> and the authority of his Anointed One. ✛

Psalm 45:10-12,16

**R. The queen stands at your right hand,
arrayed in gold.**

The queen takes her place at your right hand
> in gold of Ophir. **R.**

Hear, O daughter, and see; turn your ear,
> forget your people and your father's house. **R.**

So shall the king desire your beauty;
> for he is your lord. **R.**

They are borne in with gladness and joy;

they enter the palace of the king. **R.**

† *1 Corinthians 15:20-27*
Christ, the firstfruits; then those who belong to him.

Brothers and sisters:
Christ has been raised from the dead,
 the firstfruits of those who have fallen asleep.
For since death came through man,
 the resurrection of the dead came also through man.
For just as in Adam all die,
 so too in Christ shall all be brought to life,
 but each one in proper order:
 Christ the firstfruits;
 then, at his coming, those who belong to Christ;
 then comes the end,
 when he hands over the kingdom to his God and Father,
 when he has destroyed every sovereignty
 and every authority and power.
For he must reign until he has put all his enemies under his feet.
The last enemy to be destroyed is death,
 for "he subjected everything under his feet." +

R. Alleluia, alleluia.
Mary is taken up to heaven;
a chorus of angels exults. **R.**

† *Luke 1:39-56*
The Mighty One has done great things for me: he has raised up the lowly.

Mary set out
 and traveled to the hill country in haste
 to a town of Judah,
 where she entered the house of Zechariah
 and greeted Elizabeth.
When Elizabeth heard Mary's greeting,
 the infant leaped in her womb,
 and Elizabeth, filled with the Holy Spirit,
 cried out in a loud voice and said,
 "Blessed are you among women,
 and blessed is the fruit of your womb.
And how does this happen to me,

that the mother of my Lord should come to me?
For at the moment the sound of your greeting reached my ears,
the infant in my womb leaped for joy.
Blessed are you who believed
that what was spoken to you by the Lord
would be fulfilled."

And Mary said:
"My soul proclaims the greatness of the Lord;
my spirit rejoices in God my Savior
for he has looked upon his lowly servant.
From this day all generations will call me blessed:
the Almighty has done great things for me,
and holy is his Name.
He has mercy on those who fear him
in every generation.
He has shown the strength of his arm,
and has scattered the proud in their conceit.
He has cast down the mighty from their thrones,
and has lifted up the lowly.
He has filled the hungry with good things,
and the rich he has sent away empty.
He has come to the help of his servant Israel
for he has remembered his promise of mercy,
the promise he made to our fathers,
to Abraham and his children forever."

Mary remained with her about three months
and then returned to her home. ✢

THURSDAY, AUGUST 16
WEEKDAY, ST. STEPHEN OF HUNGARY

† *Joshua 3:7-11,13-17*
The ark of the Lord God will precede you across the Jordan.

The Lord said to Joshua, "Today I will begin to exalt you in the sight of all Israel, that they may know I am with you, as I was with Moses. Now command the priests carrying the ark of the covenant to come to a halt in the Jordan when they reach the edge of the waters."

So Joshua said to the Israelites, "Come here and listen to

the words of the Lord, your God." He continued: "This is how you will know that there is a living God in your midst, who at your approach will dispossess the Canaanites. The ark of the covenant of the Lord of the whole earth will precede you into the Jordan. When the soles of the feet of the priests carrying the ark of the Lord, the Lord of the whole earth, touch the water of the Jordan, it will cease to flow; for the water flowing down from upstream will halt in a solid bank."

The people struck their tents to cross the Jordan, with the priests carrying the ark of the covenant ahead of them. No sooner had these priestly bearers of the ark waded into the waters at the edge of the Jordan, which overflows all its banks during the entire season of the harvest, than the waters flowing from upstream halted, backing up in a solid mass for a very great distance indeed, from Adam, a city in the direction of Zarethan; while those flowing downstream toward the Salt Sea of the Arabah disappeared entirely. Thus the people crossed over opposite Jericho. While all Israel crossed over on dry ground, the priests carrying the ark of the covenant of the Lord remained motionless on dry ground in the bed of the Jordan until the whole nation had completed the passage. ✛

Psalm 114:1-6
R. Alleluia.
When Israel came forth from Egypt,
　　the house of Jacob from a people of alien tongue,
Judah became his sanctuary,
　　Israel his domain. **R.**
The sea beheld and fled;
　　Jordan turned back.
The mountains skipped like rams,
　　the hills like the lambs of the flock. **R.**
Why is it, O sea, that you flee?
　　O Jordan, that you turn back?
You mountains, that you skip like rams?
　　You hills, like the lambs of the flock? **R.**

James 1:21

R. Alleluia, alleluia.

Receive and submit to the word planted in you;
it can save your souls.

† *Matthew 18:21—19:1*
I did not say to you to forgive seven times, but seventy times seven.

Peter came up to Jesus and asked him, "Lord, when my brother wrongs me, how often must I forgive him? Seven times?" "No," Jesus replied, "not seven times; I say, seventy times seven times. That is why the reign of God may be said to be like a king who decided to settle accounts with his officials. When he began his auditing, one was brought in who owed him a huge amount. As he had no way of paying it, his master ordered him to be sold, along with his wife, his children, and all his property, in payment of the debt. At that the official prostrated himself in homage and said, 'My lord, be patient with me and I will pay you back in full.' Moved with pity, the master let the official go and wrote off the debt. But when that same official went out he met a fellow servant who owed him a mere fraction of what he himself owed. He seized him and throttled him. 'Pay back what you owe,' he demanded. His fellow servant dropped to his knees and began to plead with him, 'Just give me time and I will pay you back in full.' But he would hear none of it. Instead, he had him put in jail until he paid back what he owed. When his fellow servants saw what had happened they were badly shaken, and went to their master to report the whole incident. His master sent for him and said, 'You worthless wretch! I canceled your entire debt when you pleaded with me. Should you not have dealt mercifully with your fellow servant, as I dealt with you?' Then in anger the master handed him over to the torturers until he paid back all that he owed. My heavenly Father will treat you in exactly the same way unless each of you forgives his brother from his heart."

When Jesus had finished this discourse, he left Galilee and came to the district of Judea across the Jordan. ✝

FRIDAY, AUGUST 17
WEEKDAY

† *Joshua 24:1-13*

I brought your father from Mesopotamia,
out of the land of Egypt and took you to your own land.

Joshua gathered together all the tribes of Israel at Shechem, summoning their elders, their leaders, their judges and their officers. When they stood in ranks before God, Joshua addressed all the people: "Thus says the Lord, the God of Israel: In times past your fathers, down to Terah, father of Abraham and Nahor, dwelt beyond the River and served other gods. But I brought your father Abraham from the region beyond the River and led him through the entire land of Canaan. I made his descendants numerous, and gave him Isaac. To Isaac I gave Jacob and Esau. To Esau I assigned the mountain region of Seir in which to settle, while Jacob and his children went down to Egypt.

"Then I sent Moses and Aaron, and smote Egypt with the prodigies which I wrought in her midst. Afterward I led you out of Egypt, and when you reached the sea, the Egyptians pursued your fathers to the Red Sea with chariots and horsemen. Because they cried out to the Lord, he put darkness between your people and the Egyptians, upon whom he brought the sea so that it engulfed them. After you witnessed what I did to Egypt, and dwelt a long time in the desert, I brought you into the land of the Amorites who lived east of the Jordan. They fought against you, but I delivered them into your power. You took possession of their land, and I destroyed them [the two kings of the Amorites] before you. Then Balak, son of Zippor, king of Moab, prepared to war against Israel. He summoned Balaam, son of Beor, to curse you; but I would not listen to Balaam. On the contrary, he had to bless you, and I saved you from him. Once you crossed the Jordan and came to Jericho, the men of Jericho fought against you, but I delivered them also into your power. And I sent the hornets ahead of you which drove them [the Amorites, Perizzites, Canaanites, Hittites, Girgashites, Hivites and Jebusites] out of your way; it was not your sword or your bow.

"I gave you a land which you had not tilled and cities which you had not built, to dwell in; you have eaten of vineyards and olive groves which you did not plant." ✝

Psalm 136:1-3,16-18, 21-22, 24
R. His love is everlasting. (*or* **Alleluia.**)
Give thanks to the Lord, for he is good,
    for his mercy endures forever;
Give thanks to the God of gods,
    for his mercy endures forever;
Give thanks to the Lord of lords,
    for his mercy endures forever. **R.**
Who led his people through the wilderness,
    for his mercy endures forever;
Who smote great kings,
    for his mercy endures forever;
And slew powerful kings,
    for his mercy endures forever. **R.**
And made their land a heritage,
    for his mercy endures forever;
The heritage of Israel his servant,
    for his mercy endures forever;
And freed us from our foes,
    for his mercy endures forever. **R.**

James 1:21
R. Alleluia, alleluia.
Receive and submit to the word planted in you;
it can save your souls. **R.**

✝ *Matthew 19:3-12*
Because of the hardness of your hearts Moses permitted you to divorce your wives, but it was not like this from the beginning.

Some Pharisees came up to Jesus and said, to test him, "May a man divorce his wife for any reason whatever?" He replied, "Have you not read that at the beginning the Creator made them male and female and declared, 'For this reason a man shall leave his father and mother and cling to his wife, and the two shall become as one'? Thus they are no longer two but one flesh. Therefore, let no man separate what God has joined." They said to him, "Then why did Moses command divorce and the promulgation of a divorce decree?" "Because of your stubbornness Moses let you divorce your wives," he replied; "but at the beginning it was not that way. I now say to you whoever divorces his wife (lewd conduct is a separate case) and marries another commits adultery, and the man who marries a divorced woman commits adultery."

His disciples said to him, "If that is the case between man and wife, it is better not to marry." He said, "Not everyone can accept this teaching, only those to whom it is given to do so. Some men are incapable of sexual activity from birth; some have been deliberately made so; and some there are who have freely renounced sex for the sake of God's reign. Let him accept this teaching who can." ✛

SATURDAY, AUGUST 18
WEEKDAY, ST. JANE DE CHANTAL

† Joshua 24:14-29
Choose today whom you wish to serve.

Joshua said to the people, "Fear the Lord and serve him completely and sincerely. Cast out the gods your fathers served beyond the River and in Egypt, and serve the Lord. If it does not please you to serve the Lord, decide today whom you will serve, the gods your fathers served beyond the River or the gods of the Amorites in whose country you are dwelling. As for me and my household, we will serve the Lord.

But the people answered, "Far be it from us to forsake the Lord for the service of other gods. For it was the Lord, our God, who brought us and our fathers up out of the land of Egypt, out of a state of slavery. He performed those great miracles before our very eyes and protected us along our entire journey and among all the peoples through whom we passed. At our approach the Lord drove out [all the peoples, including] the Amorites who dwelt in the land. Therefore we also will serve the Lord, for he is our God.

Joshua in turn said to the people, "You may not be able to serve the Lord, for he is a holy God; he is a jealous God who will not forgive your transgressions or your sins. If, after the good he has done for you, you forsake the Lord and serve strange gods, he will do evil to you and destroy you."

But the people answered Joshua, "We will still serve the

Lord." Joshua therefore said to the people, "You are your own witnesses that you have chosen to serve the Lord." They replied, "We are, indeed!" [Joshua continued:] "Now, therefore, put away the strange gods that are among you and turn your hearts to the Lord, the God of Israel." Then the people promised Joshua, "We will serve the Lord, our God, and obey his voice."

So Joshua made a covenant with the people that day and made statutes and ordinances for them at Shechem, which he recorded in the book of the law of God. Then he took a large stone and set it up there under the oak that was in the sanctuary of the Lord. And Joshua said to all the people, "This stone shall be our witness, for it has heard all the words which the Lord spoke to us. It shall be a witness against you, should you wish to deny your God." Then Joshua dismissed the people, each to his own heritage.

After these events, Joshua, son of Nun, servant of the Lord, died at the age of a hundred and ten. ✝

Psalm 16:1-2, 5, 7-8, 11
R. You are my inheritance, O Lord.
Keep me, O God, for in you I take refuge;
    I say to the Lord, "My Lord are you.
    Apart from you I have no good."
O Lord, my allotted portion and my cup,
    you it is who hold fast my lot. **R.**
I bless the Lord who counsels me;
    even in the night my heart exhorts me.
I set the Lord ever before me;
    with him at my right hand I shall not be disturbed. **R.**
You will show me the path to life,
    fullness of joys in your presence,
    the delights at your right hand forever. **R.**

James 1:21
R. Alleluia, alleluia.
Receive and submit to the word planted in you;
it can save your souls. **R.**

✝ *Matthew 19:13-15*

*Do not prevent the little children from coming
to me: to them belongs the kingdom of heaven.*

Children were brought to Jesus so that he could place his hands on them in prayer. The disciples began to scold them, but Jesus said, "Let the children come to me. Do not hinder them. The kingdom of God belongs to such as these." And he laid his hands on their heads before he left that place. ✝

AUGUST 19
TWENTIETH SUNDAY IN ORDINARY TIME

✝ *Jeremiah 38:4-6, 8-10*

A man of strife and contention to all the land.

In those days, the princes said to the king:
"Jeremiah ought to be put to death;
he is demoralizing the soldiers who are left in this city,
and all the people, by speaking such things to them;
he is not interested in the welfare of our people,
but in their ruin."
King Zedekiah answered: "He is in your power";
for the king could do nothing with them.
And so they took Jeremiah
and threw him into the cistern of Prince Malchiah,
which was in the quarters of the guard,
letting him down with ropes.
There was no water in the cistern, only mud,
and Jeremiah sank into the mud.

Ebed-melech, a court official,
went there from the palace and said to him:
"My lord king,
these men have been at fault
in all they have done to the prophet Jeremiah,
casting him into the cistern.
He will die of famine on the spot,
for there is no more food in the city."
Then the king ordered Ebed-melech the Cushite
to take three men along with him,
and draw the prophet Jeremiah out of the cistern before
he should die. ✝

Psalm 40:2-4,18

R. Lord, come to my aid!

I have waited, waited for the LORD,
  and he stooped toward me. **R.**

The LORD heard my cry.

He drew me out of the pit of destruction,
  out of the mud of the swamp;

he set my feet upon a crag;
  he made firm my steps. **R.**

And he put a new song into my mouth,
  a hymn to our God.

Many shall look on in awe
  and trust in the LORD. **R.**

Though I am afflicted and poor,
  yet the LORD thinks of me.

You are my help and my deliverer;
  O my God, hold not back! **R.**

† *Hebrews 12:1-4*

Let us persevere in running the race that lies before us.

Brothers and sisters:

Since we are surrounded by so great a cloud of witnesses,
  let us rid ourselves of every burden and sin that clings to us
  and persevere in running the race that lies before us
  while keeping our eyes fixed on Jesus,
  the leader and perfecter of faith.

For the sake of the joy that lay before him
  he endured the cross, despising its shame,
  and has taken his seat at the right of the throne of God.

Consider how he endured such opposition from sinners,
  in order that you may not grow weary and lose heart.

In your struggle against sin
  you have not yet resisted to the point of shedding blood. ✛

John 10:27

R. Alleluia, alleluia.

My sheep hear my voice, says the Lord;
I know them, and they follow me. **R.**

† *Luke 12:49-53*
I have come not to establish peace, but rather division.

Jesus said to his disciples:
"I have come to set the earth on fire,
and how I wish it were already blazing!
There is a baptism with which I must be baptized,
and how great is my anguish until it is accomplished!
Do you think that I have come to establish peace on the earth?
No, I tell you, but rather division.
From now on a household of five will be divided,
three against two and two against three;
a father will be divided against his son
and a son against his father,
a mother against her daughter
and a daughter against her mother,
a mother-in-law against her daughter-in-law
and a daughter-in-law against her mother-in-law." ✛

MONDAY, AUGUST 20
St. Bernard

† *Judges 2:11-19*
The Lord God appointed judges for them,
but they would not listen to them.

The Israelites offended the Lord by serving the Baals. Abandoning the Lord, the God of their fathers, who had led them out of the land of Egypt, they followed the other gods of the various nations around them, and by their worship of these gods provoked the Lord.

Because they had thus abandoned him and served Baal and the Ashtaroth, the anger of the Lord flared up against Israel, and he delivered them over to plunderers who despoiled them. He allowed them to fall into the power of their enemies round about whom they were no longer able to withstand. Whatever they undertook, the Lord turned into disaster for them, as in his warning he had sworn he would do, till they were in great distress. Even when the Lord raised up judges to deliver them from the power of their despoilers, they did not listen to their judges, but abandoned themselves to the worship of other gods. They were quick to stray from the way their fathers had taken, and did not follow their example of obedience to the commandments of the Lord. Whenever the Lord raised up judges for them, he would be with the judge and save them from the power of their enemies as long as the judge lived; it was thus the Lord took pity on their distressful cries of affliction under their oppressors. But when the judge died, they would relapse and do worse than their fathers, following other gods in service and worship, relinquishing none of their evil practices or stubborn conduct. ✛

Psalm 106:34-37, 39-40, 43-44
R. Lord, remember us,
   for the love you bear your people.
They did not exterminate the peoples,
   as the Lord had commanded them,
But mingled with the nations
   and learned their works. **R.**
They served their idols,
   which became a snare for them.
They sacrificed their sons
   and their daughters to demons. **R.**
They became defiled by their works,
   and wanton in their crimes.
And the Lord grew angry with his people,
   and abhorred his inheritance. **R.**
Many times did he rescue them,
   but they embittered him with their counsels.
Yet he had regard for their affliction
   when he heard their cry. **R.**

1 Peter 1:25
R. Alleluia, alleluia.
The word of the Lord stands for ever;
it is the word given to you, the Good News. **R.**

† *Matthew 19:16-22*
If you wish to be perfect, sell what you own,
and your treasure will be in heaven.

A man came up to Jesus and said, "Teacher, what good must I do to possess everlasting life?" He answered, "Why do you question me about what is good? There is One who is good. If you wish to enter into life, keep the commandments." "Which ones?" he asked. Jesus replied, "'You shall not kill'; 'You shall not commit adultery'; 'You shall not steal'; 'You shall not bear false witness'; 'Honor your father and your mother'; and 'Love your neighbor as yourself.'" The young man said to him, "I have kept all these; what do I need to do further?" Jesus told him, "If you seek perfection, go, sell your possessions, and give to the poor. You will then have treasure in heaven. After that, come back and follow me." Hearing these words, the young man went away sad, for his possessions were many. ✛

TUESDAY, AUGUST 21
POPE PIUS X

† *Judges 6:11-24*
Gideon, you will free Israel. Do I not send you?

The angel of the Lord came and sat under the terebinth in Ophrah that belonged to Joash the Abiezrite. While his son Gideon was beating out wheat in the wine press to save it from the Midianites, the angel of the Lord appeared to him and said, "The Lord is with you, O champion!" "My lord," Gideon said to him, "if the Lord is with us, why has all this happened to us? Where are his wondrous deeds of which our fathers told us when they said, 'Did not the Lord bring us up from Egypt?' For now the Lord has abandoned us and has delivered us into the power of Midian." The Lord turned to him and said, "Go with the strength you have and save Israel from the power of Midian. It is I who send you." But he answered him, "Please, my lord, how can I save Israel? My family is the meanest in Manasseh, and I am the most insignificant in my father's house." "I shall be with you," the Lord said to him, "and you will cut down Midian to the last man." He answered him, "If I find favor with you, give me a sign that you are speaking with me. Do not depart from here, I pray you, until I come back to you and bring out my offering and set it before you." He answered, "I will await your return."

So Gideon went off and prepared a kid and an ephah of flour in the form of unleavened cakes. Putting the meat in a basket and the broth in a pot, he brought them out to him under the terebinth and presented them. The angel of God said to him, "Take the meat and unleavened cakes and lay them on this rock; then pour out the broth." When he had done so, the angel of the Lord stretched out the tip of the staff he held, and touched the meat and unleavened cakes. Thereupon a fire came up from the rock which consumed the meat and unleavened cakes, and the angel of the Lord disappeared from sight. Gideon, now aware that it had been the angel of the Lord, said, "Alas, Lord God, that I have seen the angel of the Lord face to face!" The Lord answered him, "Be calm, do not fear. You shall not die." So Gideon built there an altar to the Lord and called it Yahweh-shalom. ✛

Psalm 85:9,11-14
R. The Lord speaks of peace to his people.
I will hear what God proclaims;
    the Lord—for he proclaims peace
To his people, and to his faithful ones,
    and to those who put in him their hope. **R.**
Kindness and truth shall meet;
    justice and peace shall kiss.
Truth shall spring out of the earth,
    and justice shall look down from heaven. **R.**
The Lord himself will give his benefits;
    our land shall yield its increase.
Justice shall walk before him,
    and salvation, along the way of his steps. **R.**

1 Peter 1:25
R. Alleluia, alleluia.
The word of the Lord stands for ever;
it is the word given to you, the Good News. **R.**

† *Matthew 19:23-30*

*It is easier for a camel to pass through the eye of a
needle than for a rich man to enter the kingdom of heaven.*

Jesus said to his disciples: "I assure you, only with difficulty will a rich man enter into the kingdom of God. I repeat what I said: it is easier for a camel to pass through a needle's eye than for a rich man to enter the kingdom of God." When the disciples heard this they were completely overwhelmed, and exclaimed, "Then who can be saved?" Jesus looked at them and said, "For man it is impossible; but for God all things are possible." Then it was Peter's turn to say to him: "Here we have put everything aside to follow you. What can we expect from it?" Jesus said to them: "I give you my solemn word, in the new age when the Son of Man takes his seat upon a throne befitting his glory, you who have followed me shall likewise take your places on twelve thrones to judge the twelve tribes of Israel. Moreover, everyone who has given up home, brothers or sisters, father or mother, wife or children or property for my sake will receive many times as much and inherit everlasting life. Many who are first shall come last, and the last shall come first." ✝

WEDNESDAY, AUGUST 22
THE QUEENSHIP OF MARY

† Judges 9:6-15
It is said, the king will reign over us,
when the Lord God reigns among you (1 Samuel 12:12).

All the citizens of Shechem and all Beth-millo came together and proceeded to make Abimelech king by the terebinth at the memorial pillar in Shechem.

When this was reported to him, Jotham went to the top of Mount Gerizim, and standing there, cried out to them in a loud voice: "Hear me, citizens of Shechem, that God may then hear you! Once the trees went to anoint a king over themselves. So they said to the olive tree, 'Reign over us.' But the olive tree answered them, 'Must I give up my rich oil, whereby men and gods are honored, and go to wave over the trees?' Then the trees said to the fig tree, 'Come; you reign over us!' But the fig tree answered them, 'Must I give up my sweetness and my good fruit, and go to wave over the trees?' Then the trees said to the vine, 'Come you, and reign over us.' But the vine answered them, 'Must I give up my wine that cheers gods and men, and go to wave over the trees?' Then all the trees said to the buckthorn, 'Come you reign over us!' But the buckthorn replied to the trees, 'If you wish to anoint me king over you in good faith, come and take refuge in my shadow. Otherwise, let fire come from the buckthorn and devour the cedars of Lebanon.'" ✝

Psalm 21:2-7
R. Lord, your strength gives joy to the king.
O Lord, in your strength the king is glad;
  in your victory how greatly he rejoices!
You have granted him his heart's desire;
  you refused not the wish of his lips. **R.**
For you welcomed him with goodly blessings,
  you placed on his head a crown of pure gold.
He asked life of you: you gave him
  length of days forever and ever. **R.**
Great is his glory in your victory;
  majesty and splendor you conferred upon him.
For you made him a blessing forever;
  you gladdened him with the joy of your presence. **R.**

1 Peter 1:25
R. Alleluia, alleluia.
The word of the Lord stands for ever;
it is the word given to you, the Good News. **R.**

† *Matthew 20:1-16*
Are you jealous because I am generous?

Jesus told his disciples this parable: "The reign of God is like the case of the owner of an estate who went out at dawn to hire workmen for his vineyard. After reaching an agreement with them for the usual daily wage, he sent them out to his vineyard. He came out about midmorning and saw other men standing around the marketplace without work, so he said to them, 'You too go along to my vineyard and I will pay you whatever is fair.' At that they went away. He came out again around noon and midafternoon and did the same. Finally, going out in late afternoon he found still others standing around. To these he said, 'Why have you been standing here idle all day?' 'No one has hired us,' they told him. He said, 'You go to the vineyard too.' When evening came the owner of the vineyard said to his foreman, 'Call the workmen and give them their pay, but begin with the last group and end with the first.' When those hired late in the afternoon came up they received a full day's pay, and when the first group appeared they supposed they would get more; yet they received the same daily wage. Thereupon they complained to the owner, 'This last group did only an hour's work, but you have put them on the same basis as us who have worked a full day in the scorching heat.' 'My friend,' he said to one in reply, 'I do you no injustice. You agreed on the usual wage, did you not? Take your pay and go home. I intend to give this man who was hired last the same pay as you. I am free to do as I please with my money, am I not? Or are you envious because I am generous?' Thus the last shall be first and the first shall be last." ✝

THURSDAY, AUGUST 23
WEEKDAY, ST. ROSE OF LIMA

† *Judges 11:29-39*
Whoever first comes from the door of
my house I will offer up as a holocaust.

The spirit of the Lord came upon Jephthah. He passed through Gilead and Manasseh, and through Mizpah-Gilead as well, and from there he went on to the Ammonites. Jephthah made a vow to the Lord. "If you deliver the Ammonites into my power," he said, "whoever comes out of the doors of my house to meet me when I return in triumph from the Ammonites shall belong to the Lord. I shall offer him up as a holocaust."

Jephthah then went on to the Ammonites to fight against them, and the Lord delivered them into his power, so that he inflicted a severe defeat on them, from Aroer to the approach of Minnith (twenty cities in all) and as far as Abel-keramin. Thus were the Ammonites brought into subjection by the Israelites. When Jephthah returned to his house in Mizpah, it was his daughter who came forth, playing the tambourines and dancing. She was an only child: he had neither son nor daughter besides her. When he saw her, he rent his garments and said, "Alas, daughter, you have struck me down and brought calamity upon me. For I have made a vow to the Lord and I cannot retract." "Father," she replied, "you have made a vow to the Lord. Do with me as you have vowed, because the Lord has wrought vengeance for you on your enemies the Ammonites." Then she said to her father, "Let me have this favor. Spare me for two months, that I may go off down the mountains to mourn my virginity with my companions." "Go," he replied, and sent her away for two months. So she departed with her companions and mourned her virginity on the mountains. At the end of the two months she returned to her father, who did to her as he had vowed. ✛

Psalm 40:5, 7-10
**R. Here am I, Lord;
I come to do your will.**
Happy the man who makes the Lord his trust;
  who turns not to idolatry
  or to those who stray after falsehood. **R.**
Sacrifice or oblation you wished not,
  but ears open to obedience you gave me.
Holocausts or sin-offerings you sought not;
  then said I, "Behold I come"; **R.**
"In the written scroll it is prescribed for me
  to do your will, O my God, is my delight,
  and your law is within my heart!" **R.**
I announced your justice in the vast assembly;
  I did not restrain my lips, as you, O Lord, know. **R.**

1 Peter 1:25
R. Alleluia, alleluia.
The word of the Lord stands for ever;
it is the word given to you, the Good News. **R.**

† *Matthew 22:1-14*
Go out and find whomever you can, and invite them to the wedding.

Jesus began to address the chief priests and elders of the people, once more using parables. "The reign of God may be likened to a king who gave a wedding banquet for his son. He dispatched his servants to summon the invited guests to the wedding, but they refused to come. A second time he sent other servants, saying: 'Tell those who are invited, See, I have my dinner prepared! My bullocks and corn-fed cattle are killed; everything is ready. Come to the feast.' Some ignored the invitation and went their way, one to his farm, another to his business. The rest laid hold of his servants, insulted them, and killed them. At this the king grew furious and sent his army to destroy those murderers and burn their city. Then he said to his servants: 'The banquet is ready, but those who were invited were unfit to come. That is why you must go out into the byroads and invite to the wedding anyone you come upon.' The servants then went out into the byroads and rounded up everyone they met, bad as well as good. This filled the wedding hall with banqueters.

"When the king came in to meet the guests, however, he caught sight of a man not properly dressed for a wedding feast. 'My friend,' he said, 'how is it you came in here not properly dressed?' The man had nothing to say. The king then said to the attendants, 'Bind him hand and foot and throw him out into the night to wail and grind his teeth.' The invited are many, the elect are few." ✦

FRIDAY, AUGUST 24
St. Bartholomew

† *Revelation 21:9-14*
On the foundations are the names of the twelve Apostles of the Lamb.

An angel said to me, "Come, I will show you the woman who is the bride of the Lamb." He carried me away in spirit to the top of a very high mountain and showed me the holy city Jerusalem coming down out of heaven from God. It gleamed with the splendor of God. The city had the radiance of a precious jewel that sparkled like a diamond. Its wall, massive and high, had twelve gates at which twelve angels were stationed. Twelve names were written on the gates, the names of the twelve tribes of Israel. There were three gates facing east, three north, three south, and three west. The wall of the city had twelve courses of stones as its foundation, on which were written the names of the twelve apostles of the Lamb. ✦

Psalm 145:10-13, 17-18
R. Your friends tell the glory of your kingship, Lord.
Let all your works give you thanks, O Lord,
    and let your faithful ones bless you.
Let them discourse of the glory of your kingdom
    and speak of your might. **R.**
Making known to men your might
    and the glorious splendor of your kingdom.
Your kingdom is a kingdom for all ages,

and your dominion endures through all generations. **R.**
The Lord is just in all his ways
  and holy in all his works.
The Lord is near to all who call upon him,
  to all who call upon him in truth. **R.**

John 1:49
R. Alleluia, alleluia.
Master, you are the Son of God,
you are the king of Israel. **R.**

† *John 1:45-51*
There is a true Israelite, in whom there is no deceit.

Philip sought out Nathanael and told him, "We have found the one Moses spoke of in the law—the prophets too—Jesus, son of Joseph, from Nazareth." Nathanael's response to that was, "Can anything good come from Nazareth?" and Philip replied, "Come, see for yourself." When Jesus saw Nathanael coming toward him, he remarked: "This man is a real Israelite. There is no guile in him." "How do you know me?" Nathanael asked him. "Before Philip called you," Jesus answered, "I saw you under the fig tree." "Rabbi," said Nathanael, "you are the Son of God; you are the king of Israel." Jesus responded: "Do you believe just because I told you I saw you under the fig tree? You will see much greater things than that."

He went on to tell them, "I solemnly assure you, you shall see the sky opened and the angels of God ascending and descending on the Son of Man." ✝

SATURDAY, AUGUST 25
WEEKDAY, ST. LOUIS, ST. JOSEPH OF CALASANZ

† *Ruth 2:1-3, 8-11; 4:13-17*
The Lord has not left your family without a successor.
This was the father of David's father.

Naomi had a prominent kinsman named Boaz, of the clan of her husband Elimelech. Ruth the Moabite said to Naomi, "Let me go and glean ears of grain in the field of anyone who will allow me that favor." Naomi said to her, "Go, my daughter," and she went. The field she entered to glean after the harvesters happened to be the section belonging to Boaz of the clan of Elimelech.

Boaz said to Ruth, "Listen, my daughter! Do not go to glean in anyone else's field; you are not to leave here. Stay here with my woman servants. Watch to see which field is to be harvested, and follow them; I have commanded the young men to do you no harm. When you are thirsty, you may go and drink from the vessels the young men have filled." Casting herself prostrate upon the ground, she said to him, "Why should I, a foreigner, be favored with your notice?" Boaz answered her: "I have had a complete account of what you have done for your mother-in-law after your husband's death; you have left your father and your mother and the land of your birth, and have come to a people whom you did not know previously."

Boaz took Ruth. When they came together as man and wife, the Lord enabled her to conceive and she bore a son. Then the women said to Naomi, "Blessed is the Lord who has not failed to provide you today with an heir! May he become famous in Israel! He will be your comfort and the support of your old age, for his mother is the daughter-in-law who loves you. She is worth more to you than seven sons!" Naomi took the child, placed him on her lap, and became his nurse. And the neighbor women gave him his name, at the news that a grandson had been born to Naomi. They called him Obed. He was the father of Jesse, the father of David. ✛

Psalm 128:1-5
R. See how the Lord blesses those who fear him.
Happy are you who fear the Lord,
    who walk in his ways!
For you shall eat the fruit of your handiwork;
    happy shall you be, and favored. **R.**
Your wife shall be like a fruitful vine
    in the recesses of your home;
Your children like olive plants
    around your table. **R.**
Behold, thus is the man blessed
    who fears the Lord. **R.**
The Lord bless you from Zion:
    may you see the prosperity of Jerusalem
    all the days of your life. **R.**

1 Peter 1:25

R. Alleluia, alleluia.

The word of the Lord stands for ever;
it is the word given to you, the Good News. **R.**

† *Matthew 23:1-12*

They speak, but do not practice what they preach.

Jesus told the crowds and his disciples: "The scribes and the Pharisees have succeeded Moses as teachers; therefore, do everything and observe everything they tell you. But do not follow their example. Their words are bold but their deeds are few. They bind up heavy loads, hard to carry, to lay on other men's shoulders, while they themselves will not lift a finger to budge them. All their works are performed to be seen. They widen their phylacteries and wear huge tassels. They are fond of places of honor at banquets and the front seats in synagogues, of marks of respect in public and of being called 'Rabbi.' As to you, avoid the title 'Rabbi.' One among you is your teacher, the rest are learners. Do not call anyone on earth your father. Only one is your father, the One in heaven. Avoid being called teachers. Only one is your teacher, the Messiah. The greatest among you will be the one who serves the rest. Whoever exalts himself shall be humbled, but whoever humbles himself shall be exalted." ✛

AUGUST 26
TWENTY-FIRST SUNDAY IN ORDINARY TIME

† *Isaiah 66:18-21*

They shall bring all your brothers and sisters from all the nations.

Thus says the LORD:
I know their works and their thoughts,
and I come to gather nations of every language;
    they shall come and see my glory.
I will set a sign among them;
    from them I will send fugitives to the nations:
    to Tarshish, Put and Lud, Mosoch, Tubal and Javan,
    to the distant coastlands
    that have never heard of my fame, or seen my glory;
    and they shall proclaim my glory among the nations.

They shall bring all your brothers and sisters
     from all the nations
   as an offering to the LORD,
   on horses and in chariots, in carts, upon mules
         and dromedaries,
   to Jerusalem, my holy mountain, says the LORD,
   just as the Israelites bring their offering
   to the house of the LORD in clean vessels.
Some of these I will take as priests and Levites, says the LORD. ✛

Psalm 117:1-2
R. Go out to all the world
   and tell the Good News. *(or* **Alleluia.***)*
Praise the LORD, all you nations;
   glorify him, all you peoples! **R.**
For steadfast is his kindness toward us,
   and the fidelity of the LORD endures forever. **R.**

† Hebrews 12:5-7, 11-13
Those whom the Lord loves, he disciplines.

Brothers and sisters,
You have forgotten the exhortation addressed to you as chil-
     dren:
   "My son, do not disdain the discipline of the Lord
      or lose heart when reproved by him;
   for whom the Lord loves, he disciplines;
      he scourges every son he acknowledges."
Endure your trials as "discipline";
   God treats you as sons.
For what "son" is there whom his father does not discipline?
At the time,
   all discipline seems a cause not for joy but for pain,
   yet later it brings the peaceful fruit of righteousness
   to those who are trained by it.

So strengthen your drooping hands and your weak knees.
Make straight paths for your feet,
   that what is lame may not be disjointed but healed. ✛

John 14:6

R. Alleluia, alleluia.

I am the way, the truth and the life, says the Lord;
no one comes to the Father, except through me. **R.**

† *Luke 13:22-30*

*They will come from east and west and
recline at table in the kingdom of God.*

Jesus passed through towns and villages,
 teaching as he went and making his way to Jerusalem.
Someone asked him,
 "Lord, will only a few people be saved?"
He answered them,
 "Strive to enter through the narrow gate,
 for many, I tell you, will attempt to enter
 but will not be strong enough.
After the master of the house has arisen and locked the door,
 then will you stand outside knocking and saying,
 'Lord, open the door for us.'
He will say to you in reply,
 'I do not know where you are from.'
And you will say,
 'We ate and drank in your company and you taught in our
  streets.'
Then he will say to you,
 'I do not know where you are from.
Depart from me, all you evildoers!'
And there will be wailing and grinding of teeth
 when you see Abraham, Isaac, and Jacob
 and all the prophets in the kingdom of God
 and you yourselves cast out.
And people will come from the east and the west
 and from the north and the south
 and will recline at table in the kingdom of God.
For behold, some are last who will be first,
 and some are first who will be last." ✛

MONDAY, AUGUST 27
St. Monica

✝ *1 Thessalonians 1:2-5,8-10*
You converted to God from idolatry,
expecting his Son whom he raised from the dead.

We constantly remember you in our prayers, for we are mindful before our God and Father of the way you are proving your faith, laboring in love, and showing constancy in hope in our Lord Jesus Christ. We know, too, brothers beloved of God, how you were chosen. Our preaching of the gospel proved not a mere matter of words for you but one of power; it was carried on in the Holy Spirit and out of complete conviction. You know as well as we do what we proved to be like when, while still among you, we acted on your behalf.

This is true not only in Macedonia and Achaia; throughout every region your faith in God is celebrated, which makes it needless for us to say anything more. The people of those parts are reporting what kind of reception we had from you and how you turned to God from idols, to serve him who is the living and true God and to await from heaven the Son he raised from the dead—Jesus, who delivers us from the wrath to come. ✝

Psalm 149:1-6, 9
R. The Lord takes delight in his people. *(or* **Alleluia.***)*
Sing to the Lord a new song
   of praise in the assembly of the faithful.
Let Israel be glad in their maker,
   let the children of Zion rejoice in their king. **R.**
Let them praise his name in the festive dance,
   let them sing praise to him with timbrel and harp.
For the Lord loves his people,
   and he adorns the lowly with victory. **R.**
Let the faithful exult in glory;
   let them sing for joy upon their couches;
   let the high praises of God be in their throats.
This is the glory of all his faithful. Alleluia. **R.**

Philippians 2:15-16
R. Alleluia, alleluia.
Shine on the world like bright stars;
you are offering it the word of life. **R.**

† *Matthew 23:13-22*
Woe to you, blind leaders.

Jesus said, "Woe to you scribes and Pharisees, you frauds! You shut the doors of the kingdom of God in men's faces, neither entering yourselves nor admitting those who are trying to enter. Woe to you scribes and Pharisees, you frauds! You travel over sea and land to make a single convert, but once he is converted you make a devil of him twice as wicked as yourselves. It is an evil day for you, blind guides! You declare, 'If a man swears by the temple it means nothing, but if he swears by the gold of the temple he is obligated.' Blind fools! Which is more important, the gold or the temple which makes it sacred? Again you declare, 'If a man swears by the altar it means nothing, but if he swears by the gift on the altar he is obligated.' How blind you are! Which is more important, the offering or the altar which makes the offering sacred? The man who swears by the altar is swearing by it and by everything on it. The man who swears by the temple is swearing by it and by him who dwells there. The man who swears by heaven is swearing by God's throne and by him who is seated on that throne." ✛

TUESDAY, AUGUST 28
ST. AUGUSTINE

† *1 John 4:7-16*
If we love one another, God will live in us.

Beloved,
let us love one another
because love is of God;
everyone who loves is begotten of God
and has knowledge of God.
The man without love has known nothing of God
for God is love.
God's love was revealed in our midst in this way:

he sent his only Son to the world
that we might have life through him.
Love, then, consists of this:
not that we have loved God,
but that he has loved us
and has sent his Son as an offering for our sins.
Beloved,
if God has loved us so,
we must have the same love for one another.
God has never yet been seen.
Yet if we love one another
God dwells in us,
and his love is brought to perfection in us.
The way we know we remain in him
and he in us
is that he has given us of his Spirit.
We have seen for ourselves, and can testify,
that the Father has sent the Son as savior of the world.
When anyone acknowledges that Jesus is the Son of God,
God dwells in him
and he in God.
We have come to know and enter fully
    into the love God has for us.
God is love,
and he who lives in love
lives in God
and God in him. ✛

Psalm 139:1-6
**R. You have searched me
and you know me, Lord.**
O Lord, you have probed me and you know me;
    you know when I sit and when I stand;
    you understand my thoughts from afar.
My journeys and my rest you scrutinize,
    with all my ways you are familiar. **R.**
Even before a word is on my tongue,
    behold, O Lord, you know the whole of it.
Behind me and before, you hem me in
    and rest your hand upon me.

Such knowledge is too wonderful for me;
    too lofty for me to attain. **R.**

Philippians 2:15-16
R. Alleluia, alleluia.
Shine on the world like bright stars;
you are offering it the word of life. **R.**

† *Matthew 23:8-12*
*You must not allow yourselves to be called teachers,
for you have only one teacher, the Christ.*

Jesus said to his disciples: "Avoid the title 'Rabbi.' One among you is your teacher, the rest are learners. Do not call anyone on earth your father. Only one is your father, the One in heaven. Avoid being called teachers. Only one is your teacher, the Messiah. The greatest among you will be the one who serves the rest. Whoever exalts himself shall be humbled, but whoever humbles himself shall be exalted. ✛

WEDNESDAY, AUGUST 29
THE MARTYRDOM OF JOHN THE BAPTIST

† *Jeremiah 1:17-19*
Say to them everything that I tell you; do not be afraid of their presence.

The word of the Lord said to me:
Do you gird your loins;
    stand up and tell them
    all that I command you.
Be not crushed on their account,
    as though I would leave you crushed before them;
For it is I this day
    who have made you a fortified city,
A pillar of iron, a wall of brass,
    against the whole land:
Against Judah's kings and princes,
    against its priests and people.
They will fight against you, but not prevail over you,
    for I am with you to deliver you, says the Lord. ✛

Psalm 71:1-6, 15, 17
R. I will sing of your salvation.
In you, O Lord, I take refuge;
    let me never be put to shame.
In your justice rescue me, and deliver me;
    incline your ear to me, and save me. **R.**
Be my rock of refuge,
    a stronghold to give me safety,
    for you are my rock and my fortress.
O my God, rescue me from the hand of the wicked. **R.**
For you are my hope, O Lord:
    my trust, O God, from my youth.
On you I depend from birth;
    from my mother's womb you are my strength. **R.**
My mouth shall declare your justice,
    day by day your salvation.
O God, you have taught me from my youth,
    and till the present I proclaim your wondrous deeds. **R.**

Matthew 5:10
R. Alleluia, alleluia.
Happy are they who suffer persecution for justice' sake;
the kingdom of heaven is theirs. **R.**

† *Mark 6:17-29*
I want you to give me the head of John the Baptist on a dish.

Herod was the one who had ordered John arrested, chained, and imprisoned on account of Herodias, the wife of his brother Philip, whom he had married. That was because John had told Herod, "It is not right for you to live with your brother's wife." Herodias harbored a grudge against him for this and wanted to kill him but was unable to do so. Herod feared John, knowing him to be an upright and holy man, and kept him in custody. When he heard him speak he was very much disturbed; yet he felt the attraction of his words. Herodias had her chance one day when Herod held a birthday dinner for his court circle, military officers, and the leading men of Galilee. Herodias' own daughter came in at one point and performed a dance which delighted Herod and his guests. The king told the girl, "Ask for anything you want and I will give it to you." He went so far as to swear to her: "I will grant you whatever you ask, even to half my kingdom!" She went out and said to her mother, "What shall I ask for?" The mother answered, "The head of John the Baptizer." At that the girl hurried back to the king's presence and made her request: "I want you to give me, at once, the head of John the Baptizer on a platter." The king bitterly regretted the request; yet because of his oath and the presence of the guests, he did not want to refuse her. He promptly dispatched an executioner, ordering him to bring back the Baptizer's head. The man went and beheaded John in the prison. He brought in the head on a platter and gave it to the girl, and the girl gave it to her mother. Later, when his disciples heard about this, they came and carried his body away and laid it in a tomb. ✝

THURSDAY, AUGUST 30
WEEKDAY

† 1 Thessalonians 3:7-13
May the Lord be generous in increasing
your love for one another and for the whole human race.

We have been much consoled by your faith throughout our distress and trial—so much so that we shall continue to flourish only if you stand firm in the Lord!

What thanks can we give to God for all the joy we feel in his presence because of you, as we ask him fervently night and day that we may see you face to face and remedy any shortcomings in your faith? May God himself, who is our Father, and our Lord Jesus make our path to you a straight one! And may the Lord increase you and make you overflow with love for one another and for all, even as our love does for you. May he strengthen your hearts, making them blameless and holy before our God and Father at the coming of our Lord Jesus with all his holy ones. ✝

Psalm 90:3-4, 12-14, 17
R. **Fill us with your love, O Lord,**
   and we will sing for joy!
You turn man back to dust,
   saying, "Return, O children of men."

For a thousand years in your sight
    are as yesterday, now that it is past,
    or as a watch of the night. **R.**
Teach us to number our days aright,
    that we may gain wisdom of heart.
Return, O Lord! How long?
    Have pity on your servants! **R.**
Fill us at daybreak with your kindness,
    that we may shout for joy and gladness all our days.
And may the gracious care of the Lord our God be ours;
    prosper the work of our hands for us!
    [Prosper the work of our hands!] **R.**

Philippians 2:15-16
R. Alleluia, alleluia.
Shine on the world like bright stars;
you are offering it the word of life. **R.**

✝ *Matthew 24:42-51*
Stay awake and be ready.

Jesus said to his disciples: "Stay awake, therefore! You cannot know the day your Lord is coming.

"Be sure of this: if the owner of the house knew when the thief was coming he would keep a watchful eye and not allow his house to be broken into. You must be prepared in the same way. The Son of Man is coming at the time you least expect. Who is the faithful, far-sighted servant whom the master has put in charge of his household to dispense food at need? Happy that servant whom his master discovers at work on his return! I assure you, he will put him in charge of all his property. But if the servant is worthless and tells himself, 'My master is a long time in coming,' and begins to beat his fellow servants, to eat and drink with drunkards, that man's master will return when he is not ready and least expects him. He will punish him severely and settle with him as is done with hypocrites. There will be wailing then and grinding of teeth." ✝

FRIDAY, AUGUST 31
WEEKDAY

† 1 Thessalonians 4:1-8
This is the will of God, your holiness.

Now, my brothers, we beg and exhort you in the Lord Jesus that, even as you learned from us how to conduct yourselves in a way pleasing to God—which you are indeed doing—so you must learn to make still greater progress. You know the instructions we gave you in the Lord Jesus. It is God's will that you grow in holiness: that you abstain from immorality, each of you guarding his member in sanctity and honor, not in passionate desire as do the Gentiles who know not God; and that each refrain from overreaching or cheating his brother in the matter at hand; for the Lord is an avenger of all such things, as we once indicated to you by our testimony. God has not called us to immorality but to holiness; hence, whoever rejects these instructions rejects, not man, but God "who sends his holy Spirit upon you." ✛

Psalm 97:1-2, 5-6, 10-12
R. **Let good men rejoice in the Lord.**
The Lord is king; let the earth rejoice;
    let the many isles be glad.
Justice and judgment are the foundation of his throne. **R.**
The mountains melt like wax before the Lord,
    before the Lord of all the earth.
The heavens proclaim his justice,
    and all peoples see his glory. **R.**
The Lord loves those that hate evil;
    he guards the lives of his faithful ones;
    from the hand of the wicked he delivers them. **R.**
Light dawns for the just;
    and gladness, for the upright of heart.
Be glad in the Lord, you just,
    and give thanks to his holy name. **R.**

Philippians 2:15-16
R. **Alleluia, alleluia.**
Shine on the world like bright stars;
you are offering it the word of life. **R.**

✝ *Matthew 25:1-13*
The bridegroom is here, go out and meet him.

Jesus told this parable to his disciples: "The reign of God can be likened to ten bridesmaids who took their torches and went out to welcome the groom. Five of them were foolish, while the other five were sensible. The foolish ones, in taking their torches, brought no oil along, but the sensible ones took flasks of oil as well as their torches. The groom delayed his coming, so they all began to nod, then to fall asleep. At midnight someone shouted, 'The groom is here! Come out and greet him!' At the outcry all the virgins woke up and got their torches ready. The foolish ones said to the sensible, 'Give us some of your oil. Our torches are going out.' But the sensible ones replied, 'No, there may not be enough for you and us. You had better go to the dealers and buy yourselves some.' While they went off to buy it the groom arrived, and the ones who were ready went in to the wedding with him. Then the door was barred. Later the other bridesmaids came back. 'Master, master!' they cried. 'Open the door for us.' But he answered, 'I tell you, I do not know you.' The moral is: keep your eyes open, for you know not the day or the hour." ✝

SATURDAY, SEPTEMBER 1
WEEKDAY

✝ *1 Thessalonians 4:9-12*
You have learned from God himself to love one another.

As regards brotherly love, there is no need for me to write you. God himself has taught you to love one another, and this you are doing with respect to all the brothers throughout Macedonia. Yet we exhort you to even greater progress, brothers. Make it a point of honor to remain at peace and attend to your own affairs. Work with your hands as we directed you to do, so that you will give good example to outsiders and want for nothing. ✝

Psalm 98:1, 7-9
R. The Lord comes to rule the earth with justice.
Sing to the Lord a new song,
    for he has done wondrous deeds;

His right hand has won victory for him,
 his holy arm. **R.**
Let the sea and what fills it resound,
 the world and those who dwell in it;
Let the rivers clap their hands,
 the mountains shout with them for joy. **R.**
Before the Lord, for he comes,
 for he comes to rule the earth;
He will rule the world with justice
 and the peoples with equity. **R.**

Philippians 2:15-16
R. Alleluia, alleluia.
Shine on the world like bright stars;
you are offering it the word of life. **R.**

† *Matthew 25:14-30*
You have been faithful in small things, enter into the joy of your Master.

Jesus told this parable to his disciples: "A certain man was going on a journey. He called in his servants and handed his funds over to them according to each man's abilities. To one he disbursed five thousand silver pieces, to a second two thousand, and to a third a thousand. Then he went away. Immediately the man who received the five thousand went to invest it and made another five. In the same way, the man who received the two thousand doubled his figure. The man who received the thousand went off instead and dug a hole in the ground, where he buried his master's money. After a long absence, the master of those servants came home and settled accounts with them. The man who had received the five thousand came forward bringing the additional five. 'My lord,' he said, 'you let me have five thousand. See, I have made five thousand more.' His master said to him, 'Well done! You are an industrious and reliable servant. Since you were dependable in a small matter I will put you in charge of larger affairs. Come, share your master's joy!' The man who had received the two thousand then stepped forward. 'My lord,' he said, 'you entrusted me with two thousand and I have made two thousand more.' His master said to him, 'Cleverly done! You too are an industrious and reliable servant. Since you were dependable in a small matter I will put you in charge of larger affairs. Come, share your master's joy!'

"Finally the man who had received the thousand stepped forward. 'My lord,' he said, 'I knew you were a hard man. You reap where you did not sow and gather where you did not scatter, so out of fear I went off and buried your thousand silver pieces in the ground. Here is your money back.' His master exclaimed: 'You worthless, lazy lout! You know I reap where I did not sow and gather where I did not scatter. All the more reason to deposit my money with the bankers, so that on my return I could have had it back with interest. You, there! Take the thousand away from him and give it to the man with the ten thousand. Those who have, will get more until they grow rich, while those who have not, will lose even the little they have. Throw this worthless servant into the darkness outside, where he can wail and grind his teeth.'" ✦

SEPTEMBER 2
TWENTY-SECOND SUNDAY IN ORDINARY TIME

† *Sirach 3:17-18, 20, 28-29*
Humble yourself and you will find favor with God.

My child, conduct your affairs with humility,
    and you will be loved more than a giver of gifts.
Humble yourself the more, the greater you are,
    and you will find favor with God.
What is too sublime for you, seek not,
    into things beyond your strength search not.
The mind of a sage appreciates proverbs,
    and an attentive ear is the joy of the wise.
Water quenches a flaming fire,
    and alms atone for sins. ✦

Psalm 68:4-7, 10-11
**R. God, in your goodness,
you have made a home for the poor.**
The just rejoice and exult before God;
    they are glad and rejoice.
Sing to God, chant praise to his name;
    whose name is the LORD. **R.**

The father of orphans and the defender of widows
  is God in his holy dwelling.
God gives a home to the forsaken;
  he leads forth prisoners to prosperity. **R.**
A bountiful rain you showered down, O God,
    upon your inheritance;
  you restored the land when it languished;
your flock settled in it;
    in your goodness, O God, you provided it for the needy. **R.**

† Hebrews 12:18-19, 22-24a

You have approached Mount Zion and the city of the living God.

Brothers and sisters:
You have not approached that which could be touched
  and a blazing fire and gloomy darkness
  and storm and a trumpet blast
  and a voice speaking words such that those who heard
  begged that no message be further addressed to them.
No, you have approached Mount Zion
  and the city of the living God, the heavenly Jerusalem,
  and countless angels in festal gathering,
  and the assembly of the firstborn enrolled in heaven,
  and God the judge of all,
  and the spirits of the just made perfect,
  and Jesus, the mediator of a new covenant,
  and the sprinkled blood that speaks more eloquently
    than that of Abel. ✠

Matthew 11:29ab
R. Alleluia, alleluia.
Take my yoke upon you, says the Lord,
and learn from me, for I am meek and humble of heart. **R.**

† Luke 14:1, 7-14

Everyone who exalts himself will be humbled,
everyone who humbles himself will be exalted.

On a sabbath Jesus went to dine
  at the home of one of the leading Pharisees,
  and the people there were observing him carefully.

He told a parable to those who had been invited,

noticing how they were choosing the places of honor at the table.

"When you are invited by someone to a wedding banquet,
do not recline at table in the place of honor.
A more distinguished guest than you may have been invited by him,
and the host who invited both of you may approach you and say,
'Give your place to this man,'
and then you would proceed with embarrassment
to take the lowest place.
Rather, when you are invited,
go and take the lowest place
so that when the host comes to you he may say,
'My friend, move up to a higher position.'
Then you will enjoy the esteem of your companions at the table.
For everyone who exalts himself will be humbled,
but the one who humbles himself will be exalted."
Then he said to the host who invited him,
"When you hold a lunch or a dinner,
do not invite your friends or your brothers
or your relatives or your wealthy neighbors,
in case they may invite you back and you have repayment.
Rather, when you hold a banquet,
invite the poor, the crippled, the lame, the blind;
blessed indeed will you be because of their inability to repay you.
For you will be repaid at the resurrection of the righteous." ✛

MONDAY, SEPTEMBER 3
St. Gregory the Great

† 1 Thessalonians 4:13-18
The Lord himself will lead all who are asleep in Jesus with him.

We would have you be clear about those who sleep in death, brothers; otherwise you might yield to grief, like those who have no hope. For if we believe that Jesus died and rose, God will bring forth with him from the dead those also who have fallen asleep believing in him. We say to you, as if the Lord himself had said it, that we who live, who survive until his coming, will in no way have an advantage over those who have fallen asleep. No, the Lord himself will come down from heaven at the word of command, at the sound of the archangel's voice and God's trumpet; and those who have died in Christ will rise first. Then we, the living, the survivors, will be caught up with them in the clouds to meet the Lord in the air. Thenceforth we shall be with the Lord unceasingly. Console one another with this message. ✛

Psalm 96:1, 3-5, 11-13
R. The Lord comes to judge the earth.
Sing to the Lord a new song;
    sing to the Lord, all you lands.
Tell his glory among the nations;
    among all peoples, his wondrous deeds. **R.**
For great is the Lord and highly to be praised;
    awesome is he, beyond all gods.
For all the gods of the nations are things of nought,
    but the Lord made the heavens. **R.**
Let the heavens be glad and the earth rejoice;
    let the sea and what fills it resound;
    let the plains be joyful and all that is in them!
Then shall all the trees of the forest exult. **R.**
Before the LORD, for he comes;
    for he comes to rule the earth.
He shall rule the world with justice
    and the peoples with his constancy. **R.**

Psalm 119:88
R. Alleluia, alleluia.
Give me life, O Lord,
and I will do your commands. **R.**

† *Luke 4:16-30*

He has sent me to bring the Good News to the poor.
No prophet is ever accepted in his own country.

Jesus came to Nazareth where he had been reared, and entering the synagogue on the sabbath as he was in the habit of doing, he stood up to do the reading. When the book of the prophet Isaiah was handed him, he unrolled the scroll and

found the passage where it was written:
"The spirit of the Lord is upon me;
    therefore he has anointed me.
He has sent me to bring glad tidings to the poor,
    to proclaim liberty to captives,
Recovery of sight to the blind
    and release to prisoners,
To announce a year of favor from the Lord."
Rolling up the scroll, he gave it back to the assistant and sat down. All in the synagogue had their eyes fixed on him. Then he began by saying to them, "Today this Scripture passage is fulfilled in your hearing." All who were present spoke favorably of him; they marveled at the appealing discourse which came from his lips. They also asked, "Is not this Joseph's son?"

He said to them, "You will doubtless quote me the proverb, 'Physician, heal yourself,' and say, 'Do here in your own country the things we have heard you have done in Capernaum.' But in fact," he went on, "no prophet gains acceptance in his native place. Indeed, let me remind you, there were many widows in Israel in the days of Elijah when the heavens remained closed for three and a half years and a great famine spread over the land. It was to none of these that Elijah was sent, but to a widow of Zarephath near Sidon. Recall, too, the many lepers in Israel in the time of Elisha the prophet; yet not one was cured except Naaman the Syrian."

At these words the whole audience in the synagogue was filled with indignation. They rose up and expelled him from the town, leading him to the brow of the hill on which it was built and intending to hurl him over the edge. But he went straight through their midst and walked away. ✛

TUESDAY, SEPTEMBER 4
WEEKDAY

† *1 Thessalonians 5:1-6,9-11*
Christ has died for us, that we might live.

As regards specific times and moments, brothers, we do not need to write you; you know very well that the day of the Lord is coming like a thief in the night. Just when people are saying,

"Peace and security," ruin will fall on them with the suddenness of pains overtaking a woman in labor, and there will be no escape. You are not in the dark, brothers, so that the day might catch you off guard, like a thief. No, all of you are children of light and of the day. We belong neither to darkness nor to night; therefore let us not be asleep like the rest, but awake and sober!

God has not destined us for wrath but for acquiring salvation through our Lord Jesus Christ. He died for us that all of us, whether awake or asleep, together might live with him. Therefore, comfort and upbuild one another, as indeed you are doing. ✛

Psalm 27:1, 4, 13-14
R. I believe that I shall see the good things of the Lord in the land of the living.
The Lord is my light and my salvation;
   whom should I fear?
The Lord is my life's refuge;
   of whom should I be afraid? **R.**
One thing I ask of the Lord;
   this I seek:
To dwell in the house of the Lord
   all the days of my life,
That I may gaze on the loveliness of the Lord
   and contemplate his temple. **R.**
I believe that I shall see the bounty of the Lord
   in the land of the living.
Wait for the Lord with courage;
   be stouthearted, and wait for the Lord. **R.**

Psalm 119:88
R. Alleluia, alleluia.
Give me life, O Lord,
and I will do your commands. **R.**

✝ Luke 4:31-37
I know who you are, the Holy One of God.

Jesus went down to Capernaum, a town of Galilee, where he began instructing the people on the sabbath day. They were spellbound by his teaching, for his words had authority.

In the synagogue there was a man with an unclean spirit, who shrieked in a loud voice: "Leave us alone! What do you want of us, Jesus of Nazareth? Have you come to destroy us? I know who you are: the Holy One of God." Jesus said to him sharply, "Be quiet! Come out of him." At that, the demon threw him to the ground before everyone's eyes and came out of him without doing him any harm. All were struck with astonishment, and they began saying to one another: "What is there about his speech? He commands the unclean spirits with authority and power, and they leave." His renown kept spreading through the surrounding country. ✝

WEDNESDAY, SEPTEMBER 5
WEEKDAY

✝ *Colossians 1:1-8*
The Good News which has reached you is spreading all over the world.

Paul, an apostle of Christ Jesus by the will of God, and Timothy our brother, to the holy ones at Colossae, faithful brothers in Christ. May God our Father give you grace and peace.

We always give thanks to God, the Father of our Lord Jesus Christ, in our prayers for you because we have heard of your faith in Christ Jesus and the love you bear toward all the saints—moved as you are by the hope held in store for you in heaven. You heard of this hope through the message of truth, the gospel, which has come to you, has borne fruit, and has continued to grow in your midst as it has everywhere in the world. This has been the case from the day you first heard it and comprehended God's gracious intention through the instructions of Epaphras, our dear fellow slave, who represents us as a faithful minister of Christ. He it was who told us of your love in the Spirit. ✝

Psalm 52:10-11
R. I trust in the kindness of God forever.
I, like a green olive tree
    in the house of God,
Trust in the kindness of God
    forever and ever. **R.**
I will thank you always for what you have done,

and proclaim the goodness of your name
before your faithful ones. **R.**

Psalm 119:88
R. Alleluia, alleluia.
Give me life, O Lord,
and I will do your commands. **R.**

† *Luke 4:38-44*
*I must preach the Good News to other towns as well,
because that is what I was sent to do.*

On leaving the synagogue, Jesus entered the house of Simon.
Simon's mother-in-law was in the grip of a severe fever, and
they interceded with him for her. He stood over her and
addressed himself to the fever, and it left her. She got up
immediately and waited on them.

At sunset, all who had people sick with a variety of diseases
took them to him, and he laid hands on each of them and cured
them. Demons departed from many, crying out as they did so,
"You are the son of God!" He rebuked them and did not allow
them to speak because they knew that he was the Messiah.

The next morning he left the town and set out into the open
country. The crowds went in search of him, and when they
found him they tried to keep him from leaving them. But he
said to them, "To other towns I must announce the good news
of the reign of God, because that is why I was sent." And he
continued to preach in the synagogues of Judea. ✛

THURSDAY, SEPTEMBER 6
WEEKDAY

† *Colossians 1:9-14*
*He has taken us out of the power of darkness and
created a place for us in the kingdom of his Son.*

Ever since we heard this we have been praying for you
unceasingly and asking that you may attain full knowledge of
his will through perfect wisdom and spiritual insight. Then
you will lead a life worthy of the Lord and pleasing to him in
every way. You will multiply good works of every sort and grow
in the knowledge of God. By the might of his glory you will be
endowed with the strength needed to stand fast, even to

endure joyfully whatever may come, giving thanks to the
Father for having made you worthy to share the lot of the
saints in light. He rescued us from the power of darkness and
brought us into the kingdom of his beloved Son. Through him
we have redemption, the forgiveness of our sins. ✛

Psalm 98:2-6
R. The Lord has made known his salvation.
The Lord has made his salvation known:
    in the sight of the nations he has revealed his justice.
He has remembered his kindness and his faithfulness
    toward the house of Israel. **R.**
All the ends of the earth have seen
    the salvation by our God.
Sing joyfully to the Lord, all you lands;
    break into song; sing praise. **R.**
Sing praise to the Lord with the harp,
    with the harp and melodious song.
With trumpets and the sound of the horn
    sing joyfully before the King, the Lord. **R.**

Psalm 119:88
R. Alleluia, alleluia.
Give me life, O Lord,
and I will do your commands. **R.**

† *Luke 5:1-11*
They left everything and followed him.

As the crowd pressed in on Jesus to hear the word of God, he
saw two boats moored by the side of the lake; the fishermen
had disembarked and were washing their nets. He got into one
of the boats, the one belonging to Simon, and asked him to pull
out a short distance from the shore; then, remaining seated, he
continued to teach the crowds from the boat. When he had
finished speaking he said to Simon, "Put out into deep water
and lower your nets for a catch." Simon answered, "Master, we
have been hard at it all night long and have caught nothing;
but if you say so, I will lower the nets." Upon doing this they
caught such a great number of fish that their nets were at the
breaking point. They signaled to their mates in the other boat
to come and help them. These came, and together they filled

the two boats until they nearly sank.

At the sight of this, Simon Peter fell at the knees of Jesus saying, "Leave me, Lord. I am a sinful man." For indeed, amazement at the catch they had made seized him and all his shipmates, as well as James and John, Zebedee's sons, who were partners with Simon. Jesus said to Simon, "Do not be afraid. From now on you will be catching men." With that they brought their boats to land, left everything, and became his followers. ✢

FRIDAY, SEPTEMBER 7
WEEKDAY

† *Colossians 1:15-20*
All things were created through him and for him.

Christ is the image of the invisible God, the first-born of all creatures. In him everything in heaven and on earth was created, things visible and invisible, whether thrones or domi-nations, principalities or powers; all were created through him and for him. He is before all else that is. In him everything continues in being. It is he who is head of the body, the church; he who is the beginning, the first-born of the dead, so that primacy may be his in everything. It pleased God to make absolute fullness reside in him and, by means of him, to reconcile everything in his person, everything, I say, both on earth and in the heavens, making peace through the blood of his cross. ✢

Psalm 100:1-5
R. Come with joy into the presence of the Lord.
Sing joyfully to the Lord, all you lands;
> serve the Lord with gladness;
> come before him with joyful song. **R.**
Know that the Lord is God;
> he made us, his we are;
> his people, the flock he tends. **R.**
Enter his gates with thanksgiving,
> his courts with praise;
Give thanks to him; bless his name. **R.**
The Lord is good,
> the Lord, whose kindness endures forever,
> and his faithfulness, to all generations. **R.**

Psalm 119:88

R. Alleluia, alleluia.

Give me life, O Lord,
and I will do your commands. **R.**

† *Luke 5:33-39*
When the bridegroom is taken from them, then they will fast.

The scribes and Pharisees said to Jesus: "John's disciples fast frequently and offer prayers; the disciples of the Pharisees do the same. Yours, on the contrary, eat and drink freely." Jesus replied: "Can you make guests of the groom fast while the groom is still with them? But when the days come that the groom is removed from their midst, they will surely fast in those days."

He then proposed to them this figure: "No one tears a piece from a new coat to patch an old one. If he does he will only tear the new coat, and the piece taken from it will not match the old. Moreover, no one pours new wine into old wineskins. Should he do so, the new wine will burst the old skins, the wine will spill out, and the skins will be lost. New wine should be poured into fresh skins. No one, after drinking old wine, wants new. He says, 'I find the old wine better.'" ✛

SATURDAY, SEPTEMBER 8
THE BIRTH OF MARY

† *Micah 5:1-4* (or *Romans 8:28-30*)
This is the time when she who is in labor is to give birth.

You, Bethlehem-Ephrathah,
    too small to be among the clans of Judah,
From you shall come forth for me
    one who is to be ruler in Israel;
Whose origin is from of old,
    from ancient times.
(Therefore the Lord will give them up, until the time
    when she who is to give birth has borne,
And the rest of his brethren shall return
    to the children of Israel.)
He shall stand firm and shepherd his flock
    by the strength of the Lord,
    in the majestic name of the Lord, his God;

And they shall remain, for now his greatness
    shall reach to the ends of the earth;
    he shall be peace. ✛

Psalm 13:6
R. With delight I rejoice in the Lord.
Though I trusted in your kindness,
    let my heart rejoice in your salvation. **R.**
Let me sing of the Lord, "He has been good to me." **R.**

R. Alleluia, alleluia.
Happy are you, holy Virgin Mary, deserving of all praise;
from you arose the sun of justice, Christ the Lord. **R.**

      ✝ *Matthew 1:18-23* (or *Matthew 1:1-16, 18-23*)
        She has conceived what is in her by the Holy Spirit.

Now this is how the birth of Jesus Christ came about. When his mother Mary was engaged to Joseph, but before they lived together, she was found with child through the power of the Holy Spirit. Joseph her husband, an upright man unwilling to expose her to the law, decided to divorce her quietly. Such was his intention when suddenly the angel of the Lord appeared in a dream and said to him: "Joseph, son of David, have no fear about taking Mary as your wife. It is by the Holy Spirit that she has conceived this child. She is to have a son and you are to name him Jesus because he will save his people from their sins." All this happened to fulfill what the Lord had said through the prophet:
    "The virgin shall be with child
    and give birth to a son,
    and they shall call him Emmanuel,"
a name which means "God is with us." ✛

SEPTEMBER 9
Twenty-third Sunday in Ordinary Time

      ✝ *Wisdom 9:13-18b*
      Who can conceive what the Lord intends?

Who can know God's counsel,
    or who can conceive what the Lord intends?
For the deliberations of mortals are timid,

and unsure are our plans.
For the corruptible body burdens the soul
and the earthen shelter weighs down the mind
that has many concerns.
And scarce do we guess the things on earth,
and what is within our grasp we find with difficulty;
but when things are in heaven, who can search them out?
Or who ever knew your counsel, except you had given wisdom
and sent your holy spirit from on high?
And thus were the paths of those on earth made straight. ✛

Psalm 90:3-6,12-17
R. In every age, O Lord, you have been our refuge.
You turn man back to dust,
saying, "Return, O children of men."
For a thousand years in your sight
are as yesterday, now that it is past,
or as a watch of the night. **R.**
You make an end of them in their sleep;
the next morning they are like the changing grass,
which at dawn springs up anew,
but by evening wilts and fades. **R.**
Teach us to number our days aright,
that we may gain wisdom of heart.
Return, O LORD! How long?
Have pity on your servants! **R.**
Fill us at daybreak with your kindness,
that we may shout for joy and gladness all our days.
And may the gracious care of the Lord our God be ours;
prosper the work of our hands for us!
Prosper the work of our hands! **R.**

† *Philemon 9-10,12-17*
Receive him no longer as a slave but as a beloved brother.

I, Paul, an old man,
and now also a prisoner for Christ Jesus,
urge you on behalf of my child Onesimus,
whose father I have become in my imprisonment;
I am sending him, that is, my own heart, back to you.
I should have liked to retain him for myself,
so that he might serve me on your behalf

in my imprisonment for the gospel,
but I did not want to do anything without your consent,
so that the good you do might not be forced but voluntary.
Perhaps this is why he was away from you for a while,
that you might have him back forever,
no longer as a slave
but more than a slave, a brother,
beloved especially to me, but even more so to you,
as a man and in the Lord.
So if you regard me as a partner, welcome him as you would
me. ✝

Psalm 119:135
R. Alleluia, alleluia.
Let your face shine upon your servant;
and teach me your laws. **R.**

✝ *Luke 14:25-33*
*Anyone of you who does not renounce all
possessions cannot be my disciple.*

Great crowds were traveling with Jesus,
and he turned and addressed them,
"If anyone comes to me
without hating his father and mother,
wife and children, brothers and sisters,
and even his own life,
he cannot be my disciple.
Whoever does not carry his own cross and come after me
cannot be my disciple.
Which of you wishing to construct a tower
does not first sit down and calculate the cost
to see if there is enough for its completion?
Otherwise, after laying the foundation
and finding himself unable to finish the work
the onlookers should laugh at him and say,
'This one began to build but did not have the resources to
finish.'
Or what king marching into battle would not first sit down
and decide whether with ten thousand troops
he can successfully oppose another king
advancing upon him with twenty thousand troops?

But if not, while he is still far away,
he will send a delegation to ask for peace terms.
In the same way,
anyone of you who does not renounce all his possessions
cannot be my disciple." ✛

MONDAY, SEPTEMBER 10
WEEKDAY

† *Colossians 1:24—2:3*
*I am the servant of the Church to make known
the word of God, a mystery hidden for generations.*

Even now I find my joy in the suffering I endure for you. In
my own flesh I fill up what is lacking in the sufferings of Christ
for the sake of his body, the church. I became a minister of this
church through the commission God gave me to preach among
you his word in its fullness, that mystery hidden from ages and
generations past but now revealed to his holy ones. God has
willed to make known to them the glory beyond price which
this mystery brings to the Gentiles—the mystery of Christ in
you, your hope of glory. This is the Christ we proclaim while we
admonish all men and teach them in the full measure of
wisdom, hoping to make every man complete in Christ. For
this I work and struggle, impelled by that energy of his which
is so powerful a force within me.

I want you to know how hard I am struggling for you and for
the Laodiceans and the many others who have never seen me in
the flesh. I wish their hearts to be strengthened and themselves
to be closely united in love, enriched with full assurance by their
knowledge of the mystery of God—namely Christ—in whom
every treasure of wisdom and knowledge is hidden. ✛

Psalm 62:6-7, 9
R. In God is my safety and my glory.
Only in God be at rest, my soul,
for from him comes my hope.
He only is my rock and my salvation,
my stronghold; I shall not be disturbed. **R.**
Trust in him at all times, O my people!
Pour out your hearts before him;
God is our refuge! **R.**

See Acts 16:14

R. Alleluia, alleluia.

Open our hearts, O Lord,
to listen to the words of your Son. **R.**

† *Luke 6:6-11*
They watched him to see if he would cure a man on the sabbath.

On a sabbath Jesus came to teach in a synagogue where there was a man whose right hand was withered. The scribes and Pharisees were on the watch to see if he would perform a cure on the sabbath so that they could find a charge against him. He knew their thoughts, however, and said to the man whose hand was withered, "Get up and stand here in front." The man rose and remained standing. Jesus said to them, "I ask you, is it lawful to do good on the sabbath—or evil? To preserve life—or destroy it?" He looked around at them all and said to the man, "Stretch out your hand." The man did so and his hand was perfectly restored.

At this they became frenzied and began asking one another what could be done to Jesus. ✛

TUESDAY, SEPTEMBER 11
WEEKDAY

† *Colossians 2:6-15*
You must live your life in Christ, who has given you all forgiveness.

Continue to live in Christ Jesus the Lord, in the spirit in which you received him. Be rooted in him and built up in him, growing ever stronger in faith as you were taught, and overflowing with gratitude. See to it that no one deceives you through any empty, seductive philosophy that follows mere human traditions, a philosophy based on cosmic powers rather than on Christ.

In Christ the fullness of deity resides in bodily form. Yours is a share of this fullness, in him who is the head of every principality and power. You were also circumcised in him, not with the circumcision administered by hand but with Christ's circumcision, which strips off the carnal body completely. In baptism you were not only buried with him but also raised to life with him because you believed in the power of God who raised him from the dead. Even when you were dead in sin and your flesh was uncircumcised, God gave you new life in company with Christ. He pardoned all our sins. He canceled the bond that stood against us with all its claims, snatching it up and nailing it to the cross. Thus did God disarm the principalities and powers. He made a public show of them and, leading them off captive, he triumphed in the person of Christ. ✝

Psalm 145:1-2, 8-11
R. The Lord is compassionate to all his creatures.
I will extol you, O my God and King,
  and I will bless your name forever and ever.
Every day will I bless you,
  and I will praise your name forever and ever. **R.**
The Lord is gracious and merciful,
  slow to anger and of great kindness.
The Lord is good to all
  and compassionate toward all his works. **R.**
Let all your works give you thanks, O Lord,
  and let your faithful ones bless you.
Let them discourse of the glory of your kingdom
  and speak of your might. **R.**

See Acts 16:14
R. Alleluia, alleluia.
Open our hearts, O Lord,
to listen to the words of your Son. **R.**

† *Luke 6:12-19*
*He spent the night in prayer. He chose twelve
from his disciples and called them Apostles.*

Jesus went out to the mountain to pray, spending the night in communion with God. At daybreak he called his disciples and selected twelve of them to be his apostles: Simon, to whom he gave the name Peter, and Andrew his brother, James and John, Philip and Bartholomew, Matthew and Thomas, James son of Alphaeus, and Simon called the Zealot, Judas son of James, and Judas Iscariot, who turned traitor.
  Coming down the mountain with them, he stopped at a level stretch where there were many of his disciples; a large crowd of people was with them from all Judea and Jerusalem and the coast of Tyre and Sidon, people who came to hear him and be

healed of their diseases. Those who were troubled with unclean spirits were cured; indeed, the whole crowd was trying to touch him because power went out from him which cured all. ✛

WEDNESDAY, SEPTEMBER 12
WEEKDAY

† Colossians 3:1-11
You must die with Christ; put to death
everything in you that belongs to earthly life.

Since you have been raised up in company with Christ, set your heart on what pertains to higher realms where Christ is seated at God's right hand. Be intent on things above rather than on things of earth. After all, you have died! Your life is hidden now with Christ in God. When Christ our life appears, then you shall appear with him in glory.

Put to death whatever in your nature is rooted in earth: fornication, uncleanness, passion, evil desires, and that lust which is idolatry. These are the sins which provoke God's wrath. Your own conduct was once of this sort, when these sins were your very life. You must put that aside now: all the anger and quick temper, the malice, the insults, the foul language. Stop lying to one another. What you have done is put aside your old self with its past deeds and put on a new man, one who grows in knowledge as he is formed anew in the image of his Creator. There is no Greek or Jew here, circumcised or uncircumcised, foreigner, Scythian, slave, or freeman. Rather Christ is everything in all of you. ✛

Psalm 145:2-3, 10-13
R. **The Lord is compassionate to all his creatures.**
Every day will I bless you,
    and I will praise your name forever and ever.
Great is the Lord and highly to be praised;
    his greatness is unsearchable. **R.**
Let all your works give you thanks, O Lord,
    and let your faithful ones bless you.
Let them discourse of the glory of your kingdom
    and speak of your might. **R.**
Making known to men your might
    and the glorious splendor of your kingdom.

Your kingdom is a kingdom for all ages,
and your dominion endures through all generations. **R.**

See Acts 16:14
R. Alleluia, alleluia.
Open our hearts, O Lord,
to listen to the words of your Son. **R.**

✝ *Luke 6:20-26*
Happy are the poor. Woe to you who are rich.

Jesus raised his eyes to his disciples and said:
"Blest are you poor; the reign of God is yours.
Blest are you who hunger; you shall be filled.
Blest are you who are weeping; you shall laugh.

Blest shall you be when men hate you, when they ostracize you and insult you and proscribe your name as evil because of the Son of Man. On the day they do so, rejoice and exult, for your reward shall be great in heaven. Thus it was that their fathers treated the prophets.

"But woe to you rich, for your consolation is now.
Woe to you who are full; you shall go hungry.
Woe to you who laugh now; you shall weep in your grief.
Woe to you when all speak well of you. Their fathers treated the false prophets in just this way." ✝

THURSDAY, SEPTEMBER 13
ST. JOHN CHRYSOSTOM

✝ *Colossians 3:12-17*
Have charity, which is the bond of perfection.

Because you are God's chosen ones, holy and beloved, clothe yourselves with heartfelt mercy, with kindness, humility, meekness, and patience. Bear with one another; forgive whatever grievances you have against one another. Forgive as the Lord has forgiven you. Over all these virtues put on love, which binds the rest together and makes them perfect. Christ's peace must reign in your hearts, since as members of the one body you have been called to that peace. Dedicate yourselves to thankfulness. Let the word of Christ, rich as it is, dwell in you. In wisdom made perfect, instruct and admonish one another. Sing gratefully to God from your hearts in psalms, hymns, and inspired songs. Whatever you do, whether in speech or in action, do it in the name of the Lord Jesus. Give thanks to God the Father through him. ✝

Psalm 150:1-6

R. Let everything that breathes praise the Lord!
(or **Alleluia.***)*

Praise the Lord in his sanctuary,
    praise him in the firmament of his strength.
Praise him for his mighty deeds,
    praise him for his sovereign majesty. **R.**
Praise him with the blast of the trumpet,
    praise him with lyre and harp,
Praise him with timbrel and dance,
    praise him with strings and pipe. **R.**
Praise him with sounding cymbals,
    praise him with clanging cymbals.
Let everything that has breath
    praise the Lord! Alleluia. **R.**

See Acts 16:14

R. Alleluia, alleluia.
Open our hearts, O Lord,
to listen to the words of your Son. **R.**

✝ *Luke 6:27-38*
Be merciful, as your Father is merciful.

Jesus said to his disciples: 'To you who hear me, I say: Love your enemies, do good to those who hate you; bless those who curse you and pray for those who maltreat you. When someone slaps you on one cheek, turn and give him the other; when someone takes your coat, let him have your shirt as well. Give to all who beg from you. When a man takes what is yours, do not demand it back. Do to others what you would have them do to you. If you love those who love you, what credit is that to you? Even sinners love those who love them. If you do good to those who do good to you, how can you claim any credit? Sinners do as much. If you lend to those from whom you expect repayment, what merit is there in it for you? Even sinners lend to sinners, expecting to be repaid in full.

"Love your enemy and do good; lend without expecting repayment. Then will your recompense be great. You will rightly be called sons of the Most High, since he himself is good to the ungrateful and the wicked.

"Be compassionate, as your Father is compassionate. Do not judge, and you will not be judged. Do not condemn, and you will not be condemned. Pardon, and you shall be pardoned. Give, and it shall be given to you. Good measure pressed down, shaken together, running over, will they pour into the fold of your garment. For the measure you measure with will be measured back to you." ✛

FRIDAY, SEPTEMBER 14
THE EXALTATION OF THE HOLY CROSS

† *Numbers 21:4b-9*
*Whenever anyone who had been bitten
by a serpent looked at the bronze serpent, he lived.*

With their patience worn out by the journey,
    the people complained against God and Moses,
    "Why have you brought us up from Egypt to die in this
        desert,
    where there is no food or water?
    We are disgusted with this wretched food!"

In punishment the LORD sent among the people saraph serpents,
    which bit the people so that many of them died.
Then the people came to Moses and said,
    "We have sinned in complaining against the LORD and you.
    Pray the LORD to take the serpents from us."
So Moses prayed for the people, and the LORD said to Moses,
    "Make a saraph and mount it on a pole,
    and if any who have been bitten look at it, they will live."
Moses accordingly made a bronze serpent and mounted it on
        a pole,
    and whenever anyone who had been bitten by a serpent
    looked at the bronze serpent, he lived. ✛

Psalm 78:1-2, 34-38
R. Do not forget the works of the Lord!
Hearken, my people, to my teaching;
    incline your ears to the words of my mouth.
I will open my mouth in a parable,
    I will utter mysteries from of old. **R.**

While he slew them they sought him
and inquired after God again,
remembering that God was their rock
and the Most High God, their redeemer. **R.**
But they flattered him with their mouths
and lied to him with their tongues,
though their hearts were not steadfast toward him,
nor were they faithful to his covenant. **R.**
Yet he, being merciful, forgave their sin
and destroyed them not;
often he turned back his anger
and let none of his wrath be roused. **R.**

† *Philippians 2:6-11*
He humbled himself; because of this God greatly exalted him.

Brothers and sisters:
Christ Jesus, though he was in the form of God,
did not regard equality with God
something to be grasped.
Rather, he emptied himself,
taking the form of a slave,
coming in human likeness;
and found human in appearance,
he humbled himself,
becoming obedient to the point of death,
even death on a cross.
Because of this, God greatly exalted him
and bestowed on him the name
which is above every name,
that at the name of Jesus
every knee should bend,
of those in heaven and on earth and under the earth,
and every tongue confess that
Jesus Christ is Lord,
to the glory of God the Father. ✝

R. Alleluia, alleluia.
We adore you, O Christ, and we bless you,
because by your Cross you have redeemed the world. **R.**

† *John 3:13-17*
So the Son of Man must be lifted up.

Jesus said to Nicodemus:
"No one has gone up to heaven
except the one who has come down from heaven,
the Son of Man.
And just as Moses lifted up the serpent in the desert,
so must the Son of Man be lifted up,
so that everyone who believes in him
may have eternal life."

For God so loved the world that he gave his only Son,
so he who believes in him might not perish
but might have eternal life.
For God did not send his Son into the world to condemn the
world,
but that the world might be saved through him. ✛

SATURDAY, SEPTEMBER 15
OUR LADY OF SORROWS

† *Hebrews 5:7-9*
He learned obedience and became the source of eternal salvation.

In the days when Christ was in the flesh, he offered prayers
and supplications with loud cries and tears to God, who was
able to save him from death, and he was heard because of his
reverence. Son though he was, he learned obedience from what
he suffered; and when perfected, he became the source of
eternal salvation for all who obey him. ✛

Psalm 31:2-6, 15-16, 20
R. Save me, O Lord, in your steadfast love.
In you, O Lord, I take refuge;
    let me never be put to shame.
In your justice rescue me,
    incline your ear to me,
        make haste to deliver me! **R.**
Be my rock of refuge,
    a stronghold to give me safety.
You are my rock and my fortress;
    for your name's sake you will lead and guide me. **R.**

You will free me from the snare they set for me,
for you are my refuge.
Into your hands I commend my spirit;
you will redeem me, O Lord, O faithful God. **R.**
But my trust is in you, O Lord;
I say, "You are my God."
In your hands is my destiny; rescue me
from the clutches of my enemies and my persecutors. **R.**
How great is the goodness, O Lord,
which you have in store for those who fear you,
And which, toward those who take refuge in you,
you show in the sight of men. **R.**

R. Alleluia, alleluia.
Happy are you, O Blessed Virgin Mary;
without dying you won the martyr's crown beside the cross of
the Lord. **R.**

✝ John 19:25-27 (or Luke 2:33-35)
How that loving mother was pierced with grief
and anguish when she saw the sufferings of her son.

Near the cross of Jesus there stood his mother, his mother's
sister, Mary the wife of Clopas, and Mary Magdalene. Seeing
his mother there with the disciple whom he loved, Jesus said
to his mother, "Woman, there is your son." In turn he said to
the disciple, "There is your mother." From that hour onward,
the disciple took her into his care. ✝

SEPTEMBER 16
TWENTY-FOURTH SUNDAY IN ORDINARY TIME

✝ Exodus 32:7-11,13-14
The Lord relented in the punishment he
had threatened to inflict on his people.

The LORD said to Moses,
"Go down at once to your people,
whom you brought out of the land of Egypt,
for they have become depraved.
They have soon turned aside from the way I pointed out to them,
making for themselves a molten calf and worshiping it,
sacrificing to it and crying out,

'This is your God, O Israel,
who brought you out of the land of Egypt!'
"I see how stiff-necked this people is, " continued the LORD to
Moses.
Let me alone, then,
that my wrath may blaze up against them to consume them.
Then I will make of you a great nation."

But Moses implored the LORD, his God, saying,
"Why, O LORD, should your wrath blaze up against your own
people,
whom you brought out of the land of Egypt
with such great power and with so strong a hand?
Remember your servants Abraham, Isaac, and Israel,
and how you swore to them by your own self, saying,
'I will make your descendants
as numerous as the stars in the sky;
and all this land that I promised,
I will give your descendants as their perpetual heritage.'"
So the LORD relented in the punishment
he had threatened to inflict on his people. ✛

Psalm 51:3-4, 12-13, 17, 19
R. I will rise and go to my father.
Have mercy on me, O God, in your goodness;
in the greatness of your compassion wipe out my offense.
Thoroughly wash me from my guilt
and of my sin cleanse me. **R.**
A clean heart create for me, O God,
and a steadfast spirit renew within me.
Cast me not out from your presence,
and your holy spirit take not from me. **R.**
O Lord, open my lips,
and my mouth shall proclaim your praise.
My sacrifice, O God, is a contrite spirit;
a heart contrite and humbled, O God, you will not spurn. **R.**

† *1 Timothy 1:12-17*
Christ came to save sinners.

Beloved:
I am grateful to him who has strengthened me, Christ Jesus

our Lord,
because he considered me trustworthy
in appointing me to the ministry.
I was once a blasphemer and a persecutor and arrogant,
but I have been mercifully treated
because I acted out of ignorance in my unbelief.
Indeed, the grace of our Lord has been abundant,
along with the faith and love that are in Christ Jesus.
This saying is trustworthy and deserves full acceptance:
Christ Jesus came into the world to save sinners.
Of these I am the foremost.
But for that reason I was mercifully treated,
so that in me, as the foremost,
Christ Jesus might display all his patience as an example
for those who would come to believe in him for everlasting
life.
To the king of ages, incorruptible, invisible, the only God,
honor and glory forever and ever. Amen. ✝

2 Corinthians 5:19
R. Alleluia, alleluia.
God was reconciling the world to himself in Christ
and entrusting to us the message of reconciliation. **R.**

*✝ **Luke 15:1-32** (or Luke 15:1-10)*
There will be great joy in heaven over one sinner who repents.

Tax collectors and sinners were all drawing near
to listen to Jesus,
but the Pharisees and scribes began to complain, saying,
"This man welcomes sinners and eats with them."
So to them he addressed this parable.
"What man among you having a hundred sheep and losing one
of them
would not leave the ninety-nine in the desert
and go after the lost one until he finds it?
And when he does find it,
he sets it on his shoulders with great joy
and, upon his arrival home,
he calls together his friends and neighbors and says to
them,

'Rejoice with me because I have found my lost sheep.'
I tell you, in just the same way
   there will be more joy in heaven over one sinner who repents
   than over ninety-nine righteous people
   who have no need of repentance.

"Or what woman having ten coins and losing one
   would not light a lamp and sweep the house,
   searching carefully until she finds it?
And when she does find it,
   she calls together her friends and neighbors
   and says to them,
   'Rejoice with me because I have found the coin that I lost.'
In just the same way, I tell you,
   there will be rejoicing among the angels of God
   over one sinner who repents."

Then he said,
   "A man had two sons, and the younger son said to his father,
   'Father give me the share of your estate that should come
      to me.'
So the father divided the property between them.
After a few days, the younger son collected all his belongings
   and set off to a distant country
   where he squandered his inheritance on a life of dissipation.
When he had freely spent everything,
   a severe famine struck that country,
   and he found himself in dire need.
So he hired himself out to one of the local citizens
   who sent him to his farm to tend the swine.
And he longed to eat his fill of the pods on which the swine fed,
   but nobody gave him any.
Coming to his senses he thought,
   'How many of my father's hired workers
   have more than enough food to eat,
   but here am I, dying from hunger.
I shall get up and go to my father and I shall say to him,
   "Father, I have sinned against heaven and against you.
I no longer deserve to be called your son;
   treat me as you would treat one of your hired workers."'
So he got up and went back to his father.

While he was still a long way off,
    his father caught sight of him,
    and was filled with compassion.
He ran to his son, embraced him and kissed him.
His son said to him,
    'Father, I have sinned against heaven and against you;
    I no longer deserve to be called your son.'
But his father ordered his servants,
    'Quickly bring the finest robe and put it on him;
    put a ring on his finger and sandals on his feet.
Take the fattened calf and slaughter it.
Then let us celebrate with a feast,
    because this son of mine was dead, and has come to life again;
    he was lost, and has been found.'
Then the celebration began.
Now the older son had been out in the field
    and, on his way back, as he neared the house,
    he heard the sound of music and dancing.
He called one of the servants and asked what this might mean.
The servant said to him,
    'Your brother has returned
    and your father has slaughtered the fattened calf
    because he has him back safe and sound.'
He became angry,
    and when he refused to enter the house,
    his father came out and pleaded with him.
He said to his father in reply,
    'Look, all these years I served you
    and not once did I disobey your orders;
    yet you never gave me even a young goat to feast on with
        my friends.
    But when your son returns,
    who swallowed up your property with prostitutes,
    for him you slaughter the fattened calf.'
He said to him,
    'My son, you are here with me always;
    everything I have is yours.
But now we must celebrate and rejoice,
    because your brother was dead and has come to life again;
    he was lost and has been found.'" ✛

MONDAY, SEPTEMBER 17
Weekday, St. Robert Bellarmine

✝ *1 Timothy 2:1-8*
There should be prayers offered to God
for everyone; he wants everyone to be saved.

First of all, I urge that petitions, prayers, intercessions, and thanksgivings be offered for all men, especially for kings and those in authority, that we may be able to lead undisturbed and tranquil lives in perfect piety and dignity. Prayer of this kind is good, and God our savior is pleased with it, for he wants all men to be saved and come to know the truth. And the truth is this:

"God is one.
One also is the mediator between God and men,
the man Christ Jesus,
who gave himself as a ransom for all."

This truth was attested at the fitting time. I have been made its herald and apostle (believe me, I am not lying but speak the truth), the teacher of the nations in the true faith.

It is my wish, then, that in every place the men shall offer prayers with blameless hands held aloft, and be free from anger and dissension. ✝

Psalm 28:2, 7-9
R. Blest be the Lord for he has heard my prayer.
Hear the sound of my pleading, when I cry to you,
lifting up my hands toward your holy shrine. **R.**
The Lord is my strength and my shield.
In him my heart trusts, and I find help;
Then my heart exults, and with my song I give him thanks. **R.**
The Lord is the strength of his people,
the saving refuge of his anointed.
Save your people, and bless your inheritance;
feed them, and carry them forever! **R.**

Hebrews 4:12
R. Alleluia, alleluia.
The word of God is living and active;
it probes the thoughts and motives of our heart. **R.**

† *Luke 7:1-10*
Not even in Israel have I found such faith.

When Jesus had finished his discourse in the hearing of the people, he entered Capernaum. A centurion had a servant he held in high regard, who was at that moment sick to the point of death. When he heard about Jesus he sent some Jewish elders to him, asking him to come and save the life of his servant. Upon approaching Jesus they petitioned him earnestly. "He deserves this favor from you," they said, "because he loves our people, and even built our synagogue for us." Jesus set out with them. When he was only a short distance from the house, the centurion sent friends to tell him: "Sir, do not trouble yourself, for I am not worthy to have you enter my house. That is why I did not presume to come to you myself. Just give the order and my servant will be cured. I too am a man who knows the meaning of an order, having soldiers under my command. I say to one, 'On your way,' and off he goes; to another, 'Come here,' and he comes; to my slave, 'Do this,' and he does it." Jesus showed amazement on hearing this, and turned to the crowd which was following him to say, "I tell you, I have never found so much faith among the Israelites." When the deputation returned to the house, they found the servant in perfect health. ✛

TUESDAY, SEPTEMBER 18
WEEKDAY

† *1 Timothy 3:1-13*
The bishop must be blameless; deacons also must
be conscientious believers in the mystery of the faith.

You can depend on this: whoever wants to be a bishop aspires to a noble task. A bishop must be irreproachable, married only once, of even temper, self-controlled, modest, and hospitable. He should be a good teacher. He must not be addicted to drink. He ought not to be contentious but, rather, gentle, a man of peace. Nor can he be someone who loves money. He must be a good manager of his own household, keeping his children under control without sacrificing his dignity; for if a man does not know how to manage his own house, how can he take care of the church of God? He should not be a new convert, lest he become conceited and thus incur the punishment once meted out to the devil. He must also be well thought of by those outside the church, to ensure that he not fall into disgrace and the devil's trap. In the same way, deacons must be serious, straightforward, and truthful. They may not overindulge in drink, or give in to greed. They must hold fast to the divinely revealed faith with a clear conscience. They should be put on probation first; then, if there is nothing against them, they may serve as deacons. The women, similarly, should be serious, not slanderous gossips. They should be temperate and entirely trustworthy. Deacons may be married but once and must be good managers of their children and their households. Those who serve well as deacons gain a worthy place for themselves and much assurance in their faith in Christ Jesus. ✝

Psalm 101:1-3, 5-6
R. I will walk with blameless heart.
Of kindness and judgment I will sing;
    to you, O Lord, I will sing praise.
I will persevere in the way of integrity;
    when will you come to me? **R.**
I will walk in the integrity of my heart,
    within my house;
I will not set before my eyes
    any base thing. **R.**
Whoever slanders his neighbor in secret,
    him will I destroy.
The man of haughty eyes and puffed-up heart
    I will not endure. **R.**
My eyes are upon the faithful of the land,
    that they may dwell with me.
He who walks in the way of integrity
    shall be in my service. **R.**

Hebrews 4:12
R. Alleluia, alleluia.
The word of God is living and active;
it probes the thoughts and motives of our heart. **R.**

† *Luke 7:11-17*
Young man, I tell you, arise.

Jesus went to a town called Naim, and his disciples and a large crowd accompanied him. As he approached the gate of the town a dead man was being carried out, the only son of a widowed mother. A considerable crowd of townsfolk were with her. The Lord was moved with pity upon seeing her and said to her, "Do not cry." Then he stepped forward and touched the litter; at this, the bearers halted. He said, "Young man, I bid you get up." The dead man sat up and began to speak. Then Jesus gave him back to his mother. Fear seized them all and they began to praise God. "A great prophet has risen among us," they said; and, "God has visited his people." This was the report that spread about him throughout Judea and the surrounding country. ✛

WEDNESDAY, SEPTEMBER 19
Weekday, St. Januarius

† *1 Timothy 3:14-16*
The mystery of our religion is very deep.

Although I hope to visit you soon, I am writing you about these matters so that if I should be delayed you will know what kind of conduct befits a member of God's household, the church of the living God, the pillar and bulwark of truth. Wonderful, indeed, is the mystery of our faith, as we say in professing it:
"He was manifested in the flesh,
vindicated in the Spirit;
Seen by the angels;
preached among the Gentiles,
Believed in throughout the world,
taken up into glory." ✛

Psalm 111:1-6
R. How great are the works of the Lord! *(or **Alleluia.**)*
I will give thanks to the Lord with all my heart
in the company and assembly of the just.
Great are the works of the Lord,
exquisite in all their delights. **R.**
Majesty and glory are his work,

and his justice endures forever.
He has won renown for his wondrous deeds;
    gracious and merciful is the Lord. **R.**
He has given food to those who fear him;
    he will forever be mindful of his covenant.
He has made known to his people the power of his works,
    giving them the inheritance of the nations. **R.**

Hebrews 4:12
R. Alleluia, alleluia.
The word of God is living and active;
it probes the thoughts and motives of our heart. **R.**

✛ *Luke 7:31-35*
*We played the pipes for you, and you wouldn't
dance; we sang dirges, and you wouldn't cry.*

Jesus said: "What comparison can I use for the men of today?
What are they like? They are like children squatting in the city
squares and calling to their playmates,
    'We piped you a tune but you did not dance,
    We sang you a dirge but you did not wail.'
I mean that John the Baptizer came neither eating bread nor
drinking wine, and you say, 'He is mad!' The Son of Man came
and he both ate and drank, and you say, 'Here is a glutton and
a drunkard, a friend of tax collectors and sinners!' God's
wisdom is vindicated by all who accept it." ✛

THURSDAY, SEPTEMBER 20
ANDREW TAEGON, PAUL HASANG & COMPANIONS

✛ *1 Timothy 4:12-16*
*Take care about what you do and teach;
in this way you will save both yourself and those who listen to you.*

Let no one look down on you because of your youth, but be a
continuing example of love, faith and purity to believers. Until
I arrive, devote yourself to the reading of Scripture, to preaching and teaching. Do not neglect the gift you received when, as
a result of prophecy, the presbyters laid their hands on you.
Attend to your duties; let them absorb you, so that everyone
may see your progress. Watch yourself and watch your teaching. Persevere at both tasks. By doing so you will bring to
salvation yourself and all who hear you. ✛

Psalm 111:7-10

R. How great are the works of the Lord! *(or* **Alleluia.***)*
The works of his hands are faithful and just;
  sure are all his precepts,
Reliable forever and ever,
  wrought in truth and equity. **R.**
He has sent deliverance to his people;
  he has ratified his covenant forever;
  holy and awesome is his name. **R.**
The fear of the Lord is the beginning of wisdom;
  prudent are all who live by it.
His praise endures forever. **R.**

Hebrews 4:12
R. Alleluia, alleluia.
The word of God is living and active;
it probes the thoughts and motives of our heart. **R.**

† *Luke 7:36-50*
Her many sins must have been forgiven her, because she loved much.

There was a certain Pharisee who invited Jesus to dine with him. Jesus went to the Pharisee's home and reclined to eat. A woman known in the town to be a sinner learned that he was dining in the Pharisee's home. She brought in a vase of perfumed oil and stood behind him at his feet, weeping so that her tears fell upon his feet. Then she wiped them with her hair, kissing them and perfuming them with the oil. When his host, the Pharisee, saw this, he said to himself, "If this man were a prophet, he would know who and what sort of woman this is that touches him—that she is a sinner." In answer to his thoughts, Jesus said to him, "Simon, I have something to propose to you." "Teacher," he said, "speak."

"Two men owed money to a certain moneylender; one owed a total of five hundred coins, the other fifty. Since neither was able to repay, he wrote off both debts. Which of them was more grateful to him?" Simon answered, "He, I presume, to whom he remitted the larger sum." Jesus said to him, "You are right."

Turning then to the woman, he said to Simon: "You see this woman? I came to your home and you provided me with no water for my feet. She has washed my feet with her tears and wiped them with her hair. You gave me no kiss, but she has not ceased kissing my feet since I entered. You did not anoint my head with oil, but she has anointed my feet with perfume. I tell you, that is why her many sins are forgiven—because of her great love. Little is forgiven the one whose love is small."

He said to her then, "Your sins are forgiven," at which his fellow guests began to ask among themselves, "Who is this that he even forgives sin?" Meanwhile he said to the woman, "Your faith has been your salvation. Now go in peace." ✛

FRIDAY, SEPTEMBER 21
St. Matthew

✝ Ephesians 4:1-7, 11-13
It was his gift that some should be apostles, others evangelists.

I plead with you, as a prisoner for the Lord, to live a life worthy of the calling you have received, with perfect humility, meekness, and patience, bearing with one another lovingly. Make every effort to preserve the unity which has the Spirit as its origin and peace as its binding force. There is but one body and one Spirit, just as there is but one hope given all of you by your call. There is one Lord, one faith, one baptism; one God and Father of all, who is over all, and works through all, and is in all.

Each of us has received God's favor in the measure in which Christ bestows it.

It is he who gave apostles, prophets, evangelists, pastors, and teachers in roles of service for the faithful to build up the body of Christ, till we become one in faith and in the knowledge of God's Son, and form that perfect man who is Christ come to full stature. ✛

Psalm 19:2-5
R. Their message goes out through all the earth.
The heavens declare the glory of God,
    and the firmament proclaims his handiwork.
Day pours out the word to day,
    and night to night imparts knowledge. **R.**
Not a word nor a discourse
    whose voice is not heard;
Through all the earth their voice resounds,
    and to the ends of the world, their message. **R.**

R. Alleluia, alleluia.
We praise you, God; we acknowledge you as Lord;
your glorious band of apostles extols you. **R.**

† *Matthew 9:9-13*
Follow me. And standing up, he followed him.

As Jesus moved on, he saw a man named Matthew at his post where taxes were collected. He said to him, "Follow me." Matthew got up and followed him. Now it happened that, while Jesus was at table in Matthew's house, many tax collectors and those known as sinners came to join Jesus and his disciples at dinner. The Pharisees saw this and complained to his disciples, "What reason can the Teacher have for eating with tax collectors and those who disregard the law?" Overhearing the remark, he said: "People who are in good health do not need a doctor; sick people do. Go and learn the meaning of the words, 'It is mercy I desire and not sacrifice.' I have come to call, not the self-righteous, but sinners." ✛

SATURDAY, SEPTEMBER 22
WEEKDAY

† *1 Timothy 6:13-16*
Do all that you have been told until the appearance of our Lord Jesus Christ.

Before God, who gives life to all, and before Christ Jesus, who in bearing witness made his noble profession before Pontius Pilate, I charge you to keep God's command without blame or reproach until our Lord Jesus Christ shall appear. This appearance God will bring to pass at his chosen time. He is the blessed and only ruler, the King of kings and Lord of lords who alone has immortality and who dwells in inapproachable light, whom no human being has ever seen or can see. To him be honor and everlasting rule! Amen. ✛

Psalm 100:2-5
R. Come with joy into the presence of the Lord.
Serve the Lord with gladness;
    come before him with joyful song. **R.**
Know that the Lord is God;
    he made us, his we are;
    his people, the flock he tends. **R.**
Enter his gates with thanksgiving,

his courts with praise;
Give thanks to him; bless his name. **R.**
For he is good:
the Lord, whose kindness endures forever,
and his faithfulness, to all generations. **R.**

Hebrews 4:12
R. Alleluia, alleluia.
The word of God is living and active;
it probes the thoughts and motives of our heart. **R.**

† *Luke 8:4-15*

As for the seed in good ground, this is the people who have heard the word and take it to themselves and yield a harvest through their perseverance.

A large crowd was gathering, with people resorting to Jesus from one town after another. He spoke to them in a parable: "A farmer went out to sow some seed. In the sowing, some fell on the footpath where it was walked on and the birds of the air ate it up. Some fell on rocky ground, sprouted up, then withered through lack of moisture. Some fell among briers, and the thorns growing up with it stifled it. But some fell on good soil, grew up, and yielded grain a hundred-fold."

As he said this he exclaimed: "Let everyone who has ears attend to what he has heard." His disciples began asking him what the meaning of this parable might be. He replied, "To you the mysteries of the reign of God have been confided, but to the rest in parables that,

'Seeing they may not perceive,
and hearing they may not understand.'

This is the meaning of the parable. The seed is the word of God. Those on the footpath are people who hear, but the devil comes and takes the word out of their hearts lest they believe and be saved. Those on the rocky ground are the ones who, when they hear the word, receive it with joy. They have no root; they believe for a while, but fall away in time of temptation. The seed fallen among briers are those who hear, but their progress is stifled by the cares and riches and pleasures of life and they do not mature. The seed on good ground are those who hear the word in a spirit of openness, retain it, and bear fruit through perseverance." ✛

SEPTEMBER 23
TWENTY-FIFTH SUNDAY IN ORDINARY TIME

† *Amos 8:4-7*
Against those who buy the poor for money.

Hear this, you who trample upon the needy
and destroy the poor of the land!
"When will the new moon be over," you ask,
"that we may sell our grain,
and the sabbath, that we may display the wheat?
We will diminish the ephah,
add to the shekel,
and fix our scales for cheating!
We will buy the lowly for silver,
and the poor for a pair of sandals;
even the refuse of the wheat we will sell!"
The LORD has sworn by the pride of Jacob:
Never will I forget a thing they have done! ✛

Psalm 113:1-2, 4-8
R. Praise the Lord, who lifts up the poor.
(or **Alleluia.***)*
Praise, you servants of the LORD,
praise the name of the LORD.
Blessed be the name of the Lord
both now and forever. **R.**
High above all nations is the LORD;
above the heavens is his glory.
Who is like the LORD, our God, who is enthroned on high
and looks upon the heavens and the earth below? **R.**
He raises up the lowly from the dust;
from the dunghill he lifts up the poor
to seat them with princes,
with the princes of his own people. **R.**

† *1 Timothy 2:1-8*
Let prayers be offered for everyone to God who wills everyone to be saved.

Beloved:
First of all, I ask that supplications, prayers,
petitions, and thanksgivings be offered for everyone,

for kings and for all in authority,
that we may lead a quiet and tranquil life
in all devotion and dignity.
This is good and pleasing to God our savior,
who wills everyone to be saved
and to come to knowledge of the truth.
For there is one God.
There is also one mediator between God and men,
the man Christ Jesus,
who gave himself as ransom for all.
This was the testimony at the proper time.
For this I was appointed preacher and apostle
—I am speaking the truth, I am not lying—,
teacher of the Gentiles in faith and truth.

It is my wish, then, that in every place the men should pray,
lifting up holy hands, without anger or argument. ✝

cf. 2 Corinthians 8:9
R. Alleluia, alleluia.
Though our Lord Jesus Christ was rich, he became poor,
so that by his poverty you might become rich. **R.**

† Luke 16:1-13 (or Luke 16:10-13)
You cannot serve both God and mammon.

Jesus said to his disciples,
"A rich man had a steward
who was reported to him for squandering his property.
He summoned him and said,
'What is this I hear about you?
Prepare a full account of your stewardship,
because you can no longer be my steward.'
The steward said to himself, 'What shall I do,
now that my master is taking the position of steward away
from me?
I am not strong enough to dig and I am ashamed to beg.
I know what I shall do so that,
when I am removed from the stewardship,
they may welcome me into their homes.'
He called in his master's debtors one by one.
To the first he said,

'How much do you owe my master?'
He replied, 'One hundred measures of olive oil.'
He said to him, 'Here is your promissory note.
Sit down and quickly write one for fifty.'
Then to another the steward said, 'And you, how much do you
    owe?'
He replied, 'One hundred kors of wheat.'
The steward said to him, 'Here is your promissory note;
    write one for eighty.'
And the master commended that dishonest steward
    for acting prudently.

"For the children of this world
    are more prudent in dealing with their own generation
    than are the children of light.
I tell you, make friends for yourselves with dishonest wealth,
    so that when it fails, you will be welcomed into eternal
        dwellings.
The person who is trustworthy in very small matters
    is also trustworthy in great ones;
    and the person who is dishonest in very small matters
    is also dishonest in great ones.
If, therefore, you are not trustworthy with dishonest wealth,
    who will trust you with true wealth?
If you are not trustworthy with what belongs to another,
    who will give you what is yours?
No servant can serve two masters.
He will either hate one and love the other,
    or be devoted to one and despise the other.
You cannot serve both God and mammon." ✛

MONDAY, SEPTEMBER 24
WEEKDAY

† Ezra 1:1-6
These are the people of the Lord who went to
Jerusalem to build the temple of the Lord God.

In the first year of Cyrus, king of Persia, in order to fulfill the
word of the Lord spoken by Jeremiah, the Lord inspired King
Cyrus of Persia to issue this proclamation throughout his
kingdom, both by word of mouth and in writing: "Thus says
Cyrus, king of Persia: 'All the kingdoms of the earth the Lord,

the God of heaven, has given to me, and he has also charged me to build him a house in Jerusalem, which is in Judah. Whoever, therefore, among you belongs to any part of his people, let him go up, and may his God be with him! Let everyone who has survived, in whatever place he may have dwelt, be assisted by the people of that place with silver, gold, goods, and cattle, together with free-will offerings for the house of God in Jerusalem.'"

Then the family heads of Judah and Benjamin and the priests and Levites—everyone, that is, whom God had inspired to do so—prepared to go up to build the house of the Lord in Jerusalem. All their neighbors gave them help in every way, with silver, gold, goods, and cattle, and with many precious gifts besides all their free-will offerings. ✛

Psalm 126:1-6
R. The Lord has done marvels for us.
When the Lord brought back the captives of Zion,
    we were like men dreaming.
Then our mouth was filled with laughter,
    and our tongue with rejoicing. **R.**
Then they said among the nations,
    "The Lord has done great things for them."
The Lord has done great things for us;
    we are glad indeed. **R.**
Restore our fortunes, O Lord,
    like the torrents in the southern desert.
Those that sow in tears
    shall reap rejoicing. **R.**
Although they go forth weeping,
    carrying the seed to be sown,
They shall come back rejoicing,
    carrying their sheaves. **R.**

See Ephesians 1:17-18
R. Alleluia, alleluia.
May the Father of our Lord Jesus Christ
enlighten the eyes of our heart
that we might see how great is the hope
to which we are called. **R.**

† *Luke 8:16-18*
Place your light on a stand so that the people may see it when they enter.

Jesus said to the crowds: "No one lights a lamp and puts it under a bushel basket or under a bed; he puts it on a lampstand so that whoever comes in can see it. There is nothing hidden that will not be exposed, nothing concealed that will not be known and brought to light. Take heed, therefore, how you hear: to the man who has, more will be given; and he who has not, will lose even the little he thinks he has." ✚

TUESDAY, SEPTEMBER 25
WEEKDAY

† *Ezra 6:7-8,12,14-20*
They completed the temple of God, and ate the passover.

King Darius issued an order to the officials of West-of-Euphrates: "Let the governor and the elders of the Jews continue the work on that house of God; they are to rebuild it on its former site. I also issue this decree concerning your dealing with these elders of the Jews in the rebuilding of that house of God: From the royal revenue, the taxes of West-of-Euphrates, let these men be repaid for their expenses, in full and without delay. I, Darius, have issued this decree; let it be carefully executed."

The elders of the Jews continued to make progress in the building, supported by the message of the prophets, Haggai and Zechariah, son of Iddo. They finished the building according to the command of the God of Israel and the decrees of Cyrus and Darius [and of Artaxerxes, king of Persia]. They completed this house on the third day of the month Adar, in the sixth year of the reign of King Darius. The Israelites—priests, Levites, and the other returned exiles—celebrated the dedication of this house of God with joy. For the dedication of this house of God, they offered one hundred bulls, two hundred rams, and four hundred lambs, together with twelve he-goats as a sin-offering for all Israel, in keeping with the number of the tribes of Israel. Finally, they set up the priests in their classes and the Levites in their divisions for the service of God in Jerusalem, as is prescribed in the book of Moses.

The exiles kept the Passover on the fourteenth day of the

first month. The Levites, every one of whom had purified himself for the occasion, sacrificed the Passover for the rest of the exiles, for their brethren the priests, and for themselves. ✛

Psalm 122:1-5
**R. I rejoiced when I heard them say:
let us go to the house of the Lord.**
I rejoiced because they said to me,
   "We will go up to the house of the Lord."
And now we have set foot
   within your gates, O Jerusalem— **R.**
Jerusalem, built as a city
   with compact unity.
To it the tribes go up,
   the tribes of the Lord, **R.**
According to the decree for Israel,
   to give thanks to the name of the Lord.
In it are set up judgment seats,
   seats for the house of David. **R.**

See Ephesians 1:17-18
R. Alleluia, alleluia.
May the Father of our Lord Jesus Christ
enlighten the eyes of our heart
that we might see how great is the hope
to which we are called. **R.**

† *Luke 8:19-21*
*My mother and my brothers are those who
hear the word of God and put it into practice.*

The mother and brothers of Jesus came to be with him, but they could not reach him because of the crowd. He was informed, "Your mother and your brothers are standing outside and wish to see you." He told them in reply, "My mother and my brothers are those who hear the word of God and act upon it." ✛

WEDNESDAY, SEPTEMBER 26
WEEKDAY, STS. COSMAS AND DAMIAN

† *Ezra 9:5-9*
Our God has not forgotten us in our slavery.

At the time of the evening sacrifice, I Ezra rose in my wretchedness, and with cloak and mantle torn I fell on my knees, stretching out my hands to the Lord my God.

I said: "My God, I am too ashamed and confounded to raise my face to you, O my God, for our wicked deeds are heaped up above our heads and our guilt reaches up to heaven. From the time of our fathers even to this day great has been our guilt, and for our wicked deeds we have been delivered over, we and our kings and our priests, to the will of the kings of foreign lands, to the sword, to captivity, to pillage, and to disgrace, as is the case today.

"And now, but a short time ago, mercy came to us from the Lord our God, who left us a remnant and gave us a stake in his holy place; thus our God has brightened our eyes and given us relief in our servitude. For slaves we are, but in our servitude our God has not abandoned us; rather, he has turned the good will of the kings of Persia toward us. Thus he has given us new life to raise again the house of our God and restore its ruins, and has granted us a fence in Judah and Jerusalem." ✛

Tobit 13:2-4, 6-8
R.   Blessed be God, who lives forever.

He scourges and then has mercy;
> he casts down to the depths of the nether world,
> and he brings up from the great abyss.

No one can escape his hand. **R.**

For though he has scattered you among the Gentiles,
> he has shown you his greatness even there.

Exalt him before every living being,
> because he is the Lord our God,
> our Father and God forever. **R.**

So now consider what he has done for you,
> and praise him with full voice.

Bless the Lord of righteousness,
> and exalt the King of ages. **R.**

As for me, I exalt my God,

and my spirit rejoices in the King of heaven.
Let all men speak of his majesty,
and sing his praises in Jerusalem. **R.**
"Turn back, you sinners! Do the right before him:
perhaps he may look with favor upon you
and show you mercy." **R.**

See Ephesians 1:17-18
R. Alleluia, alleluia.
May the Father of our Lord Jesus Christ
enlighten the eyes of our heart
that we might see how great is the hope
to which we are called. **R.**

† *Luke 9:1-6*
He sent them to proclaim the kingdom of God and to heal the sick.

Jesus called the Twelve together and gave them power and authority to overcome all demons and to cure diseases. He sent them forth to proclaim the reign of God and heal the afflicted. Jesus advised them: "Take nothing for the journey, neither walking staff nor traveling bag; no bread, no money. No one is to have two coats. Stay at whatever house you enter and proceed from there. When people will not receive you, leave that town and shake its dust from your feet as a testimony against them." So they set out and went from village to village, spreading the good news everywhere and curing diseases. ✛

THURSDAY, SEPTEMBER 27
St. Vincent de Paul

† *Haggai 1:1-8*
Build the temple and you will be acceptable to me.

In the second year of King Darius, the word of the Lord came through the prophet Haggai to the governor of Judah, Zerubbabel, son of Shealtiel, and to the high priest Joshua, son of Jehozadak:

Thus says the Lord of hosts: This people says: "Not now has the time come to rebuild the house of the Lord." (Then this word of the Lord came through Haggai, the prophet:) Is it time for you to dwell in your own paneled houses, while this house lies in ruins?

Now thus says the Lord of hosts:
Consider your ways!
You have sown much, but have brought in little;
you have eaten, but have not been satisfied;
You have drunk, but have not been exhilarated;
have clothed yourselves, but not been warmed;
And he who earned wages
earned them for a bag with holes in it.

Thus says the Lord of hosts:
Consider your ways!
Go up into the hill country;
bring timber, and build the house
That I may take pleasure in it
and receive my glory, says the Lord. ✛

Psalm 149:1-6, 9
R. The Lord takes delight in his people.
Sing to the Lord a new song
of praise in the assembly of the faithful.
Let Israel be glad in their maker,
let the children of Zion rejoice in their king. **R.**
Let them praise his name in the festive dance,
let them sing praise to him with timbrel and harp.
For the Lord loves his people,
and he adorns the lowly with victory. **R.**
Let the faithful exult in glory;
let them sing for joy upon their couches;
let the high praises of God be in their throats.
This is the glory of all his faithful. Alleluia. **R.**

See Ephesians 1:17-18
R. Alleluia, alleluia.
May the Father of our Lord Jesus Christ
enlighten the eyes of our heart
that we might see how great is the hope
to which we are called. **R.**

† *Luke 9:7-9*
I beheaded John, so who is this I hear so much about?

Herod the tetrarch heard of all that Jesus was doing and he was perplexed, for some were saying, "John has been raised from the dead"; others, "Elijah has appeared"; and still others, "One of the prophets of old has risen." But Herod said, "John I beheaded. Who is this man about whom I hear all these reports?" He was very curious to see him. ✦

FRIDAY, SEPTEMBER 28
WEEKDAY, ST. WENCESLAUS, ST. LAWRENCE RUIZ AND COMPANIONS

† Haggai 1:15—2:9
A little while and I shall fill the temple with glory.

In the second year of King Darius, on the twenty-first day of the seventh month, the word of the Lord came through the prophet Haggai: Tell this to the governor of Judah, Zerubbabel, son of Shealtiel, and to the high priest Joshua, son of Jehozadak, and to the remnant of the people:
Who is left among you
    that saw this house in its former glory?
And how do you see it now?
    Does it not seem like nothing in your eyes?
But now take courage, Zerubbabel, says the Lord,
    and take courage, Joshua, high priest, son of Jehozadak,
And take courage, all you people of the land,
    says the Lord, and work!
For I am with you, says the Lord of hosts.
This is the pact that I made with you
    when you came out of Egypt,
And my spirit continues in your midst;
    do not fear!

For thus says the Lord of hosts:
One moment yet, a little while,
    and I will shake the heavens and the earth,
    the sea and the dry land.
I will shake all the nations,
    and the treasures of all the nations will come in,
And I will fill this house with glory,
    says the Lord of hosts.
Mine is the silver and mine the gold
    says the Lord of hosts.
Greater will be the future glory of this house
    than the former, says the Lord of hosts;

And in this place I will give peace,
   says the Lord of hosts! ✛

Psalm 43:1-4
**R. Hope in God; I will praise him,
   my savior and my God.**
Do me justice, O God, and fight my fight
   against a faithless people;
   from the deceitful and impious man rescue me. **R.**
For you, O God, are my strength.
   Why do you keep me so far away?
Why must I go about in mourning,
   with the enemy oppressing me? **R.**
Send forth your light and your fidelity;
   they shall lead me on
And bring me to your holy mountain,
   to your dwelling-place. **R.**
Then will I go in to the altar of God,
   the God of my gladness and joy;
Then will I give you thanks upon the harp,
   O God, my God! **R.**

See Ephesians 1:17-18
R. Alleluia, alleluia.
May the Father of our Lord Jesus Christ
enlighten the eyes of our heart
that we might see how great is the hope
to which we are called. **R.**

† *Luke 9:18-22*
You are the Christ of God. The Son of Man must suffer much.

One day when Jesus was praying in seclusion and his disciples
were with him, he put the question to them, "Who do the crowds
say that I am?" "John the Baptizer," they replied, "and some say
Elijah, while others claim that one of the prophets of old has
returned from the dead." "But you—who do you say that I am?"
he asked them. Peter said in reply, "The Messiah of God." He
strictly forbade them to tell this to anyone. "The Son of Man," he
said, "must first endure many sufferings, be rejected by the
elders, the high priests and the scribes, and be put to death, and
then be raised up on the third day." ✛

SATURDAY, SEPTEMBER 29
ARCHANGELS MICHAEL, GABRIEL & RAPHAEL

✝ *Daniel 7:9-10, 13-14 (or Revelation 12:7-12)*
Countless thousands ministered to him.

As Daniel watched:
Thrones were set up
    and the Ancient One took his throne.
His clothing was snow bright,
    and the hair on his head as white as wool;
His throne was flames of fire,
    with wheels of burning fire.
A surging stream of fire
    flowed out from where he sat;
Thousands upon thousands were ministering to him,
    and myriads upon myriads attended him.
    The court was convened, and the books were opened. As
the visions during the night continued, I saw
One like a son of man coming,
    on the clouds of heaven;
When he reached the Ancient One
    and was presented before him,
He received dominion, glory, and kingship;
    nations and peoples of every language serve him.
His dominion is an everlasting dominion
    that shall not be taken away,
    his kingship shall not be destroyed. ✝

Psalm 138:1-5
**R. In the sight of the angels
I will sing your praises, Lord.**
I will give thanks to you, O Lord, with all my heart,
    [for you have heard the words of my mouth;]
    in the presence of the angels I will sing your praise;
I will worship at your holy temple
    and give thanks to your name, **R.**
Because of your kindness and your truth;
    for you have made great above all things
    your name and your promise.
When I called, you answered me;
    you built up strength within me. **R.**

All the kings of the earth shall give thanks to you, O Lord,
   when they hear the words of your mouth;
And they shall sing of the ways of the Lord:
   "Great is the glory of the Lord." **R.**

Psalm 103:21
R. Alleluia, alleluia.
Bless the Lord, all you his angels,
his ministers who do his will. **R.**

† *John 1:47-51*
*Above the Son of Man you will see the
angels of God ascending and descending.*

When Jesus saw Nathanael coming toward him, he remarked: "This man is a real Israelite. There is no guile in him."
"How do you know me?" Nathanael asked him. "Before Philip
called you," Jesus answered, "I saw you under the fig tree."
"Rabbi," said Nathanael, "you are the Son of God; you are the
king of Israel." Jesus responded: "Do you believe just because
I told you I saw you under the fig tree? You will see much
greater things than that."

   He went on to tell them, "I solemnly assure you, you shall
see the sky opened and the angels of God ascending and
descending on the Son of Man." ✢

SEPTEMBER 30
TWENTY-SIXTH SUNDAY IN ORDINARY TIME

† *Amos 6:1a, 4-7*
Their wanton revelry shall be done away with.

Thus says the LORD, the God of hosts:
Woe to the complacent in Zion!
Lying upon beds of ivory,
   stretched comfortably on their couches,
they eat lambs taken from the flock,
   and calves from the stall!
Improvising to the music of the harp,
   like David, they devise their own accompaniment.
They drink wine from bowls
   and anoint themselves with the best oils;
   yet they are not made ill by the collapse of Joseph!
Therefore, now they shall be the first to go into exile,

and their wanton revelry shall be done away with. ✛

Psalm 146:7-10

R. Praise the Lord, my soul! *(or **Alleluia.**)*

Blessed he who keeps faith forever,
    secures justice for the oppressed,
    gives food to the hungry. **R.**

The LORD sets captives free.
The LORD gives sight to the blind;
    the LORD raises up those who were bowed down.
The LORD loves the just;
    the LORD protects strangers. **R.**

The fatherless and the widow he sustains,
    but the way of the wicked he thwarts.
The LORD shall reign forever;
    your God, O Zion, through all generations. Alleluia. **R.**

† *1 Timothy 6:11-16*

Keep the commandment until the appearance of the Lord Jesus Christ.

But you, man of God, pursue righteousness,
    devotion, faith, love, patience, and gentleness.
Compete well for the faith.
Lay hold of eternal life, to which you were called
    when you made the noble confession in the presence of
        many witnesses.
I charge you before God, who gives life to all things,
    and before Christ Jesus,
    who gave testimony under Pontius Pilate for the noble
        confession,
    to keep the commandment without stain or reproach
    until the appearance of our Lord Jesus Christ
    that the blessed and only ruler
    will make manifest at the proper time,
    the King of kings and Lord of lords,
    who alone has immortality, who dwells in unapproachable
        light,
    and whom no human being has seen or can see.
To him be honor and eternal power. Amen. ✛

cf. 2 Corinthians 8:9
R. Alleluia, alleluia.

Though our Lord Jesus Christ was rich, he became poor,
so that by his poverty you might become rich. **R.**

† *Luke 16:19-31*

You received what was good, Lazarus what was bad;
now he is comforted, whereas you are tormented.

Jesus said to the Pharisees:
"There was a rich man who dressed in purple garments
          and fine linen
and dined sumptuously each day.
And lying at his door was a poor man named Lazarus, covered
          with sores,
     who would gladly have eaten his fill of the scraps
     that fell from the rich man's table.
Dogs even used to come and lick his sores.
When the poor man died,
     he was carried away by angels to the bosom of Abraham.
The rich man also died and was buried,
     and from the netherworld, where he was in torment,
     he raised his eyes and saw Abraham far off
     and Lazarus at his side.
And he cried out, 'Father Abraham, have pity on me.
Send Lazarus to dip the tip of his finger in water and cool my
          tongue,
     for I am suffering torment in these flames.'
Abraham replied,
     'My child, remember that you received
     what was good during your lifetime
     while Lazarus likewise received what was bad;
     but now he is comforted here, whereas you are tormented.
Moreover, between us and you a great chasm is established
     to prevent anyone from crossing who might wish to go
     from our side to yours or from your side to ours.'
He said, 'Then I beg you, father,
     send him to my father's house, for I have five brothers,
     so that he may warn them,
     lest they too come to this place of torment.'
But Abraham replied, 'They have Moses and the prophets.
Let them listen to them.'
He said, 'Oh no, father Abraham,

but if someone from the dead goes to them, they will repent.'
Then Abraham said, 'If they will not listen to Moses and the
prophets,
neither will they be persuaded if someone should rise from
the dead.'" ✛

MONDAY, OCTOBER 1
St. Therese of the Child Jesus

† *Zechariah 8:1-8*
I will save my people from the east and the west.

This word of the Lord of hosts came: Thus says the Lord of
hosts:
I am intensely jealous for Zion,
    stirred to jealous wrath for her.
Thus says the Lord:
I will return to Zion,
    and I will dwell within Jerusalem;
Jerusalem shall be called the faithful city,
    and the mountain of the Lord of hosts,
    the holy mountain.
Thus says the Lord of hosts: Old men and old women, each with
staff in hand because of old age, shall again sit in the streets
of Jerusalem. The city shall be filled with boys and girls
playing in her streets. Thus says the Lord of hosts: Even if this
should seem impossible in the eyes of the remnant of this
people, shall it in those days be impossible in my eyes also, says
the Lord of hosts. Thus says the Lord of hosts: Lo, I will rescue
my people from the land of the rising sun, and from the land
of the setting sun. I will bring them back to dwell within
Jerusalem. They shall be my people, and I will be their God,
with faithfulness and justice. ✛

Psalm 102:16-23, 29
R. **The Lord will build up Zion again,**
    and appear in all his glory.
And the nations shall revere your name, O Lord,
    and all the kings of the earth your glory,
When the Lord has rebuilt Zion
    and appeared in his glory;

When he has regarded the prayer of the destitute,
  and not despised their prayer. **R.**
Let this be written for the generation to come,
  and let his future creatures praise the Lord:
"The Lord looked down from his holy height,
  from heaven he beheld the earth,
To hear the groaning of the prisoners,
  to release those doomed to die." **R.**
The children of your servants shall abide,
  and their posterity shall continue in your presence.
That the name of the Lord may be declared in Zion;
  and his praise, in Jerusalem,
When the peoples gather together,
  and the kingdoms, to serve the Lord. **R.**

John 14:5
Alleluia, alleluia.
I am the way, the truth, and the life, says the Lord;
no one comes to the Father, except through me. **R.**

† *Luke 9:46-50*
The least among you all is the one who is great.

A discussion arose among the disciples as to which of them was the greatest. Jesus, who knew their thoughts, took a little child and placed it beside him, after which he said to them, "Whoever welcomes this little child on my account welcomes me, and whoever welcomes me welcomes him who sent me; for the least one among you is the greatest."

It was John who said, "Master, we saw a man using your name to expel demons, and we tried to stop him because he is not of our company." Jesus told him in reply, "Do not stop him, for any man who is not against you is on your side." †

TUESDAY, OCTOBER 2
THE GUARDIAN ANGELS

† *Exodus 23:20-23*
My angel will go before you.

The Lord said: "See, I am sending an angel before you, to guard you on the way and bring you to the place I have prepared. Be attentive to him and heed his voice. Do not rebel against him, for he will not forgive your sin. My authority resides in him. If you heed his voice and carry out all I tell you, I will be an enemy to your enemies and a foe to your foes.

"My angel will go before you and bring you to the Amorites, Hittites, Perizzites, Canaanites, Hivites and Jebusites; and I will wipe them out." ✛

Psalm 91:1-6, 10-11
**R. He has put his angels in charge of you,
to guard you in all your ways.**
You who dwell in the shelter of the Most High,
    who abide in the shadow of the Almighty,
Say to the Lord, "My refuge and my fortress,
    my God, in whom I trust." **R.**
For he will rescue you from the snare of the fowler,
    from the destroying pestilence.
With his pinions he will cover you,
    and under his wings you shall take refuge. **R.**
His faithfulness is a buckler and a shield.
    You shall not fear the terror of the night
    nor the arrow that flies by day;
Not the pestilence that roams in darkness
    nor the devastating plague at noon. **R.**
No evil shall befall you,
    nor shall affliction come near your tent,
For to his angels he has given command about you
    that they guard you in all your ways. **R.**

Psalm 103:21
R. Alleluia, alleluia.
Bless the Lord, all you his angels,
his ministers who do his will. **R.**

† Matthew 18:1-5,10
*Their angels in heaven are always in the
presence of my Father, who is in heaven.*

The disciples came up to Jesus with the question, "Who is of greatest importance in the kingdom of God?" He called a little child over and stood him in their midst and said: "I assure you, unless you change and become like little children, you will not enter the kingdom of God. Whoever makes himself lowly, becoming like this child, is of greatest importance in that heavenly reign. Whoever welcomes one such child for my sake welcomes me.

"See that you never despise one of these little ones. I assure you, their angels in heaven constantly behold my heavenly Father's face." ✢

WEDNESDAY, OCTOBER 3
WEEKDAY

† Nehemiah 2:1-8
*If it pleases the king, send me to the city of
my ancestors and I will rebuild it.*

In the month Nisan of the twentieth year of King Artaxerxes, when the wine was in my charge, I Nehemiah took some and offered it to the king. As I had never before been sad in his presence, the king asked me, "Why do you look sad? If you are not sick, you must be sad at heart." Though I was seized with great fear, I answered the king: "May the king live forever! How could I not look sad when the city where my ancestors are buried lies in ruins, and its gates have been eaten out by fire?" The king asked me, "What is it, then, that you wish?" I prayed to the God of heaven and then answered the king: "If it please the king, and if your servant is deserving of your favor, send me to Judah, to the city of my ancestors' graves, to rebuild it." Then the king, and the queen seated beside him, asked me how long my journey would take and when I would return. I set a date that was acceptable to him, and the king agreed that I might go.

I asked the king further: "If it please the king, let letters be given to me for the governors of West-of-Euphrates, that they may afford me safe-conduct till I arrive in Judah; also a letter for Asaph, the keeper of the royal park, that he may give me wood for timbering the gates of the temple-citadel and for the city wall and the house that I shall occupy." The king granted my requests, for the favoring hand of my God was upon me. ✢

Psalm 137:1-6
R. Let my tongue be silenced, if I ever forget you!
By the streams of Babylon
    we sat and wept

when we remembered Zion.
On the aspens of that land
  we hung up our harps. **R.**
Though there our captors asked of us
  the lyrics of our songs,
And our despoilers urged us to be joyous:
  "Sing for us the songs of Zion!" **R.**
How could we sing a song of the Lord
  in a foreign land?
If I forget you, Jerusalem,
  may my right hand be forgotten! **R.**
May my tongue cleave to my palate
  if I remember you not,
If I place not Jerusalem
  ahead of my joy. **R.**

John 14:5
R. Alleluia, alleluia.
I am the way, the truth, and the life, says the Lord;
no one comes to the Father, except through me. **R.**

† *Luke 9:57-62*
I will follow you wherever you go.

As Jesus and his disciples were making their way along, someone said to Jesus, "I will be your follower wherever you go." Jesus said to him, "The foxes have lairs, the birds of the sky have nests, but the Son of Man has nowhere to lay his head." To another he said, "Come after me." The man replied, "Let me bury my father first." Jesus said to him, "Let the dead bury their dead; come away and proclaim the kingdom of God." Yet another said to him, "I will be your follower, Lord, but first let me take leave of my people at home." Jesus answered him, "Whoever puts his hand to the plow but keeps looking back is unfit for the reign of God." ✛

THURSDAY, OCTOBER 4
St. Francis of Assisi

† *Nehemiah 8:1-12*
*Ezra opened the book of the law, blessed the people,
and they responded, Amen! Amen!*

The whole people gathered as one man in the open space before the Water Gate, and they called upon Ezra the scribe to bring forth the book of the law of Moses which the Lord prescribed for Israel. On the first day of the seventh month, therefore, Ezra the priest brought the law before the assembly, which consisted of men, women, and those children old enough to understand. Standing at one end of the open place that was before the Water Gate, he read out of the book from daybreak until midday, in the presence of the men, the women, and those children old enough to understand; and all the people listened attentively to the book of the law. Ezra the scribe stood on a wooden platform that had been made for the occasion.

Ezra opened the scroll so that all the people might see it (for he was standing higher up than any of the people); and, as he opened it, all the people rose. Ezra blessed the Lord, the great God, and all the people, their hands raised high, answered, "Amen, amen!" Then they bowed down and prostrated themselves before the Lord, their faces to the ground. As the people remained in their places Ezra read plainly from the book of the law of God, interpreting it so that all could understand what was read. Then [Nehemiah, that is, His Excellency, and] Ezra the priest-scribe [and the Levites who were instructing the people] said to all the people: "Today is holy to the Lord your God. Do not be sad, and do not weep" — for all the people were weeping as they heard the words of the law. He said further: "Go, eat rich foods and drink sweet drinks, and allot portions to those who had nothing prepared; for today is holy to our Lord. Do not be saddened this day, for rejoicing in the Lord must be your strength!" [And the Levites quieted all the people, saying, "Hush, for today is holy, and you must not be saddened."] Then all the people went to eat and drink, to distribute portions, and to celebrate with great joy, for they understood the words that had been expounded to them. ✛

Psalm 19:8-11

R. The precepts of the Lord give joy to the heart.

The law of the Lord is perfect,
  refreshing the soul;
The decree of the Lord is trustworthy,
  giving wisdom to the simple. **R.**
The precepts of the Lord are right,
  rejoicing the heart;
The command of the Lord is clear,
  enlightening the eye; **R.**
The fear of the Lord is pure,
  enduring forever;
The ordinances of the Lord are true,
  all of them just. **R.**
They are more precious than gold,
  than a heap of purest gold;
Sweeter also than syrup
  or honey from the comb. **R.**

John 14:5

R. Alleluia, alleluia.

I am the way, the truth, and the life, says the Lord;
no one comes to the Father, except through me. **R.**

† *Luke 10:1-12*
Your peace will rest on them.

Jesus appointed a further seventy-two and sent them in pairs before him to every town and place he intended to visit. He said to them: "The harvest is rich but the workers are few; therefore ask the harvest-master to send workers to his harvest. Be on your way, and remember: I am sending you as lambs in the midst of wolves. Do not carry a walking staff or traveling bag; wear no sandals and greet no one along the way. On entering any house, first say, 'Peace to this house.' If there is a peaceable man there, your peace will rest on him; if not, it will come back to you. Stay in the one house eating and drinking what they have, for the laborer is worth his wage. Do not move from house to house.

"Into whatever city you go, after they welcome you, eat what they set before you, and cure the sick there. Say to them, 'The reign of God is at hand.' If the people of any town you enter do not welcome you, go into its streets and say, 'We shake the dust of this town from our feet as testimony against you. But know that the reign of God is near.' I assure you, on that day the fate of Sodom will be less severe than that of such a town." ✢

FRIDAY, OCTOBER 5
WEEKDAY

✝ Baruch 1:15-22
We have sinned in the sight of the Lord and have not believed.

Justice is with the Lord, our God; and we today are flushed with shame, we men of Judah and citizens of Jerusalem, that we, with our kings and rulers and priests and prophets, and with our fathers, have sinned in the Lord's sight and disobeyed him. We have neither heeded the voice of the Lord, our God, nor followed the precepts which the Lord set before us. From the time the Lord led our fathers out of the land of Egypt until the present day, we have been disobedient to the Lord, our God, and only too ready to disregard his voice. And the evils and the curse which the Lord enjoined upon Moses, his servant, at the time he led our fathers forth from the land of Egypt to give us the land flowing with milk and honey, cling to us even today. For we did not heed the voice of the Lord, our God, in all the words of the prophets whom he sent us, but each one of us went off after the devices of his own wicked heart, served other gods, and did evil in the sight of the Lord, our God. ✢

Psalm 79:1-5, 8-9
R. For the glory of your name,
   O Lord, deliver us.
O God, the nations have come into your inheritance;
   they have defiled your holy temple,
   they have laid Jerusalem in ruins.
They have given the corpses of your servants
   as food to the birds of heaven,
   the flesh of your faithful ones to the beasts of the earth. **R.**
They have poured out their blood like water
   round about Jerusalem,
   and there is no one to bury them.
We have become the reproach of our neighbors,
   the scorn and derision of those around us.

O Lord, how long? Will you be angry forever?
Will your jealousy burn like fire? **R.**
Remember not against us the iniquities of the past;
may your compassion quickly come to us,
for we are brought very low. **R.**
Help us, O God our savior,
because of the glory of your name;
Deliver us and pardon our sins
for your name's sake. **R.**

John 14:5
R. Alleluia, alleluia.
I am the way, the truth, and the life, says the Lord;
no one comes to the Father, except through me. **R.**

† *Luke 10:13-16*
He who rejects me, rejects him who sent me.

Jesus said: "It will go ill with you, Chorazin! And just as ill with you, Bethsaida! If the miracles worked in your midst had occurred in Tyre and Sidon, they would long ago have reformed in sackcloth and ashes. It will go easier on the day of judgment for Tyre and Sidon than for you. And as for you, Capernaum, 'Are you to be exalted to the skies? You shall be hurled down to the realm of death!'

"He who hears you, hears me. He who rejects you, rejects me. And he who rejects me, rejects him who sent me." ✛

SATURDAY, OCTOBER 6
WEEKDAY, ST. BRUNO, BL. MARIE-ROSE DUROCHER

† *Baruch 4:5-12, 27-29*
He who delivered you to your enemies will rescue you and give you eternal joy.

Fear not, my people!
Remember, Israel,
You were sold to the nations
not for your destruction;
It was because you angered God
that you were handed over to your foes.
For you provoked your Maker

with sacrifices to demons, to no-gods;
You forsook the Eternal God who nourished you,
and you grieved Jerusalem who fostered you.
She indeed saw coming upon you
the anger of God; and she said:

"Hear, you neighbors of Zion!
God has brought great mourning upon me,
For I have seen the captivity
that the Eternal God has brought
upon my sons and daughters.
With joy I fostered them;
but with mourning and lament I let them go.
Let no one gloat over me, a widow,
bereft of many:
For the sins of my children I am left desolate,
because they turned from the law of God.

Fear not, my children; call out to God!
He who brought this upon you will remember you.
As your hearts have been disposed to stray from God,
turn now ten times the more to seek him;
For he who has brought disaster upon you
will, in saving you, bring you back enduring joy." ✛

Psalm 69:33-37
R. The Lord listens to the poor.
"See, you lowly ones, and be glad;
you who seek God, may your hearts be merry!
For the Lord hears the poor,
and his own who are in bonds he spurns not.
Let the heavens and the earth praise him,
the seas and whatever moves in them!" **R.**
For God will save Zion
and rebuild the cities of Judah.
They shall dwell in the land and own it,
and the descendants of his servants shall inherit it,
and those who love his name shall inhabit it. **R.**

John 14:5
R. Alleluia, alleluia.
I am the way, the truth, and the life, says the Lord;

no one comes to the Father, except through me. **R.**

✝ *Luke 10:17-24*
Rejoice because your names are written in heaven.

The seventy-two disciples returned in jubilation, saying, "Master, even the demons are subject to us in your name." He said in reply: "I watched Satan fall from the sky like lightning. See what I have done; I have given you power to tread on snakes and scorpions and all the forces of the enemy, and nothing shall ever injure you. Nevertheless, do not rejoice so much in the fact that the devils are subject to you as that your names are inscribed in heaven."

At that moment Jesus rejoiced in the Holy Spirit and said: "I offer you grateful praise, O Father, Lord of heaven and earth, because what you have hidden from the learned and the clever you have revealed to the merest children.

"Yes, Father, you have graciously willed it so. Everything has been given over to me by my Father. No one knows the Son except the Father and no one knows the Father except the Son—and anyone to whom the Son wishes to reveal him."

Turning to his disciples he said to them privately: "Blest are the eyes that see what you see. I tell you, many prophets and kings wished to see what you see but did not see it, and to hear what you hear but did not hear it." ✛

OCTOBER 7
TWENTY-SEVENTH SUNDAY IN ORDINARY TIME

✝ *Habakkuk 1:2-3; 2:2-4*
The just one, because of his faith, shall live.

How long, O LORD? I cry for help
  but you do not listen!
I cry out to you, "Violence!"
  but you do not intervene.
Why do you let me see ruin;
  why must I look at misery?
Destruction and violence are before me;
  there is strife, and clamorous discord.
Then the LORD answered me and said:
  Write down the vision clearly upon the tablets,

so that one can read it readily.
For the vision still has its time,
  presses on to fulfillment, and will not disappoint;
if it delays, wait for it,
  it will surely come, it will not be late.
The rash one has no integrity;
  but the just one, because of his faith, shall live. ✢

Psalm 95:1-2, 6-9
**R. If today you hear his voice,
  harden not your hearts.**
Come, let us sing joyfully to the LORD;
  let us acclaim the Rock of our salvation.
Let us come into his presence with thanksgiving;
  let us joyfully sing psalms to him. **R.**
Come, let us bow down in worship;
  let us kneel before the LORD who made us.
For he is our God,
  and we are the people he shepherds, the flock he guides. **R.**
Oh, that today you would hear his voice:
  "Harden not your hearts as at Meribah,
  as in the day of Massah in the desert,
where your fathers tempted me;
  they tested me though they had seen my works." **R.**

† 2 Timothy 1:6-8,13-14
Do not be ashamed of your testimony to our Lord.

Beloved:
I remind you, to stir into flame
  the gift of God that you have through the imposition of my
    hands.
For God did not give us a spirit of cowardice
  but rather of power and love and self-control.
So do not be ashamed of your testimony to our Lord,
  nor of me, a prisoner for his sake;
  but bear your share of hardship for the gospel
  with the strength that comes from God.

Take as your norm the sound words that you heard from me,
  in the faith and love that are in Christ Jesus.
Guard this rich trust with the help of the Holy Spirit
  that dwells within us. ✢

1 Peter 1:25
R. Alleluia, alleluia.
The word of the Lord remains for ever.
This is the word that has been proclaimed to you. **R.**

✝ *Luke 17:5-10*
If you have faith!

The apostles said to the Lord, "Increase our faith."
The Lord replied,
 "If you have faith the size of a mustard seed,
 you would say to this mulberry tree,
 'Be uprooted and planted in the sea,' and it would obey you.

"Who among you would say to your servant
 who has just come in from plowing or tending sheep in the
  field,
 'Come here immediately and take your place at table'?
Would he not rather say to him,
 'Prepare something for me to eat.
Put on your apron and wait on me while I eat and drink.
You may eat and drink when I am finished'?
Is he grateful to that servant because he did what was
  commanded?
So should it be with you.
When you have done all you have been commanded,
 say, 'We are unprofitable servants;
 we have done what we were obliged to do.'" ✝

MONDAY, OCTOBER 8
WEEKDAY

✝ *Jonah 1:1—2:1, 11*
Jonah rose up and fled from the face of the Lord.

This is the word of the Lord that came to Jonah, son of
Amittai: "Set out for the great city of Nineveh, and preach
against it; their wickedness has come up before me." But
Jonah made ready to flee to Tarshish away from the Lord. He
went down to Joppa, found a ship going to Tarshish, paid the
fare, and went aboard to journey with them to Tarshish, away
from the Lord.

 The Lord, however, hurled a violent wind upon the sea, and
in the furious tempest that arose the ship was on the point of

breaking up. Then the mariners became frightened and each one cried to his god. To lighten the ship for themselves, they threw its cargo into the sea. Meanwhile, Jonah had gone down into the hold of the ship, and lay there fast asleep. The captain came to him and said, "What are you doing asleep? Rise up, call upon your God! Perhaps God will be mindful of us so that we may not perish."

Then they said to one another, "Come, let us cast lots to find out on whose account we have met with this misfortune." So they cast lots, and thus singled out Jonah. "Tell us," they said, "what is your business? Where do you come from? What is your country, and to what people do you belong?" "I am a Hebrew," Jonah answered them; "I worship the Lord, the God of heaven, who made the sea and the dry land."

Now the men were seized with great fear and said to him, "How could you do such a thing!"—They knew that he was fleeing from the Lord, because he had told them.—"What shall we do with you," they asked, "that the sea may quiet down for us?" For the sea was growing more and more turbulent. Jonah said to them, "Pick me up and throw me into the sea, that it may quiet down for you; since I know it is because of me that this violent storm has come upon you."

Still the men rowed hard to regain the land, but they could not, for the sea grew ever more turbulent. Then they cried to the Lord: "We beseech you, O Lord, let us not perish for taking this man's life; do not charge us with shedding innocent blood, for you, Lord, have done as you saw fit." Then they took Jonah and threw him into the sea, and the sea's raging abated. Struck with great fear of the Lord, the men offered sacrifice and made vows to him.

But the Lord sent a large fish, that swallowed Jonah; and he remained in the belly of the fish three days and three nights. Then the Lord commanded the fish to spew Jonah upon the shore. ✛

Jonah 2:2-5, 8
R. You will rescue my life from the pit, O Lord.
From the belly of the fish Jonah said
this prayer to the Lord, his God: **R.**
Out of my distress I called to the Lord,
    and he answered me;

From the midst of the nether world I cried for help,
and you heard my voice. **R.**
For you cast me into the deep, into the heart of the sea,
and the flood enveloped me;
All your breakers and your billows
passed over me. **R.**
Then I said, "I am banished from your sight!
yet would I again look upon your holy temple." **R.**
When my soul fainted within me,
I remembered the Lord;
My prayer reached you
in your holy temple. **R.**

John 17:17
R. Alleluia, alleluia.
Your word, O Lord, is truth;
make us holy in the truth. **R.**

✝ *Luke 10:25-37*
Who is my neighbor?

On one occasion a lawyer stood up to pose to Jesus this problem: "Teacher, what must I do to inherit everlasting life?" Jesus answered him: "What is written in the law? How do you read it?" He replied:
"You shall love the Lord your God
with all your heart,
with all your soul,
with all your strength,
and with all your mind;
and your neighbor as yourself."
Jesus said, "You have answered correctly. Do this and you shall live." But because he wished to justify himself he said to Jesus, "And who is my neighbor?" Jesus replied: "There was a man going down from Jerusalem to Jericho who fell in with robbers. They stripped him, beat him, and then went off leaving him half-dead. A priest happened to be going down the same road; he saw him but continued on. Likewise there was a Levite who came the same way; he saw him and went on. But a Samaritan who was journeying along came on him and was moved to pity at the sight. He approached him and dressed his wounds, pouring in oil and wine. He then hoisted him on his

own beast and brought him to an inn, where he cared for him. The next day he took out two silver pieces and gave them to the innkeeper with the request: 'Look after him, and if there is any further expense I will repay you on my way back.'

"Which of these three, in your opinion, was neighbor to the man who fell in with the robbers?" The answer came, "The one who treated him with compassion." Jesus said to him, "Then go and do the same." ✢

TUESDAY, OCTOBER 9
WEEKDAY, ST. DENIS AND COMPANIONS, ST. JOHN LEONARDI

† *Jonah 3:1-10*
Nineveh was converted from its evil ways and was spared by the Lord.

The word of the Lord came to Jonah a second time: "Set out for the great city of Nineveh, and announce to it the message that I will tell you." So Jonah made ready and went to Nineveh, according to the Lord's bidding. Now Nineveh was an enormously large city; it took three days to go through it. Jonah began his journey through the city, and had gone but a single day's walk, announcing, "Forty days more and Nineveh shall be destroyed," when the people of Nineveh believed God; they proclaimed a fast and all of them, great and small, put on sackcloth.

When the news reached the king of Nineveh, he rose from his throne, laid aside his robe, covered himself with sackcloth, and sat in the ashes. Then he had this proclaimed throughout Nineveh, by decree of the king and his nobles: "Neither man nor beast, neither cattle nor sheep, shall taste anything; they shall not eat, nor shall they drink water. Man and beast shall be covered with sackcloth and call loudly to God; every man shall turn from his evil way and from the violence he has in hand. Who knows, God may relent and forgive, and withhold his blazing wrath, so that we shall not perish." When God saw by their actions how they turned from their evil way, he repented of the evil that he had threatened to do to them; he did not carry it out. ✢

Psalm 130:1-4, 7-8
**R. If you, O Lord, laid bare our guilt,
who could endure it?**

Out of the depths I cry to you, O Lord;
  Lord, hear my voice!
Let your ears be attentive
  to my voice in supplication. **R.**
If you, O Lord, mark iniquities,
  Lord, who can stand?
But with you is forgiveness,
  that you may be revered. **R.**
Let Israel wait for the Lord,
For with the Lord is kindness
  and with him is plenteous redemption;
And he will redeem Israel
  from all their iniquities. **R.**

John 17:17
R. Alleluia, alleluia.
Your word, O Lord, is truth;
make us holy in the truth. **R.**

✝ *Luke 10:38-42*
Martha took up the duties in the house. Mary chose the better part.

Jesus entered a village where a woman named Martha welcomed him to her home. She had a sister named Mary, who seated herself at the Lord's feet and listened to his words. Martha, who was busy with all the details of hospitality, came to him and said, "Lord, are you not concerned that my sister has left me all alone to do the household tasks? Tell her to help me"

The Lord in reply said to her: "Martha, Martha, you are anxious and upset about many things; one thing only is required. Mary has chosen the better portion and she shall not be deprived of it." ✝

WEDNESDAY, OCTOBER 10
WEEKDAY

✝ *Jonah 4:1-11*
*Jonah, you worry over a plant. Am I not to
feel sorry for the great city Nineveh?*

Jonah was greatly displeased and became angry that God did not carry out the evil he threatened [against Nineveh]. "I beseech you, Lord," he prayed, "is not this what I said while I was still in my own country? This is why I fled at first to Tarshish. I knew that you are a gracious and merciful God, slow to anger, rich in clemency, loathe to punish. And now, Lord, please take my life from me; for it is better for me to die than to live." But the Lord asked, "Have you reason to be angry?"

Jonah then left the city for a place to the east of it, where he built himself a hut and waited under it in the shade, to see what would happen to the city. And when the Lord God provided a gourd plant, that grew up over Jonah's head, giving shade that relieved him of any discomfort, Jonah was very happy over the plant. But the next morning at dawn God sent a worm which attacked the plant, so that it withered. And when the sun arose, God sent a burning east wind; and the sun beat upon Jonah's head till he became faint. Then he asked for death, saying, "I would be better off dead than alive."

But God said to Jonah, "Have you reason to be angry over the plant?" "I have reason to be angry," Jonah answered, "angry enough to die." Then the Lord said, "You are concerned over the plant which cost you no labor and which you did not raise; it came up in one night and in one night it perished. And should I not be concerned over Nineveh, the great city, in which there are more than a hundred and twenty thousand persons who cannot distinguish their right hand from their left, not to mention the many cattle?" ✛

Psalm 86:3-6, 9-10
R. Lord, you are tender and full of love.
You are my God; have pity on me, O Lord,
    for to you I call all the day.
Gladden the soul of your servant,
    for to you, O Lord, I lift up my soul. **R.**
For you, O Lord, are good and forgiving,
    abounding in kindness to all who call upon you.
Hearken, O Lord, to my prayer
    and attend to the sound of my pleading. **R.**
All the nations you have made shall come
    and worship you, O Lord,
    and glorify your name.
For you are great, and you do wondrous deeds;
    you alone are God. **R.**

John 17:17
R. Alleluia, alleluia.
Your word, O Lord, is truth;
make us holy in the truth. **R.**

✝ *Luke 11:1-4*
Lord, teach us to pray.

One day Jesus was praying in a certain place. When he had finished, one of his disciples asked him, "Lord, teach us to pray as John taught his disciples." He said to them, "When you pray, say:
'Father,
hallowed be your name,
your kingdom come.
Give us each day our daily bread.
Forgive us our sins,
for we too forgive all who do us wrong;
and subject us not to the trial.'" ✝

THURSDAY, OCTOBER 11
WEEKDAY

✝ *Malachi 3:13-20*
The day is coming now like a burning furnace.

You have defied me in word, says the Lord,
yet you ask, "What have we spoken against you?"
You have said, "It is vain to serve God,
and what do we profit by keeping his command,
And going about in penitential dress
in awe of the Lord of hosts?
Rather must we call the proud blessed;
for indeed evildoers prosper,
and even tempt God with impunity."
Then they who fear the Lord spoke with one another,
and the Lord listened attentively;
And a record book was written before him
of those who fear the Lord and trust in his name.
And they shall be mine, says the Lord of hosts,
my own special possession, on the day I take action.
And I will have compassion on them,

as a man has compassion on his son who serves him.
Then you will again see the distinction
   between the just and the wicked;
Between him who serves God,
   and him who does not serve him.
For lo, the day is coming, blazing like an oven,
   when all the proud and all evildoers will be stubble,
And the day that is coming will set them on fire,
   leaving them neither root nor branch,
   says the Lord of hosts.
But for you who fear my name, there will arise
   the sun of justice with its healing rays. ✛

Psalm 1:1-4, 6
R. Happy are they who hope in the Lord.
Happy the man who follows not
   the counsel of the wicked
Nor walks in the way of sinners,
   nor sits in the company of the insolent,
But delights in the law of the Lord
   and meditates on his law day and night. **R.**
He is like a tree
   planted near running water,
That yields its fruit in due season,
   and whose leaves never fade.
[Whatever he does, prospers.] **R.**
Not so the wicked, not so;
   they are like chaff which the wind drives away.
For the Lord watches over the way of the just,
   but the way of the wicked vanishes. **R.**

John 17:17
R. Alleluia, alleluia.
Your word, O Lord, is truth;
make us holy in the truth. **R.**

† *Luke 11:5-13*
Seek and it will be given to you.

Jesus said to his disciples: "If one of you knows someone who
comes to him in the middle of the night and says to him,
'Friend, lend me three loaves, for a friend of mine has come in

from a journey and I have nothing to offer him'; and he from inside should reply, 'Leave me alone. The door is shut now and my children and I are in bed. I can't get up to look after your needs'—I tell you, even though he does not get up and take care of the man because of friendship, he will find himself doing so because of his persistence and give him as much as he needs.

"So I say to you, 'Ask and you shall receive; seek and you shall find; knock and it shall be opened to you.'

"For whoever asks, receives; whoever seeks, finds; whoever knocks, is admitted. What father among you will give his son a snake if he asks for a fish, or hand him a scorpion if he asks for an egg? If you, with all your sins, know how to give your children good things, how much more will the heavenly Father give the Holy Spirit to those who ask him." ✛

FRIDAY, OCTOBER 12
WEEKDAY

† *Joel 1:13-15; 2:1-2*
The day of the Lord God is coming, a day of darkness and gloom.

Gird yourselves and weep, O priests!
    wail, O ministers of the altar!
Come, spend the night in sackcloth,
    O ministers of my God!
The house of your God is deprived
    of offering and libation.
Proclaim a fast,
    call an assembly;
Gather the elders,
    all who dwell in the land,
Into the house of the Lord, your God,
    and cry to the Lord!

Alas, the day!
    for near is the day of the Lord,
    and it comes as ruin from the Almighty.

Blow the trumpet in Zion,
    sound the alarm on my holy mountain!
Let all who dwell in the land tremble,
    for the day of the Lord is coming;

Yes, it is near, a day of darkness and of gloom,
   a day of clouds and somberness!
Like dawn spreading over the mountains,
   a people numerous and mighty!
Their like has not been from of old,
   nor will it be after them,
   even to the years of distant generations. ✛

Psalm 9:2-3, 6, 8-9, 16
R. The Lord will judge the world with justice.
I will give thanks to you, O Lord, with all my heart;
   I will declare all your wondrous deeds.
I will be glad and exult in you;
   I will sing praise to your name, Most High. **R.**
You rebuked the nations and destroyed the wicked;
   their names you blotted out forever and ever.
The nations are sunk in the pit they have made;
   in the snare they set, their foot is caught. **R.**
But the Lord sits enthroned forever;
   he has set up his throne for judgment.
He judges the world with justice;
   he governs the peoples with equity. **R.**

John 17:17
R. Alleluia, alleluia.
Your word, O Lord, is truth;
make us holy in the truth. **R.**

† Luke 11:15-26
*If by the finger of God I cast out devils, the
kingdom of God has overtaken you.*

As Jesus was casting out a devil, some of the crowd said, "It is by Beelzebul, the prince of devils, that he casts out devils." Others, to test him, were demanding of him a sign from heaven.

Because he knew their thoughts, he said to them: "Every kingdom divided against itself is laid waste. Any house torn by dissension falls. If Satan is divided against himself, how can his kingdom last?—since you say it is by Beelzebul that I cast out devils. If I cast out devils by Beelzebul, by whom do your people cast them out? In such a case, let them act as your judges. But if it is by the finger of God that I cast out devils, then the reign of God is upon you.

"When a strong man fully armed guards his courtyard, his possessions go undisturbed. But when someone stronger than he comes and overpowers him, such a one carries off the arms on which he was relying and divides the spoils. The man who is not with me is against me, and the man who does not gather with me scatters.

"When an unclean spirit has gone out of a man, it wanders through arid wastes, searching for a resting place; failing to find one, it says, 'I will go back where I came from.' It then returns, to find the house swept and tidied. Next it goes out and returns with seven other spirits far worse than itself, who enter in and dwell there. The result is that the last state of the man is worse than the first." ✝

SATURDAY, OCTOBER 13
WEEKDAY

✝ *Joel 4:12-21*
Put the sickle in because the harvest is ripe.

The Lord said:
Let the nations bestir themselves and come up
    to the Valley of Jehoshaphat;
For there will I sit in judgment
    upon all the neighboring nations.

Apply the sickle,
    for the harvest is ripe;
Come and tread,
    for the wine press is full;
The vats overflow,
    for great is their malice.
Crowd upon crowd
    in the valley of decision;
For near is the day of the Lord
    in the valley of decision.
Sun and moon are darkened,
    and the stars withhold their brightness.
The Lord roars from Zion,
    and from Jerusalem raises his voice;
The heavens and the earth quake,

but the Lord is a refuge to his people,
a stronghold to the men of Israel.

Then shall you know that I, the Lord, am your God,
dwelling on Zion, my holy mountain;
Jerusalem shall be holy,
and strangers shall pass through her no more.
And then, on that day,
the mountains shall drip new wine,
and the hills shall flow with milk;
And the channels of Judah
shall flow with water:
A fountain shall issue from the house of the Lord,
to water the Valley of Shittim.
Egypt shall be a waste,
and Edom a desert waste,
Because of violence done to the people of Judah,
because they shed innocent blood in their land.
But Judah shall abide forever,
and Jerusalem for all generations.
I will avenge their blood,
and not leave it unpunished.
The Lord dwells in Zion. ✝

Psalm 97:1-2, 5-6, 11-12
R. Let good men rejoice in the Lord.
The Lord is king; let the earth rejoice;
let the many isles be glad.
Clouds and darkness are round about him,
justice and judgment are the foundation of his throne. **R.**
The mountains melt like wax before the Lord,
before the Lord of all the earth.
The heavens proclaim his justice,
and all peoples see his glory. **R.**
Light dawns for the just;
and gladness, for the upright of heart.
Be glad in the Lord, you just,
and give thanks to his holy name. **R.**

John 17:17
R. Alleluia, alleluia.

Your word, O Lord, is truth;
make us holy in the truth. **R.**

✝ *Luke 11:27-28*

*Happy the womb that bore you! Happier still
are those who hear the word of God.*

While Jesus was speaking, a woman from the crowd called out, "Blest is the womb that bore you and the breasts that nursed you!" "Rather," he replied, "blest are they who hear the word of God and keep it." ✛

OCTOBER 14
TWENTY-EIGHTH SUNDAY IN ORDINARY TIME

✝ *2 Kings 5:14-17*
Naaman returned to the man of God and acknowledged the Lord.

Naaman went down and plunged into the Jordan seven times
    at the word of Elisha, the man of God.
His flesh became again like the flesh of a little child,
    and he was clean of his leprosy.

Naaman returned with his whole retinue to the man of God.
On his arrival he stood before Elisha and said,
    "Now I know that there is no God in all the earth,
    except in Israel.
Please accept a gift from your servant."

Elisha replied, "As the LORD lives whom I serve, I will not take
    it;"
    and despite Naaman's urging, he still refused.
Naaman said: "If you will not accept,
    please let me, your servant, have two mule-loads of earth,
    for I will no longer offer holocaust or sacrifice
    to any other god except to the LORD." ✛

Psalm 98:1-4
**R. The Lord has revealed
to the nations his saving power.**
Sing to the LORD a new song,
    for he has done wondrous deeds;
his right hand has won victory for him,
    his holy arm. **R.**

The Lord has made his salvation known:
    in the sight of the nations he has revealed his justice.
He has remembered his kindness and his faithfulness
    toward the house of Israel. **R.**
All the ends of the earth have seen
    the salvation by our God.
Sing joyfully to the Lord, all you lands:
    break into song; sing praise. **R.**

† 2 Timothy 2:8-13
If we persevere we shall also reign with Christ.

Beloved:

Remember Jesus Christ, raised from the dead, a descendant of
    David:
    such is my gospel, for which I am suffering,
    even to the point of chains, like a criminal.
But the word of God is not chained.
Therefore, I bear with everything for the sake of those who are
    chosen,
    so that they too may obtain the salvation that is in Christ
    Jesus,
    together with eternal glory.
This saying is trustworthy:
    If we have died with him
        we shall also live with him;
    if we persevere
        we shall also reign with him.
    But if we deny him
        he will deny us.
    If we are unfaithful
        he remains faithful,
        for he cannot deny himself. ✢

1 Thessalonians 5:18
R. Alleluia, alleluia.
In all circumstances, give thanks,
for this is the will of God for you in Christ Jesus. **R.**

† Luke 17:11-19
None but this foreigner has returned to give thanks to God.

As Jesus continued his journey to Jerusalem,
    he traveled through Samaria and Galilee.

As he was entering a village, ten lepers met him.
They stood at a distance from him and raised their voices,
    saying,
    "Jesus, Master! Have pity on us!"
And when he saw them, he said,
    "Go show yourselves to the priests."
As they were going they were cleansed.
And one of them, realizing he had been healed,
    returned, glorifying God in a loud voice;
    and he fell at the feet of Jesus and thanked him.
He was a Samaritan.
Jesus said in reply,
    "Ten were cleansed, were they not?
Where are the other nine?
Has none but this foreigner returned to give thanks to God?"
Then he said to him, "Stand up and go;
    your faith has saved you." ✛

MONDAY, OCTOBER 15
St. Teresa of Avila

† *Romans 1:1-7*
*Through Christ we received grace and our apostolic
mission to preach the obedience of faith to the gentiles.*

Greetings from Paul, a servant of Christ Jesus, called to be an apostle and set apart to proclaim the gospel of God which he promised long ago through his prophets, as the Holy Scriptures record—the gospel concerning his Son, who was descended from David according to the flesh but was made Son of God in power, according to the spirit of holiness, by his resurrection from the dead: Jesus Christ our Lord. Through him we have been favored with apostleship, that we may spread his name and bring to obedient faith all the Gentiles, among whom are you who have been called to belong to Jesus Christ.

    To all in Rome, beloved of God and called to holiness, grace and peace from God our Father and the Lord Jesus Christ. ✛

Psalm 98:1-4
R. The Lord has made known his salvation.
Sing to the Lord a new song,
    for he has done wondrous deeds;

His right hand has won victory for him,
his holy arm. **R.**
The Lord has made his salvation known:
in the sight of the nations he has revealed his justice.
He has remembered his kindness and his faithfulness
toward the house of Israel. **R.**
All the ends of the earth have seen
the salvation by our God.
Sing joyfully to the Lord, all you lands;
break into song; sing praise. **R.**

Psalm 130:5
R. Alleluia, alleluia.
I hope in the Lord,
I trust in his word. **R.**

† *Luke 11:29-32*
*No sign will be given to this generation
except the sign of Jonah the prophet.*

While the crowds pressed around him Jesus began to speak to them in these words: "This is an evil age. It seeks a sign. But no sign will be given it except the sign of Jonah. Just as Jonah was a sign for the Ninevites, so will the Son of Man be a sign for the present age. The queen of the south will rise at the judgment along with the men of this generation, and she will condemn them. She came from the farthest corner of the world to listen to the wisdom of Solomon, but you have a greater than Solomon here. At the judgment, the citizens of Nineveh will rise along with the present generation, and they will condemn it. For at the preaching of Jonah they reformed, but you have a greater than Jonah here. ✛

TUESDAY, OCTOBER 16
WEEKDAY, ST. HEDWIG, ST. MARGARET MARY ALACOQUE

† *Romans 1:16-25*
Men have known God, yet they refused to honor him.

I am not ashamed of the gospel. It is the power of God leading everyone who believes in it to salvation, the Jew first, then the Greek. For in the gospel is revealed the justice of God which begins and ends with faith; as Scripture says, "The just man shall live by faith."

The wrath of God is being revealed from heaven against the irreligious and perverse spirit of men who, in this perversity of theirs, hinder the truth. In fact, whatever can be known about God is clear to them; he himself made it so. Since the creation of the world, invisible realities, God's eternal power and divinity, have become visible, recognized through the things he has made. Therefore these men are inexcusable. They certainly had knowledge of God, yet they did not glorify him as God or give him thanks; they stultified themselves through speculating to no purpose, and their senseless hearts were darkened. They claimed to be wise, but turned into fools instead; they exchanged the glory of the immortal God for images representing mortal man, birds, beasts and snakes. In consequence, God delivered them up in their lusts to unclean practices; they engaged in the mutual degradation of their bodies, these men who exchanged the truth of God for a lie and worshiped and served the creature rather than the Creator—blessed be he forever, amen! ✛

Psalm 19:2-5
R. The heavens proclaim the glory of God.
The heavens declare the glory of God,
   and the firmament proclaims his handiwork.
Day pours out the word to day,
   and night to night imparts knowledge. **R.**
Not a word nor a discourse
   whose voice is not heard;
Through all the earth their voice resounds,
   and to the ends of the world, their message. **R.**

Psalm 130:5
R. Alleluia, alleluia.
I hope in the Lord,
I trust in his word. **R.**

† *Luke 11:37-41*
Give alms and everything will be made clean for you.

As Jesus was speaking, a Pharisee invited him to dine at his house. He entered and reclined at table. Seeing this, the Pharisee was surprised that he had not first performed the ablutions prescribed before eating. The Lord said to him: "You Pharisees! You cleanse the outside of cup and dish, but within you are filled with rapaciousness. Fools! Did not he who made the outside make the inside too? But if you give what you have as alms, all will be wiped clean for you." ✛

WEDNESDAY, OCTOBER 17
St. Ignatius of Antioch

† Romans 2:1-11
He will repay each one according to his works,
Jews first, but Greeks as well.

Every one of you who judges another is inexcusable. By your judgment you convict yourself, since you do the very same things. "We know that God's judgment on men who do such things is just." Do you suppose, then, that you will escape his judgment, you who condemn these things in others yet do them yourself? Or do you presume on his kindness and forbearance? Do you not know that God's kindness is an invitation to you to repent? In spite of this, your hard and impenitent heart is storing up retribution for that day of wrath when the just judgment of God will be revealed, when he will repay every man for what he has done: eternal life to those who strive for glory, honor, and immortality by patiently doing right; wrath and fury to those who selfishly disobey the truth and obey wickedness. Yes, affliction and anguish will come upon every man who has done evil, the Jew first, then the Greek. But there will be glory, honor, and peace for everyone who as done good, likewise the Jew first, then the Greek. With God there is no favoritism. ✛

Psalm 62:2-3, 6-7, 9
R. Lord, you give back to every man
according to his works.
Only in God is my soul at rest;
    from him comes my salvation.
He only is my rock and my salvation,
    my stronghold; I shall not be disturbed at all. **R.**
Only in God be at rest, my soul,
    for from him comes my hope.
He only is my rock and my salvation,

my stronghold; I shall not be disturbed. **R.**
Trust in him at all times, O my people!
    Pour out your hearts before him;
    God is our refuge! **R.**

Psalm 130:5
R. Alleluia, alleluia.
I hope in the Lord,
I trust in his word. **R.**

✝ *Luke 11:42-46*
Alas for you pharisees—and you lawyers, woe to you!

The Lord said: "Woe to you Pharisees! You pay tithes on mint
and rue and all the garden plants, while neglecting justice and
the love of God. These are the things you should practice,
without omitting the others. Woe to you Pharisees! You love
the front seats in synagogues and marks of respect in public.
Woe to you! You are like hidden tombs over which men walk
unawares."

In reply one of the lawyers said to him, "Teacher, in
speaking this way you insult us too." Jesus answered: "Woe to
you lawyers also! You lay impossible burdens on men but will
not lift a finger to lighten them." ✝

THURSDAY, OCTOBER 18
St. Luke

✝ *2 Timothy 4:9-17*
Luke alone is with me.

Do your best to join me soon, for Demas, enamored of the
present world, has left me and gone to Thessalonica. Crescens
has gone to Galatia and Titus to Dalmatia. I have no one with
me but Luke. Get Mark and bring him with you, for he can be
of great service to me. Tychicus I have sent to Ephesus. When
you come, bring the cloak I left in Troas with Carpus, and the
books, especially the parchments.

Alexander the coppersmith did me a great deal of harm;
the Lord will repay him according to his deeds. Meanwhile,
you too had better be on guard, for he has strongly resisted our
preaching. At the first hearing of my case in court, no one took
my part. In fact everyone abandoned me. May it not be held

against them! But the Lord stood by my side and gave me strength, so that through me the preaching task might be completed and all the nations might hear the gospel. ✢

Psalm 145:10-13, 17-18
R. Your friends tell the glory of your kingship, Lord.
Let all your works give you thanks, O Lord,
    and let your faithful ones bless you.
Let them discourse of the glory of your kingdom
    and speak of your might. **R.**
Making known to me your might
    and the glorious splendor of your kingdom.
Your kingdom is a kingdom for all ages,
    and your dominion endures through all generations. **R.**
The Lord is just in all his ways
    and holy in all his works.
The Lord is near to all who call upon him,
    to all who call upon him in truth. **R.**

John 15:16
R. Alleluia, alleluia.
I have chosen you from the world says the Lord,
to go and bear fruit that will last. **R.**

✝ *Luke 10:1-9*
The harvest is plentiful but the laborers are few.

The Lord appointed a further seventy-two and sent them in pairs before him to every town and place he intended to visit. He said to them: "The harvest is rich but the workers are few; therefore ask the harvest-master to send workers to his harvest. Be on your way, and remember: I am sending you as lambs in the midst of wolves. Do not carry a walking staff or traveling bag; wear no sandals and greet no one along the way. On entering any house, first say, 'Peace to this house.' If there is a peaceable man there, your peace will rest on him; if not, it will come back to you. Stay in the one house eating and drinking what they have, for the laborer is worth his wage. Do not move from house to house.

"Into whatever city you go, after they welcome you, eat what they set before you, and cure the sick there. Say to them, 'The reign of God is at hand.'" ✢

FRIDAY, OCTOBER 19
STS. ISAAC JOGUES, JOHN DE BREBEUF AND COMPANIONS

† *Romans 4:1-8*
Abraham believed in God, and his faith justified him.

What shall we say of Abraham our ancestor according to the flesh? Certainly if Abraham was justified by his deeds he has grounds for boasting, but not in God's view, for what does Scripture say? "Abraham believed God, and it was credited to him as justice." Now, when a man works, his wages are not regarded as a favor but as his due. But when a man does nothing, yet believes in him who justifies the sinful, his faith is credited as justice. Thus David congratulates the man to whom God credits justice without requiring deeds:

"Blest are they whose iniquities are forgiven,
   whose sins are covered over.
Blest is the man to whom the Lord imputes no guilt." ✤

Psalm 32:1-2, 5, 11
**R. I turn to you, Lord, in time of trouble,
and you fill me with the joy of salvation.**
Happy is he whose fault is taken away,
   whose sin is covered.
Happy the man to whom the Lord imputes not guilt,
   in whose spirit there is no guile. **R.**
Then I acknowledged my sin to you,
   my guilt I covered not.
I said, "I confess my faults to the Lord,"
   and you took away the guilt of my sin. **R.**
Be glad in the Lord and rejoice, you just;
   exult, all you upright of heart. **R.**

Psalm 130:5
R. Alleluia, alleluia.
I hope in the Lord,
I trust in his word. **R.**

† *Luke 12:1-7*
Every hair on your head has been numbered.

A crowd of thousands had gathered, so dense that they were treading on one another. Jesus began to speak first to his disciples: "Be on guard against the yeast of the Pharisees, which is hypocrisy. There is nothing concealed that will not be revealed, nothing hidden that will not be made known. Everything you have said in the dark will be heard in the daylight; what you have whispered in locked rooms will be proclaimed from the rooftops.

"I say to you who are my friends: Do not be afraid of those who kill the body and can do no more. I will show you whom you ought to fear. Fear him who has power to cast into Gehenna after he has killed. Yes, I tell you, fear him. Are not five sparrows sold for a few pennies? Yet not one of them is neglected by God. In very truth, even the hairs of your head are counted! Fear nothing, then. You are worth more than a flock of sparrows." ✝

SATURDAY, OCTOBER 20
WEEKDAY, ST. PAUL OF THE CROSS

† *Romans 4:13, 16-18*
In hope he believed against hope.

The promise made to Abraham and his descendants that they would inherit the world did not depend on the law; it was made in view of the justice that comes from faith. Hence all depends on faith, everything is a grace. Thus the promise holds true for all Abraham's descendants, not only for those who have the law but for all who have his faith. He is the father of us all, which is why Scripture says, "I have made you father of many nations." Yes, he is our father in the sight of God in whom he believed, the God who restores the dead to life and calls into being those things which had not been. Hoping against hope, Abraham believed and so became the father of many nations, just as it was once told him, "Numerous as this shall your descendants be." ✝

Psalm 105:6-9, 42-43

R. **The Lord remembers his covenant forever.**
(*or* **Alleluia.**)
You descendants of Abraham, his servants,
    sons of Jacob, his chosen ones!
He, the Lord, is our God;
    throughout the earth his judgments prevail. **R.**
He remembers forever his covenant

which he made binding for a thousand generations—
Which he entered into with Abraham
   and by his oath to Isaac. **R.**
For he remembered his holy word
   to his servant Abraham.
And he led forth his people with joy;
   with shouts of joy, his chosen ones. **R.**

Psalm 130:5
R. Alleluia, alleluia.
I hope in the Lord,
I trust in his word. **R.**

✝ *Luke 12:8-12*
When the time comes the Holy Spirit will teach you what you must say.

Jesus said to his disciples: "I tell you, whoever acknowledges me before men—the Son of Man will acknowledge him before the angels of God. But the man who has disowned me in the presence of men will be disowned in the presence of the angels of God. Anyone who speaks against the Son of Man will be forgiven, but whoever blasphemes the Holy Spirit will never be forgiven. When they bring you before synagogues, rulers and authorities, do not worry about how to defend yourselves or what to say. The Holy Spirit will teach you at that moment all that should be said." ✙

OCTOBER 21
TWENTY-NINTH SUNDAY IN ORDINARY TIME

✝ *Exodus 17:8-13*
As long as Moses kept his hands raised up,
Israel had the better of the fight.

In those days, Amalek came and waged war against Israel.
Moses, therefore, said to Joshua,
   "Pick out certain men,
   and tomorrow go out and engage Amalek in battle.
I will be standing on top of the hill
   with the staff of God in my hand."
So Joshua did as Moses told him:
   he engaged Amalek in battle
   after Moses had climbed to the top of the hill with Aaron

and Hur.
As long as Moses kept his hands raised up,
 Israel had the better of the fight,
 but when he let his hands rest,
 Amalek had the better of the fight.
Moses' hands, however, grew tired;
 so they put a rock in place for him to sit on.
Meanwhile Aaron and Hur supported his hands,
 one on one side and one on the other,
 so that his hands remained steady till sunset.
And Joshua mowed down Amalek and his people
 with the edge of the sword. ✛

Psalm 121:1-8

R. Our help is from the Lord,
who made heaven and earth.

I lift up my eyes toward the mountains;
 whence shall help come to me?
My help is from the Lord,
 who made heaven and earth. **R.**

May he not suffer your foot to slip;
 may he slumber not who guards you:
indeed he neither slumbers nor sleeps,
 the guardian of Israel. **R.**

The Lord is your guardian; the Lord is your shade;
 he is beside you at your right hand.
The sun shall not harm you by day,
 nor the moon by night. **R.**

The Lord will guard you from all evil;
 he will guard your life.
The Lord will guard your coming and your going,
 both now and forever. **R.**

† *2 Timothy 3:14-4:2*

One who belongs to God may be competent, equipped for every good work.

Beloved:
Remain faithful to what you have learned and believed,
 because you know from whom you learned it,
  and that from infancy you have known the sacred Scrip
   tures,
 which are capable of giving you wisdom for salvation

through faith in Christ Jesus.
All Scripture is inspired by God
and is useful for teaching, for refutation, for correction,
and for training in righteousness,
so that one who belongs to God may be competent,
equipped for every good work.

I charge you in the presence of God and of Christ Jesus,
who will judge the living and the dead,
and by his appearing and his kingly power:
proclaim the word;
be persistent whether it is convenient or inconvenient;
convince, reprimand, encourage through all patience and
teaching. ✛

Hebrews 4:12
R. Alleluia, alleluia.
The word of God is living and effective,
discerning reflections and thoughts of the heart. **R.**

† *Luke 18:1-8*
God will secure the rights of his chosen ones who call out to him.

Jesus told his disciples a parable
about the necessity for them to pray always without becom
ing weary.
He said, "There was a judge in a certain town
who neither feared God nor respected any human being.
And a widow in that town used to come to him and say,
'Render a just decision for me against my adversary.'
For a long time the judge was unwilling, but eventually he
thought,
'While it is true that I neither fear God nor respect any
human being,
because this widow keeps bothering me
I shall deliver a just decision for her
lest she finally come and strike me.'"
The Lord said, "Pay attention to what the dishonest judge says.
Will not God then secure the rights of his chosen ones
who call out to him day and night?
Will he be slow to answer them?
I tell you, he will see to it that justice is done for them speedily.

But when the Son of Man comes, will he find faith on earth?" ✛

MONDAY, OCTOBER 22
WEEKDAY

✝ *Romans 4:20-25*
It was written for us when it says that our faith in him will be counted.

Abraham never questioned or doubted God's promise; rather, he was strengthened in faith and gave glory to God, fully persuaded that God could do whatever he had promised. Thus his faith was credited to him as justice.

The words, "It was credited to him," were not written with him alone in view; they were intended for us too. For our faith will be credited to us also if we believe in him who raised Jesus our Lord from the dead, the Jesus who was handed over to death for our sins and raised up for our justification. ✛

Luke 1:69-75
**R. Blessed be the Lord God of Israel,
for he has visited his people.**
He has raised a horn of saving strength for us
in the house of David his servant,
As he promised through the mouths of his holy ones,
the prophets of ancient times. **R.**
Salvation from our enemies
and from the hands of all our foes.
He has dealt mercifully with our fathers
and remembered the holy covenant he made. **R.**
The oath he swore to Abraham our father he would grant us:
that, rid of fear and delivered from the enemy,
We should serve him devoutly and through all our days
be holy in his sight. **R.**

Psalm 119:35, 29
R. Alleluia, alleluia.
Turn my heart to do your will;
teach me your law, O God. **R.**

✝ *Luke 12:13-21*
What good are your possessions?

Someone in the crowd said to Jesus, "Teacher, tell my brother to give me my share of our inheritance." He replied, "Friend, who has set me up as your judge or arbiter?" Then he said to the crowd, "Avoid greed in all its forms. A man may be wealthy, but his possessions do not guarantee him life."

He told them a parable in these words: "There was a rich man who had a good harvest. 'What shall I do?' he asked himself. 'I have no place to store my harvest. I know!' he said. 'I will pull down my grain bins and build larger ones. All my grain and my goods will go there. Then I will say to myself: You have blessings in reserve for years to come. Relax! Eat heartily, drink well. Enjoy yourself.'

But God said to him, 'You fool! This very night your life shall be required of you. To whom will all this piled-up wealth of yours go?' That is the way it works with the man who grows rich for himself instead of growing rich in the sight of God." ✝

TUESDAY, OCTOBER 23
WEEKDAY, ST. JOHN OF CAPISTRANO

✝ *Romans 5:12,15,17-21*
*If death reigns from one man's sin, how much more
will those who receive the gift of grace reign.*

Just as through one man sin entered the world and with sin death, so death came to all men inasmuch as all sinned. For if by the offense of the one man, all died, much more did the grace of God and the gracious gift of the one man, Jesus Christ, abound for all. If death began its reign through one man because of his offense, much more shall those who receive the overflowing grace and gift of justice live and reign through the one man, Jesus Christ.

To sum up, then: just as a single offense brought condemnation to all men, a single righteous act brought all men acquittal and life. Just as through one man's disobedience all became sinners, so through one man's obedience all shall become just.

Despite the increase of sin, grace has far surpassed it, so that, as sin reigned through death, grace may reign by way of justice leading to eternal life, through Jesus Christ our Lord. ✝

Psalm 40:7-10, 17
**R. Here am I, Lord;
I come to do your will.**
Sacrifice or oblation you wished not,

but ears open to obedience you gave me.
Holocausts or sin-offerings you sought not;
then said I, "Behold I come." **R.**
"In the written scroll it is prescribed for me,
To do your will, O my God, is my delight,
and your law is within my heart!" **R.**
I announced your justice in the vast assembly;
I did not restrain my lips, as you, O Lord, know. **R.**
But may all who seek you
exult and be glad in you,
And may those who love your salvation
say ever, "The Lord be glorified." **R.**

Psalm 119:35, 29
R. Alleluia, alleluia.
Turn my heart to do your will;
teach me your law, O God. **R.**

† *Luke 12:35-38*
Happy those servants whom the master finds awake when he comes.

Jesus said to his disciples: "Let your belts be fastened around your waists and your lamps be burning ready. Be like men awaiting their master's return from a wedding, so that when he arrives and knocks, you will open for him without delay. It will go well with those servants whom the master finds wide-awake on his return. I tell you, he will put on an apron, seat them at table, and proceed to wait on them. Should he happen to come at midnight or before sunrise and find them prepared, it will go well with them." **+**

WEDNESDAY, OCTOBER 24
WEEKDAY, ST. ANTHONY MARY CLARET

† *Romans 6:12-18*
Offer yourselves to God as dead men brought back to life.

Do not, therefore, let sin rule your mortal body and make you obey its lusts; no more shall you offer the members of your body to sin as weapons for evil. Rather, offer yourselves to God as men who have come back from the dead to life, and your bodies to God as weapons for justice. Sin will no longer have power over you; you are now under grace, not under the law.

What does all this lead to? Just because we are not under the law but under grace, are we free to sin? By no means! You must realize that, when you offer yourselves to someone as obedient slaves, you are the slave of the one you obey, whether yours is the slavery of sin, which leads to death, or of obedience, which leads to justice. Thanks be to God, though once you were slaves of sin, you sincerely obeyed that rule of teaching which was imparted to you; freed from your sin, you became slaves of justice. ✝

Psalm 124:1-8
R. Our help is in the name of the Lord.
Had not the Lord been with us,
    let Israel say,
    had not the Lord been with us—
When men rose up against us,
    then would they have swallowed us alive.
When their fury was inflamed against us. **R.**
Then would the waters have overwhelmed us;
The torrent would have swept over us;
    over us then would have swept
    the raging waters.
Blessed be the Lord, who did not leave us
    a prey to their teeth. **R.**
We were rescued like a bird
    from the fowlers' snare;
Broken was the snare,
    and we were freed.
Our help is in the name of the Lord,
    who made heaven and earth. **R.**

Psalm 119:35, 29
R. Alleluia, alleluia.
Turn my heart to do your will;
teach me your law, O God. **R.**

† *Luke 12:39-48*
From the man who has received much, much will be demanded.

Jesus said to his disciples: "You know as well as I that if the head of the house knew when the thief was coming he would not let him break into his house. Be on guard, therefore. The

Son of Man will come when you least expect him."

Peter said, "Do you intend this parable for us, Lord, or do you mean it for the whole world?" The Lord said, "Who in your opinion is that faithful, farsighted steward whom the master will set over his servants to dispense their ration of grain in season? That servant is fortunate whom his master finds busy when he returns. Assuredly, his master will put him in charge of all his property. But if the servant says to himself, 'My master is taking his time about coming,' and begins to abuse the housemen and servant girls, to eat and drink and get drunk, that servant's master will come back on a day when he does not expect him, at a time he does not know. He will punish him severely and rank him among those undeserving of trust. The slave who knew his master's wishes but did not prepare to fulfill them will get a severe beating, whereas the one who did not know them and who nonetheless deserved to be flogged will get off with fewer stripes. When much has been given a man, much will be required of him. More will be asked of a man to whom more has been entrusted." ✢

THURSDAY, OCTOBER 25
WEEKDAY

† *Romans 6:19-23*
Now that you have been freed from sin, you have been made slaves of God.

I use the following example from human affairs because of your weak human nature. Just as formerly you enslaved your bodies to impurity and licentiousness for their degradation, make them now the servants of justice for their sanctification. When you were slaves of sin, you had freedom from justice. What benefit did you then enjoy? Things you are now ashamed of, all of them tending toward death. But now that you are freed from sin and have become slaves of God, your benefit is sanctification as you tend toward eternal life. The wages of sin is death, but the gift of God is eternal life in Christ Jesus our Lord. ✢

Psalm 1:1-4, 6
R. **Happy are they who hope in the Lord.**
Happy the man who follows not
    the counsel of the wicked
Nor walks in the way of sinners,

nor sits in the company of the insolent,
But delights in the law of the Lord
and meditates on his law day and night. **R.**
He is like a tree
planted near running water,
That yields its fruit in due season,
and whose leaves never fade.
[Whatever he does, prospers.] **R.**
Not so the wicked, not so;
they are like chaff which the wind drives away.
For the Lord watches over the way of the just,
but the way of the wicked vanishes. **R.**

Psalm 119:35, 29
R. Alleluia, alleluia.
Turn my heart to do your will;
teach me your law, O God. **R.**

† *Luke 12:49-53*
I have not come to bring peace, but separation.

Jesus said to his disciples: "I have come to light a fire on the earth. How I wish the blaze were ignited! I have a baptism to receive. What anguish I feel till it is over! Do you think I have come to establish peace on the earth? I assure you, the contrary is true; I have come for division. From now on, a household of five will be divided three against two and two against three; father will be split against son and son against father, mother against daughter and daughter against mother, mother-in- law against daughter-in-law, daughter-in-law against mother-in-law." ✛

FRIDAY, OCTOBER 26
WEEKDAY

† *Romans 7:18-25*
Who will rescue me from this body of death?

I know that no good dwells in me, that is, in my flesh; the desire to do right is there but not the power. What happens is that I do, not the good I will to do, but the evil I do not intend. But if I do what is against my will, it is not I who do it, but sin which dwells in me. This means that even though I want to do what is right, a law that leads to wrongdoing is always ready to hand. My inner self agrees with the law of God, but I see in my body's members another law at war with the law of my mind; this makes me the prisoner of the law of sin in my members. What a wretched man I am! Who can free me from this body under the power of death? All praise to God, through Jesus Christ our Lord. ✛

Psalm 119:66, 68, 76-77, 93-94
R. Teach me your laws, O Lord.
Teach me wisdom and knowledge,
    for in your commands I trust. **R.**
You are good and bountiful;
    teach me your statutes. **R.**
Let your kindness comfort me
    according to your promise to your servants. **R.**
Let your compassion come to me that I may live,
    for your law is my delight. **R.**
Never will I forget your precepts,
    for through them you give me life. **R.**
I am yours; save me,
    for I have sought your precepts. **R.**

Psalm 119:35, 29
R. Alleluia, alleluia.
Turn my heart to do your will;
teach me your law, O God. **R.**

† *Luke 12:54-59*
*You know how to interpret the face of the earth and
the sky. How is it you do not know how to interpret these times?*

Jesus said to the crowds: "When you see a cloud rising in the west, you say immediately that rain is coming — and so it does. When the wind blows from the south, you say it is going to be hot — and so it is. You hypocrites! If you can interpret the portents of earth and sky, why can you not interpret the present time? Tell me, why do you not judge for yourselves what is just? When you are going with your opponent to appear before a magistrate, try to settle with him on the way lest he turn you over to the judge, and the judge deliver you up to the jailer, and the jailer throw you into prison. I warn you, you will not be released from there until you have paid the last penny." ✛

SATURDAY, OCTOBER 27
WEEKDAY

† *Romans 8:1-11*
The Spirit of him who raised Jesus from the dead lives in you.

There is no condemnation now for those who are in Christ Jesus. The law of the spirit, the spirit of life in Christ Jesus, has freed you from the law of sin and death. The law was powerless because of its weakening by the flesh. Then God sent his Son in the likeness of sinful flesh as a sin offering, thereby condemning sin in the flesh, so that the just demands of the law might be fulfilled in us who live, not according to the flesh, but according to the spirit. Those who live according to the flesh are intent on the things of the flesh, those who live according to the spirit, on those of the spirit. The tendency of the flesh is toward death but that of the spirit toward life and peace. The flesh in its tendency is at enmity with God; it is not subject to God's law. Indeed, it cannot be; those who are in the flesh cannot please God. But you are not in the flesh; you are in the spirit, since the Spirit of God dwells in you. If anyone does not have the Spirit of Christ, he does not belong to Christ. If Christ is in you, the body is indeed dead because of sin, while the spirit lives because of justice. If the Spirit of him who raised Jesus from the dead dwells in you, then he who raised Christ from the dead will bring your mortal bodies to life also through his Spirit dwelling in you. ✛

Psalm 24:1-6
R. Lord, this is the people that longs to see your face.
The Lord's are the earth and its fullness;
    the world and those who dwell in it.
For he founded it upon the seas
    and established it upon the rivers. **R.**
Who can ascend the mountain of the Lord?
    or who may stand in his holy place?
He whose hands are sinless, whose heart is clean,
    who desires not what is vain. **R.**
He shall receive a blessing from the Lord,
    a reward from God his savior.

Such is the race that seeks for him,
    that seeks the face of the God of Jacob. **R.**

Psalm 119:35, 29
R. Alleluia, alleluia.
Turn my heart to do your will;
teach me your law, O God. **R.**

† *Luke 13:1-9*
Unless you repent, you will all perish as they did.

Persons were present who told Jesus about the Galileans whose blood Pilate had mixed with their sacrifices. He said in reply: "Do you think that these Galileans were the greatest sinners in Galilee just because they suffered this? By no means! But I tell you, you will all come to the same end unless you reform. Or take those eighteen who were killed by a falling tower in Siloam. Do you think they were more guilty than anyone else who lived in Jerusalem? Certainly not! But I tell you, you will all come to the same end unless you reform."

Jesus spoke this parable: "A man had a fig tree growing in his vineyard, and he came out looking for fruit on it but did not find any. He said to the vinedresser, 'Look here! For three years now I have come in search of fruit on this fig tree and found none. Cut it down. Why should it clutter up the ground?' In answer, the man said, 'Sir, leave it another year, while I hoe around it and manure it; then perhaps it will bear fruit. If not, it shall be cut down.'" ✛

OCTOBER 28
THIRTIETH SUNDAY IN ORDINARY TIME

† *Sirach 35:12-14,16-18*
The prayer of the lowly pierces the clouds.

The LORD is a God of justice,
    who knows no favorites.
Though not unduly partial toward the weak,
    yet he hears the cry of the oppressed.
The Lord is not deaf to the wail of the orphan,
    nor to the widow when she pours out her complaint.
The one who serves God willingly is heard;

his petition reaches the heavens.
The prayer of the lowly pierces the clouds;
it does not rest till it reaches its goal,
nor will it withdraw till the Most High responds,
judges justly and affirms the right,
and the Lord will not delay. ✝

Psalm 34:2-3, 17-19, 23
R. The Lord hears the cry of the poor.
I will bless the LORD at all times;
his praise shall be ever in my mouth.
Let my soul glory in the LORD;
the lowly will hear me and be glad. **R.**
The LORD confronts the evildoers,
to destroy remembrance of them from the earth.
When the just cry out, the LORD hears them,
and from all their distress he rescues them. **R.**
The LORD is close to the brokenhearted;
and those who are crushed in spirit he saves.
The LORD redeems the lives of his servants;
no one incurs guilt who takes refuge in him. **R.**

✝ 2 Timothy 4:6-8,16-18
From now on, the crown of righteousness awaits me.

Beloved:
I am already being poured out like a libation,
and the time of my departure is at hand.
I have competed well; I have finished the race;
I have kept the faith.
From now on the crown of righteousness awaits me,
which the Lord, the just judge,
will award to me on that day, and not only to me,
but to all who have longed for his appearance.

At my first defense no one appeared on my behalf,
but everyone deserted me.
May it not be held against them!
But the Lord stood by me and gave me strength,
so that through me the proclamation might be completed
and all the Gentiles might hear it.
And I was rescued from the lion's mouth.

The Lord will rescue me from every evil threat
    and will bring me safe to his heavenly kingdom.
To him be glory forever and ever. Amen. ✛

2 Corinthians 5:19
R. Alleluia, alleluia.
God was reconciling the world to himself in Christ,
and entrusting to us the message of salvation. **R.**

† *Luke 18:9-14*
The tax collector, not the Pharisee, went home justified.

Jesus addressed this parable
    to those who were convinced of their own righteousness
    and despised everyone else.
"Two people went up to the temple area to pray;
    one was a Pharisee and the other was a tax collector.
The Pharisee took up his position and spoke this prayer to
        himself,
    'O God, I thank you that I am not like the rest of humanity—
    greedy, dishonest, adulterous—or even like this tax collec
        tor.
I fast twice a week, and I pay tithes on my whole income.'
But the tax collector stood off at a distance
    and would not even raise his eyes to heaven
    but beat his breast and prayed,
    'O God, be merciful to me a sinner.'
I tell you, the latter went home justified, not the former;
    for whoever exalts himself will be humbled,
    and the one who humbles himself will be exalted." ✛

MONDAY, OCTOBER 29
WEEKDAY

† *Romans 8:12-17*
The Spirit you received is the spirit of
sons and it makes us cry out: Abba, Father.

We are debtors, then, my brothers—but not to the flesh, so
that we should live according to the flesh. If you live according
to the flesh, you will die; but if by the spirit you put to death
the evil deeds of the body, you will live.

    All who are led by the Spirit of God are sons of God. You did not receive a spirit of slavery leading you back into fear, but a spirit of adoption through which we cry out, "Abba!" (that is, "Father"). The Spirit himself gives witness with our spirit that we are children of God. But if we are children, we are heirs as well: heirs of God, heirs with Christ, if only we suffer with him so as to be glorified with him. ✝

Psalm 68:2, 4, 6-7, 20-21
R. Our God is the God of salvation.
God arises; his enemies are scattered,
    and those who hate him flee before him.
But the just rejoice and exult before God;
    they are glad and rejoice. **R.**
The father of orphans and the defender of widows
    is God in his holy dwelling.
God gives a home to the forsaken;
    he leads forth prisoners to prosperity. **R.**
Blessed day by day be the Lord,
    who bears our burdens; God, who is our salvation.
God is a saving God for us;
    the Lord, my Lord, controls the passageways of death. **R.**

James 1:21
R. Alleluia, alleluia.
Receive and submit to the word planted in you;
it can save your souls. **R.**

† Luke 13:10-17
*This daughter of Abraham, was it
not right to untie her on the sabbath day?*

On a sabbath day Jesus was teaching in one of the synagogues. There was a woman there who for eighteen years had been possessed by a spirit which drained her strength. She was badly stooped—quite incapable of standing erect. When Jesus saw her, he called her to him and said, "Woman, you are free of your infirmity." He laid his hand on her, and immediately she stood up straight and began thanking God.

The chief of the synagogue, indignant that Jesus should have healed on the sabbath, said to the congregation, "There are six days for working. Come on those days to be cured, not on the sabbath." The Lord said in reply, "O you hypocrites! Which of you does not let his ox or ass out of the stall on the sabbath to water it? Should not this daughter of Abraham here who has been in the bondage of Satan for eighteen years have been released from her shackles on the sabbath?" At these words, his opponents were covered with confusion; meanwhile, everyone else rejoiced at the marvels Jesus was accomplishing. ✠

TUESDAY, OCTOBER 30
WEEKDAY

† *Romans 8:18-25*
The whole creation is eagerly waiting for God to reveal his sons.

I consider the sufferings of the present to be as nothing compared with the glory to be revealed in us. Indeed, the whole created world eagerly awaits the revelation of the sons of God. Creation was made subject to futility, not of its own accord but by him who once subjected it; yet not without hope, because the world itself will be freed from its slavery to corruption and share in the glorious freedom of the children of God. Yes, we know that all creation groans and is in agony even until now. Not only that, but we ourselves, although we have the Spirit as first fruits, groan inwardly while we await the redemption of our bodies. In hope we were saved. But hope is not hope if its object is seen; how is it possible for one to hope for what he sees? And hoping for what we cannot see means awaiting it with patient endurance. ✠

Psalm 126:1-6
R. The Lord has done marvels for us.
When the Lord brought back the captives of Zion,
    we were like men dreaming.
Then our mouth was filled with laughter,
    and our tongue with rejoicing. **R.**
Then they said among the nations,
    "The Lord has done great things for them."
The Lord has done great things for us;
    we are glad indeed. **R.**
Restore our fortunes, O Lord,
    like the torrents in the southern desert.
Those that sow in tears

shall reap rejoicing. **R.**
Although they go forth weeping,
   carrying the seed to be sown,
They shall come back rejoicing,
   carrying their sheaves. **R.**

James 1:21
R. Alleluia, alleluia.
Receive and submit to the word planted in you;
it can save your souls. **R.**

✝ *Luke 13:18-21*
The seed grew and became a mighty tree.

Jesus said: "What does the reign of God resemble? To what shall I liken it? It is like mustard seed which a man took and planted in his garden. It grew and became a large shrub and the birds of the air nested in its branches."

He went on: "To what shall I compare the reign of God? It is like yeast which a woman took to knead into three measures of flour until the whole mass of dough began to rise." ✛

WEDNESDAY, OCTOBER 31
WEEKDAY

✝ *Romans 8:26-30*
All things work to the good for those who love God.

The Spirit too helps us in our weakness, for we do not know how to pray as we ought; but the Spirit himself makes intercessions for us with groanings which cannot be expressed in speech. He who searches hearts knows what the Spirit means, for the Spirit intercedes for the saints as God himself wills.

We know that God makes all things work together for the good of those who have been called according to his decree. Those whom he foreknew he predestined to share the image of his Son, that the Son might be the first-born of many brothers. Those he predestined he likewise called; those he called he also justified; and those he justified he in turn glorified. ✛

Psalm 13:4-6
**R. All my hope, O Lord,
is in your loving kindness.**

Look, answer me, O Lord, my God!
　Give light to my eyes that I may not sleep in death
Lest my enemy say, "I have overcome him";
　　lest my foes rejoice at my downfall. **R.**
Though I trusted in your kindness,
　　let my heart rejoice in your salvation;
　　let me sing of the Lord, "He has been good to me." **R.**

James 1:21
R. Alleluia, alleluia.
Receive and submit to the word planted in you;
it can save your souls. **R.**

† *Luke 13:22-30*
*Men from east and west will take their places
at the feast in the kingdom of God.*

Jesus went through cities and towns teaching—all the while
making his way toward Jerusalem. Someone asked him, "Lord,
are they few in number who are to be saved?" He replied: "Try
to come in through the narrow door. Many, I tell you, will try
to enter and be unable. When once the master of the house has
risen to lock the door and you stand outside knocking and
saying, 'Sir, open for us,' he will say in reply, 'I do not know
where you come from.' Then you will begin to say, 'We ate and
drank in your company. You taught in our streets.' But he will
answer, 'I tell you, I do not know where you come from. Away
from me, you evildoers!'

　"There will be wailing and grinding of teeth when you see
Abraham, Isaac, Jacob, and all the prophets safe in the kingdom of God, and you yourselves rejected. People will come from
the east and the west, from the north and the south, and will
take their place at the feast in the kingdom of God. Some who
are last will be first and some who are first will be last." ✛

THURSDAY, NOVEMBER 1
ALL SAINTS

† *Revelation 7:2-4, 9-14*
*I had a vision of a great multitude, which no one
could count, from every nation, race, people and tongue.*

I, John, saw another angel come up from the East,

holding the seal of the living God.
He cried out in a loud voice to the four angels
    who were given power to damage the land and the sea,
    "Do not damage the land or the sea or the trees
    until we put the seal on the foreheads of the servants of our
        God."
I heard the number of those who had been marked with the seal,
    one hundred and forty-four thousand marked
    from every tribe of the Israelites.

After this I had a vision of a great multitude,
    which no one could count,
    from every nation, race, people, and tongue.
They stood before the throne and before the Lamb,
    wearing white robes and holding palm branches in their
        hands.
They cried out in a loud voice:
    "Salvation comes from our God,
        who is seated on the throne,
    and from the Lamb."
All the angels stood around the throne
    and around the elders and the four living creatures.
They prostrated themselves before the throne,
    worshiped God, and exclaimed:
    "Amen. Blessing and glory, wisdom and thanksgiving,
        honor, power, and might
        be to our God forever and ever. Amen."
Then one of the elders spoke up and said to me,
    "Who are these wearing white robes, and where did they
        come from?"
I said to him, "My lord, you are the one who knows."
He said to me,
    "These are the ones who have survived the time of great
        distress;
    they have washed their robes
    and made them white in the blood of the Lamb." ✛

Psalm 24:1-6
R. Lord, this is the people that longs to see your face.
The LORD's are the earth and its fullness;
    the world and those who dwell in it.

For he founded it upon the seas
>and established it upon the rivers. **R.**
Who can ascend the mountain of the LORD?
>or who may stand in his holy place?
One whose hands are sinless, whose heart is clean,
>who desires not what is vain. **R.**
He shall receive a blessing from the LORD,
>a reward from God his savior.
Such is the race that seeks for him,
>that seeks the face of the God of Jacob. **R.**

† 1 John 3:1-3
We shall see God as he is.

Beloved:
See what love the Father has bestowed on us
>that we may be called the children of God.
Yet so we are.
The reason the world does not know us
>is that it did not know him.
Beloved, we are God's children now;
>what we shall be has not yet been revealed.
We do know that when it is revealed we shall be like him,
>for we shall see him as he is.
Everyone who has this hope based on him makes himself pure,
>as he is pure. ✛

Matthew 11:28
R. Alleluia, alleluia.
Come to me, all you who labor and are burdened
and I will give you rest, says the Lord. **R.**

† Matthew 5:1-12a
Rejoice and be glad, for your reward will be great in heaven.

When Jesus saw the crowds, he went up the mountain,
>and after he had sat down, his disciples came to him.
He began to teach them, saying:
>"Blessed are the poor in spirit,
>>for theirs is the kingdom of heaven.
>Blessed are they who mourn,
>>for they will be comforted.

Blessed are the meek,
  for they will inherit the land.
Blessed are they who hunger and thirst for righteousness,
  for they will be satisfied.
Blessed are the merciful,
  for they will be shown mercy.
Blessed are the clean of heart,
  for they will see God.
Blessed are the peacemakers,
  for they will be called children of God.
Blessed are they who are persecuted for the sake of
    righteousness,
  for theirs is the kingdom of heaven.
Blessed are you when they insult you and persecute you
  and utter every kind of evil against you falsely because
    of me.
Rejoice and be glad,
  for your reward will be great in heaven." ✛

FRIDAY, NOVEMBER 2
ALL SOULS

(Other readings from Masses for the Dead: Job 19:1, 23-27 • Lamentations 3:17-26 • Wisdom 4:7-14 • Isaiah 25:6-9 • 2 Maccabees 12:43-46 • Daniel 12:1-3 • Romans 5:17-21 • Romans 8:31-35 • Romans 14:7-12 • Psalm 23:1-6 • Psalm 25:6-7, 17-18, 20-21 • Psalms 42:2-3, 5; 43:3-5 • Matthew 5:1-12 • Matthew 25:1-13 • Matthew 25:31-46)

✝ _Wisdom 3:1-9_ _(or Wisdom 3:1-6, 9)_
As sacrificial offerings he took them to himself.

The souls of the just are in the hand of God,
  and no torment shall touch them.
They seemed, in the view of the foolish, to be dead;
  and their passing away was thought an affliction
  and their going forth from us, utter destruction.
But they are in peace.
For if in the sight of others, indeed they be punished,
  yet is their hope full of immortality;
chastised a little, they shall be greatly blessed,
  because God tried them
  and found them worthy of himself.
As gold in the furnace, he proved them,

and as sacrificial offerings he took them to himself.
In the time of their visitation they shall shine,
  and shall dart about as sparks through stubble;
they shall judge nations and rule over peoples,
  and the LORD shall be their King forever.
Those who trust in him shall understand truth,
  and the faithful shall abide with him in love:
because grace and mercy are with his holy ones,
  and his care is with his elect. ✢

Psalm 27:1, 4, 7, 8b, 9a, 13-14
R. The Lord is my light and my salvation.
(or **R. I believe that I shall see the good things of the Lord in the land of the living.**)
The LORD is my light and my salvation;
  whom should I fear?
The LORD is my life's refuge;
  of whom should I afraid? **R.**
One thing I ask of the LORD;
  this I seek:
to dwell in the house of the LORD
  all the days of my life,
that I may gaze on the loveliness of the LORD
  and contemplate his temple. **R.**
Hear, O LORD, the sound of my call;
  have pity on me and answer me.
Your presence, O LORD, I seek!
  Hide not your face from me. **R.**
I believe I shall see the bounty of the LORD
  in the land of the living.
Wait for the LORD with courage;
  be stouthearted and wait for the LORD! **R.**

† *Romans 6:3-9*
Let us walk in newness of life.

Are you unaware that we who were baptized into Christ Jesus
  were baptized into his death?
We were indeed buried with him through baptism into death,
  so that, just as Christ was raised from the dead
  by the glory of the Father,
  we too might live in newness of life

For if we have grown into union with him through a death like
  his,
  we shall also be united with him in the resurrection.
We know that our old self was crucified with him,
  so that our sinful body might be hone away with,
  that we might no longer be in slavery to sin.
For a dead person has been absolved from sin.
If, then, we have died with Christ,
  we believe that we shall also live with him.
We know that Christ, raised from the dead, dies no more;
  death no longer has power over him. ✛

Matthew 25:34
R. Alleluia, alleluia.
Come, you who are blessed by my Father;
inherit the kingdom prepared for you
from the foundation of the world. **R.**

†*Matthew 11:25-30*
Come to me . . . and I will give you rest.

At that time Jesus exclaimed:
  "I give praise to you, Father, Lord of heaven and earth,
  for although you have hidden these things
  from the wise and the learned
  you have revealed them to little ones.
Yes, Father, such has been your gracious will.
All things have been handed over to me by my Father.
No one knows the Son except the Father,
  and no one knows the Father except the Son
  and anyone to whom the Son wishes to reveal him."

"Come to me, all you who labor and are burdened,
  and I will give you rest.
Take my yoke upon you and learn from me,
  for I am meek and humble of heart;
  and you will find rest for yourselves.
For my yoke is easy, and my burden light." ✛

SATURDAY, NOVEMBER 3
WEEKDAY, ST. MARTIN DE PORRES

† *Romans 11:1-2, 11-12, 25-29*
*If the loss of the Jews brings reconciliation to the world,
what can we assume but that life comes from death?*

I ask, then, has God rejected his people? Of course not! I myself am an Israelite, descended from Abraham, of the tribe of Benjamin. No, God has not rejected his people whom he foreknew.

I further ask, does their stumbling mean that they are forever fallen? Not at all! Rather, by their transgressions salvation has come to the Gentiles to stir Israel to envy. But if their transgression and their diminishing have meant riches for the Gentile world, how much more their full number!

Brothers, I do not want you to be ignorant of this mystery lest you be conceited: blindness has come upon part of Israel until the full number of Gentiles enter in, and then all Israel will be saved. As Scripture says: "Out of Zion will come the deliverer who shall remove all impiety from Jacob; and this is the covenant I will make with them when I take away their sins." In respect to the gospel, the Jews are enemies of God for your sake; in respect to the election, they are beloved by him because of the patriarchs. God's gifts and his call are irrevocable. ✛

Psalm 94:12-15, 17-18
R. The Lord will not abandon his people.
Happy the man whom you instruct, O Lord,
   whom by your law you teach,
Giving him rest from evil days. **R.**
For the Lord will not cast off his people,
   nor abandon his inheritance;
But judgment shall again be with justice,
   and all the upright of heart shall follow it. **R.**
Were not the Lord my help,
   I would soon dwell in the silent grave.
When I say, "My foot is slipping,"
   your kindness, O Lord, sustains me. **R.**

James 1:21
R. Alleluia, alleluia.
Receive and submit to the word planted in you;
it can save your souls. **R.**

✝ *Luke 14:1, 7-11*
*Everyone who exalts himself will be humbled,
and the man who humbles himself will be exalted.*

When Jesus came on a sabbath to eat a meal in the house of one of the leading Pharisees, they observed him closely. He went on to address a parable to the guests, noticing how they were trying to get the places of honor at the table: "When you are invited by someone to a wedding party, do not sit in the place of honor in case some greater dignitary has been invited. Then the host might come and say to you, 'Make room for this man,' and you would have to proceed shamefacedly to the lowest place. What you should do when you have been invited is go and sit in the lowest place, so that when your host approaches you he will say, 'My friend, come up higher.' This will win you the esteem of your fellow guests. For everyone who exalts himself shall be humbled, and he who humbles himself shall be exalted." ✝

NOVEMBER 4
THIRTY-FIRST SUNDAY IN ORDINARY TIME

✝ *Wisdom 11:22—12:2*
You have mercy on all because you love all things that are.

Before the LORD the whole universe is as a grain from a
    balance
    or a drop of morning dew come down upon the earth.
But you have mercy on all, because you can do all things;
    and you overlook people's sins that they may repent.
For you love all things that are
    and loathe nothing that you have made;
    for what you hated, you would not have fashioned.
And how could a thing remain, unless you willed it;
    or be preserved, had it not been called forth by you?
But you spare all things, because they are yours,
    O LORD and lover of souls,
    for your imperishable spirit is in all things!

Therefore you rebuke offenders little by little,
  warn them and remind them of the sins
    they are committing,
  that they may abandon their wickedness
  and believe in you, O LORD! ✛

Psalm 145:1-2, 8-11,13-14
**R. I will praise your name forever,
  my king and my God.**
I will extol you, O my God and King,
  and I will bless your name forever and ever.
Every day will I bless you,
  and I will praise your name forever and ever. **R.**
The LORD is gracious and merciful,
  slow to anger and of great kindness.
The LORD is good to all
  and compassionate toward all his works. **R.**
Let all your works give you thanks, O LORD,
  and let your faithful ones bless you.
Let them discourse of the glory of your kingdom
  and speak of your might. **R.**
The LORD is faithful in all his words
  and holy in all his works.
The LORD lifts up all who are falling
  and raises up all who are bowed down. **R.**

† *2 Thessalonians 1:11—2:2*
May the name of Christ be glorified in you and you in him.

Brothers and sisters:
We always pray for you,
  that our God may make you worthy of his calling
  and powerfully bring to fulfillment every good purpose
  and every effort of faith,
  that the name of our Lord Jesus may be glorified in you,
  and you in him,
  in accord with the grace of our God and Lord Jesus Christ.

We ask you, brothers and sisters,
  with regard to the coming of our Lord Jesus Christ
  and our assembling with him,
  not to be shaken out of your minds suddenly, or to be alarmed

either by a "spirit, " or by an oral statement,
or by a letter allegedly from us
to the effect that the day of the Lord is at hand. ✛

John 3:16
R. Alleluia, alleluia.
God so loved the world that he gave his only Son,
so that everyone who believes in him might have eternal life. **R.**

† *Luke 19:1-10*
The Son of Man has come to seek and to save what was lost.

At that time, Jesus came to Jericho and intended to pass
through the town.
Now a man there named Zacchaeus,
who was a chief tax collector and also a wealthy man,
was seeking to see who Jesus was;
but he could not see him because of the crowd,
for he was short in stature.
So he ran ahead and climbed a sycamore tree
in order to see Jesus,
who was about to pass that way.
When he reached the place, Jesus looked up and said,
"Zacchaeus, come down quickly,
for today I must stay at your house."
And he came down quickly and received him with joy.
When they all saw this, they began to grumble, saying,
"He has gone to stay at the house of a sinner."
But Zacchaeus stood there and said to the Lord,
"Behold, half of my possessions, Lord, I shall give to the
poor,
and if I have extorted anything from anyone
I shall repay it four times over."
And Jesus said to him,
"Today salvation has come to this house
because this man too is a descendant of Abraham.
For the Son of Man has come to seek
and to save what was lost." ✛

MONDAY, NOVEMBER 5
WEEKDAY

† *Romans 11:29-36*
God has consigned all men to disobedience only to show mercy to them.

God's gifts and his call are irrevocable. Just as you were once disobedient to God and now have received mercy through their disobedience, so they have become disobedient—since God wished to show you mercy—that they too may receive mercy. God has imprisoned all in disobedience that he might have mercy on all.

How deep are the riches and the wisdom and the knowledge of God! How inscrutable his judgments, how unsearchable his ways! For "who has known the mind of the Lord? Or who has ever been his counselor? Who has given him anything so as to deserve return?" For from him and through him and for him all things are: To him be glory forever. Amen. ✛

Psalm 69:30-31, 33-34, 36-37
R. Lord, in your great love, answer me.
But I am afflicted and in pain;
　　let your saving help, O God, protect me.
I will praise the name of God in song,
　　and I will glorify him with thanksgiving. **R.**
"See, you lowly ones, and be glad;
　　you who seek God, may your hearts be merry!
For the Lord hears the poor,
　　and his own who are in bonds he spurns not." **R.**
For God will save Zion
　　and rebuild the cities of Judah.
They shall dwell in the land and own it,
　　and the descendants of his servants shall inherit it,
　　and those who love his name shall inhabit it. **R.**

1 Peter 1:25
R. Alleluia, alleluia.
The word of the Lord stands forever;
it is the word given to you, the Good News. **R.**

† *Luke 14:12-14*
Do not invite just your friends, but the poor and the crippled.

Jesus said to the chief of the Pharisees who had invited him to dinner: "Whenever you give a lunch or dinner, do not invite your friends or brothers or relatives or wealthy neighbors. They might invite you in return and thus repay you. No, when you have a reception, invite beggars and the crippled, the lame and the blind. You should be pleased that they cannot repay you, for you will be repaid in the resurrection of the just." +

TUESDAY, NOVEMBER 6
WEEKDAY

† *Romans 12:5-16*
We form one body and as parts of it we belong to each other.

We, though many, are one body in Christ and individually members one of another. We have gifts that differ according to the favor bestowed on each of us. One's gift may be prophecy; its use should be in proportion to his faith. It may be the gift of ministry; it should be used for service. One who is a teacher should use his gift for teaching; one with the power of exhortation should exhort. He who gives alms should do so generously; he who rules should exercise his authority with care; he who performs works of mercy should do so cheerfully.

Your love must be sincere. Detest what is evil, cling to what is good. Love one another with the affection of brothers. Anticipate each other in showing respect. Do not grow slack but be fervent in spirit; he whom you serve is the Lord. Rejoice in hope, be patient under trial, persevere in prayer. Look on the needs of the saints as your own; be generous in offering hospitality. Bless your persecutors; bless and do not curse them. Rejoice with those who rejoice, weep with those who weep. Have the same attitude toward all. +

Psalm 131:1-3
R. In you, Lord, I have found my peace.
O Lord, my heart is not proud,
    nor are my eyes haughty;
I busy not myself with great things,
    nor with things too sublime for me. **R.**

Nay rather, I have stilled and quieted
   my soul like a weaned child.
Like a weaned child on its mother's lap,
   [so is my soul within me.] **R.**
O Israel, hope in the Lord,
   both now and forever. **R.**

1 Peter 1:25
R. Alleluia, alleluia.
The word of the Lord stands forever;
it is the word given to you, the Good News. **R.**

† *Luke 14:15-24*
Go to the highway and force people to come that my house will be filled.

One of the guests at a party said to Jesus, "Happy is he who eats bread in the kingdom of God." Jesus responded: "A man was giving a large dinner and he invited many. At dinner time he sent his servant to say to those invited, 'Come along, everything is ready now.' But they began to excuse themselves, one and all. The first one said to the servant, 'I have bought some land and must go out and inspect it. Please excuse me.' Another said, 'I have bought five yoke of oxen and I am going out to test them. Please excuse me.' A third said, 'I am newly married and so I cannot come.' The servant, returning, reported all this to his master. The master of the house grew angry at the account. He said to his servant, 'Go out quickly into the streets and alleys of the town and bring in the poor and crippled, the blind and the lame.' The servant reported, after some time, 'Your orders have been carried out, my lord, and there is still room.' The master then said to the servant, 'Go out into the highways and along the hedgerows and force them to come in. I want my house to be full, but I tell you that not one of those invited shall taste a morsel of my dinner.'" ✝

WEDNESDAY, NOVEMBER 7
WEEKDAY

† *Romans 13:8-10*
You fulfill the law if you love your neighbor.

Owe no debt to anyone except the debt that binds us to love another. He who loves his neighbor has fulfilled the law. The commandments, "You shall not commit adultery; you shall not murder; you shall not steal; you shall not covet," and any other commandment there may be are all summed up in this, "You shall love your neighbor as yourself." Love never does any wrong to the neighbor, hence love is the fulfillment of the law. ✝

Psalm 112:1-2, 4-5, 9
**R. Happy the man who is merciful
and lends to those in need.**
Happy the man who fears the Lord,
    who greatly delights in his commands.
His posterity shall be mighty upon the earth;
    the upright generation shall be blessed. **R.**
He dawns through the darkness, a light for the upright;
    he is gracious and merciful and just.
Well for the man who is gracious and lends,
    who conducts his affairs with justice. **R.**
Lavishly he gives to the poor;
    his generosity shall endure forever;
    his horn shall be exalted in glory. **R.**

1 Peter 1:25
R. Alleluia, alleluia.
The word of the Lord stands forever;
it is the word given to you, the Good News. **R.**

✝ *Luke 14:25-33*
He who does not give up all his possessions cannot be my disciple.

On one occasion when a great crowd was with Jesus, he turned to them and said, "If anyone comes to me without turning his back on his father and mother, his wife and his children, his brothers and sisters, indeed his very self, he cannot be my follower. Anyone who does not take up his cross and follow me cannot be my disciple. If one of you decides to build a tower, will he not first sit down and calculate the outlay to see if he has enough money to complete the project? He will do that for fear of laying the foundation and then not being able to complete the work; at which all who saw it would then jeer at him, saying, 'That man began to build what he could not finish.'

"Or if a king is about to march on another king to do battle with him, will he not sit down first and consider whether, with ten thousand men, he can withstand an enemy coming against him with twenty thousand? If he cannot, he will send a delegation while the enemy is still at a distance, asking for terms of peace. In the same way, none of you can be my disciple if he does not renounce all his possessions." ✝

THURSDAY, NOVEMBER 8
WEEKDAY

✝ Romans 14:7-12
If we live, we live for the Lord; if we die, we die for the Lord.

None of us lives as his own master and none of us dies as his own master. While we live we are responsible to the Lord, and when we die we die as his servants. Both in life and in death we are the Lord's. That is why Christ died and came to life again, that he might be Lord of both the dead and the living. But you, how can you sit in judgment on your brother? Or you, how can you look down on your brother? We shall all have to appear before the judgment seat of God. It is written, "As surely as I live, says the Lord, every knee shall bend before me and every tongue shall give praise to God."

Every one of us will have to give an account of himself before God. ✝

Psalm 27:1, 4, 13-14
**R. I believe that I shall see the good things
of the Lord in the land of the living.**
The Lord is my light and my salvation;
　　whom should I fear?
The Lord is my life's refuge;
　　of whom should I be afraid? **R.**
One thing I ask of the Lord;
　　this I seek:
To dwell in the house of the Lord
　　all the days of my life,
That I may gaze on the loveliness of the Lord
　　and contemplate his temple. **R.**
I believe that I shall see the bounty of the Lord
　　in the land of the living.
Wait for the Lord with courage;
　　be stouthearted, and wait for the Lord. **R.**

1 Peter 1:25

R. Alleluia, alleluia.

The word of the Lord stands forever;
it is the word given to you, the Good News. **R.**

✛ *Luke 15:1-10*

There will be great rejoicing in heaven over one repentant sinner.

The tax collectors and sinners were all gathering around to hear Jesus, at which the Pharisees and the scribes murmured, "This man welcomes sinners and eats with them." Then he addressed this parable to them: "Who among you, if he has a hundred sheep and loses one of them, does not leave the ninety-nine in the wasteland and follow the lost one until he finds it? And when he finds it, he puts it on his shoulders in jubilation. Once arrived home, he invites friends and neighbors in and says to them, 'Rejoice with me because I have found my lost sheep.' I tell you, there will likewise be more joy in heaven over one repentant sinner than over ninety-nine righteous people who have no need to repent.

"What woman, if she has ten silver pieces and loses one, does not light a lamp and sweep the house in a diligent search until she has retrieved what she lost? And when she finds it, she calls in her friends and neighbors to say, 'Rejoice with me! I have found the silver piece I lost.' I tell you, there will be the same kind of joy before the angels of God over one repentant sinner." ✛

FRIDAY, NOVEMBER 9
THE DEDICATION OF THE LATERAN BASILICA

✛ *Ezekiel 47:1-2, 8-9, 12*

I saw water flowing from the temple,
and all who were touched by it were saved.

The angel brought me
back to the entrance of the temple,
and I saw water flowing out
from beneath the threshold of the temple toward the east,
for the facade of the temple was toward the east;
the water flowed down from the southern side of the temple,
south of the altar.

He led me outside by the north gate,
and around to the outer gate facing the east,
where I saw water trickling from the southern side.
He said to me,
"This water flows into the eastern district down upon the
Arabah,
and empties into the sea, the salt waters, which it makes
fresh.
Wherever the river flows,
every sort of living creature that can multiply shall live,
and there shall be abundant fish,
for wherever this water comes the sea shall be made fresh.
Along both banks of the river, fruit trees of every kind shall grow;
their leaves shall not fade, nor their fruit fail.
Every month they shall bear fresh fruit,
for they shall be watered by the flow from the sanctuary.
Their fruit shall serve for food, and their leaves for medicine." ✛

Psalm 84:3, 4, 5-6, 8-9

**R. The waters of the river gladden the city of God,
the holy dwelling of the Most High.**
God is our refuge and our strength,
an ever-present help in distress.
Therefore we fear not, though the earth be shaken
and mountains plunge into the depths of the sea. **R.**
There is a stream whose runlets gladden the city of God,
the holy dwelling of the Most High.
God is in its midst; it shall not be disturbed;
God will help it at the break of dawn. **R.**
The LORD of hosts is with us;
our stronghold is the God of Jacob.
Come! behold the deeds of the Lord,
the astounding things he has wrought on earth. **R.**

† *1 Corinthians 3:9c-11, 16-17*
You are God's temple.

Brothers and sisters:
You are God's building.
According to the grace of God given to me,
like a wise master builder I laid a foundation,
and another is building upon it.

But each one must be careful how he builds upon it,
for no one can lay a foundation other than the one that is
there,
namely, Jesus Christ.

Do you not know that you are the temple of God,
and that the Spirit of God dwells in you?
If anyone destroys God's temple,
God will destroy that person;
for the temple of God, which you are, is holy. ✚

2 Chronicles 7:16
R. Alleluia, alleluia.
I have chosen and consecrated this house, says the Lord,
that my name may be there forever. **R.**

✝ *John 2:13-22*
Jesus was speaking about the temple of his body.

Since the Passover of the Jews was near,
Jesus went up to Jerusalem.
He found in the temple area those who sold oxen, sheep, and
doves,
as well as the money changers seated there.
He made a whip out of cords
and drove them all out of the temple area, with the sheep
and oxen,
and spilled the coins of the money changers
and overturned their tables,
and to those who sold doves he said,
"Take these out of here,
and stop making my Father's house a marketplace."
His disciples recalled the words of Scripture,
Zeal for your house will consume me.
At this the Jews answered and said to him,
"What sign can you show us for doing this?"
Jesus answered and said to them,
"Destroy this temple and in three days I will raise it up."
The Jews said,
"This temple has been under construction for forty-six
years,
and you will raise it up in three days?"

But he was speaking about the temple of his body.
Therefore, when he was raised from the dead,
  his disciples remembered that he had said this,
  and they came to believe the Scripture
  and the word Jesus had spoken. ✝

SATURDAY, NOVEMBER 10
POPE LEO THE GREAT

✝ *Romans 16:3-9, 16, 22-27*
Greet each other with a holy kiss.

Give my greetings to Prisca and Aquila; they were my fellow workers in the service of Christ Jesus and even risked their lives for the sake of mine. Not only I but all the churches of the Gentiles are grateful to them. Remember me also to the congregation that meets in their house. Greetings to my beloved Epaenetus; he is the first offering that Asia made to Christ. My greetings to Mary, who has worked hard for you, and to Andronicus and Junias, my kinsmen and fellow prisoners; they are outstanding apostles, and they were in Christ even before I was. Greetings to Ampliatus, who is dear to me in the Lord; to Urbanus, our fellow worker in the service of Christ; and to my beloved Stachys. Greet one another with a holy kiss. All the churches of Christ send you greetings.

I, Tertius, who have written this letter, send you my greetings in the Lord. Greetings also from Gaius, who is host to me and to the whole church. Erastus, the city treasurer, and our brother Quartus wish to be remembered to you.

Now to him who is able to strengthen you in the gospel which I proclaim when I preach Jesus Christ, the gospel which reveals the mystery hidden for many ages but now manifested through the writings of the prophets, and, at the command of the eternal God, made known to all the Gentiles that they may believe and obey — to him, the God who alone is wise, may glory be given through Jesus Christ unto endless ages. Amen. ✝

Psalm 145:2-5, 10-11
R. **I will praise your name forever, Lord.**
Every day will I bless you,
  and I will praise your name forever and ever.
Great is the LORD and highly to be praised;

his greatness is unsearchable. **R.**
Generation after generation praises your works
and proclaims your might.
They speak of the splendor of your glorious majesty
and tell of your wondrous works. **R.**
Let all your works give you thanks, O LORD,
and let your faithful ones bless you.
Let them discourse of the glory of your kingdom
and speak of your might. **R.**

1 Peter 1:25
R. Alleluia, alleluia.
The word of the Lord stands forever;
it is the word given to you, the Good News. **R.**

✝ *Luke 16:9-15*
If you cannot be trusted with money,
who will trust you with the true riches?

[**J**esus said to his disciples:] "Make friends for yourselves through your use of this world's goods, so that when they fail you, a lasting reception will be yours. If you can trust a man in little things, you can also trust him in greater; while anyone unjust in a slight matter is also unjust in greater. If you cannot be trusted with elusive wealth, who will trust you with lasting? And if you have not been trustworthy with someone else's money, who will give you what is your own?

"No servant can serve two masters. Either he will hate the one and love the other or be attentive to the one and despise the other. You cannot give yourself to God and money." The Pharisees, who were avaricious men, heard all this and began to deride him. He said to them: "You justify yourselves in the eyes of men, but God reads your hearts. What man thinks important, God holds in contempt." ✛

NOVEMBER 11
THIRTY-SECOND SUNDAY IN ORDINARY TIME

✝ *2 Maccabees 7:1-2, 9-14*
The King of the world will raise us up to live again forever.

It happened that seven brothers with their mother were
arrested

and tortured with whips and scourges by the king,
to force them to eat pork in violation of God's law.
One of the brothers, speaking for the others, said:
"What do you expect to achieve by questioning us?
We are ready to die rather than transgress the laws of our
ancestors."

At the point of death he said:
"You accursed fiend, you are depriving us of this present
life,
but the King of the world will raise us up to live again
forever.
It is for his laws that we are dying."

After him the third suffered their cruel sport.
He put out his tongue at once when told to do so,
and bravely held out his hands, as he spoke these noble
words:
"It was from Heaven that I received these;
for the sake of his laws I disdain them;
from him I hope to receive them again."
Even the king and his attendants marveled at the young man's
courage,
because he regarded his sufferings as nothing.

After he had died,
they tortured and maltreated the fourth brother in the
same way.
When he was near death, he said,
"It is my choice to die at the hands of men
with the hope God gives of being raised up by him;
but for you, there will be no resurrection to life." ✛

Psalm 17:1, 5-6, 8, 15
R. Lord, when your glory appears, my joy will be full.
Hear, O LORD, a just suit;
attend to my outcry;
hearken to my prayer from lips without deceit. **R.**
My steps have been steadfast in your paths,
my feet have not faltered.
I call upon you, for you will answer me, O God;
incline your ear to me; hear my word. **R.**

Keep me as the apple of your eye,
   hide me in the shadow of your wings.
But I in justice shall behold your face;
   on waking I shall be content in your presence. **R.**

✝ *2 Thessalonians 2:16-3:5*
*May the Lord encourage your hearts and
strengthen them in every good deed and word.*

Brothers and sisters:
May our Lord Jesus Christ himself and God our Father,
   who has loved us and given us everlasting encouragement
   and good hope through his grace,
   encourage your hearts and strengthen them in every good
   deed and word.

Finally, brothers and sisters, pray for us,
   so that the word of the Lord may speed forward and be
      glorified,
   as it did among you,
   and that we may be delivered from perverse and wicked
      people,
   for not all have faith.
But the Lord is faithful;
   he will strengthen you and guard you from the evil one.
We are confident of you in the Lord that what we instruct you,
   you are doing and will continue to do.
May the Lord direct your hearts to the love of God
   and to the endurance of Christ. ✛

Revelation 1:5a, 6b
R. Alleluia, alleluia.
Jesus Christ is the first born of the dead;
to him be glory and power, forever and ever. **R.**

✝ *Luke 20:27-38* (or *Luke 20:27, 34-38*)
He is not God of the dead, but of the living.

Some Sadducees, those who deny that there is a resurrection,
   came forward and put this question to Jesus, saying,
   "Teacher, Moses wrote for us,
   If someone's brother dies leaving a wife but no child,
   his brother must take the wife

and raise up descendants for his brother.
Now there were seven brothers;
    the first married a woman but died childless.
Then the second and the third married her,
    and likewise all the seven died childless.
Finally the woman also died.
Now at the resurrection whose wife will that woman be?
For all seven had been married to her."
Jesus said to them,
    "The children of this age marry and remarry;
    but those who are deemed worthy to attain to the coming age
    and to the resurrection of the dead
    neither marry nor are given in marriage.
They can no longer die,
    for they are like angels;
    and they are the children of God
    because they are the ones who will rise.
That the dead will rise
    even Moses made known in the passage about the bush,
    when he called out 'Lord,'
    the God of Abraham, the God of Isaac, and the God of Jacob;
    and he is not God of the dead, but of the living,
    for to him all are alive." ✝

MONDAY, NOVEMBER 12
St. Josaphat

✝ *Wisdom 1:1-7*
Wisdom is a spirit, a friend of man;
the Spirit of the Lord fills the whole world.

Love justice, you who judge the earth;
    think of the Lord in goodness,
    and seek him in integrity of heart;
Because he is found by those who test him not,
    and he manifests himself to those who do not disbelieve him.
For perverse counsels separate a man from God,
    and his power, put to the proof, rebukes the foolhardy;
Because into a soul that plots evil wisdom enters not,
    nor dwells she in a body under debt of sin.
For the holy spirit of discipline flees deceit

and withdraws from senseless counsels;
and when injustice occurs it is rebuked.
For wisdom is a kindly spirit,
yet she acquits not the blasphemer of his guilty lips;
Because God is the witness of his inmost self
and the sure observer of his heart
and the listener to his tongue.
For the spirit of the Lord fills the world,
is all-embracing, and knows what man says. ✝

Psalm 139:1-10
R. Guide me, Lord, along the everlasting way.
O Lord, you have probed me and you know me;
you know when I sit and when I stand;
you understand my thoughts from afar.
My journeys and my rest you scrutinize,
with all my ways you are familiar. **R.**
Even before a word is on my tongue,
behold, O Lord, you know the whole of it.
Behind me and before, you hem me in
and rest your hand upon me.
Such knowledge is too wonderful for me;
too lofty for me to attain. **R.**
Where can I go from your spirit?
from your presence where can I flee?
If I go up to the heavens, you are there;
if I sink to the nether world, you are present there. **R.**
If I take the wings of the dawn,
if I settle at the farthest limits of the sea,
Even there your hand shall guide me,
and your right hand hold me fast. **R.**

John 6:64, 69
R. Alleluia, alleluia.
Your words, Lord, are spirit and life,
you have the words of everlasting life. **R.**

† *Luke 17:1-6*
*If your brother returns to you seven times a day
and says, I am sorry, you must forgive him.*

J esus said to his disciples: "Scandals will inevitably arise, but woe to him through whom they come. He would be better off thrown into the sea with a millstone around his neck than giving scandal to one of these little ones.

"Be on your guard. If your brother does wrong, correct him; if he repents, forgive him. If he sins against you seven times a day, and seven times a day turns back to you saying, 'I am sorry,' forgive him."

The apostles said to the Lord, "Increase our faith," and he answered: "If you had faith the size of a mustard seed, you could say to this sycamore, 'Be uprooted and transplanted into the sea,' and it would obey you." ✝

TUESDAY, NOVEMBER 13
St. Frances Xavier Cabrini

† Wisdom 2:23—3:9
In the eyes of fools they were dead, but they are at peace.

For God formed man to be imperishable;
  the image of his own nature he made him.
But by the envy of the devil, death entered the world,
  and they who are in his possession experience it.
But the souls of the just are in the hands of God,
  and no torment shall touch them.
They seemed, in the view of the foolish, to be dead;
  and their passing away was thought an affliction
  and their going forth from us, utter destruction.
But they are in peace.
For if before men, indeed, they be punished,
  yet is their hope full of immortality;
Chastised a little, they shall be greatly blessed,
  because God tried them
  and found them worthy of himself.
As gold in the furnace, he proved them,
  and as sacrificial offerings he took them to himself.
In the time of their visitation they shall shine,
  and shall dart about as sparks through stubble;
They shall judge nations and rule over peoples,
  and the Lord shall be their king forever.
Those who trust in him shall understand truth,
  and the faithful shall abide with him in love:

Because grace and mercy are with his holy ones,
and his care is with his elect. ✛

Psalm 34:2-3, 16-19
R. I will bless the Lord at all times.
I will bless the Lord at all times;
his praise shall be ever in my mouth.
Let my soul glory in the Lord;
the lowly will hear me and be glad. **R.**
The Lord has eyes for the just,
and ears for their cry.
The Lord confronts the evildoers,
to destroy remembrance of them from the earth. **R.**
When the just cry out, the Lord hears them,
and from all their distress he rescues them.
The Lord is close to the brokenhearted;
and those who are crushed in spirit he saves. **R.**

John 6:64, 69
R. Alleluia, alleluia.
Your words, Lord, are spirit and life,
you have the words of everlasting life. **R.**

† *Luke 17:7-10*
We are only servants: we have done our duty.

The Lord said: "If one of you had a servant plowing or herding
sheep and he came in from the fields, would you say to him,
'Come and sit down at table'? Would you not rather say,
'Prepare my supper. Put on your apron and wait on me while
I eat and drink. You can eat and drink afterward'? Would he
be grateful to the servant who was only carrying out his
orders? It is quite the same with you who hear me. When you
have done all you have been commanded to do, say, 'We are
useless servants. We have done no more than our duty.'" ✛

WEDNESDAY, NOVEMBER 14
WEEKDAY

† *Wisdom 6:2-11*
Listen, kings, that you may learn wisdom.

Hear, therefore, kings, and understand;
learn, you magistrates of the earth's expanse!

Hearken, you who are in power over the multitude
  and lord it over throngs of peoples!
Because authority was given you by the Lord
  and sovereignty by the Most High,
  who shall probe your works and scrutinize your counsels!
Because, though you were ministers of his kingdom, you
    judged not rightly,
  and did not keep the law,
  nor walk according to the will of God,
Terribly and swiftly shall he come against you,
  because judgment is stern for the exalted—
For the lowly may be pardoned out of mercy
  but the mighty shall be mightily put to the test.
For the Lord of all shows no partiality,
  nor does he fear greatness,
Because he himself made the great as well as the small,
  and he provides for all alike;
  but for those in power a rigorous scrutiny impends.
To you, therefore, O princes, are my words addressed
  that you may learn wisdom and that you may not sin.
For those who keep the holy precepts hallowed
    shall be found holy,
  and those learned in them will have ready a response.
Desire therefore my words;
  long for them and you shall be instructed. ✛

Psalm 82:3-4, 6-7
R. Rise up, O God, bring judgment to the earth.
Defend the lowly and the fatherless;
  render justice to the afflicted and the destitute.
Rescue the lowly and the poor;
  from the hand of the wicked deliver them. **R.**
"I said: You are gods,
  all of you sons of the Most High;
Yet like men you shall die,
  and fall like any prince." **R.**

John 6:64, 69
R. Alleluia, alleluia.
Your words, Lord, are spirit and life,
you have the words of everlasting life. **R.**

† *Luke 17:11-19*

It seems that no one has come back to
God to give praise, except this foreigner.

On his journey to Jerusalem Jesus passed along the borders of Samaria and Galilee. As he was entering a village, ten lepers met him. Keeping their distance, they raised their voices and said, "Jesus, Master, have pity on us!" When he saw them, he responded, "Go and show yourselves to the priests." On their way there they were cured. One of them, realizing that he had been cured, came back praising God in a loud voice. He threw himself on his face at the feet of Jesus and spoke his praises. This man was a Samaritan.

Jesus took the occasion to say, "Were not all ten made whole? Where are the other nine? Was there no one to return and give thanks to God except this foreigner?" He said to the man, "Stand up and go your way; your faith has been your salvation." ✛

THURSDAY, NOVEMBER 15
Weekday, St. Albert the Great

† *Wisdom 7:22—8:1*

Wisdom is a reflection of eternal light,
a spotless mirror of the majesty of God.

In Wisdom is a spirit
     intelligent, holy, unique,
Manifold, subtle, agile,
     clear, unstrained, certain,
Not baneful, loving the good, keen,
     unhampered, beneficent, kindly,
Firm, secure, tranquil,
     all-powerful, all-seeing,
And pervading all spirits,
     though they be intelligent, pure, and very subtle.
For Wisdom is mobile beyond all motion,
     and she penetrates and pervades all things
          by reason of her purity.
For she is an aura of the might of God
     and a pure effusion of the glory of the Almighty;
     therefore nought that is sullied enters into her.

For she is the refulgence of eternal light,
  the spotless mirror of the power of God,
  the image of his goodness.
And she, who is one, can do all things,
  and renews everything while herself perduring;
And passing into holy souls, from age to age,
  she produces friends of God and prophets.
For there is nought God loves, be it not one
  who dwells with Wisdom.
For she is fairer than the sun
  and surpasses every constellation of the stars.
Compared to light, she takes precedence;
  for that, indeed, night supplants,
  but wickedness prevails not over Wisdom.
Indeed, she reaches from end to end mightily
  and governs all things well. ✛

Psalm 119:89-91, 130, 135, 175
R. Your word is forever, O Lord.
Your word, O Lord, endures forever;
  it is firm as the heavens. **R.**
Through all generations your truth endures;
  you have established the earth, and it stands firm. **R.**
According to your ordinances they still stand firm:
  all things serve you. **R.**
The revelation of your words sheds light,
  giving understanding to the simple. **R.**
Let your countenance shine upon your servant,
  and teach me your statutes. **R.**
Let my soul live to praise you,
  and may your ordinances help me. **R.**

John 6:64, 69
R. Alleluia, alleluia.
Your words, Lord, are spirit and life,
you have the words of everlasting life. **R.**

† *Luke 17:20-25*
The kingdom of God is among you.

Jesus, on being asked by the Pharisees when the reign of God
would come, replied: "You cannot tell by careful watching

when the reign of God will come. Neither is it a matter of reporting that it is 'here' or 'there.' The reign of God is already in your midst."

He said to the disciples: "A time will come when you will long to see one day of the Son of Man but will not see it. They will tell you he is to be found in this place or that. Do not go running about excitedly. The Son of Man in his day will be like the lightning that flashes from one end of the sky to the other. First, however, he must suffer much and be rejected by the present age." ✛

FRIDAY, NOVEMBER 16
WEEKDAY, ST. MARGARET OF SCOTLAND, ST. GERTRUDE THE GREAT

† *Wisdom 13:1-9*
If they are able to investigate the world,
how have they been so slow to find its master?

For all men were by nature foolish
    who were in ignorance of God,
and who from the good things seen did not succeed in
    knowing him who is,
and from studying the works did not discern the artisan:
But either fire, or wind, or the swift air,
    or the circuit of the stars, or the mighty water,
    or the luminaries of heaven, the governors of the world,
        they considered gods.
Now if out of joy in their beauty they thought them gods,
    let them know how far more excellent
        is the Lord than these;
    for the original source of beauty fashioned them.
Or if they were struck by their might and energy,
    let them from these things realize how much more power
        ful is he who made them.
For from the greatness and the beauty of created things
    their original author, by analogy, is seen.
But yet, for these the blame is less;
For they indeed have gone astray perhaps,
    though they seek God and wish to find him.
For they search busily among his works,
    but are distracted by what they see,

because the things seen are fair.
But again, not even these are pardonable.
For if they so far succeeded in knowledge
   that they could speculate about the world,
   how did they not more quickly find its Lord? ✢

Psalm 19:2-5
R. The heavens proclaim the glory of God.
The heavens declare the glory of God,
   and the firmament proclaims his handiwork.
Day pours out the word to day,
   and night to night imparts knowledge. **R.**
Not a word nor a discourse
   whose voice is not heard;
Through all the earth their voice resounds,
   and to the ends of the world, their message. **R.**

John 6:64, 69
R. Alleluia, alleluia.
Your words, Lord, are spirit and life,
you have the words of everlasting life. **R.**

† *Luke 17:26-37*
It will be the same when the day comes the Son of Man is revealed.

Jesus said to his disciples: As it was in the days of Noah, so will it be in the days of the Son of Man. They ate and drank, they took husbands and wives, right up to the day Noah entered the ark—and when the flood came, it destroyed them all. It was much the same in the days of Lot: they ate and drank, they bought and sold, they built and planted. But on the day Lot left Sodom, fire and brimstone rained down from heaven and destroyed them all.

    "It will be like that on the day the Son of Man is revealed. On that day, if a man is on the rooftop and his belongings are in the house, he should not go down to get them; neither should the man in the field return home. Remember Lot's wife. Whoever tries to spare his life will lose it; whoever seems to forfeit it will keep it. I tell you, on that night there will be two men in one bed; one will be taken and the other left. Two women will be grinding grain together; one will be taken and the other left." "Where, Lord?" they asked him, and he an-

swered, "Wherever the carcass is, there will the vultures
gather." ✦

SATURDAY, NOVEMBER 17
St. Elizabeth of Hungary

† *Wisdom 18:14-16;19:6-9*
*It appeared over the Red Sea, the way was
opened and they rejoiced like lambs.*

For when peaceful stillness compassed everything
and the night in its swift course was half spent,
Your all-powerful word from heaven's royal throne
bounded, a fierce warrior, into the doomed land,
bearing the sharp sword of your inexorable decree.
And as he alighted, he filled every place with death;
he still reached to heaven, while he stood upon the earth.

For all creation, in its several kinds, was being made over anew,
serving its natural laws,
that your children might be preserved unharmed.
The cloud overshadowed their camp;
and out of what had before been water,
dry land was seen emerging:
Out of the Red Sea an unimpeded road,
and a grassy plain out of the mighty flood.
Over this crossed the whole nation sheltered by your hand,
after they beheld stupendous wonders.
For they ranged about like horses,
and bounded about like lambs,
praising you, O Lord! their deliverer. ✦

Psalm 105:2-3, 36-37, 42-43
R. Remember the marvels the Lord has done.
*(or **Alleluia.**)*
Sing to him, sing his praise,
proclaim all his wondrous deeds.
Glory in his holy name;
rejoice, O hearts that seek the Lord! **R.**
Then he struck every first-born throughout their land,
the firstfruits of all their manhood.
And he led them forth laden with silver and gold,
with not a weakling among their tribes. **R.**

For he remembered his holy word
   to his servant Abraham.
And he led forth his people with joy;
   with shouts of joy, his chosen ones. **R.**

John 6:64, 69
R. Alleluia, alleluia.
Your words, Lord, are spirit and life,
you have the words of everlasting life. **R.**

† *Luke 18:1-8*
God will see justice done to his chosen who cry to him.

Jesus told his disciples a parable on the necessity of praying always and not losing heart: "Once there was a judge in a certain city who respected neither God nor man. A widow in that city kept coming to him saying, 'Give me my rights against my opponent.' For a time he refused, but finally he thought, 'I care little for God or man, but this widow is wearing me out. I am going to settle in her favor or she will end by doing me violence.'" The Lord said, "Listen to what the corrupt judge has to say. Will not God then do justice to his chosen who call out to him day and night? Will he delay long over them, do you suppose? I tell you, he will give them swift justice. But when the Son of Man comes, will he find any faith on the earth?" ✛

NOVEMBER 18
THIRTY-THIRD SUNDAY IN ORDINARY TIME

† *Malachi 3:19-20a*
The sun of justice will shine on you.

Lo, the day is coming, blazing like an oven,
   when all the proud and all evildoers will be stubble,
and the day that is coming will set them on fire,
   leaving them neither root nor branch,
   says the LORD of hosts.
But for you who fear my name, there will arise
   the sun of justice with its healing rays. ✛

Psalm 98:5-9
R. The Lord comes to rule the earth with justice.
Sing praise to the LORD with the harp,

with the harp and melodious song.
With trumpets and the sound of the horn
    sing joyfully before the King, the LORD. **R.**
Let the sea and what fills it resound,
    the world and those who dwell in it;
let the rivers clap their hands,
    the mountains shout with them for joy. **R.**
Before the LORD, for he comes,
    for he comes to rule the earth;
he will rule the world with justice
    and the peoples with equity. **R.**

✝ *2 Thessalonians 3:7-12*
If anyone is unwilling to work, neither should that one eat.

Brothers and sisters:
You know how one must imitate us.
For we did not act in a disorderly way among you,
    nor did we eat food received free from anyone.
On the contrary, in toil and drudgery, night and day
    we worked, so as not to burden any of you.
Not that we do not have the right.
Rather, we wanted to present ourselves as a model for you,
    so that you might imitate us.
In fact, when we were with you,
    we instructed you that if anyone was unwilling to work,
    neither should that one eat.
We hear that some are conducting themselves among you
    in a disorderly way,
    by not keeping busy but minding the business of others.
Such people we instruct and urge in the Lord Jesus Christ to
    work quietly
    and to eat their own food. ✝

Luke 21:28
R. Alleluia, alleluia.
Stand erect and raise your heads
because your redemption is at hand. **R.**

† *Luke 21:5-19*

By your perseverance you will secure your lives.

While some people were speaking about
 how the temple was adorned with costly stones and votive
  offerings,
 Jesus said, "All that you see here—
 the days will come when there will not be left
 a stone upon another stone that will not be thrown down."

Then they asked him,
 "Teacher, when will this happen?
And what sign will there be when all these things are about to
  happen?"
He answered,
 "See that you not be deceived,
  for many will come in my name, saying,
  'I am he, 'and 'The time has come.'
Do not follow them!
When you hear of wars and insurrections,
  do not be terrified; for such things must happen first,
  but it will not immediately be the end."
Then he said to them,
 "Nation will rise against nation, and kingdom against
  kingdom.
There will be powerful earthquakes, famines, and plagues
  from place to place;
  and awesome sights and mighty signs will come from the
  sky.

"Before all this happens, however,
 they will seize and persecute you,
 they will hand you over to the synagogues and to prisons,
 and they will have you led before kings and governors
 because of my name.
It will lead to your giving testimony.
Remember, you are not to prepare your defense beforehand,
 for I myself shall give you a wisdom in speaking
 that all your adversaries will be powerless to resist or refute.
You will even be handed over by parents, brothers,
  relatives,and friends,
 and they will put some of you to death.

You will be hated by all because of my name,
but not a hair on your head will be destroyed.
By your perseverance you will secure your lives." ✝

MONDAY, NOVEMBER 19
WEEKDAY

✝ *1 Maccabees 1:10-15, 41-43, 54-57, 62-63*
A dreadful wrath visited Israel.

There sprang a sinful offshoot, Antiochus Epiphanes, son of King Antiochus, once a hostage at Rome. He became king in the year one hundred and thirty-seven of the kingdom of the Greeks.

In those days there appeared in Israel men who were breakers of the law, and they seduced many people, saying: "Let us go and make an alliance with the Gentiles all around us; since we separated from them, many evils have come upon us." The proposal was agreeable; some from among the people promptly went to the king, and he authorized them to introduce the way of living of the Gentiles. Thereupon they built a gymnasium in Jerusalem according to the Gentile custom. They covered over the mark of their circumcision and abandoned the holy covenant; they allied themselves with the Gentiles and sold themselves to wrongdoing.

Then the king wrote to his whole kingdom that all should be one people, each abandoning his particular customs. All the Gentiles conformed to the command of the king, and many Israelites were in favor of his religion; they sacrificed to idols and profaned the sabbath.

On the fifteenth day of the month Chislev, in the year one hundred and forty-five, the king erected the horrible abomination upon the altar of holocausts, and in the surrounding cities of Judah they built pagan altars. They also burnt incense at the doors of houses and in the streets. Any scrolls of the law which they found they tore up and burnt. Whoever was found with a scroll of the covenant, and whoever observed the law, was condemned to death by royal decree. But many in Israel were determined and resolved in their hearts not to eat anything unclean; they preferred to die rather than to be defiled with unclean food or to profane the holy covenant; and they did die. Terrible affliction was upon Israel. ✝

Psalm 119:53, 61, 134, 150, 155, 158
**R. Give me life, O Lord,
and I will do your commands.**
Indignation seizes me because of the wicked
who forsake your law. **R.**
Though the snares of the wicked are twined about me,
your law I have not forgotten. **R.**
Redeem me from the oppression of men,
that I may keep your precepts. **R.**
I am attacked by malicious persecutors
who are far from your law. **R.**
Far from sinners is salvation,
because they seek not your statutes. **R.**
I beheld the apostates with loathing,
because they kept not to your promise. **R.**

Psalm 95:8
R. Alleluia, alleluia.
If today you hear his voice,
harden not your hearts. **R.**

✝ *Luke 18:35-43*
What do you want me to do? Lord, that I may see.

As Jesus drew near Jericho a blind man sat at the side of the road begging. Hearing a crowd go by the man asked, "What is that?" The answer came that Jesus of Nazareth was passing by. He shouted out, "Jesus, Son of David, have pity on me!" Those in the lead sternly ordered him to be quiet, but he cried out all the more, "Son of David, have pity on me!" Jesus halted and ordered him to be brought to him. When he had come close, Jesus asked him, "What do you want me to do for you?" "Lord," he answered, "I want to see." Jesus said to him, "Receive your sight. Your faith has healed you." At that very moment he was given his sight and began to follow him, giving God the glory. All the people witnessed it and they too gave praise to God. ✝

TUESDAY, NOVEMBER 20
WEEKDAY

✝ *2 Maccabees 6:18-31*
I have left the young an example of how to die
a good death for the venerable and holy laws.

Eleazar, one of the foremost scribes, a man of advanced age and noble appearance, was being forced to open his mouth to eat pork. But preferring a glorious death to a life of defilement, he spat out the meat, and went forward of his own accord to the instrument of torture, as men ought to do who have the courage to reject the food which it is unlawful to taste even for love of life. Those in charge of that unlawful ritual meal took the man aside privately, because of their long acquaintance with him, and urged him to bring meat of his own providing, such as he could legitimately eat, and to pretend to be eating some of the meat of the sacrifice prescribed by the king; in this way he would escape the death penalty, and be treated kindly because of their old friendship with him. But he made up his mind in a noble manner, worthy of his years, the dignity of his advanced age, the merited distinction of his gray hair, and of the admirable life he had lived from childhood; and so he declared that above all he would be loyal to the holy laws given by God.

He told them to send him at once to the abode of the dead, explaining: "At our age it would be unbecoming to make such a pretense; many young men would think the ninety-year-old Eleazar had gone over to an alien religion. Should I thus dissimulate for the sake of a brief moment of life, they would be led astray by me, while I would bring shame and dishonor on my old age. Even if, for the time being, I avoid the punishment of men, I shall never, whether alive or dead, escape the hands of the Almighty. Therefore, by manfully giving up my life now, I will prove myself worthy of my old age, and I will leave to the young a noble example of how to die willingly and generously for the revered and holy laws."

He spoke thus, and went immediately to the instrument of torture. Those who shortly before had been kindly disposed, now became hostile toward him because what he had said seemed to them utter madness. When he was about to die under the blows, he groaned and said: "The Lord in his holy knowledge knows full well that, although I could have escaped death, I am not only enduring terrible pain in my body from this scourging, but also suffering it with joy in my soul because of my devotion to him." This is how he died, leaving in his death a model of courage and an unforgettable example of virtue not only for the young but for the whole nation. ✛

Psalm 3:2-8
R. The Lord upholds me.
O Lord, how many are my adversaries!
 Many rise up against me!
Many are saying of me,
 "There is no salvation for him in God." **R.**
But you, O Lord, are my shield;
 my glory, you lift up my head!
When I call out to the Lord,
 he answers me from his holy mountain. **R.**
When I lie down in sleep,
 I wake again, for the Lord sustains me.
I fear not the myriads of people
 arrayed against me on every side.
Rise up, O Lord!
 Save me, my God! **R.**

Psalm 95:8
R. Alleluia, alleluia.
If today you hear his voice,
harden not your hearts. **R.**

† *Luke 19:1-10*
The Son of Man has come to seek out and save what was lost.

On entering Jericho, Jesus passed through the city. There was a man there named Zacchaeus, the chief tax collector and a wealthy man. He was trying to see what Jesus was like, but being small of stature, was unable to do so because of the crowd. He first ran on in front, then climbed a sycamore tree which was along Jesus' route, in order to see him. When Jesus came to the spot he looked up and said, "Zacchaeus, hurry down. I mean to stay at your house today." He quickly descended, and welcomed him with delight. When this was observed, everyone began to murmur, "He has gone to a sinner's house as a guest." Zacchaeus stood his ground and said to the Lord: "I give half my belongings, Lord, to the poor. If I have defrauded anyone in the least, I pay him back fourfold." Jesus said to him: "Today salvation has come to this house, for this is what it means to be a son of Abraham. The Son of Man has come to search out and save what was lost." ✛

WEDNESDAY, NOVEMBER 21
THE PRESENTATION OF MARY

✝ *2 Maccabees 7:1, 20-31*
The creator of the world will give you breath and life.

Seven brothers with their mother were arrested and tortured with whips and scourges by the king, to force them to eat pork in violation of God's law.

Most admirable and worthy of everlasting remembrance was the mother, who saw her seven sons perish in a single day, yet bore it courageously because of her hope in the Lord. Filled with a noble spirit that stirred her womanly heart with manly courage, she exhorted each of them in the language of their forefathers with these words: "I do not know how you came into existence in my womb; it was not I who gave you the breath of life, nor was it I who set in order the elements of which each of you is composed. Therefore, since it is the Creator of the universe who shapes each man's beginning, as he brings about the origin of everything, he, in his mercy, will give you back both breath and life, because you now disregard yourselves for the sake of his law."

Antiochus, suspecting insult in her words, thought he was being ridiculed. As the youngest brother was still alive, the king appealed to him, not with mere words, but with promises on oath, to make him rich and happy if he would abandon his ancestral customs: he would make him his Friend and entrust him with high office. When the youth paid no attention to him at all, the king appealed to the mother, urging her to advise her boy to save his life. After he had urged her for a long time, she went through the motions of persuading her son. In derision of the cruel tyrant, she leaned over close to her son and said in their native language: "Son, have pity on me, who carried you in my womb for nine months, nursed you for three years, brought you up, educated and supported you to your present age. I beg you, child, to look at the heavens and the earth and see all that is in them; then you will know that God did not make them out of existing things; and in the same way the human race came into existence. Do not be afraid of this executioner, but be worthy of your brothers and accept death, so that in the time of mercy I may receive you again with them."

She had scarcely finished speaking when the youth said: "What are you waiting for? I will not obey the king's command. I obey the command of the law given to our forefathers through Moses. But you, who have contrived every kind of affliction for the Hebrews, will not escape the hands of God." ✛

Psalm 17:1, 5-6, 8, 15
R. Lord, when your glory appears,
my joy will be full.
Hear, O Lord, a just suit;
    attend to my outcry;
    hearken to my prayer from lips without deceit. **R.**
My steps have been steadfast in your paths,
    my feet have not faltered.
I call upon you, for you will answer me, O God;
    incline your ear to me; hear my word. **R.**
Hide me in the shadow of your wings.
But I in justice shall behold your face;
    on waking, I shall be content in your presence. **R.**
    Psalm 95:8
R. Alleluia, alleluia.
If today you hear his voice,
harden not your hearts. **R.**

† *Luke 19:11-28*
Why did you not put my money in the bank?

While the disciples were listening Jesus went on to tell a parable, because he was near Jerusalem where they thought that the reign of God was about to appear. He said: "A man of noble birth went to a faraway country to become its king, and then return. He summoned ten of his servants and gave them sums of ten units each, saying to them, 'Invest this until I get back.' But his fellow citizens despised him, and they immediately sent a deputation after him with instructions to say, 'We will not have this man rule over us.' He returned, however, crowned as king. Then he sent for the servants to whom he had given the money, to learn what profit each had made. The first presented himself and said, 'Lord, the sum you gave me has earned you another ten.' 'Good man!' he replied. 'You showed yourself capable in a small matter. For that you can take over ten villages.' The second came and said, 'Your investment, my lord, has netted you five.' His word to him was, 'Take over five villages.' The third came in and said: 'Here is your money, my lord, which I hid for safekeeping. You see, I was afraid of you because you are a hard man. You withdraw what you never deposited. You reap what you never sowed.' To him the king said: 'You worthless lout! I intend to judge you on your own evidence. You knew I was a hard man, withdrawing what I never deposited, reaping what I never sowed! Why, then, did you not put my money out on loan, so that on my return I could get it back with interest?' He said to those standing around, 'Take from him what he has, and give it to the man with the ten.' 'Yes, but he already has ten,' they said. He responded with, 'The moral is: whoever has will be given more, but the one who has not will lose the little he has. Now about those enemies of mine who did not want me to be king, bring them in and slay them in my presence.'"

Having spoken thus he went ahead with his ascent to Jerusalem. ✛

THURSDAY, NOVEMBER 22
St. Cecilia, Thanksgiving Day
(Below are the Mass readings proper for Thanksgiving Day. If the Thanksgiving Mass is not celebrated, readings for St. Cecilia Memorial Mass are: 2 Chronicles 24:18-22 • Psalm 31:3-4, 6-8, 17, 21 • Matthew 10:17-22)

† Zephaniah 3:14-15
The Lord, the King of Israel, is in your midst.

Shout for joy, O daughter Zion!
sing joyfully, O Israel!
Be glad and exult with all your heart,
O daughter Jerusalem!
The Lord has removed the judgment against you
he has turned away your enemies;
The King of Israel, the Lord, is in your midst,
you have no further misfortune to fear. ✛

Psalm 113:1-8

**R. Blessed be the name of the Lord
both now and forever.**

Praise you, servants of the Lord,
    praise the name of the Lord.
Blessed be the name of the Lord
    both now and forever. **R.**
From the rising to the setting of the sun
    is the name of the Lord to be praised.
High above all nations is the Lord;
    above the heavens is his glory. **R.**
Who is like the Lord, our God, who is enthroned on high
    and looks upon the heavens and the earth below? **R.**
He raises up the lowly from the dust;
    from the dunghill he lifts up the poor
To seat them with princes,
    with the princes of his own people. **R.**

† *1 Corinthians 1:3-9*
I give thanks always to my God for you.

Grace and peace from God our Father and the Lord Jesus Christ.

I continually thank my God for you because of the favor he has bestowed on you in Christ Jesus, in whom you have been richly endowed with every gift of speech and knowledge. Likewise, the witness I bore to Christ has been so confirmed among you that you lack no spiritual gift as you wait for the revelation of our Lord Jesus Christ. He will strengthen you to the end, so that you will be blameless on the day of our Lord Jesus [Christ]. God is faithful, and it was he who called you to fellowship with his Son, Jesus Christ our Lord. ✛

1 Thessalonians 5:18

R. Alleluia, alleluia.
Rejoice always, never cease praying,
render constant thanks;
such is God's will for you in Christ Jesus. **R.**

✝ *Mark 5:18-20*
Announce what great things the Lord has done for you.

As Jesus was getting into the boat, the man who had been possessed was pressing to accompany him. Jesus did not grant his request, but told him instead: "Go home to your family and make it clear to them how much the Lord in his mercy has done for you." At that the man went off and began to proclaim throughout the Ten Cities what Jesus had done for him. They were all amazed at what they heard. ✛

FRIDAY, NOVEMBER 23
WEEKDAY, POPE CLEMENT I, ST. COLUMBAN, BL. MIGUEL AGUSTIN PRO

✝ *1 Maccabees 4:36-37, 52-59*
They offered with joy a sacrifice on the
new altar which they had dedicated.

Judas and his brothers said, "Now that our enemies have been crushed, let us go up to purify the sanctuary and rededicate it." So the whole army assembled, and went up to Mount Zion.

Early in the morning on the twenty-fifth day of the ninth month, that is, the month of Chislev, in the year one hundred and forty-eight, they arose and offered sacrifice according to the law on the new altar of holocausts that they had made. On the anniversary of the day on which the Gentiles had defiled it, on that very day it was re consecrated with songs, harps, flutes, and cymbals. All the people prostrated themselves and adored and praised Heaven, who had given them success.

For eight days they celebrated the dedication of the altar and joyfully offered holocausts and sacrifices of deliverance and praise. They ornamented the facade of the temple with gold crowns and shields; they repaired the gates and the priests' chambers and furnished them with doors. There was great joy among the people now that the disgrace of the Gentiles was removed. Then Judas and his brothers and the entire congregation of Israel decreed that the days of the dedication of the altar should be observed with joy and gladness on the anniversary every year for eight days, from the twenty-fifth day of the month Chislev. ✛

1 Chronicles 29:10-12
R. We praise your glorious name, O mighty God.
Blessed may you be, O Lord,
   God of Israel our father,
   from eternity to eternity. **R.**
Yours, O Lord, are grandeur and power,
   majesty, splendor, and glory.
For all in heaven and on earth is yours; **R.**
Yours, O Lord, is the sovereignty;
   you are exalted as head over all.
Riches and honor are from you. **R.**
And you have dominion over all,
   in your hand are power and might;
   it is yours to give grandeur and strength to all. **R.**

Psalm 95:8
R. Alleluia, alleluia.
If today you hear his voice,
harden not your hearts. **R.**

† *Luke 19:45-48*
You have turned the house of the Lord into a robber's den.

Jesus entered the temple and began ejecting the traders saying "Scripture has it,
   'My house is meant for a house of prayer' but you have made it 'a den of thieves.'"
   He was teaching in the temple area from day to day. The chief priests and scribes meanwhile were looking for a way to destroy him, as were the leaders of the people, but they had no idea how to achieve it, for indeed, the entire populace was listening to him and hanging on his words. ✛

SATURDAY, NOVEMBER 24
St. Andrew Dung-Lac & Companions

† *1 Maccabees 6:1-13*
*On account of the evil I did in Jerusalem,
I have suffered great misfortunes.*

As King Antiochus was traversing the inland provinces, he heard that in Persia there was a city called Elymias, famous for its wealth in silver and gold, and that its temple was very rich, containing gold helmets, breastplates, and weapons left there by Alexander, son of Philip, king of Macedon, the first king of the Greeks. He went therefore and tried to capture and pillage the city. But he could not do so, because his plan became known to the people of the city who rose up in battle against him. So he retreated and in great dismay withdrew from there to return to Babylon.

While he was in Persia, a messenger brought him news that the armies sent into the land of Judah had been put to flight; that Lysias had gone at first with a strong army and been driven back by the Israelites; that they had grown strong by reason of the arms, men, and abundant possessions taken from the armies they had destroyed; that they had pulled down the Abomination which he had built upon the altar in Jerusalem; and that they had surrounded with high walls both the sanctuary, as it has been before, and his city of Beth-zur.

When the king heard this news, he was struck with fear and very much shaken. Sick with grief because his designs had failed, he took to his bed. There he remained many days, overwhelmed with sorrow, for he knew he was going to die.

So he called in all his Friends and said to them: "Sleep has departed from my eyes, for my heart is sinking with anxiety. I said to myself: 'Into what tribulation have I come, and in what floods of sorrow am I now! Yet I was kindly and beloved in my rule.' But I now recall the evils I did in Jerusalem, when I carried away all the vessels of gold and silver that were in it, and for no cause gave orders that the inhabitants of Judah be destroyed. I know that this is why these evils have overtaken me; and now I am dying, in bitter grief, in a foreign land." +

Psalm 9:2-4 ,6, 16, 19
R. I will rejoice in your salvation, O Lord.
I will give thanks to you, O Lord, with all my heart;
I will declare all your wondrous deeds.
I will be glad and exult in you;
I will sing praise to your name, Most High. **R.**
Because my enemies are turned back,
overthrown and destroyed before you.
You rebuked the nations and destroyed the wicked;
their name you blotted out forever and ever. **R.**
In the snare they set, their foot is caught;

for the needy shall not always be forgotten,
nor shall the hope of the afflicted forever perish. **R.**

Psalm 95:8
R. Alleluia, alleluia.
If today you hear his voice,
harden not your hearts. **R.**

† *Luke 20:27-40*
He is God not of the dead, but of the living.

Some Sadducees came forward (the ones who claim there is no resurrection) to pose this problem to Jesus: "Master, Moses prescribed that if a man's brother dies leaving a wife and no child, the brother should marry the widow and raise posterity to his brother. Now there were seven brothers. The first one married and died childless. Next, the second brother married the widow, then the third, and so on. All seven died without leaving her any children. Finally the widow herself died. At the resurrection, whose wife will she be? Remember, seven married her."

Jesus said to them: "The children of this age marry and are given in marriage, but those judged worthy of a place in the age to come and of resurrection from the dead do not. They become like angels and are no longer liable to death. Sons of the resurrection, they are sons of God. Moses in the passage about the bush showed that the dead rise again when he called the Lord the God of Abraham, and the God of Isaac, and the God of Jacob. God is not the God of the dead but of the living. All are alive for him."

Some of the scribes responded, "Well said, Teacher." They did not dare ask him anything else. ✛

SUNDAY, NOVEMBER 25
CHRIST THE KING

† *2 Samuel 5:1-3*
They anointed David king of Israel.

In those days, all the tribes of Israel came to David in Hebron
and said:
"Here we are, your bone and your flesh.

In days past, when Saul was our king,
it was you who led the Israelites out and brought them
back.
And the LORD said to you,
'You shall shepherd my people Israel
and shall be commander of Israel.'"
When all the elders of Israel came to David in Hebron,
King David made an agreement with them there before the
LORD,
and they anointed him king of Israel. ✛

Psalm 122:1-5
R. Let us go rejoicing to the house of the Lord.
I rejoiced because they said to me,
"We will go up to the house of the LORD."
And now we have set foot
within your gates, O Jerusalem. **R.**
Jerusalem, built as a city
with compact unity.
To it the tribes go up,
the tribes of the LORD. **R.**
According to the decree for Israel,
to give thanks to the name of the LORD.
In it are set up judgment seats,
seats for the house of David. **R.**

† *Colossians 1:12-20*
He transferred us to the kingdom of his beloved Son.

Brothers and sisters:
Let us give thanks to the Father,
who has made you fit to share
in the inheritance of the holy ones in light.
He delivered us from the power of darkness
and transferred us to the kingdom of his beloved Son,
in whom we have redemption, the forgiveness of sins.

He is the image of the invisible God,
the firstborn of all creation.
For in him were created all things in heaven and on earth,
the visible and the invisible,
whether thrones or dominions or principalities or

powers;
all things were created through him and for him.
He is before all things,
and in him all things hold together.
He is the head of the body, the church.
He is the beginning, the firstborn from the dead,
that in all things he himself might be preeminent.
For in him all the fullness was pleased to dwell,
and through him to reconcile all things for him,
making peace by the blood of his cross
through him, whether those on earth or those in
heaven. ✝

Mark 11:9, 10
R. Alleluia, alleluia.
Blessed is he who comes in the name of the Lord!
Blessed is the kingdom of our father David that is to come! **R.**

† *Luke 23:35-43*
Lord, remember me when you come into your kingdom.

The rulers sneered at Jesus and said,
"He saved others, let him save himself
if he is the chosen one, the Christ of God."
Even the soldiers jeered at him.
As they approached to offer him wine they called out,
"If you are King of the Jews, save yourself."
Above him there was an inscription that read,
"This is the King of the Jews."

Now one of the criminals hanging there reviled Jesus, saying,
"Are you not the Christ?
Save yourself and us."
The other, however, rebuking him, said in reply,
"Have you no fear of God,
for you are subject to the same condemnation?
And indeed, we have been condemned justly,
for the sentence we received corresponds to our crimes,
but this man has done nothing criminal."
Then he said,
"Jesus, remember me when you come into your kingdom."
He replied to him,
"Amen, I say to you,

today you will be with me in Paradise." ✛

MONDAY, NOVEMBER 26
WEEKDAY

† Daniel 1:1-6, 8-20
They have not found the equal of Daniel, Hananiah, Mishael, and Azariah.

In the third year of the reign of Jehoiakim, king of Judah, King Nebuchadnezzar of Babylon came and laid siege to Jerusalem. The Lord handed over to him Jehoiakim, king of Judah, and some of the vessels of the temple of God, which he carried off to the land of Shinar, and placed in the temple treasury of his god.

The king told Ashpenaz, his chief chamberlain, to bring in some of the Israelites of royal blood and of the nobility, young men without any defect, handsome, intelligent and wise, quick to learn, and prudent in judgment, such as could take their place in the king's palace; they were to be taught the language and literature of the Chaldeans; after three years' training they were to enter the king's service. The king allotted them a daily portion of food and wine from the royal table. Among these were men of Judah: Daniel, Hananiah, Mishael, and Azariah.

But Daniel was resolved not to defile himself with the king's food or wine; so he begged the chief chamberlain to spare him this defilement. Though God had given Daniel the favor and sympathy of the chief chamberlain, he nevertheless said to Daniel, "I am afraid of my lord the king; it is he who allotted your food and drink. If he sees that you look wretched by comparison with the other young men of your age, you will endanger my life with the king." Then Daniel said to the steward whom the chief chamberlain had put in charge of Daniel, Hananiah, Mishael, and Azariah, "Please test your servants for ten days. Give us vegetables to eat and water to drink. Then see how we look in comparison with the other young men who eat from the royal table, and treat your servants according to what you see." He acceded to this request, and tested them for ten days; after ten days they looked healthier and better fed than any of the young men who ate from the royal table. So the steward continued to take away the food and wine they were to receive, and gave them vegetables.

To these four young men God gave knowledge and proficiency in all literature and science, and to Daniel the understanding of all visions and dreams. At the end of the time the king had specified for their preparation, the chief chamberlain brought them before Nebuchadnezzar. When the king had spoken with all of them, none was found equal to Daniel, Hananiah, Mishael, and Azariah; and so they entered the king's service. In any question of wisdom or prudence which the king put to them, he found them ten times better than all the magicians and enchanters in his kingdom. ✛

Daniel 3:52-56
R. Glory and praise forever!
Blessed are you, O Lord, the God of our fathers,
 praiseworthy and exalted above all forever;
And blessed is your holy and glorious name,
 praiseworthy and exalted above all for all ages. **R.**
Blessed are you in the temple of your holy glory,
 praiseworthy and glorious above all forever. **R.**
Blessed are you on the throne of your kingdom,
 praiseworthy and exalted above all forever. **R.**
Blessed are you who look into the depths
 from your throne upon the cherubim,
 praiseworthy and exalted above all forever. **R.**
Blessed are you in the firmament of heaven,
 praiseworthy and glorious forever. **R.**

Luke 21:28
R. Alleluia, alleluia.
Lift up your heads and see;
your redemption is near at hand. **R.**

✛ Luke 21:1-4
He saw the poor widow give two small coins.

Jesus glanced up and saw the rich putting their offerings into the treasury, and also a poor widow putting in two copper coins. At that he said: "I assure you, this poor widow has put in more than all the rest. They make contributions out of their surplus, but she from her want has given what she could not afford—every penny she had to live on." ✛

TUESDAY, NOVEMBER 27
WEEKDAY

† *Daniel 2:31-45*

The God of heaven will set up a kingdom which will never
be destroyed, and it will absorb all the kingdoms of the world.

Daniel said to Nebuchadnezzar: "In your vision, O king, you saw a statue, very large and exceedingly bright, terrifying in appearance as it stood before you. The head of the statue was pure gold, its chest and arms were silver, its belly and thighs bronze, the legs iron, its feet partly iron and partly tile. While you looked at the statue, a stone which was hewn from a mountain without a hand being put to it, struck its iron and tile feet, breaking them in pieces. The iron, tile, bronze, silver, and gold all crumbled at once, fine as the chaff on the threshing floor in summer, and the wind blew them away without leaving a trace. But the stone that struck the statue became a great mountain and filled the whole earth.

"This was the dream; the interpretation we shall also give in the king's presence. You, O king, are the king of kings; to you the God of heaven has given dominion and strength, power and glory; men, wild beasts, and birds of the air, wherever they may dwell, he has handed over to you, making you ruler over them all; you are the head of gold. Another kingdom shall take your place, inferior to yours, then a third kingdom, of bronze, which shall rule over the whole earth. There shall be a fourth kingdom, strong as iron; it shall break in pieces and subdue all these others, just as iron breaks in pieces and crushes everything else. The feet and toes you saw, partly of potter's tile and partly of iron, mean that it shall be a divided kingdom, but yet have some of the hardness of iron. As you saw the iron mixed with clay tile, and the toes partly iron and partly tile, the kingdom shall be partly strong and partly fragile. The iron mixed with clay tile means that they shall seal their alliances by intermarriage, but they shall not stay united, any more than iron mixes with clay. In the lifetime of those kings the God of heaven will set up a kingdom that shall never be destroyed or delivered up to another people; rather, it shall break in pieces all these kingdoms and put an end to them, and it shall stand forever. That is the meaning of the stone you saw hewn from the mountain without a hand being put to it, which broke in pieces the tile, iron, bronze, silver, and gold. The great God has revealed to the king what shall be in the future; this is exactly what you dreamed, and its meaning is sure." ✛

Daniel 3:57-61
R. Give glory and eternal praise to him.
Bless the Lord, all you works of the Lord,
    praise and exalt him above all forever. **R.**
Angels of the Lord, bless the Lord,
    praise and exalt him above all forever. **R.**
You heavens, bless the Lord,
    praise and exalt him above all forever. **R.**
All you waters above the heavens, bless the Lord,
    praise and exalt him above all forever. **R.**
All you hosts of the Lord, bless the Lord;
    praise and exalt him above all forever. **R.**

Luke 21:28
R. Alleluia, alleluia.
Lift up your heads and see;
your redemption is near at hand. R.

† *Luke 21:5-11*
Not a single stone will be left on the other.

People were speaking of how the temple was adorned with precious stones and votive offerings. Jesus said, "These things you are contemplating — the day will come when not one stone will be left on another, but it will all be torn down." They asked him, "When will this occur, Teacher? And what will be the sign it is going to happen?" He said, "Take care not to be misled. Many will come in my name saying, 'I am he' and 'The time is at hand.' Do not follow them. Neither must you be perturbed when you hear of wars and insurrections. These things are bound to happen first, but the end does not follow immediately."

He said to them further: "Nation will rise against nation and kingdom against kingdom. There will be great earthquakes, plagues and famines in various places, and in the sky fearful omens and great signs." ✛

WEDNESDAY, NOVEMBER 28
WEEKDAY

† *Daniel 5:1-6, 13-14, 16-17, 23-28*
The fingers of a human hand appeared and began to write on the wall.

King Belshazzar gave a great banquet for a thousand of his lords, with whom he drank. Under the influence of the wine, he ordered the gold and silver vessels which Nebuchadnezzar, his father, had taken from the temple in Jerusalem, to be brought in so that the king, his lords, his wives and his entertainers might drink from them. When the gold and silver vessels taken from the house of God in Jerusalem had been brought in, and while the king, his lords, his wives and his entertainers were drinking wine from them, they praised their gods of gold and silver, bronze and iron, wood and stone.

Suddenly, opposite the lampstand, the fingers of a human hand appeared, writing on the plaster of the wall in the king's palace. When the king saw the wrist and hand that wrote, his face blanched; his thoughts terrified him, his hip joints shook, and his knees knocked.

Then Daniel was brought into the presence of the king. The king asked him, "Are you the Daniel, the Jewish exile, whom my father, the king, brought from Judah? I have heard that the spirit of God is in you, that you possess brilliant knowledge and extraordinary wisdom. But I have heard that you can interpret dreams and solve difficulties; if you are able to read the writing and tell me what it means, you shall be clothed in purple, wear a gold collar about your neck, and be third in the government of the kingdom."

Daniel answered the king: "You may keep your gifts, or give your presents to someone else; but the writing I will read for you, O king, and tell you what it means. You have rebelled against the Lord of heaven. You had the vessels of his temple brought before you, so that you and your nobles, your wives and your entertainers, might drink wine from them; and you praised the gods of silver and gold, bronze and iron, wood and stone, that neither see nor hear nor have intelligence. But the God in whose hand is your life breath and the whole course of your life, you did not glorify. By him were the wrist and hand sent, and the writing set down.

"This is the writing that was inscribed: MENE, TEKEL, and PERES. These words mean: MENE, God has numbered your kingdom and put an end to it; TEKEL, you have been weighed on the scales and found wanting; PERES, your kingdom has been divided and given to the Medes and Persians." ✝

Daniel 3:62-67
R. Give glory and eternal praise to him.
Sun and moon, bless the Lord;
 praise and exalt him above all forever. **R.**
Stars of heaven, bless the Lord;
 praise and exalt him above all forever. **R.**
Every shower and dew, bless the Lord;
 praise and exalt him above all forever. **R.**
All you winds, bless the Lord;
 praise and exalt him above all forever. **R.**
Fire and heat, bless the Lord;
 praise and exalt him above all forever. **R.**
[Cold and chill, bless the Lord;
 praise and exalt him above all forever.] **R.**

Luke 21:28
R. Alleluia, alleluia.
Lift up your heads and see;
your redemption is near at hand. **R.**

✝ *Luke 21:12-19*
*You will be hated by all men because of my name,
but not a hair of your head will be lost.*

Jesus said to his disciples: "People will manhandle and persecute you, summoning you to synagogues and prisons, bringing you to trial before kings and governors, all because of my name. You will be brought to give witness on account of it. I bid you resolve not to worry about your defense beforehand, for I will give you words and a wisdom which none of your adversaries can take exception to or contradict. You will be delivered up even by your parents, brothers, relatives and friends, and some of you will be put to death. All will hate you because of me, yet not a hair of your head will be harmed. By patient endurance you will save your lives." ✝

THURSDAY, NOVEMBER 29
WEEKDAY

† *Daniel 6:12-28*
God sent his angels to seal the lions' jaws.

Men rushed into the upper chamber of Daniel's home and found him praying and pleading before his God. Then they went to remind the king about the prohibition: "Did you not decree, O king, that no one is to address a petition to god or man for thirty days, except to you, O king; otherwise he shall be cast into a den of lions?" The king answered them, "The decree is absolute, irrevocable under the Mede and Persian law." To this they replied, "Daniel, the Jewish exile, has paid no attention to you, O king, or to the decree you issued; three times a day he offers his prayer." The king was deeply grieved at this news and he made up his mind to save Daniel; he worked till sunset to rescue him. But these men insisted. "Keep in mind, O king," they said, "that under the Mede and Persian law every royal prohibition or decree is irrevocable." So the king ordered Daniel to be brought and cast into the lions' den. To Daniel he said, "May your God, whom you serve so constantly, save you." To forestall any tampering, the king sealed with his own ring and the rings of the lords the stone that had been brought to block the opening of the den.

Then the king returned to his palace for the night; he refused to eat and he dismissed the entertainers. Since sleep was impossible for him, the king rose very early the next morning and hastened to the lions' den. As he drew near, he cried out to Daniel sorrowfully, "O Daniel, servant of the living God, has the God whom you serve so constantly been able to save you from the lions?" Daniel answered the king: "O king, live forever! My God has sent his angel and closed the lions' mouths so that they have not hurt me. For I have been found innocent before him; neither to you have I done any harm, O king!" This gave the king great joy. At his order Daniel was removed from the den, unhurt because he trusted in his God. The king then ordered the men who had accused Daniel, along with their children and their wives, to be cast into the lions' den. Before they reached the bottom of the den, the lions overpowered them and crushed all their bones.

Then King Darius wrote to the nations and peoples of every language, wherever they dwell on the earth: "All peace to you! I decree that throughout my royal domain the God of Daniel is to be reverenced and feared:

"For he is the living God, enduring forever;
   his kingdom shall not be destroyed,
   and his dominion shall be without end.
He is a deliverer and savior,
   working signs and wonders in heaven and on earth,
   and he delivered Daniel from the lions' power." ✝

Daniel 3:68-74
R. Give glory and eternal praise to him.
Dew and rain, bless the Lord;
   praise and exalt him above all forever. **R.**
Frost and chill, bless the Lord;
   praise and exalt him above all forever. **R.**
Ice and snow, bless the Lord;
   praise and exalt him above all forever. **R.**
Nights and days, bless the Lord;
   praise and exalt him above all forever. **R.**
Light and darkness, bless the Lord;
   praise and exalt him above all forever. **R.**
Lightnings and clouds, bless the Lord;
   praise and exalt him above all forever. **R.**
Let the earth bless the Lord,
   praise and exalt him above all forever. **R.**

Luke 21:28
R. Alleluia, alleluia.
Lift up your heads and see;
your redemption is near at hand. **R.**

✝ *Luke 21:20-28*
*Jerusalem will be desolate and the people
will be led captive to every nation.*

Jesus said to his disciples: "When you see Jerusalem encircled by soldiers, know that its devastation is near. Those in Judea at the time must flee to the mountains; those in the heart of the city must escape it; those in the country must not return. These indeed will be days of retribution, when all that is written must be fulfilled.

"The women who are pregnant or nursing at the breast will fare badly in those days! The distress in the land and the wrath against this people will be great. The people will fall before the sword; they will be led captive in the midst of the Gentiles. Jerusalem will be trampled by the Gentiles, until the times of the Gentiles are fulfilled.

"There will be signs in the sun, the moon and the stars. On the earth, nations will be in anguish, distraught at the roaring of the sea and the waves. Men will die of fright in anticipation of what is coming upon the earth. The powers in the heavens will be shaken. After that, men will see the Son of Man coming on a cloud with great power and glory. When these things begin to happen, stand up straight and raise your heads, for your ransom is near at hand." ✚

FRIDAY, NOVEMBER 30
St. Andrew

† *Romans 10:9-18*
Faith comes from what is heard and what is heard comes from the preaching of Christ.

If you confess with your lips that Jesus is Lord, and believe in your heart that God raised him from the dead, you will be saved. Faith in the heart leads to justification, confession on the lips to salvation. Scripture says, "No one who believes in him will be put to shame." Here there is no difference between Jew and Greek; all have the same Lord, rich in mercy toward all who call upon him. "Everyone who calls on the name of the Lord will be saved."

But how shall they call on him in whom they have not believed? And how can they believe unless they have heard of him? And how can they hear unless there is someone to preach? And how can men preach unless they are sent? Scripture says, "How beautiful are the feet of those who announce good news!" But not all have believed the gospel. Isaiah asks, "Lord, who has believed what he has heard from us?" Faith, then, comes through hearing, and what is heard is the word of Christ. I ask you, have they not heard? Certainly they have, for "their voice has sounded over the whole earth, and their words to the limits of the world." ✚

Psalm 19:2-5

R. Their message goes out through all the earth.

The heavens declare the glory of God,
    and the firmament proclaims his handiwork,
Day pours out the word to day,
    and night to night imparts knowledge. **R.**
Not a word nor a discourse
    whose voice is not heard;
Through all the earth their voice resounds,
    and to the end of the world, their message. **R.**

Matthew 4:19

R. Alleluia, alleluia.

Come follow me, says the Lord,
and I will make you fishers of men. **R.**

† *Matthew 4:18-22*
Immediately they left their nets and followed him.

As Jesus was walking along the Sea of Galilee he watched two brothers, Simon now known as Peter, and his brother Andrew, casting a net into the sea. They were fishermen. He said to them, "Come after me and I will make you fishers of men." They immediately abandoned their nets and became his followers. He walked along farther and caught sight of two other brothers, James, Zebedee's son, and his brother John. They too were in their boat, getting their nets in order with their father, Zebedee. He called them, and immediately they abandoned boat and father to follow him. ✛

SATURDAY, DECEMBER 1
WEEKDAY

† *Daniel 7:15-27*
Kingdoms and power will be given to the people of the Most High.

I, Daniel, found my spirit anguished within its sheath of flesh, and I was terrified by the visions of my mind. I approached one of those present and asked him what all this meant in truth; in answer, he made known to me the meaning of the things: "These four great beasts stand for four kingdoms which shall arise on the earth. But the holy ones of the Most High shall receive the kingship, to possess it forever and ever."

But I wished to make certain about the fourth beast, so very terrible and different from the others, devouring and crushing with its iron teeth and bronze claws, and trampling with its feet what was left; about the ten horns on its head, and the other one that sprang up, before which three horns fell; about the horn with the eyes and the mouth that spoke arrogantly, which appeared greater than its fellows. For, as I watched, that horn made war against the holy ones and was victorious until the Ancient One arrived; judgment was pronounced in favor of the holy ones of the Most High, and the time came when the holy ones possessed the kingdom. He answered me thus:
"The fourth beast shall be a fourth kingdom on earth,
  different from all the others;
It shall devour the whole earth,
  beat it down, and crush it.
The ten horns shall be ten kings
  rising out of that kingdom;
  another shall rise up after them,
Different from those before him,
  who shall lay low three kings.
He shall speak against the Most High
  and oppress the holy ones of the Most High,
  thinking to change the feast days and the law.
They shall be handed over to him
  for a year, two years, and a half-year.
But when the court is convened,
  and his power is taken away
  by final and absolute destruction,
Then the kingship and dominion and majesty
  of all the kingdoms under the heavens
  shall be given to the holy people of the Most High,
Whose kingdom shall be everlasting:
  all dominions shall serve and obey him." ✦

Daniel 3:82-87
R. Give glory and eternal praise to him.
You sons of men, bless the Lord;
  praise and exalt him above all forever. **R.**
O Israel, bless the Lord;
  praise and exalt him above all forever. **R.**

Priests of the Lord, bless the Lord;
  praise and exalt him above all forever. **R.**
Servants of the Lord, bless the Lord;
  praise and exalt him above all forever. **R.**
Spirits and souls of the just, bless the Lord;
  praise and exalt him above all forever. **R.**
Holy men of humble heart, bless the Lord;
  praise and exalt him above all forever. **R.**

Luke 21:28
R. Alleluia, alleluia.
Lift up your heads and see;
your redemption is near at hand. **R.**

† *Luke 21:34-36*
*Stay awake, that you might have the strength
to survive all that is going to happen.*

Jesus said to his disciples: "Be on guard lest your spirits become bloated with indulgence and drunkenness and worldly cares. The great day will suddenly close in on you like a trap. The day I speak of will come upon all who dwell on the face of the earth. So be on the watch. Pray constantly for the strength to escape whatever is in prospect, and to stand secure before the Son of Man." ✛